Forensic Evidence in Court

Forensic Evidence in Court

A Case Study Approach

SECOND EDITION

Christine Beck Lissitzyn

Marc Wm. Vallen

Carolina Academic Press

Durham, North Carolina

Library of Congress Cataloging-in-Publication Data

Names: Lissitzyn, Christine Beck, author. | Vallen, Marc Wm., author.
Title: Forensic evidence in court : a case study approach / Christine Beck
    Lissitzyn and Marc Wm. Vallen.
Description: Second edition. | Durham, North Carolina : Carolina Academic
    Press, LLC, [2017] | Includes bibliographical references and index.
Identifiers: LCCN 2017024140 | ISBN 9781531002237 (alk. paper)
Subjects: LCSH: Evidence, Expert--United States. | Forensic sciences--United
    States. | Evidence, Criminal--United States.
Classification: LCC KF9674 .L55 2017 | DDC 363.25--dc23
LC record available at https://lccn.loc.gov/2017024140

eISBN 978-1-53100-451-4

Carolina Academic Press, LLC
700 Kent Street
Durham, NC 27701
Telephone (919) 489-7486
Fax (919) 493-5668
www.cap-press.com

Printed in the United States of America

Contents

Table of Cases

List of Figures

Acknowledgments

Thank you to the University of Hartford, where I first developed the course in forensic evidence in court, from which this text is developed. I am grateful to my colleague, Marc Vallen, who generously accepted my request to lend his expertise in digital forensics to the preparation of this second edition, and who later agreed to update our chapter on eyewitness identification and add a chapter on firearms and toolmarks. And I wish to thank Lawrence Lissitzyn, my husband and an attorney, who read and re-read chapters, researched Confrontation Clause issues, and was helpful in innumerable ways.

—CBL

I wish to thank, first and foremost, my darling wife Erica, who in addition to providing much needed moral support, tolerated me throughout this project, particularly as deadlines approached. Much gratitude to my children, Marc, Olivia, and Tessa, each of whom is an inspiration in their own way. Many thanks to my friend, colleague, and co-author, Christine Lissitzyn, for asking me to be involved in this project. My friend and colleague Gary Blake provided much needed assistance and support. Judge Holly Abery-Wetstone kindly shared her time and experiences, and helped me put a realistic slant on some otherwise esoteric subject matter. I am indebted to the National Computer Forensics Institute for all their assistance in educating me on the topics at hand, and to the Connecticut Forensic Science Laboratory, particularly Jill Theriault in the Firearms and Toolmarks section for her, and their, invaluable assistance. Finally, thanks to all those who kindly allowed the use of their photography, without which a much more lackluster presentation would obtain.

—MWV

Introduction

This textbook is designed to examine the process by which forensic evidence is used in the court system through case studies and the case law that has resulted when forensic evidence has been introduced. The text is designed for any student of law, criminal justice, or political science who wishes to understand both the power and the limitations of forensic evidence. The primary focus will be on criminal trials, in which forensic evidence is frequently introduced to prove one of two critical issues: (1) is the defendant the perpetrator of the crime, or (2) what happened at the crime scene?

As you will see, forensic evidence is frequently more reliable in excluding a defendant as the perpetrator (for example, the fingerprint on the weapon is not the defendant's or the blood at the scene is not the defendant's) than in positively identifying the defendant (for example, the hair sample or shoeprint at the scene is "consistent with" a class of individuals that includes the defendant but also many other individuals).

You will also learn how the rules of the U.S. court system limit the ways forensic evidence may be introduced in a trial, the types of expert "opinions" that may be offered in evidence, and the limitations on the ability of an appellate court to use its own judgment in deciding whether forensic evidence should have been introduced or excluded.

The public fascination with forensic evidence was captured with the advent of DNA testing. DNA evidence was introduced in 1995 in the trial of O.J. Simpson, in which a jury failed to convict Simpson of the murder of his wife, Nicole, and Ron Goldman, a waiter, despite a mass of DNA evidence pointing to his guilt. Due in part to the introduction of evidence that some DNA evidence may have been deliberately planted and testimony about a racist detective, the jury concluded there was "reasonable doubt" about Simpson's guilt. A different jury, in a subsequent civil trial, on virtually the same evidence, found based on a "preponderance of the evidence" that Simpson was liable in monetary damages for killing Nicole and Ron Goldman. This may be due in part to the fact that the standard of proof that a criminal jury uses requires a higher level of proof than that of a civil jury.

Television shows such as *CSI* depict detectives processing forensic evidence and getting a "hit" on a suspect. In most jurisdictions, the personnel who process forensic evidence hold degrees in chemistry or other scientific studies and work separately from the police force. Several types of forensic evidence, such as DNA and fingerprints, are either processed by commercial laboratories, as in the case of DNA, or are processed in part by computer systems that yield reports that must be read and evaluated by a fingerprint expert before a "match" can be declared. DNA, in particular, is almost never processed overnight and the DNA backlogs in many states have led to substantial questions about the justice system's ability to render a speedy verdict.

However, juries may expect forensic evidence and this expectation, sometimes called the "*CSI* effect" may present problems at trial, similar to earlier tendencies of juries to simply accept as fact the opinion of an expert witness due to the "White Coat Effect." Today juries are sophisticated enough to realize that both the prosecution and the defense pay for their expert witnesses, who often give conflicting reports. However, many defendants who rely on public defenders may not be able to afford to pay an expert witness, which presents another access to justice issue.

In 1993, the use of forensic evidence in court was radically changed by the U.S. Supreme Court in a civil case involving whether a drug caused birth defects. This case, *Daubert v. Merrell Dow Pharmaceuticals*,[1] stated that in deciding whether to admit scientific testimony under the Federal Rules of Evidence, the party proposing to offer the evidence must show that it meets certain tests that demonstrate that it is based on the scientific method, tested, and reliable. This test subsequently was incorporated into a revised federal rule of evidence and subsequently adopted in most state rules of evidence. Therefore, it applies in almost all federal and state criminal cases today. This inquiry often requires attorneys and judges to understand the scientific method and statistics, which many do not.

Although *Daubert* was a civil case, the language of the Supreme Court opinion applies to any case — civil or criminal — in which forensic evidence is proffered. And it set off thousands of subsequent court hearings on admissibility and appeals based on convictions where the defendant contended that the evidence either should or should not have been admitted under the *Daubert* standard.

One important issue we will examine is the Supreme Court's "alternate test" that scientific evidence can also be admitted if it is "generally accepted" in the scientific community. This has led to a dispute over defining the scientific community. Is it composed of academics or law enforcement? Another dispute is whether "generally accepted" is the same thing as "generally admitted." As you will see when we examine handwriting analysis, expert opinions as to who wrote a questioned document have been admitted routinely for years (for example, in the trial of the Lindbergh baby kidnapping in 1935) but that does not mean that handwriting analysis has ever been subjected to the scientific method. It has been generally admitted (and continues to be) but it is not generally accepted as scientifically reliable.

Forensic evidence almost always requires an "expert witness," someone who either processed the evidence and testifies to what he or she concluded, or an expert hired

---

1. 509 U.S. 579 (1993).

to evaluate the work or report of a forensic laboratory and give an opinion about what the test results mean. The expert witness must be qualified by training and/or experience before he or she can testify, which is another battleground we will examine.

The language of the opinion permitted by courts varies based on history and the ability of a jury to look at the evidence and draw their own conclusions. For example, historically, fingerprint experts have been permitted to declare that a fingerprint they have examined is a "match" to the defendant's fingerprint and that it was made by the defendant and no one other than the defendant. Yet DNA experts typically give an opinion, for example, that the chance a DNA sample taken from a rape kit matches anyone other than the defendant is 1 in 300 million. Why this difference? You will see that in part it is because fingerprint experts were permitted to give their "match" opinion long before DNA evidence was available. The other reason is that fingerprint evidence is not used for anything other than criminal investigations, whereas DNA evidence resulted from rigorous scientific studies as the human genome was mapped. Finally, a jury is frequently shown a picture of the crime scene fingerprint and the defendant's fingerprint. They can see for themselves the similarities. Of course, the crime scene print is frequently smudged and incomplete, so the ability of a jury to make a meaningful comparison is often impaired.

We will also look at areas of forensics that are considered "junk science," rather than true science. Junk science is a term used for a type of forensic evidence that has not been subjected to scientific testing and validation. As we will see, the question of how much testing is sufficient is not a bright line. Polygraph, for example, is generally viewed as reliable in measuring blood pressure and sweat. But can these physical measurements correspond to truthfulness? Does the fact that polygraph reliability varies widely based on the training and experience of the person who formulates the questions mean that it is not science because it cannot be replicated by anyone? Bitemark analysis is an example of something that sounds like science, but has never been tested. Can bitemarks conclusively identify a person? Unlike fingerprints, which have been subjected to a test (albeit flawed) of 50,000 fingerprints, bitemarks have never been tested at all. Can a person be identified by his smell? This is another topic that may or may not be reliable. Do MRIs of certain areas of the brain indicate the defendant is violent or dangerous? We will examine these and similar contentions.

The U.S. Constitution bears on a number of important issues relating to forensic evidence. A major issue is whether a defendant has the right to confront and cross-examine the individual who processed a forensic sample. In the case of DNA, for example, the prosecutor generally offers a report conducted by an outside laboratory and asks an independent expert to explain its significance. The issue arose in 2009 in a case called *Melendez-Diaz v. Massachusetts*,[2] in which the U.S. Supreme Court held that a criminal defendant has a constitutional right to confront the lab technician who ran a forensic test used as evidence against him. The particular facts related to a test of a white substance found on the defendant and identified by a laboratory report

---

2. 557 U.S. 305 (2009).

entered into evidence as cocaine. In this case, the results of the report were admitted to prove a fact in issue — that the powder was cocaine — but the defendant was not able to cross-examine the analyst who tested the powder to determine what test was performed or whether the analyst used any judgment in interpreting the results.

The Supreme Court stated that forensic evidence is not immune from manipulation, particularly by scientists who may feel pressure from a law enforcement official to alter evidence in a manner favorable to the prosecution. It cited a commentator whose research showed over 60% of overturned criminal convictions involved invalid forensic testimony.[3] Finally, it said that the ability to confront and cross-examine the analyst could expose incompetent analysts:

> Contrary to respondent's and the dissent's suggestion, there is little reason to believe that confrontation will be useless in testing analysts' honesty, proficiency, and methodology — the features that are commonly the focus in the cross-examination of experts.[4]

This case could have far-reaching implications for an already-overburdened forensic laboratory system if individual lab technicians must leave work to testify in court. Following *Melendez-Diaz*, the Supreme Court has held that the Confrontation Clause also requires the analyst who tests blood alcohol levels[5] to be present for cross-examination, but rejected the argument that the analyst who tests a DNA sample at an outside laboratory must appear. Although the U.S. Supreme Court in *Williams v. Illinois*[6] later held in a plurality opinion that DNA test results were not "testimonial" and therefore did not trigger the Confrontation Clause, at least one court has restricted that opinion to its unusual facts and declined to follow it, holding that at least certain personnel involved in DNA testing must be present to testify. This issue can be expected to have widespread implications in the future.

In 2009, the National Research Council of the National Academies released a report entitled *Strengthening Forensic Science in the United States: A Path Forward* (referred to in this text as the NRC Report).[7] The report resulted from a congressional mandate to the National Academy of the Sciences to study both research and the technical practice of the forensic science community. It was influenced, no doubt, by a widely reported decision by a federal court in Philadelphia that banned a fingerprint expert on the ground that fingerprint matching was not sufficiently scientifically reliable. Although the opinion was later withdrawn, calls for research about fingerprinting promptly ensued.

The NRC Report stated that fingerprinting and 11 other areas of forensic evidence (other than DNA) had not been sufficiently scientifically validated. It also concluded

---

3. Brandon L. Garrett and Peter J. Neufeld, "Invalid Forensic Science Testimony and Wrongful Convictions," *Virginia Law Review* 95, no. 1 (2009): 14.

4. *Melendez-Diaz, supra* at 321.

5. *Bullcoming v. New Mexico*, 564 U.S. 647 (2011).

6. 132 S. Ct. 2221 (2012).

7. The National Academies Press, Washington, D.C., www.nap.edu.

that testing and training in forensic examination varied widely among the states. It made 13 recommendations, including the creation of a federal agency to "establish and enforce best practices for forensic science professionals and laboratories," to be called the National Institute of Forensic Science. It called for standardized laboratory reports and terminology and the development of quantifiable measures of uncertainty in the conclusions of forensic analyses.

The report highlighted a "major problem" in the forensic science community:

> The simple reality is that the interpretation of forensic evidence is not always based on scientific studies to determine its validity. This is a serious problem. Although research has been done in some disciplines, there is a notable dearth of peer-reviewed published studies establishing the scientific bases and validity of many forensic methods.[8]

Substantial funds will have to be found to conduct peer-reviewed scientific studies, studies that may be of use only to the crime enforcement community. Without support from the academic scientific community, it may be difficult to achieve the type of scientific testing this board recommended.

Subsequent to this report, Congress established an Office of Forensic Science Improvement and Support (OFSIS) to direct forensic science-related research and standard-setting. The Department of Justice is to direct accreditation, certification, and compliance enforcement of the standards set by OFSIS. As of June 26, 2014, the Department of Justice and the U.S. Commerce Department's National Institute of Standards and Technology had named 17 academic researchers and forensic science experts to a Forensic Science Standards Board. And by May 2016, this board had issued some standards for public comment as well as a number of calls for research studies, including one for Forensic Document Examination Friction Ridge (fingerprint) analysis, and Firearms and Toolmarks.

This text will present a number of case studies in which forensic evidence was presented and contested in court. Some, such as the O.J. Simpson case, the Amanda Knox case, and the JonBenét Ramsey case may be familiar to you. Others, such as the kidnapping and murder of the Lindbergh baby, the Sam Shepherd murder trial, and the Richard Crafts "wood-chipper murder" took place before DNA profiling, yet involved forensic issues such as blood spatter analysis, crime reconstruction, and handwriting analysis. We will also refer frequently to a Connecticut "cold case," *State v. Edward Grant*, in which Grant was convicted of murdering Penney Serra twenty-five years after the crime. The arrest and conviction were triggered by a routine run of fingerprints in cold cases through the AFIS computer fingerprint matching system.

Here is a short summary of the case of *State v. Grant*.[9] Edward Grant was convicted in 2002 for the 1973 murder of Concetta "Penney" Serra in a New Haven, Connecticut, garage. Serra had driven her car into the garage and parked on the top floor. At some

---

8. NRC Report, p 8.
9. A detailed case record appears in the Appendix to this text.

point, her attacker got into her car, a fight ensued with a knife, and his blood, which was Type O, was left in the car (and in a trail throughout the garage, believed to have been left by the attacker as he looked on foot for his own car after the crime). The blood was typed but DNA profiling was not yet invented. Serra then fled across the lot and tried to escape up a staircase, which was locked at the top. Her body was found stabbed at the foot of the stairs. She was not raped and nothing was taken from her car. Based on these facts, investigators believed the murder was a "crime of passion" by someone Serra knew. They interviewed three former boyfriends and put them in a lineup for possible identification by some people who had been in the garage. A prior boyfriend of the victim was identified the following day in a lineup, but he was ruled out based on his blood type. Another was arrested and charged with the crime, but charges were dropped on the eve of trial when it turned out his blood type did not match the Type O blood trail either.

Investigators lifted one clear fingerprint from a tissue box on the floor behind the driver's seat. The print did not match any of the fingerprints on card files in New Haven at the time. (The Automated Fingerprint Identification System, AFIS, was not yet in operation.) They also found a handkerchief four flights down in the garage, which they initially thought was unconnected to the crime. They later connected it based on a blood trail in the garage, which they believed was the attacker's as he searched the garage trying to find his own car. Blood typing showed the victim's blood type — A — was found where Serra was killed, but Type O blood, believed to be the attacker's, was present in the trail and in the car.

The case remained a "cold case" for almost twenty-five years until Chris Grice, a fingerprint examiner in the Connecticut State Forensic Laboratory (who had been involved as one of the investigators in New Haven twenty-five years prior), did a cold case run of the fingerprint from the tissue box through AFIS. As we will see in the "Fingerprint Analysis" chapter, the AFIS report was a series of numbers identifying people. Grice then needed to pull actual prints and visually compare them. Ed Grant was not number 1 on the list. However, Grice eliminated the higher numerical "matches" and identified Grant as the print on the box.

The *Grant* case is unique in that the defendant was convicted based on two pieces of forensic evidence and virtually nothing else. There was no evidence that he had ever met Penney Serra. No one saw the fight in the car, Penney's flight to the stairs, or the stabbing. The few witnesses at the time — other drivers and the garage ticket taker — were inconsistent in their descriptions of a man driving erratically in the garage. The ticket taker said he was handed a bloody parking ticket by a driver in a car that did not match any Grant ever owned and the man spoke with a foreign accent. Grant had no accent.

Grant's attorneys did not deny that the forensic tests were accurate, but argued that there was no evidence to prove that the fingerprint was impressed on the tissue box at the time of the crime, so even if it was Grant's, it didn't prove he was in the car the day Serra was murdered. Nor was there any testimony that proved the handkerchief was Grant's or that it was dropped at the time of the crime. They also questioned how only one small spot of "blood" could have remained testable after years of investigators moving the handkerchief from place to place under conditions that deteriorated the rest of the spots beyond testing. None of these arguments were persuasive to the jury.

Grant's main argument on appeal was that his arrest warrant lacked probable cause because it was based on a fingerprint on a moveable object — the tissue box in the car — and there was no proof that the fingerprint was placed on the tissue box at the time of the crime. The court was not persuaded and denied Grant's appeal:

> In most of the cases relied on by the defendant, the courts held that fingerprint evidence with a possible innocent explanation was insufficient to support a finding of guilt *beyond a reasonable doubt.* The mere possibility of an innocent explanation for evidence connecting a defendant with a crime does not, however, preclude a finding of probable cause.[10]

This text will examine the *Grant* case and many other court cases where forensic evidence has been contested in the following primary areas:

- DNA
- Fingerprints
- Firearms and Ballistics
- Toolmarks
- Computer Forensics
- Eyewitness Identification
- Blood Spatter
- Handwriting

This text will also discuss these questions:

- How does the way crime scene investigators handle evidence affect whether it is admissible in court?
- What is circumstantial evidence? Is it as good as direct evidence? Is forensic evidence direct evidence or circumstantial?
- Does a jury have to believe a forensic expert witness?
- Why does an appeals court allow an evidence ruling of a trial court to stand, even where the appeals court disagrees with the decision of the trial court?
- How can a prisoner who believes he is innocent get access to crime scene DNA for post-conviction testing?
- Is the judge better than the jury in deciding whether scientific testimony is reliable? Why not just let all forensic evidence in and let the lawyers cross-examine the opposing experts?

---

10. 286 Conn. 499, 518, 944 A.2d 947, 962 (2008).

- How does the Constitution apply to the defendant's right to confront and cross-examine experts who tested forensic evidence?
- When does the possible prejudice to a defendant of introducing evidence justify excluding it?
- How does the fact that a forensic fingerprint examiner must use his subjective judgment in comparing fingerprint samples affect its admissibility?
- When must an expert simply present forensic evidence to a jury (such as handwriting) and let the jury decide if it matches, rather than giving an opinion?
- How have evidentiary principles been applied to digital evidence?
- Is firearm and toolmark evidence appropriate for expert testimony?
- How have advances in psychological sciences affected the admissibility of both eyewitness identification and expert testimony on eyewitness identification?

Forensic Evidence in Court

Chapter 1

Using Forensic Evidence to Prove Ultimate Issues

Overview

What is the nature of forensic evidence? What does it "prove"? How can it be used to prove issues in a criminal trial? Is all forensic evidence "circumstantial"? What role does the law of probability play in forensic evidence? What types of "expert opinions" can forensic experts offer? When should the jury be able to look at the evidence and come to its own conclusions about the meaning of the evidence? Are some types of forensic evidence so powerful that they can unduly sway or "prejudice" a jury? We will examine these questions in detail.

Forensic evidence is any evidence based on science, technique, or expert evaluation entered into evidence at trial. It frequently requires an expert to explain the evidence to the jury. The expert's "opinion" is valuable to the party who presents the expert because it often links the evidence to an issue the jury must decide. The danger that the jury will be unduly impressed by the expert is called the "white coat" effect.

The jury must find all "elements" of a crime by a standard of beyond a reasonable doubt. For the crime of murder, depending on the state or federal crime, there are generally three elements:

- the defendant is the perpetrator,
- the defendant intended to cause death, and
- the defendant's acts caused the victim's death.

These three findings are the "ultimate issues" in a prosecution for murder.

Forensic evidence can also be classified depending on whether it is based on a class characteristic or an individual characteristic. For example, if a size 10 shoeprint is found at a crime scene and a suspect wears a size 10 shoe that looks similar, the shoeprint is only a class characteristic. In order to become an individual characteristic, the shoeprint at the crime scene must have some unique feature (such as a wear pattern, a tack stuck in the sole, etc.) that makes the shoeprint unique. Otherwise, the suspect's shoe is simply in a class of prints that are included in the crime scene print. If, on the other hand, the suspect wears a size 7 shoe, the suspect can be excluded as the source of the print. Class characteristics are useful primarily to exclude.

An individual characteristic is a DNA match at all 13 loci tested in a typical DNA test. As we will see in the DNA chapter, such a "match" means that it is virtually certain the suspect is the source of the DNA (but not necessarily proof of how the DNA was deposited at the site or when). Chapter 4, "The Scientific Method and 'Junk Science,'" explains more about forms of forensic evidence and what they can prove.

Most forensic evidence is circumstantial evidence. That means it may prove a fact from which the jury will need to infer or conclude another fact in order to reach a decision about guilt or innocence. The jury is not required to find that each circumstantial fact is true beyond a reasonable doubt, as long as the cumulative evidence proves guilt beyond a reasonable doubt. The level of certainty for *beyond a reasonable doubt* is not 100%. Proof beyond a reasonable doubt is proof that precludes every reasonable hypothesis except guilt and is inconsistent with any other rational conclusion.

Hearsay evidence is evidence of statements made by someone who is not in court to testify or be cross-examined about the statement. It is generally not admissible. Reports of forensic tests that contain conclusions are considered hearsay. They may not be admitted in court without the person who made the conclusions being available to be cross-examined. The Confrontation Clause of the U.S. Constitution also requires that a defendant be able to cross-examine all witnesses against him, including any forensic analyst whose report is "testimonial" in nature. We will consider the Confrontation Clause in Chapter 2, "The Court Process."

Forensic evidence requires an expert to explain the significance of the evidence to the jury. The jury is free to accept or reject the testimony of an expert witness, just as for any other witness. There are rules of court that govern experts. At the federal level, the rules are Federal Rules of Evidence 702, 703, and 705, which govern the admission of forensic evidence in all federal trial courts. Most states have similar rules. You will learn about other rules governing trials in the chapter called "The Court Process."

Chapter Objectives

Based on this chapter, students will be able to:

1. Define forensic evidence.
2. Understand the standard of evidence for a verdict.
3. Understand Federal Rules of Evidence 702, 703, and 705.
4. Appreciate the jury's role as finder of fact.
5. Understand court instructions that explain a jury is free to reject an expert opinion.
6. Distinguish between direct and circumstantial evidence.

7. Describe the ultimate issues in a criminal trial and be able to identify their relationship to the legal elements of a crime.

8. Define the hearsay rule and the exception in the *Crafts* case.

9. Identify the legal standard of proof for ultimate issues determined by one or more inferences from circumstantial evidence.

What Is Forensic Evidence?

The term "forensic" does not mean "scientific." It means "of or used in legal proceedings or formal debate."[1] Forensic evidence consists of any physical thing that can be used in a court of law as evidence of a fact in issue. Although we think of forensic evidence as relating only to criminal trials, it also applies to civil matters, such as whether a particular drug causes injury. Forensic psychology is used to determine which parent would be best suited to have custody. Forensic accounting is used to determine the value of business assets.

> Forensic evidence consists of any physical thing that can be used in a court of law as evidence of a fact in issue.

How Is Forensic Evidence Used in Criminal Trials?

As we will discuss, forensic evidence is evidence resulting from a scientific test or analysis to be used in a criminal trial. This includes: physical items discovered in the course of investigating a crime, such as a gun, knife, document, photograph, piece of clothing, etc. The evidence to be admitted must be "authenticated" by a witness who can identify it and explain its "chain of custody," which means how it got from the crime scene to the courthouse. See Chapter 3, "Crime Scene Investigation." It also includes the results of tests conducted by investigators, such as tests of DNA, fingerprints, fiber, hair, or dental records. Finally, it may involve the results of experiments designed to reconstruct a crime or crime scene, involving the forensic science of ballistics or blood spatter. See Chapter 3.

In 2009, The National Research Council published a report (the NRC Report) called *Strengthening Forensic Science in the United States*.[2] It examined the scientific reliability of many areas of forensics, as follows:

- fingerprints
- firearms examination
- tool marks
- bite marks
- impressions (tires, footwear)

---

1. *The American Heritage Dictionary*, 4th ed., Dell Publishing, 2001, "forensic."
2. *Strengthening Forensic Science in the United States, A Path Forward*, National Research Council, The National Academies Press, http://www.nap.edu/catalog/12589.html.

- bloodstain pattern analysis
- handwriting
- hair
- DNA
- coatings (e.g., paint)
- chemicals (including drugs)
- materials (including fibers)
- fluids
- serology
- fire and explosive analysis
- digital evidence

The NRC Report recommended further testing to show scientific reliability in each of these areas of forensic evidence except DNA. Even for DNA, it recommended standards for training, laboratories, and reporting. We will review many of these in the chapters to come.

Proof of Ultimate Issues

Forensic evidence, by itself, does not prove guilt. It is admitted to prove or disprove a fact in a criminal trial that may lead to a finding of guilt. The two most frequent facts are:

1. The identity of the perpetrator.

2. What happened at the crime scene.

"Ultimate issues" are issues which the jury must decide in order to determine its verdict.

"Ultimate issues" are issues which the jury must decide in order to determine its verdict. They are generally determined by the definition of the crime. For the crime of murder, the ultimate issues are the legal elements of the crime. These include generally (1) whether the defendant is the person who committed the crime, (2) whether the defendant acted with the intent required for the specific crime, and (3) whether, in accordance with that intent, the defendant carried out the act or acts necessary to commit the crime.

The Federal Rules of Evidence prohibit an expert from giving an opinion about an ultimate issue, although the opinion may "embrace" an ultimate issue:

Rule 704. Opinion on an Ultimate Issue

(a) In General—Not Automatically Objectionable. An opinion is not objectionable just because it embraces an ultimate issue.

(b) Exception. In a criminal case, an expert witness must not state an opinion about whether the defendant did or did not have a mental state or condition that constitutes an element of the crime charged or of a defense. Those matters are for the trier of fact alone.

Standard of Proof

The jury is not required to find that each fact is true beyond a reasonable doubt, as long as the cumulative evidence proves guilt beyond a reasonable doubt. The level of certainty for *beyond a reasonable doubt* is not 100%. Proof beyond a reasonable doubt is proof that precludes every reasonable hypothesis except guilt and is inconsistent with any other rational conclusion.

Typically, forensic evidence, by itself, will not prove guilt or innocence. The jury reaches a verdict: guilty or not guilty. It makes that one decision and is not required to explain what other facts it decided were true or not. For example, a jury could reject the defendant's alibi evidence and still conclude that the prosecution had not proved its case beyond a reasonable doubt. We rarely know what facts a criminal jury has determined to be true in giving its verdict.

> Proof beyond a reasonable doubt is proof that precludes every reasonable hypothesis except guilt and is inconsistent with any other rational conclusion.

Identification

Identifying a suspect can result from eyewitness identification. It can also result indirectly from DNA, fingerprinting, and handwriting analysis. Examples of the type of forensic evidence used to identify a perpetrator are as follows:

1. DNA in a sperm kit that matches the defendant's DNA.
2. Defendant's fingerprint on a weapon he owns and that was used to kill the victim.
3. Defendant's shoeprint in blood at the crime scene.
4. Hair collected from the crime scene that matches the defendant.

As we will discuss below while examining the concept of circumstantial evidence, none of this evidence proves the defendant committed a crime. For example, defendant may say the sex in #1 was consensual. Defendant may say in #2 that his fingerprint is on the gun from a prior occasion, but someone stole his gun to commit the crime and wore gloves. In #3, defendant may admit his shoe matches the print, but so do 300,000 other people who own that shoe. In #4 defendant may admit he has the same type of hair, but so does 20% of the population (I'm assuming no hair root for DNA testing).

Proving What Happened

Typically, forensic evidence can be used to help reconstruct a crime, which is relevant to the ultimate issue of whether the defendant, with the appropriate level of intent, did the "act" set out in the legal elements of the crime. Attempting to prove "what happened" may involve evaluating a pattern of bloodstains, tool marks on a doorway, or fingerprints on a weapon. This has led to the concept of crime scene analysis. Again, some forensic evidence is better than others. In general, the more science based, the more reliable. For example, the trajectory of a bullet can be measured by scientific means. An expert can state the place the shooter must have been standing when the bullet was fired. Blood spatter can be measured. Its size and shape will prove the velocity and type of weapon.

But crime scene analysis involves many, many steps and not all will be consistent. For example, in the *Grant* case, investigators first decided a handkerchief found on a lower level of the garage was not related to the crime. The criminologist Henry Lee agreed when he was asked to review the evidence at the time of the crime. Then they came up with a new hypothesis that involved Grant running through different floors of the garage looking for his car, finally finding it, and dropping his handkerchief four floors below where the crime took place. The theory was that Grant then left in his car; hence, the handkerchief and the keys to Serra's car, both of which were on that level, did not make any sense without that hypothesis. The DNA on that handkerchief was crucial in convicting Grant. What is important to note is that the crime scene analysis required a number of subjective judgments before the handkerchief could even be connected to the crime.

Individual vs. Class Characteristics

One way of examining the value of forensic evidence is to ask whether it proves an individual or a class characteristic. An individual characteristic requires that the form of forensic evidence be unique to the suspect. For example, DNA and fingerprints prove an individual characteristic if we accept the scientific hypothesis that no two people share the same DNA or the same fingerprints. As we will see, this conclusion is only valid if there is sufficient scientific testing to prove statistically that a match proves individuality.

Individual characteristics are those characteristics in evidence that conclusively identify a suspect.

Individual characteristics are those characteristics in evidence that conclusively identify a suspect. For example, in fingerprint identification, the examiner can determine positive identification by comparing a fingerprint left at a crime scene with the suspect's fingerprint. This assumes that the crime scene print is clear and complete enough to make a valid comparison.

Shoeprints, fiber, toolmarks, and many other forms of forensic evidence prove only a class characteristic. In other words, the evidence includes a suspect along with many other people. However, class evidence can effectively exclude a suspect. If, for example, the hair sample is blonde straight hair and the defendant has black curly hair, the evidence excludes the defendant. Class evidence can do no more than "include" the suspect in a class of people who share that type of evidence.

Class evidence can do no more than "include" the suspect in a class of people who share that type of evidence.

Hair is an example. Even if a hair from the crime scene under magnification looks exactly like the suspect's, there is no scientific basis for concluding that the hair from the crime scene actually came from the defendant, unless the hair is tested for DNA. In other words, assume 30% of the population has the exact same color and quality of hair. In the *Crafts* case, the hair found on the hillside where witnesses saw the wood chipper looked under a microscope to be identical to a hair belonging to Helle Crafts that had been found in her bedroom. However, science does not support the conclusion that each person's hair is unique. Therefore, the most an expert could say is that the hair from the site was "consistent" with the hair of Helle Crafts. This is the typical expert opinion given for a class characteristic.

One case demonstrating the results of an improper opinion on a class characteristic is the conviction of Mark Reid in Connecticut for sexual assault and kidnapping. In that case, an expert testified that he compared a hair recovered from the victim's clothes to a sample from the defendant and found "that the characteristics of the known hairs from the defendant were similar to the characteristics of those recovered from the victim's clothing."[3] This was a proper opinion about a class characteristic, but it was wrong, because the hair was ultimately determined not to be either a pubic hair or negroid. You will see in Chapter 7, on DNA, that Reid on appeal was able to show that the hair was not his, based on mitochondrial DNA testing.

The same is true for shoeprints. The suspect may own a pair of shoes that creates an identical print to that found at the crime scene; however, so may 100,000 other people. In order to "individuate" the defendant, the prosecution would have to prove that the defendant's shoes were one of a kind, or that some mark on them, such as a tack stuck in the sole in a particular location, made such a rare mark that it could only be defendant's.

This does not mean that footprint evidence is inadmissible. However, an expert cannot testify that it absolutely identifies the defendant. The *Mahone* case below involves this issue.

United States v. Mahone, 328 F. Supp. 2d 77 (D. Maine 2004)

While footwear impression evidence may appear to the Defendant a simple matching process not requiring any specialized skill, and Ms. Homer's testimony will "provide undeserved weight to a comparison which the jury as fact finder is equally qualified to make," it is apparent the process requires a critically trained eye to ensure accurate results.

The Defendant's contention that any lay person can perform the comparisons presumes any lay person will know what to look for and how to apply the information — the significant versus insignificant markings and the weight to ascribe each. In this way, the examiner functions like a radiologist, directing attention to the relevant aspects of the impression or medical image. That the conclusion is readily apparent after the professional explains the image more likely speaks to the effectiveness of the professional, not the simplicity of the science.

Further, even if the Court accepts the Defendant's contention that a lay person could arrive at the conclusion for herself, Ms. Homer's testimony is admissible under Rule 702 because it will undoubtedly assist the trier of fact

---

3. *State v. Reid*, 254 Conn. 540 (2000), pet. for new trial granted, CV020818851 2003 Conn. Super. LEXIS 1496 (Conn. Sup. 2003).

in determining whether the impressions from the crime scene match those from the shoes.

Science vs. Junk Science

Forensic evidence is also only as valuable as the tests to prove it is scientifically valid. Bite marks, for example, have never been scientifically tested. That is, no one has tested whether a bite mark can conclusively identify a person or even an animal. Therefore, bite mark matching is what is called "Junk Science." That doesn't mean that prosecutors will not try to introduce it at trial or find an expert who will give an opinion that it matches the defendant's teeth. As you will see in the Chapter 4, "The Scientific Method and 'Junk Science,'" courts have admitted bite mark evidence in the past, but a 2016 report from the President's Council of Advisors on Science and Technology stated that bite mark matching is not valid science: "available scientific evidence strongly suggests that examiners cannot consistently agree on whether an injury is a human bitemark and cannot identify the source of a bitemark with reasonable accuracy."[4]

Qualifications of the Forensic Expert and Freedom from Bias

Finally, an important issue is who did the testing and who is testifying. In the case of DNA, two large independent laboratories run DNA tests. They are given no information about the source of the DNA, the identity of any suspects, or the nature of the crime. In the case of fingerprinting, fingerprints are frequently run through a computer system called AFIS to see if there is a print on file with "ridge characteristics" in the same location, but the final match must be made by an expert who visually compares two prints, thus introducing a subjective element. Any time a subjective element is required, two examiners could differ in their opinion. And any time this is possible, the results veer from pure science, which requires that given the same data, the same result will invariably occur.

Once law enforcement is involved in the testing, or the crime scene reconstruction, a potential element of bias is introduced, which can affect the results. This is why DNA is viewed as the "gold standard" of forensic evidence. First, it was developed by the scientific community for reasons unrelated to law enforcement. Second, if the DNA testing is performed by Profiler or Cellmark, the two commercial laboratories used by the FBI, the laboratory personnel do not know anything about the crime or the suspect and are employees unrelated to law enforcement. Fingerprint analysis, by contrast, is primarily used for identification by law enforcement. Although fingerprints are frequently sent to a federal database called AFIS for an initial list of

---

4. Jordan Smith, "White House Report Concludes that Bite Mark Analysis Is Junk Science," *The Intercept*, September 7, 2016, https://theintercept.com/2016/09/07/white-house-report-concludes-that-bite-mark-analysis-is-junk-science.

possible matches, a fingerprint examiner, typically part of law enforcement, must visually inspect any possible matching fingerprints and use his or her training and judgment to decide: positive identification, inconclusive, or elimination. See Chapter 6 on "Fingerprint Analysis." Any time the process is conducted by law enforcement, there is therefore the possibility of bias and in the worst case, fraud. A number of cases have been overturned due to revelations that DNA results, where the testing was handled by law enforcement, were deliberately falsified. See Chapter 8, "Firearms and Toolmarks."

Eyewitness Identification

Many prisoners have been convicted on the strength of a positive identification by a victim. Eyewitness identification is direct evidence, someone stating that he or she saw a crime being committed by the defendant. It is powerful. And it is sometimes wrong. Some of these prisoners have been exonerated by DNA, even though the victim still believes that his or her visual identification was correct. Besides the fact that many people *do* look alike, there are other factors that may show visual identifications are particularly "unscientific." We will examine these in Chapter 10, "Eyewitness Identification." You will see that the scientific proposition that a suspect of a violent crime will be able to categorically identify the perpetrator even when the crime takes place for only a few minutes and under extraordinary stress has been seriously undermined by testing and research.

Rules Governing Admitting a Forensic Expert's Testimony

An expert is a witness who, because of his knowledge, skill, experience, training, or education, may testify to assist the trier of fact, usually the jury, to understand the evidence or to determine a fact in issue. An expert opinion is the testimony of an expert as to the significance of the evidence to a fact in issue.

The Federal Rules of Evidence, and related rules applicable in state courts, have specific sections, Rules 702, 703, and 705, that pertain to expert testimony.

Rule 702 was amended after a U.S. Supreme Court case called *Daubert v. Merrell Dow* (discussed in Chapter 5 on the *Daubert* rule) to require that expert opinion testimony be scientifically reliable. It was most recently amended in 2011, and currently reads as follows:

Rule 702. Testimony by Experts

A witness who is qualified as an expert by knowledge, skill, experience, training, or education may testify in the form of an opinion or otherwise if:

(a) the expert's scientific, technical, or other specialized knowledge will help the trier of fact to understand the evidence or to determine a fact in issue;

(b) the testimony is based on sufficient facts or data;

(c) the testimony is the product of reliable principles and methods; and

(d) the expert has reliably applied the principles and methods to the facts of the case.

Many states have adopted language similar to Rule 702. Some retain an older test that allows expert testimony on scientific or technical topics if the area of testimony is "generally accepted" by the scientific community. Many of the cases we will read involve challenges to an expert's qualifications, sometimes because he or she lacks experience and sometimes because the "expert" works for law enforcement and the defendant argues the expert may be biased (this is covered by (a) above). Others involve a challenge to the area of testimony as lacking scientific reliability, which is covered in (b)–(d) above.

Federal Rules of Evidence 703 and 705

These rules require an expert to disclose the basis for his or her opinion and any facts or data upon which the expert relied:

Rule 703. Bases of Opinion Testimony by Experts

The facts or data in the particular case upon which an expert bases an opinion or inference may be those perceived by or made known to the expert at or before the hearing. If of a type reasonably relied upon by experts in the particular field in forming opinions or inferences upon the subject, the facts or data need not be admissible in evidence.

Rule 705. Disclosure of Facts or Data Underlying Expert Opinions

The expert may testify in terms of opinion or inference and give reasons therefore without first testifying to the underlying facts or data, unless the court requires otherwise. The expert may in any event be required to disclose the underlying facts or data on cross-examination.

As mentioned earlier, Federal Rule of Evidence 702 was the subject of an important United States Supreme Court case, *Daubert v. Merrell Dow*, in 1993. In this case, the U.S. Supreme Court required that the trial court hold a hearing before trial and outside the presence of the jury to determine if expert forensic testimony was valid "science." The case listed criteria the trial court should use in making that decision. It also decided that Rule 702 superseded an earlier federal court case that set down a different rule for accepting expert testimony. This case is discussed in detail elsewhere. There is no federal rule that requires that experts have any specific training or experience in order to testify.

There is no federal rule that requires that experts have any specific training or experience in order to testify.

However, the attorney offering the expert will ask about the expert's qualifications in the presence of the jury, and would be foolish to offer a witness without qualification. Opposing counsel would destroy the expert's credibility on cross-examination. Experts frequently rely on textbooks or other "learned articles" in their area of expertise. Where the expert has not done any independent research but relies only on the expertise of others, some courts have held the expert is not qualified. Generally, the expert must establish independent knowledge in the area of testimony. The expert must also have personally examined the evidence to give an opinion.

An expert cannot give an opinion as to who committed the crime, but only an opinion as to the forensic facts. For example, in the *Grant* case, Chris Grice, the fingerprint expert, testified that in his expert opinion, the latent fingerprint lifted from the tissue box found in Penney Serra's car was made by Edward Grant. However, he could not testify as to when the fingerprint was placed on the tissue box. He could not testify that, in his opinion, Grant had been in Penney Serra's car. After all, the print could have been deposited before the box got in the car. He also could not testify that in his opinion, Grant murdered Serra. The jury could infer that Grant was in the car; the jury could further infer that he was in the car on the day of the murder and that he was, therefore, the murderer. The forensic evidence in that case, however, does not prove those facts.

Chain of Custody

Finally, to the extent that a forensic expert testifies about a piece of concrete evidence (for example, a gun or a piece of clothing), counsel must offer evidence establishing a chain of custody of the item. For example, in the *Grant* case, the jury heard testimony about a latent fingerprint lifted from a tissue box that was found in the back seat of Penney Serra's car. In order for the fingerprint expert to testify, counsel must establish that the box was taken by law enforcement officers at the scene and logged in under proper procedures. Moreover, the article must have been stored properly, and it must have been logged in and logged out by anyone who handled the evidence. In general, its presence, and the conditions of its storage, must be accounted for from the time it was found to its presentation at trial. The prosecution must be able to establish the entire "chain of custody" by testimonial or documentary evidence. In fact, the defense objected to the chain of custody because the Serra evidence had been kept in a basement for years where it was said to have deteriorated. The court disagreed and admitted the evidence.

The prosecution must be able to establish the entire "chain of custody" by testimonial or documentary evidence.

The Expert "Opinion"

Generally, a piece of forensic evidence requires an expert to explain its significance to the jury. The expert usually testifies to three things:

- What the forensic evidence consists of.
- The process the expert used to evaluate the forensic evidence.
- The expert's "opinion" as to the significance of the evidence to a fact in issue at trial.

We will examine at length the various types of opinions the courts will allow. However, it is the ultimate opinion that is of primary value to the party presenting the evidence. That party hopes to convince the jury that if an expert comes to a certain opinion, then that opinion has more weight, and therefore is more likely to be true,

Expert Opinion. An expert is a witness who, because of his knowledge, skill, experience, training, or education, may testify to assist the trier of fact, usually the jury, to understand the evidence or to determine a fact in issue. An expert opinion is the testimony of an expert as to the significance of the evidence to a fact in issue.

than if the evidence were simply offered to the jury without an opinion. This is called the "white coat effect," the hope that the aura of respectability and superior knowledge of the expert will convince the jury to accept this opinion.

Jury Instructions on Expert Testimony

A jury is free to accept or reject an expert opinion. The judge will tell the jury at the end of trial during jury instructions. Here is an example from the *Grant* trial:

> You have heard some testimony of witnesses who have testified as expert witnesses. Expert witnesses are witnesses who, because of their training, skill, education and experience, are permitted not only to testify about facts that they have personally observed, but to state their opinions.
>
> In making your decision whether to believe an expert's opinion, you should consider the expert's education, training and experience in the particular field, the information available to the expert, including the facts the expert had and the documents or other physical evidence available to the expert, the expert's opportunity and ability to examine those things, the completeness or incompleteness of the expert's report, the expert's ability to recollect the facts that form the basis for the opinion, and the expert's ability to tell you accurately about the basis for the opinion.
>
> You should ask yourselves about the methods employed by the expert and the reliability of the result. You should further consider whether the opinions stated by the expert have a rational and reasonable basis in the evidence.
>
> Based on all of these things together with your general observation and assessment of the witness, it's up to you to decide whether or not to accept the opinion. You may believe all, some or none of the testimony of an expert witness. An expert's testimony is subject to your review like that of any other witness.[5]

Forensic Evidence Is Circumstantial Evidence

Direct evidence is evidence that can be used to prove a disputed fact directly — eyewitness testimony, for example. When an eyewitness says "the man sitting at that table is the man I saw shoot the victim," that testimony is direct evidence of the act of homicide. Circumstantial evidence is evidence that is probative of a fact indirectly in that it can prove one fact from which the finder of fact can conclude another fact is true. For example, evidence that the defendant owned a gun of the same type that killed the victim *may* mean that the defendant shot the victim, but only if the jury makes a number of additional inferences based on that fact.

Let's say investigators recover a gun from the crime scene. The gun is forensic evidence. If investigators then introduce evidence that the defendant owns the gun

A jury is free to accept or reject an expert opinion.

"[T]he fact that a witness has qualified as an expert does not mean that you have to accept that witness's opinion. You could accept an expert witness's opinion or reject it in whole or in part."

Circumstantial evidence is evidence that is probative of a fact indirectly in that it can prove one fact from which the finder of fact can conclude another fact is true.

---

5. Transcript, May 22, 2002, at 160–1.

found at the crime scene, this fact does not prove also that the defendant was the person who fired the gun. However, the first fact is "probative," because based on that fact, perhaps along with other facts, the jury may determine that the defendant fired the gun at the crime scene. A fact is "probative" if the jury would find it relevant in determining the truth or falsehood of some fact in issue in a case. Forensic evidence is therefore generally circumstantial evidence because it requires the jury to *find another fact or facts based upon it* in order to conclude guilt or innocence.

From this example, you can see that most forensic evidence is circumstantial evidence. Although defense attorneys often try to convince a jury that it is wrong to convict a defendant based on circumstantial evidence, because circumstantial evidence is somehow not good evidence, or of lesser value than direct evidence, it is the rare trial where a jury does not make inferences from some evidence to determine ultimate issues and guilt or innocence.

In the *Grant* case, for example, the presence of Type O blood at a crime scene may have convinced the jury to conclude that Grant was present in the garage and bled on the garage floor at the time of the murder. However, as the defense pointed out, there is no way to "date" when the blood was put there, and it is possible to "plant" blood, as the jurors in the O.J. Simpson apparently concluded the police did. The jury, as finder of fact, was therefore free to conclude from the evidence of Type O blood that the blood came from Grant or that it did not. In that sense, the Type O blood was circumstantial evidence of the presence of Grant in the garage. It was also circumstantial evidence of *when* Grant was in the garage and of *how* his blood got there.

Circumstantial evidence therefore is proof of a fact from which the jury[6] can infer another fact. The trial judge in *Grant* gave the jury a standard instruction to explain what circumstantial evidence is:

> You may consider both direct and circumstantial evidence. Direct evidence is testimony by a witness about what that witness personally saw or heard or did. Circumstantial evidence is evidence involving inferences reasonably and logically drawn from proven facts.
>
> Let me give you an example of what I mean by direct and circumstantial evidence. If you wake up in the morning and see water on the sidewalk, that is direct evidence that there is water on the sidewalk. It is also circumstantial evidence that it rained during the night. Of course, other evidence such as a turned on garden hose may explain the water on the sidewalk.[7]

The instruction given under Ohio law on circumstantial evidence in the trial of Sam Sheppard, convicted in 1955 for the murder of his wife, was somewhat different:

> It is for you to determine how much of circumstantial evidence adduced in this case is credible and what fair inferences are to be drawn from it. You

Probative.
A fact is probative if the jury would find it relevant to prove an issue in the case.

---

6. I will refer to the finder of fact as the "jury," although a judge in certain circumstances can also be a finder of fact.

7. Transcript, May 22, 2002, p. 134.

are instructed that any inference drawn must in every instance be drawn from a proven or established fact. In other words, you are not to draw a second or further inference upon an inference but that is not to say that you are confined to drawing only one inference from one fact.

There is no limit to the number of independent inferences that may be drawn from a fact. The rule is simply that every inference must be drawn from, and based on, a fact and that once having drawn an inference one may not draw a second inference from the first.

It is necessary that you keep in mind, and you are so instructed, that where circumstantial evidence is adduced it, together with all other evidence, must convince you on the issue involved beyond a reasonable doubt and that where circumstantial evidence alone is relied upon in the proof of any element essential to a finding of guilt such evidence, together with any and all other evidence in the case, and with all the facts and circumstances of the case as found by you must be such as to convince you beyond a reasonable doubt and be consistent only with the theory of guilt and inconsistent with any theory of innocence. If evidence is equally consistent with the theory of innocence as it is with the theory of guilt it is to be resolved in favor of the theory of innocence.[8]

The jury in the *Sheppard* case was told that they were not permitted to draw one inference based on another inference. Yet, as you can see from the list of inferences presented below for the *Crafts* case, a jury typically needs to make multiple inferences from certain facts in order to determine guilt. An appeals court in the *Crafts* case held that an instruction like the one in *Sheppard* violated the law. It held that the law does not require that any fact be determined by a standard of beyond a reasonable doubt. Only guilt must be found beyond a reasonable doubt.

Assuming a jury believes a fingerprint expert when he testifies that a print lifted from a crime scene "matches" or "identifies" the defendant, what does that mean? Does it mean that the defendant was at the crime scene? Absent an unusual circumstance, such as someone taking an imprint of the defendant's finger and deliberately planting it at the crime scene, yes, the testimony proves that the defendant left his print at the scene. But does it prove *when* the defendant left the print? No, it does not. Fingerprint experts agree that a fingerprint cannot be "dated." Does it prove that the defendant committed the crime, say a burglary, at the scene? For the fingerprint to be proof of the defendant's guilt, the jury must *infer* from the presence of the fingerprint at the crime scene that the defendant was there at the time of the crime and further, that he committed the crime.

Say the defendant has an alibi. He proves that he was in the hospital on the date of the burglary. Now what can the jury infer? It must infer that the fingerprint was placed at the scene on some other date and does *not* tend to prove the defendant was

---

8. *Ohio v. Sheppard*, 165 Ohio St. 293, 300–301 (Ohio 1956).

the burglar. Although the public tends to believe that forensic evidence "proves" guilt, this is rarely the case.

Even the presence of the defendant's semen in a rape victim does not "prove" the defendant raped the victim. The sex may have been consensual. The sex may have taken place up to 12 hours before the rape, which can be proved by determining if the cells are still active or "motile," which can occur for up to twelve hours. Perhaps the victim has semen from more than one source in her vagina. These were some of the defenses in the Kobe Bryant trial. It was reported that DNA tests showed the victim was sexually active shortly after the time she reported the rape had occurred.[9] What seems "open and shut" can often be highly speculative.

What alternative theories might prevent the jury from "jumping to conclusions" based on inferences from circumstantial evidence? For example, the Simpson jury could well have found that the bloodstains at Nicole Simpson's home were O.J. Simpson's. That fact would be probative on the issue of whether he was the source of the blood. The jury could also have found that the blood was planted at the scene and did not result from O.J. Simpson having been actually present at the murder site. Likewise, they may have concluded that Nicole's blood was on O.J.'s sock without necessarily concluding that the blood got on the sock during O.J.'s murder of Nicole. Any of these conclusions would have prevented the fact of the presence of Simpson's blood from implicating him in the murder of Nicole Brown Simpson.

Here are some examples of ultimate issues that a jury may infer from circumstantial forensic evidence. Each "therefore" below is an inference from the preceding fact.

- Is the defendant the person who did the act?

  The presence of blood matching the defendant's DNA profile can be used to conclude that the defendant was the source of the blood. Therefore, the defendant was at the crime scene at some point. Therefore, the defendant was at the crime scene at the time of the crime. Therefore, the defendant was the perpetrator.

  The latent fingerprint lifted from the crime scene can be used to conclude that the defendant was the source of the fingerprint. Therefore, the defendant was at the crime scene at some point. Therefore, the defendant was at the crime scene at the time of the crime. Therefore, the defendant was the perpetrator.

  The defendant's handwriting appears on the ransom note. Therefore, the defendant wrote the note. Therefore, the defendant was the kidnapper.

- What happened and did the defendant do it?

  The blood spatter pattern shows where the assailant was standing, the angle of the blows, the force of the blows, etc.

  The gunpowder residue shows how close the gun was to the target.

---

9. Patrick A. Tuite, "Kobe Case Offered Lessons in Greed and Sordidness," *Chicago Lawyer*, April 2005.

Each of these "what happened" facts must then be linked to the defendant if the jury is to find him guilty.

Case Study in Circumstantial Evidence: The Richard Crafts Case

On November 19, 1986, a flight attendant named Helle Crafts was reported missing. A Connecticut jury later convicted her husband, Richard Crafts, of murdering his wife, putting her body in a freezer, renting a wood chipper, and chopping up her body in the chipper. The case was a major event because it was the first time in Connecticut that a jury was asked to convict someone of murder without a dead body.

A review of the facts introduced in evidence illustrates the difference between direct and circumstantial evidence.

Here is what the direct evidence showed:

- On November 17, Crafts picked up a new freezer.
- Crafts told a witness that his old freezer had stopped working and he had taken it to the dump.
- On November 19 at 6 a.m., Crafts put his children in his car to go to his sister's house in Westport. It was snowing and the children were not dressed for the weather.
- Crafts later told witnesses he went to his sister's house because his house had no heat.
- Crafts' house had kerosene heaters, fireplaces, and a generator.
- Crafts told his children that his wife, Helle, had already gone to his sister's house.
- Helle was not at his sister's house and was never seen again.
- On November 20, Crafts rented a truck and a wood chipper, as demonstrated by receipts.
- Between 3 and 4 a.m. on the night of November 21, witnesses saw a man in the vicinity of a steel bridge in Newtown, Connecticut, operating a wood chipper.
- At 4 a.m. on November 21, Crafts told a co-worker in the parking lot of the Town of Southbury offices that he rented the wood chipper to clean up limbs from the November 18 storm.
- There were no limbs down on Crafts' property after the November 18 storm.
- On November 21, Crafts returned the truck and wood chipper.
- The state began to investigate Helle's disappearance.
- Crafts made a number of conflicting statements as to where Helle was, such as at her sister's in Europe.

- When Crafts learned that state divers were looking for Helle's body, he told his brother-in-law, "Let them dive. There's no body. It's gone."
- Investigators found the following evidence near the bridge: an envelope with Helle's name on it; blue fabric consistent with her uniform, pieces of bone and tissue, a human fingernail painted with fingernail polish consistent with that used by Helle, and crowns to some teeth.
- The crowns were identified as Helle's through dental records.
- Investigators found a chain saw in the water with blood, tissue, hair, and cotton fiber. The blood, tissue, and hair were consistent with Helle's blood type and a hair found in her home.
- Helle had told several witnesses before she disappeared that if she suddenly disappeared, it would not be of her own free will.

Each of these pieces of evidence is direct evidence — statements made, items rented, tests on hair and fiber. But the jury needed to make inferences from each piece of evidence to determine whether Crafts killed his wife. Therefore, the direct evidence was circumstantial evidence of another fact and *that* fact was circumstantial evidence of guilt of the crime.

Here are a few examples of the inferences the jury would need to draw from the evidence it heard to the issues required to determine guilt of murder.

1. Purchase of new freezer and absence of old one. The jury could infer that Crafts put his wife's body in the old freezer, lied about it being broken, showing evidence of guilt, and bought a new one to falsely demonstrate the old one was broken.

2. Rental of the wood chipper. The jury could infer that it was Crafts that witnesses saw at 3 a.m. on the hill, that Crafts was cutting up his wife whom he had previously murdered and stuffed in the freezer, and that he had premeditated the crime by renting the wood chipper in advance. The rental of the wood chipper is circumstantial evidence of those facts.

3. Presence of Helle's tooth crown on hill. The jury could infer that the tooth got there when her body was being cut up, that Crafts was the one operating the chipper and that Crafts killed her.

The cumulative power of all of the direct and circumstantial evidence was overpowering. On appeal, the court affirmed the conviction.[10] Crafts is still incarcerated.

Were Helle's Statements Admissible under the Hearsay Rule?

The statements Helle made to friends about her fear of Crafts' killing her would normally not be admitted. Any statement made by a witness who is not in court, and therefore cannot be cross-examined, is hearsay and is not admissible to prove that

---

10. *State v. Crafts*, 226 Conn. 237 (1993).

Hearsay.
A statement, other than one made by the declarant while testifying at the trial or hearing, offered in evidence to prove the truth of the matter asserted.

the statement was true. Here is the definition of hearsay under the Federal Rules of Evidence:

(c) Hearsay. "Hearsay" means a statement that:

(1) the declarant does not make while testifying at the current trial or hearing; and

(2) a party offers in evidence to prove the truth of the matter asserted in the statement.[11]

The purpose of the hearsay rule is to guard against testimony that may not be true, where the opposing party has no opportunity to cross-examine the person who made the statement in order to test whether or not it is true. As Helle was definitely not available to testify, her statement could not be admitted to prove that because she said she was afraid Crafts might kill her, it was likely that he did kill her. Nicole Brown Simpson's diary in which she stated her fear that her husband might kill her was kept out of evidence because of the hearsay rule.[12]

However, the court ruled that the statement could come in under one of the many exceptions to the Hearsay Rule. In general, statements that are hearsay can sometimes be admitted into court if their purpose is not to prove that the statement was true — for example, that Helle was afraid Crafts would kill her — but for a different purpose — in this case, to prove that Helle would not have left her home and children voluntarily. The court would probably still not have allowed the statement, as it was highly prejudicial to Crafts, but Crafts himself had argued before the court that Helle had left voluntarily. Therefore, Crafts "opened the door" to letting the prosecution introduce Helle's statements to counter or "impeach" Crafts' assertion that Helle left voluntarily.

Dissent.
An opinion written by one or more judges in an appeal in which they disagree with the decision of the majority opinion.

Although the majority of the appellate court judges voted to affirm Crafts' conviction, two judges wrote a strong dissent opposing the admission of Helle's statements. They argued that her statement that if she suddenly disappeared, it would not be voluntary on her part, could just as easily be proof that she *did* run away in fear of Crafts. They would have excluded the statement.

Fingernail, Hair, Fiber, Tooth, and Tissue

The fingernail, hair, fiber, tooth crown, and tissue were all forensic evidence. If the jury chose to believe the forensic experts, they could conclude that all this forensic evidence came from Helle. But that is all the forensic experts could say. They could give no opinion about how the items came to be there or whether Crafts was guilty of murder. Some of the evidence, such as the strand of hair, were consistent with Helle's hair, but not unique. It was up to the jury to draw inferences from the forensic

---

11. Federal Rule of Evidence 801.

12. Neal A. Hudders, "The Problem of Using Hearsay in Domestic Violence Cases: Is a New Exception the Answer?," *Duke Law Journal* 49 (February 2000): 1041, 1067.

evidence. If body parts of Helle's were found near a bridge where a man was seen with a wood chipper at night, what could they infer? They could infer that Helle was dead; they could infer that she was chipped into small pieces, and they could infer that Crafts did it. All the forensic evidence was circumstantial evidence for these three important conclusions.

Standard of Proof Where One Inference Depends on Another

Crafts' first trial resulted in a hung jury. At his second trial, he was convicted and sentenced to fifty years in prison. He appealed, arguing that the jury was required to find *each fact* necessary to build upon another fact by the standard of "beyond a reasonable doubt." The Connecticut Supreme Court heard this appeal in 1993 and denied Crafts' claim. Even though Crafts' conviction rested almost exclusively on circumstantial evidence, the court held that the jury had used the correct legal instructions and upheld the conviction. Here is part of the opinion:

State v. Crafts, 226 Conn. 237 (1993)[13]

The principal issue in this criminal appeal is the sufficiency of largely circumstantial evidence to support a conviction for the crime of murder. The state charged the defendant, Richard B. Crafts, with having committed the crime of murder in violation of General Statutes § 53a-54a, by killing his wife, Helle Crafts.

After an earlier trial resulted in a mistrial because of the jury's inability to arrive at a verdict, the state retried the defendant and a jury found him guilty of murder. The trial court then rendered a judgment sentencing the defendant to a term of fifty years' imprisonment. The defendant appeals his conviction to this court pursuant to General Statutes § 51-199(b)(3). We affirm.

At the trial, the state's theory of the offense was that the defendant had intentionally killed the victim as a result of the deterioration of their marriage. To conceal detection of the crime, the defendant had allegedly devised and executed an elaborate plan to destroy the victim's body. In support of this proposition, the state presented extensive, but primarily circumstantial, evidence describing the couple's marital troubles as well as the defendant's actions during the fall and winter of 1986–1987 to establish that the defendant, with the requisite intent, had murdered the victim. The defendant maintained, to the contrary, that he had not killed his wife, but that he nonetheless did not know her present whereabouts.

The jury could reasonably have found the following facts. Because of the defendant's continued extramarital affairs, the victim contacted an attorney

---

13. Throughout this text, I have edited cases by omitting certain sections, deleting citations and footnotes, and altering paragraphing in order to improve clarity in reading. I have included some footnotes that appeared in the original court opinions, marked without the original footnote numbers, but indicated as [footnote].

and began divorce proceedings against him. She hired a private detective, who carried out surveillance of the defendant. The detective confirmed that the defendant was involved with another woman, and presented the victim with photographs of the defendant's activities. Not only was the defendant himself aware of the victim's intention to divorce him, but she also had told a number of people of her plans.

The victim's marital troubles would not, however, have led to her voluntary departure from her home and family. The victim was extremely devoted to her children, was planning to seek their custody in the divorce proceedings, and would not under any circumstances have left them voluntarily. Furthermore, the victim warned several people that, if anything unusual were to happen to her, they should not believe that such an event was of her own making.

The victim was last seen or heard from on November 18, 1986, as she was dropped off at her home by a coworker. On the morning of November 19, 1986, the defendant ushered the children and the family's live-in au pair helper from the home at 6 a.m. to leave for his sister's house in Westport purportedly, according to what the defendant told the au pair helper at the time, because of the lack of heat due to a power failure during a snowstorm the night before.

The defendant's home, however, had alternative sources of heat, including kerosene heaters, a fireplace, and a generator. The victim was not present, and at that time the defendant explained that she had left earlier, probably to go to his sister's house. In his rush to leave the house, the defendant made no attempt to dress the children for the severe weather and drove through difficult conditions to leave the children with his sister in Westport.

Although the victim was not at the sister's house, the defendant neither mentioned her absence nor inquired regarding her whereabouts. The jury could reasonably have inferred that, in light of all of the evidence, the defendant had already killed the victim during the night and was proceeding with the execution of his plan to conceal the crime.

Thereafter, the defendant offered to different parties various stories regarding his wife's whereabouts, all of which were demonstrated to be incorrect. In addition to the explanation for the victim's absence on the morning of November 19 offered as he brought his children to his sister's house, he initially told several of the victim's friends that in fact she had gone to Denmark to be with her ill mother. He later began to tell acquaintances that the victim might be visiting her friends overseas. In an interview with the police on December 4, 1986, the defendant indicated that he had last seen the victim on November 19, 1986, but that, at the time of the interview, she might be visiting a friend in the Canary Islands.

Besides numerous inaccurate and contradictory statements regarding the victim's whereabouts, the defendant also made several incriminating remarks to acquaintances regarding the police investigation, which the jury could reasonably have found to indicate further a consciousness of guilt. For instance, when advised by his brother-in-law of the state police diving efforts, the defendant replied, "Let them dive. There's no body. It's gone."

Relying on this evidentiary showing, the jury hearing the defendant's case found him guilty of murder as charged. The defendant's appeal challenges his conviction on five grounds. He claims that the trial court improperly:

(1) denied his motion for acquittal because his conviction, resting primarily on circumstantial evidence, was the result of impermissible inferences that were not supported by proof beyond a reasonable doubt, thereby denying his right to due process;

(2) instructed the jury that it might infer specific intent to commit murder from the mere fact of the death of the victim, thus denying his right to due process;

(3) refused to instruct the jury on three lesser included homicides not requiring a finding of intent to kill;

(4) admitted into evidence out-of-court statements made by the victim to others; and

(5) denied him a fair trial because of extensive pretrial publicity implicating, again, his right to due process.

We are unpersuaded.

...

In light of the state's presentation of extensive circumstantial evidence, the principal issue raised by this claim is whether special procedural rules govern the validity of the jury's ultimate findings regarding each element of the crime of murder if, in making these findings, the jury presumably relied upon sets of multiple inferences, in other words, inferences derived from previous inferences.

The defendant maintains that recourse to multiple inferences potentially leads to speculative ultimate findings. From this premise, he contends that due process requires that a verdict of guilty depending on such inferences cannot be sustained unless each successive inference is itself established beyond a reasonable doubt. We reject this contention.

Due process requires that the state prove each element of an offense beyond a reasonable doubt. It follows that insufficiency of the evidence to support a jury's ultimate findings on each of these elements requires acquittal.

...

Due process does not, however, require that each subordinate conclusion established by or inferred from evidence, or even from other inferences, be proved beyond a reasonable doubt. We have regularly held that a jury's

Due process does not require that each subordinate conclusion established by or inferred from evidence, or even from other inferences, be proved beyond a reasonable doubt.

factual inferences that support a guilty verdict need only be reasonable. Equally well established is our holding that a jury may draw factual inferences on the basis of already inferred facts.

...

The defendant's argument that a special standard of proof is required to guard against attenuated probabilities associated with inferences based on inferences is, however, an argument the basis of which we have previously considered and rejected. More than seventy years ago, we concluded, in *Sliwowski v. New York*, that "there is, in fact, no rule of law that forbids the resting of one inference upon facts whose determination is the result of other inferences...."

It is but a rule of caution; its true function is to guide the court in the exercise of its judgment in determining whether or not evidence offered is too remote ... or, in making its final decision, in deciding whether the plaintiff has established a reasonable probability."

We have adhered to that position, noting that "it is not one fact, but the cumulative impact of a multitude of facts which establishes guilt in a case involving substantial circumstantial evidence."

... As we explained, however, in *State v. McDonough*, "Where a group of facts are relied upon for proof of an element of the crime, it is their cumulative impact that is to be weighed in deciding whether the standard of proof beyond a reasonable doubt has been met and each individual fact need not be proved in accordance with that standard. It is only where a single fact is essential to proof of an element ... such as identification by means of fingerprint evidence, that such evidence must support the inference of that fact beyond a reasonable doubt."

...

[The Hearsay Objection]

The defendant claims that the trial court incorrectly allowed the state to introduce into evidence certain statements made by the victim tending to show the victim's belief that, if something should "happen" to her, it would not be the result of her own actions. He claims that the statements were inadmissible because they were hearsay, irrelevant and prejudicial. We find no reason to overturn the trial court's rulings.

Over the defendant's objections, the state presented the testimony of five witnesses who offered statements made by the victim during the fall of 1986. Diane Andersen, the victim's attorney handling the divorce proceeding, testified that the victim had told her that "if something should happen to her I should not assume that it was an accident." Lee Ficheroulle, a coworker and friend, testified that the victim had told her that "her husband would find her wherever she went ... [and that] he would have an alibi and a well thought out plan."

. . .

Our review of claims of alleged error in evidentiary rulings is limited. The issue before us is whether the trial court's admission of this testimony was an abuse of its discretion.

The defendant initially claims that these out-of-court statements were hearsay. An out-of-court statement is hearsay, however, only if it is offered to prove the truth of the matter asserted in the statement. As the trial court correctly observed, because the state offered the evidence to establish only the victim's state of mind, the statements were not hearsay.

A statement that is offered to establish circumstantially the state of mind of the declarant is not offered for the truth of the statement.

. . .

In the present case, similarly, the victim's state of mind became relevant when the defendant questioned whether the victim was in fact dead, or was merely missing or in hiding. Although not overtly adopted as a "theory of defense" at trial and although disavowed on appeal, the defendant's assertion that he was not guilty because the "victim" had voluntarily left the country or had otherwise disappeared without leaving a trace appears repeatedly in the trial record.

Additionally, the defendant at trial challenged not only the state's assertion that the human fragments in evidence at trial proved that a person had died, but also its claim that the human fragments were those of an identifiable victim, his wife. This evidence of the victim's state of mind, therefore, was probative of whether she was likely to leave. From this evidence the jury could have concluded that, despite the victim's concern for her safety, she intended to remain with her family.

. . .

The defendant claims that the testimony regarding the five statements by the victim referring to the defendant was unduly prejudicial because the jury may have focused on the alleged accusatory aspect of the statements and, despite the court's curative instructions, may have impermissibly considered them as probative of the defendant's conduct rather than as evidentiary of the victim's state of mind.

We recognize the risk of prejudice in allowing surrogates to speak for the victim "pointing back from the grave." We conclude, nonetheless, that the defendant has not established that the trial court, which carefully evaluated the statements, noted the absence of any direct accusations of the defendant and determined that in this case the statements were not unduly prejudicial, abused its discretion by admitting them into evidence.

The judgment is affirmed.

A statement that is offered to establish circumstantially the state of mind of the declarant is not offered for the truth of the statement.

The defendant claims that the testimony regarding the five statements by the victim referring to the defendant was unduly prejudicial because the jury may have focused on the alleged accusatory aspect of the statements. . . .

DISSENT:

Berdon, J., dissenting....

I would reverse on the ground that the trial court abused its discretion by admitting into evidence the hearsay statements of the alleged victim, Helle Crafts. Helle Crafts' lawyer and friends were permitted to testify, over the defendant's objection, that Helle had stated that if anything happened to her they should not believe it was an accident and that the defendant would have a well-planned alibi. The majority justifies the admission of these statements on the ground that they were not offered to prove the truth of the matter asserted, but merely to show Helle Crafts' state of mind. But how is her state of mind relevant in this case? The majority concludes that her state of mind is relevant to disprove the "theory" of the defendant's defense — that is, Helle Crafts is still alive.

To me, the victim's fear of the defendant, if relevant at all, would tend to support the opposite conclusion — that she ran off out of fear. The logic of the state's argument, that Helle's fear and apprehension show that she would not have left voluntarily — eludes me. How could one logically conclude that, because she feared the defendant and was apprehensive about him, she was dead. In *State v. Duntz*, dealing with the precise issue of whether the deceased's hearsay statements of fear may be admitted into evidence, we held the admission of such evidence to be reversible error. "The victim's alleged fear of the defendant was not relevant, and therefore ... the testimony was not admissible under the state of mind exception to the hearsay rule. Evidence is relevant only if it has some tendency 'to establish the existence of a material fact.'"

...

Furthermore, the claim that Helle Crafts was still alive was not the "theory of defense" in the defendant's second trial. The defendant did not testify at the second trial; rather, the state introduced the defendant's testimony from the first trial, thereby raising this issue. Similarly, defense counsel did not argue this theory to the jury in closing argument. The majority merely passes this off by stating that although it was "not overtly adopted," it was in the record. It was in the record, but only because the state put it there.

...

To admit into evidence these hearsay statements, which tend to prove the crime for which the defendant was charged, violates the defendant's constitutional rights "to be confronted by the witnesses against him" and to due process of law.

Circumstantial Evidence in the *Grant* Case

The two major pieces of forensic evidence against Ed Grant were both circumstantial. The fingerprint on the tissue box, identified as belonging to Grant, proved only that Grant had touched the tissue box sometime before the crime was committed, as the fingerprint was under a bloodstain, presumably put on the box during the crime. In order to use this "fact" to convict Grant, the jury needed to draw the following inferences:

- Grant was present at some point in Serra's car;
- Grant reached for and touched the tissue box at some point when he was in the car;
- Grant subsequently touched the same part of the tissue box and smeared his blood on it;
- Grant then placed the tissue box on the floor behind the driver's seat of Serra's car;
- Grant had a reason for picking up the box, presumably to get a tissue or tissues;
- Grant used the tissue or tissues and then removed them from Serra's car and took them with him when he left the garage;
- Grant was bleeding as a result of a fight with Serra, presumably as a result of a cut with the same knife that was used to kill Serra, which was never found;
- Grant used the knife to kill Serra in the stairwell of the garage.

The Handkerchief

The second piece of forensic evidence was the handkerchief, which expert Henry C. Lee concluded in 1989 was not connected with the crime. He later revised his opinion when he had learned that a DNA test of genetic material on the handkerchief had identified Grant. In order to conclude that the DNA test proved Grant murdered Serra, the jury would have to make the following circumstantial conclusions:

- The handkerchief belonged to Grant.
- The blood spot on the handkerchief that identified Grant was placed on the handkerchief in the garage at the time of the murder.
- The blood spot resulted from a fight between Grant and Serra in which Grant was cut with a knife that he used in the murder.
- Grant dropped the handkerchief on the 7th floor of the garage after driving Serra's car around looking for his own car, leaving her car on level 8, proceeding on foot until he found his car on level 7, and then throwing out both Serra's car keys and his own handkerchief before fleeing.
- One blood spot on the handkerchief survived 23 years of being moved around for testing and being subjected to heat and other conditions likely to degrade the DNA.
- The presence of Grant's bloodstained handkerchief in the garage proved that he was in a fight with Serra that resulted in his bleeding on the handkerchief at the time of the crime, and therefore he murdered Serra.

The jury doubtless did not move step-by-step through this logic. Absent any strong alternative explanations, they concluded that the forensic evidence put Grant at the crime scene and so Grant committed the crime. The defense argued that Grant may have touched the tissue box at the Pathmark before it was purchased. They also argued that it was too incredible that one blood spot on the handkerchief could survive degradation over time. The jury was apparently not convinced by either argument.

Summary

Forensic evidence is any evidence based on science, technique, or expert evaluation entered into evidence at trial. It frequently requires an expert to explain the evidence to the jury. The expert's "opinion" is valuable to the party who presents the expert because it often links the evidence to an issue the jury must decide. The danger that the jury will be unduly impressed by the expert is called the "white coat" effect.

The admission of forensic expert testimony in federal court is governed by Federal Rules of Evidence 702, 703, and 705. These rules require that the expert show the methodology to be testified to is scientifically reliable. Similar rules of evidence have been adopted by state courts, although some state courts retain an older test of scientific reliability which requires only "general acceptance" by the scientific community.

Forensic evidence does not, by itself, prove ultimate issues, which are the legal elements of any crime. For example, one legal element of murder is whether the defendant is the person who did the act. Forensic evidence of defendant's DNA or fingerprints at the crime scene *may* be used by the jury to conclude that ultimate issue, but the jury can choose not to accept the expert's opinion or can conclude another innocent explanation for the presence of the evidence.

Most forensic evidence is circumstantial evidence. It may tend to prove a fact from which the jury will need to infer or conclude another fact in order to reach a decision about guilt or innocence. The jury must find all "elements" of a crime by a standard of beyond a reasonable doubt. This standard is more than a *preponderance of the evidence*, but it does not require 100% certainty.

The legal test is that the jury must find guilt beyond a reasonable doubt, but this does not mean the jury must find each circumstantial "fact" to be true beyond a reasonable doubt. In the *Crafts* case, these elements were whether Crafts was the perpetrator, whether he intended the act, and whether that act resulted in Helle's death. In *State v. Crafts*, the Connecticut Supreme Court held that the jury can find individual facts based on circumstantial evidence by a standard of a "preponderance of the evidence." It rejected Crafts' argument that each circumstantial fact must be proved by a standard of beyond a reasonable doubt.

Hearsay evidence is evidence of a statement made out of court by a witness who is not present to be cross-examined and which is admitted to prove a fact or conclusion in the statement. Hearsay was an issue in the Crafts trial. Statements made by Helle, his wife, that she feared he might kill her were admitted even though they were hearsay under one of the exceptions to the rule. A report of a forensic expert's opinion qualifies as hearsay. Therefore, the expert who made the opinion must be present in court to be available for cross-examination.

Discussion Questions

1. What does the term "forensic" mean? Before you began this course, what did you think it meant?

2. Why does forensic evidence generally require an expert at trial to introduce and explain it?

3. What is the white coat effect? Do you believe juries today are influenced by it?

4. What is the difference between forensic evidence, proof of ultimate issues, and a finding of guilt?

5. What are individual v. class characteristics?

6. What does it mean for the jury to be a finder of fact?

7. What are Federal Rules of Evidence 702, 703, and 705 and how do they affect the admission of an expert's opinion testimony?

8. How is an expert "qualified" at trial to testify?

9. Is a jury required to accept an expert's opinion? Why or why not?

10. What is chain of custody and why is it important?

11. What is the difference between circumstantial and direct evidence?

12. What is the standard of proof the court used in the *Crafts* case for the proof of issues based on multiple inferences from circumstantial evidence?

13. What is the difference between beyond a reasonable doubt and a preponderance of the evidence?

14. Why do the rules of evidence prohibit hearsay evidence? What exception was used to admit statements made by Helle Crafts? Do you believe the court decided Crafts' objection to this testimony rightly or wrongly? Why?

Chapter 2

The Court Process: Procedure, Law, and Rules of Evidence

Overview

There are separate court systems for federal prosecutions and state prosecutions. There are federal courts in all states and they are all bound to follow one set of federal rules governing trial procedure and evidence. Each state also has its own court system with its own set of rules. These may be patterned after the federal rules or may be different. Therefore, it is important to determine whether a crime will be prosecuted in a federal or state court. Sometimes, both courts can prosecute the same underlying conduct if that conduct violates a federal law and a state law.

Forensic evidence cannot be admitted in trial before a trial judge or a jury unless the party who wishes to introduce the evidence follows the proper court process, including all applicable rules of evidence. These rules are contained in the Federal Rules of Evidence for cases in federal court and in similar laws adopted by each state for trials held in those states. We will primarily discuss the Federal Rules of Evidence, as they apply in federal courts in all states.

Most crimes have a defined set of legal elements that appear in state or federal statutes. The jury must find each legal element by a preponderance of the evidence (51% or more). It must find guilt, however, by the standard of beyond a reasonable doubt. This does not mean 100% certainty. Proof beyond a reasonable doubt precludes every reasonable hypothesis except guilt and is inconsistent with any other rational conclusion. We will review a typical jury instruction of the standard of proof for a crime.

The jury is the sole finder of fact, but it must apply the law as given to it by the judge. At the trial's conclusion, the judge will give the jury instructions about how to apply the law to the facts. Usually, each side in a trial will "propose" a set of jury instructions favorable to their view of the law. The judge must then decide which specific instructions to give. Take the crime of murder, for example. The legal elements of murder are legal tests to which the jury must apply the facts.

Rules of evidence are designed to safeguard all parties against the introduction of unreliable or impermissibly prejudicial evidence. Evidence must be relevant to the legal issues in the case. If prejudice would result to the defendant from the introduction of the evidence, the court may exclude that evidence. The rules of evidence contain separate rules for admitting testimony by experts, which we reviewed in Chapter 1. These rules govern forensic testimony and provide that testimony by a qualified expert is admissible only if it will assist the jury to understand the evidence or determine a fact in issue.

"Judicial Notice" means that a trial court may accept a fact as having been proved without either party putting on evidence. The reliability of the science of DNA has been the subject of judicial notice, meaning that a party does not have to put on proof of what DNA or DNA testing consists of. The jury may still refuse to accept a fact that is judicially noticed or any other evidence.

The Confrontation Clause of the U.S. Constitution has been held to apply to forensic testimony. If any report of forensic investigation performed by someone not in court is attempted to be introduced, the defendant will likely object that the person who performed the test be available to testify. The courts are still testing the limits of this rule, in particular as it may relate to various personnel involved in DNA testing. If the report is "testimonial" in nature, the court is likely to rule the writer of the report must testify.

Court decisions in federal courts are binding precedent on the courts below them. For example, a decision by a federal circuit court is binding on all the federal courts in that circuit. This is called "precedent," meaning the courts must all follow the decision. The U.S. Supreme Court decisions are binding on all federal courts (if on a matter of federal law) and on all states as well (if the decision involves a question under the U.S. Constitution). We will read cases from both state and federal courts, so it is important to ask what the precedential value of the case may be.

Both state and federal courts maintain trial courts, intermediate appellate courts, and a supreme court. Typically, a defendant may appeal as of right (assuming he meets time requirements and presents a "question of law" that was raised at trial) to the intermediate appellate court. The supreme court generally takes a final appeal only if it chooses to. Finally, both state and federal prisoners may bring a habeas corpus action before a federal trial court on the issue of whether his imprisonment violates the U.S. Constitution.

Appellate courts do not take evidence or determine facts. They are bound by the trial record as to facts. Their job is to determine if an error of law was made by the trial court that justifies reversing a conviction. They defer to decisions of the trial court, unless there was an abuse of its discretion. They may note an error took place, but affirm a conviction regardless if it was "harmless error," meaning that there is sufficient evidence of guilt without looking at the evidence that is tainted by an error to conclude a reasonable jury would have found the defendant guilty.

Chapter Objectives

Based on this chapter, students will be able to:

1. Explain the difference between state and federal courts.

2. Describe the difference between trial and appellate courts.

3. Understand the concept of double jeopardy.

4. Identify the legal elements of the crime of murder in their state.

5. Understand the concept of relevance and the Federal Rules 401 and 402.

6. Describe Federal Rule of Evidence 403 and the balancing test used to keep prejudicial evidence out of the trial.

7. Evaluate the federal rules relating to evidence of prior crimes or bad acts in terms of possible prejudice to a defendant.

8. Explain the concept of judicial notice and how it applies to forensic evidence.

9. Understand the appellate and habeas corpus procedure and the standards of review in each.

10. Describe how the U.S. Constitution Confrontation Clause affects what forensic analysts must testify in court.

The Rules of Evidence Govern the Admission of Evidence

State and Federal Courts Have Different Rules

This country has a dual system of courts: each state has its own court system and the federal government also has an entirely separate court system. Crimes that violate state law are heard in state trial courts. Crimes that violate federal law are heard in federal courts. In the federal system, the trial court is called a "district court": The United States District Court for the Southern District of New York is an example. There are 94 separate judicial districts in the United States. In Connecticut, the trial court is called the Superior Court for the Judicial District (county) in which the trial takes place: The Superior Court for the Judicial District of New Haven is an example.

Both state and federal trial courts have written rules which govern procedure, what types of evidence are admissible, and the appropriate admission procedure. The defendant has a right to a trial before a jury in both court systems. (The defendant may waive that right, and have his or her case tried by a judge without a jury. A trial before a judge without a jury is called a court trial or a bench trial.) Therefore, the first question in determining whether certain evidence will be admissible is whether the matter is being heard in state or federal court.

The elements of a crime that must be proved will be found in either the state code of criminal law or in a federal statute making a certain act a crime. (We will discuss

> Crimes that violate state law are heard in state trial courts. Crimes that violate federal law are heard in federal courts.

> A trial before a judge without a jury is called a court trial or a bench trial.

later acts that can be both a state and federal crime.) Once the elements of the crime are known, the prosecution then must present evidence on each of the elements (unless the parties have agreed beforehand or "stipulated" to a fact or element). The prosecution goes first. It must introduce evidence to prove each of the elements of the alleged crime. The defendant does not need to present a defense, testify, or otherwise refute the prosecution's case. He is not required to offer an alibi or an alternate theory of how the crime occurred. The burden is entirely on the prosecution.

The Role of the Courts in Admitting Evidence

When the prosecution or the defense seeks to admit evidence, the attorney will "offer" the item in evidence. It will then be marked as an exhibit and given a number. Generally, the prosecution and defense have exchanged lists of evidence prior to the trial so there are no surprises when an item is offered. If the other side objects to the evidence on a legal ground, that party must state the objection before the court, which generally will rule immediately on whether the evidence can be admitted. If it is admitted "over a party's objection," that objection remains in the trial record and can form the basis for a later motion to dismiss or an appeal.

> If evidence is admitted "over a party's objection," that objection remains in the trial record and can form the basis for a later motion to dismiss or an appeal.

The courts rule on the admissibility of forensic evidence at two levels: the trial court and the appellate court. The trial court is where the jury hears evidence, finds facts, and decides the ultimate questions, such as whether defendant is liable for a plaintiff's injuries in a civil trial or whether defendant is guilty of the offense charged in a criminal trial.

Motions

Motions are a significant part of the trial process in criminal and civil cases in both court systems. A motion is a request by an attorney for a party in a case that the court take an action or refrain from taking an action. A motion may be as significant as a request that the trial court dismiss an entire case. On the other hand, a motion may be as mundane as a request for a two-day extension of time to complete a court-ordered task. Motions are most frequently submitted to the court in written form with a copy of the submission to the lawyers for the opposing parties. In turn, the lawyers for the opposing parties submit a written response after which the court makes a decision called a ruling. Often, the court will hold a separate hearing on a motion involving the taking of testimony and admission of other evidence. One example is a motion to exclude evidence on the theory that it was obtained without a warrant in violation of the defendant's constitutional rights.

> A motion is a request by an attorney for a party in a case that the court take an action or refrain from taking an action.

When forensic experts are involved, if an opposing party challenges the introduction of expert testimony on a scientific issue, he may request the trial court to hold a hearing outside the presence of the jury before the trial begins to determine whether the subject of the expert's testimony is reliable and is based on good science. If the court refuses to hold such a hearing, this may form the basis for appeal.

Frequently, these rulings are accompanied by a written opinion. If the court rules against the moving party, that party can appeal the issue after the conclusion of the trial to an appellate court.

Motions in the *Grant* Case

Grant's Motion to Exclude DNA Evidence

Grant made many motions to exclude particular pieces of evidence. The defense wanted the DNA evidence excluded on the ground that the form of DNA testing known as Short Tandem Repeat ("STR") testing was not yet proven reliable. The court denied that motion. The defense also moved unsuccessfully to exclude the handkerchief bearing a sample of Grant's DNA on the ground that it had been moved from place to place since 1973 without a proper "chain of custody." That motion also was denied.

The DNA evidence identified Grant based on statistics cited by Dr. Carll Ladd that the chance of someone other than Grant being the source of the genetic material on the handkerchief was less than one out of 300 million. Public Defender Brian Carlow argued that the DNA profile was fatally flawed because it failed to detect certain "gene pairs" in blood on the handkerchief and because there was DNA from multiple sources on the sample. The court ruled against the defense and allowed the evidence following a detailed hearing in which it examined the Short Tandem Repeat form of DNA testing and found it to be reliable.

Grant's Motion to Exclude His Statement to Police

Grant made the following comment to investigators at the police barracks prior to formal questioning and his Miranda warnings:

> "Did you read about the guy in Texas who killed all those people? They got him on a fingerprint, too."[1]

Prosecutors wanted the jury to hear the statement because it appeared that Grant acknowledged that he was guilty "too." Grant's lawyers argued Grant's statement was not a knowing and intelligent waiver of the defendant's privilege against self-incrimination. The judge disagreed and admitted the statement.

Grant had also told investigators about his working in a family auto body shop in Waterbury in the 1970s and apparently stated that he had suffered frequent blackouts due to an Army injury and sometimes couldn't remember where he had been or what he had done.[2] Grant lost his motion to keep this statement from the jury.

The defense won its motion to allow the jury to hear that the police had investigated both Philip DeLieto, Serra's ex-fiance, and Selman Topciu, a former restauranteur whose dental bills had been found in Serrra's car. In support of its point, the defense

---

1. Christa Lee Rock, "'Too' Key Word in Slay Case," *New Haven Register*, January 12, 2002.
2. *Id.*

argued that one of the eyewitnesses, Gary Hryb, had identified DeLieto out of a lineup within 12 hours of the murder.

Grant's Motion during Trial for a "Mistrial"

A mistrial is a trial rendered invalid through a serious error in the court proceedings which irreparably affects the jury's ability to return a fair verdict.

A mistrial is a trial rendered invalid through a serious error in the court proceedings which irreparably affects the jury's ability to return a fair verdict. Mistrials are largely restricted to jury cases in which, for example, the jury mistakenly hears a damning piece of inadmissible evidence the effect of which cannot be cured by a corrective instruction to the jury by the trial judge. For example, when retired New Haven Police Detective Vincent Perricone testified that the fingerprint on the tissue box had been "fresh" and told the jury that there are factors you can use to approximate how long ago a suspect left his prints behind, the defense moved for a mistrial on the ground that the state was offering an expert opinion from Perricone without giving the defense notice of its expert, which it is required to do. The defense also argued that there was no scientific proof that a fingerprint could be dated. The court denied the motion.[3]

Grant's Motion for New Trial

Following the verdict, Grant's attorneys moved for a new trial, citing such errors as the prosecution's offering a possible motive in their closing statement that Grant was trying to steal Serra's car, although no evidence to that effect had been introduced. The motion also argued that the prosecution had impermissibly stated that the jury would have to believe two investigators had lied to acquit. Finally, it asserted error because of the judge's failure to sanction the state for losing significant pieces of evidence.[4] The motion was denied.

General Principles of Law Applicable to Criminal Trials

The Effect of a Not Guilty Verdict

An acquittal means only that the jury concluded that prosecution failed to establish the defendant's guilt by a standard of beyond a reasonable doubt.

In a criminal case, if a defendant is found "not guilty" this does not mean that the defendant is "innocent" of the crime charged. Said another way, an acquittal means only that the jury concluded that prosecution failed to establish the defendant's guilt by a standard of beyond a reasonable doubt. Also, a defendant cannot use a verdict of "not guilty" to prove his innocence in a later civil trial arising out of the same set of facts.

---

3. Christa Lee Rock, "Mistrial Denied," *New Haven Register*, May 3, 2002.
4. Christa Lee Rock, "Citing Misconduct, Grant's Lawyers Seek New Trial," *New Haven Register*, June 4, 2002.

More than One Trial Can Result from the Same Set of Facts

As discussed earlier, in the O.J. Simpson case, the jury acquitted Simpson of murder in the criminal case. Thereafter, the families of Nicole Brown and Ron Goldman sued Simpson in a civil court case to recover damages from Simpson for the "wrongful death" of the two victims. Simpson was found liable in that second case, and ordered to pay the two plaintiffs over $35 million in compensatory and punitive damages. In short, a defendant may be either convicted or acquitted of a crime and then sued in civil court for damages based on the same acts.

A defendant can be convicted of both state and federal crimes resulting from the same set of facts. Mayor Philip Giordano of Waterbury, Connecticut, was being investigated by wiretap for corruption by federal officials when they discovered that his phone conversations included making arrangements with a woman to have sex with her young nieces. He was convicted in federal court of depriving the two children of their due process liberty right to be free from sexual abuse and of conspiracy to use a facility of interstate commerce for the purpose of enticing a person under the age of sixteen to engage in sex.[5] Following sentencing, he was then tried by the state of Connecticut for sexual assault in the first degree, risk of injury to a minor, and conspiracy to commit sexual assault.[6] Giordano was convicted of the second crime as well.

> A defendant can be convicted of both state and federal crimes resulting from the same set of facts.

Double Jeopardy Applies Only to Acquittal of the Same Crime

The Double Jeopardy Clause appears in the Fifth Amendment to the U.S. Constitution. It provides that "No person shall ... be subject for the same offence to be twice put in jeopardy of life or limb." Most states have the same guarantee for defendants appearing in separate state constitutions.

The clause includes three basic protections for individuals against prosecutions in state and federal courts. In summary they prohibit a second prosecution for the same offense after an acquittal, a second prosecution for the same offense after a guilty verdict, and multiple punishments for the same offense in the same forum. The clause is not a bar to a new trial when the defendant successfully appeals his conviction as the conviction is then "reversed." A defendant can also be re-tried for the same crime if the first case results in a mistrial.

Same Offense: There are a vast number of criminal statutes in the state and federal systems. Only a careful comparison of the language of the statute under which the first prosecution took place with the language of statute of involved in the second prosecution will determine whether the offenses are the same.

There is never a double jeopardy issue with a later civil trial in a case, just as in the *Simpson* case, because the second trial was not a trial for a "crime." Also, the

---

5. *United States v. Giordano*, 172 Fed. Appx. 340 (2d Cir. 2006).
6. *State v. Giordano*, CR403319736, 2004 Conn. Super. LEXIS 1538 (2004).

standard of proof in a civil trial is different. Instead of beyond a reasonable doubt, the jury needs only to find a preponderance of the evidence that the defendant committed the act: in this case homicide. A preponderance of the evidence has been held to be anything over 50% of the evidence admitted for consideration.

Why wasn't the second *Giordano* criminal case barred by the Double Jeopardy Clause in both the Connecticut and U.S. constitutions? In the two successive *Giordano* criminal cases, the defendant was tried for two separate crimes, so the second criminal trial did not violate the double jeopardy provision.

Note that the prosecution does not have the right to appeal if the defendant is found not guilty.[7]

The Effect of the U.S. Confrontation Clause on Which Witnesses Must Testify

The Confrontation Clause is that part of the Sixth Amendment which states that a criminal defendant has the right "to be confronted with the witnesses against him."

The U.S. Constitution bears on a number of important issues relating to forensic evidence. A major issue is whether a defendant has the right to confront and cross-examine the individual who processed a forensic sample. The Confrontation Clause is that part of the Sixth Amendment which states that a criminal defendant has the right "to be confronted with the witnesses against him." This applies to the states through the Fourteenth Amendment.

In the case of DNA, for example, the prosecutor generally offers a report conducted by an outside laboratory and asks an independent expert to explain its significance. The issue arose in 2009 in a case called *Melendez-Diaz v. Massachusetts*,[8] in which the U.S. Supreme Court held that a criminal defendant has a constitutional right to confront the lab technician who ran a forensic test used as evidence against him. The particular facts related to a test of a white substance found on the defendant and identified by a laboratory report entered into evidence as cocaine. In this case, the results of the report were admitted to prove a fact in issue — that the powder was cocaine — but the defendant was not able to cross-examine the analyst who tested the powder to determine what test was performed or whether the analyst used any judgment in interpreting the results.

The Supreme Court stated that forensic evidence is not immune from manipulation, particularly by scientists who may feel pressure from a law enforcement official to alter evidence in a manner favorable to the prosecution. It cited a commentator whose research showed over 60% of overturned criminal convictions involved invalid forensic testimony.[9] Finally, it said that the ability to confront and cross-examine the analyst could expose incompetent analysts:

7. *Martinez v. Illinois,* 134 S.Ct. 2070 (2014).

8. 557 U.S. 305 (2009).

9. Brandon L. Garrett and Peter J. Neufeld, "Invalid Forensic Science Testimony and Wrongful Convictions," *Virginia Law Review* 95, no. 1 (2009): 14.

Contrary to respondent's and the dissent's suggestion, there is little reason to believe that confrontation will be useless in testing analysts' honesty, proficiency, and methodology—the features that are commonly the focus in the cross-examination of experts.[10]

Following *Melendez-Diaz*, the Supreme Court has held that the Confrontation Clause also requires the analyst who tests blood alcohol levels to be present for cross-examination, but rejected the argument that the analyst who tests a DNA sample at an outside laboratory must appear. In *Williams v. Illinois*,[11] the Supreme Court said that a forensic specialist from the Illinois State Police lab could testify that she matched a DNA profile produced by an outside lab, Cellmark, to a profile that the state lab produced using a sample of the defendant's blood. Even though she stated that the Cellmark sample came from a vaginal swab from the victim, the court said that "fact" was merely a premise she assumed to be true in giving her report of the match.

Following *Melendez-Diaz*, the Confrontation Clause requirement has been argued to require cross-examination of forensic analysts in other areas, among them blood-alcohol testing and DNA testing. The case of *Bullcoming v. New Mexico*[12] provides a helpful illustration of an appellate court's disapproval of the presentation of forensic evidence at the trial court level. In that case, the issue was whether the prosecution may introduce a forensic laboratory report of a blood alcohol test through the testimony of a scientist who did not certify or observe the tests without violating the Confrontation Clause of the U.S. Constitution, which guarantees the right to "confront" and examine witnesses against the defendant. Testimony of this sort is called "surrogate testimony."

Bullcoming was arrested and charged with driving while intoxicated after he was involved in an automobile collision. A sample of his blood was submitted to a state laboratory to determine its alcohol content. The test was actually performed by Curtis Caylor, a laboratory analyst, who concluded that Bullcoming's blood-alcohol level was well above the minimum level required for charging aggravated DWI. Caylor was later placed on administrative leave and did not testify at Bullcoming's trial. In Caylor's place, the state offered the testimony of another analyst from the state laboratory who was familiar with the testing procedures and the science of blood-alcohol testing. But that analyst had not participated in testing Bullcoming's blood sample.

The Supreme Court rejected the state's "surrogate testimony" by the second analyst as insufficient to satisfy the Confrontation Clause. The Court reasoned that that Bullcoming could not adequately explore mistakes or lies in the testing unless he could cross-examine Caylor, the person who actually performed the test. The guilty verdict was reversed and remanded to the trial court with instructions to the lower court that if the state chose to retry Bullcoming, it may not introduce the results of

"[T]here is little reason to believe that confrontation will be useless in testing analysts' honesty, proficiency, and methodology—the features that are commonly the focus in the cross-examination of experts."

---

10. *Melendez-Diaz, supra* at 320.
11. 132 S.Ct 221 (2012).
12. 564 U.S. 647 (2011).

the laboratory test through the testimony of a person who did not participate in its performance.

Following *Bullcoming*, the U.S. Supreme Court held in *Williams v. Illinois*[13] that a DNA analyst did not need to testify under the Confrontation Clause because the DNA report was not testimonial in nature. The opinion was a plurality as only four justices signed it. The dissenting justices strongly disagreed. Following *Williams*, some courts have decided that it should be restricted to its unique set of facts (see Chapter 7 on DNA), and have refused to follow it.

In a more recent case, *People v. M.F.*[14] in New York state court, the court held that some of the DNA testing personnel must be present to be examined and it restricted the U.S. Supreme Court's opinion in *Williams* to its "narrowest grounds," which included that the DNA test was performed before the defendant was a suspect and submitted to a judge in a non-jury trial. It looked at the entire spectrum of people involved in the DNA test process to determine which ones must be present at trial.

> Despite the supervising analyst's credentials and role in this case, the defense contends that each individual who conducted a task must be called because of the risk of contamination and the presumptions technicians make at each step of the testing process. This argument essentially represents the view of at least some of the dissenting Justices in *Williams,* namely that the practical difficulties of calling at trial every person in the testing process, regardless of his or her role, should be secondary to the defendant's confrontation rights.[15]

In this case, which involved a rape where the victim was unable to identify her assailant, the court decided that the first analyst, who made decisions about the evidence in the DNA rape kit, must be present to testify, as a supervisor had no direct knowledge of those decisions, which the court found to be "testimonial" in nature. The court decided that the initial analyst must be present, but those who did the computer-testing did not:

> Given a laboratory with well-established protocols, in-court testimony of every analyst who operated machinery is unnecessary. The People have made a sufficient offer of proof that a qualified expert from the laboratory that produced the report will be called to testify and be subject to challenge on her findings and conclusions ...
>
> ...
>
> In sum, the motion to bar admission of the DNA report in the absence of laboratory witnesses is separated into three distinct components: a) the initial analysis, in which the initial analyst took the alleged victim's cervical sample, b) the machine driven testing performed by several technicians and

---

13. ___ U.S. ___, 132 S. Ct. 2221, 2227, 2244, 183 L. Ed. 2d 89 (2012) (plurality opinion).
14. *People v. M.F.*, 51 Misc.3d 327 (Sup. Ct. 2016).
15. *Id.* at 333.

c) the analysis of the data and the report's conclusions as found by the supervising analyst. The initial analyst's work is deemed to be testimonial *and* the technical preparation of the DNA graphs is presumed not to be testimonial subject to contrary evidence elicited at trial. The data resulting from the testing protocols will be admissible through the testimony of the witness the People have proffered, the supervising analyst.[16]

The dispute over what the *Williams* opinion really means will probably not be resolved unless and until the U.S. Supreme Court takes up the issue again.

The Meaning of Precedent

Although many of the rules governing admission of evidence in court are written in "codes" or "statutes" adopted by the federal or state legislature, the interpretation of those laws are made by the courts. Rulings by an appellate court become "precedent," which means they are binding law on any inferior court in its jurisdiction.

> Rulings by an appellate court become "precedent," which means they are binding law on any inferior court in its jurisdiction.

This means that a ruling by the U.S. Supreme Court, for example, is binding on all federal courts below it, and if it is a ruling on U.S. constitutional law, it will also be binding on states if they have adopted laws in conflict with the Supreme Court opinion. For example, the famous desegregation case, *Brown v. Board of Education*,[17] was a U.S. Supreme Court case that had been brought based on a lower court ruling about the school system in Kansas. However, it stated that "separate but equal" in public schools violated the U.S. Constitution. Therefore, it was binding on every school in every state, even though the case involved only one state.

The U.S. Supreme Court ruling in *Daubert v. Merrill Dow* addressed the standards required for admission of technical or scientific testimony by experts in federal courts. We will consider it in a separate chapter. That ruling applied to all federal courts because it was an interpretation of what Federal Rule of Evidence 702 "meant." However, state courts were free to adopt their own test for admission of technical or scientific testimony. Some adopted the *Daubert* standard; others did not.

As we review cases throughout this text, bear in mind that federal appellate decisions at the circuit court level are precedent only for federal trial courts in that circuit. It is not uncommon for there to be a conflict in the circuit courts, with one circuit ruling one way and another a different way. Sometimes the U.S. Supreme Court will take an appeal from a circuit court decision precisely in order to "resolve a conflict" within the circuits, although it has no duty to do so.

At the state court level, a state supreme court ruling is precedent on appellate and trial courts only in that state. You will see presented in this text a number of cases which come to different conclusions on the same issue of forensic testimony. How important this difference is will be governed, in part, by how high a court has rendered the decision.

---

16. 51 Misc. 3d at 334.
17. 347 U.S. 483 (1954).

The Jury Is the Finder of Fact

If the judge refuses to give a defendant's proposed instruction, this may later form the basis for an appeal based on an "error of law."

The judge will instruct the jury that it is the sole finder of fact, but must use the law as given by the judge to apply to the facts.

At the end of trial, the trial judge gives "jury instructions" to the jury, some of which are general to all trials and some of which have been tailored to the specifics of the case. Generally, each side "proposes" certain instructions to the judge that they want the judge to give. If the judge refuses to give a defendant's proposed instruction, this may later form the basis for an appeal based on an "error of law."

The judge will instruct the jury that it is the sole finder of fact, but must use the law as given by the judge to apply to the facts. Here are the instructions given in the *Grant* trial, which illustrate that distinction:

> You are the sole judges of the facts. It's your duty to find the facts. You are to recollect and weigh the evidence and form your own conclusion as to what the facts are. You may not go outside the evidence presented in court to find the facts. You may not resort to guess work, conjecture, suspicion or speculation, and you must not be influenced by any personal likes or dislikes, prejudice or sympathy. You must carefully consider all of the evidence presented and the claims of each party.

> The evidence from which you are to decide what the facts are consists of the sworn testimony of witness, the exhibits that have been received into evidence as full exhibits and your observations at the view.

> The testimonial evidence includes both what was said on direct examination and what was said on cross-examination without regard to which party called the witness.[18]

Rules of Evidence Governing What Evidence Can Be Admitted

In the next several paragraphs, we will review admissibility of evidence at trial using the Federal Rules of Evidence because they apply in the federal courts in every state. Bear in mind that state rules may differ.

Pretrial Procedure

Before the start of trial, the prosecution and the defense exchange lists of all witnesses which each side anticipates calling to testify. Each party will also be required to submit a list of exhibits which it anticipates introducing. Jurisdictions vary on the degree of specificity required in the witness and exhibit lists.

Generally, witnesses are divided into two categories: Fact witnesses and expert witnesses. A fact witness is a person who has personal knowledge of events relating to the case based on what that individual has personally observed or witnessed in

---

18. Transcript, May 22, 2003, p. 132–3.

the broadest sense of those two words: that is, what the person actually saw, felt, heard, or smelled. They may not offer opinions.

In contrast, an expert witness is a person who is a specialist in a particular discipline or subject, frequently one of the sciences, who may present an opinion about a relevant fact, without having personally witnessed any aspect of the case. It is an exception to the general rule barring witnesses from offering an opinion. The expert witness performs two primary functions: (1) the scientific function — collecting, testing, and evaluating evidence and forming an opinion as to that evidence; and (2) the forensic function — communicating that opinion and its basis to the judge and jury.

We have considered the Federal Rules of Evidence governing expert forensic testimony in federal courts in Chapter 1.

If a party objects to the introduction of certain evidence proposed by the opposing side, that objection is made to the judge before the trial begins or during the trial if that is the point at which the issue arises. Frequently objections are made and resolved outside the presence of the jury. If a party disagrees with the ruling and loses the trial, that party may later appeal on that issue.

The federal rules of evidence require that admissible evidence must be relevant, and not unduly prejudicial to the defendant. Obviously, all evidence which the prosecution offers is prejudicial to the accused in that it tends to show that the defendant committed the crime alleged. But "unduly" prejudicial means that certain evidence may tend to inflame the jury more than it tends to prove an element of the crime.

> The federal rules of evidence require that admissible evidence must be relevant, and not unduly prejudicial to the defendant.

Relevance

Federal Rule 401. Definition of Relevant Evidence.

Relevant evidence means evidence having any tendency to make the existence of any fact that is of consequence to the determination of the action more probable or less probable than it would be without the evidence.

Federal Rule 402. Relevant Evidence Generally Admissible; Irrelevant Evidence Inadmissible.

All relevant evidence is admissible, except as otherwise provided by the Constitution of the United States, by Act of Congress, by these rules, or by other rules prescribed by the Supreme Court pursuant to statutory authority. Evidence which is not relevant is not admissible.

The test for relevance is fairly broad. "Any tendency" to prove a fact gives wide discretion to the party offering the testimony and the judge deciding its admissibility.

In the *Grant* case, evidence of the kind of car Grant drove was relevant, because the parking ticket attendant, Christopher Fagan, described the car as a dark blue or brown GM or Chrysler. However, where Grant bought his car or how he financed it is irrelevant. Those facts cannot possibly help a jury decide whether Grant's car was at the scene of the crime.

Although courts sometimes state that evidence must be "relevant, probative, and material," those words are very closely related to the concept of "relevance" under the Federal Rules which do not use those two terms. "Probative" means tending to prove or disprove an issue. "Material" means evidence that has more than a minor relationship to a legal issue in dispute. The current definition of "relevant" incorporates these concepts. It requires that the evidence have any tendency to make the existence of any fact that is of consequence to the determination of the action more probable or less probable than it would be without the evidence. The phrase "any fact that is of consequence" includes the concept of materiality. The phrase "more probable or less probable" includes the concept of "probative."

"Probative" means tending to prove or disprove an issue.

Undue Prejudice

But even if certain evidence is relevant, a court may still exclude it. Federal Rule 403 deals with this subject.

Federal Rule 403. Exclusion of Relevant Evidence on Grounds of Prejudice, Confusion, or Waste of Time.

Although relevant, evidence may be excluded if its probative value is substantially outweighed by the danger of unfair prejudice, confusion of the issues, or misleading the jury, or by considerations of undue delay, waste of time, or needless presentation of cumulative evidence.

Rule 403 is designed to balance the jury's need for all relevant evidence with judicial concern that the jury may be unduly swayed against the defendant by certain types of evidence.

Rule 403 is designed to balance the jury's need for all relevant evidence with judicial concern that the jury may be unduly swayed against the defendant by certain types of evidence. For example, Grant was arrested because a routine submission of unmatched fingerprints into an Automated Fingerprint Identification System (AFIS) by the Connecticut Forensic Science Laboratory turned up a match to fingerprints of Grant's that had been entered into the database as a result of an earlier domestic dispute. If the jury heard that Grant had been involved in a domestic dispute, what would it conclude? Would it think that a defendant who was involved in a domestic dispute would be more likely to have been the murderer? One juror stated after the trial that once she knew this fact, it convinced her that her verdict had been right. So this was a very significant piece of evidence, but it was excluded because it was also impermissibly prejudicial.

Some experts argue that giving the trial judge the right to exclude certain expert testimony from the jury deprives the jury of its right to be a "finder of fact." Certainly, jurors are rightly upset when they learn of evidence after a trial that they did not hear in court. The jurors in the O.J. Simpson case made this very clear:

Like everyone else, I've heard a lot of things that we didn't get to hear during sequestration.... What I hate is that a lot of that information I did not receive I think would have been important information to me. I'm not saying that the same reasonable doubt issues may not have come up, but I think I would have weighed them a little bit differently.... [Amanda Cooley]

The ten thousand dollars, the passport, the fake beard, the fibers from the Bronco, Nicole's words from her diary, all those things I believe should have been presented to the jury ... I have a problem with the judicial system presenting itself — presenting the truth, the whole truth, and nothing but the truth. The whole truth was not an issue. And to put those people in that position to say make a decision based on the evidence and only giving them a part of the evidence was very unfair to the jury. [Jeanette Harris][19]

Was a Prosecution's DNA Testimony Unduly Prejudicial?

In 1997, a defendant appealed his conviction for murder based on the admission of DNA testing.[20] The expert, Vick, testified that the chances of someone other than the defendant matching the bands from the swab on three probes was 1 in 500,000. The defendant claimed the testimony should be excluded because it was prejudicial.

Having determined that the statistical portion of the DNA profiling evidence was both relevant and reliable, we must also consider whether the evidence is inadmissible because its probative value was substantially outweighed by the danger of unfair prejudice. As we have stated, "prejudice, in this context, means more than simply damage to the opponent's cause. A party's case is always damaged by evidence that the facts are contrary to his contention; but that cannot be ground for exclusion. What is meant here is an undue tendency to move the tribunal to decide on an improper basis ..."

...

Although the DNA statistics could be considered prejudicial, they are not unfairly so, and in no event did unfair prejudice substantially outweigh the probative value of this evidence. The DNA statistical evidence was relevant and reliable, and the court committed no error in admitting the evidence against Fleming.

Evidence of Prior Crimes Is Generally Not Admissible

Rule 404(b). Other Crimes, Wrongs, or Acts

Evidence of other crimes, wrongs, or acts is not admissible to prove the character of a person in order to show action in conformity therewith.

It may, however, be admissible for other purposes, such as proof of motive, opportunity, intent, preparation, plan, knowledge, identity, or absence of mistake or accident ...

19. Amanda Cooley, Carrie Bess, and Marsha Rubin-Jackson, *Madam Foreman: A Rush to Judgment?* (Dove Books, 1995), 196–7.

20. *State v. Fleming*, 698 A.2d 503 (Sup Ct Me 1997).

We start with a general proposition to which there are complicated exceptions: in criminal trials in both the state and federal courts, evidence of crimes or wrongs previously committed by a defendant is not admissible to prove that the defendant is more likely to have committed the crime charged at trial. Though not defined by the Federal Rules, it is generally accepted that character evidence consists of any testimony or document offered to prove that a person (the defendant) acted in a particular way based on his character or disposition.[21] For example, in a criminal case involving the charge of burglary, the prosecution might try to introduce evidence of the defendant's prior conviction of burglary to establish in the jury's mind that he is the kind of person likely to have committed the crime charged in the pending case. On those facts alone, that is not permissible.

But the prosecution may introduce character evidence for certain limited purposes *after* the defendant has done so. That is to say, after the defendant has "opened the door" by introducing evidence of, for example, her good character. Therefore, a defendant must think carefully if he or she chooses to introduce evidence of good character.

Evidence of crimes or wrongs previously committed by a defendant is not admissible to prove that the defendant is more likely to have committed the crime charged at trial.

The Defendant Is Not Required to Testify

Ed Grant did not take the stand. As he had no alibi defense, there was no reason for him to testify. And his attorneys didn't want him to be cross-examined. By the time of trial, Grant was a rather feeble-looking older man who did not look capable of murder. But he also had very little personality or "affect" so he did not appear sympathetic to jurors. This was his lawyers' advice.

Although the jury did not hear the possibly prejudicial evidence that Grant's fingerprint was obtained from an arrest for domestic abuse in 1994, they also did not hear the possibly positive fact that he had never been convicted of a crime or committed any act of violence. Two ex-wives of Grant refused to testify about his alleged abusive past.[22] Grant had no criminal record and neighbors said he was quiet and loved fishing and fixing cars, but the jury never heard about it.

George Oliver, a friend of Grant's, stated out of court that Grant was in Groton, not New Haven, the day Serra was killed. However, he did not testify as an alibi witness for Grant.[23] However, Grant's attorneys did not believe this was a credible alibi. This left the jury with no possible explanation of where Grant had been on the day of the murder.

In the same case we examined above, in which David Fleming was convicted of rape and murder based in part on DNA testing, Fleming also appealed based on

21. Cornell University Law School, Legal Information Institute, "Notes of Advisory Committee on Proposed Rules."
22. Christa Lee Rock, "Portrait of a Complex Suspect," *New Haven Register*, April 28, 2002.
23. *Id.*

evidence of prior DNA testing of his blood. He argued that the jury would assume the prior testing involved an earlier crime, and that this was prejudicial to him as evidence of a prior "bad act." The court rejected this claim:

> Fleming contends that testimony relating to prior DNA testing of his blood was improperly admitted as evidence of a prior bad act. Although he did not object to the admission of this evidence, he argues that, by its admission, the jurors were forced to conclude that he had raped or murdered another person. When the defense fails to object or otherwise preserve an error, we review for obvious error affecting substantial rights. Obvious error is error that is so highly prejudicial and so taints the proceedings as to virtually deprive the defendant of a fair trial.
>
> At the trial Fleming vigorously cross-examined all the expert witnesses on their labeling of the evidentiary samples. At a sidebar conference that occurred during the cross-examination of Vick, the State warned defense counsel that he was opening the door for the State to dispel any confusion about the mislabeling of the samples. After Fleming's counsel replied, "well, go ahead and do it," the court told the prosecution that it was entitled to clear up opposing counsel's "improper spin" on redirect.
>
> During the ensuing redirect examination of Vick, the State elicited testimony that a sample of Fleming's blood had been submitted to him "earlier on a prior occasion," that he had already run the sample through the DNA testing procedure. [Further, Vick testified] that he would be able to lay the test results produced on the [earlier] occasion over the test results produced in this case to establish that there was no inconsistency between Fleming's known sample and the other samples he had received. Defendant offered no objection.
>
> The State then requested a sidebar conference and obtained the court's permission to have Vick compare the test results. The State then asked Vick to compare one of Fleming's test results in this case with a comparable test result obtained on a "separate occasion," and he subsequently testified that the band patterns lined up perfectly. The State then offered the other test result into evidence without objection.
>
> The jury only heard testimony that Vick had obtained Fleming's whole blood sample on a "separate occasion." Fleming's contention that the jury was then forced to conclude that he had raped or murdered another person [was held to be] without merit. [The court reasoned that] there was no evidence that a whole blood sample is only obtained by the FBI in rape and murder cases. The jury was free to conclude that the FBI obtained two whole blood samples from Fleming solely as a result of this case. Contrary to Fleming's assertion, the court did not commit obvious error.[24]

---

24. *Id.* at 508–9.

In the *Grant* case, some would argue that the prior domestic dispute is not relevant to whether Grant killed Serra, who as far as anyone knows he had never met. Others would argue that the domestic incident shows that Grant is violent toward women and therefore would be more likely to commit a crime of violence against a woman. But regardless of whether the evidence is relevant, it is clearly prejudicial. This shows that the court must balance the desire of the prosecution to present all relevant evidence with the desire of the defendant to receive a fair trial free of undue prejudice.

There is always *some* prejudice in every trial. For example, even though Grant had a constitutional right not to testify and the judge so directed the jury, many jurors conclude that a defendant does not take the stand because he is hiding something.

Rules Relating to Forensic Expert Testimony

We have discussed the Federal Rules of Evidence that govern expert testimony in Chapter 1. They include Rules 702, 703, and 704.

Judicial Notice

Judicial notice simply means that the parties do not need to "prove" the area of science to the jury.

Once a court has determined that an area of science is valid and reliable, the court can take "judicial notice" of this as a fact. Judicial notice simply means that the parties do not need to "prove" the area of science to the jury. Judicial notice is not actually a form of evidence, but serves to save time by avoiding the need to prove an accepted fact over and over in trials. For example, the defense in the *Grant* case challenged the validity of the "STR" method of DNA testing. The trial judge held a hearing, heard from the experts outside the presence of the jury, and ruled that the area of science was valid and reliable. Therefore, the parties did not need to put on any further proof of this issue at the trial.

The Model Federal Jury Instructions for Criminal Cases contain a sample or "Pattern" Jury Instruction concerning judicial notice as follows:

Pattern Instruction 2.04 Judicial Notice (Fed. R. Evid. 201)

Even though no evidence has been introduced about it, I have decided to accept as proved the fact that, [for example, DNA evidence is scientifically based and reliable] I believe this fact [is of such common knowledge] [can be so accurately and readily determined from (name accurate source)] that it cannot reasonably be disputed. You may therefore treat this fact as proved, even though no evidence was brought out on the point. As with any fact, however, the final decision whether or not to accept it is for you to make and you are not required to agree with me.

A recent Connecticut case stated that the court will take judicial notice of a scientific principle only if it is "considered so reliable within the relevant [medical] community that there is little or no real debate as to its validity."[25] For example, the courts have

---

25. *Maher v. Quest Diagnostics*, 269 Conn. 154 (2004).

taken judicial notice of the fact that the Horizontal Gaze Nystagmus test is reliable in determining alcohol level for cases involving driving under the influence. Another example is judicial recognition of the ability of a blood test to accurately prove or disprove paternity.

Courts have taken judicial notice of the "science of DNA testing."[26] For a discussion of whether judicial notice of DNA testing as scientifically reliable in identifying a defendant amounts to prejudice in emphasizing DNA over other forms of evidence of identity, see Chapter 7 on DNA.

Appeals

Appeals are also governed by state procedural laws in state courts and federal procedural rules in federal court. These rules can be as mundane as setting deadlines for filing notices and papers and as sophisticated as what standards must be used by the reviewing court in deciding how to rule on an appeal.

Federal Court System

In the federal system, the first level appellate review takes place before what is called a circuit court. They are the intermediate appellate courts in the federal court system between the federal district court (trial court) and the U.S. Supreme Court.

The federal courts of appeals are among the most powerful courts in the United States. Because the U.S. Supreme Court chooses to review less than 1% of the more than 10,000 cases filed with it annually, the circuit courts of appeals serve as the final decision maker on most federal cases which are the subject of appeal.

There are thirteen circuit courts of appeal in the federal system. Eleven of those circuits are geographically based and are numbered. The United States Court of Appeals for the Second Circuit, for example, includes all of the federal district courts physically located in Connecticut, New York, and Vermont. The Second Circuit hears appeals from trial court decisions of just those federal district courts. Similarly, Florida, Alabama, and Georgia are in the Eleventh Circuit. Appeals from decisions of the district courts located in those states are heard by that circuit. All of the circuit courts operate under a system of what is called mandatory review, which means they *must* hear all appeals from the lower courts in that circuit. In contrast, the U.S. Supreme Court does not have to hear an appeal from a circuit court: it chooses the cases which it wishes to hear and declines the others. Decisions of the courts of appeals are

---

26. In *U.S. v. Shea*, the court stated: "The theory and techniques used in PCR are sufficiently established that a court may take judicial notice of their general reliability. *See Beasley*, 102 F.3d at 1448 (taking judicial notice of general reliability of PCR testing); *see also United States v. Martinez*, 3 F.3d 1191, 1197 (8th Cir. 1993) (taking judicial notice of general reliability of DNA testing), cert. denied, 510 U.S. 1062, 114 S. Ct. 734, 126 L. Ed. 2d 697 (1994); *U.S. v. Jakobetz*, 955 F.2d at 799 (taking judicial notice of reliability of DNA testing).

published by the private company West Publishing in a separate reporter called the *Federal Reporter.*

State Courts

In most state courts, there is a similar two-tier appellate system: an intermediate appellate court and a supreme court. For example, in the Connecticut state court system, there is an intermediate appellate court called the Connecticut Appellate Court located in Hartford, Connecticut, and a Connecticut Supreme Court, also in Hartford. With minor exceptions, all appeals from superior court decisions are taken to the appellate court, which is required to accept them and render a decision. A party who is dissatisfied with a ruling by the Appellate Court may attempt to take an appeal to the Connecticut Supreme Court. As with the U.S. Supreme Court, the Connecticut Supreme Court selects the cases which it will hear, so an appeal to that forum is not a matter of right.

In general, there are a few over-riding rules governing appellate practice:

1. An appeals court does not review the trial record as if it were the trial court. The appellate court will reverse a decision generally only if there has been an error of law that is "harmful," if the trial court has "abused its discretion" in conducting the trial, or if there has been some constitutional error that equals manifest injustice.

2. An appeals court is "bound by the trial record." It does not take testimony or admit any new evidence.

3. All grounds for appeal must have been challenged during trial and "preserved in the record." With certain important exceptions, an appeal court will not reverse an error that was not objected to at trial.

4. The prosecution does not get to appeal a verdict of "not guilty."

A party who appeals must include all facts found by the trial court relevant to the appeal by citing to the trial record in his or her appeal brief. Appellate court judges read the verbatim written transcript that says exactly what happened in trial court. They also read and review the "record" (all of the pleadings and the trial judge's rulings that were filed with the clerk of the trial court). Then, they review the law that applies to the controversy that has prompted the appeal. Finally, they determine whether errors of law occurred in the trial court, and whether those errors are serious enough that the judgment of the trial court should be reversed.

It is important to understand that an appeal is not at all a second trial. The appellate court does not allow or consider any new evidence or take any testimony. It is "bound" by the record of proceedings that took place in the trial court. Therefore, if the jury rejects the conclusion of a forensic expert, this is not a ground for appeal. Appeals must present a "question of law." In the example above, say the prosecutor wanted to introduce a weapon that the police found in the defendant's home, which they searched without a warrant. The appellate court may decide that the police did not

> The appellate court will reverse a decision generally only if there has been an error of law that is "harmful," if the trial court has "abused its discretion" in conducting the trial, or if there has been some constitutional error that equals manifest injustice.

> Appeals must present a "question of law."

search the home without a warrant. That is a fact established by the evidence presented in the trial court, but it may decide whether a warrantless search was unconstitutional (a question of law). If the appellate court concludes that the search was unconstitutional, it would reverse the guilty verdict and remand the case for retrial before the lower court with instructions to exclude the evidence relating to the weapon which was impermissibly seized.

Harmless Error Rule and Abuse of Discretion Standard

There are two big hurdles that the appellant (the party taking the appeal from an unfavorable ruling or verdict in the lower court) faces on appeal. The first is that the appeals court will "defer to," or let stand, many decisions made by the trial judge during the course of the trial, so long as the trial court acted reasonably. The standard for appeal on such issues is whether the trial court "abused its discretion."

So, for example, in decisions on whether to admit the testimony of an expert witness, the appellate court may review the record and believe that the expert was not as qualified as it thinks he should be. But unless the trial court admitted the expert's opinion without a showing of any qualifications at all, the appellate court will not challenge the decision. The ruling was, as the appellate courts say, "within the discretion of the trial court."

The second big hurdle is that even if the appeals court finds that there was an error of law at the trial level, the appeals court will not reverse the conviction or grant a new trial if it decides that the error was "harmless error." For example, the appeals court may agree with Grant that the prosecutor should not have told the jury in closing that Grant may have been trying to steal Serra's car. But it may also decide that there was sufficient evidence without that comment for the jury to convict. Therefore, any error by the trial judge will be found "harmless" as it was not crucial to the conviction.

> The appeals court will "defer to," or let stand, many decisions made by the trial judge during the course of the trial, so long as the trial court acted reasonably.

> The appeals court will not reverse the conviction or grant a new trial if it decides that the error was "harmless error."

Possible Rulings on Appeal

If the appeals court finds that the trial court did not err, or that the errors were not serious enough to warrant a reversal, they will "affirm" the trial court's decision. The judges' decision, in written form, analyzes the parties' arguments, declares what law controls the case, and rules on how that law applies to the facts of the case. The written decision of the court of appeals becomes "the law" for that particular district. It also becomes "precedent" in that jurisdiction. Alternatively, if the appeals court concludes that there was a serious error of law in the trial, the appeals court can reverse the lower court's judgment, and remand the case to the trial court with instructions that it must hold a new trial and exclude the evidence in question.

If the intermediate appellate court agrees with the ruling or action of the trial court and affirms its decision, the losing party may then petition to the highest appellate court: the U.S. Supreme Court in a federal case or the state supreme court in a state court litigation. However, as noted above, the acceptance of an appeal is discretionary with both of the highest appellate courts. Each supreme court can take the appeal if it wishes, but it is not required to do so.

For example, at the federal court level, there were 54,697 appeals filed in the year 2000 at the circuit court level. There were 5,633 petitions for appeal to the U.S. Supreme Court, called petitions for a writ of certiorari, of which the Supreme Court granted only 99.[27]

Habeas Corpus Appeals

A habeas corpus petition is a petition to a federal trial court that can be made only after all regular appeals have been exhausted. It is based on the argument that continuing to hold the petitioner in prison violates the U.S. Constitution. Under 28 U.S.C. § 2254, a federal court must entertain a claim by a state prisoner that he or she is being held in "custody in violation of the Constitution or laws or treaties of the United States." The petitioner must show that the evidence in support of his state conviction was insufficient to have led a rational trier of fact to find guilt beyond a reasonable doubt.

The U.S. Supreme Court has ruled that the standard for granting a habeas corpus action is where the reviewing court finds that upon the record of the evidence at the trial no rational trier of fact could have found proof of guilt beyond a reasonable doubt. In *Jackson v. Virginia*, a 1979 case, the U.S. Supreme Court held:

> [T]he Due Process Clause of the Fourteenth Amendment protects a defendant in a criminal case against conviction "except upon proof beyond a reasonable doubt of every fact necessary to constitute the crime with which he is charged."
>
> ...
>
> The standard of proof of beyond a reasonable doubt, said the Court, "plays a vital role in the American scheme of criminal procedure," because it operates to give "concrete substance" to the presumption of innocence, to ensure against unjust convictions, and to reduce the risk of factual error in a criminal proceeding. At the same time, by impressing upon the fact finder the need to reach a subjective state of near certitude of the guilt of the accused, the standard symbolizes the significance that our society attaches to the criminal sanction and thus to liberty itself.
>
> The constitutional standard recognized in the *Winship* case was expressly phrased as one that protects an accused against a conviction except on "proof beyond a reasonable doubt...." In subsequent cases discussing the reasonable-doubt standard, we have never departed from this definition of the rule or from the *Winship* understanding of the central purposes it serves.

A habeas corpus petition is a petition to a federal trial court that can be made only after all regular appeals have been exhausted. It is based on the argument that continuing to hold the petitioner in prison violates the U.S. Constitution.

The petitioner must show that the evidence in support of his state conviction was insufficient to have led a rational trier of fact to find guilt beyond a reasonable doubt.

---

27. Frank A. Schubert, *Introduction to Law and the Legal System*, 8th ed., (Houghton Mifflin, 2003), 152.

A "reasonable doubt," at a minimum, is one based upon "reason." Yet a properly instructed jury may occasionally convict even when it can be said that no rational trier of fact could find guilt beyond a reasonable doubt, and the same may be said of a trial judge sitting as a jury. In a federal trial, such an occurrence has traditionally been deemed to require reversal of the conviction.

After *Winship* the critical inquiry on review of the sufficiency of the evidence to support a criminal conviction must be not simply to determine whether the jury was properly instructed, but to determine whether the record evidence could reasonably support a finding of guilt beyond a reasonable doubt.

But this inquiry does not require a court to "ask itself whether it believes that the evidence at the trial established guilt beyond a reasonable doubt." Instead, the relevant question is whether, after viewing the evidence in the light most favorable to the prosecution, any rational trier of fact could have found the essential elements of the crime beyond a reasonable doubt.

This familiar standard gives full play to the responsibility of the trier of fact fairly to resolve conflicts in the testimony, to weigh the evidence, and to draw reasonable inferences from basic facts to ultimate facts. Once a defendant has been found guilty of the crime charged, the fact finder's role as weigher of the evidence is preserved through a legal conclusion that upon judicial review all of the evidence is to be considered in the light most favorable to the prosecution.

Under 28 U.S.C. § 2254, a federal court must entertain a claim by a state prisoner that he or she is being held in "custody in violation of the Constitution or laws or treaties of the United States." Under the *Winship* decision, it is clear that a state prisoner who alleges that the evidence in support of his state conviction cannot be fairly characterized as sufficient to have led a rational trier of fact to find guilt beyond a reasonable doubt has stated a federal constitutional claim. Thus, assuming that state remedies have been exhausted, see 28 U.S.C. § 2254 (b), and that no independent and adequate state ground stands as a bar, it follows that such a claim is cognizable in a federal habeas corpus proceeding.

We hold that in a challenge to a state criminal conviction brought under 28 U.S.C. § 2254 — if the settled procedural prerequisites for such a claim have otherwise been satisfied — the applicant is entitled to habeas corpus relief if it is found that upon the record evidence adduced at the trial no rational trier of fact could have found proof of guilt beyond a reasonable doubt.

. . .

Under the standard established in this opinion as necessary to preserve the due process protection recognized in *Winship*, a federal habeas corpus court faced with a record of historical facts that supports conflicting inferences

"A federal habeas corpus court faced with a record of historical facts that supports conflicting inferences must presume — even if it does not affirmatively appear in the record — that the trier of fact resolved any such conflicts in favor of the prosecution, and must defer to that resolution."

must presume — even if it does not affirmatively appear in the record — that the trier of fact resolved any such conflicts in favor of the prosecution, and must defer to that resolution. Applying these criteria, we hold that a rational trier of fact could reasonably have found that the petitioner committed murder in the first degree under Virginia law. [28]

Summary

Forensic evidence cannot be admitted in front of a jury unless all applicable rules of evidence are met. There are separate court systems for federal prosecutions and state prosecutions. There are federal courts in all states and they are all bound to follow one set of federal rules governing trial procedure and evidence. Each state also has its own court system with its own set of rules. These may be patterned after the federal rules or may be different. Therefore, it is important to determine whether a crime will be prosecuted in a federal or state court. Sometimes, both courts can prosecute the same underlying conduct if that conduct violates a federal law and a state law.

Forensic evidence cannot be admitted in trial before a trial judge or a jury unless the party who wishes to introduce the evidence follows the proper court process, including all applicable rules of evidence. These rules are contained in the Federal Rules of Evidence for cases in federal court and in similar laws adopted by each state for trials held in those states.

Most crimes have a defined set of legal elements that appear in state or federal statutes. The jury must find each legal element by a preponderance of the evidence (51% or more). It must find guilt, however, by the standard of beyond a reasonable doubt. This does not mean 100% certainty. Proof beyond a reasonable doubt precludes every reasonable hypothesis except guilt and is inconsistent with any other rational conclusion.

The jury is the sole finder of fact, but it must apply the law as given to it by the judge. At the trial's conclusion, the judge will give the jury instructions about how to apply the law to the facts. Usually, each side in a trial will "propose" a set of jury instructions favorable to their view of the law. The judge must then decide which specific instructions to give. Take the crime of murder, for example. The legal elements of murder are legal tests to which the jury must apply the facts.

Rules of evidence are designed to safeguard all parties against the introduction of unreliable or impermissibly prejudicial evidence. Evidence must be relevant to the legal issues in the case. If prejudice would result to the defendant from the introduction of the evidence, the court may exclude that evidence. The rules of evidence contain separate rules for admitting testimony by experts, which we reviewed in Chapter 1. These rules govern forensic testimony and provide that testimony by a qualified

---

28. *Jackson v. Virginia*, 443 U.S. 307 (1979).

expert is admissible only if it will assist the jury to understand the evidence or determine a fact in issue.

Judicial notice means that a trial court may accept a fact as having been proved without either party putting on evidence. The reliability of the science of DNA has been the subject of judicial notice. The jury may still refuse to accept a fact that is judicially noticed. The Confrontation Clause of the U.S. Constitution has been held to apply to forensic testimony. If any report of forensic investigation performed by someone not in court is attempted to be introduced, the defendant will likely object that the person who performed the test be available to testify. The courts are still testing the limits of this rule, in particular as it may relate to various personnel involved in DNA testing. If the report is "testimonial" in nature, the court is likely to rule the writer of the report must testify.

Court decisions in federal courts are binding precedent on the courts below them. For example, a decision by a federal circuit court is binding on all the federal courts in that circuit. This is called "precedent," meaning the courts must all follow the decision. The U.S. Supreme Court decisions are binding on all federal courts (if on a matter of federal law) and on all states as well (if the decision involves a question under the U.S. Constitution). We will read cases from both state and federal courts, so it is important to ask what the precedential value of the case may be.

Both state and federal courts maintain trial courts, intermediate appellate courts, and a supreme court. Typically, a defendant may appeal as of right (assuming he meets time requirements and presents a "question of law" that was raised at trial) to the intermediate appellate court. The supreme court generally takes a final appeal only if it chooses to. Finally, both state and federal prisoners may bring a habeas corpus action before a federal trial court on the issue of whether his imprisonment violates the U.S. Constitution.

Appellate courts do not take evidence or determine facts. They are bound by the trial record as to facts. Their job is to determine if an error of law was made by the trial court that justifies reversing a conviction. They defer to decisions of the trial court, unless there was an abuse of its discretion. They may note an error took place, but affirm a conviction regardless if it was "harmless error," meaning that there is sufficient evidence of guilt without looking at the evidence that is tainted by an error to conclude a reasonable jury would have found the defendant guilty.

Discussion Questions

1. What is the purpose of having rules of evidence?

2. What is the difference between relevant and material evidence?

3. What is the relationship between the federal rules of evidence and state rules of evidence?

4. How can the same facts be used to convict a defendant of a crime in state and federal court? Why doesn't this violate the rule against double jeopardy?

5. What is precedent? Why is it important?

6. What does Federal Rule of Evidence 403 say? Why did the court in the *Fleming* case decide that admission of DNA evidence did not violate this rule?

7. What other kinds of evidence would be so prejudicial to the defendant that they should be excluded, even though they might be relevant to a jury?

8. How does the Confrontation Clause of the U.S. Constitution affect what forensic analysts must testify at trial?

9. What are the legal standards of review that govern an appeal and why do they make it difficult for a defendant to overturn a guilty verdict?

10. What is the legal standard for winning a habeas corpus action? What must the prisoner do before he can bring the action?

11. Define the concept of judicial notice. Is a jury required to accept the truth of a fact that is subject to judicial notice?

Chapter 3

Crime Scene Investigation

Overview

Locard's Principle says that every person who comes in contact with an object or person will make a cross transfer of evidence that will identify him. This principle is why crime scene investigators examine a crime scene in detail. Forensic evidence must be collected carefully and following all laws in order to be admitted in trial. The process requires investigators to carefully document all evidence and to remain objective. An expert who testifies about the crime scene may rely on notes or drawings prepared by others, so long as they do not contain opinions or conclusions.

One of the objectives is to link forensic evidence to suspects. Forensic evidence may demonstrate either class characteristics or individual characteristics. Class characteristics will be those that will "include" the suspect, such as the same shoeprint, but individual characteristics are those that can conclusively identify a suspect, such as DNA. Both investigators and juries need to be aware of the difference.

Chain of custody requires that evidence be properly controlled and accounted for in order to be admissible at trial. Some courts refuse to admit evidence where there is a break in the chain of custody. Others admit the evidence, but allow the defendant to argue that the jury should take the break in the chain and possible tampering into consideration in their deliberations.

Courts are now mindful that juries may expect forensic evidence and have tried to avoid prejudice by questioning in voir dire and by jury instructions.

An expert may testify based on crime scene drawings or sketches prepared by someone who is not in court, unless they contain any conclusion or opinion, in which case the Confrontation Clause would require the presence of the investigator who wrote the report.

Counsel must carefully select and prepare the forensic expert in order to persuade a jury that the expert's opinion is correct. Some believe that the criminal justice system favors the prosecution in the area of expert testimony, as states have forensic laboratories and technicians to test and testify, whereas defendants must hire expensive experts to evaluate or contest the state's evidence. At least one court has held that failure to request a more expensive, "better" forensic expert constitutes "ineffective counsel," which may warrant reversing a conviction.

Chapter Objectives

Based on this chapter, students will be able to:

1. Define Locard's "Exchange Principle" and how it affects the processing of crime scenes.

2. Explain basic steps involved in securing and investigating a crime scene.

3. Describe why investigators should get a warrant to search a crime scene.

4. Distinguish the difference between class and individual characteristics in evidence.

5. Explain the importance of maintaining a chain of custody.

6. Describe the challenges in the *Grant* case to chain of custody.

7. Tell how to find and prepare an expert witness.

How Forensic Evidence Is Processed

Forensic evidence is generally collected from the crime scene by investigators working for law enforcement. Therefore, it is critical that the original crime scene investigators do their job properly. Although the actors on CSI make investigating look simple and dramatic, it is not. The actors often wade into a crime scene before it has been blocked off and secured. They almost never get a warrant before searching. They pick up and hand around pieces of evidence. And then they go back to the lab and process the evidence themselves — all in one hour!

The purpose of crime scene investigation is to recognize, preserve, collect, safeguard, interpret and reconstruct all relevant physical evidence.

Whether conducted by local law enforcement or a highly specialized team of forensic scientists, the objectives of crime scene investigation are to recognize, preserve, collect, safeguard, interpret and reconstruct all relevant physical evidence at a crime scene.[1]

Forensic processing frequently involves two important groups of people. The crime scene investigators on the scene are typically local police officers or members of a major crime unit of law enforcement officers who are trained to collect evidence and investigate crimes. In Connecticut, for example, the state maintains four major crime units that respond to all crimes involving police officers and any other crime scene if asked for help by local law enforcement. A number of the larger cities maintain their own crime scene units, but smaller towns do not. In the event that local law enforcement arrives on the scene and contaminates it in any way, this may impede the ability of the crime scene unit to process the scene. This was one of the claims made in the murder investigation of JonBenet Ramsey, which today is a cold case. This case is discussed in the chapter on Questioned Documents.

---

1. Stuart H. James and Jon J. Nordby, *Forensic Science*, 2d ed., CRC Press, 2005.

The second group is composed of laboratory technicians. These technicians typically do not travel to crime scenes to gather evidence, but instead test evidence in the laboratory. Some technicians began as law enforcement officers. Christopher Grice, for example, the fingerprint expert who identified Grant's fingerprint and testified to the match at trial, began as a detective in New Haven and is now a fingerprint expert at the Connecticut State Forensics Laboratory. Today, many forensic laboratories hire only graduates of forensic training programs, or individuals with degrees in the hard sciences.

In 2009, the NRC Report evaluated the scientific reliability of many forms of forensic evidence collected from crime scenes. It noted that crime scenes can be investigated by sophisticated teams or by a single investigator: "Crime scene evidence collectors can include uniformed officers, detectives, crime scene investigators, criminalists, forensic scientists, coroners, medical examiners, hospital personnel, photographers, and arson investigators. Thus, the nature and process of crime scene investigation varies dramatically across jurisdictions, with the potential for inconsistent policies and procedures and bias.... [T]here remains great variability in crime scene investigation practices, along with persistent concerns that the lack of standards and proper training at the crime scene can contribute to the difficulties of drawing accurate conclusions once evidence is subjected to forensic laboratory methods."[2]

> The nature and process of crime scene investigation varies dramatically across jurisdictions, with the potential for inconsistent policies and procedures and bias.

Locard's Exchange Principle

This principle states that whenever two objects come into contact, there will be a mutual exchange of matter. This means that the suspect will leave something of himself at the crime scene and will take something of the scene away with him. Of course, these items may be microscopic, but the investigator's job is to find them. The investigator seeks to link the victim and the crime scene to a suspect and/or objects identified with the suspect.

> Locard's Exchange Principle. At every crime scene, a person who comes in contact with an object or person will make a cross transfer of evidence to the scene.

On-Site Investigation

The steps in on-site crime scene investigation must be done in order:

1. Ensure that the victim is not present or in need of help.

2. Ensure that the scene is safe and no suspects are present.

3. Block off the scene.

4. Detain all witnesses. Establish a security log to document all people who come in and out.

5. Observe and take notes.

---

2. NRC Report at 56.

6. Determine if the scene is the primary or a secondary crime scene.

7. Photograph the scene; videotape the scene.

8. Draw a sketch of the scene and add to notes.

9. Collect evidence, bag it and seal it for transport to the lab.

When the crime scene is on private property, detectives should obtain a warrant rather than relying on the consent of the owner for the search. Consent can be revoked. A warrant ensures legal validity of the search. Although police can search legally without a warrant in emergencies or to prevent the immediate loss or destruction of evidence, the U.S. Supreme Court has reversed some convictions based on searches that took place without a warrant. In one such case,[3] an undercover policeman entered the defendant's apartment during a drug raid and was killed. Police thereafter searched the apartment without a warrant over the next four days, and found bullets, drugs and other items entered in evidence at trial against the defendant. The court reversed the conviction, stating:

> There was no indication that evidence would be lost, destroyed or removed during the time required to obtain a search warrant. Indeed, the police guard at the apartment minimized that possibility. And there is no suggestion that a search warrant could not easily and conveniently have been obtained. We decline to hold that the seriousness of the offense under investigation itself creates exigent circumstances of the kind that under the Fourth Amendment justify a warrantless search.

A sketch of the crime scene is essential to the process. The sketch indicates the scale of the crime scene, so that photographs then relate to their actual location and size. Photographs of small items are taken with a ruled scale in the photograph to indicate actual size. Videotape is an important tool because it can capture three dimensional views that otherwise cannot be seen later.

Investigators will review the scene to determine if it is the primary crime scene or a secondary crime scene. The primary scene is where the crime took place, whereas a secondary scene may be where evidence has been removed, or where a victim may have been taken. For example, if a murder victim is placed in an unnatural position, investigators will look for the original site of the murder. If there is no evidence of bloodstain or blood spatter, investigators may conclude the victim was murdered elsewhere.

Evidence such as blood-stained items must be bagged in paper rather than plastic. Plastic will cause wet items to decay and bacteria to grow. Wrapping paper, manila envelopes or paper bags allow the items to breathe. However, charred debris from a suspected arson must be stored in an airtight container to avoid evaporation of a possible accelerant. Each item must be packaged separately to avoid contamination, breakage, evaporation, scratching or bending.

Search Warrant. A search warrant is issued by a court based on a finding of probable cause, and ensures that a search of a scene is legal and the evidence can be introduced against the defendant.

The crime sketch puts the pieces of evidence into visual perspective.

---

3. *Mincey v. Arizona*, 437 U.S. 385 (1978).

Investigators search the entire scene systematically. They may use a grid approach, dividing the scene into small squares and searching each one. Other patterns include the link, line or strip, zone, wheel or ray, and spiral.[4] Investigators mark, but do not touch, items until they are documented. Here are the types of information that can be learned from the crime scene:

- Information about the victim, placement of the body, whether the body was moved after death, the apparent cause of death, based on physical appearance and time of death, based on morbidity and lividity.[5]

- Information about possible modus operandi of the crime can be obtained by checking method of entry, whether cash or valuables appear missing, any damage to the scene, etc.

- Linkage of people and objects to the scene.

- Credibility of initial witness statements.

- Identification of possible suspects.

- Identification of unknown substances, such as fluids, drugs, and fingerprints.

- Reconstruction of the crime can be determined by examining blood spatter patterns, possible weapons and other details.

The investigator will generally write a formal police report, sometimes with the aid of or at the request of local law enforcement.

Laboratory Testing

After the evidence has been collected, it goes to the crime laboratory for testing. The lab will need control samples for some of its testing. This is not necessary for gun shot residue or evidence of drugs. However, fingerprints cannot be matched without "rolled" prints taken from suspects; likewise DNA cannot be matched without a DNA sample from the suspect. The same holds true for examination of hair or fiber.

Laboratory testing can be time-consuming. Fingerprint testing can take an hour if the lab technician is free. However, most of them are backed up and the incoming fingerprint takes its turn in line.[6]

DNA testing may take from three weeks to longer. The process is laborious and expensive. In 2009, The National Research Council stated that there were more than 175 publicly funded forensic laboratories and approximately 30 private laboratories that conduct hundreds of thousands of DNA analyses annually in the United States.[7] And the decision to add DNA profiles of all prisoners into the national database has resulted in backlogs in many labs. In the view of one commentator, the scope of

4. James and Nordby, *Forensic Science*, supra, at 177.
5. Morbidity is the extent of rigor mortis; lividity is the coloring caused by pooling of blood post mortem.
6. Interview with Christopher Grice, 2006.
7. NRC Report at 41.

DNA database profiles, including those of prisoners required by many state laws, puts further pressure on the DNA laboratory process:

> In 1994, the Director of the FBI was authorized to establish an index of: 1) DNA identification records; 2) analyses of DNA samples recovered from crime scenes; 3) analyses of DNA samples recovered from unidentified human remains; and 4) analyses of DNA samples voluntarily contributed from relatives of missing persons. The national DNA database relies on the FBI's CODIS software, which provides a central database of the DNA profiles from all public forensic DNA laboratories throughout the country. The FBI provides CODIS software for free to all public forensic laboratories, but each laboratory is responsible for their own computer hardware and all support software. CODIS is comprised of two indexes: 1) convicted offender index of DNA profiles from convicted criminals or arrestees pursuant to individual state statutes, and 2) forensic index of DNA profiles from crime scene evidence. DNA samples from victims are not permitted in CODIS. An individual's DNA profile must be promptly expunged from the national DNA database if his or her conviction was overturned or if the charge has been dismissed, resulted in an acquittal, or if no charge was filed.

> Local laboratories can maintain their own local DNA index system (LDIS) and then upload approved profiles to the state database. The state DNA index system (SDIS) contains profiles from local laboratories in that state, profiles analyzed by the state laboratory itself, and profiles from convicted offenders and mere arrestees (depending on specific state statutes). In addition, the FBI is responsible for obtaining samples in the federal prison system and entering those profiles into CODIS. In this sense the FBI is functioning as a state laboratory. Profiles from the states and the FBI are then uploaded into the national DNA index system (NDIS).[8]

Blood spatter analysis is tedious, in particular if investigators attempt to reconstruct the trajectory of the blood. It may involve stringing multiple strings from the spatter marks back to a common point of origin. Trace evidence, such as hair and fiber, is difficult to collect, and must be separated onto different slides for microscopic examination.

Fingerprints, particular latent prints, which are not visible, must be lifted, transferred, preserved and then either visually compared to hard copy fingerprint cards or scanned into a computer for comparison with an AFIS database. If the technician is sure what finger he or she is looking for, this shortens the time the database must search. A full ten finger search can take up to an hour before a written report of possible matches prints out.[9] That is just the first step. Then the examiner must visually view all likely matches and form an opinion. This process must be

---

8. Candice Roman-Santos "Concerns Associated with Expanding DNA Databases," 2 *Hastings Sci. & Tech. L.J.* 267 (Summer 2010).

9. Based on an interview with Christopher Grice, Connecticut Forensic Laboratory, July 2005.

repeated by another examiner. In addition, fingerprint identification must generally wait behind a long line of prints waiting to be evaluated.

Do Juries Expect Forensic Evidence?

The popularity of crime scene shows on television has led some commentators to believe juries expect forensic evidence and may be reluctant to convict without it. One court[10] may have confused jurors by the following comments made during voir dire before trial:

> In the jury selection process, the trial judge asked every potential juror a variant of the following question:
>
> > It's expected that the Commonwealth will not introduce DNA or fingerprint evidence to link the defendant to the crime scene. The Commonwealth will allege that it possesses other evidence to demonstrate that the defendant committed the crimes. Would the absence of DNA or fingerprint evidence prevent you from fairly evaluating the evidence in this case?
>
> … The phrasing of this question occasionally confused jurors, and in clarifying, the judge once asked a juror if he would be able to "focus solely" on the State's evidence, and another whether she would be able to "[p]ut aside the DNA and the fingerprint evidence."… As the SJC observed, the trial judge's goal was probably weeding out the so-called "CSI effect," the theory that because of the proliferation of crime investigation television dramas, jurors hold prosecutors to an unrealistic standard of proof and require that every crime be proven irrefutably by high-tech gadgetry and scientific analysis. Indeed, the trial judge dismissed one juror who stated that she would be unable to find a defendant guilty without DNA or fingerprint evidence of his guilt.… Defense counsel objected to both the voir dire questions and the excusal of that juror.

The "CSI effect": The theory that because of the proliferation of crime investigation television dramas, jurors hold prosecutors to an unrealistic standard of proof.

> The petitioner's argument here is that the judge's CSI-effect voir dire questioning implied to jurors that it was not significant that the prosecution lacked scientific support for its case, in effect encouraging them to ignore what could be a weakness of proof sufficient to raise a reasonable doubt about the defendant's guilt. As a result, he argues, the level of proof required for a conviction was lessened for jurors, in violation of his due process right not to be convicted except on proof beyond a reasonable doubt.
>
> …

The court held that the judge's instructions were not improper:

> The SJC's conclusion that the voir dire CSI-effect questions "did not amount to a command to ignore the lack of scientific evidence, … is an eminently

---

10. *Gray v. Gelb and Coakley*, 2015 WL 6870048 (D. Mass. 11/06/2015).

reasonable one that was not "contrary to, or ... an unreasonable application of, clearly established Federal law ...

In a similar case,[11] The Third Circuit heard a challenge to a jury instruction argued by the defendant to be an "anti-CSI" instruction:

> In his closing, Gorny's counsel highlighted the fact that no fingerprints were recovered from the gun or the bags and that the officers did not test these items for DNA because they did not want to "develop evidence against themselves," and he urged the jury to find that the Government had not met its burden of proof. After summation and over Gorny's objection, the District Court gave a so-called "anti-CSI" instruction, telling the jury that:

> > Although the government is required to prove Mr. Gorny guilty beyond a reasonable doubt, the government is not required to present all possible evidence related to the case or to produce all possible witnesses who might have some knowledge about the facts of the case.

> > During the trial, you heard testimony of witnesses and argument by counsel that the government did not use specific investigative techniques, such as DNA analysis, the use of audio or video recording devices, or the taking of photographs. You may consider these facts in deciding whether the government has met its burden of proof because, as I told you, you should look to all of the evidence or lack of evidence in deciding whether the defendant is guilty. However, there is no legal requirement that the government use any of these specific investigative techniques or all possible techniques to prove its case. As such, there is no requirement that the officers conduct DNA analysis, use audio or video recording devices, or take photographs.

"[T]here is no legal requirement that the government use any of these specific investigative techniques or all possible techniques to prove its case."

The court held that this instruction was not reversible error:

> ... the District Court expressly stated that reasonable doubt may be found based on the *lack* of evidence admitted: "it is proper for the defense to point to [a] lack of evidence and you, the jury, may consider same in determining whether the government met its burden to prove the defendant's guilt beyond a reasonable doubt." ... Thus, the District Court's instructions made clear that the jury was free to find that even if the Government is not *required* to present, say, DNA evidence, the absence of such evidence could raise a reasonable doubt demanding acquittal.

Crime Scene Drawings

Can the jury be shown the crime scene drawings or report if the officer who did the work is not present for cross-examination? If the crime scene sketch contains "conclusions" or is testamentary in nature, it would seem to trigger the Confrontation

---

11. *U.S. v. Gorny*, 2016 WL 3689063 (3rd Cir. 2016).

Clause issue discussed in Chapter 2. However, one court held that such drawings are admissible if they do not contain conclusions.[12] But where the trooper's report contained a sketch interpreting gouge marks on the road, the report was held inadmissible in his absence.[13]

Can a crime scene expert rely on notes and records collected by someone else? By definition, the defense expert must rely on the records collected by police in challenging the prosecution's theory of what happened at the crime scene. In *Gonzalez-Perez v. Gomez-Aquila*,[14] a civil suit based on a police shooting, the court said:

> David G. Townshend ("Townshend") is plaintiffs' crime scene investigation and analysis expert. The defendants move to excluded his testimony from trial arguing that Townshend did not make an actual reconstruction of the scene, did not gather any evidence, and did not test the physical evidence obtained by those present at the scene. It is further claimed that Townshend's opinion consists only of general observations and complaints regarding some discrepancies arising from the physical evidence and the way in which said evidence has been interpreted by the experts who produced those reports. In essence, the defendants' contend that Townshend's opinion is not supported by his independent testing and therefore, does not satisfy the *Daubert–Kumho* requirements of relevance and reliability ... Defendants object to the blood pattern analysis on the grounds that Townshend has admitted that he is not an expert in that field and that his knowledge consists of a four-hour segment of a conference by the Association of Crime Scene Reconstruction.

> The plaintiffs argue to the contrary. They claim that the testimony of this experienced crime scene investigator and firearms expert will aid the jury. According to plaintiffs, he can testify as to the evidence gathered at the scene and its congruence with the police version. Townshend's methodology, plaintiffs claim, is explained at length in his report as well as in his deposition and it references the methods used by investigators both at the scene and for those who are not present. It is further asserted by the plaintiffs that what Townshend performed is a crime scene evaluation which consists of a review of the available documentation on the physical evidence, statements and other evidence. Mr. Townshend's experience qualifies him to testify about the wounds on Anthony's body, the number of shots fired, and to explain the use of weapons and the patterns in which they appeared at the scene. Finally, the plaintiffs argue that there is no support in the case law for defendants' proposition that an expert of Townshend's experience must be disqualified simply because he was not present at the scene.

> ... The defendants fail to provide any support for the proposition that Townshend's testimony must be excluded simply because he bases his opinion

If the crime scene sketch contains "conclusions" or is testamentary in nature, it would seem to trigger the Confrontation Clause.

---

12. *Joines v.Moffitt,* 739 S.E.2d 177, 181 (N.C. App. 2013).
13. *Seay v. Snyder,* 638 S.E.2d 584, 181 N.C. App. 248 (2007).
14. 296 F. Supp. 2d 110, 116 (D. Puerto Rico 2003).

on an evaluation of the evidence gathered by persons other than him. After all,[u]nder Rule 702, a qualified expert witness may testify "in the form of an opinion, or otherwise, if (1) the testimony is based upon sufficient facts or data, (2) the testimony is the product of reliable principles and methods, and (3) the witness has applied the principles and methods reliably to the facts of the case."*United States v. Mooney,* 315 F.3d 54, 62 (1st Cir.2002). Any flaws in Townshend's otherwise reliable methodology go to the weight and credibility of the evidence and not to its admissibility.

In *Brower v. Secretary for the Department of Corrections,*[15] petitioner's habeas appeal was denied. He argued that failure of counsel to call witnesses who would have questioned the prosecution's theory of what happened at the crime scene constituted ineffective counsel. The court disagreed:

> Brower also argues he was denied effective assistance of counsel when his trial counsel did not call two witnesses. One of the witnesses, a forensic expert, would have provided testimony that, based on the trajectory of the bullets, the shots must have been fired by a taller person. This witness would have also called into question the veracity of the information gleaned from the crime scene investigation. The other witness would have impeached the testimony of the government's star witness. Brower argues that he suffered prejudice because this testimony would have undermined the government's circumstantial evidence of his guilt.

> As discussed above, an appellant must show both incompetence and prejudice in order to succeed with a claim of ineffective assistance of counsel. We agree with the state habeas court and the district court that Brower cannot show prejudice. "[T]he absence of exculpatory witness testimony from a defense is more likely prejudicial when a conviction is based on little record evidence of guilt." *Fortenberry v. Haley,* 297 F.3d 1213, 1228 (11th Cir. 2002) (rejecting petitioner's ineffective assistance of counsel argument on lack of prejudice grounds despite "no conclusive forensic or eyewitness evidence" because of petitioner's "multiple uncoerced confessions"). As the court of appeals stated on direct appeal, Brower's guilt was supported by "overwhelming evidence." *Brower v. State,* 684 So. 2d 1378, 1378 (Fla. 4th DCA 1996).

For similar reasons, the court in *U.S. v. Fultz*[16] rejected a petitioner's claim that additional literature supporting his expert's offer to testify about a shooting scene reconstruction equaled "newly discovered evidence" justifying granting a habeas petition. Most important of the tests for granting a new trial based on newly discovered evidence is that the evidence would "probably" result in acquittal. The court decided the testimony would not have resulted in an acquittal.

"[A]n appellant must show both incompetence and prejudice in order to succeed with a claim of ineffective assistance of counsel."

Most important of the tests for granting a new trial based on newly discovered evidence is that the evidence would "probably" result in acquittal.

---

15. 137 Fed. Appx. 260 (11th Cir. 2005).
16. 18 F. Supp. 3d 748 (E.D.Va. 2014).

Although the general rule is that crime scene photos are admissible, the defense can object if the crime scene photos are inflammatory on the ground that they are prejudicial. One commentator reviewed a number of cases that made this argument and concluded:

> Courts have determined that gruesome crime scene videotapes were improperly admitted under a variety of circumstances, although their admission has been upheld in a substantial majority of cases. In *State v. Loza* (1994, Ohio) 641 N.E.2d 1082, the court held that a videotape from the crime scene was properly admitted to rebut the defendant's claim that the absence of blood on the clothes he wore showed that he could not have committed the murders. The court emphasized that the videotape, as well as photographs, were particularly illustrative of the fact that the victims' wounds involved the splattering of very little blood, and concluded that the gruesome nature of the exhibits was not sufficient to render them per se inadmissible.[17]

Failures in crime scene processing can result in a failed investigation altogether. The well-known case of the murder of JonBenet Ramsey, which occurred in 1996 in her Colorado home, has never been solved. We examine the ransom note in the chapter on Handwriting and Questioned Documents. But from the outset, questions were raised about errors in crime scene investigation process, including the fact that the crime scene was not immediately sealed by investigators and the fact that John Ramsey, her father, was permitted to search the house after investigators arrived in response to a call that he had found a ransom note.

Chain of Custody

Forensic evidence cannot be introduced at trial by the attorney for either the prosecution or the defense without a witness on the stand who can identify the evidence and assure the court that it is reliable. How do we know that the firearm introduced into evidence is in fact the firearm taken from the crime scene many weeks, months, or sometimes years ago? And even if the crime scene investigator were on the stand, what are the chances he or she could look at the firearm and absolutely identify it as the one found in connection with this particular crime?

The process of authenticating forensic evidence involves proving a formal "chain of custody," starting with the crime scene investigator and ending with the location where the evidence has been stored immediately before being introduced. This involves keeping the evidence in a sealed container of some type and requiring any person who removes it to sign, stating the dates and times of removal and replacement.

In a case involving a drug arrest in Guatemala,[18] the prosecution sought to admit a note that it said was taken from the defendant's wallet that had the letters "DEA"

---

17. 37 A.L.R.5th 515 (Originally published in 1996).
18. *U.S. v. Mejia*, 597 F.3d 1329 (D.C. Cir. 2010).

on it with names of DEA officials. Because the initial arrest took place outside the country, the foreign officials who found the wallet were unable to testify and there was a ten-minute "gap" between finding the wallet and handing it to U.S. officials. The court held that the general rule that prohibits introduction of evidence without a clear chain of custody would be relaxed to allow the evidence to be admitted, with the defense permitted to make the chain of custody argument to the jury. In other words, the evidence would be admitted, subject to the jury considering the weight of the evidence.

As noted earlier, shortly after Mejia (along with Morales, Bran and the informant Cortez) arrived at his third and final meeting, several Salvadoran police officers entered the restaurant where the three co-conspirators and Cortez were meeting and arrested them. DEA Agent Fraga did not witness the arrest because at the time he was in an automobile parked several blocks away from the scene. He testified that he arrived at the restaurant about ten minutes after the arrest, at which point he was given a bag from a Salvadoran police officer he presumed to be the leader of the arrest team. The bag contained Mejia's personal effects. The Salvadoran officer who seized Mejia's belongings did not testify and the government did not identify him; in fact, the government did not call any witness who took part in Mejia's arrest and the seizure of his property. Neither did it introduce a return or other official document listing the items seized from Mejia upon arrest. Agent Fraga testified that among the items included in the bag the Salvadoran officer gave him was Mejia's wallet and inside the wallet he found a folded, handwritten note with "DEA" and a list of names on it. The names included at least five agents stationed in the DEA's Guatemala City office. The paper did not include Mejia's name or signature and no handwriting or fingerprint evidence was introduced to link Mejia to it. In short, Mejia's chain-of-custody objection to the admission of the list — that it was given to Agent Fraga by "[s]omeone who's not present here and we don't know what happened to it [before Agent Fraga obtained it]," Trial Tr., Mar. 3, 2008 (P.M.) at 102 — is fundamentally correct.

. . .

See *Novak v. District of Columbia,* 160 F.2d 588, 588-89 (D.C.Cir.1947) (citing *Smith v. United States,* 157 F.2d 705 (D.C.Cir.1946)). In *Novak,* a police officer testified that he had obtained a urine sample from the defendant, labeled the bottle and delivered it to the laboratory for analysis; a lab chemist also testified as to the alcohol content of a urine sample in a bottle labeled with the defendant's name and confirming lab records were introduced. The government did not establish, however, that the bottle the arresting officer labeled and initialed was the same one the lab chemist analyzed. We concluded that the evidence was "missing a necessary link in the chain of identification" and reversed Novak's conviction.

"[A] challenge to the chain of custody goes to weight rather than admissibility."

We have since retreated somewhat from *Novak,* holding that a challenge to the chain of custody goes to weight rather than admissibility. *See United*

States v. Stewart, 104 F.3d 1377, 1383 (D.C. Cir. 1997) (evidence of delay in testing lab sample "went to the weight to be ascribed to the drug evidence by the jury, not its admissibility"). Indeed, we held in *Stewart* that the government's burden "only requires it to demonstrate that, 'as a matter of reasonable probability,' possibilities of misidentification and adulteration have been eliminated."

One commentator, who is a defense lawyer, gave the following advice on challenging chain of custody:

> Firsthand knowledge is at the center of chain of custody disputes. Someone with personal, hands-on, and visual experience with the evidence can testify to its maintenance from when it entered his or her hands to when it left. Then, someone else has to continue the chain of custody with his or her own firsthand knowledge. Usually, the party alleging that a "solid" chain exists either hasn't attempted to find everyone in the chain or cannot identify them. The witness also may be unable to testify that the proper procedures were implemented throughout each layer of the chain of custody.

> Next, attack the recordkeeping, which is always vulnerable if no one can defend each and every record. Imagine a sample of temperature-sensitive evidence, passing through several hands before it reaches its destination. Records of who received it and when and how it was maintained could be in triplicate affidavits—but unless they address the temperature issue, they are relatively meaningless. Even if the records address temperature, they are weak if no one has personal knowledge of specific refrigeration efforts. Personal knowledge is key.

> There are many ways evidence could have been contaminated, allowed to degrade, or tampered with. You or your expert should conjure up the different scenarios. When jurors consider the issues and potential unaccounted-for problems, the chain of custody will look like a circus.[19]

House v. Bell,[20] a U.S. Supreme Court case, was not strictly speaking about chain of custody and crime scene investigation, but it involved the consequence of a pre-DNA blood test that wrongfully implicated the defendant. The evidence of murder, including a nightgown and the defendant's pants, were put in one box in the trunk of a car along with a vial of the victim's blood and driven ten hours to an FBI lab. The Supreme Court agreed with the defendant House's contention that the blood on the pants may well have come from a leak in the sample of the murdered woman's blood that was packed in vials with the evidence. There was also seepage of her blood in one corner of the packing box. We will look at this case in more detail in the chapter on Exonerations of the Wrongfully Convicted.

"Usually, the party alleging that a 'solid' chain exists either hasn't attempted to find everyone in the chain or cannot identify them."

---

19. Shannon Pennock, "Missing Links in the Chain of Custody," *Trial* 52 (June 2016).
20. 126 S. Ct. 2064 (2006).

The Chain of Custody in the *Grant* Case

The defense contended that various items of evidence should not be introduced into trial because some items had been lost, such as Serra's keys and the bloody parking ticket, and because evidence had been moved from place to place and stored under improper conditions.

Here is the decision of the court on the Chain of Custody motion to exclude evidence:

State v. Grant, 2002 Conn. Super. LEXIS 1127

. . .

The factual backdrop of these motions has been discussed in a number of prior decisions. On July 16, 1973, the body of Concetta ("Penny") Serra was found in a stairway of the Temple Street parking garage in New Haven. The medical examiner determined that she died as the result of a stab wound to the heart. No one was apprehended at the scene. There was, however, a substantial amount of blood at the scene, and some of this blood is thought to be that of the killer.

(Serra's blood was Type A; the blood thought to be that of the perpetrator is Type O.) Edward Grant, the defendant herein, was arrested for Serra's murder in 1999, largely on the basis of the State's allegation that the blood found at the scene is consistent with a DNA profile of Grant's blood.

… Grant, who is about to be tried, understandably wishes to exclude the DNA evidence that the State seeks to introduce. On January 4, 2002, he filed a motion to preclude evidence because of an assertedly insufficient chain of custody. On February 4, 2002, he filed a separate motion to preclude all evidence relating to STR testing. (No. 74.) The motions were the subject of evidentiary hearings held over the course of several days in January and February 2002.

Numerous witnesses testified at the chain of custody hearing. The sole witness at the STR hearing was Dr. Carll Ladd, the supervisor of the forensic biology unit of the State Forensic Science Laboratory ("Laboratory"). The motions were argued on April 5, 2002.

Although the chain of custody motion facially seeks exclusion of numerous items of evidence, Grant has narrowed its scope considerably in his post-hearing briefs. He presently seeks to exclude only

- "Item 6" (a handkerchief found at the crime scene) and
- "Item 12" (blood on tape lifts taken from inside an automobile belonging to John Serra, also found at the crime scene).

The evidentiary importance of these items is primarily related to scientific testing that has been performed on them.

. . .

The State has met its burden of showing an appropriate chain of custody with respect to "Item 6" as well. The evidence shows appropriate preservation and custody of that item, and there is no possibility that intermeddlers somehow tampered with that item to contaminate it with material containing Grant's DNA.

The only real question with respect to "Item 6" is whether the handling of that item by a variety of testers over the years has compromised the DNA material remaining on that item to the point where the State's DNA testing can no longer be considered reliable. After a full consideration of all of the evidence, the court is convinced that the answer to this question is no. Grant's factual assertions involving contamination and degradation of the DNA material on "Item 6" go to the weight rather than the admissibility of the evidence.

The court denied Grant's motions to preclude evidence.

"[T]here is no possibility that intermeddlers somehow tampered with that item to contaminate it with material containing Grant's DNA."

Linking Forensic Evidence to Witness Statements

Many investigators develop ideas about possible theories of the crime after the initial crime scene has been processed. Even before laboratory work begins or is finished, they have located potential witnesses and begun to question them. All suspects should be treated initially as witnesses, even though investigators are often influenced by what they know about patterns of crimes. For example, they know most burglaries are committed by someone who knows the house — a workman, friend of a family member, or other regular guest. Initial witness lists consist of such people. However, the investigator must always remain objective, and question witnesses with a view to ruling them out as a suspect, rather than to "solve the crime."

Crime scene officers try to be objective in determining whether a crime has been committed, and who the perpetrator might be. This is often difficult, particularly as officers are aware that statistics show that most crimes fit a pattern. For example, most murders take place between people who know each other. Most burglaries are committed by someone who had access to the home.

Just as important as collecting forensic evidence is tying that evidence to a witness, who may become a suspect and ultimately a perpetrator. Crime scene officers are trained in questioning strategy. They also can frequently tell if a witness is hiding something. For example,[21] if an innocent person is accused of something he did not do, he will usually be angry at being falsely accused and will remain angry throughout an interview. A guilty person, by contrast, will initially act angry, because he thinks

---

21. Interview with Detective Peter Valentin, Connecticut Fourth District Major Crime Unit, October 2006.

that is what he should do, but will eventually forget or be unable to continue the "act." This same theory is used by the polygraphist in dealing with witnesses who try to use "countermeasures" in an attempt to influence the results of the polygraph. Most witnesses cannot consistently apply their attempted countermeasure over time.

Some detectives ask each witness to recount every moment of the day. An innocent person can sometimes be excluded based on the written statement. Frequently, he will often divide the day into equal parts—for example, before lunch, lunch until mid-afternoon, and so forth, whereas the guilty person will skip over the timeframe when the crime occurred, resulting in an unnatural break in the timeline.[22]

Missing Evidence

The Grant team was unsuccessful is dismissing the case because of the missing keys and bloody parking ticket. Clearly, if two pieces of evidence had been lost, they could potentially have exonerated Grant or at least pointed to another possible defendant. Unfortunately, there was no evidence that the Connecticut Forensics Laboratory had lost the evidence due to poor procedures, or even fraud.

Expert Qualifications

All forensic witnesses are not created equal. Obviously, a party wants to find an expert who is well-qualified in his or her field, someone who has published in scientific journals, and is an authority in an area of science. The expert should also be someone willing to review the evidence and become thoroughly familiar with the case. A big name may impress the jury, but an expert who is not prepared will alienate them more.

Scientists tend to speak a different language, so the attorney may have to spend time helping the expert to speak in terms the jury can understand. The jury in the O.J. Simpson case, for example, were annoyed that the DNA expert talked down to them as if they were children. Scientists also tend to want to answer the question they think the examining attorney *should be* asking, not the one the attorney is actually asking. In other words, the scientist wants to educate everyone, including the opponent. Getting an expert to listen carefully to the question and not volunteer any information on cross examination can be extremely difficult.

A good attorney will always ask his expert on direct examination if he is being paid and how much.

Most experts are paid to prepare and to testify. The only experts who are not paid are those who work for the state. In the Grant trial, Chris Grice, the fingerprint expert, was not paid to testify, as he worked for the forensic lab. Dr. Henry Lee, by contrast, was an outside expert at that point and was paid. A good attorney will always ask his expert on direct examination if he is being paid and how much. This gets the issue in front of the jury and avoids embarrassment on cross examination. Does being

22. *Id.*

paid create potential bias? Of course it does. But as the experts on both sides are generally both being paid, the bias tends to cancel itself out.

Experienced attorneys know that it helps to find an expert who has testified before and read the transcript of the earlier testimony. An expert can be severely discredited on cross examination if the opposing attorney can point to a prior inconsistent opinion. This is called "impeaching" a witness. Experts who become rattled or arrogant on cross examination are a poor choice, as even the expert who is absolutely right will not be believed by a jury if he is unlikable. In the Grant case, the defense attorney referred to a joke that expert Henry Lee made during his testimony. This prompted an unpleasant exchange between attorneys and the judge, alternately attacking and defending Lee. The expert should never become a personality rather than a source of expert testimony.

> An expert can be severely discredited on cross examination if the opposing attorney can point to a prior inconsistent opinion. This is called "impeaching" a witness.

In criminal cases, the experts for the prosecution tend to be criminalists and forensic scientists who work for the state. The defendant generally must locate and pay for his own experts. Particularly for poor defendants, this can create an unfair system. There have been a number of appeals based on defendants arguing that inadequate resources were used to prepare for their defense. These appeals generally fail, unless the defendant can prove that his counsel's performance was so deficient that it prejudiced the defense. For example, the decision of an attorney not to pursue psychological testing for his client was not prejudicial because the appeals court held that there was overwhelming evidence of guilt and the defendant failed to show there was a reasonable probability that, but for the challenged errors, he would have been acquitted.[23]

Slowly, courts are coming to the realization that a defendant is prejudiced by the inability to obtain and independently test forensic evidence. For example, many states now provide that prisoners may petition for DNA evidence on a claim of actual innocence.

No Experts for the Defense

The Grant defense did not call any expert witnesses. They cross-examined Christopher Grice, who said that the fingerprint he identified as Grant's from the tissue box could have been placed on the box prior to the time of the crime. They also cross examined Carll Ladd, the DNA expert, on various technical issues about the DNA alleles from the handkerchief. He also agreed that he could not say when the genetic material was placed on the handkerchief.

Finally, the defense cross-examined Dr. Lee in an effort to discredit him by showing that in 1989, he had concluded that the handkerchief was not a part of the crime scene. Dr. Lee succeeded in stating both that he changed his mind once he knew that Grant's DNA was on the handkerchief *and* that he made his decision about the

---

23. *Link v. Luebbers*, 469 F.3d 1197 (8th Cir. 2006).

handkerchief being connected to the crime without resort to anything other than the crime scene itself.[24]

Therefore, the jury was not left to decide which of two opposing experts to believe. Although experts for the prosecution and defense typically disagree, this does not justify the defendant in claiming on appeal that the prosecution's expert presented "false testimony":

> Gimenez presents a battle between experts who have different opinions about how Priscilla died. Introducing expert testimony that is contradicted by other experts, whether at trial or at a later date, doesn't amount to suborning perjury or falsifying documents; it's standard litigation. Accordingly, Gimenez can't obtain relief under section 2244(b)(2)(B)(ii) on the theory that the prosecution introduced false testimony at trial.[25]

Claims of Ineffective Counsel Based on Crime Scene Experts

A claim of ineffective counsel is generally raised on *habeas corpus,* as it would be a Constitutional violation. The general rule is that such arguments will not succeed unless counsel presents no defense. If the reviewing court finds there is other evidence of guilt, the claim will also fail. In *Brower v. Secretary for the Dept. of Corrections,*[26] the prisoner said his counsel did not call an expert witness who would have testified that the shots in question must have been fired by a taller person and would otherwise have contradicted information from the crime scene investigation. His counsel was also denied access to the crime scene. The Appellate Court held that this did not amount to ineffective counsel, where there was overwhelming evidence of the petitioner's guilt, including multiple confessions.

But the U.S. Supreme Court held in a 2014 case[27] that failure to request a more expensive, "better" forensic expert constitutes "ineffective counsel," which may warrant reversing a conviction. In that case, counsel did not properly research state law. If he had, he would have learned that he could apply for any expenses "reasonably incurred," rather than the maximum of $1,000 which he believed the law required and which would pay only for an inexperienced expert who was discredited at trial. The case involved a restaurant manager who was shot to death in a robbery of his restaurant. The only testimony linking defendant to the crime scene was testimony of two government experts that bullets fired from his .38 caliber gun "matched" those recovered at the crime scene and the eye witness testimony of a witness. The defendant's alibi was corroborated by witnesses. The defendant was convicted and sentenced to death. The U.S. Supreme Court stated that if the lawyer had hired better-qualified experts in a case where the evidence

"Introducing expert testimony that is contradicted by other experts, whether at trial or at a later date, doesn't amount to suborning perjury or falsifying documents; it's standard litigation."

---

24. Transcript, May 9, 2002, p. 36.
25. *Gimenez v. J.T. Ochoa,* 821 F.3d 1136 (2015).
26. 137 Fed. Appx. 260 (11th Cir. 2005).
27. *Hinton v. Alabama,* 134 S. Ct. 1081 (2014).

was so slim to begin with, it might well have led to a different result. The court reversed and remanded for reconsideration of whether counsel's performance was prejudicial.[28]

Summary

Forensic evidence must be collected carefully and follow all laws in order to be admitted in trial. The process requires investigators to carefully document all evidence and to remain objective. One of their objectives is to link forensic evidence to suspects. Forensic evidence may demonstrate either class characteristics or individual characteristics. The nature of the forensic expert's opinion will differ, depending on the type of evidence. Counsel must carefully select and prepare the forensic expert in order to persuade a jury that the expert's opinion is correct.

Locard's Principle says that every person who comes in contact with an object or person will make a cross transfer of evidence that will identify him. This principle is why crime scene investigators examine a crime scene in detail. Forensic evidence must be collected carefully and following all laws in order to be admitted in trial. The process requires investigators to carefully document all evidence and to remain objective. An expert who testifies about the crime scene may rely on notes or drawings prepared by others, so long as they do not contain opinions or conclusions.

One of the objectives is to link forensic evidence to suspects. Forensic evidence may demonstrate either class characteristics or individual characteristics. Class characteristics will be those that will "include" the suspect, such as the same shoeprint, but individual characteristics are those that can conclusively identify a suspect, such as DNA. Both investigators and juries need to be aware of the difference.

Chain of custody requires that evidence be properly controlled and accounted for in order to be admissible at trial. Some courts refuse to admit evidence where there is a break in the chain of custody. Others admit the evidence, but allow the defendant to argue that the jury should take the break in the chain and possible tampering into consideration in their deliberations.

Courts are now mindful that juries may expect forensic evidence and have tried to avoid prejudice by questioning in voir dire and by jury instructions.

An expert may testify based on crime scene drawings or sketches prepared by someone who is not in court, unless they contain any conclusion or opinion, in which case the Confrontation Clause would require the presence of the investigator who wrote the report.

Counsel must carefully select and prepare the forensic expert in order to persuade a jury that the expert's opinion is correct. Some believe that the criminal justice system favors the prosecution in the area of expert testimony, as states have forensic

---

28. *Id.* at 1083.

laboratories and technicians to test and testify, whereas defendants must hire expensive experts to evaluate or contest the state's evidence.

Discussion Questions

1. Why is it important to secure the crime scene and to collect evidence as quickly as possible?

2. Name the steps to investigating a crime scene. Why is it important to do the steps in the order given? What would happen if the investigators left out or varied one of the steps?

3. How does what the crime scene investigator does or does not do affect the admissibility of evidence at trial?

4. Watch an episode of CSI and explain anything you saw the actors do that a real crime scene investigator would not do.

5. Why is a sketch of the scene better than photographs or video alone?

6. What procedures ensure that the prosecution can establish a "chain of custody" of forensic evidence at trial?

7. Why did Grant lose his chain of custody challenge? Do you agree?

8. What are the ways that an expert witness can show his qualifications to testify?

9. Find the following website: truthsleuth.com. What does this tell you about how investigators use witness statements?

10. What is the difference between a primary crime scene and a secondary crime scene? How does this apply to the *Grant* case?

11. How can an expert satisfy the burden of proving his or her qualifications?

12. How might a petitioner on *habeas corpus* succeed in an argument that his attorney provided ineffective counsel by failing to call an expert witness?

Chapter 4

The Scientific Method and "Junk Science"

Overview

Following the U.S. Supreme Court case in 1993 called *Daubert v. Merrell Dow Pharmaceuticals, Inc.*[1] all areas of forensic expert testimony were required to establish that they were scientifically "reliable." The first inquiry in establishing reliability is whether the area of forensic evidence meets the "scientific method." *Daubert* set down several non-exclusive tests to determine scientific reliability, including (1) whether the underlying method can be or has been tested; (2) whether the method has been subject to peer review and publication; (3) the method's known or potential error rate; and (4) the level of the method's acceptance within the relevant discipline.

In NRC Report, published in 2009, made various recommendations for more testing in forensic disciplines and validation of conclusions in almost all areas of forensics except DNA. We will examine this report and its conclusions in this chapter.

The term "junk science" was coined to refer to theories that do not meet the scientific method. This does mean that such a theory might not be later proved scientifically valid. It may mean simply that the theory has not yet been tested. For example, there is much brain research currently being done that has shown incapacity to form criminal intent and that may ultimately prove lack of "guilty knowledge" or propensity to commit certain crimes. This area, called neuroimaging, has not yet achieved general acceptance in the scientific community and despite arguments that it meets the *Daubert* tests for scientific reliability, it has been rejected by many courts:

> ... [D]efense lawyers have rushed to bring brain scans into courtrooms. Some of what they propose is out-and-out chicanery; some may hold real value; whatever the case, the job of piloting the public through the complex neuroscientific maze — in order that potential jurors may better judge whether a violent offender should be condemned to death, to a long or life sentence in America's barbaric present-day prison system, or should have their

---

1. 509 U.S. 579 (1993).

sentences reduced or changed because of a brain irregularity or insult—is vital to society.[2]

We will discuss neuroimaging as one of the areas of supposed "junk science."

The area of junk science that is most difficult to prove by the scientific method are hypotheses that exposure to certain chemicals or forces causes a specific disease. The reason is because in order to prove causation, the scientist must rule out all other possible causes. Isolating one particular agent to the exclusion of all others is a daunting scientific task. *Daubert* involved just such an hypothesis, namely, that ingesting the drug Bendectin caused birth defects.

For our purposes, we will concentrate on the forensic disciplines used in criminal cases. The science underlying these disciplines is generally directed either toward identifying an individual based on evidence such as fingerprints, DNA, handwriting, or the like, or demonstrating what likely occurred at a crime scene, for example, through examining blood spatter patterns or the trajectory of ballistics.

The NRC Report highlighted a number of problems that affect the scientific reliability of most forms of forensic evidence today:

> With more and better educational programs, accredited laboratories, certified forensic practitioners, sound operational principles and procedures, and serious research to establish the limits and measures of performance in each discipline, forensic science experts will be better able to analyze evidence and coherently report their findings in the courts. The current situation, however, is seriously wanting, both because of the limitations of the judicial system and because of the many problems faced by the forensic science community.[3]

The scientific method requires that two different examiners must arrive at the same conclusion, assuming all variables are constant. This requirement of "replicability" is key to science. However, there are a number of areas of forensics that require subjective examination and conclusion, which precludes replicability.

In the area of forensics, there are a number of techniques that have not been proven under the scientific method to be reliable as a form of individual identification. These include bite-mark identification, lip print identification, palm print identification, bullet identification through lead composition, and neuroimaging, as well as more creative theories such as whether one can be identified by smell.

Chapter Objectives

Based on this chapter, students will be able to:

1. Explain the scientific method.

---

2. "Brains Take the Stand," Caleb Carr, *The New York Times Book Review*, March 12, 2017.
3. NRC Report at 13.

2. Identify the scientific hypotheses underlying fingerprints, DNA testing, eyewitness identification, firearm and tool mark identification, lip print and palm print identification, and neuroimaging.

3. Understand the concept of "error rate" in science.

4. Describe the concept of junk science.

5. Identify the reason various types of junk science fail to qualify under the scientific method.

6. Appreciate the difference in proving causation in a personal injury civil case and proving identity in a criminal case.

7. Articulate the arguments for and against admission of neuroimaging technology to prove mental state.

What Is the Scientific Method?

The dictionary definition of "science" is "the observation, identification, description, experimental investigation, and theoretical explanation of phenomena."[4] In essence, a scientific "theory" results from the observation of phenomena, the creation of a hypothesis, and the testing of that hypothesis to explain or disprove the phenomena in question. A scientist and his or her colleagues create tests or experiments to try to test the validity of the hypothesis.

"Science" is "the observation, identification, description, experimental investigation, and theoretical explanation of phenomena."

The National Research Council defined the scientific method as follows:

> Scientists continually observe, test, and modify the body of knowledge. Rather than claiming absolute truth, science approaches truth either through breakthrough discoveries or incrementally, by testing theories repeatedly. Evidence is obtained through observations and measurements conducted in the natural setting or in the laboratory. In the laboratory, scientists can control and vary the conditions in order to isolate exclusive effects and thus better understand the factors that influence certain outcomes. Typically, experiments or observations must be conducted over a broad range of conditions before the roles of specific factors, patterns, or variables can be understood. Methods to reduce errors are part of the study design, so that, for example, the size of the study is chosen to provide sufficient statistical power to draw conclusions with a high level of confidence or to understand factors that might confound results. Throughout scientific investigations, the investigator must be as free from bias as possible, and practices are put in place to detect biases (such as those from measurements, human interpretation) and to minimize their effects on conclusions.[5]

"Typically, experiments or observations must be conducted over a broad range of conditions before the roles of specific factors, patterns, or variables can be understood."

4. *The American Heritage Dictionary*, 4th ed., Dell Publishing, 2001.
5. NRC Report at 112.

Following the *Daubert* decision, in an effort to help federal judges assess scientific evidence, the Federal Judicial Center published an extensive *Reference Manual on Scientific Evidence*.[6] David Goodstein, in his article "What Is Science," which appears in the manual, says:

> If one asks a scientist the question, What is science?, the answer will almost surely be that science is a process, a way of examining the natural world and discovering important truths about it. In short, the essence of science is the scientific method.

Another author of the manual defined "good science" as follows:

> Good science is usually described as dependent upon qualities such as falsifiable hypotheses, replication, verification, peer-review and publication, general acceptance, consensus, communalism, universalism, organized skepticism, neutrality, experiment/empiricism, objectivity, dispassionate observation, naturalistic explanation, and use of the scientific method.[7]

The scientific method requires these steps:

1. Hypothesis.
2. Observation and/or experimentation to prove the hypothesis false.
3. Sufficient sample size to draw valid conclusions.
4. Elimination of any alternative hypothesis for the results.
5. Explanation for any contradictions of the evidence.

The National Research Council prepared a detailed analysis of many forms of forensic evidence in 2009, and recommended more uniformity of training, common standards for forensic laboratories, and in particular, more scientific testing to establish scientific reliability for every area of forensic evidence it examined, except DNA. These include:

- fingerprints
- firearms examination
- tool marks
- bite marks
- impressions (tires, footwear)
- bloodstain pattern analysis
- handwriting
- hair
- DNA
- coatings (e.g., paint)
- chemicals (including drugs)
- materials (including fibers)
- fluids
- serology

---

6. Available at http://www.fjc.gov.
7. *Id.* at 13.

- fire and explosive analysis
- digital evidence

Defining the Relevant Scientific Community

One important issue is who has done the scientific testing, whether they have any bias, and whether their results have been peer-viewed and accepted by other objective scientists. The *Daubert* case included as one test for reliability whether the science was "generally accepted in the scientific community." Yet, with the exception of DNA, law enforcement has generally been involved in developing forensic evidence testing without submitting their results to universities or outside laboratories for verification. This creates the question of whether the science has been tested and proven to the "Relevant Scientific Community." For example, in evaluating polygraph reliability, should a court look at the studies conducted by the American Polygraph Association? If they did, the reliability statistics would approach 80%.[8] On the other hand, if the court looked at the myriad of websites that claim they can teach someone how to fool a polygraph in ten hours,[9] it might come to the opposite conclusion.

> With the exception of DNA, law enforcement has generally been involved in developing forensic evidence testing without submitting their results to universities or outside laboratories for verification.

Determining the Error Rate

The word "error" in law means that a court has made a mistake — something no court being reviewed on appeal wants to hear. The word "error" in science is intrinsic to any process of measurement. Scientists expect error and, indeed, search for it. In fact, one of the hallmarks of science is that an "error rate" can be ascribed to the results of testing. That is why you hear plus or minus x% as an error rate. Error can result from two causes: mistakes that occur in the testing process as a random event and human error.

> "Error" in science is intrinsic to any process of measurement.

In addition to the elements of hypothesis, experimentation, and falsification are certain "ideal standards of conduct" that should govern scientific inquiry in order legitimize it. The scientist should be unbiased, self-critical, and open-minded. Edmond and Mercer, in "Trashing Junk Science" put it this way:

> There have been a number of attempts to formulate the ideal standards of conduct (norms) and institutional imperatives of science. Robert Merton provided the most famous formulation of these imperatives, categorizing them under the four headings of communalism, universalism, disinterestedness, and organized skepticism.[10]

Note that some commentators reject the notion that there is one all-purpose scientific method. For example, Edmond and Mercer say:

---

8. Raymond Nelson, "Scientific Basis for Polygraph Testing," http://www.polygraph.org /scientific-basis-for-polygraph.

9. http://www.wikihow.com/Cheat-a-Polygraph-Test (Lie-Detector).

10. Gary Edmond and David Mercer, "Trashing 'Junk Science,'" *Stanford Technology Law Review* 3 (1998): 25, 29.

The notion that there is a simple, identifiable, universal scientific method used in some kind of standard way by scientists to distinguish science from non-science is difficult to support on any kind of empirical basis. One of the factors which illustrate the implausibility of this contention is the sheer diversity of activities which can be placed beneath the umbrella of modern science. Given such diversity, various branches of scientific knowledge rely, to different degrees, upon observational practices, experimental tests, mathematical proofs, and so on.

For instance, in some branches of industrial chemistry, test situations can be established where there are strong linkages between theory, practice and phenomena. In contrast, other areas of science rely upon situations intrinsically difficult to test. These situations, then, may rely on statistical methods, new, sensitive measuring devices, and phenomena not easily modeled in the laboratory. The latter is true in many areas of atmospheric physics, ecology, and epidemiology.[11]

Science does not proceed smoothly in properly sequential "baby steps." To the contrary, it appears to advance is large "jumps." Whereas science may have been a "gentlemen's calling" in the 1800s, characterized by collecting and cataloging butterflies and rocks, today it involves peer review and publication, government grants, prestige, and money in form of prizes, such as the Nobel Prize.[12] It may also result in discoveries of enormous economic value, such as patents and appearances on television shows.

The "Science" of Inclusion, Exclusion, and Identification

The purpose of forensic evidence is to identify the suspect and no one other than the suspect as the person linked to the crime.

As we discussed in Chapter 1, forensic evidence can be critical in linking a particular person to a crime or a crime site. The purpose of such evidence is to identify the suspect and no one other than the suspect as the person linked to the crime. Yet of the variety of types of forensic evidence, some can only "include" the defendant in a class of people that may have contributed the sample. This is true for blood (based on blood type), most tool marks, hair (based on microscopic examination, not DNA), footwear (unless there is some unique identifier on it) and fiber. "Identification" requires that every other source of the evidence be eliminated. This is true only for DNA and fingerprints. As we will see, even in the case of DNA, the typical expert "opinion" is expressed in terms of statistical probabilities of someone other than the defendant being the source of the sample (referred to as the chance of a "random match"). And although fingerprint examiners are permitted to give a positive identification opinion, the subjective element in fingerprint identification calls into question whether such an opinion is scientifically reliable. See Chapter 6, on fingerprint identification.

---

11. Edmund and Mercer, *supra* at 29.

12. The 2006 scandal in Korea over falsified data and the subsequent resignation of its chief scientist shows the pressure to publish results is international in scope. See Nicholas Wade, "University Panel Faults Cloning Co-Author," *New York Times*, February 11, 2006.

Replicability and Absence of Subjective Judgment

Under the scientific method, one scientist should be able to replicate the results of another. In other words, the subjective judgment of the scientist should not be involved in setting up or analyzing the results of the experiment. Therefore, whenever there is a subjective judgment to be made, the training and experience, to say nothing of bias, of one examiner may lead to a different conclusion by one than by another. By definition, this disqualifies as "science."

Let's look at eyewitness identification and handwriting identification. The purpose of these two types of forensics, like DNA and fingerprinting, is identification, that is, an opinion that the suspect and only the suspect is identified. As we will see when we examine eyewitness identification, there are serious problems with reliability, some of which have been demonstrated in studies. And handwriting relies on even more subjectivity on the part of the examiner than does fingerprint examination because there is no agreement among handwriting experts about which similarities are most important, which should be evaluated first, and how many points of similarity are required to declare a "match." In essence, the handwriting examiner decides what features are important and what ones are not, which again can differ among examiners.

What Is the Scientific Hypothesis?

In evaluating the scientific reliability of all of these types of evidence, it is useful to first determine what scientific principles underlie the identification. Then we can see if they have actually been tested. There is one basic scientific hypothesis that underlies the identification forensics we will review, which is the concept of "uniqueness," that the item being tested is unique between individuals:

> There is one basic scientific hypothesis that underlies the identification forensics we will review, which is the concept of "uniqueness."

- Each person's fingerprints are unique, so a fingerprint match will identify a person to the exclusion of all others.
- Each person's DNA is unique, so a DNA profile will identify a person to the exclusion of all others (except an identical twin).
- No two people look exactly alike, so an eyewitness identification is reliable in identifying a suspect.
- No two people write exactly alike, so an examination of samples of handwriting will reveal if a person has written another document.

Fingerprints

Let's examine fingerprint matching to see how the scientific reliability inquiry works. The validity of a fingerprint identification rests on two hypotheses:

- first, that fingerprints are unique, and
- second, that the methodology of identification is sufficient to distinguish one print from another.

How do we *know* that each person's fingerprints are unique? We obviously cannot take fingerprints from everyone in the world and compare them. So scientists examine a sample of people to see if the fingerprints in that sample are unique. This presents the first obstacle to evaluating scientific accuracy. How many fingerprints are enough to prove the hypothesis? You would agree that looking at the prints of ten people would not be useful. Even if they were all unique, there might be other people who shared the same fingerprints. Scientists must therefore combine a representative sample with sufficient sample size, using the laws of statistics to generalize to the general population.[13] Depending on the size of the sample, scientists may give a level of confidence to their conclusion that is less than 100%.

Scientists must therefore combine a representative sample with sufficient sample size, using the laws of statistics to generalize to the general population.

For example, if scientists looked at the fingerprints of only white males, someone might question if the sample were representative. What if white females had a different pattern in their fingerprints? What if race made a difference? The job of the scientist is to think up as many explanations for why the theory might be wrong as possible and then test those theories.

As a result of fingerprint testing and the use of databases in which the three basic patterns of all prints — arch, loop, and whorl — have been entered, scientists conclude that 65% of all people have a loop pattern, 30% have a whorl, and 5% have an arch.[14] Based on these three features of fingerprints, there would be no way to identify a person simply by finding a loop, whorl, or arch on his print, as, for example, someone with a whorl print would have the same pattern — and therefore be indistinguishable from — 30% of the population.

The next step is for scientists to look at smaller patterns within the patterns. They identified approximately ten "ridge characteristics," smaller patterns such as a ridge ending, an island or a crossover line. As each fingerprint has up to 200 of these characteristics, the statistical chances of someone else having the exact same characteristics in the same specific locations on his or her fingerprint is astronomically small.

But *how* small? Scientists do not know. No one has yet studied a random population to determine how many ridge endings, islands, or crossovers occur. Of the 200 characteristics, do 80% of people have crossovers, but only 20% have islands on a print? We do not know. In addition, are the characteristics spread over a fingerprint randomly, or do islands appear in the upper left quadrant of 90% of the population? We don't know that either.

The "science" behind fingerprint matching is not perfect. Scientists do not match prints by overlaying a photograph of one perfect fingerprint over another on a computer screen that then displays the word MATCH! This is a scene made to

---

13. You will learn in the fingerprint identification chapter that the only test of uniqueness of fingerprints involved 50,000 white male FBI employees and that the test involved matching "clean" fingerprints, not partial or smudged prints, which are typically lifted at crime scenes.

14. Andre A. Moenssens, James E. Starrs, Carol E. Henderson, and Fred E. Inbau, *Scientific Evidence in Civil and Criminal Cases*, 4th ed. (Foundation Press, 1995), 506.

entertain television audiences in shows such as *CSI: Crime Scene Investigation*. Examiners do most of their work looking under magnification at small, blurred, and splotchy lines, trying to determine if there are any dissimilarities. As with all scientists, they work first to exclude, and then to include.

Although a national computer database is often used in fingerprint matching, it generates only a list of fingerprints with the highest number of ridge characteristics to the lowest. The examiner must then view the photographs of the fingerprints matching those numbers. As you will see in the fingerprint identification chapter, the number one "hit" is not always the print chosen by the examiner as the match! Fingerprint examiners in some states are permitted to declare that a partial fingerprint lifted from a crime site absolutely identifies a suspect if the expert finds only 10 ridge characteristics in common. Is this adequate to absolutely identify someone? The FBI has no minimum number of points required to declare a match. Law enforcement points to the fact that there are almost no errors reported; hence, the system must be valid. But this is not a scientific experiment.

The lack of scientific validity between the number of ridge characteristics matched and the lack of data about the distribution of ridge characteristics in the population led one court to reject fingerprint analysis as being unreliable.[15] The court agreed with the hypothesis that no two fingerprints are alike, but disagreed that the methodology of identification had controlling standards, peer review, and other evidence of reliability. We will discuss this in detail in Chapter 6, "Fingerprint Analysis."

The NRC Report in 2009 made two recommendations about fingerprint identification:

- first, it acknowledged the subjective element involved and said that the examiner should be required to document the subjective process used in fingerprint matching, and
- second, it called for additional research into "ridge flow and crease pattern distributions on the hands and feet."[16]

DNA

Because DNA typing was developed after scientists had mapped the entire human genome, there was already a database showing the proportion of genetic variations at each site tested in a DNA profile. As we will see in the chapter on DNA, DNA profiles do *not* create a person's total DNA profile. In fact, as with fingerprints, DNA profiling looks at only 13 of a possible 2,000 places where DNA variations occur with no known association with a genetic trait. But because scientists know the relative proportions of variations at those 13 locations, they can create statistical probabilities of the likelihood of a "random match." No such statistical probabilities have ever been developed for fingerprinting.

---

15. *U.S. v. Llera Plaza*, 179 F.Supp.2d (E.D. Pa. 2002), vacated, 1888 F. Supp.2d 549 (2002).
16. NRC Report at 144.

Eyewitness Identification

Prisoners have been exonerated by DNA, even though the victim still believes that his or her visual identification was correct.

Many prisoners have been convicted solely on the strength of a positive visual identification by a victim. Some of these prisoners have been exonerated by DNA, even though the victim still believes that his or her visual identification was correct! Besides the fact that many people *do* look alike, there are other factors that may show visual identifications are particularly "unscientific." We will examine these in the chapter on eyewitness identification. You will see that the scientific proposition that a victim of a violent crime will be able to categorically identify the perpetrator even when the crime takes place for only a few minutes and under extraordinary stress, has been seriously undermined by testing and research.

These examples show that proof of a scientific hypothesis rests on many subsidiary scientific hypotheses and testing of those hypotheses is needed to establish validity.

What Is Junk Science?

Junk science is a conclusion presented as a scientific "truth" that has been derived without using the scientific method as its source.

The term "junk science" was coined in the late 1980s and early 1990s. Peter Huber, of the Manhattan Institute, promoted the term through a number of publications, including one called "Gallileo's Revenge: Junk Science in the Courtroom."[17] His point was that scientific theories are promoted by special interest groups, entrepreneurial scientists, and the press—eager to "explain" various phenomena to the public.

Some critics argue that the courtroom, with its emphasis on an adversarial system and cross-examination of experts to impeach their credibility over their credentials and method of experiment, actually promote junk science. Scientists who might otherwise be willing to admit error rates or other problems with experimental results are also forced to overstate certainty as a result of the process. Others argue that the court system is the best possible place to test scientific conclusions because it is an adversarial system.

The *Daubert* case in 1993 involved a claim that a drug, Bendectin, caused birth defects. This is a very different type of science from that used in criminal trials because it involves proof of *causation* as opposed to proof of *association*. In order to prove a drug causes a certain effect, the scientist must exclude all other possible factors. This is typically not an issue in criminal forensic disciplines. However, the explosion in society of claims that certain products cause injury shows how the public can be swayed by what sound like scientific claims.

The following is an example of a scientific conclusion that was formerly accepted and now is viewed as "junk science" hypothesis: Anthropometry Can Conclusively Identify a Person. Anthropometry was developed in 1879 by Alphonse Bertillon, a Parisian law enforcement officer.[18] It was the practice of measuring specific body parts to identify an individual. Bertillon's scientific hypothesis was that each person's

---

17. Peter W. Huber, "Gallileo's Revenge," New York: Basic Books, Harper Collins 1991.
18. Ed German, "The History of Fingerprints," ONIN, http://www.onin.com/fp/fphistory.html.

body was unique, so that a series of specific bodily measurements would absolutely identify an individual. One purpose was to identify a person who had been recently arrested and compare it to records made at an earlier arrest to establish the existence of a prior record. This would avoid the use of false identities to conceal one's true identity.

Bertillon used calipers to measure the hands, head, limbs, torso and face of an individual. Here are some examples of the detailed measurements contained with anthropometry:

1. length and width of the head
2. left middle finger, left foot, and left forearm
3. height, span of arms, trunk, right ear
4. profile of head
5. ear
6. front view of face
7. ridge and base of nose and nose dimensions
8. left eye
9. eye pigmentation

Bertillon believed that individual body parts, such an ear, were unique. In his book, *Signaletic Instructions: Including the Theory and Practice of Anthropometrical Identification*, published in 1896,[19] he presented detailed measurements of all parts of the ear. Bertillon proposed his method of measurement as a way to identify former prisoners who were subsequently arrested and gave an assumed name.

The Bertillon system of anthropometric measurements was abandoned worldwide because it failed to provide reliable and unique measurements and was too cumbersome to administer in a uniform manner. Moreover, it never relied on a single measurement of any part of the body for identifying a specific individual.[20]

Today, we can't imagine how it could have been seriously contemplated that each of us has a set of unique body measurements, and certainly that they would not change over time. But certain aspects of anthropometry are used today for a variety of respected medical tasks, such as identifying disease based on a lack of proportion between the head and other body parts. Also, NASA uses anthropometry in designing space capsules to fit human proportions.[21] Cranofacial anthropometry — measurements of the skull and face — can help diagnose plagiocephaly, a condition in infants that may require surgery.[22] Anthropometry evolved into the science of measuring just one body part — the fingerprint — in order to distinguish individuals.

The Bertillon system of anthropometric measurements was abandoned world-wide because it failed to provide reliable and unique measurements and was too cumbersome to administer in a uniform manner.

---

19. *See* http://www.forensic-evidence.com/site/ID/ID_bertillion.html.

20. *Id.*

21. National Aeronautics and Space Administration, "Anthropometry and Biomechanics," *Man-Systems Integration Standards* 1, http://msis.jsc.nasa.gov/sections/section03.htm.

22. International Society for Pediatric Neurosurgery, "Presentation of Positional Plagiocephaly in Children," http://ispn.guide/book/The%20ISPN%20Guide%20to%20Pediatric%20Neurosurgery/

Although anthropometry was not tested using the scientific method, perhaps the presence of particular "instruments" for measurement, combined with a detailed set of measurements coupled with a chart of results, led people to believe it was science simply because it "looked like science." Again, keep this idea in mind as we review some more recent methods that propose they can be used for identification, but which lack sufficient testing and therefore should be called "junk science."

Forensic Evidence that Lacks Sufficient Scientific Studies

In 2009, the NRC Report recommended more scientific testing in all areas of forensic evidence it examined, except for DNA. And for any type of testing that involves subjective judgment, it recommended detailed written findings by the examiner.

The following are areas where courts have sometimes accepted forensic evidence, although there are insufficient scientific studies to validate it as a means of identification under the scientific method. Remember that such evidence may have value used as class evidence, particularly as a method of excluding the suspect (for example the shoeprint is size 10 and the suspect wears a size 7) but identification requires scientific reliability, proof of uniqueness, and evaluation of the testing method being used (and as we know that each pair of shoes is not unique, the value of a "matching" shoeprint must be compared with the known universe of how many of those shoes in that size are in the relevant population).

- firearms and toolmarks
- bite marks
- knife marks
- shoeprints
- palm prints and foot prints
- lip prints
- polygraph
- smell
- neuroimaging

Firearms and Toolmarks

Both firearms and toolmarks depend on the same hypothesis and are variations on "impression" evidence, as are shoeprints, lip prints, and palm prints.

The scientific hypothesis is that an examiner can tell what tool (including a firearm) made certain markings on an object (such as a bullet or cartridge) and therefore "match" the tool to the mark. See Chapter 8, "Firearms and Toolmarks." Both firearms and toolmarks depend on the same hypothesis and are variations on "impression" evidence, as are shoeprints, lip prints, and palm prints. However, there is a big difference between firearm analysis and other forms of impression evidence. This is

---

Congenital%20Disorders%20of%20the%20Nervous%20System/Positional%20Plagiocephaly/presentation-p.

because there is an impressive databank of firearm images, both bullet and cartridge case markings, which can be accessed for a possible match. The National Integrated Ballistic Information Network (NIBIN) contains these images. There have also been tests of specific firearms to support the theory that each firearm leaves particular striations on the bullet and/or casing. But even there, the NRC Report said that the scientific knowledge is "fairly limited."[23]

However, there is no corresponding database for marks made by different tools for obvious reasons. Tools can range from crowbars to screwdrivers to any conceivable object that is used in a burglary, homicide, or other crime. The hypothesis that every tool leaves a unique mark has never been tested. In fact, it seems obvious that the best an expert could ever opine is that a particular tool is consistent with a particular impression.

The NRC Report noted that in the early 1990s, the FBI and the Bureau of Alcohol, Tobacco, Firearms, and Explosives developed separate databases of images of bullet and cartridge case markings which could be consulted to look for a match. But the National Research Council cautioned "[k]nowing the extent of agreement in marks made by different tools, and the extent of variation in marks made by the same tool, is a challenging task."[24] And even with newer image-based measurement data, there is still a subjective judgment made by the examiner. "Even with more training and experience using newer techniques, the decision of the toolmark examiner remains a subjective decision based on unarticulated standards and no statistical foundation for the estimation of error rates."[25] The combination of use of subjective judgment with lack of statistical data means that this form of identification does not qualify as "reliable science."

The NRC Report also pointed to the fact that, even for firearms, the AFTE has adopted a theory of identification, but lacks a specific protocol and does not specify how many points of similarity are necessary for an opinion of identification. However, courts have accepted expert opinions that a particular firearm or tool was used in a crime, without restricting the opinion to "could have been used" or requiring a *Daubert* hearing on the scientific reliability of the testimony.

In its summary, the council concluded:

> Because not enough is known about the variabilities among individual tools and guns, we are not able to specify how many points of similarity are necessary for a given level of confidence in the result. Sufficient studies have not been done to understand the reliability and repeatability of the methods ... additional studies should be performed to make the process of individualization more precise and repeatable.[26]

"Even with more training and experience using newer techniques, the decision of the toolmark examiner remains a subjective decision based on unarticulated standards and no statistical foundation for the estimation of error rates."

---

23. NRC Report at 153.
24. *Id.*
25. *Id.*
26. *Id.* at 154.

Another area of firearms testimony involves the lead composition of bullets, as some experts have testified that the lead composition of a bullet can be matched to other bullets found in a suspect's weapon. In a decision by the Kentucky Supreme Court, testimony by a forensic scientist that the metallurgical composition of a bullet that killed the victim was identical to bullets found in the defendant's rifle was ruled inadmissible. The appellate court said that the trial court should have rejected the testimony because FBI studies showed that bullets manufactured at different times and different places may have the same lead composition.[27] In this respect the court's view was similar to that which requires a shoeprint expert to opine only that a shoeprint is "consistent with" the defendant's. The issue of how many other people may wear the same shoe then goes to the weight of the evidence.

Similarly, an expert was not permitted to testify that a defendant had recently fired a gun, handled a gun or been near a gun when it was fired, because the standard for the number of gunshot residue (GSR) particles that indicates a positive result is not agreed.[28] "Based on the testimony of both the state's expert and the defendant's expert, it is clear that significant questions exist in the relevant scientific community concerning how many particles are required ... [I]t is also clear that scientists agree that the results will not determine if a person fired a gun, was present when a gun was fired or handled contaminated guns or ammunition. The scientists agree a positive test will only conclude a person has been in an environment of gunshot residue."[29]

These cases involving firearms show the courts grappling with the level of scientific testing of the hypothesis of identification from impression evidence, coupled with a concern that any time a subjective analysis is required by the expert, this opinion cannot be grounded on pure science.

Bite Marks

Although dental records have been used for decades to identify people, the matching of a person's "bite" to a bite mark on a victim has raised similar issues to toolmarks. There are no standards for what constitutes a full bite mark and there are no scientific studies to show if each person's bite mark is unique. Nevertheless, bite mark "experts" have been permitted to testify.

A defendant convicted of murder contested the introduction of a computer-enhanced image that matched his teeth to the bite mark on the victim's breast. He contended that the evidence required an expert. His attorney stated "This is nascent technology. It's brand-new. It was imperative that the defendant had an opportunity to explore how it works."[30] The Connecticut Supreme Court disagreed, holding that

---

27. *Ragland v. Kentucky*, 191 S.W.3d 569 (Sup. Kentucky 2006).
28. *Minn. v. Moua*, No. K5-05-7335 (Minn Dist. 2006).
29. *Id.*
30. Lynne Tuohy, "Murder Appeal Centers on Technology," *Hartford Courant*, September 27, 2003.

the defendant had an opportunity to cross-examine and that even if there were error, it was harmless.[31]

Similarly, a petitioner brought a habeas corpus petition[32] contending that introduction of expert testimony that his dentition matched a bite mark on the inner thigh of the victim was grounds to vacate his conviction. The court disagreed. However, it is important to remember that the issue on habeas was whether a constitutional violation had occurred, not whether the expert should have been permitted to testify to begin with.

> [Defendant] Milone argues that the science of forensic odontology was in its infancy at the time of his trial and that it was therefore error to admit testimony from the state's expert to the effect that his dentition matched the mark found on Sally's thigh. Milone reasons that such testimony fails both the *Frye* and the *Daubert* tests for the admissibility of scientific evidence in federal courts.
>
> …
>
> It is clear that the probative value of the odontology evidence presented by the state was not so outweighed by its prejudice to Milone as to deny him a fundamentally fair trial. With respect to its probative value, while the science of forensic odontology might have been in its infancy at the time of trial, as Milone asserts, certainly there is some probative value to comparing an accused's dentition to bite marks found on the victim. With respect to the prejudice to Milone caused by the admission of what he claims was unreliable evidence, he had ample opportunity to persuade the trial judge to discount the testimony of the state's expert: Milone was able to cross-examine the state's expert both in regard to his credentials and in regard to the general reliability of the science of bite mark identification, and Milone presented several experts of his own to testify that he could not have made the mark found on Sally's thigh. Accordingly, it was not constitutional error for Illinois to have allowed the admission of the bite mark evidence.

In *Starks v. City of Waukegan*, another habeas petition, the court came to the same conclusion without evaluating the science of bite mark analysis: even if dentists gave false or mistaken testimony with respect to their analysis of bite marks on the rape victim, that did not amount to a due process violation.[33]

The National Research Council said of bite marks in 2009:

> Despite the inherent weaknesses involved in bite mark comparison, it is reasonable to assume that the process can sometimes reliably exclude suspects. Although the methods of collection of bite mark evidence are relatively noncontroversial, there is considerable dispute about the value and reliability

"It is clear that the probative value of the odontology evidence presented by the state was not so outweighed by its prejudice to Milone as to deny him a fundamentally fair trial."

---

31. *State v. Swinton*, 268 Conn. 781 (2004).
32. *Milone v. Camp*, 22 F.3d 693 (1994).
33. 123 F. Supp. 3d 1036 (2015).

of the collected data for interpretation. Some of the key areas of dispute include the accuracy of human skin as a reliable registration material for bite marks, the uniqueness of human dentition, the techniques used for analysis, and the role of examiner bias.... Although the majority of forensic odontologists are satisfied that bite marks can demonstrate sufficient detail for positive identification, no scientific studies support this assessment, and no large population studies have ever been conducted.[34]

However, in 2016, this view that bite marks may be valid was apparently rejected by the President's Council of Advisors on Science and Technology:

"[F]orensic bite-mark evidence is not scientifically valid and is unlikely ever to be validated."

... forensic bite-mark evidence is not scientifically valid and is unlikely ever to be validated, according to a draft report obtained by *The Intercept*. The report, titled "Forensic Science in Criminal Courts: Ensuring Scientific Validity of Feature-Comparison Methods," is marked as a "predecisional" draft created August 26 [2016].

The report reviews a handful of common forensic practices, so called feature-comparison disciplines, or pattern-matching practices — bite-mark analysis, fingerprint and firearm analysis, shoe tread analysis, and DNA mixture analysis — each of which involves an "expert" looking at a piece of evidence and eyeballing whether it matches a particular image, person, or object.

In the case of bite-mark evidence, the report is especially critical. "PCAST finds that bitemark analysis does not meet the scientific standards for foundational validity, and is far from meeting such standards," it reads. "To the contrary, available scientific evidence strongly suggests that examiners cannot consistently agree on whether an injury is a human bitemark and cannot identify the source of [a] bitemark with reasonable accuracy."

Bite-mark analysis is conducted by forensic dentists and relies on two foundational premises: first, that human dentition is unique — as unique as DNA — and second, that human skin (or another malleable substrate) is a suitable medium on which to record such an impression. The problem is that neither premise has been proved.[35]

The news report added that a prisoner, Bill Richards, who was in prison for nearly 23 years based on dubious bite-mark evidence, had been released in June of 2016.[36]

The evolving analysis of bite mark analysis is a hopeful sign that more scientific rigor is being applied to areas that may have been accepted as "common wisdom"

---

34. NRC Report at 176.

35. Jordan Smith, "White House Report Concludes that Bite Mark Analysis Is Junk Science," *The Intercept*, September 7, 2016, https://www.theintercept.com/2016/09/07/white-house-report-concludes-that-bite-mark-analysis-is-junk-science.

36. *Id.*

but that are actually junk science in the sense that they do not meet the standards set by the Supreme Court in *Daubert*.

Knife Prints

Knife prints are also a form of impression evidence and knife print matching rests on the hypothesis that a particular knife can be definitely linked to a wound. This hypothesis suffers from the same impediments as bite mark testimony. A Florida court rejected a crime technician's opinion that a particular knife definitely caused a wound and reversed defendant's conviction. Using the *Frye* test that requires "general acceptance" in the scientific community, it said there was no evidence to show that a specific knife can be identified by the marks made on cartilage.[37]

There was no evidence to show that a specific knife can be identified by the marks made on cartilage.

A more common reason for excluding knife print testimony is the lack of training or experience of the examiner, which relieves the court of having to decide about scientific reliability. Arguably, when there is a subjective judgment of the examiner required to declare a "match," the burden of training and experience should increase. This was the case in *U.S. v. Smallwood*,[38] in which the government appealed a ruling before trial that a knife mark examiner would not be permitted to testify:

> In excluding Gerber's testimony in this case, the district court reasoned that she "does not have the 'skill and experience' with knife marks to reliably make the required subjective determination." The government argues that the district court abused its discretion because it read the standard promulgated by the Association of Firearms and Toolmark Examiners ("AFTE") too narrowly when it required that Gerber have extensive experience in examining toolmarks left by knives in order to be qualified as an expert witness in the area of toolmark examination. According to the government, although the AFTE theory lacks an objective standard, competent firearms toolmark examiners still operate under standards controlling their profession, and the fact that Gerber has less experience with knife toolmarks than with firearms toolmarks is not a valid reason to preclude her testimony. We find the government's argument unconvincing.

> The AFTE guidelines provide that a qualified examiner may determine that there is a match between a tool and a tool mark when there is "sufficient agreement" in the pattern of two sets of marks. *Theory of Identification*, 30 AFTE J. 86, 86 (1998). "Agreement is significant when it exceeds the best agreement demonstrated between toolmarks known to have been produced by different tools and is consistent with agreement demonstrated by toolmarks known to have been produced by the same tool." *Id.* (using "sufficient" and "significant" interchangeably). Because such determinations

"The AFTE guidelines provide that a qualified examiner may determine that there is a match between a tool and a tool mark when there is 'sufficient agreement' in the pattern of two sets of marks."

---

37. *Ramirez v. Florida*, 810 So. 2d 836 (Fla. Sup. 2002).
38. 456 Fed. Appx. 563 (6th Cir. 2012).

"involve subjective qualitative judgments ... the accuracy of [an] examiner['s] assessment[ ] is highly dependant on [her] skill and training."

Shoeprints

As with other areas of impression evidence (including fingerprints), matching shoeprints requires a subjective conclusion by an expert, based on knowledge of the universe of possible matching shoes and a knowledge of statistics. "Matching" shoeprints are generally at best a class characteristic, meaning that they can exclude a defendant if they do not match, but they cannot conclusively identify a defendant, unless the shoeprint is so unique or rare that the likelihood of anyone else having the identical shoeprint is virtually impossible. A shoeprint could become unique if it were worn in an unusual pattern, but the expert would have to demonstrate knowledge of wear patterns in shoes generally and, again, be able to identify statistical probabilities. This is almost never done in shoeprint testimony.

Furthermore, the expert would need to refer to a database of similar shoes. Identifying a shoeprint as an Adidas size 7 "Edge Bounce Runner" running shoe requires proof that the sole of an Adidas "Edge Bounce Runner" running shoe is unique among all other running shoes. So far, there is no database of all soles of all running shoes in America, so this premise lacks proof. Britain, by contrast, launched a database of thousands of shoes and shoe types, similar to the DNA databases, in order to help identify criminals. Dr. Romelle Piercy, of the Forensic Science Service in London, said "footwear marks at the scene are the second biggest evidence type behind blood and DNA."[39] The archive will include shoe type, color, branding, and marks as well as demographic information. It already contains over 1,000 distinguishing marks on Nike training shoes alone.[40]

Shoeprints are not an individual characteristic unless they are so unique that no other person could have the same print.

However, some courts have refused to require shoeprint matching to prove it is scientifically reliable. In one case, a criminologist with the state crime lab used a side-by-side comparison of shoeprints found in powder at a laundry where $2,000 was stolen with the defendant's shoes. The trial court said the testimony was not "scientific,"[41] and therefore did not require a *Daubert* hearing. Nevertheless, the appellate court said that a hearing held by the trial court in which the expert described her methods satisfied the requirements of *Daubert* anyway. Even where the expert had limited training and experience, a trial court accepted shoeprint testimony.

In a 2011 case in the Eastern District of Virginia, *U.S. v. Council*,[42] the court conducted a day-long hearing on defendant's motion to exclude a Maine police lab forensic scientist from testifying that footwear impressions taken inside a credit union matched defendant's shoe. The trial court ruled her testimony satisfied *Daubert*. She testified the defendant's shoe made the impressions found on the stairway and teller

---

39. Patricia Reaney, "Shoe Database to Help Forensic Investigators," Reuters, January 29, 2007.
40. *Id.*
41. *Ratliff v. Alaska*, 110 P.3d 982 (Ct. App. Alas. 2005).
42. *U.S. v. Mahone*, 453 F.3d 68 (1st Cir. 2006).

counter. On appeal, the court agreed that the expert was qualified even though she lacked a voluntary certification through the IAI. The defendant argued, however, that her testimony was not scientific because:

> there is no set number of clues which dictate a match between an impression and a particular shoe; 2) there is no objective standard for determining whether a discrepancy between an impression and a shoe is major or minor; and 3) the government provided "absolutely no scientific testing of the premises underlying ACE-V."[43]

The appellate court held that this argument was without merit, using fingerprint as a comparison because it is also impression evidence. It held that because the ACE-V (analysis, comparison, evaluation, and verification) method of fingerprint analysis has met *Daubert*, so should matching shoeprints. However, the court failed to recognize that fingerprinting rests on the scientific premise that no two fingerprints are alike, which has at least some scientific support, coupled with many years of successful use by law enforcement and a very small error rate. Shoeprint analysis has no database and has never proved uniqueness. In fact, it is common knowledge that a manufacturer sells thousands of a particular shoe, all of which hit the stream of commerce looking identical.

Palmprints

Although some experts have testified that a palm print "matches" a suspect, this area of testimony suffers from similar problems as other impression evidence. It may at first appear as if a palm print is as unique as a fingerprint (and scientists may well determine this in scientific studies) but without proof of the hypothesis, palm print matching lacks proof and requires a totally subjective judgment on how much of a palm print is required and how many matching points the analyst must find. Nonetheless, in 2011, the federal trial court in Virginia[44] allowed an expert to testify to a palm print match, finding her testimony to be sufficiently reliable.

Lip Prints

Are lip prints unique? There are no studies on this topic. How much of a lip print is required for identification? Again, there are no studies. Nevertheless, experts have been permitted to testify about lip print "matches." One website states there are five basic types of lip prints that can be used for identification, but admits the credibility of lip prints has not been firmly established.[45] What about ear prints? One commentator says it currently has "non-status as an identification science."[46]

---

43. *Id.*
44. *U.S. v. Council*, 777 F. Supp. 2d 1006 (E.D. Va. 2011).
45. http://www.geocities.com/Athens/Atrium/5924/lipprintsbackground.htm.
46. http://www.forensic-evidence.com/site/ID/ID_bertillion.html.

Polygraph

Polygraph is a strange hybrid. It measures changes in sweat, blood pressure, and heart-rate while a subject is answering questions posed by a polygrapher. While the physiological changes are not disputed, the point of polygraph is to correlate those changes to "guilty knowledge," commonly called a lie detector. This process involves carefully posed questions — neutral, control, and relevant. An examiner must use subjective judgment in interpreting the polygraph results. For this reason, most scientists would call polygraph "junk science." In addition, polygraph can be highly prejudicial, as it is designed to detect whether a person committed a crime. For this reason, most states ban it from being introduced in court. Nevertheless, polygraph was the subject of two cases which examined its scientific reliability in detail. The first in 1923, was the *Frye* case. The court held a precursor of polygraph was not admissible because it was not "generally accepted" by the scientific community. This case set the standard for forensic expert testimony for many years and is still the test in some states, including New York.

> An examiner must use subjective judgment in interpreting polygraph results.

A second more recent case also dealt with polygraph. *State v. Porter*[47] in Connecticut examined polygraph more carefully and seemed to be persuaded that polygraph might meet the *Daubert* tests. However, the court decided to maintain its rule that polygraph is inadmissible in court because of the possible prejudice to the defendant. In essence, the court feared that a jury, confronted with scientific evidence that proved the defendant told the truth when he said he had no involvement in an arson, would substitute the polygraph for its own judgment instead of weighing all of the other facts.

The *Porter* case contains an excellent explanation of exactly how polygraph works:

> Modern polygraph theory rests on two assumptions:
>
> > (1) there is a regular relationship between deception and certain emotional states; and
> >
> > (2) there is a regular relationship between those emotional states and certain physiological changes in the body that can be measured and recorded.
>
> These physiological changes include fluctuations in heart rate and blood pressure, rate of breathing, and flow of electrical current through the body, and they are measured by a cardiosphygmograph, a pneumograph and a galvanometer, respectively. These instruments, bundled together, form the basis of most modern polygraphs.
>
> There is no question that a high quality polygraph is capable of accurately measuring the relevant physical characteristics. Even polygraph advocates, however, acknowledge that "no known physiological response or pattern of responses is unique to deception."

---

47. 241 Conn. 57, 698 A.2d 739 (1997).

Indeed, "there is no reason to believe that lying produces distinctive physiological changes that characterize it and only it.... There is no set of responses — physiological or otherwise — that humans emit only when lying or that they produce only when telling the truth.... No doubt when we tell a lie many of us experience an inner turmoil, but we experience similar turmoil when we are falsely accused of a crime, when we are anxious about having to defend ourselves against accusations, when we are questioned about sensitive topics — and, for that matter, when we are elated or otherwise emotionally stirred.

Thus, while a polygraph machine can accurately gauge a subject's physiological profile, it cannot, on its own, determine the nature of the underlying psychological profile. "The instrument cannot itself detect deception."[48]

New Mexico is the one state that admits polygraph and it has adopted strict rules that must be followed. The federal courts do not ban polygraph *per se*, or automatically, but most cases reject it unless both parties have agreed in advance of the test that the results will be admissible.

Is "Neuroimaging" a More Scientific Form of Measuring Knowledge?

Like polygraph, neuroimaging, the measurement of brain function through MRI, CT-scan, and the like, is scientifically valid as a measurement of brain function. But linking that brain function to a conclusion about a specific person's ability to form intent or to be psychologically able to form a defense is a different matter. Nonetheless, neuroimaging may be one area where "junk science" will evolve into accepted science.

> Neuroimaging may be one area where "junk science" will evolve into accepted science.

One commentator, who has argued that neuroimaging meets *Daubert* and should be admissible, concedes that so far, courts have refused to accept the testimony, usually concluding that it is not relevant or not probative. Therefore, they have not addressed the scientific reliability issue:

> In *United States v. Mezvinsky*, PET scan evidence was introduced to show that the defendant, who was accused of multiple counts of fraud, was incapable of intentionally deceiving a person or institution, which was the requisite mens rea for his crime. The district court found the scans unhelpful and irrelevant since they could not provide concrete information concerning the defendant's capacity to deceive. Accordingly, the PET scans were inadmissible for lack of reliability and for irrelevance to the specific legal question at issue.
>
> Similarly, in *United States v. Puerto*, the Eleventh Circuit affirmed the lower court's decision to exclude the defendant's expert under a *Daubert* analysis. In an attempt to demonstrate that the defendant could not have formed the mens rea necessary for fraud and money laundering, the

---

48. *State v. Porter*, 241 Conn. 57, 60–73, 698 A.2d 739, 743–749 (1996).

defendant sought to introduce expert testimony about his diagnoses of progressive vascular dementia. The defendant wanted to show a brain scan indicating that a region of his brain was "cavitated out" and the brain tissue was replaced by fluid, indicating damage to numerous brain functions, including comprehension and executive planning.[49]

Although the court in the second case referred to *Daubert*, the appellate court made clear that the primary reason for excluding the expert was relevance, not reliability:

> The Eleventh Circuit affirmed, finding that the experts were unable to testify "with any medical certainty" that the defendant lacked the requisite intent at the time of the offenses and that the evidence could not "help the jury decide a factual dispute." In both *Mezvinsky* and *Puerto*, functional brain scans were excluded under *Daubert* for lack of relevance.[50]

More recently, another commentator in 2016[51] argued in favor of separating out different forms of neuroimaging and analyzing each for its scientific reliability. The authors reviewed over 100 cases in which neuroimaging testimony was proffered in court, often on the issue of whether the defendant was able to form the specific intent required for the crime charged. They referred to the trial of John Hinkley, Jr. as the first case where neuroimaging evidence was introduced to prove a defense of insanity. (Hinkley was released in the fall of 2016, upon a finding that he was no longer a danger to himself or others.)[52]

The authors found one case in 1978 in which an appellate court agreed that the defendant was improperly denied the expert evidence that would show his lack of intent:

> In the 1978 case of *United States v. Erskine* the defendant sought to admit brain scan evidence and expert testimony to establish that he was unable to form the specific intent required to violate 18 U.S.C. § 1014 (i.e., making a false statement for the purpose of influencing a bank). The trial court excluded the evidence but the appellate court found the defendant's brain scan evidence was improperly denied admission. The court stated, "[w]e express no opinion on whether Dr. Saidy was qualified to give such an opinion on the defendant's mental condition, but we do hold that the defendant was entitled to introduce competent evidence pertaining to the defense of lack of specific intent. While the competence and persuasiveness of the offered testimony can be questioned, the relevance of the subject matter cannot be.[53]

"[W]e do hold that the defendant was entitled to introduce competent evidence pertaining to the defense of lack of specific intent."

---

49. Adam Teitcher, "Weaving Functional Brain Imaging into the Tapestry of Evidence: A Case for Functional Neuroimaging in Federal Criminal Courts," *Fordham Law Review* 80 (October 2011): 355.

50. *Id.*

51. Jason Kerkmans and Lyn Gaudet, "*Daubert* on the Brain: How New Mexico's *Daubert* Standard Should Inform Its Handling of Neuroimaging Evidence," *New Mexico Law Review* 46 (Summer 2016): 383.

52. Spencer S. Hsu and Ann E. Marimow, "Would-Be Reagan Assassin John Hinkley Jr. to Be Freed after Thirty-Eight Years," *Washington Post*, July 27, 2016.

53. *Id.* at 403.

The court in *Booth v. Kit*,[54] came to a similar conclusion, holding that the specific type of MRI called diffusion tensor imaging had been tested, was subject to peer-review, lacked a high error rate, and was generally accepted in the scientific community for measuring the integrity of the white matter of the brain. It held that any perceived weakness in the expert's testimony could be attacked on cross-examination or by a contradictory expert opinion. However, this was a civil case for damages caused by carbon monoxide, so the causal connection between the neuroimaging evidence and the damage alleged was at issue. We can expect to continue to see objections to the relevance of neuroimaging to issues of criminal intent.

Another type of brain imaging has been offered as a form of polygraph — a very different purpose than forming intent. "Brain mapping" or "brain fingerprinting" is a process that uses electronic measurement of brain waves arguably to detect guilty knowledge. Brain mapping can supposedly detect whether a suspect recognizes elements about a crime scene that someone not involved in the crime would not know. The theory is that certain parts of the brain respond when someone recognizes something he or she already knows There is apparently no way to circumvent this process, as it is involuntary. "Brain fingerprinting" as it is called by Dr. Lawrence A. Farwell, its inventor,[55] is a process in which a suspect is shown a series of words or pictures relevant to a crime along with other irrelevant words or pictures. Electrical brain response (called MERMER) is measured through a headband equipped with sensors. The theory is that the brain will involuntarily "recognize" the words or pictures and the MERMER will show this recognition. The responses are coded by a computer, thereby theoretically removing human observational error.[56]

> Brain mapping can supposedly detect whether a suspect recognizes elements about a crime scene that someone not involved in the crime would not know.

The *New York Times* reported on Farwell's ideas in a 2001 article[57] and spoke with his thesis advisor:

> Dr. Donchin, who was Dr. Farwell's thesis adviser at the University of Illinois and now teaches at the University of South Florida in Tampa, calls Mermer "business nonsense." Some brain wave researchers complain that Dr. Farwell's search for real-world applications that appear to prove the value of the technology is diverting attention from the need to do more research like the peer-reviewed 1991 paper.

> But Dr. Donchin and others say that p300 testing may one day be as valuable as Dr. Farwell currently claims if more research into how to present the right questions or other stimuli. Dr. John J. B. Allen, a psychologist at the University of Arizona, said the technique demanded extremely effective detective work to prepare the test. "You have to be quite confident that an

---

54. *Booth v. Kit*, 2009 WL 4263615 (D.N. Mex. 2009).
55. "Farwell Brain Fingerprinting Executive Summary," http://www.larryfarwell.com/brain-fingerprinting-executive-summary-dr-larry-farwell-dr-lawrence-farwell.html.
56. *Id.*
57. Barnaby J. Feder, "Truth and Justice, by the Blip of a Brainwave," *New York Times*, October 9, 2001.

innocent person wouldn't have any access to the material and that the guilty person would," he said.

Farwell is not the only scientist involved in studying whether brain waves can uncover guilty knowledge. Researchers at the University of Pennsylvania have published extensively on their research on the measurement of functional magnetic resource imaging,[58] or fMRI, and the topic was discussed at a symposium of the American Academy of Science in Boston on February 2, 2007. As stated by Ronald Barndollar, a former FBI polygrapher who has reviewed some of this experimental work: "fMRI has the potential to do for lie detection what DNA did for forensic serology."[59]

"fMRI has the potential to do for lie detection what DNA did for forensic serology."

Scientists from the Department of Psychiatry, University of Pennsylvania, working on fMRI published the results of a comparison of polygraph with fMRI that took place between 2008 and 2009[60] and concluded:

> In this prospective and blind comparison, fMRI was significantly more likely to detect deception than polygraphy. The fact that a decision rule that incorporated lie determinations from both modalities (fMRI and polygraphy) made no errors upon reaching consensus suggests that sequential polygraphy and fMRI examinations may have the potential to minimize false-positive lie determinations, a critical feature for any legal application. This study sets the stage for the more comprehensive trials that would include a control group of nondeceptive participants, manipulate the risk and benefit of deception in an ecologically valid fashion, and use algorithm-driven polygraph and fMRI testing and data analysis. While the jury remains out on whether fMRI will become a forensic tool, these data certainly justify further investigation of its potential.

This study will no doubt be cited if any when expert testimony on fMRI is sought to be introduced, probably by a defendant to prove his innocence.

Psychological Expert Testimony

Psychological testimony introduced to explain a person's actions or reactions is frequently rejected by the court.

Other, more creative, views of science involving psychological evidence have generally been rejected by the courts in which motions under state rules of evidence similar to *Daubert* or *Frye* have been upheld on appeal. For example, a teenaged defendant in a murder trial sought to introduce an expert to testify about false

---

58. Daniel D. Langleben, James W. Loughead, Warren B. Bilker, Kosha Ruparel, Anna Rose Childress, Samantha I. Busch, and Ruben C. Gur, "Telling Truth from Lie in Individual Subjects with Fast Event-Related fMRI," Wiley InterScience, September 13, 2005, www.interscience.wiley.com.

59. Interview with the author, March 20, 2007.

60. Daniel D. Langleben, et al., "Polygraphy and Functional Magnetic Resonance Imaging in Lie Detection: A Controlled Blind Comparison Using the Concealed Information Test," *Journal of Clinical Psychiatry* 77, no. 10 (2016): 1372–1380, http://www.psychiatrist.com/JCP/article/Pages/2016/v77 n10/v77n1027.aspx.

confessions and their alleged presence among juveniles. In an extended *Daubert* hearing, the court held that although the expert was qualified in the study of false confessions, he could not point to any test to determine whether a false confession had occurred.[61]

Other psychological testimony was rejected in a New Jersey case. There the court refused to permit a witness in a criminal trial whose recollection was "hypnotically refreshed," because such testimony was suspect. The court pointed out that guidelines for conducting witness hypnosis to ensure that the results are reliable no longer outweigh the potential harm of the testimony.[62]

Similarly, Connecticut rejected testimony by a psychologist that a teenage defendant had limited ability to understand his *Miranda* rights. An expert proposed to testify that the defendant was unable to understand his rights, based on an evaluation, an interview, IQ testing, personality testing, and general achievement testing. The Connecticut Supreme Court agreed with the trial court that this test was an innovative scientific technique that should be subject to a *Daubert* analysis. The only articles the expert submitted in support of the scientific validity of the "Grisso test" were published by Grisso himself, which the court held to be self-promotion and not peer evaluation.[63]

Psychological testimony about whether a sex offender who had a history of assaulting young girls was highly motivated to reoffend was admitted. In that case, the Pennsylvania court decided that as the expert was applying a "statutory formula" designed to determine whether the offender must register as a sex offender under "Megan's Law," the science was not novel and did not require a *Frye* hearing.[64]

Post-Mortem Hair Banding

In a New York rape and murder trial, the defendants tried to introduce an expert who would testify that a hair of the victim had been planted in their van. The testimony involved post-mortem "hair banding" and the amount of time it would take for this to occur. The court held that the theory of post-mortem hair banding is generally accepted under *Frye*. Defense experts testified that it generally takes two days for post-mortem hair banding to occur. Because the state argued that the defendants disposed of the body shortly after placing it in their van, their theory of hair banding would support their argument that someone planted the hair belonging to the victim in their van. The court held that the theory of microscopic analysis of hair shafts is grounded in science.[65]

---

61. *Edmonds v. Mississippi*, No. 2004-KA-02081, 2006 LEXIS 88 (Miss App. 2006).
62. *N.J. v. Moore*, 902 A.2d 1212 (N.J. Sup. 2006).
63. *Conn. v. Griffin*, 869 A.2d 640 (Conn. Sup. 2004).
64. *Pa. v. Dengler*, 890 A.2d 372 (Pa. Sup. 2005).
65. *N.Y. v. Kogut*, 806 N.Y.S.2d 353 (Supreme Ct. 2005).

Can Your Smell Identify You?

The news reported that researchers have begun analyzing traces of scent that people leave behind them, hoping to develop a forensic technique to exploit one's smell as an identification device for airline security. The report states that researchers have isolated chemicals that evaporate off the body using an "electronic nose" that breaks the scent into chemical components:

> Researchers examined body odor samples of about 200 adults from Carinthia, a village in the Austrian Alps, chosen because no one from outside had settled there for many generations and the residents were mainly members of big families and genetically similar. Despite this the analysis showed each individual had a unique scent signature.... Dr. Silva Valussi, of the Forensic Science Service, said: "You can tell a lot about a person's lifestyle from the chemical markers in sweat. Getting it to a level of reliability where it can be used as evidence is the challenge."[66]

Can a Computer Identify Your Handwriting?

Researchers at the State University of New York at Buffalo have been working for some years on a computer system that analyzes specified handwriting characteristics in an effort to demonstrate scientifically both that handwriting is unique and that it can be distinguished by computer. See Chapter 12, "Handwriting and Questioned Documents."

Both these areas may lead courts of the future to resolve the controversy over reliability by applying the *Daubert* tests to these emerging technologies.

Summary

In order to ensure that scientific or technical expert testimony is reliable, the court must first examine if the area of testimony is "science." Science is defined as a specific methodology of inquiry that involves developing a hypothesis, testing, replicating results, developing further hypotheses, and ruling out alternative explanations. The one form of forensic evidence that clearly adheres to the scientific method is DNA analysis. Other methods of forensic identification, such as fingerprint analysis, firearm and tool mark analysis, shoeprint, bite mark, lip print, and palm print matching, are based on scientific hypotheses, but the process of identification often has no tests to establish uniqueness and also requires the subjective judgment of the examiner, which cannot be an element in a scientific experiment. The scientific method assumes that the results of an experiment can be replicated by any other scientist using the same methodology. This is one reason why courts have struggled with applying the *Daubert*

---

66. Richard Gray, "Scientists Learn What Every Dog Knows — That We All Have a Unique Smell," Telegraph.co.uk, January 21, 2007.

tests to areas such as handwriting, where there is no set protocol for analysis, and various forms of impression evidence. The President's Council on Science has recently indicated that it has concluded bite mark matching is not science and cannot meet *Daubert*.

Much of the impression evidence may be useful in excluding a suspect. These methods can determine a class characteristic but cannot individualize a particular person.

Even areas of forensic evidence that are scientifically trustworthy will be rejected by the courts if the expert is not qualified or attempts to testify to an experiment that does not meet the scientific method.

Junk science can become either rejected as a method of identification or perhaps evolve into genuine science by experiment and time. Anthropometry was once thought to be a method of absolutely identification, but has now been disproven. Neuroimaging, by contrast, is still in its infancy as a method of determining mental states or knowledge.

Scientists are developing computer models to evaluate handwriting, which would remove the subjective element and identify which aspects of handwriting can distinguish one writer's handwriting from another.

Discussion Questions

1. What is the scientific method and how does it operate?

2. Why is the scientific hypothesis associated with causation of injury so much more difficult than forensic evidence associated with identification?

3. What is the scientific hypothesis of identification through fingerprints, DNA, dental records, shoeprints, or lip prints? How can these hypotheses be proved?

4. Why is it important for scientists to try to prove a scientific hypothesis is wrong?

5. What is anthropometry? What was its scientific hypothesis? How might a jury assess the credibility of the science at trial?

6. Explain the issues with proving that various forms of impression evidence, from bullet and casing matching to bite mark matching are scientific. What would a proponent need to show in order to get such evidence before a jury? Should an expert ever be permitted to testify to an absolute "match" or should the expert be required to give only a "consistent with" opinion?

7. If the President's Council has rejected bite mark matching as junk science, what do you think should happen to prisoners who have been convicted based on bite mark evidence? Would your opinion change if there were other evidence of guilt that would lead a reasonable jury to convict?

8. What are the scientific objections to polygraph? Do you agree or disagree with the states that refuse to admit polygraph? Would you admit MERMER results of a "guilty knowledge" test as better science than polygraph? Why or why not?

9. Under what circumstances do you think a court should refuse to allow an expert to testify if the expert lacks formal training or certification from any relevant organization? Do you think the jury should get to hear the testimony anyway and allow it to make up its own mind about the credibility of the expert?

Chapter 5

The General Acceptance Rule and the *Daubert* Case

Overview

The admissibility of forensic evidence based on science was governed in the federal courts by the General Acceptance Rule first stated in the case of *Frye v. United States*, decided in 1923. Shortly after Congress passed the Federal Rule of Evidence 702, governing admissibility of expert opinions, the Supreme Court ruled in 1993 that Rule 702 had superseded the *Frye* test. In this case, *Daubert v. Merrrell Dow*, the Court held that scientific testimony should be admissible if it meets alternate tests of reliability, such as a scientific hypothesis, publication and peer review, and error rate. This ruling governs the admissibility of expert opinions about forensic evidence in all federal courts.

The *Daubert* test was soon adopted in some state courts, but not in all. Some states retain the *Frye* test, and some use other tests. The *Daubert* test requires the trial court to act as a gatekeeper and decide outside the hearing of the jury whether the forensic expert testimony is admissible or not.

The *Kuhmo* case decided that the *Daubert* test should apply to experts testifying about a technique — such as examination of a tire to determine any defect — as well as science. The *General Electric* case held that an appeals court must defer to the trial court's gatekeeper decision, unless the trial court abused its discretion. After *Daubert*, courts have expanded the gatekeeper questions to include such issues as whether the science was developed specifically for litigation.

We examine the courts' reaction to the *Daubert* case in different chapters in this text. As a general matter, courts frequently cite the *Daubert* tests but rarely apply them step-by-step to the proposed expert testimony. Many courts make their decision to accept or exclude based on the training and experience of the expert or a review of other courts that have accepted similar experts, rather than the scientific reliability of the testimony. They apparently admit expert testimony based on whether it has been "generally admitted" rather than on the *Daubert* question of whether it has been "generally accepted" by the relevant scientific community. Commentators have pointed out that courts much more frequently allow a prosecution expert and exclude one proposed by the defense.

The National Research Council in its 2009 report stated "*Daubert* and its progeny have engendered confusion and controversy ... judicial dispositions of *Daubert*-type questions in criminal cases have been criticized by some lawyers and scholars who thought that the Supreme Court's decision would be applied more rigorously."[1]

Chapter Objectives

Based on this chapter, student will be able to:

1. Explain the General Acceptance Test from the *Frye* case.

2. Describe how the case of *Daubert v. Merrell Dow* changed the *Frye* test.

3. Identify the elements of the *Daubert* tests.

4. Explain what happened to the plaintiffs' case in *Daubert* after the case was remanded back to the trial court.

5. Detail the role of the court in conducting gatekeeper hearings.

6. Explain the facts of the case of *Kuhmo Tire* and how it expanded the *Daubert* case.

7. Understand whether state courts were required to follow *Daubert*.

8. Describe the Connecticut state case of *State v. Porter* and its relationship to the *Daubert* case.

9. Identify the standard of appellate review of gatekeeper hearings in federal court under the *General Electric v. Joiner* case.

10. Identify issues courts have confronted in applying *Daubert*.

The General Acceptance Test

In 1923, Congress had not yet adopted the rules about expert witnesses referred to in the prior chapter. So the question of what standard to use in admitting forensic evidence was left to each individual court to decide. The Court of Appeals for the District of Columbia, a federal appeals court, made an important ruling in the case of *Frye v. United States*.[2] In this case, the court adopted a standard to be applied by all federal trial courts in the District of Columbia in determining whether an expert could testify. This standard was called the "general acceptance test." In effect, the court was guarding against letting juries hear "junk science" by requiring that any scientific expert could testify only about a scientific theory that was "generally accepted" by all scientists in the same field. The *Frye* case involved whether the jury could hear an expert opinion about a test similar to a polygraph. The court refused, on the ground that the science had not been proven. Here is part of its reasoning:

---

1. NRC Report at 11.
2. 293 F. 1013 (Ct. App. D.C., 1923).

***Frye v. United States,* 293 F. 1013 (Ct. App. D.C. 1923)**

. . .

A single assignment of error is presented for our consideration. In the course of the trial counsel for defendant offered an expert witness to testify to the result of a deception test made upon defendant. The test is described as the systolic blood pressure deception test. It is asserted that blood pressure is influenced by change in the emotions of the witness, and that the systolic blood pressure rises are brought about by nervous impulses sent to the sympathetic branch of the autonomic nervous system.

Scientific experiments, it is claimed, have demonstrated that fear, rage, and pain always produce a rise of systolic blood pressure, and that conscious deception or falsehood, concealment of facts, or guilt of crime, accompanied by fear of detection when the person is under examination, raises the systolic blood pressure in a curve, which corresponds exactly to the struggle going on in the subject's mind, between fear and attempted control of that fear, as the examination touches the vital points in respect of which he is attempting to deceive the examiner.

In other words, the theory seems to be that truth is spontaneous, and comes without conscious effort, while the utterance of a falsehood requires a conscious effort, which is reflected in the blood pressure. The rise thus produced is easily detected and distinguished from the rise produced by mere fear of the examination itself. In the former instance, the pressure rises higher than in the latter, and is more pronounced as the examination proceeds, while in the latter case, if the subject is telling the truth, the pressure registers highest at the beginning of the examination, and gradually diminishes as the examination proceeds.

Prior to the trial defendant was subjected to this deception test, and counsel offered the scientist who conducted the test as an expert to testify to the results obtained. The offer was objected to by counsel for the government, and the court sustained the objection. Counsel for defendant then offered to have the proffered witness conduct a test in the presence of the jury. This also was denied.

Counsel for defendant, in their able presentation of the novel question involved, correctly state in their brief that no cases directly in point have been found. The broad ground, however, upon which they plant their case, is succinctly stated in their brief as follows:

"The rule is that the opinions of experts or skilled witnesses are admissible in evidence in those cases in which the matter of inquiry is such that inexperienced persons are unlikely to prove capable of forming a correct judgment upon it, for the reason that the subject-matter so far partakes of a science, art, or trade as to require a previous habit or experience or study in it, in order to acquire a knowledge of it. When the question involved does not lie within the range of common experience or common knowledge, but requires special experience or special knowledge, then the opinions of witnesses skilled in that particular science, art, or trade to which the question relates are admissible in evidence."

Numerous cases are cited in support of this rule. Just when a scientific principle or discovery crosses the line between the experimental and demonstrable stages is difficult to define. Somewhere in this twilight zone the evidential force of the principle must be recognized, and while courts will go a long way in admitting expert testimony deduced from a well-recognized scientific principle or discovery, the thing from which the deduction is made must be sufficiently established to have gained general acceptance in the particular field in which it belongs.

The General Acceptance Test: "The thing from which the deduction is made must be sufficiently established to have gained general acceptance in the particular field in which it belongs."

We think the systolic blood pressure deception test has not yet gained such standing and scientific recognition among physiological and psychological authorities as would justify the courts in admitting expert testimony deduced from the discovery, development, and experiments thus far made.

The judgment is affirmed.

The *Frye* case was subsequently referred to as the source of the General Acceptance Test. Following the *Frye* case, many courts — both state courts and federal courts in other appellate circuits — adopted the general acceptance test for scientific experts. When Congress enacted Federal Rule of Evidence 702, however, it was not clear whether Congress intended the rule to change the general acceptance test. The United States Supreme Court answered this question in 1993, in the case of *Daubert v. Merrell Dow*.

The *Daubert* Rule

In 1993, the Supreme Court issued a landmark decision in the case of *Daubert v. Merrell Dow*. This case was not a criminal case. It was a civil liability case for damages. Although many students think of forensic evidence only in the criminal context, this is not the case. In fact, the three major U.S. Supreme Court cases about forensic evidence, which are discussed in this chapter, were all civil liability cases.

In *Daubert*, the issue was whether Bendectin, a drug manufactured by Merrell Dow, caused birth defects. The plaintiff's expert was prepared to testify that it did, based on test-tube and live-animal studies and pharmacological studies, as well as a reanalysis of previously published studied. The defendant objected on the ground that no published epidemiological (human statistical) study had demonstrated a statistically significant association between Bendectin and birth defects. In effect, the defendant argued that there was no "general acceptance" in the medical community that Bendectin caused birth defects.

The plaintiff was relying in large part on a re-analysis of data that had previously concluded that Bendectin did not cause birth defects. This was called a meta-data test.

A meta-analysis is defined as follows:

The term "meta-analysis" refers to "the process or technique of synthesizing research results by using various statistical methods to retrieve, select, and combine results from previous separate but related studies" …"With the help of a relatively new procedure, the meta-analysis, we are now in a position to statistically compare the results of a large number of experiments."[3]

The trial court refused to accept the plaintiffs' expert testimony, finding that its conclusions were not "generally accepted" in the scientific community. The U.S. Supreme Court determined that Rule 702 had superseded the *Frye* case. As a result, it stated that the test to admit scientific expert testimony had changed to include more factors than just "general acceptance." It remanded the case back to the appellate, with instructions to apply a new test about the admissibility of the expert testimony. The new rule required a more liberal test for admissibility than the general acceptance standard set forth in *Frye*. The Court acknowledged that general acceptance was one test for admissibility, but it added others that could be used even if general acceptance was not met. These included:

- whether the science had been tested,
- whether it had a known error rate, and
- whether it had been subject to peer review and publication.

The court's reasoning was that juries should be able to hear cutting edge science, even if the general scientific community had not yet accepted it, as long as the evidence followed the scientific method and had other signs of reliability, such as being published and critiqued by other scientists. Here is an excerpt of the *Daubert* opinion:

Daubert v. Merrell Dow Pharmaceuticals, 509 U.S. 579 (1993)[4]

In this case we are called upon to determine the standard for admitting expert scientific testimony in a federal trial.

Petitioners Jason *Daubert* and Eric Schuller are minor children born with serious birth defects. They and their parents sued respondent in California state court, alleging that the birth defects had been caused by the mothers' ingestion of Bendectin, a prescription anti-nausea drug marketed by respondent. Respondent removed the suits to federal court on diversity grounds.

After extensive discovery, respondent moved for summary judgment, contending that Bendectin does not cause birth defects in humans and that petitioners would be unable to come forward with any admissible evidence that it does. In support of its motion, respondent submitted an affidavit of Steven H. Lamm, physician and epidemiologist, who is a well-credentialed expert on the risks from exposure to various chemical substances. Doctor Lamm stated that he had reviewed all the literature on Bendectin and human

---

3. *New York v. Legrand*, 747 N.Y.S. 2d 733 (2002).
4. Affirmed on remand by *Daubert v. Merrell Dow*, 43 F.3d 1311 (9th Cir. 1995).

birth defects — more than 30 published studies involving over 130,000 patients. No study had found Bendectin to be a human teratogen (i.e., a substance capable of causing malformations in fetuses).

On the basis of this review, Doctor Lamm concluded that maternal use of Bendectin during the first trimester of pregnancy has not been shown to be a risk factor for human birth defects.

Petitioners did not (and do not) contest this characterization of the published record regarding Bendectin. Instead, they responded to respondent's motion with the testimony of eight experts of their own, each of whom also possessed impressive credentials. These experts had concluded that Bendectin can cause birth defects. Their conclusions were based upon "in vitro" (test tube) and "in vivo" (live) animal studies that found a link between Bendectin and malformations; pharmacological studies of the chemical structure of Bendectin that purported to show similarities between the structure of the drug and that of other substances known to cause birth defects; and the "reanalysis" of previously published epidemiological (human statistical) studies....

In the 70 years since its formulation in the *Frye* case, the "general acceptance" test has been the dominant standard for determining the admissibility of novel scientific evidence at trial. Although under increasing attack of late, the rule continues to be followed by a majority of courts, including the Ninth Circuit.

[The court then explained the holding of the *Frye* case.] The merits of the *Frye* test have been much debated, and scholarship on its proper scope and application is legion. Petitioners' primary attack, however, is not on the content but on the continuing authority of the rule. They contend that the *Frye* test was superseded by the adoption of the Federal Rules of Evidence. We agree.

We interpret the legislatively enacted Federal Rules of Evidence as we would any statute.... Rule 402 provides the baseline:

> "All relevant evidence is admissible, except as otherwise provided by the Constitution of the United States, by Act of Congress, by these rules, or by other rules prescribed by the Supreme Court pursuant to statutory authority. Evidence which is not relevant is not admissible."

...

Nothing in the text of this Rule establishes "general acceptance" as an absolute prerequisite to admissibility. Nor does respondent present any clear indication that Rule 702 or the Rules as a whole were intended to incorporate a "general acceptance" standard. The drafting history makes no mention of *Frye,* and a rigid "general acceptance" requirement would be at odds with the "liberal thrust" of the Federal Rules and their "general approach of relaxing the traditional barriers to 'opinion' testimony."....

Rule 702 further requires that the evidence or testimony "assist the trier of fact to understand the evidence or to determine a fact in issue." This condition goes primarily to relevance. "Expert testimony which does not relate to any issue in the case is not relevant and, ergo, non-helpful.".... The study of the phases of the moon, for example, may provide valid scientific "knowledge" about whether a certain night was dark, and if darkness is a fact in issue, the knowledge will assist the trier of fact. However (absent creditable grounds supporting such a link), evidence that the moon was full on a certain night will not assist the trier of fact in determining whether an individual was unusually likely to have behaved irrationally on that night. Rule 702's "helpfulness" standard requires a valid scientific connection to the pertinent inquiry as a precondition to admissibility.

… Ordinarily, a key question to be answered in determining whether a theory or technique is scientific knowledge that will assist the trier of fact will be whether it can be (and has been) tested.

> "Scientific methodology today is based on generating hypotheses and testing them to see if they can be falsified; indeed, this methodology is what distinguishes science from other fields of human inquiry." …

Another pertinent consideration is whether the theory or technique has been subjected to peer review and publication. Publication (which is but one element of peer review) is not a *sine qua non* of admissibility; it does not necessarily correlate with reliability, and in some instances well-grounded but innovative theories will not have been published. Some propositions, moreover, are too particular, too new, or of too limited interest to be published. But submission to the scrutiny of the scientific community is a component of "good science," in part because it increases the likelihood that substantive flaws in methodology will be detected....

Additionally, in the case of a particular scientific technique, the court ordinarily should consider the known or potential rate of error, and the existence and maintenance of standards controlling the technique's operation. Finally, "general acceptance" can yet have a bearing on the inquiry. A "reliability assessment does not require, although it does permit, explicit identification of a relevant scientific community and an express determination of a particular degree of acceptance within that community." Widespread acceptance can be an important factor in ruling particular evidence admissible, and "a known technique which has been able to attract only minimal support within the community."

The inquiries of the District Court and the Court of Appeals focused almost exclusively on "general acceptance," as gauged by publication and the decisions of other courts.

Accordingly, the judgment of the Court of Appeals is vacated, and the case is remanded for further proceedings consistent with this opinion.

The *Daubert* Tests. In deciding whether to admit scientific testimony under FRE 702, the trial judge should ask:

a. Is it based on a scientific methodology?

b. Is the methodology published and peer reviewed?

c. Does it have a known or potential error rate?

d. Is it generally accepted in the scientific community?

Remand of the *Daubert* Case

The case was remanded back to the circuit court of appeal. That court declined to send the case back to the trial court for a gatekeeper hearing, but instead reviewed the expert testimony from the trial record under the new standard set out by the Supreme Court. It decided that the testimony failed to qualify under *Daubert* and therefore affirmed the trial court's original grant of summary judgment.[5]

It is largely because the opinions proffered by plaintiffs' experts run counter to the substantial consensus in the scientific community that we affirmed the district court's grant of summary judgment the last time the case appeared before us. The standard for admissibility of expert testimony in this circuit at the time was the so-called *Frye* test: Scientific evidence was admissible if it was based on a scientific technique generally accepted as reliable within the scientific community. We found that the district court properly applied this standard, and affirmed. The Supreme Court reversed, holding that *Frye* was superseded by Federal Rule of Evidence 702, and remanded for us to consider the admissibility of plaintiffs' expert testimony under this new standard.

First, however, we address plaintiffs' argument that we should simply remand the case so the district court can make the initial determination of admissibility under the new standard announced by the Supreme Court. There is certainly something to be said for this position, as the district court is charged with making the initial determination whether to admit evidence. In the peculiar circumstances of this case, however, we have determined that the interests of justice and judicial economy will best be served by deciding those issues that are properly before us and, in the process, offering guidance on the application of the *Daubert* standard in this circuit.

The district court already made a determination as to admissibility, albeit under a different standard than we apply on remand, and granted summary judgment based on its exclusion of plaintiffs' expert testimony. A grant of summary judgment may be sustained on any basis supported by the record, so we shall consider whether the district court's grant of summary judgment can be sustained under the new standard announced by the Supreme Court.

Our review here is, of course, very narrow: We will affirm the summary judgment only if, as a matter of law, the proffered evidence would have to be excluded at trial. The district court's power is far broader; were we to conclude that the expert testimony is not per se inadmissible, the district court on remand would nevertheless have discretion to reject it under Rule 403 or 702. Such a ruling would be reviewed under the deferential abuse of discretion standard.

---

5. *Id.*

... [T]he question is whether plaintiffs adduced enough admissible evidence to create a genuine issue of material fact as to whether Bendectin caused their injuries. It is to that question we now turn.

Plaintiffs have made no such showing. As noted above, plaintiffs rely entirely on the experts' unadorned assertions that the methodology they employed comports with standard scientific procedures. In support of these assertions, plaintiffs offer only the trial and deposition testimony of these experts in other cases. While these materials indicate that plaintiffs' experts have relied on animal studies, chemical structure analyses and epidemiological data, they neither explain the methodology the experts followed to reach their conclusions nor point to any external source to validate that methodology. We've been presented with only the experts' qualifications, their conclusions and their assurances of reliability. Under *Daubert*, that's not enough.

As the district court properly found below, "the strongest inference to be drawn for plaintiffs based on the epidemiological evidence is that Bendectin could *possibly* have caused plaintiffs' injuries." The same is true of the other testimony derived from animal studies and chemical structure analyses — these experts "testify to a possibility rather than a probability." Plaintiffs do not quantify this possibility, or otherwise indicate how their conclusions about causation should be weighted, even though the substantive legal standard has always required proof of causation by a preponderance of the evidence.

Unlike these experts' explanation of their methodology, this is not a shortcoming that could be corrected on remand ... Plaintiffs' experts must, therefore, stand by the conclusions they originally proffered, rendering their testimony inadmissible under the second prong of Fed. R. Evid. 702.

Daubert Requires Gatekeeper Hearings

Daubert was viewed as a "landmark" decision for two reasons:

- It rejected the old "general acceptance" test as the only test for admissibility and proposed some new tests that would make it easier to admit scientific testimony about a science which might not have reached general acceptance.

- It established the trial judge as a "gatekeeper" to evaluate a list of factors in order to decide whether the expert could testify at all.

The role of the trial court in evaluating the reliability of the scientific testimony before it is presented to the jury has been called the "gatekeeper" role. The trial court may open or close the gate to allow the testimony to reach the jury. On remand, the Ninth Circuit court explained that *Daubert* requires a trial court to engage in a two-part analysis:

First, we must determine nothing less than whether the experts' testimony reflects "scientific knowledge," whether their findings are "derived by the

Gatekeeper. The role of the trial court in determining if scientific or technical evidence is admissible under Federal Rule of Evidence 702 or a similar state rule.

scientific method," and whether their work product amounts to "good science."

Second, we must ensure that the proposed expert testimony is "relevant to the task as hand," i.e., that it logically advances a material aspect of the proposing party's case. The Supreme Court referred to this second prong of the analysis as the "fit" requirement.[6]

Rule 702. A witness who is qualified as an expert by knowledge, skill, experience, training, or education may testify thereto in the form of an opinion or otherwise, if

(1) the expert's scientific, technical, or other specialized knowledge will assist the trier of fact to understand the evidence or to determine a fact in issue,

(2) the testimony is based upon sufficient facts or data,

(3) the testimony is the product of reliable principles and methods, and

(4) the expert has applied the principles and methods to the facts of the case.

Congress amended Rule 702 on December 1, 2000, to reflect the Supreme Court's holding (a subsequent amendment was made in 2011 to streamline the language).

Note that the revised rule 702 does not specifically refer to a "gatekeeping" function by the trial judge, who must decide whether the witness is qualified to testify in the first instance. However, by stating specific criteria for when a witness is "qualified as an expert," and requiring that the testimony be based on "sufficient facts or data" which is the product of "reliable principles and methods," the rule in effect requires the trial judge to evaluate the science behind the expert's proposed testimony.

Federal Rule of Evidence 702 does not incorporate any of the specific *Daubert* tests, such as publication and peer review, error rate, etc. In part, this is because the Supreme Court's list of *Daubert* tests were meant to be nonexclusive guidelines. Congress chose to keep Rule 702 more general, thus giving more discretion to the trial judge.

But exactly how is the trial court to ensure that scientific testimony is reliable? As the Ninth Circuit stated after the remand of *Daubert*:

> The Court held.... that federal judges perform a "gatekeeping role; to do so they must satisfy themselves that scientific evidence meets a certain standard of reliability before it is admitted. This means that the expert's bald assurance of validity is not enough. Rather, the party presenting the expert must show that the expert's findings are based on sound science, and this will require some objective, independent validation of the expert's methodology.[7]

The judge is generally in a better position to evaluate evidence and determine questions of admissibility. Judges make such rulings every day and therefore are familiar with the rules of evidence. The *Daubert* hearing allows the judge to become educated on an issue before ruling on admissibility. As certain areas of testimony in criminal cases will occur repeatedly, such as DNA, fingerprints, handwriting, eyewitness identification and blood stain analysis, judges will build up expertise which can be applied to subsequent hearings. Although each expert will present different issues, a trial judge will know the questions to consider, such as whether the expert has omitted certain variables from his scientific hypothesis or whether internal inconsistencies appear in his testimony.

---

6. 43 F.3d 1311 at 1315.
7. *Id.* at 1316.

Judges must know enough about a subject to identify indicia of reliability and to apply them competently. Beyond this threshold level of knowledge, the judiciary's expertise is in deconstructing an argument: assessing the logic of the argument, the validity of its premises, the rigor with which the witness applied the technique, the faithfulness of the witness's application of the methodology to her description of it, the magnitude of the inference drawn by the witness in forming her opinion and the sufficiency of the facts to support the inference. Parties' identification of contested issues and potential weaknesses in a proffered expert's methodology or reasoning should assist judges in this endeavor.[8]

The Gatekeeper Process

So how exactly is the trial court to act as a gatekeeper? Must it hear testimony outside the hearing of the jury? Must it hold a hearing if neither party objects to the expert witness? The trial judge has broad latitude in holding pretrial hearings, and an appeals court will generally not reverse unless the trial judge has clearly abused its discretion. This makes a high hurdle for parties who try to challenge the court's decision at a *Daubert* hearing.

The trial court need not hold a full pretrial hearing in every case. This was shown by the trial court's decision to affirm summary judgment on the remand of the *Daubert* case without holding a gatekeeper hearing. Some courts have held *Daubert* hearings by reviewing the trial transcript of the *Daubert* hearing held in another, similar case.[9] The courts have also stated that a party waives the right to argue on appeal that expert testimony should not have been admitted if he does not request a *Daubert* hearing at trial. In one case where a defendant failed to object to testimony that a mark found in a photograph of a corpse was the defendant's tooth pattern, the appellate court denied a new trial because the defendant had not objected to the testimony at trial. However, defendant was successful on a habeas corpus petition that his counsel's failure to raise the issue was a denial of his right to counsel.[10] Trial courts frequently bend over backwards to avoid being reversed on appeal. For this reason, if a party requests a *Daubert* hearing, most trials will grant the motion.

The *Reference Manual on Scientific Evidence* made a number of predictions of the outcome of *Daubert* on criminal trials:

[C]hallenges to reliability have been raised with regard to numerous techniques of forensic identification, such as fingerprinting, handwriting analysis, ballistics, and bite-mark analysis. DNA typing may well be the only area of forensic identification in which research has been conducted in

---

8. "Reliable Evaluation of Expert Testimony," *Harvard Law Review* 116 (May 2003): 2142, 2150.

9. See *U.S. v. Llera Plaza*, 179 F.Supp.2d 492 (E.D.Pa. 2002); vacated, 188 F. Supp. 2d 549 (E.D. Pa. 2002).

10. *Ege v. Yukins*, 380 F. Supp. 2d 852 (E.D. Mich. 2006).

accordance with conventional scientific standards. In other areas, experts have in large measure relied on their experience to arrive at subjective conclusions that either have not been validated or are not objectively verifiable.

The post-*Daubert* challenges to forensic identification have been largely unsuccessful if looked at solely in terms of rulings on admissibility. Courts have by and large refused to exclude prosecution experts.... That courts continued to allow forensic identification experts to testify is not, however, the whole story. It is clear that in the aftermath of *Daubert*, empirical research has begun to examine the foundation of some forensic sciences.[11]

In the *Grant* case, the defendants requested a *Daubert* hearing on whether the DNA testimony was reliable. The trial court took extensive testimony and wrote a separate opinion after the hearing, stating specific findings for a reviewing court to consider if the holding was appealed. This issue is not included in Grant's appeal.

As *Kuhmo* made clear, the trial judge has flexibility in what standards to apply in a gatekeeper hearing: "In sum, Rule 702 grants the district judge the discretionary authority, reviewable for its abuse, to determine reliability in light of the particular facts and circumstances of the particular case."[12] Trial judges also have discretion to use court-appointed experts, special masters, and specially trained law clerks, and to narrow the issues in dispute at pretrial hearing and conferences.

The supreme court in Nebraska[13] described the gatekeeper process as follows:

Under our recent *Daubert/Schafersman* jurisprudence, the trial court acts as a gatekeeper to ensure the evidentiary relevance and reliability of an expert's opinion. Most recently, we described a trial court's evaluation of the admissibility of expert testimony as essentially a four-step process.

First, the court must determine whether the witness is qualified to testify as an expert.

If the expert is and it is necessary for the court to conduct a *Daubert* analysis, the court must next determine whether the reasoning or methodology underlying the expert testimony is scientifically valid and reliable.

Once the reasoning or methodology has been found to be reliable, the court must next determine whether the methodology was properly applied to the facts in issue.

---

11. Margaret A. Berger, "Supreme Court's Trilogy on Admissibility of Expert Testimony," *Reference Manual on Scientific Evidence*, 31, *supra*.

12. *Id*. at 158.

13. *Epp v. Lauby*, 715 N.W.2d 501 (Sup. Neb. 2006).

Finally, the court determines whether the evidence and opinions related thereto are more probative than prejudicial, as required under Neb. Evid. R. 403.[14]

How State Courts Reacted to *Daubert*

Following the *Daubert* decision, many states decided to adopt the *Daubert* approach. This was not required by the *Daubert* decision, as it applied only to the Federal Rules of Evidence. Each state is free to make its own rules, so long as they do not violate the federal constitution. Connecticut, for example, adopted the *Daubert* rule in a case called *State v. Porter*, discussed below. The Connecticut rule of evidence governing expert testimony is numbered Rule 7-2 and appears below:

> A witness qualified as an expert by knowledge, skill, experience, training, education or otherwise may testify in the form of an opinion or otherwise concerning scientific, technical or other specialized knowledge, if the testimony will assist the trier of fact in understanding the evidence or in determining a fact in issue.

In *State v. Porter*,[15] Connecticut reviewed its long-standing application of *Frye* and adopted the *Daubert* standard. In *Porter*, the defendant appealed the judgment of the Appellate Court affirming his conviction for first degree arson. Prior to trial, Porter underwent a polygraph examination and, in the opinion of the expert polygraphist, was truthful when he answered "no" to a series of questions relating to his guilty knowledge of any participation in the burning of his home. When Porter moved to have the trial court admit the results of the polygraph test, his motion was denied and Porter was convicted of first degree arson.

On appeal, Porter claimed that the trial court erred when it refused to admit the results of his polygraph test. In affirming the decision of the trial court, the Appellate Court addressed the issue of Connecticut's per se rule that polygraph evidence is inadmissible at trial. In granting Porter's petition for certification to appeal, the Connecticut Supreme Court limited its review to whether Connecticut should adopt *Daubert* as the standard for admissibility of scientific evidence. In its decision, the court held that "*Daubert* provides the proper threshold standard for the admissibility of scientific evidence in Connecticut."[16]

The *Porter* Test. Connecticut adopted the *Daubert* test in *State v. Porter*, so its test is called the *Porter* test.

To date some states still retain the *Frye* approach, some have adopted the *Daubert* approach, and others have different rules altogether.[17]

---

14. *Id.* at 508.

15. 241 Conn. 57 (1997).

16. The Court also held that Connecticut should not abandon its per se rule that polygraph evidence is admissible at trial, thereby affirming the lower court's conviction of Porter.

17. "The Demise of *Daubert* in State Courts," *Mealey's Daubert Report*, (June 2005): 3, www.lexis.com/research.

Standard of Appellate Review Is Abuse of Discretion

Shortly after *Daubert*, the Supreme Court heard another case called *General Electric Co. v. Joiner*.[18] The issue was whether the plaintiff, who had small-cell lung cancer, could sue for exposure to polycholorinated biphenyls (PCBs) on the theory that it had promoted his cancer. This case was important because it established that the appellate court must affirm the trial court's gatekeeping decision unless it was an "abuse of discretion," a very high standard of proof to meet. In effect, it meant that the appellate courts will defer to the trial court, which had the opportunity to see the expert and hear the testimony about the various *Daubert* tests.

One court defined abuse of discretion this way:

> An abuse of discretion can occur where the district court applies the wrong law, follows the wrong procedure, bases its decision on clearly erroneous facts, or commits a clear error in judgment.[19]

Kuhmo Extends *Daubert* to "Technical" Testimony

In *Kuhmo Tire Co. v. Carmichael*,[20] the plaintiffs sued Kuhmo Tire Company for injuries sustained when the tire on their van blew out. Kuhmo contended that the blowout was caused by the plaintiff's putting too little air in the rear tires. This resulted in overdeflection, which consists of underinflating the tire so that it carries too much weight and generates heat that can cause it to unravel. The plaintiff's expert, Carlson, contended that the tire was defective and that the blowout was caused by a manufacturing or design defect. He based his testimony on his visual inspection of the tire and his experience as a tire inspector for Michelin.

The Supreme Court did not doubt the expert's qualifications. However, it said that the *Daubert* factors would apply to this technical testimony, although not necessarily all of the factors would be relevant. In affirming the trial court's decision to exclude plaintiffs' expert, the Court decided that the methodology used by the expert in analyzing certain data obtained by his visual inspection, such as the wear on the tire treads, was unreliable and "fell outside the range where experts might reasonably differ."[21]

> … the specific issue before the court was not the reasonableness *in general* of a tire expert's use of a visual and tactile inspection to determine whether overdeflection had caused the tire's tread to separate from its steel-belted carcass. Rather, it was the reasonableness of using such an approach, along with Carlson's particular method of analyzing the data thereby obtained, to

18. 522 U.S. 136 (1997).

19. *United States v. Brown*, 415 F.3d 1257, 1266 (11th Cir. 2005), cert. den., 126 S. Ct.1570 (2006).

20. 526 U.S. 137 (1999).

21. *Id.* at 153.

draw a conclusion regarding *the particular matter to which the expert testimony was directly relevant.*

The trial court had found that none of the *Daubert* factors, including general acceptance, were satisfied by Carlson's testimony and therefore excluded it as unreliable. The appellate court reversed. On appeal to the Supreme Court, it found that the decision by the trial court was not an "abuse of discretion." Finally, the Court stated that the *Daubert* factors apply to both scientific and technical testimony, but that the factors must be "flexible" and that not all factors will apply in all cases:

> Carlson testified precisely that in the absence of at least two of four signs of abuse (proportionately greater tread wear on the shoulder; signs of grooves caused by the beads; discolored sidewalls; marks on the rim flange) he concludes that a defect caused the separation. And his analysis depended upon acceptance of a further implicit proposition, namely, that his visual and tactile inspection could determine that the tire before him had not been abused despite some evidence of the presence of the very signs for which he looked (and two punctures).

> . . .

> [T]he transcripts of Carlson's depositions support both the trial court's initial uncertainty and its final conclusion. Those transcripts cast considerable doubt upon the reliability of both the explicit theory (about the need for two signs of abuse) and the implicit proposition (about the significance of visual inspection in this case). Among other things, the expert could not say whether the tire had traveled more than 10, or 20, or 30, or 40, or 50 thousand miles, adding that 6,000 miles was "about how far" he could "say with any certainty." The court could reasonably have wondered about the reliability of a method of visual and tactile inspection sufficiently precise to ascertain with some certainty the abuse-related significance of minute shoulder/center relative tread wear differences, but insufficiently precise to tell "with any certainty" from the tread wear whether a tire had traveled less than 10,000 or more than 50,000 miles.

> . . .

> The particular issue in this case concerned the use of Carlson's two-factor test and his related use of visual/tactile inspection to draw conclusions on the basis of what seemed small observational differences. We have found no indication in the record that other experts in the industry use Carlson's two-factor test or that tire experts such as Carlson normally make the very fine distinctions about, say, the symmetry of comparatively greater shoulder tread wear that were necessary, on Carlson's own theory, to support his conclusions. Nor, despite the prevalence of tire testing, does anyone refer to any articles or papers that validate Carlson's approach.

> . . .

The *Daubert* test extends to technical as well as scientific testimony.

[T]he court ultimately based its decision upon Carlson's failure to satisfy either *Daubert*'s factors or any other set of reasonable reliability criteria. In light of the record as developed by the parties, that conclusion was within the District Court's lawful discretion.[22]

In the year 2000, the Supreme Court again addressed a procedural question: if the appellate court found that the expert testimony had been admitted against the defendant in violation of *Daubert*, could the court simply enter judgment in favor of the defendant or did it have to send the case back to the trial court to let plaintiff try the case again without the expert testimony? In *Weisgram v. Marley*,[23] the Supreme Court reversed a jury verdict in a wrongful death action based on plaintiff's claim that a heater manufactured by the defendant had been defective and caused a fire that resulted in the death of his mother. The circuit appellate court held that the plaintiffs' expert opinions were speculative and not scientifically sound. The Supreme Court recognized that an appellate court has the discretion to remand the case for a new trial, but stated that it is not required to do so where it decides that the remaining evidence that had been properly introduced at trial was legally insufficient to support the verdict.

One of the requirements of the *Daubert* test is to show peer review and publication within the scientific community. Yet, as personal injury claims continue to expand into new areas of possible dangers — mold, electromagnetic force fields, breast implants, etc., plaintiffs' lawyers have begun to commission their own "scientific" studies for use in court.

Post-*Daubert* Issues

Is "Science" Developed Specifically for Litigation Suspect?

As courts have tried to perform their gatekeeping function, they have developed several other tests to determine if purported expert forensic testimony should be admitted. One of these is whether the evidence was developed for a purpose other than litigation. The theory is that the evidence will be more objective and reliable if the researchers did not undertake the research hoping for a favorable outcome in litigation.

When this test is applied to many standard forms of forensic science, such as fingerprints, handwriting analysis, ballistics, blood spatter, footprint, tire print, or fiber analysis, the proposing party cannot argue that any of these forensic methods were developed for a purpose other than investigating crime and for use in the criminal justice system. In this context, it would seem that the test of whether the science was developed for an independent use seems pointless.

---

22. *Id.* at 155–158.
23. 528 U.S. 440 (2000).

However, this inquiry is worthwhile when applied to the many personal injury civil lawsuits that depend upon an expert opinion establishing the element of causation. A court will justifiably inquire whether the studies that show that the crucial element of causation was developed independently by researchers in medicine, or whether they were commissioned especially for litigation. Given the multi-billion dollar verdicts that tantalize personal injury lawyers — think of the $3.2 billion verdict against Dow for what was believed to be causation of failure of the autoimmune systems of women who had breast implants — such lawyers might choose to arrange studies with a friendly "expert" specifically to use in litigation.

The *Daubert* case itself was an example of litigation-generated testimony.[24] There, the plaintiffs' counsel commissioned an expert to "review" the studies previously performed by Merrell Dow, which did not show a tetragenic effect, i.e., the existing tests had disproved causation. The plaintiffs' experts performed a "meta analysis" and concluded that the data actually did show a link between Bendectin and birth defects. "After the Supreme Court remanded the case, … the Ninth Circuit discussed the difference in reliability between independent research and litigation research. But the circuit court did not automatically exclude the plaintiffs' study."[25] However, the circuit court said that additional evidence must be offered to show that the test was based on valid scientific principles, specifically peer review and publication through the process of normal scientific research. Here are just a few of the plaintiffs-generated studies that have been reported:

- A study that linked the MMR vaccine and autism, published by a researcher who had received $90,000 from the plaintiffs' law firm to investigate the link.

- A link between insecticide and birth defects, published by an expert witness for plaintiffs for over twenty years in all of the similar cases. The expert had not published her protocols, reasoning, or methodology. This deficiency meant it was impossible to replicate her work, which is an important element in determining the validity of the "science" and, thus, its admissibility.

- A study that showed asbestos in schools caused a variety of illness.[26]

Although the Supreme Court in *Daubert* did not make this point, the circuit court on remand stated that one important factor is whether the science involved in expert testimony was developed for a purpose other than litigation. Such studies create concerns about bias and undue influence by a particular sponsor.

Courts should be particularly wary of studies of the effect of substances on animals when the dosage is much higher than that to which any human would likely to be exposed. Other examples of biased scientific research include using in vivo (animal) or in vitro (laboratory cell tests) to propose a link between a substance and a human

Additional *Daubert* questions: Was the "science" developed specifically for litigation? Does the expert use the science for any purpose outside the courtroom?

---

24. William L. Anderson and Barry M. Parsons, "The Growing Role of Litigation-Generated Science," *Mealey's Daubert Report* 10, no. 1 (January 2006).

25. *Id.*

26. *Id.*

disease. Furthermore, experts that try to use studies of one substance to establish a point by arguing that another chemical has a similar composition are likewise regarded as suspect science.

The temptation to achieve the hoped-for result may prove irresistible. Scientists see large dollars and lucrative contracts on the horizon. In 2005, a South Korean researcher named Dr. Hwang Woo Suk was discredited after being caught forging evidence of human stem cell cloning, which many believe was a result of pressure to gain publicity and fame.[27]

Is General Acceptance Alone Sufficient for Admissibility?

The cases after *Daubert* have shown that courts still routinely admit certain types of expert testimony without requiring a *Daubert* analysis. For example, handwriting experts testify although there have never been any scientific tests cited in court to establish what characteristics will absolutely identify a person's handwriting or what error rates occur in identifying handwriting. Prior to the *Kuhmo* decision that said *Daubert* applied to "technical" as well as scientific testimony, one court stated that handwriting analysis would definitely not pass the *Daubert* test, but because it was technical and not scientific, it could be admitted. After the *Kuhmo* court stated that *Daubert* applied to technical as well as scientific testimony, the courts have continued to admit handwriting testimony, but now on the theory that it is "generally accepted." But there is a difference between "generally admitted" and "generally accepted." A long history of admitting certain evidence does not mean that it is scientifically sound.

Another area of testimony that is admitted as "generally accepted" is fingerprint analysis. Experts agree that fingerprints are unique and that matching "ridge characteristics" of fingerprints will yield a very high rate of accuracy, at least if a sufficient number of ridge characteristics are found in common. However, no studies have been completed to show exactly what number of points in common are required to make a "match." One trial court refused to admit a fingerprint examiner's testimony about a fingerprint match after a full *Daubert* hearing; however, the court later retracted its opinion on less than satisfactory grounds. We will examine this case in detail in Chapter 6, on fingerprints.

It is unlikely that the Supreme Court meant for courts to admit expert testimony simply because it had always been admitted in the past. In effect, by using the phrase "generally accepted," courts can sidestep a genuine examination of whether the science or technique is based on a reliable scientific hypothesis that has been subjected to review, critique, and duplication by other scientists.

---

27. Nicholas Wade, "University Panel Faults Cloning Co-Author," *New York Times*, February 11, 2006.

Although *Daubert* used general acceptance as one of the tests for admitting expert testimony, it seems unlikely that the court meant that science that is generally accepted but does *not* meet the other criteria stated in the test should be admitted. As the Ninth Circuit stated on the second *Daubert* appeal:

> Under *Frye*, the party proffering scientific evidence had to show it was based on the method generally accepted in the scientific community. The focus under *Daubert* is on the reliability of the methodology, and in addressing that question the court and the parties are not limited to what is generally accepted; methods accepted by a minority in the scientific community may well be sufficient.
>
> However, the party proffering the evidence must explain the expert's methodology and demonstrate in some objectively verifiable way that the expert has both chosen a reliable scientific method and followed it faithfully. Of course, the fact that one party's experts use a methodology accepted by only a minority of scientists would be a proper basis for impeachment at trial.[28]

How Well Do Trial Judges Understand Science?

Daubert hearings can be lengthy and complex. Experts for each side come prepared with scientific theories and experiments. The consequences for the litigating parties of refusing to allow expert testimony can be devastating. Yet, most judges are not trained in science. How can they possibly evaluate the competing theories?

In 2000, the Federal Judicial Center published an extensive *Reference Manual on Scientific Evidence*[29] for federal judges, explaining the science behind many types of forensic testimony. Here is the assessment by one scientist[30] of the relationship of the *Daubert* decision to the process of scientific research:

> The presentation of scientific evidence in a court of law is a kind of shot gun marriage between the two disciplines. Both are forced to some extent to yield to the central imperatives of the other's way of doing business, and it is likely that neither will be shown in its best light. The *Daubert* decision is an attempt (not the first, of course) to regulate that encounter. Judges are asked to decide the "evidential reliability" of the intended testimony, based not on the conclusions to be offered, but on the methods used to reach those conclusions. In particular, the methods should be judged by the following four criteria:

---

28. 43 F.3d 1311, n.11.
29. Available at http://www.fjc.gov.
30. David Goodstein, "How Science Works," *Reference Manual on Scientific Evidence*, 81–82, *supra*.

- The theoretical underpinnings of the methods must yield testable predictions by means of which the theory could be falsified.

- The methods should preferably be published in a peer-reviewed journal.

- There should be a known rate of error that can be used in evaluating the results.

- The methods should be generally accepted within the relevant scientific community.

The doctrine of falsification is supplemented by a bow to the institution of peer review, an acknowledgment of the scientific meaning of error, and a paradigm check (really, an inclusion of the earlier *Frye* standard).

All in all, I would score the decision a pretty good performance. The justices ventured into the treacherous crosscurrents of the philosophy of science — where even most scientists fear to tread — and emerged with at least their dignity intact. Falsifiability may not be a good way of doing science, but it's not the worst a posteriori way to judge science, and that's all that's required here.

Post-*Daubert* Decisions

Few courts have held *Daubert* gatekeeper hearings in which they evaluate testimony based on each of the *Daubert* factors.

We will review the courts' rulings on expert testimony based on the *Daubert* test and its adoption in federal and state evidence codes, as well as the states that retain the *Frye* test, in chapters on individual forms of forensic evidence. As a general matter, however, few courts have held *Daubert* gatekeeper hearings in which they evaluate testimony based on each of the *Daubert* factors. You can see the results of one such hearing on fingerprint analysis in the *Llera Plaza* case (see Chapter 6, "Fingerprint Analysis") and one on polygraph in the *Porter* case (discussed in Chapter 4, "The Scientific Method and 'Junk Science'"). Many courts have continued to admit expert testimony on one of three theories:

- The testimony has been admitted in other courts in its jurisdiction.

- The expert is qualified by training and experience.

- The issue of reliability can go to the jury to consider in weighing the evidence.

The first argument confuses "generally admitted' with "generally accepted." The fact that courts have admitted an area before does not mean that the science is reliable. One example of this is bite marks, discussed in Chapter 4, "The Scientific Method and 'Junk Science.'" Courts have admitted bite mark matching in the past, but a 2016 report by a national council has stated its conclusion that bite mark matching has no scientific support.[31]

---

31. See Chapter 4, pp. 91–92.

The fact that an expert is well qualified similarly does not bootstrap an area of testimony that is not science into science. An example is handwriting matching. There are handwriting experts who have practiced this process and been certified by associations. But as they cannot point to any step-by-step process, any agreed number of points of similarity, or any external scientific support, handwriting analysis would appear to be more a subjective process than a scientific one. See Chapter 12, "Handwriting and Questioned Documents."

Finally, asking the jury to weigh the scientific reliability of an area of scientific testimony is passing the buck. If the judge is unwilling to submit the testimony to scientific rigor, how can the jury be expected to do so? This is exacerbated by the fact that the prosecution typically presents expert testimony, but the defendant frequently does not, due largely to issues of cost. Without rigorous cross-examination, the jury cannot be expected to understand the issues with scientific reliability.

In 2009, the National Research Council acknowledged many of these problems:

> Federal appellate courts have not with any consistency or clarity imposed standards ensuring the application of scientifically valid reasoning and reliable methodology in criminal cases involving *Daubert* questions.... [T]rial judges exercise great discretion in deciding whether to admit or exclude expert testimony, and their judgments are subject only to a highly deferential "abuse of discretion" standard of review.
>
> ...
>
> The adversarial process relating to the admission and exclusion of scientific evidence is not suited to the task of finding "scientific truth." The judicial system is encumbered by, among other things, judges and lawyers who generally lack the scientific expertise necessary to comprehend and evaluate forensic evidence in an informed manner ... Judicial review, by itself, will not cure the infirmities of the forensic science community.... With more and better educational programs, accredited laboratories, certified forensic practitioners, sound operational principles and procedures, and serious research to establish the limits and measures of performance in each discipline, forensic science experts will be better able to analyze evidence and coherently report their findings in the courts.[32]

Summary

The admissibility of forensic evidence based on science was governed in the federal courts by the General Acceptance Test from the case of *Frye v. United States*, decided in 1923. Shortly after Congress passed the Federal Rule of Evidence 702, governing admissibility of expert opinions, the Supreme Court ruled in 1993 that Rule 702 had

---

32. NRC Report at 11, 13.

The fact that an expert is well qualified similarly does not bootstrap an area of testimony that is not science into science.

"With more and better educational programs, accredited laboratories, certified forensic practitioners, sound operational principles and procedures, and serious research to establish the limits and measures of performance in each discipline, forensic science experts will be better able to analyze evidence and coherently report their findings in the courts."

superseded the *Frye* test. In this case, *Daubert v. Merrrell Dow*, the Court held that scientific testimony should be admissible if it meets alternate tests of reliability, such as a scientific hypothesis, publication and peer review, and error rate.

The *Daubert* test was soon adopted in some state courts, but not in all. Some states retain the *Frye* test. The *Daubert* test requires the trial court to act as a gatekeeper and decide outside the hearing of the jury whether the forensic expert testimony is admissible or not. However, the court will conduct a gatekeeper hearing only if a party objects to the admission of expert testimony. It has no independent obligation to hold such a hearing. If the opposing party does not challenge the testimony, he generally cannot raise the issue on appeal.

The *Kuhmo* case decided that the *Daubert* test should apply to experts testifying about a technique — such as examination of a tire to determine any defect — as well as science. The *General Electric* case held that an appeals court must defer to the trial court's gatekeeper decision, unless the trial court abused its discretion. After *Daubert*, courts have expanded the gatekeeper questions to include such issues as whether the science was developed specifically for litigation.

As a general matter, courts frequently cite the *Daubert* tests but rarely apply them step-by-step to the proposed expert testimony. Many courts make their decision to accept or exclude based on the training and experience of the expert or a review of other courts that have accepted similar experts, rather than the scientific reliability of the testimony. They seem to admit expert testimony based on whether it has been "generally admitted" rather than on the *Daubert* question of whether it has been "generally accepted" by the relevant scientific community. Commentators have pointed out that courts much more frequently allow a prosecution expert and exclude one proposed by the defense.

The National Research Council in its 2009 report stated "*Daubert* and its progeny have engendered confusion and controversy ... judicial dispositions of *Daubert*-type questions in criminal cases have been criticized by some lawyers and scholars who thought that the Supreme Court's decision would be applied more rigorously."[33]

Discussion Questions

1. How does the *Frye* test differ from the *Daubert* test? Give an example of evidence that might be excluded under the *Frye* test but included under the *Daubert* test?

2. What happened to the plaintiffs' case in *Daubert* after the Supreme Court vacated the Court of Appeals judgment and remanded the case back to the circuit appeals court? Did the trial court hold a *Daubert* hearing? Why or why not?

3. Was the *Daubert* case likely to result in the admissibility of more scientific evidence or less? Why?

---

33. NRC Report at 11.

4. What would have to happen for a court to conclude that bite-mark identification is admissible under *Frye*? Under *Daubert*?

5. Were all state courts required to change to the *Daubert* test after the case was decided? Why or why not?

6. What are three questions a trial court should ask in conducting a *Daubert* hearing?

7. What is your state's test for the admissibility of scientific testimony?

8. What was the effect of the changes Congress made to FRE 702 after the *Daubert* decision? Does FRE 702 specifically require a gatekeeping hearing?

9. How did the court extend the *Daubert* decision in the case of *Kuhmo Tire v. Carmichael*?

10. How did the opinion in *General Electric v. Joiner* affect gatekeeper hearings? Did this decision make it harder or easier for the losing party to get the appellate court to overturn the trial court's *Daubert* ruling on admissibility of forensic testimony?

11. What is the definition of "abuse of discretion"? What do you think a trial court would have to do in a gatekeeper hearing to show an abuse of discretion?

12. Do you believe that the *Daubert* decision means a trial court should refuse to admit forensic testimony *solely* because it has been generally accepted by the scientific community? What if the testimony otherwise would fail to meet the other tests in *Daubert*?

13. What reforms did the National Research Council recommend in 2009 that may improve the application of *Daubert* in the courtroom? What do you see as impediments to achieving those reforms?

Chapter 6

Fingerprint Analysis

Overview

The science of fingerprint identification rests upon two hypotheses:

- All fingerprints are permanent and unique and therefore can identify one individual compared with another.

- By visually examining certain detail on less than a complete fingerprint or a completely clear fingerprint, examiners can conclusively identify a subject.

Fingerprints are formed in utero by the fingers of a fetus moving through amniotic fluid. For this reason, even the prints of identical twins, who share the same DNA, are different. Most scientists agree that fingerprints are unique, that they do not change over time, and that they cannot be easily altered. A typical fingerprint has approximately 200 distinguishing features, called ridge characteristics, which can appear in any one of a number of configurations. Fingerprint identification uses a combination of automated search based on an algorithm coupled with visual inspection and confirmation, called the ACE-V approach (Analysis, Comparison, Evaluation, and Verification). The basis for matching requires a conclusion that a latent fingerprint lifted from a crime scene have no visible characteristics that differ from an exemplar print taken from a suspect and possess a number of characteristics that appear identical in size, shape, and location.

Fingerprint identification has been accepted as forensic evidence since the early 1900s.[1] Not until quite recently has there been any challenge to its reliability. However, a few scholars as well as one federal district court argued that fingerprint identification did not pass the *Daubert* tests for reliability because no scientific studies had been conducted outside the fingerprint community to verify the required minimum number of comparison points to declare a match.[2]

This 2002 case was later retracted, but it spawned a number of subsequent challenges to fingerprint identification under *Daubert* and similar state statutes. These challenges uniformly failed.

---

1. *People v. Jennings*, 252 Ill. 534 (1911).
2. *U.S. v. Llera Plaza*, 179 F. Supp. 2d 492 (E.D. Pa. 2002); vacated, 188 F. Supp. 2d 549 (E.D. Pa. 2002). The two cases will be referred to as *Llera Plaza I* and *Llera Plaza II*.

The NRC Report in 2009, however, led to another spate of challenges, as it concluded that fingerprint identification needed better documentation for each step of the ACE-V process and that error rate needed further study:

> [A]dditional research is also needed into ridge flow and crease pattern distributions on the hands and feet. This information could be used to limit the possible donor population of a particular print in a statistical approach ... Additionally, more research is needed regarding the discriminating value of the various ridge formations and clusters of ridge formations.[3]
>
> The NRC Report also called for more research on the various factors that affect the quality of latent prints such as condition of the skin, residue, and mechanics of touch. And because the print examiner uses his or her subjective judgment in declaring a match between a latent print and an exemplar from a suspect, the NRC also recommended that the examiner document the basis for subjective conclusions.

Although challenges based on the NRC Report that fingerprint matching fails *Daubert* have not succeeded, they have led at least one commentator to criticize the NRC Report and refute its contentions about problems with fingerprinting.[4]

There have been almost no reported cases of fingerprint identification errors, other than mechanical errors such as copying the wrong person's name on a file. One highly publicized fingerprint identification error took place in 2004, in which a fingerprint that appeared on a piece of luggage in Madrid at the site of a train station bombing was incorrectly reported as identifying an attorney in Seattle, Washington, who happened to be a Muslim.[5] Most people believe this error was the result more of cutting corners in the haste to find a terrorist than any fault in fingerprint identification methods.

Chapter Objectives

Based on this chapter, students will be able to:

1. Explain the scientific principle underlying fingerprint identification.

2. Appreciate the difference between class and individual characteristics of fingerprints and the three levels of detail in fingerprints.

3. Understand the process of lifting and comparing latent and exemplar fingerprints.

4. Explain the ACE-V process.

5. Understand the use of computers using an AFIS database.

---

3. NRC Report at 144.

4. Wayne G. Plumtree, "A Perspective on the Appropriate Weight to Be Given to the National Academy of Sciences' Report on Forensics in Evidentiary Hearings: The Significance of Continued Court Acceptance of Fingerprint Evidence," *Southwester Law Review* 42 (2013): 605.

5. John Leyden, "FBI Apology for Madrid Bomb Fingerprint Fiasco," *The Register*, May 26, 2004.

6. Explain the history of using fingerprints in court.

7. Apply each of the *Daubert* tests to fingerprint identification.

8. Evaluate the NRC recommendations for further fingerprint research and form an opinion as to whether these recommendations are valid.

9. Identify errors in the initial identification of fingerprints in the Madrid bombing case.

The Evolution of Fingerprint Identification

Fingerprinting is one of the oldest forms of forensic evidence, and has been routinely admitted in court to prove identity. Its predecessor was anthropometry, which is discussed in Chapter 4, "The Scientific Method and 'Junk Science.'" Anthropometry was a system developed by Alphonse Bertillon in which measurements of body dimensions, including the size of ears, were thought to create a unique profile of an individual's physical characteristics that could identify him to the exclusion of all others. Although anthropometry did not prove discriminating enough for this task, the use of fingerprint comparison is based on the same principle: that no two people share the exact same fingerprints.

Scientists today agree that fingerprints are unique. This is based, in part, on the knowledge that fingerprints are formed in utero by the movement of the fetus' hands through amniotic fluid. For this reason, the fingerprints of even identical twins (who share the same DNA) are different, which shows that fingerprints are not a genetic trait. The uniqueness of fingerprints was confirmed by a government study in which 50,000 fingerprints consisting of all loop patterns from all white males were compared. The study found that no two were identical:

> The goal of this study, which was comprised of two separate tests, was to determine the probability that fingerprints of two people could be identical. Donald Ziesig, an algorithmist at Lockheed Martin Information Systems who played an important role in developing the FBI's computer-based fingerprint system (the Automated Fingerprint Identification System, or AFIS), was a developer of the 50k x 50k study and explained in detail how it operated. The result of the first test, in which full-sized, one inch fingerprints were compared with each other, was that the probability of finding two people with identical fingerprints was one in ten to the ninety-seventh power.
>
> In the second test, the rolled prints were artificially cropped to the average size of latent prints so that only the center 21.7% of the rolled prints was analyzed, with the resultant conclusion that the probability of finding two different, partial fingerprints to be identical was one in ten to the twenty-seventh power.[6]

---

6. *Llera Plaza I*, at 497.

Fingerprint Patterns

Radial or **Ulnar**

Loops

Characterized by one or more free recurving friction ridges and one delta. (When the hand from which the loop pattern originated is known, you may determine if the recurving ridges originate from the little finger side (ulnar loop) or the thumb side (radial loop).)

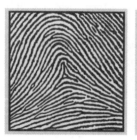 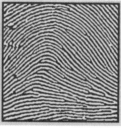

Tented   **Plain**

Arches

Characterized by friction ridges lying one above the other in a general arching formation.

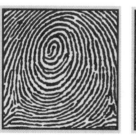 

Plain   **Double Looped**

Central Pocket Loop   **Accidental**

Whorls

Characterized by one or more free recurving friction ridges and two points of delta.

Ridge Characteristics

1. **Bifurcation** — The point at which one friction ridge divides into two friction ridges
2. **Enclosure** — A single friction ridge that bifurcates and rejoins after a short course and continues as a single friction ridge
3. **Ending Ridge** — A single friction ridge that terminates within the friction ridge structure
4. **Short Ridge** — A single friction ridge that only travels a short distance before terminating
5. **Ridge Dot** — An isolated ridge unit whose length approximates its width in size

© 2004 WARD'S Natural Science

Some critics noted that this sample was restricted, and did not cover a wide spectrum of the population. However, no one has disproved the hypothesis that fingerprints are unique. Scientists have also concluded that most wounds will not eradicate a fingerprint; at most, a deep cut into the dermis layer may result in a scar, but the rest of the fingerprint will remain the same.

If you look at your own fingers, you will be able to see that each finger bears one of three primary patterns: loop, arch, or whorl, of which there are subgroups. There are two types of arches and loops and four types of whorls. There have been a number of studies done to determine the distribution of these major patterns in the population. In general, loop pattern is most common — about 60% of people have this pattern. The whorl accounts for about 35% and the arch for about 5%.[7] These characteristics are therefore "class" characteristics. You can be excluded if your fingers all have loops and the print from the crime scene is a whorl. But if the crime scene print is a loop, that alone does not mean it is yours. It could belong is 60 out of 100 people chosen

Class characteristics in fingerprints are the loop, arch, and whorl and their variations.

7. Andre Moenssens, James Starrs, Carol E. Henderson, and Fred E. Inbau, *Scientific Evidence in Civil and Criminal Cases*, 4th ed., (Foundation Press, 1995), 506.

at random. Fingerprints also have fixed reference points called "deltas," seen in loops and whorls, and "cores" seen in loops.

The principle that can identify a person in fingerprint analysis depends upon much smaller characteristics that are called ridge characteristics or Galton points (after Sir Francis Galton, who identified them in the late 1800s). These are the patterns made by the raised lines on each print. Each fingerprint has from between 75 and 175 of these ridge characteristics on each finger.[8] Fingerprint examiners refer to three primary types of ridge characteristics: ending ridge, bifurcation, and ridge dot. Variations, such as an enclosure, island, crossover, bridge, or trifurcation are combinations of the three major patterns. The chart below taken from Ward's Natural Sciences includes five ridge characteristics:

- Bifurcation — where one friction ridge divides into two.
- Enclosure — a single friction ridge that bifurcates and rejoins to continue as a single ridge.
- Ending Ridge — a single friction ridge that terminates.
- Short Ridge — a single friction ridge that travels a short distance and terminates.
- Ridge Dot — an isolated ridge unit whose length is approximately equal to its width.

Level two and level three detail are used to individualize, or identify, fingerprints. Ridge characteristics such as bifurcations, ridge endings, and ridge dots are level two detail. Pores are level three detail.

Examiners also compare a final intricate level of detail — level three detail — which includes sweat pores and their structures.

The Process of Fingerprint Identification

Obtaining the Crime Scene Print

Plastic fingerprints are those impressed in soft material, such as wax, putty, or dust. Visible prints are those plainly identifiable because they appear in colored substances such as blood, grease, or ink. Latent prints, which are not visible to the human eye, constitute the third type of prints.

Fingerprint examiners obtain latent prints in a variety of ways. Since the 1900s, fingerprint examiners have recovered these prints by powdering surfaces, and then dusting the powder off with a small brush so as to differentiate the fingerprint image from its background. Light-colored powder was used for dark surfaces, while dark-colored powder was used for light surfaces. The process of lifting the print can result in damaging or destroying the print. The most common is pressure distortion, which occurs when the print is being deposited. The shape of the surface on which the print has been deposited and the process used to develop and lift the print can cause other types of distortion.

---

8. *Id.*

Investigators then photograph the resulting image, lift the powdered image, and transfer it to paper using clear tape. After classifying the fingerprint according to the prevailing classification system, examiners compare the ridge characteristics and minutia of the exemplar image with those of the latent print.

Crime scene prints are often "latent," which means not visible to the human eye. They are colored to make them visible and then lifted and preserved for evaluation.

Getting Prints from a Suspect

Fingerprints are taken from criminal suspects using a two-part method. First, law enforcement officers apply ink to the suspect's finger and roll the inked finger on a piece of paper with boxes labeled for each finger of both the left and right hand.

Next, plain impressions are taken by pressing inked fingertips directly against the paper below the labeled boxes. This step insures against manual error and serves as a backup impression should the rolled print become smudged. New technology is improving the process of taking prints from a suspect by using live scan computers.

Comparing Ridge Characteristics and Minutiae

The process of identifying ridge characteristics and minutiae in one print and comparing them to another is how fingerprint examiners determine identification. If an examiner has two full prints which are clearly visible to compare, he can visually inspect them under magnification and decide if they match. Obviously, even one difference would disqualify the match, so he will search first for differences.

Even one difference between two finger-prints would disqual-ify an identification.

Although fingerprint identification today is frequently aided by computer searches, the basic search process can be done by visual inspection. The technician looks for four different elements:

- Likeness of general pattern type,
- Qualitative likeness of the friction ridge characteristics,
- Quantitative likeness of those characteristics, and
- Likeness of location of the characteristics.

The two most difficult challenges for the examiner are in determining when he has enough of a print from the crime scene for a valid comparison and how many characteristics to find in common to make an identification. Prints from a crime scene are frequently partial, badly blurred, or smudged. You can see this on the prints from the Madrid bombing. Examiners use their skill and experience to make this judgment call. There is no agreed amount of a crime scene print—for example one-third or one-half of a total print—deemed acceptable for fingerprint identification among state and federal examiners.

There is also no agreed number of comparison points that must be found in common. "By tradition, though not by empirical studies, latent print examiners in the United States have required a matching of at east six to eight characteristics in both prints for identity, though most experts prefer at least 10–12 concordances."[9] The FBI has no required minimum number for an identification. This fact led to one federal court to decide that fingerprint identification was not scientifically reliable because it lacked an agreed standard number of comparison points to make an identification.

> Take an example where a latent print that possesses 8 matching points with a subject's inked print is compared by different examiners. The first examiner's criterion for identification is 8 points so he makes a positive identification. The second examiner's criteria is 9 points, therefore he is unable to make a positive identification. Is it wrong for the second examiner to report his findings? Many examiners feel that the second examiner should report that since he did not make a positive identification, the print is of no value.

> Is it wrong for the second examiner to provide detail that he found a significant number of matching points even though he did not make a positive identification? It would be better practice to state the facts of a comparison, i.e., the print lacked the criteria for 100% positive identification, however 7 or 8 points match and there is a degree of probability the print was made by a particular person, rather than totally disregarding the print.[10]

Although it is possible for an overly eager or unscrupulous examiner to call an identification based on a crime scene print with inadequate detail for evaluation, this does not invalidate the process of fingerprint identification. The same charges have been made about fraudulent DNA reports. When one watches a fingerprint examination, as I did, many of the theoretical objections that the court considered are put into perspective. In "real life," examiners typically compare far more points of similarity than 8 or 10.

In 1970, long before the legal challenge to fingerprinting in 2003 or the NRC Report in 2009, the fingerprint community had set up a Standardization Committee, composed of 11 members with total experience of 250 years. After three years of work, it concluded:

"The decision on whether two prints under examination are made by the same digit is one that must be made . . . on the basis of the expert's experience and background."

> there exists no valid basis, at this time, for requiring a predetermined minimum number of friction ridge characteristics in two impressions in order to establish positive identification. The decision on whether two prints under examination are made by the same digit is one that must be made . . . on the basis of the expert's experience and background, taking into account, along with the number of matching characteristics, other factors such as clarity of the impressions, types of characteristics found, location of the characteristics in relation to the core or delta, etc.[11]

The question then becomes: how many points of similarity are enough to call a match? Again, even one point of dissimilarity is enough to rule out a match. The question

---

9. *Id.* at 513–14.
10. *Id.* at 514.
11. *Id.* at 516.

of the right number of points for a match was a major issue in a case we will examine that held fingerprint identification was unreliable under *Daubert*. In that case, the court decided that the fact that there was no standard "required" number of points of similarity to declare a match meant that the process of fingerprint identification lacked standards and was therefore unreliable:

> In some state jurisdictions in the United States, and in some foreign jurisdictions, fingerprint examiners must find a minimum number of Galton points (characteristics on the fingerprint ridges) in common before they can declare a match with absolute certainty. The FBI switched from relying on a mandatory minimum number of points to no minimum number in the late 1940s. Mr. Meagher discussed the absence of a uniform standard prescribing a minimum number of points in common as a precondition of finding a match.
>
> Meagher testified that there is no single quantifiable standard for reaching an identification opinion because of differences in both the quantity of characteristics shown in the latent print and the quality of the image. For example, if a latent print shows a relatively small portion of a fingerprint but has a very clear image — one that allows clear identification of level three detail such as the shapes of ridges, locations of pores, and the like, a reliable identification may still be possible even with relatively few level two "points."[12]

I asked Christopher Grice, the fingerprint examiner in the *Grant* case, to respond to the controversy over looking for a specific number of ridge characteristics in common. "Two bifurcations appearing in prints being compared is not a point of identification," he says," unless they have the same shape. A bifurcation can be "y" shaped or wine-glass shaped. It can have an acute angle or an obtuse angle. There is a myriad of shapes involving the width of the ridges themselves and in impressions of great clarity, even pore shapes."[13]

The ACE-V Method of Fingerprint Comparison

Analysis

The examiner must first analyze the crime scene print to determine if it is sufficient for identification purposes. Is it enough of a print and does it show enough clear ridge characteristics to be compared? What ridge characteristics can be identified on the print? Here are portions of testimony by an FBI expert in explaining the ACE-V method:

> In comparing latent and rolled prints, fingerprint examiners employ a process known as "ridgeology" or ACE-V, an acronym for "analysis,"

The ACE-V method consists of the following four steps:
1. Analysis
2. Comparison
3. Evaluation
4. Verification

---

12. *Llera Plaza I*, at 499–500.
13. Christopher Grice, interview March 12, 2007.

comparison," "evaluation," and "verification." Sergeant Ashbaugh testified that, during the analysis stage, examiners look at the unknown, or latent, print and note both the "anatomical aspects" of the fingerprint and the clarity of the print. He described the analysis stage in some detail: Does it have first, second and third level detail or a combination? What is the clarity of the print? We would then look at all the ridge paths, all the ridge arrangements. We'd explore ridge shapes and we would note any red flags.

Red flags — I'll be very brief with this because it is a very large area — we would look for any lines running in the print that could have been caused by pressure, substraight [sic] or matrix smears. We would look for areas of fat ridges, possibly that could be caused by overlapping ridges. We'd look for differing amounts of pressure. We'd look for similar ridge characteristics close to each other. This could mean a double tap, two pressures and a [sic] again, an overlapping print. We'd look for shadows, shadow ridges in the furrows, which also could mean two prints deposited.

We'd look for misaligned ridges protruding into the furrow. We'd look for crossover ridges running through the furrow and, of course, we'd look for inappropriate print outline.[14]

Comparison of Prints

The examiner will compare the crime scene print with the rolled print to determine if they match. Before the introduction of computer technology, the examiner visually compared prints side by side under a magnifier. Examiners have never used a method in which one print is superimposed on another to determine a match. This is simply TV theatrics. At the time of the Serra murder, for example, police detectives examined the latent print from the tissue box against the entire base of approximately 70,000 fingerprint cards in New Haven. No match was found.

In the *Llera Plaza* case, the expert in the *Daubert* hearing said:

After analysis: We move on to comparison, and comparison is carried out in sequence or systematically and we start — first of all, we would look at first level detail, is the overall pattern configuration in agreement. And then we would look at — start at an area that is common to both the unknown and the known print. And we would start at a common area and we start systematically comparing all the various friction ridge arrangements and friction ridge shapes, including relative pore position, if it's at all possible.

The comparison is something that is very objective. We're dealing with physical evidence and if I discuss something in the ridge arrangement, I should be able to point to it, so it's a very objective process.[15]

---

14. *Llera Plaza I*, at 498.
15. *Id.*

Evaluation

Once the comparison is complete, and we recommend that the whole print be compared, the next thing that we would do is then evaluate what we saw during comparison as far as agreement of the various ridge formations. And I break it down into actually two separate areas. The first area is, do I have agreement? If you say yes to that, if you form the opinion you have agreement, then you have to ask yourself, is there sufficient unique detail present to individualize?

That final decision is a subjective decision. It's based on your knowledge and experience and your ability. And that, if you say yes, I feel there's enough to individualize, then you formed an opinion of identification.

The conclusions that we recommend that are available to you at the end of identification, would be elimination, which usually would start very early in the identification process, identification, a situation where you have sufficient volume of unique details to individualize. And a situation where you have agreement, but you're unable to individualize or eliminate. And, in other words, you can't differentiate from others. And those are the three conclusions that we recommend that you can form.[16]

Verification

[All fingerprint identifications must be repeated by a second, independent investigator, who does not know the results of the first test.]

From there we move into the very last box, which deals with the verification, which is a form of peer review, and it is part of the scientific process. From this point the person actually starts right at the beginning and goes through the same questions.

Opinion

After utilizing the ACE-V and quantitative/qualitative processes, an examiner is ready to make a determination with respect to the latent print in question. The three opinions that the examiner has are described in one of two ways:

(1) identification, elimination, or "agreement but not enough to individualize — not enough to eliminate," or

(2) "absolutely him, absolutely not him, and absolutely I don't know."

Whichever terminology is used, the result is the same — an examiner who makes a positive identification is determining that the latent fingerprint necessarily came from the individual in question, "to the exclusion of all other fingers in the world."[17]

An examiner can give one of three opinions:

1. identification,

2. elimination, or

3. inconclusive.

---

16. *Id.*
17. *Id.*

Automated Fingerprint Identification System (AFIS) Matching[18]

The advent of computer technology has made the process of matching fingerprints quicker and it has expanded the number and geographic area of prints that can be searched. However, it has not eliminated visual examination by a human — both at the outset and after the computer gives its "results." The only step in the ACE-V process that does not depend upon the judgment and experience of the examiner is the "C" piece — Comparison. And it is important to note that even the computer comparison process requires the examiner to code information that goes into the computer and use his judgment in evaluating the scores the computer generates. The AFIS system does not generate one fingerprint "match." It generates a list of likely candidates in order of numerical score. The examiner can set the system to generate any number of candidates. The Connecticut Forensic Science Laboratory, for example, is set to generate 50 candidates.

The process of matching a latent print with prints in the database through an automated fingerprint index system (AFIS) combines computer technology that marks all ridge characteristics (here called "minutiae") on a fingerprint (without regard to the type of minutiae). Early systems converted this data into an algorithm based on the number of characteristics on the field using an x/y axis. More modem systems can do a 360-degree search even if a print is scanned in upside down. It then searches its database of fingerprints that have been similarly coded and put into the system using the same algorithm.[19]

The fingerprints in the database come from inked fingerprint cards, referred to as "tenprints," that have been taken in conjunction with criminal investigations. Some databases also include prints taken by applicants for employment.

The FBI maintains an AFIS base of approximately 70 million cards. As each card contains 10 fingerprints, it contains 700 million prints. Most states have their own database on a computer system so that they can search within their own state. However, in order to search through the FBI database, states must adopt compatible software.

Isolating the Print

The first step in matching a print is to get a copy of a latent print from a crime site. It is usually sent to the forensic lab by the officers who investigated the site. Once the print has been lifted, the examiner will scan it into a computer system and enter certain data that he obtains by visually examining the print, such as what finger the print came from or whether it is an arch, whorl, or loop. Typically, a latent print will

---

18. This section is based on an interview at the Connecticut Forensic Science Laboratory with Christopher Grice and demonstration of fingerprint analysis using an AFIS system, August, 2007.

19. Grice interview, *supra*.

appear along with other prints — sometimes superimposed on other prints or partially masked. The latent print will typically not be straight up and down, as will the rolled print. It may be smudged and barely visible. It may be impossible to tell what finger it is from. The examiner will view the scanned print on a screen and isolate the portion that he wishes to match. Once isolated, this portion is then enlarged by the computer screen.

Identifying the Ridge Characteristics

Once the print to be matched has been scanned in, the computer will automatically identify with yellow circles every minutiae point it identifies (ridge ending, branch, breaks, island, etc.). A typical print will have as many as 100 or more detectable minutiae points. The circle will have a "tail" pointing in the direction from which the minutiae is running, for example, in the direction of a ridge that ends with a ridge ending. It will also identify with a red circle what it sees as the "core," or center of the print and with a green triangle where it sees the "delta," which is a triangular area determined by the ridge flow.

When I observed a fingerprint comparison at the Connecticut Forensic Science Laboratory, the computer identified approximately 60 of these points on the first print the examiner entered into the system. The system will also identify the "ridge count," which is the number of ridges between one minutiae to another. For example, if there are four ridges between a ridge ending and an island, the computer will mark this spatial relationship. The FBI database requires ridge counts for matching; the Connecticut system does not.

The examiner then looks at the latent print and removes yellow circles which in his judgment are not really minutiae, and he relocates yellow circles to the proper point of certain minutiae, again, using his judgment and experience. By restricting the search to the most prominent and strongest minutiae, the examiner reduces the amount of scanning the computer must do. Again, this is judgment made based on the examiner's knowledge of typical patterns and decisions about where the computer has made a "mistake," possibly based on misreading woodgrain or scratches as being ridges.

The system then asks the examiner if he wants to search the latent print against any particular finger in the inked cards in the database. Only when the examiner is relatively sure that he is looking at a particular finger will he elect to restrict the search this way. It will also ask if the examiner wants to search prints with a certain direction of ridges.

The Computer Search

In the print examination process that I watched, after the examiner had deleted and moved minutiae the computer had identified, there were 55 minutiae marked on the latent print and submitted for a match. It took about ten minutes to process.

AFIS Screens

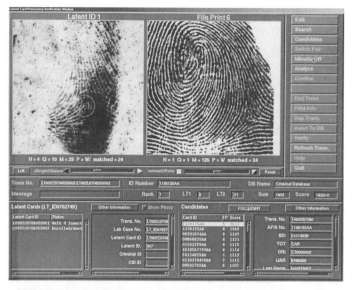

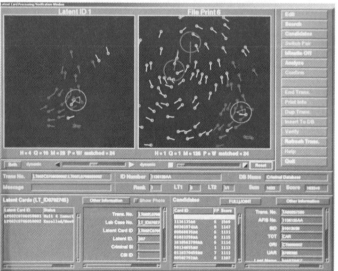

Courtesy of Connecticut State Forensic Laboratory

The screen produced the top ten prints, with "scores" ranging from 2914 to 1010. Christopher Grice of the Connecticut Forensic Science Laboratory estimates that the first candidate is the match about 75% of the time.[20]

In the case I observed, the latent print had 55 minutiae; the inked print had 94; 43 of the minutiae matched. See photograph called AFIS Screens.

The examiner first looks at the number one print generated by the system and visually compares it to the latent print on the screen, and also to the actual latent

---

20. Grice interview, *supra*.

AFIS Printout

CANDIDATE LISTS FOR LATENT SEARCH TRANSACTION

Searched Latent Data:

```
            Trans. No.: LT002L0507290005
             AFIS No.:
         Lab Case No.: LT_ID05016901
        Latent Card ID: LT002C0507290004
           Latent ID.: 001-L1
          Criminal SI:
               CSI ID:
                  ORI: CT0000003
       Submitting ORI:
             Examiner: cwg
              User ID: 1737
         Time Created: CURRENT
       Update User ID: 0
         Time Updated:
           Receipt ID:
    Miscellaneous No.:
                Memo.: Theft from Auto
        Date of Crime:
           Crime Code: LFS
                  Sex: U
           Birth Year: 0
             TLI Flag:
        Contract Info:
         Pattern Type:
        Finger Number: 0
         Adj. Pttn. L:
         Adj. Pttn. R:
        Internal flag: 0
```

Tenprint Candidates:

RANK	TRANS. NO	FP#	SCORE
1	01042468AA	2	2914
2	01042468AB	2	2092
3	20201432AA	4	1085
4	00226529AA	3	1062
5	00508916AA	4	1037
6	00294793AA	4	1032
7	20215023AA	4	1029
8	50117925AA	1	1024
9	59911923AA	1	1022
10	0410609752AA	4	1010
11	00232070AA	3	1009
12	0710675863AA	4	998
13	0110246844AA	3	996
14	00841993AA	5	993
15	00419075AA	1	988
16	0110420790AA	4	987
17	1610712034AB	1	979
18	00326599AA	4	978
19	0110478931AA	4	978
20	00298249AA	1	974

Unsolved Latent Candidates:

RANK	TRANS. NO	FP#	SCORE

Print Time: 2005-07-29 15:02:43 (CAFIS -- Cogent Systems, Inc.)

Courtesy of Connecticut State Forensic Laboratory

print viewed through a magnifying glass. The list of prints in order of score helps speed up the search process, but the examiner may need to look at ten, twenty, or all fifty possible candidates in the comparison process.

One defendant appealed on the ground that the entire list of possible fingerprint matches had not been provided to his counsel in pre-trial discovery. The defendant had been the "second best" match and neither he nor the first match had a high score. The court held that the error was harmless as it would not have affected the outcome of the trial.[21]

A second example I watched did not result in a match. Although the computer found 10 prints with similar minutiae, the examiner could see on visual inspection (and so could I) that the spatial relationship was slightly off, or one minutia was on one print and not the other. Although the number 1 print had a score similar to the number of ridge characteristic matches in the first case, on visual inspection, it was not a match. The examiner reviewed prints in order down to number 10, at which point the score had dropped to a very low number. He determined that there was no match in the system.

I watched two latent prints searched in the database; the entire process took about an hour and a half. Computer processing time is longer if the system is searching every finger; shorter if a particular finger is identified. The time is also shorter if the number 1 match is clearly the print; otherwise the examiner must review a number of potential matches.

Any latent print that cannot be matched is put in the "unsolved latent database" and is checked weekly against new prints that come into the AFIS system. Juvenile prints do not go into the system until the juvenile becomes 16.

It is obvious from this demonstration that it would be impossible for the computer to identify a match by itself — it does not identify minutiae by type and it does not distinguish between "important" minutiae and common ones. This is where the judgment of the examiner is important.

History of Use of Fingerprints in Court

The first use of fingerprints in a criminal case was in England in 1902. The first such use in the United States occurred in 1911 in *People v. Jennings*.[22] The *Jennings* case actually held that fingerprints were "in such general common use" that the courts would take "judicial notice" of fingerprints as a method of identification. Here is a fairly typical analysis of the process many courts have used to determine that fingerprint expert testimony is admissible as generally accepted science:

---

21. *People v. Tims*, A092799, 2002 Cal. App. LEXIS 4154 (February 7, 2002).
22. *People v. Jennings, supra*.

***United States v. Abreu*, 406 F.3d 1304 (11th Cir. 2005)**

Appellant Jose Manuel Abreu appeals his conviction of possession with intent to distribute marijuana, in violation of 21 U.S.C. §841, arguing that the district court erred in affirming the magistrate judge's order denying his motion to preclude expert testimony regarding fingerprint evidence, because the government failed to demonstrate that the testimony met the requirements of Rule 702 of the Federal Rules of Evidence. For the reasons that follow, we affirm.

… Abreu contends that the government failed to establish that its expert's testimony was the product of reliable principles and methods as required by Rule 702, and the district court should have at least held an evidentiary hearing on the issue…. Abreu maintains that the admission of the expert testimony was "severely prejudicial" and was the most damaging evidence relied on by the government, since it was the only direct evidence that placed Abreu in the storage room with the marijuana plants.

In the present case, there is no dispute as to the qualifications of the expert or that the expert's testimony is relevant. Abreu, however, argues that the government failed to establish the reliability of the expert opinion.

To assess the reliability of an expert opinion, the court considers a number of factors, including those listed by the Supreme Court in *Daubert*:

(1) whether the expert's theory can be and has been tested;

(2) whether the theory has been subjected to peer review and publication;

(3) the known or potential rate of error of the particular scientific technique; and

(4) whether the technique is generally accepted in the scientific community.

The *Daubert* factors are only illustrative and may not all apply in every case. The district court has wide latitude in deciding how to determine reliability.

This court has not published an opinion regarding the admissibility and reliability of fingerprint evidence under *Daubert*. Other circuits, however, have found that fingerprint evidence is sufficiently reliable and meets the standards of Fed. R. Evid. 702.

We agree with the decisions of our sister circuits and hold that the fingerprint evidence admitted in this case satisfied *Daubert*. Moreover, since district courts are given broad latitude in deciding how to determine the reliability of an expert opinion, we conclude from the record that the district court did not clearly err in giving greater weight to the general acceptance factor, as did the magistrate judge. Additionally, the magistrate judge considered information presented by the government detailing the uniform practice through which fingerprint examiners match fingerprints and the error rate of fingerprint comparison. As a result, based on our review of the record, the district court correctly found that the magistrate judge did not apply the wrong legal standard or make a clear error of judgment. Further, because the other evidence presented during Abreu's trial is sufficient to support the jury's verdict, any error committed by the district court in admitting the expert testimony regarding fingerprint evidence is not reversible error. Accordingly, we affirm Abreu's conviction.

Because most courts consider fingerprint identification to be generally accepted, they have not subjected it to the other factors in *Daubert*. The *Llera Plaza* case and the *Mitchell* case before it were the first to conduct a full *Daubert* hearing on each of the specific tests of reliability.

The *Llera Plaza* Case in 2002

In this case, a federal trial court in Philadelphia ruled, based on an extended *Daubert* hearing about fingerprint reliability, that an expert could not give an opinion about a fingerprint identification. This created quite a stir, as the ruling was unprecedented. The court examined each element of the *Daubert* test and decided that fingerprint testing failed. However, three months later, it reversed itself on the dubious grounds that the fingerprint methodology in the UK has changed. The first decision was based on a "cold record" of a similar *Daubert* hearing held in 1988 in a case called *U.S. v. Mitchell*.[23]

Although this case holding was withdrawn, the case is important to read in detail, as the record of the *Mitchell* case is one of the few detailed, step-by-step examinations of fingerprint matching based on the *Daubert* standards.

In 1998, Byron Mitchell was arrested for robbery. The arrest was supported by the apparent match of his fingerprints with small portions of two fingerprints found on the getaway car. His public defenders argued that the fingerprint comparison techniques did not meet the five criteria for admissibility established by the U.S. Supreme Court in the *Daubert* decision, particularly the fifth, that the potential rate of error is known. The *Mitchell* defense petitioned the court for a *Daubert* hearing to determine the admissibility of a fingerprint match as scientific evidence.

At issue in *Mitchell* were two latent fingerprints that the government recovered from the getaway car. In response to Mitchell's *Daubert* challenge, the government sent the two latent prints along with the ten-print card, to fifty-three different law enforcement agencies, requesting those agencies to select court-qualified examiners to compare the prints and to determine whether any identification could be made. In making this request, the government did not advise the agencies of the fact that the FBI had already determined that the latent prints could be matched to Mitchell's left and right thumbs. Of the thirty-four agencies that responded, nine reported they had not identified either one of the latent prints with any of the fingers on Mitchell's ten print card.

Although the *Daubert* hearing appeared to expose many weaknesses in the fingerprint identification system, the *Mitchell* court held that fingerprinting met the

---

23. *United States v. Mitchell*, 199 F. Supp. 2d 262 (E.D. Pa 2002), aff'd 365 F.3d 215 (3d Cir. 2004).

necessary criteria for admissibility as evidence. Fingerprinting, it held, is an established science, subjected to peer review and publication, with general acceptance and standards for its practice. Error rates are difficult to measure because they are so low.

Llera Plaza involved three defendants charged with committing four separate murders for hire in Puerto Rico and Pennsylvania. The murders were allegedly committed in furtherance of a gang-related drug conspiracy. The FBI recovered several latent prints on evidence connected to the murders. This evidence included fingerprints found in two separate vehicles allegedly used in the course of the crimes. In addition, latent prints were obtained from weapons and ammunition found in one of the vehicles.

Judge Pollack held a *Daubert* hearing using a "cold record" from *Mitchell*, but came to the opposite conclusion. He ruled for the first time that fingerprint evidence did not meet the federal evidentiary standard established in *Daubert*. The court determined that the government's experts could testify to the permanency and uniqueness of fingerprints. The experts could also point out places of comparison between the two sets of fingerprints. However, the fingerprint experts could not testify that the latent fingerprints matched those of the defendants. The prosecution relied upon the "match" testimony to convince juries of identification. Without this testimony, this ruling was a significant setback for the prosecution. The judge analyzed each of the following *Daubert* factors:

- Has the theory of fingerprint analysis been scientifically tested?
- Have the experiments been peer reviewed?
- Is there a quantifiable error rate?
- Are there controlling standards governing the process?
- Is fingerprint matching generally accepted by the scientific community?

Whether the Theory or Technique Can Be Tested

This required agreed standards. The basic problem the court found is that not all agencies agreed on the minimum number of ridge characteristics in common needed to make a match. The court reasoned that if the FBI used one standard and a state used a different one, then the "science" behind fingerprint identification was suspect.

The court was also troubled by the fact that fingerprint analysis contained a "subjective" evaluation in which the examiner looked at both prints and used his or her judgment to decide if they matched. The testimony at the *Mitchell* hearing used the term "subjective":

The significance of the fact that the determinations are "subjective" was explained by the further testimony of Dr. Stoney:

> Now, by subjective I mean that it [a fingerprint identification determination] is one that is dependent on the individual's expertise, training, and the consensus of their agreement of other individuals in the field. By not scientific, I mean that there is not an objective standard that has been tested; nor is

there a subjective process that has been objectively tested. It is the essential feature of a scientific process that there be something to test, that when that something is tested the test is capable of showing it to be false.[24]

Christopher Grice, the fingerprint analyst from the *Grant* case, objects to the word "subjective" on the ground that it sounds as if the examiner makes arbitrary decisions:

Fingerprint identification is "subjective" insofar as it depends upon the experience, training, and judgment of the examiner.

> My opinion on who the best candidate for president is would be subjective. The print itself is a physical item that can be enlarged and studied and in that sense it is an object and objective. It is impossible to take subjective factors out of the thought process. Two doctors looking at the same cancerous tumor may give opposite treatments and diagnoses based on their training and experience. This does not mean that there is something unscientific about it if they both observed, studied and investigated the actual physical object, the tumor.[25]

Peer Review

The prosecution argued that publications by examiners themselves about human error rates and the use of fingerprint testimony in courts equal "peer review." The court did not accept the argument. Peer review means review of the science, reasoned the court, not a review of error rates.

The prosecution also argued that fingerprint matching is peer reviewed because each examiner's test must be repeated by a second examiner. The court decided that peer review required review and replication by the scientific community, not the fingerprinting community, and therefore decided there was no peer review.

Peer review means a review by the scientific community, not fingerprint examiners, or a second fingerprint opinion.

> In his *Mitchell* testimony, Sergeant Ashbaugh voiced the same view. ACE-V "verification," he said, "is a form of peer review, and it is part of the scientific process." The difficulty is that if the opinion announced by a fingerprint examiner — "ident, non-ident," as Mr. Meagher expressed it — is, as both Mr. Meagher and Sergeant Ashbaugh acknowledged, "subjective," another opinion rendered by another examiner, whether in corroboration or in refutation, does little to put a "scientific" gloss on the first opinion, much less constitute "peer review" as described by Dr. Stoney.[26]

Rate of Error

The government argued that fingerprint identification, if done correctly, has an error rate of zero. However, it admitted that there is a risk of error by the examiner. The court reviewed a test relied upon in the *Mitchell* case in which the same prints were sent for evaluation by 53 law enforcement agencies. Thirty-four responded, and

---

24. *Llera Plaza I*, at 507–8.
25. Grice interview, *supra*.
26. *Llera Plaza I*, at 509.

of those, 9 could not make an identification. The court decided this was too high an error rate.

Controlling Standards

The court held that this *Daubert* requirement was also not met. How could there be controlling standards if different agencies could use a different number of Galton points for a match? In addition, the determination involved a subjective judgment, over which there could be no control. Finally, the court said that the lack of a standard certification process meant that some fingerprint examiners could have learned on the job without any process for determining their proficiency. Therefore, there were no controlling standards to be a fingerprint examiner.

As described by the *Havvard* court, "there is no single quantifiable standard for rendering an identification opinion because of differences in both the quantity of characteristics shown in the latent print and the quality of the image." While there may be good reason for not relying on a minimum point standard — or for requiring a minimum number, as some state and foreign jurisdictions do — it is evident that there is no one standard "controlling the technique's operation...."[27]

Controlling standards: "there is no single quantifiable standard for rendering an identification opinion because of differences in both the quantity of characteristics shown in the latent print and the quality of the image."

General Acceptance

Judge Pollack agreed that fingerprint matching is generally accepted in the "technical community" of examiners. However, he read the term to require a general acceptance in the scientific community. As scientific studies had not been done, he decided that the testimony failed this test too:

> Since the court finds that ACE-V does not meet *Daubert*'s testing, peer review, and standards criteria, and that information as to ACE-V's rate of error is in limbo, the expected conclusion would be that the government should be precluded from presenting any fingerprint testimony. But that conclusion — apparently putting at naught a century of judicial acquiescence in fingerprint identification processes — would be unwarrantably heavy-handed. The *Daubert* difficulty with the ACE-V process is by no means total.

> The difficulty comes into play at the stage at which, as experienced fingerprint specialists Ashbaugh and Meagher themselves acknowledge, the ACE-V process becomes "subjective" — namely, the evaluation stage. By contrast, the antecedent analysis and comparison stages are, according to the testimony, "objective": analysis of the rolled and latent prints and comparison of what the examiner has observed in the two prints.

> Up to the evaluation stage, the ACE-V fingerprint examiner's testimony is descriptive, not judgmental. Accordingly, this court will permit the

government to present testimony by fingerprint examiners who, suitably qualified as "expert" examiners by virtue of training and experience, may

- describe how the rolled and latent fingerprints at issue in this case were obtained,

- identify and place before the jury the fingerprints and such magnifications thereof as may be required to show minute details, and

- point out observed similarities (and differences) between any latent print and any rolled print the government contends are attributable to the same person.

What such expert witnesses will not be permitted to do is to present "evaluation" testimony as to their "opinion" (Rule 702) that a particular latent print is in fact the print of a particular person.

The defendants will be permitted to present their own fingerprint experts to counter the government's fingerprint testimony, but defense experts will also be precluded from presenting "evaluation" testimony. Government counsel and defense counsel will, in closing arguments, be free to argue to the jury that, on the basis of the jury's observation of a particular latent print and a particular rolled print, the jury may find the existence, or the non-existence, of a match between the prints.[28]

Three months later, the judge reconsidered his decision after a live *Daubert* hearing with fingerprint experts. His main reason for changing his mind was that the United Kingdom had abandoned its number of Galton points and now requires no set number to declare a match. The UK had therefore adopted the same standard as used by the FBI. As to the subjective element of fingerprint evaluation, the judge simply said "on further reflection, I disagree with myself."[29] The second opinion did not rely on any new facts, except the change in UK fingerprint procedures. As the court did not give any reason for changing its opinion on testing, peer review, or error rate, the reversal appeared to rest primarily on the question of whether there was uniformity in the number of ridge characteristics required to make an identification.

Cases on Fingerprints after *Llera Plaza* and before the NRC Report

Following the *Llera Plaza* cases, a number of defendants tried to convince courts to reject fingerprint identifications. These requests have uniformly failed. For example, the Seventh Circuit federal court accepted fingerprint testimony over an objection by the defendant that it could not be effectively tested:

---

28. *Id.* at 516.
29. *Llera Plaza II.*

While an actual print taken in the field cannot be objectively tested, we are satisfied that the method in general can be subjected to objective testing to determine its reliability in application.[30]

A number of defendants relied on the March 2000 solicitation by the National Institute of Justice for research to "determine the scientific validity of individuality in friction ridge examination based on measurement of features, quantification, and statistical analysis" to argue that the government admitted there is no scientific proof of the process of fingerprint identification. This argument was rejected.[31]

The NRC Report in 2009

The NRC Report in 2009 led to another spate of challenges, as the NRC Report concluded that fingerprint identification needed better documentation for each step of the ACE-V process and that error rate needed further study:

> [A]dditional research is also needed into ridge flow and crease pattern distributions on the hands and feet. This information could be used to limit the possible donor population of a particular print in a statistical approach ... Additionally, more research is needed regarding the discriminating value of the various ridge formations and clusters of ridge formations.[32]

The report noted that the examiner must use subjective judgment to evaluate seven different issues:

1. Condition of the skin.

2. Type of residue, amount, where it accumulates.

3. Mechanics of touch, including flexibility of ridges, furrows, and creases, distance between ridges, rotation of ridge systems during torsion.

4. Nature of the surface touches, including texture, flexibility, condition, and background colors and patterns.

5. Development technique.

6. Capture technique, including photograph or lifting with different materials.

7. Size of the latent print or percentage of the surface available for comparison.[33]

The NRC Report also called for more research on the various factors that affect the quality of latent prints such as condition of the skin, residue, and mechanics of touch. And because the print examiner uses his or her subjective judgment in declaring a match between a latent print and an exemplar from a suspect, the NRC also recommended that the examiner document the basis for subjective conclusions.

The NRC Report concluded that fingerprint identification needed better documentation for each step of the ACE-V process and that error rate needed further study.

The NRC Report also called for more research on the various factors that affect the quality of latent prints such as condition of the skin, residue, and mechanics of touch.

---

30. *United States v. Mustapha*, 363 F.3d 666, 672 (7th Cir. 2004).
31. *United States v. Havvard*, 260 F.3d 597 (7th Cir. 2001).
32. NRC Report at 144.
33. NRC Report at 137–38.

These issues understandably formed the basis for challenge of fingerprint testimony. Where the fingerprint expert did not disclose the number of points he found for his identification, an appellate court held this was "error," although it did not justify reversal because there was other overwhelming evidence of guilt.[34] By contrast, in *U.S. v. Campbell*,[35] the court referred to a detailed report by the fingerprint examiner, which explained his process in detail, including the verification step, in which a second examiner repeated the process with no knowledge of the individualizing features the first examiner used. The court concluded:

> Indeed, while "there is no scientifically determined error rate, the examiner's conclusions must be verified by a second examiner, which reduces, even if it does not eliminate, the potential for incorrect matches," and "[t]he ACE–V method has been used for over 20 years, and is generally accepted within the community of fingerprint experts."

> . . .

> Indeed, "[w]here, as here, the challenged form of expertise is familiar, and no novel objection is raised, justice does not require a pre-trial hearing."

A 2015 Seventh Circuit case[36] considered a challenge to a fingerprint expert in which the defendant specifically argued the NRC Report supported exclusion due to unreliability. The court disagreed:

> [Defendant] Rivas's counsel was allowed to use, and used repeatedly, conclusions from the National Academy of Sciences regarding the fallibility of fingerprint analysis. In light of Rottman's testimony that the latent fingerprint he examined could have only been made by Rivas, defense counsel asked Rottman whether he was familiar with the report by the National Academy of Sciences regarding fingerprint analysis, and in particular its statement that claims that these analyses have zero error rates are not scientifically plausible. Rottman acknowledged he was aware of this conclusion. Rottman also acknowledged that although the ACE-V method was widely used in the fingerprint examining community, he was not aware of studies that had validated the ACE-V method.

The expert, Rottman, also admitted a very small part of a fingerprint on one person could be similar to a very small portion of another person's. However, when the defendant tried to introduce testimony about the error in the *Mayfield* case, described below, the court refused: "[T]his is just a sideshow and it is going to go and delay this trial ... to start going into the merits of testing done in another case is not appropriate here."[37]

---

34. *U.S. v. Saunders and Bounds*, 2016 WL 3213039 (7th Cir. January 22, 2015).
35. 2012 WL 2374528 (N.D. Ga. July 2, 2012).
36. *U.S. v. Rivas*, 2016 WL 4151217 (7th Cir. Sept. 16, 2015).
37. *Id.*

In 2007, a Baltimore County circuit judge refused to allow a fingerprint analyst to testify that a latent print identified a defendant in a death penalty case.[38] Although some saw this case as beginning a trend following the *Llera Plaza* cases, this has not occurred. There have been many challenges to the reliability of fingerprinting, based more on the NRC Report than on the *Llera Plaza Daubert* analysis, but in almost all cases, the challenge has failed and the fingerprint examiner has been permitted to testify to identification. And because the form of identification used is the words "Positive Identification," the jury may confuse the opinion to mean that the examiner is positive, which may give the opinion more of a "white coat" effect.

One commentator examined cases following the NRC Report and found that, although defendants frequently cited the report to argue that fingerprinting was not reliable, courts generally have accepted the fingerprint expert testimony, either on the grounds that precedent had long admitted fingerprint testimony or relying on cross-examination to reveal any issues with fingerprinting.[39]

Another case said that, where the defendant did not cite any "binding authority" holding that fingerprinting was scientifically unreliable, the trial court did not abuse its discretion in allowing the testimony.[40]

Another commentator reviewed each of the NRC Report's conclusions about fingerprinting, arguing that the NRC went too far in its criticism and that stating that DNA was the "gold standard" overstated DNA and understated the foundation and capabilities of fingerprint matching:

> The NAS Committee has stated that fingerprint analyses as presently practiced do not "stand on par with nuclear DNA analysis," or do not "consistently, and with a high degree of certainty, demonstrate a connection between evidence and a specific individual" or is not "as discriminating as DNA." These statements in a National Academies of Science report imply that they were based on demonstrable evidence, but none was provided ... [41]

Changes in Fingerprint Identification Technology

As fingerprint identification technology changes, we can expect challenges similar to those that have followed changes in DNA test procedures. For example, one court held that use of a "live scan" method for taking a suspect's prints had been proven

---

38. *State of Maryland v. Bryan Rose*, In the Circuit Court for Baltimore County, Case No. K-06-545 (2007).

39. Sarah Lucy Cooper, "Challenges to Fingerprint Identification Evidence, Why the Courts Need a New Approach to Finality," *Mitchell Hamline Law Review* 42 (2016): 756.

40. *U.S. v. Dale*, 618 Fed. Appx. 494 (11th Cir. July 2, 2015).

41. Wayne G. Plumtree, "A Perspective on the Appropriate Weight to be given to the National Academy of Sciences' Report on Forensics in Evidentiary Hearings: The Significance of Continued Court Acceptance of Fingerprint Evidence," *Southwest Law Review* 42 (2013): 605.

to be reliable. The "live scan" method is essentially a digital infrared scanner, which can be used in the field. In *U.S. v. Lauder*, below, the defendant was tried for possession and distribution of illegal drugs. He was apprehended in a search of a residence and its backyard, where plastic bags containing cocaine were found buried.

United States v. Lauder, 409 F.3d 1254 (10th Cir. 2005)

...

Fingerprint Evidence

Lauder's third argument is that the district court erred in admitting fingerprint evidence tying Lauder to the cocaine buried in the backyard. Prior to trial, the government filed a motion *in limine* regarding the admissibility of fingerprint evidence it intended to use at trial. In the motion the government outlined the credentials of its fingerprint expert, Anna Zadow, and asserted her expert testimony was admissible under Federal Rules of Evidence 702 and 703....

Specifically, Lauder objected to the admission of fingerprint cards containing Lauder's known prints. The cards were created by technology referred to at trial as the "live [scan] method." In essence, the live [scan] method entails the use of a machine that records fingerprints much as a copy machine duplicates paper copies. The expert, Ms. Zadow, described it at trial:

> [It's a] digitally-captured system. It's what I will term live [scan] ... because what it is, it's a plate, it's like a glass plate, and it has technology inside of it that when your finger is placed on a glass without ink, it will capture that friction ridged skin and it will appear to have black ink on it when you look on the computer monitor, ... After you rolled your ten fingers, those are then printed out using a printer, a computer printer, and put on an 8 by 8 fingerprint card.

.... On voir dire examination, Lauder attempted to show that the live [scan] method involved new technology that lacked reliability.

Zadow admitted, for example, she was not aware of any testing done by a scientific body. Nor did she know its potential error rate, whether it has been accepted by the scientific community, or whether it had been subjected to peer review. However, Zadow stated the live [scan] method has been in use for approximately eight years and is routinely used by the FBI, DEA, United States Marshals Service, and numerous local police departments.

According to Lauder, the district court was required to make factual findings regarding the reliability of the live [scan] method, which it did not do. Lauder argues further that the court's failure to make such findings amounts to reversible error under *Daubert*. If, in fact, *Daubert* established the applicable guideposts to this case, then Lauder's argument would have some appeal.... In our view, however, Lauder's reliance on *Daubert* is misplaced. Properly framed, the admissibility of the fingerprint cards is governed by the evidentiary rules regarding foundation and authentication, not *Daubert*.

Whether the live [scan] method generated an accurate image is an authentication question unaffected by *Daubert*. The following thought experiment is illustrative: Suppose an expert relies on photographs taken by a new digital camera in forming her opinion. A district court would not be required to perform a *Daubert* analysis as to whether the photographs accurately reflected the subject matter depicted, even though digital technology is relatively new as compared to a traditional film camera.

. . .

This is not to say, in the right case, the technology underlying the data collection equipment might be sufficiently cast into doubt to require a *Daubert* hearing. But every case involving equipment — whether it be computers, cameras, or speed guns — does not automatically require a *Daubert* hearing regarding the physics behind the operation of the machine....

We ... hold that the district court did not abuse its discretion in admitting the fingerprint cards into evidence. Trial testimony by the DEA agent and the expert, Zadow, provided evidence that Lauder's known fingerprint was properly recorded, that the live [scan] method functioned properly when it recorded Lauder's print, and that the chain of custody was maintained.

Fingerprint Identification Mistakes

There will always be some level of human error in fingerprint matching. It is difficult to know how widespread this may be. One example is Rene Sanchez. In 2000, Rene Ramon Sanchez, an auto-body worker, had his fingerprints mistakenly placed on the official record of Leo Rosario. Sanchez had been arrested on three prior occasions for Rosario's crimes and once spent two months in custody before the mistake was corrected.

There have been relatively few fingerprint mistakes reported in cases, considering the widespread use of the procedure. A website called http://www.onin.com collects information about problem identifications, including the prominent example of a mistaken fingerprint identification of a Portland, Oregon, lawyer named Brandon Mayfield. His fingerprint was identified as being at the site of a Madrid railroad bombing in 2004. See photos in this chapter.

In May of 2004, the FBI issued a formal apology, stating:

Madrid Railroad Bomber Misidentification

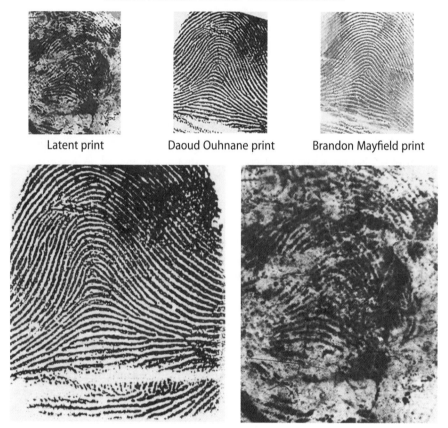

Latent print   Daoud Ouhnane print   Brandon Mayfield print

Daoud Ouhnane and latent Madrid prints enlarged

Reproduced by permission, onin.com

The FBI identification was based on an image of substandard quality, which was particularly problematic because of the remarkable number of points of similarity between Mayfield's prints and the print details in the images submitted to the FBI.[42]

A subsequent article quoting fingerprint experts, expressed concern that using computers to determine fingerprint matches might lead to increasing errors:

> No statistics exist on false fingerprint matches in the United States, but mistakes are believed to be rare, in large part because all fingerprints are checked by human examiners who make the final decision on a match. But the federal database that tied Mayfield to the plastic bag in Madrid holds tens of millions of fingerprints. The computer compares curve angles and patterns to produce a list of possible suspects.

> "Obviously, the larger the database, the greater the possibility of two fingers having roughly similar sets of coordinates," Wertheim said. "It's an

---

42. Leyden, *supra.*

issue that has troubled some of us in the business." Once a computer identifies possible matches, the science of matching is much the same as it was when fingerprints were first used in a U.S. courtroom in Chicago in 1911: It is up to humans to review two blobs of squiggly lines and decide if they are the same.[43]

According to Mayfield's attorney, Spanish authorities had notified the FBI that they did not agree with the FBI's analysis. The Spanish authorities had pointed out only 7 points in common, whereas the FBI had found 15. Mayfield's fingerprints were on file because of his Army service. A federal judge in Portland threw out a case against Mayfield, after he had been jailed for two weeks as a material witness in the bombing. In December of 2006, Mayfield won a $2 million judgment based on the incident.

An Algerian, Daoud Ouhnane, was later identified as the true source of the fingerprint found on a plastic bag containing traces of explosives and seven detonators.

According to the *New York Times*:

> Critics say the FBI has resisted using uniform standards for fingerprint identification. FBI officials say that human experience — rather than rigid and somewhat artificial indicators — is the best way to determine a fingerprint match, but critics say the FBI should insist that its examiners establish a set number of points of similarity on a print before they can declare a match.[44]

The *Seattle Times* reported on June 4, 2004, that John Massey, the retired FBI agent who made the misidentification, had been reprimanded three times for false fingerprint identifications between 1969 and 1974.[45]

In 2003, a Utah fingerprint examiner misidentified a fingerprint of the victim as that of her attacker. The problem came to light only when another examiner reviewed the prints in preparation for trial testimony:

> the staff found enough significant differences in the patterns, ridge flows, ridge counts and ridge points of the fingerprints they did not feel there was an identification of the fingerprints.[46]

Another misidentification case in Scotland led to much controversy in the fingerprint community. In 1966, the fingerprint of Detective Constable Shirley McKie was found on a candy tin inside the home of a murder victim in Scotland, despite her statement that she had not been in the home.[47] Fingerprints of one David Asbury were also found, and he was convicted of the murder. Nonetheless, McKie became an outcast among her colleagues because they felt she had undermined their case by testifying that she had not been in the house. She was subsequently charged and acquitted of perjury.

---

43. Andrew Kramer, "Fingerprint Science Not Exact, Experts Say," Associated Press, May 21, 2004.

44. Sarah Kershaw, "Spain and U.S. at Odds on Mistaken Terror Arrest," *New York Times*, June 5, 2004.

45. David Heath, "FBI's Handling of Fingerprint Case Criticized," *Seattle Times*, June 4, 2004.

46. Loretta Park, "Bloody Prints Don't Match," *Ogden Standard Examiner*, February 15, 2003.

47. Michael Specter, "Do Fingerprints Lie?" *New Yorker*, May 27, 2002.

McKie then found Allan Bayle, a forensic official at Scotland Yard, who agreed the print was not hers. He was threatened with disciplinary action, but would not back down. "[I]n the end, McKie was acquitted of perjury charges and Bayle's statement helped challenge a system that had, until then, simply been taken for granted."[48]

Fingerprints in the *Grant* Case

Ed Grant was initially identified by a "match" of a latent print taken from a tissue box found in the back of Serra's car with an inked print taken when Grant was arrested in a domestic dispute years later.

Grant's attorney pointed out that no expert could state when the fingerprint was deposited on the tissue box and that it might have occurred in a store. He did not dispute the fingerprint methodology or whether it identified Grant. The prosecution countered in its closing argument that the possibility of Grant's access to the box innocently at the Pathmark store where it was purchased was "essentially eliminated in this case."[49] There were numerous other prints in Serra's car, some of which belonged to Serra family members and some of which were not identifiable. The tissue box was found behind the driver's seat resting on the floor. Grant's counsel in his closing argument pointed out that it was improbable that Grant could have reached the box from the front seat and equally improbable that if the box had initially been in the front of the car that Grant would have placed it behind the driver's seat. His counsel also pointed out that there was another identifiable fingerprint — numbered LP4, on the exterior right window, that had never been identified.[50] The presence of so many other prints inside and outside the car, none of which could be matched to Grant, showed that he did not wipe away any prints. The question remains as to why only a single print identified to Grant was present at the crime site.

Based on that fingerprint, a blood sample from Grant was provided pursuant to court order. That was "matched" to the single spot of DNA on a handkerchief left at the crime scene. These were the two main pieces of forensic evidence used to convict Grant. One of Grant's arguments on appeal was that the fingerprint did not constitute probable cause to issue a search warrant for his blood. Grant lost this argument on appeal and his conviction was affirmed.

Should One Fingerprint Have Been Corroborated?

The Connecticut Supreme Court has held that — absent any other corroborating evidence — evidence of a single fingerprint is insufficient to identify a defendant as a perpetrator. Where a defendant was convicted of kidnapping and robbery based on two of his fingerprints found on the outside driver's window of the victim's

---

48. *Id.*
49. Transcript, May 22, 2002.
50. *Id.*

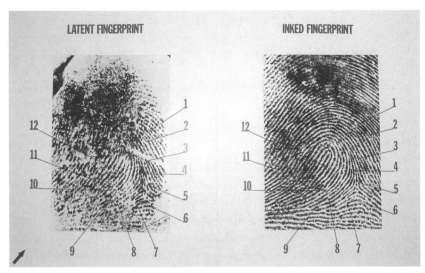

Grant's latent and inked fingerprint comparison, exhibit 55.1

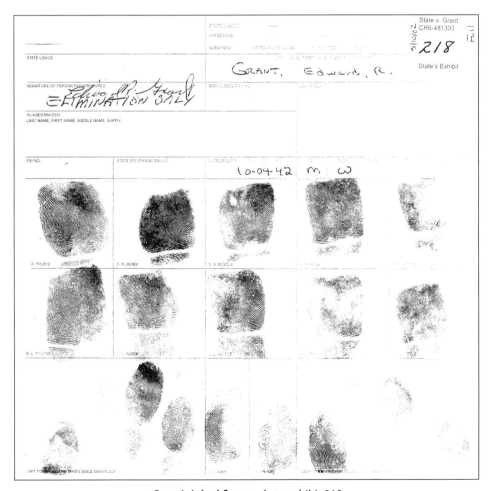

Grant's inked fingerprints, exhibit 218

car, the conviction was reserved because the only other evidence that connected the defendant to the crime scene was a general description of the perpetrator as a short, black male no more than sixteen or seventeen years old. The court agreed with the defendant's contention that the evidence against him was insufficient as a matter of law because of the "well-established rule that a conviction may not stand on fingerprint evidence alone unless the prints were found under such circumstances that they could only have been impressed at the time the crime was perpetrated."[51]

> The state was unable to present any evidence dating the defendant's fingerprints or otherwise limiting their impression to the circumstances of the crime. The state, however, has attempted to distinguish this case from those in which the rule has been applied on the ground that there was other evidence upon which the jury could have relied in reaching their verdict against the defendant. The evidence on which the state relies is the victim's description of one of the perpetrators as a short, black male no more than sixteen or seventeen years old.

> We are not persuaded by the state's argument. Although the description relied upon by the state arguably fits the defendant, it is far too general to provide any corroboration of the fingerprint evidence.[52]

Here is what another court concluded in reviewing other cases in its jurisdiction:

> Where the State has relied solely on fingerprint evidence to establish that the defendant was the perpetrator of the crimes charged, this Court has held that the defendant's motion to dismiss should have been granted. *See, e.g., State v. Bass*, 303 N.C. 267, 278 S.E.2d 209 (1981) (where the only evidence tending to show that the defendant was ever at the scene of the crime was four of defendant's fingerprints found on the frame of a window screen on the victim's home, the State produced no evidence tending to show when they were put there, and the defendant offered evidence that he was on the premises at an earlier date); *State v. Scott*, 296 N.C. 519, 251 S.E.2d 414 (1979) (where the only evidence tending to show that defendant was ever in victim's home was a thumbprint found on a metal box in the den on the day of the murder, and the niece of the deceased testified that during the week, she had no opportunity to observe who came to the house on business or to visit her uncle).

> As [was] succinctly stated in *State v. Miller*:

> These cases establish the rule that testimony by a qualified expert that fingerprints found at the scene of the crime correspond with the fingerprints of the accused, when accompanied by substantial evidence of circumstances from which the jury can find that the fingerprints could only have been impressed at the time the crime was committed, is sufficient

---

51. *State v. Payne*, 186 Conn. 179 (1982).
52. *Id.* at 184.

to withstand motion for nonsuit and carry the case to the jury. The soundness of the rule lies in the fact that such evidence logically tends to show that the accused was present and participated in the commission of the crime.[53]

The Supreme Court of Illinois agreed in a 1992 case: "defendant is correct in his assertion that in order to sustain a conviction solely on fingerprint evidence, fingerprints corresponding to those of the defendant must have been found in the immediate vicinity of the crime under circumstances as to establish beyond a reasonable doubt that they were impressed at the time the crime was committed."[54]

In *State v. Monzo*, the defendant was identified almost ten years after an assault based on a match of fingerprints left on the basement door trim of the victim's house and on her wallet to the defendant's prints in an AFIS system. The door trim had been recently painted, which was circumstantial evidence that the defendant's print had been placed on the door after it had been painted, which was shortly before the attack. An expert also testified that the print on the wallet would have been fresh, as repeated handling of the wallet would have degraded the print or left overlapping prints on it. The defendant argued that he had been legitimately present in the house before the rape, performing odd jobs for her general contractor. He also argued that during one of those jobs, he may have touched her wallet when he handed it to her so that she could pay him. The defendant was convicted, lost his appeal and then petitioned for post-conviction relief based on a claim of ineffective counsel due to failure to investigate further alibi witnesses. The Ohio Court of Appeals denied the petition, holding that it was unlikely that further alibi evidence would have affected the jury's decision.[55]

Unlike the cases discussed above, the prosecution in *Grant* did offer more than one fingerprint. It presented the DNA evidence from the handkerchief. The combination of the fingerprint and the DNA evidence would doubtless have justified a court in ruling that the fingerprint itself did not need further corroboration.

"[D]efendant is correct in his assertion that in order to sustain a conviction solely on fingerprint evidence, fingerprints corresponding to those of the defendant must have been found in the immediate vicinity of the crime...."

Summary

Fingerprint analysis is based on the hypothesis that all fingerprints are permanent and unique and that a trained examiner can compare fingerprints to determine whether or not they identify the same individual. This comparison can be made by a jury by looking at an enlarged picture of fingerprints. There are approximately 200 "level two" ridge characteristics, such as bifurcations, ridge endings, and ridge dots, that distinguish one person's fingerprint from another's. A full-size fingerprint is

---

53. *State v. Montgomery*, 461 S.E.2d 732, 736-7 (Sup. N.C. 1995).
54. *State v. Campbell*, 586 N.E.2d 1261, 1271 (Ill. 1992).
55. *State v. Monzo*, No. 97APA04-481 (1998 Ohio App. LEXIS 616, at 20 (February 17, 1998).

approximately one inch square. An examiner will give one of three opinions: (1) identification, (2) exclusion, or (3) inconclusive.

Examiners must use their judgment in matching a crime scene print that is less than complete or not completely visible. The process of lifting fingerprints from a crime scene can result in their becoming smudged or masked by other prints. An examiner typically will not attempt to identify a crime scene print of less than one-quarter of a full fingerprint or if there is insufficient detail. In addition, there is no set number of points that an examiner must find in common in order to declare a match. Although a commission in 1970 determined that such a set rule could not be established, the lack of "standards" led one district court in 2002 to declare that fingerprint identification was not reliable under *Daubert*. The court ruled that the examiner could point out similarities and differences to the jury, but could not offer an opinion about identity.

The advent of AFIS databases and computer searching has greatly decreased the time required to identify fingerprints, but it has not eliminated the need for an examiner with the training and experience to make the judgments about whether and when to determine a match. There have been almost no reports of misidentification of fingerprints. The highly publicized case in which a fingerprint was misidentified to a Seattle attorney in connection with a political bombing in Madrid, Spain, was an embarrassment to the FBI and resulted in a large dollar settlement, but probably does not undermine the integrity of the fingerprint identification system.

Fingerprint identification has been accepted as forensic evidence since the early 1900s. The ACE-V process of fingerprint identification requires analysis, comparison, evaluation, and verification. It depends upon a comparison of ridge characteristics, such as ridge endings, ridge dots, and bifurcations, which must be identical in size, shape, and location to declare a match.

When the print from a crime scene is not complete or is not completely clear, the examiner must determine exclusion if there is even one difference in ridge characteristics. If he determines that he does not have enough of a print or enough clearly visible ridge characteristics to compare, he would conclude inconclusive. Only if he is satisfied, based on his training and experience, that the prints are identical, will he give the opinion: identification.

Not until quite recently has there been any challenge to its reliability. However, a few scholars as well as one federal district court argued that fingerprint identification did not pass the *Daubert* tests for reliability because no scientific studies had been conducted outside the fingerprint community to verify the required minimum number of comparison points to declare a match.

In addition, the NRC Report in 2009 questioned the scientific reliability of fingerprint identification and called for more research. This report has been used by many defendants to challenge a fingerprint match, but these almost uniformly fail. The courts generally hold that fingerprinting has long been accepted by the courts and that cross-examination should resolve any issues about the reliability of the process. In one case where an appeals court agreed that failure to specify the number of matching points of comparison was legal error, the conviction was upheld because of overwhelming evidence of guilt in the record.

There have been almost no reported cases of fingerprint identification errors, other than mechanical errors such as copying the wrong person's name on a file. One highly publicized fingerprint identification error took place in 2004, in which a fingerprint that appeared in Madrid at the site of a train station bombing was incorrectly reported as identifying an attorney in Seattle, Washington, who was a Muslim. Most people believe this error was the result more of shortcuts taken by over-eager examiners than incorrect fingerprint identification methods.

Some cases have held that a conviction cannot be sustained on a finding of just one fingerprint but must be corroborated by other evidence. This would not have helped Ed Grant, as there was DNA evidence on the handkerchief that identified him as well as the fingerprint on the tissue box in the back of Serra's car.

Discussion Questions

1. How do we know that no two fingerprints are alike?

2. How many points of comparison of Galton points are required to match a fingerprint? How many do you think there should be?

3. Does your opinion change when you review the actual procedures used to compare fingerprints under an AFIS system such as that used in Connecticut?

4. On what grounds have courts thrown out fingerprint evidence?

5. What are some of the problems with lifting and examining latent fingerprints? Describe at least five different ridge characteristics.

6. Why did the court in *Abreu* hold that fingerprint identification met the *Daubert* standards?

7. Why did the trial court in *United States v. Llera Plaza* decide that fingerprint identification did not meet *Daubert*?

8. Why did Judge Pollack reverse himself in *Llera Plaza* and change that opinion?

9. What does the error in identifying the fingerprint in the Madrid bombing case say about possible errors in fingerprint identification?

10. Why has the NRC Report not helped defendants convince courts not to admit fingerprint evidence as unreliable?

11. How did the court in *United States v. Lauder* evaluate the "live scan" method of taking a suspect's prints under the *Daubert* standard?

12. How would you predict that future improvements in computer analysis of fingerprints, such as the possible "field testing" of fingerprints will be evaluated under *Daubert*?

13. Do you agree with Grant that the latent fingerprint found on the tissue box in Serra's car should not have been used to establish "probable cause" to issue a warrant for his blood?

14. Do you think Grant could be convicted if the DNA test on the handkerchief were excluded from the evidence at trial?

15. How does the trial in *Grant* compare with the cases that have held that a conviction may not be based on fingerprint evidence unless the evidence shows it could only have been impressed at the time the crime was perpetrated?

16. What might have happened if the jury had been told to use this standard: *You must find proof beyond a reasonable doubt that the fingerprint identified from the tissue box could only have been impressed at the time the crime was committed?*

Chapter 7

DNA

Overview

The ability of DNA profiling to identify the presence of a defendant at a crime scene has had an explosive effect on criminal trials. DNA typing is one of the newest forms of forensic identification and the most powerful. Its power stems from the wealth of knowledge scientists have generated in mapping the human genome — science for the sake of science, rather than for litigation. We can now examine a mere 13 sites on human chromosomes and, using probability statistics, identify a person with virtual certainty.

The scientific process by which DNA profiling has evolved has created pressure on other forms of forensic identification — such as fingerprints and handwriting — that rely on a scientific hypothesis, but require examiner subjectivity. What are the implications of DNA profiling for other forensic disciplines? Can any other discipline duplicate the power of DNA?

The phenomenon of reversals of convictions due to newly tested DNA is also a byproduct of DNA technology. Photos of convicts who have been cleared by DNA have caused the public to question the reliability of eyewitness identification, upon which many of the convictions have rested. Whether it will put pressure on juries to demand DNA evidence before they will convict is not yet known. However, the "*CSI* Effect," the desire of juries to want scientific evidence connecting a defendant with a crime, is probably here to stay.

Will DNA testing lead to fewer erroneous convictions and more confidence in the criminal justice system?

Although the National Research Council report in 2009 acknowledged that DNA was reliable science and did not need further testing, it called for improvements in accreditation, uniform standards across laboratories, and better training. It also noted the severe backlogs in many state laboratories, due in part to increased demand for DNA testing.

Finally, although the STR method of DNA testing and the PCR method of copying small samples of DNA are both now pretty much uniformly accepted as meeting the *Daubert* test, DNA continues to evolve new practices that result in objections from defendants. The latest development is what is called "Touch DNA" or Low Copy

Number (LCN) DNA, which is lifted typically from skin cells off weapons and the like. The objection results because greater amplification is needed than the PCR process uses, which results in DNA profiles with what is called "stutter," peaks that may not be real. No doubt this method will ultimately receive court approval, but there will probably continue to be new DNA technologies developed in the future, as the ability of DNA to link suspects to crimes is powerful. Another such development is the Rapid DNA test kits designed to create a DNA profile in ninety minutes at a crime site or police station. No doubt results from these test kits will engender objections against admissibility.

Finally, the Confrontation Clause of the U.S. Constitution has led defendants to object if every person involved in the testing of DNA, from laboratory employee to supervisor, is not available for cross-examination. Although the U.S. Supreme Court in *Williams v. Illinois*,[1] held in a plurality opinion that DNA test results were not "testimonial" and therefore did not trigger the Confrontation Clause, at least one court has restricted that opinion to its unusual facts and declined to follow it, holding that at least certain personnel involved in DNA testing must be present to testify. This issue can be expected to have widespread implications in the future.

Chapter Objectives

Based on this chapter, students will be able to:

1. Explain the science of DNA testing and why testing of 13 loci can produce absolute identity.

2. Understand why DNA can absolutely rule out a suspect.

3. Describe the product rule.

4. Explain the prosecutor's fallacy.

5. Understand how the Confrontation Clause affects what witnesses must be available to testify to the DNA testing process.

6. Explain how conditions in DNA testing laboratories can affect DNA tests.

7. Evaluate the reasons why courts have "judicially noticed" the science of DNA testing.

8. Explain how to challenge DNA test results.

9. Understand the challenges to Low Copy Number or Touch DNA results.

10. Explain Polymerase Chain Reaction and why it is important to DNA testing.

11. Explain the difference between standard DNA tests and mitochondrial DNA testing.

12. Understand the objections to "Touch DNA" as reliable science.

---

1. 132 S. Ct. 2221 (2012).

The Process of DNA Profile Analysis

What Is DNA?

The initials DNA stand for deoxyribonucleic acid, which is the material inside our chromosomes that controls our genetic makeup. All humans have 23 pairs of chromosomes — one pair inherited from the mother and one pair through the father. Both the egg and sperm contain only half the normal amount of chromosomes. The oocyte, or egg, contains 23 chromosomes and the sperm cell likewise contains 23 chromosomes. When the sperm fertilizes the egg, the cells merge and a full set of 46 chromosomes determines the genetic makeup of the offspring.

Chromosomes are made up of DNA, organized in a helix pattern, a ladder-like formation composed of sugars on each edge and four different proteins as the rungs of the ladder. These are adenine, thymine, guanine, and cytosine. Adenine pairs only with thymine and guanine pairs only with cytosine. They are organized in a pattern that repeats. These patterns vary by individual. By measuring where a pattern stops and begins a new repetition, scientists can distinguish one person's DNA from another.

At each genetic marker point on a chromosome, called a "locus," a person will have two genetic markers, called "alleles." One comes from the mother and one from the father. On the loci tested for DNA profiling, these alleles are of different lengths in different people, which is how a paternity or maternity test can identify offspring based on one set of shared chromosomes.

DNA Typing — A Quickly Changing Technology

DNA evidence has become the most respected forensic evidence in the shortest time of any forensic science. In 1944, Oswald Avery defined the concept of DNA (deoxyribonucleic acid) as the building block of human genetics. In 1953, Watson and Crick discovered the double helix model. In 1980, Botstein discovered small variations at the genetic level which he called restriction fragment length polymorphism. Shortened to its initials, it is RFLP. That technology was first applied in 1984 to detect alleles at various loci along a chain of DNA.

RFLP. Restriction Fragment Length Polymorphism—an early form of DNA testing.

The Principles of DNA Testing

DNA testing does not create a profile of the total DNA of an individual. All humans share 99.9% of their DNA in common. Of the .1% of DNA that varies, there are approximately 2,000,000 markers (called loci for the location on the chromosome) that differ from person to person. Some loci control individual characteristics, such as eye color, height, or bone structure. Of these 2,000,000, there are about 2,000 markers that do not appear to control any known genetic variable. These are called "junk DNA" because their use is unknown. These junk DNA sites are used for testing because, as far as scientists know, they are distributed randomly through the population. Of these loci (sites), only 13 are tested in the typical DNA kit. How can

Locations of DNA and MtDNA

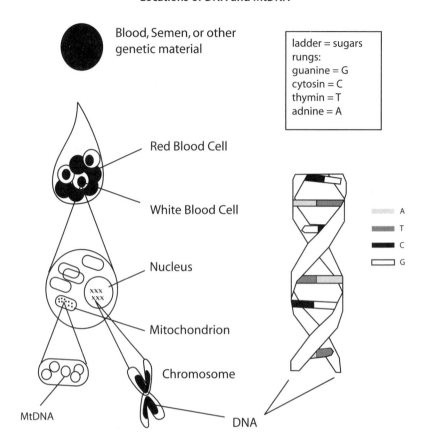

a mere 13 markers out of 2,000,000 identify a person to a certainty of 1 in 300 million? The answer lies in statistics, which is another complexity involved in explaining DNA tests to a jury.

DNA testing can absolutely rule out or exclude a suspect. In the case of rapes, hospitals take samples of fluids from the vagina for testing in what is called a rape kit. If the DNA found in a rape kit does not match the suspect's, he is absolutely excluded as the rapist, or at least as the source of the semen found in the rape kit. The fact that rape kits are routinely collected and saved is one reason why a number of convicted rapists have been exonerated due to newly tested DNA technology that did not exist at the time that the accused was tried and convicted.

If the profile of the defendant's DNA does not match the markers at all the loci tested from the crime scene, the genetic sample at the crime scene did not come from the defendant.

Today, no one disagrees that DNA is totally reliable in excluding a defendant as the source of the sample. Juries, however, are free to reject DNA evidence despite its scientific reliability.

Restriction Fragment Length Polymorphism (RFLP) Testing

Adenine pairs only with thymine and guanine pairs only with cytosine. The order of the chemical building blocks distinguishes different DNA strands. By measuring the number of repeating patterns of these four chemicals at a particular locus on the strand of DNA, scientists can create a DNA profile. And as the length of the strands differs among different people, a profile of one person's DNA strands will differ from another's. The earliest form of DNA testing looked for repeating patterns and marked the DNA whenever a repeat occurred. The chemicals are identified by their first letters; therefore a possible repeating pattern might look like this: AGCTCAATGC.

By using "restriction enzymes," scientists discovered that they could break DNA into smaller pieces at the places where a tandem repeat ended. RFLP testing involved applying an electrophoresic gel to the DNA sample. The gel would travel until it detected the end of a pattern. By using light, transfer of the pattern, and photography, scientists created a pattern that looks like a bar code in a supermarket. RFLP testing required at least a tablespoon of genetic material for testing. It was also expensive. The earliest court cases used RFLP testing and raised a number of issues about its reliability. Although RFLP testing has largely been superseded by a more efficient method called Short Tandem Repeat (STR) testing, the basic concept of identifying different length alleles is the premise of all DNA testing. Here is how one California court described the process:

> When a sample of DNA — usually in the form of hair, blood, saliva, or semen — is left at the crime scene by a perpetrator, a forensic genetic analysis is conducted. First, DNA analysts create a genetic 'profile' or 'type' of the perpetrator's DNA by determining which variants or alleles exist at several variable loci. Second, the defendant's DNA is analyzed in exactly the same manner to create a profile for comparison with the perpetrator's profile. If the defendant's DNA produces a different profile than the perpetrator's, even by only one allele, the defendant could not have been the source of the crime scene DNA, and he or she is absolutely exonerated.
>
> If, on the other hand, the defendant's DNA produces exactly the same genetic profile, the defendant could have been the source of the perpetrator's DNA — but so could any other person with the same genetic profile. Third, when the perpetrator's and the defendant's profiles are found to match, the statistical significance of the match must be explained in terms of the rarity or commonness of that profile within a particular population — that is, the number of people within a population expected to possess that particular genetic profile, or, put another way, the probability that a randomly chosen person in that population possesses that particular genetic profile. Only then can the jury weigh the value of the profile match.[2]

---

2. *People v. Pizarro*, 110 Cal. App.4th 530 (2003).

DNA Testing Improves with Short Tandem Repeats (STR)

STR. Restriction Fragment Length Polymorphism is an early form of DNA testing that has been replaced by the discovery of loci where the fragment lengths were shorter and easier to measure, thus, Short Tandem Repeats (STR).

As DNA testing progressed, scientists discovered certain loci (or locations) at which the alleles varied in length, but the variations were relatively short and easier to measure. These became known as Short Tandem Repeats. Short Tandem Repeat (STR) testing has replaced RFLP testing, not only because it is less expensive, but because once the FBI adopted STR, DNA profiles stored in its centralized CODIS database could not be "matched" by law enforcement from state agencies unless their testing used the same system.

Most examiners who use the STR process examine the length of DNA alleles at 13 different possible sites, or loci. The results at each locus will show two alleles with lengths from a range of possible allele lengths, varying from 8 possibilities (for site D13S317) to 23 possibilities (for site D18S51). The "length" of the repeats is measured using numbers from 4 to 51, which are what appear on a DNA report. A suspect will have two alleles at each locus — one from his mother and one from his father, unless both mother and father had the identical allele, in which case only one allele would appear.

Random Match Probability. The chance of selecting a random, unrelated person from the population who shares the same DNA profile found in an evidence sample.

The number associated with the length allele at each of the 13 loci determined from the suspect's genetic material is then compared with those of a sample taken from the crime scene. This comparison will either show one or more different length alleles between the samples, in which case they definitely do not match, or it will show that all tested alleles are identical. If they are identical, the next step is to calculate the likelihood of another person in the same racial group having that identical pattern of alleles at each of those 13 sites. This information then yields the likelihood of a "random match." The higher the denominator of the fraction, such as 1 over 300 million,[3] the less likely it is that anyone other than the defendant could have been the source of the DNA.

Polymerase Chain Reaction (PCR) "Copies" Small DNA Samples

PCR. Polymerase Chain Reaction is a system that copies a small piece of genetic material so that it is large enough for DNA testing.

At the same time as STR testing was developing, another process was developed that could multiply an extremely small amount of genetic material into a specimen large enough to test. This is called Polymerase Chain Reaction, or PCR. A small bit of DNA is first separated into two linear halves of a ladder. Then it is combined with free molecules of adenine, guanine, thymine, and cytosine. In a process that involves heating and then cooling the sample, the free molecules match up with their partners in the separated DNA fragment, thus creating a new fragment. This process is repeated until a "copy" of the original DNA fragment is of sufficient size to be DNA typed.

---

3. 1 in 300 million is actually a smaller number than 1 in 10 million, as the number is a fraction. However, most people look at the size of the denominator of the fraction as the indicator of the rarity of a random match.

The PCR process was a significant development. RFLP testing requires 10–50 nanograms of genetic material — roughly the amount in a clump of pulled hair. STR testing can be done with .3–.5 nanograms, or a blood drop the size of a large pinhead, which can then be duplicated by using the Polymerase Chain Reaction system to create a large enough sample to test. A single strand of hair to which the root is attached would also be sufficient because the root contains genetic material. If the only sample is a hair shaft without a root, the only method of testing available is mitochondrial DNA testing, which will identify the DNA from the subject's mother only. *See* mtDNA at the end of this chapter.

The Role of Statistics in DNA Profiling

In order to make DNA testing meaningful for identification, the scientist must first know the range of different alleles at a particular locus and how many people in the population have which allele. For example, if at a particular locus, there are 10 different variations in length of allele possible, but a test of 40,000 people showed that 99% of them had length #12, then the test is not much good for distinguishing one person from another. If you tested only the alleles at the locus D3S1358, almost 25% of the Caucasian population could be expected to have a 15 allele. So that one fact, standing alone, would "include" the suspect, but would not be specific enough to identify the suspect, as 25 Caucasians out of 100 would share the same number 15 allele.

The reason that numbers for a "random match" can get to numbers such as 1 in a trillion is because of the "product rule." This rule states that the probability of a person having the exact same allele at all of the 13 loci tested is determined by multiplying the individual probability of a match at one allele, by the probability at the next allele, by the probability at the next, and so forth.

To illustrate, assume you have a package of M&M's. The package contains 40 candies: 15 are red, 10 are yellow, 10 are green, and 5 are brown. Assume you reach into the bag, pull out an M&M, check its color, and then put it back in the bag. If you reached into the bag, the probability of pulling a red candy would be 15 divided by the total number of candies (40), or 3 in 8 (38%). If you wanted to determine the probability of drawing a red candy and then a green candy, you would need to multiply the first probability (38%) by the second probability (10 divided by 40, which is 1 in 4 or 25%). The product of 38% by 25% is 9.5% (38% times 25% is 9.5%). Multiply by the likelihood of next drawing a brown candy (12.5%) and the likelihood becomes about 1%. So, in just four probabilities, we have gone from 38% to 1%.

The "Product Rule." If two events are independent and the probabilities of each event are known, then the combined probability is calculated by multiplying the individual event probabilities together.

Table 7.1 on the next page shows the chances of a "random match" occurring between a Caucasian suspect and any other Caucasian at each locus. The chances of this occurring at all of the loci together, which is the product of multiplying each probability by the next and so forth, becomes 5.01 times 10 to the 18th power, which equates to absolute identification.

Table 7.1

Locus	Chance of Random Match
CSF1PO	0.132
D2S1338	0.027
D3S1358	0.076
D5S818	0.147
D7S820	0.063
D8S1179	0.064
D13S317	0.079
D16S539	0.097
D18S51	0.031
D19S433	0.097
D21S11	0.044
FGA	0.035
TH01	0.079
TPOX	0.188
vWA	0.066
combined	5.01×10 to the 18th power

DNA Testing of Degraded Samples

If the genetic sample is too small to be tested, degraded, or contaminated, it may be impossible to get a clear DNA reading. If this happens, one or more of the markers may not appear on the DNA test results. But the test results will not falsely identify the defendant. In other words, it is not possible for a DNA test on a poor sample to misidentify a defendant by falsely creating his DNA pattern. However, if the DNA profile shows alleles at only 3 of the 13 markers tested for, the probability of a "random match" can change markedly. This is why it is important to view the entire DNA profile. Moreover, if an evidentiary sample is contaminated with the defendant's DNA sample, the results could falsely implicate the defendant. This was one of the claims in the *Simpson* case. There have also been instances of actual fraud, where a state lab says the DNA sample identifies a suspect and lies.

Even though defense lawyers may prove to the jury that a DNA sample was contaminated (either through negligence or intentionally), or that the laboratory was poorly equipped, none of those facts will turn a genetic sample that is not the defendant's into a test result that falsely implicates him.

The Use of DNA Testimony in Court

Early Court Challenges to DNA Test Results

DNA testing was first admitted in criminal courts in the late 1980s. The issues in early appeals included whether the RFLP method of DNA testing was reliable, challenges to laboratory conditions, concerns about a DNA profile "mis-identifying" a suspect if the sample were degraded or mixed, and concerns about the population statistics unfairly creating too high a likelihood of a random match. The issue of prejudice was also raised repeatedly.

One of the early objections involved telling the jury the chances of a random match in the same racial population as the suspect. The legal argument was that the prosecution was unfairly assuming that the suspect was guilty by, for example, presenting only the likelihood of a random match in the African-American population if the defendant was African-American but the race of the perpetrator was unknown. Although early cases saw a constitutional issue with this practice,[4] this was resolved later by giving the jury the differing random match probabilities in each ethnic group.[5]

To date, both the STR method of DNA profiling and the PCR method of amplification of small quantities of DNA have been accepted by most courts as scientifically reliable. Few courts permit a *Daubert* hearing on these technologies. You can see a reference to the *Grant* case request for a *Porter* hearing (the Connecticut equivalent of *Daubert*). The court refused a hearing, finding STR reliable, but also stated its conclusions on each of the *Daubert* factors to insulate its decision from appeal.

"Judicial Notice" of DNA Testing

As DNA has become more common in courtrooms, courts have "judicially noticed" DNA as a reliable scientific test. This means that no *Daubert* or *Frye* hearing would be required in order to admit DNA results. In 1999 the Kentucky Supreme Court ruled that the reliability of RFLP and PCR methods were sufficiently established so as to no longer require a *Daubert* hearing prior to its presentation to the jury. In that case, the defendant appealed his murder and first-degree burglary conviction. The only physical evidence was his blood on one of his shoes linked to the crime scene. The court held that even though the trial court took judicial notice of the validity of the underlying science of DNA, the evidence was still subject to challenges by the defense to its credibility and significance at trial.[6]

This case is an excellent illustration of the real limitations of DNA evidence. Let's say that the defendant did legitimate plumbing work at the victim's house weeks

---

4. *People v. Pizarro*, 110 Cal. App. 4th 530 (Cal. Ap. 5th Dist. 2003).

5. *People v. Prince*, 134 Cal. App. 4th 786, 800 (Cal. App. 5th Dist 2005); depublished 42 Cal. Rptr.3d 1 (Cal. 2006) later proceedings, 2006 Cal. LEXIS 6182 (Cal. April 19, 2006).

6. *Fugate v. Kentucky*, 993 S.W.2d 931 (Sup. Ky. 1999).

before a burglary occurred. Assume further that he accidentally cut himself in the bathroom and left a bloodstain on the floor. The DNA analysis can establish that the blood on the bathroom floor came from the defendant. But in this example, the match is not incriminating. It does not tend to prove that the defendant committed the subsequent burglary. In this context, we see that although the science of DNA is now accepted and does not require a *Daubert* hearing, the significance of a "match" is always open to challenge.

A *Daubert* Hearing Is Not Required to Challenge Errors in a Particular DNA Test

The court in *Morrow* stated that challenges to errors in the DNA testing process go to the weight of the evidence, not its admissibility:

> Defendant's argument on this score [that a laboratory's past error rate requires a *Daubert* hearing] exhibits a fundamental misunderstanding of the principles of *Daubert*. The Court's concern under Rule 702 and *Daubert* is the reliability of the scientific methodology at issue, not the reliability of the laboratory performing the test. Put simply, "[a] laboratory's error rate is a measure of its past proficiency and is of little value in determining whether a test has methodological flaws." *Shea*, 957 F. Supp. at 340. What the defendant has sought to do here is challenge the proficiency of the tester rather than the reliability of the test. Such challenges go to the weight of the evidence, not its admissibility.
>
> ...
>
> *Second,* while Defendants have not challenged the adequacy of the FBI's DNA testing protocols at this point, it is possible at a hearing or at trial that Defendants may assert that the basic PCR/STR protocols employed across the board by the FBI contain a certain risk of error. The Government would then have to introduce testimony and evidence relating to its general protocols and discuss the error rate resulting from a perfect application of its guidelines. In *Ewell,* the court held a hearing relating to this type of issue, and concluded that, in the context of the FBI's PCR/STR DNA testing protocols, "[t]he testimony indicates that if an analyst follows the FBI protocol and uses properly calibrated instruments, there is essentially zero rate of error, i.e., obtaining a wrong result, within established measurement conditions."[7]

As to the possibility of human error in the laboratory that would produce false results, the court said:

---

7. *U.S. v. Morrow*, 374 F. Supp. 2d 51 (D.D.C. 2005).

… Defendants, at a potential hearing or in trial, may well (1) cross-examine the Government's DNA experts in order to discover the Government's estimated rate of human laboratory error or uncover actual human error in a specific test, and/or (2) have their DNA experts estimate the possibilities of human error. However, it is important to stress that under *Daubert*, "[l]aboratory error may only form the basis for exclusion of an expert opinion if 'a reliable methodology was *so altered … as to skew the methodology itself …*'"

The Expert Opinion in Court on a DNA "Match"

DNA is one area of forensic individuation in which experts typically have not testified that a tested sample of DNA "identifies the suspect." Rather, the expert typically gives an opinion in terms of the likelihood of a random match, as opposed to certain identification. Unlike fingerprints or handwriting, a DNA expert typically does not testify that a DNA sample found at a crime scene absolutely came from the defendant. However, more recent courts have permitted an expert to offer an opinion that a DNA match absolutely identifies a suspect. In the year 2006, one court approved an expert who testified that it can be concluded "to a reasonable scientific certainty that the evidence sample and the defendant sample came from the same person," adding that the defendant still can challenge the expert's conclusion in cross-examination.[8]

Avoiding the "Prosecutor's Fallacy"

If the DNA of the defendant matches the markers at each of the loci from the sample tested from the crime scene, the defendant is almost certainly the source of the genetic material at the crime scene. However, this does not prove that the defendant is guilty. It does not mean that the defendant was at the crime scene (the genetic material may have been planted) or that he was at the crime scene at the time of the crime. DNA testing cannot tell when or under what circumstances genetic material was deposited. After all, the defendant may have deposited DNA, for example blood, under circumstances that show he was acting in self defense, or that an accident occurred, and so forth.

However, DNA can be powerful evidence. For this reason, courts are legitimately concerned with a phenomenon known as the "prosecutor's fallacy." That is the fear that the jury will conclude that if the profile shows the chance of a random match is 1 in 300 million, that means that the chance that the defendant is innocent is also 1 in 300 million.

In the *Grant* case, the DNA expert reduced the probability of a random match to 1 in 300 million, roughly the size of the population of the United States, even

The prosecutor's fallacy. The chance that a jury will take the random match probability as representing the odds that the defendant is innocent.

---

8. *People v. Johnson*, 139 Cal. App. 4th 1135, 1146 (Cal. App. 2006).

though the actual statistics were much higher. That is a policy set by the Connecticut Forensic Science Lab in an effort to reduce the statistic to a number that the jury can grasp.

In 2010, the U.S. Supreme Court considered a habeas corpus petition[9] in which the petitioner argued that the prosecution had committed the "prosecutor's fallacy" by equating the likelihood of a random match with the likelihood of his innocence. The Court agreed that the prosecutor's fallacy had occurred. In that case, the prosecutor told the jury they could be:

> "99.999967 percent sure" [of guilt] in the case. "And when the prosecutor asked Romero, in a classic example of erroneously equating source probability with random match probability, whether 'it [would] be fair to say ... that the chances that the DNA found in the panties — the semen in the panties — and the blood sample, the likelihood that it is not Troy Brown would be .000033.... In sum, the two inaccuracies upon which this case turns are testimony equating random match probability with source probability, and an underestimate of the likelihood that one of Troy's brothers would also match the DNA left at the scene.[10]

However, the standard of review on a habeas appeal is whether no reasonable jury could have found proof of guilt beyond a reasonable doubt. Because the court found other DNA and non-DNA evidence sufficient for a verdict of guilt, it did not find that committing the prosecutor's fallacy required reversal:

> We have stated before that "DNA testing can provide powerful new evidence unlike anything known before." *District Attorney's Office for Third Judicial Dist. v. Osborne*, 557 U.S. 52, ___, 129 S. Ct. 2308, 2316, 174 L. Ed. 2d 38 (2009). Given the persuasiveness of such evidence in the eyes of the jury, it is important that it be presented in a fair and reliable manner. The State acknowledges that Romero committed the prosecutor's fallacy, Brief for Petitioners 54, and the Mueller Report suggests that Romero's testimony may have been inaccurate regarding the likelihood of a match with one of respondent's brothers. Regardless, ample DNA and non-DNA evidence in the record adduced at trial supported the jury's guilty verdict.[11]

In 2005, the District Court for the District of Columbia in *Morrow*[12] said that "best practice" is to express the opinion as a statistical probability but that using statistics can also been held to be error if it confuses the jury into believing that the probability of a "random match" is also the probability of the suspect's innocence. The court, however, said that this issue can be solved by a proper explanation to the jury:

---

9. *McDaniel v. Brown*, 130 S. Ct. 665 (2010).
10. *Id.* at 671.
11. 130 S. Ct. at 136.
12. *U.S. v. Morrow*, 374 F. Supp. 2d 51 (D. D. C. 2005).

… the Government must be "careful to frame the DNA profiling statistics presented at trial as the probability of a random match, not the probability of the defendant's innocence that is the crux of the prosecutor's fallacy." *Chischilly*, 30 F.3d at 1158. While this is a very real danger, the courts that have dealt with this potential problem have found that careful oversight by the district court and proper explanation can easily thwart this issue.[13]

"Cold Hit" DNA

Defendants will continue to challenge the admission of DNA profiles using new strategies. In 1996, a fifteen-year-old girl was abducted at knifepoint while on a pay phone and raped. She escaped and although she was unable to identify her assailant from 576 photographs, she described the truck her assailant had been driving. Investigators were unable to find a suspect. In 2001, five years later, the sexual assault kit was submitted to the Department of Justice regional laboratory CODIS (Combined DNA Index System) system, which contained more than 200,000 offender DNA profiles. The rape kit profile matched a suspect, Michael Johnson, then in prison for another crime. The victim was still unable to identify Johnson, but evidence that Johnson's truck matched the victim's description and that Johnson had tattoos matching her description was introduced in court, along with the DNA match. Johnson was convicted.

CODIS. Combined DNA Index System. The system stores profiles that can be matched to profiles created in connection with criminal investigations.

On appeal, Johnson argued that the database search presented different statistical issues than a "confirmation" match and therefore should have been excluded without a *Kelly* hearing. The court held that the CODIS search was used merely as an "investigative tool," and therefore was not subject to the *Frye* "general acceptance" standard, which was applicable in that court:

> In our view, the means by which a particular person comes to be suspected of a crime — the reason law enforcement's investigation focuses on him — is irrelevant to the issue to be decided at trial, i.e., that person's guilt or innocence, except insofar as it provides *independent* evidence of guilt or innocence. For example, assume police are investigating a robbery. The victim identifies "Joey" as the perpetrator. The means by which "Joey" becomes the focus of the investigation — the eyewitness identification — is relevant because that identification is itself evidence of guilt.

> Suppose instead that a surveillance camera captures the robbery on tape. Police use facial recognition software to check the robber's facial features against driver's license photographs. When the computer indicates a match with "Joey," officers obtain his name and address from DMV records, then go to his house and interview him. In the course of the interview, "Joey" confesses.

---

13. *Id.* at 66.

Whether the facial recognition software is discerning and accurate enough to select *the* perpetrator, or whether it declared a match involving many different people who resembled "Joey," or how many driver's license photographs were searched by the software, is immaterial: what matters is the subsequent confirmatory investigation.[14]

The court rejected Johnson's argument that the jury should hear the probability of finding his particular DNA profile in the CODIS database. It compared the DNA cold hit to the use of the CAL-ID fingerprint database.

In addition, courts have upheld state laws requiring DNA testing of prisoners, which is a growing trend and adds to the CODIS database. Once a prisoner's DNA has been entered into the CODIS database, it can potentially match an unknown suspect to DNA collected from a crime scene. However, DNA taken from victims of crime is generally exempt from entry into the CODIS database for such "cold hit" searches. In one case where a defendant's DNA taken when he was a crime victim was mistakenly entered into CODIS, the court held that the "good faith" exception to the Fourth Amendment prohibition against unreasonable searches and seizures allowed the prosecution to use the DNA where there was no evidence that such mistakes occurred regularly.[15]

DNA Evidence in the *Grant* Case

The DNA evidence in the *Grant* case was restricted to a test of one small spot on a handkerchief found in the garage next to some keys that belonged to Serra's car. The police theory was that Grant drove Serra's car looking for his own; finally found his car, and dropped both her keys and his handkerchief when he got back into his own car. The prosecution used a DNA expert to testify that one small red stain on the handkerchief was consistent with Grant and the chance of a random match was 1 in 300 million. The defense did not contest this finding.

"Something is not right about the hand-kerchief ..." Grant's counsel.

Rather, the defense concentrated on the condition of the handkerchief, its uncertain chain of custody, and the unlikely fact that only one drop of blood had not degraded beyond the point of being able to test. After the crime, the handkerchief went to local and state police labs, to a lab at Yale, to Pond Lily in New Haven, and through the mail to DuPont Corporation in Delaware. Then Detective Beausejour drove it to an army lab in Natick, Massachusetts. It then came to rest in a big box in a converted men's room with no temperature control. The state expert testified that age, heat, humidity, bacteria, and moisture all may affect a sample in degradation.[16]

Each lab cut a chunk of the handkerchief to test, so that by the time Grant was arrested, it resembled Swiss cheese. Although the defense said "something was not

---

14. *People v. Johnson*, 139 Cal. App. 4th 1135, 1150 (Cal. App 2006).
15. *U.S. v. Davis*, 690 F.3d 226 (4th Cir. 2012).
16. Transcript, May 13, 2005, p. 22.

Grant DNA report, trial exhibit 254

DNA Report Summary - II

Item	NH #	Lab #	Profiler Plus Loci -------blue-------			-------green-------			-------yellow-------			COfiler Loci -------blue-------		-------green-------		-------yellow-------		(both)
			D3S1358	vWA	FGA	D8S1149	D21S11	D18S51	D5S818	D13S317	D7S820	D3S1358	D16S539	THO1	TPOX	CSF1PO	D7S820	Amel.
E. GRANT BLOOD	:-	74-2	15,16	14,16	21,25	13,15	30,30.2	12,15	11,12	11,13	8,9	15,16	11,13	9.3	8	10,12	8,9	X,Y
Handkerchief cutting 10/01/01	6	6-1G4	15,16	14,16	21,25	13,15	30,30.2	12,15	11,12	11,13	NR	15,16	11,13	9.3	8	NR	NR	X,Y
Philip DELIETO blood	-	2004	16,18	16,19	24	8,12	29,34.2	12,18	12,13	11,13	8,10		Cofiler	Test	Not	Done		X,Y
Selman TOPCIU blood	-	1000	15,17	16,17	20,23	14,15	30,32.2	12,17	11,12	12	9,11	15,17	9,12	6,9	8,9	10,11	9,11	X,Y
Penny SERRA (blood fr/ bra)	3	3	17,18	14,18	23,25	13	29	14	11,12	11,14	8	17,18	8,9	7,8	11	10,12	8	X

NOTE: Results are combined from Profiler Plus and COfiler data. **Amelogenin** & two loci, **D3S1358** and **D7S820** are included in each kit. Results at those loci are in columns with **bold** headings.

NR = No DNA detected above the threshold for calling the alleles, due to degraded nature of the sample.

Grant electropherogram, trial exhibit 84

Electropherograms : Edward Grant Blood : Lab # 74-2
Profile Plus Loci (scale: 0-300 rfu)

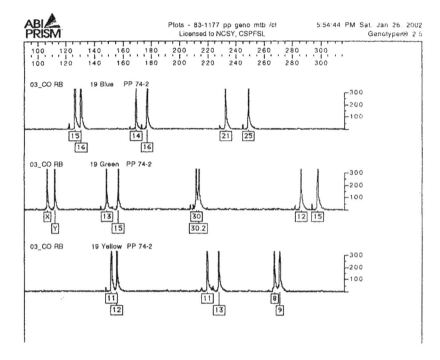

CofilerLoci (scale : 0-600 rfu)

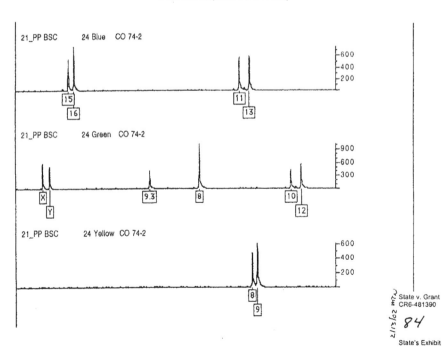

right about the handkerchief," in the closing arguments, echoing Henry Lee's testimony about the bloody glove in the O.J. Simpson case, this argument required the jury to believe that someone deliberately tampered with the blood evidence on the handkerchief. There was no testimony that anyone with access had such a motive.

Porter DNA Hearing in Grant Case

Although DNA had already been judicially noticed as valid science in Connecticut, the defense asked for a *Porter* hearing, contending that PCR/STR testing was not yet reliable. The court wrote a detailed opinion in which it held that PRC/STR met the *Porter* tests (the Connecticut equivalent of *Daubert*) and was admissible:

State v. Grant, CR 6-481390, Ct. Supr. Ct., April 9, 2002

. . .

Although the STR technique is of relatively recent vintage and has not been considered in any discovered Connecticut decision, it has already found broad acceptance in our nation's courts. Beginning with *Commonwealth v. Rosier*, numerous appellate courts have held STR evidence to be legally admissible. Three state courts of highest jurisdiction have held that the STR technique satisfies the *Daubert* test of scientific validity used in those states. A fourth state court of highest jurisdiction has held that the STR technique satisfies the 'general acceptance' test famously promulgated in *Frye v. United States* used in that state.

. . .

There is overwhelming evidence that the STR technique has gained general acceptance. This conclusion should end the court's inquiry, and the conclusions derived from that methodology should be held admissible.

In the event that a reviewing court should disagree with this conclusion, the remaining factors identified by Pappas will briefly be considered. The court makes the following additional findings.

1. The STR technique has been repeatedly tested, both by the Laboratory and by other scientific Researchers and has just as repeatedly been found reliable.

2. The technique has repeatedly been subjected to peer review and publication.

3. The known or potential rate of error is low to nonexistent when the technique is properly employed.

4. Strict, well-defined standards govern the technique's operation.

5. The prestige and background of Ladd, the expert witness supporting the evidence, is impressive.

6. The technique in question relies on objectively verifiable criteria rather than subjective interpretations and judgments by the testifying expert.

Given these specific findings, the court concludes that the STR technique used by the laboratory is valid. It is admissible under Code of Evidence § 7-2 and the *Daubert/Porter* test. The court cannot find that its probative value is outweighed by undue prejudice.

"There is overwhelming evidence that the STR technique has gained general acceptance. This conclusion should end the court's inquiry, and the conclusions derived from that methodology should be held admissible."

Professional experience and judgment are used in the analysis, but this is frequently the case with respect to scientific evidence. (As the State points out, the acceptance of X-ray technology is well established, but experts can nevertheless disagree about the meaning of a particular X-ray image.) STR analysis itself is based on objectively verifiable criteria.

7. Ladd, the testifying expert, can present the data and methodology underlying his scientific testimony in such a manner that the fact finder can reasonably and realistically draw its own conclusions there from.

8. The technique was originally developed for research purposes rather than for in-court use. It is now used for a multitude of purposes, including sexual offender data bases and the identification of human remains (as in the aftermath of the World Trade Center attack), in addition to in-court testimony.

Given these specific findings, the court concludes that the STR technique used by the Laboratory is valid. It is admissible under Code of Evidence § 7-2 and the *Daubert/Porter* test. The court cannot find that its probative value is outweighed by undue prejudice.

Challenges to New DNA Technologies

Touch DNA Evidence

Although courts almost universally accept the STR method of DNA analysis and the PCR method of duplicating small quantities of DNA, technology is constantly changing. The latest development in DNA is not a new form of testing but rather of collecting DNA. Called "touch DNA," it is collected from skin cells left on objects, such as a weapon. Because the quantity is much smaller than even the standard method of PCR can duplicate, it requires more "rounds" of PCR to get testable amounts, which also results in less clear allele patterns.

A commentator has recently raised questions about this new method of obtaining small amounts of DNA in the context of a North Carolina case, *State v. Carver*.[17]

> Touch DNA is the DNA left behind from skin cells when people touch or come into contact with an object. The method employed to test touch DNA is similar to the method used to test traditional sources of DNA, such as blood, semen, and saliva. Forensic scientists first use PCR amplification to make copies of the genes, and then analysts mix in fluorescent compounds that attach to thirteen specific locations on the DNA molecule. One primary

---

17. *State v. Carver*, 725 S.E.2d 902, 909 (N.C. Ct. App. 2012).

difference between traditional DNA and touch DNA concerns the nature of the sample that undergoes the PCR-STR testing.

Unlike traditional testing, which requires a visible sample of blood, saliva, or semen, touch DNA testing does not require a visible sample or even a bodily fluid. Instead, touch DNA testing is possible even if the sample contains "only seven or eight cells from the outermost layer of ... skin." Touch DNA sampling methods and processing procedures are highly sensitive. This sensitivity, combined with the high risk of secondary skin cell transfer, results in a greater likelihood of contamination.

2. Touch DNA Evidence in the Courtroom

Courts have been reluctant to accept touch DNA evidence. Prior to the *Carver* decision, North Carolina appellate courts had not even addressed the admissibility of inculpatory touch DNA evidence, much less its sufficiency to establish identity. In one of the few reported decisions to mention inculpatory touch DNA evidence, the Utah Court of Appeals affirmed a conviction based in part on touch DNA evidence. The court gave short shrift to the touch DNA analysis, explaining simply that:

> [The owner of the vehicle] said that the drugs, paraphernalia, and clothes were not in the car at the time she lent it to Defendant. A DNA expert testified that the combined profile from the "touch DNA" found on the bandana matched Defendant, while a randomly selected person would only have a 1 in 9,620 chance of matching the combined profile.

. . .

One of the concerns about the reliability of touch DNA as opportunity evidence concerns the difficulty of determining when an individual deposited the touch DNA sample. For example, the Arkansas Supreme Court observed that discovering touch DNA "at the crime scene and at the victim's home tends to show nothing other than that some unknown third person was present in those two places at some unknown time — it does not directly connect the unknown third person with the commission of any of these three murders." Similarly, the dissent in *Carver* expressed concern over the testimony from the State's touch DNA expert, who explained that "there is no way to tell *when* the defendant's touch DNA sample was left on the vehicle."

. . .

Perhaps the most widely known example of touch DNA exculpation occurred in the JonBenét Ramsey case. In that situation, the touch DNA exoneration did not occur in the context of post-conviction, actual innocence proceedings, but instead the touch DNA evidence cleared Ramsey family members as suspects. More than a decade after the 1996 murder of six-year-old JonBenét Ramsey, forensic testing revealed previously undiscovered touch DNA on the victim's clothing belonging to "an unexplained third party." Because investigators found the same touch DNA sample in three different places on the clothing, the prosecutor concluded that the sample belonged to the perpetrator.[18]

Another case involving small quantities of DNA called Low Copy Number (LCN) DNA[19] emphasized that errors can occur due to the magnification process:

> Law enforcement obtained three DNA swabs from the gun: one from the trigger and trigger guard; a second from the front strap, back strap, and side grip grooves; and a third from the slide grip grooves and release area. (Gov't's Mem. at 9.) An oral DNA swab was also collected from Morgan.

> At issue in this motion is OCME's report concerning the DNA testing performed on the gun swabs and the comparison of those results to Morgan's DNA profile.

> ...

> The difference in the amplification step is that HCN DNA testing employs 28 "rounds" of PCR amplification whereas LCN [Low Copy Number] DNA testing employs 31 rounds ... The small quantity of starting material in conjunction with the increased number of rounds of PCR can result in an increase in "stochastic effects," which are random errors that create inaccuracies in DNA testing ... The four most common stochastic effects, each in turn detailed below, are: allelic drop-in, allelic drop-out, stutter, and heterozygote peak imbalance.

> Allelic drop-in refers to the phenomenon that occurs when alleles not originating from the principal DNA donors show up in a DNA profile. It can arise due to the increased sensitivity of LCN testing, which leads to the detection of low levels of extraneous DNA contamination that would not normally appear in HCN testing.

> Allelic drop-out occurs when alleles from the principal DNA donors fail to appear in the DNA profile, a result frequently caused by the failure of the LCN testing to detect an allele because of the small size of the sample.

> Stutter is a phenomenon that can occur during the amplification stage: when the DNA is replicated, some of the alleles may become altered, creating a small amount of a different allele that is then detected in the analysis of the sample. Thus, when stutter occurs a false allele will be present in the resulting DNA profile that does not correspond to the donor's true DNA profile.

> Heterozygote peak imbalance is another stochastic effect that can take place during the amplification process. At any given locus, the quantity of the two alleles present should be equal. However, by reason of the increased

---

18. David Phillips, "*State v. Carver*: A Cautionary Tale About the Use of Touch DNA as Inculpatory Evidence in North Carolina," Wake Forest Law Review 49 (Winter 2014): 1545.

19. *U.S. v. Morgan*, 53 F. Supp. 3d 732 (SDNY 2014).

rounds of amplification that LCN testing entails, one allele may be amplified to a greater extent than the other allele, creating more copies of one allele in comparison to the other. Hence, it will appear that one allele is present in a much greater quantity relative to the other allele, distorting the results of the test. [citations omitted][20]

The court reviewed the laboratory that performed the analysis and found that it had conducted studies to support its methodology:

> In total, OCME examined over eight hundred DNA samples as part of its validation studies ... Based on the results of these validation studies, OCME created its interpretation guidelines, intended to allow for consistent interpretation of LCN testing results by accounting for the presence of increased stochastic effects as the quantity of DNA decreases.[21]

And the fact that the examiner needs to use subjective judgment in deciding which alleles are the result of static did not cause the court to reject the methodology under *Daubert*:

> Morgan's [the Defendant's] expert witness, suggests that some validation data allows for alternative interpretations that were not included in OCME's final protocols.... ("[T]he data allows for quite a lot of leeway in terms of interpretation.") However, under *Daubert*, the possibility that a different conclusion could be drawn from validation data does not undercut the reliability of the conclusion that was drawn, as long as the expert has "good grounds" for the chosen interpretation.

Furthermore, the fact that the FBI does not accept LCN profiles into the CODIS database did not change the court's opinion that the methodology met *Daubert*:

> Morgan also highlights that the FBI does not accept LCN samples into its CODIS database ... and that in at least one other federal jurisdiction the United States Attorney and the FBI argued that LCN results were too unreliable for admission for the purposes at issue in one case ... However, under *Daubert*, an admissible scientific technique need not be beyond substantive, legitimate debate.

Although the Southern District of New York found the validation studies of the laboratory there justified denying a *Daubert* motion to exclude the expert, the opposite result occurred the prior year in a district court in New Mexico.[22] The court denied a motion for a *Daubert* hearing on regular DNA testing, but granted the motion for LCN testing.

The touch DNA was taken from a handgun:

> Davis's report states that a DNA mixture was obtained from different parts of this handgun and magazine, and states her opinion: "To a reasonable

---

20. Morgan, *supra* at 736–37.
21. *Id.* at 738.
22. *U.S. v. McCluskey*, 954 F. Supp. 2d 1224 (D. New Mex. 2013).

degree of scientific certainty, John McCluskey is the source of the major DNA profile resolved from these mixtures." ...

In addition, Davis analyzed "Touch DNA" swabs from the steering wheel (Item 31 a) and from the gear shifter (Item 31 g) of the Haases' pickup truck....

Davis's report states that a DNA mixture was obtained from both of these items and states, with respect to both Item 31a and Item 31g: "To a reasonable degree of scientific certainty, John McCluskey is the source of the major DNA profile resolved from this mixture." Davis further states her opinion, regarding Item 31a, that Welch, Province, Linda Haas, and Gary Haas are eliminated as contributors to this DNA mixture. Regarding Item 31g, the report states that the minor DNA profile may be used for elimination purposes only, and that Welch, Province, and Linda Haas are eliminated as contributors of the minor DNA profile.... [23]

The court noted that some courts have taken judicial notice of the reliability of DNA testing. While it did not go this far, it held that normal DNA testing does not require a *Daubert* hearing and is reliable, but LCN DNA testing justifies a *Daubert* hearing to prove that it is reliable:

In determining that a separate, pretrial hearing is not required under *Daubert*, the Court observes that a number of courts have held that judicial notice of the reliability of PCR/STR DNA analysis can be taken ... The Court does not take judicial notice in this case, but rather determines on the basis of the record before the Court, that the Government's DNA evidence is admissible (with the exception of LCN evidence); however, cases holding that courts may take judicial notice of the reliability of PCR/STR DNA evidence further support the Court's determination that a separate, pretrial *Daubert* hearing is not necessary in this case.[24]

...

The Court agrees that a pretrial *Daubert* hearing is not warranted on most issues, because a sufficient record has already been presented in the hundreds of pages of briefs and thousands of pages of exhibits. On May 6 and 7, 2013, however, the Court held an evidentiary hearing on the admissibility of Low Copy Number (LCN) testing; Defendant was present at the hearing. At that hearing the Court admitted about 100 additional exhibits, for a total of about 3,500 pages of exhibits.

The Court has reviewed the parties' filings, the evidence presented, and the relevant law. The Court grants Defendant's motion to exclude the results of LCN DNA testing.[25]

---

23. *Id.* at 1230.
24. *Id.* at 1234.
25. *Id.* at 1229–30.

Rapid Testing DNA

Another new technology is a computer system that can test DNA at a crime site or elsewhere in approximately ninety minutes, versus the minimum of 24 to 72 hours on a rush basis, and weeks to months on a normal basis.[26] This technology does not require the use of a neutral laboratory, such as Bode Cellmark Forensics, which does not know who the suspect is or the nature of the crime. The possibilities for users to falsify results may be increased.

Says Steward:

> Th[e] need for a Rapid DNA scanner has been satisfied with portable DNA processing machines, including the "RapidHit 200 Human Identification System" (RapidHit 200) and the "DNAscan Rapid DNA Analysis System" (DNAscan). The RapidHit 200 is about the size of a desktop printer and can produce up to eight single-source DNA profiles within about ninety minutes, and the tabletop DNAscan processes up to five DNA single-source samples in less than eighty-five minutes. Since 2011, Rapid DNA has been slowly easing its way into the United States, as both state and federal agencies often use it to help confirm or exclude an individual as a suspect or victim of a crime.[27]

At present, DNA profiles created by rapid DNA tests cannot be uploaded to the federal CODIS database because they are not created by an accredited laboratory. Proposed legislation would resolve some of these issues:

> Many of the issues with implementing the use of Rapid DNA systems have been addressed in the Rapid DNA Act of 2015. This bill was proposed on January 13, 2015, "[t]o establish a system for integration of Rapid DNA instruments for use by law enforcement to reduce violent crime and reduce the current DNA analysis backlog." This bill would amend the DNA Identification Act of 1994 (42 U.S.C. § 14132) by inserting new provisions to allow for use of this new technology in the field by qualified agencies including, "booking stations, jails, prisons, detention centers, other law enforcement organizations and facilities outside of forensic laboratories." It proposes these agencies allow trained persons to operate "sample-to-answer" systems, fully automated systems used for Rapid DNA, rather than requiring analysis to be done by scientists in accredited laboratories. Qualified agencies would then have specific standards for compliance and testing of proficiency ... [28]

As of July of 2016 the bill was still in committee.[29]

---

26. Erin R. Steward, "Discussion and Evaluation: The Legality and Use of Rapid DNA Technologies," *UMKC L. Rev.* 84 (Summer 2016): 1133.

27. *Id.* at 1134.

28. *Id.* at 1146–47.

29. H.R.320, 114th Congress. https://www.congress.gov/bill/114th-congress/house-bill/320/all-actions?overview=closed#tabs.

Daubert Hearings on Mitochondrial DNA

A DNA profile extracted from the mitochondria in the cytoplasm outside the cell nucleus will reveal alleles inherited only from the mother. Mitochondrial DNA is found within circular structures surrounding the cellular nucleus that provide a cell with energy. DNA is found only in the nucleus of a cell; mitochondria are found in the surrounding mitochondrion. Mitochondrial DNA can be extracted from much smaller samples of genetic material, including degraded material. A hair root, for example, is required for DNA analysis, but mtDNA can be obtained from a hair shaft. It can likewise be extracted from skeletal remains. The mitochondria does not contain a full set of chromosomes; only the 23 chromosomes contributed by the mother are present. For this reason, mtDNA can exclude a defendant, but cannot be used to identify a defendant.

During his testimony about the blood spatter in the *Grant* case, Dr. Lee explained the difference between nuclear DNA testing and mitochondrial DNA. He stated that neither test had been available in 1973 to test the nasal hairs found on the handkerchief:

> Lee: You have to destroy the hair to do mitochondrial DNA, you don't have to destroy the hair to do nuclear DNA.
>
> Q: Am I correct that if you have a very small hair you may not have enough to do?
>
> A: Any DNA.
>
> Q: That's correct. Okay. If you do nuclear and you get no result, then you would be precluded from doing mitochondrial because you might not have enough?
>
> A: Nuclear, we look at tissue because in body cell we have nucleus, those nucleus basically from, one DNA from father, one from mother, when the sperm fertilize the egg, now you have two piece of DNA, so our whole body, the tissue all have the same DNA, especially in cytoplasm, the cell, the energy house, cytoplasm have something called mitochondrial DNA which only maternity link from mother, not from father because when sperm fertilize the egg, the tail stay outside, the father mitochondrial DNA is in the tail and it fall off and that's why we can't trace the father. So, with mitochondrial DNA we could only say from the mother, and all the brothers and siblings all have the same mitochondrial DNA; but nuclear DNA, everybody is different except for identical twins.[30]

Mitochondrial DNA has been admitted in court, although it has been challenged as true science, just as in the early days of DNA.

In *State v. Pappas*,[31] the Connecticut Supreme Court held that mtDNA was admissible and that questions concerning contamination and matching criteria could

---

30. Transcript, May 9, 2002, p. 60–61. Note: This is a correct transcript; Dr. Lee is not a native speaker of English.
31. *State v. Pappas*, 256 Conn. 854 (2001).

be raised before the jury as to the weight of the evidence. The police found two head hairs on a sweatshirt left near the scene of a robbery and compared the mtDNA to hairs from the defendant's head. The tests showed that the defendant could not be excluded as the source of the hairs.

In 2003, a defendant who had been convicted of rape[32] filed a motion for a new trial based on mtDNA testing of some hairs that had been offered in evidence against him at the trial.[33] The victim testified that she had been drinking at an East Hartford bar on November 8, 1996, and was accosted by the defendant, Mark Reid, as she was walking home in the early morning hours. She stated that he pulled her into a nearby park, raped her, threatened to kill her, and eventually let her go. The jury heard the victim's eyewitness identification from a photo array and testimony by a state expert about three hairs found on the victim's clothes after she was admitted to the hospital. One was on her jeans, another on a sock, and another on her panty. The expert testified that the hairs were recovered by combing or scraping down the clothing surface. The victim declined to be examined and therefore no rape kit was available.

The expert testified at trial that the three hairs were Negroid pubic hairs and were microscopically similar to those of the defendant. Reid was convicted.

In his motion for a new trial based on newly discovered evidence, Reid argued that mtDNA tests performed by Dr. Terry Melton showed that he was excluded as the source of the hairs. She stated that mtDNA "can eliminate an individual as a contributor of samples. Its primary difference from nuclear DNA testing is that mtDNA is not a unique identifier; unlike nuclear DNA which is found at the center of the human cell, and which is inherited from both parents, only maternal lineage exhibits the same mitochondrial profile."[34] Although the state argued that the pubic hairs were likely those of the victim, and therefore did not exonerate Reid, the expert admitted that neither gender nor the race of a possible contributor could be determined by mtDNA testing. However, the mtDNA did match a buccal swab taken from the victim.

In order to win the motion for a new trial, Reid had to prove that the mtDNA results were newly discovered evidence that was not available at the time of trial and that it was likely to produce a different result in a new trial. The court reviewed the trial transcript and concluded that the eyewitness identification appeared credible and not unduly influenced by the fact that the victim had been told the police had a suspect or by the fact that Reid's photo was added by the police to the photo array because one officer said the description stated by the victim "sounds like Mark Reid."

However, the only forensic evidence at trial was the three hairs:

> That evidence, stressed by the State, was, if accepted by the jury, immensely supportive of the victim's identification, and cannot be dismissed now as

32. *State v. Reid*, 254 Conn. 540 (2000).
33. *State v. Reid*, CV020818851, 2003 Conn. Super. LEXIS 1496 (May 14, 2003).
34. *Id.*

being unnecessary simply because it is impossible to quantify what weight the jury might have placed on it.

> Simply put, at the criminal trial, the identification by the victim was presented to the jury along with strong circumstantial evidence provided by the [state's] expert testimony which, if accepted, furnished powerful support for the victim's identification; guilty verdicts resulted. At a retrial, the victim's identification would not have the support of such circumstantial evidence in view of the new mtDNA evidence excluding petitioner as the source of the pubic hairs.... Although the former jury had to have accepted the victim's identification in order to convict, it did so in a proceeding where it was presented with expert testimony circumstantially supporting that identification.[35]

Reid's motion for a new trial was granted.

Mitochondrial DNA was also used in the California conviction of Scott Peterson for the murder of his wife, Laci. A strand of dark hair found on Scott Peterson's boat probably came from his dead wife, in the opinion of a DNA expert who testified at the trial. The hair was significant because Laci had apparently never been on the boat and was unaware that her husband even had bought it. Constance Fisher, the DNA expert stated: "Mitrochondrial DNA cannot be used to point to an individual to the exclusion of all others, as nuclear DNA can be.... It is less discriminating."[36]

Mitrochondrial DNA was tested because the hair did not have a root, which would have permitted standard DNA testing. The expert stated that about one out of 112 Caucasian people would have the same mitochondrial makeup. Clearly, the test would not exclude Laci. It is consistent with her DNA. The jury is free to infer that it is probative of whether Laci was on the boat, and whether she was killed on the boat.

Peterson was convicted, largely on circumstantial evidence, including testimony by his girlfriend that he had told her he was not married.

Making an Argument that DNA Was "Planted"

To convince a jury that the defendant's DNA was planted at the crime scene in order to frame him, the defendant must show both motive and means to plant evidence. In the *Grant* case, defense counsel did not argue that the DNA on the handkerchief sample was not Ed Grant's. However, Attorney Brian Carlow in summation said "something is not right with the handkerchief."[37] His objections were chiefly that the crime scene photos did not clearly show the handkerchief, that the small spot tested was the only spot on the handkerchief that had not degenerated past the point of testing, and that the chain of custody of the handkerchief did not

---

35. *Reid v. State, supra,* at 80.
36. "Peterson Testimony Focuses on Hair," Associated Press, September 9, 2004.
37. Transcript, May 22, 2003.

account for long periods when it was in a basement exposed to heat. In essence, he was hinting at a planting argument without directly asserting it.

Even if the DNA did come from Grant, Attorney Carlow pointed out that no one could testify as to when the DNA got on the handkerchief. He was raising a doubt that perhaps the police, in an effort to solve a high-profile cold case, may have had a motive to plant a drop of blood on the old handkerchief after the fingerprint on the tissue box led to the arrest of Ed Grant.

Objections Based on Poor Laboratory Procedures

Today most testing is done by a few large laboratories, including Bode Cellmark Forensics.[38] Some labs under the control of law enforcement agencies have been criticized for poor methods, lack of training, and in some cases, the outright fraudulent reporting of results in order to obtain convictions. In August of 2005, for example, the Illinois State Police canceled its contract for DNA analysis with the Bode Technology Group after finding that it failed to recognize semen on rape kit evidence in 22% of the cases that had been re-checked by police scientists.[39] The state police director notified the Justice Department and other states, at least 10 of which also had contracts with the same forensic laboratory. The canceled contract had called for payment of $7.7 million over three years.

The Houston DNA laboratory was shut down in 2003 based on findings of sloppy work, although a grand jury failed to indict anyone after reviewing 1,000 felony cases that relied on questioned DNA evidence.[40]

A federal investigation of the Massachusetts state police crime laboratory in 2007 found that the lab entered incomplete genetic profiles into its computerized databases, entered the same genetic profile under two different identification numbers, and in one case, waited nearly eight months to confirm a tentative match. The state had begun its own investigation after discovering that a technician failed to report matches to police departments in 11 sexual assault cases, making it impossible for prosecutors to pursue charges.[41]

Defendants also may object to admission of DNA where the procedures in the lab were inadequate. This objection was made in 1996 in a bank robbery case where hairs of the defendant found in a ski mask were tested by the PCR method of DNA replication. The defendant appealed his conviction arguing that the lab procedures were inadequate, that there was no external testing, the DNA samples were not "double blind" tested, and there was no record of errors made. The court decided that the PCR method was reliable and that the lab was accredited to do PCR testing

---

38. This was the case in *People v. Grant*.

39. Gretchen Ruethling, "Illinois State Police Cancels Forensic Lab's Contract, Citing Errors," *New York Times*, August 20, 2005.

40. "Grand Jury Blasts Houston Police DNA Lab," October 17, 2003, cnn.com.

41. "Federal Probe Finds Problems with State Crime Lab," Associated Press, *Boston Herald*, February 1, 2007.

and did double-reading tests of its results. Any objections about the quality of the lab went to the weight of the evidence, not its admissibility. Defendant was free to try to discredit the lab on cross-examination, but could not exclude the testimony.

In October of 2000, Professor Andre Moenssens identified an error in the United Kingdom in April of 1999 in which a suspect was arrested for a burglary based on a match in 6 loci.[42] According to Moenssens, the suspect was a man with advanced Parkinson's disease, who could not drive and could barely dress himself. He lived 200 miles from the site of the burglary. His blood sample had been taken when he was arrested, and then released, after hitting his daughter in a family dispute.

It is only when the suspect's solicitor demanded a retest using additional markers, after the suspect had been in jail for months, that further testing was done. This testing, using a total of 10 loci, showed an exclusion at the additional four loci. The interpretation of the original test's results, given by law enforcement officials, was proven to be inaccurate. The suspect was then released from custody.[43]

The British adopted a ten loci DNA test shortly thereafter.

The Confrontation Clause and the Right to Examine DNA Testers

In 2016 in *Washington v. Green Haven Correctional Facility*,[44] a New York federal court denied a habeas corpus petition based on the argument that the defendant, convicted of burglary and sexual assault, was not permitted to examine the person who actually performed the DNA analysis under the Confrontation Clause of the U.S. Constitution:

> During Washington's trial in New York State Supreme Court, Queens County, the State called Natalyn Yanoff, a DNA analyst from OCME, as an expert witness in DNA analysis and forensic biology. Although Yanoff did not personally conduct the laboratory testing to generate the DNA profiles, she prepared reports comparing the profiles derived from cells found on the bloody white shirt, the gloves, the iced-tea container, and Washington's cheek. She testified that each DNA profile matched. Yanoff further testified that the probability of this DNA profile appearing in a specific individual was one in greater than one trillion.[45]

Washington objected to the admission of Yanoff's reports and testimony because it relied on the DNA profiles generated by testing that Yanoff did not personally

---

42. Andre A. Moenssens, "A Mistaken DNA Identification? What Does It Mean?" October 20, 2000.

43. *Id.*

44. *Washington v. Green Haven Correctional Facility*, 142 F. Supp. 3d 291 (E.D.N. Y. 2016).

45. *Id.* at 293.

perform. The trial court denied the motion to examine the laboratory technician for the following reason:

> the DNA profile generated from the swab of the defendant's cheek, standing alone, shed no light on the issue of the defendant's guilt in the absence of the expert's testimony that it matched the profiles derived from the crime scene evidence.[46]

The court in reviewing the habeas petition agreed. It cited the U.S. Supreme Court, which had held in a divided opinion that DNA test results were not "testimonial," distinguishing its earlier holding that a "report" stating that a substance was cocaine that had been prepared by an out-of-court witness triggered the Confrontation Clause:

> Most recently, however, in *Williams v. Illinois*, a highly fractured Supreme Court held that a defendant's right to confrontation was not violated when the prosecution's expert witness's testimony relied on a DNA profile that the expert did not personally prepare. ___ U.S. ___, 132 S. Ct. 2221, 2227, 2244, 183 L. Ed. 2d 89 (2012) (plurality opinion). Writing for a four-justice plurality, Justice Alito opined that the Confrontation Clause was not triggered because (1) the DNA profile was an out-of-court statement that was not offered "to prove the truth of the matter asserted," and (2) the primary purpose of the DNA report "was not to accuse petitioner or to create evidence for use at trial.[47]

Justice Thomas, in a concurring opinion in *Williams*, explained why he concluded a DNA report was not testimonial:

> Thomas distinguished the testimonial certificates in *Melendez-Diaz* and *Bullcoming* by noting that the DNA profile was not sworn to before a notary, did not contain a "Certificate of Analyst" signed by the scientist who performed the testing, nor an affirmation regarding the procedures used when creating the DNA profile ...[48]

Furthermore, the court relied on language from the plurality opinion in *Williams* that stated that the technicians themselves had no idea what the result of the DNA test would be:

> [w]hen lab technicians are asked to work on the production of a DNA profile, they often have no idea what the consequences of their work will be.... The technicians who prepare a DNA profile generally have no way of knowing whether it will turn out to be incriminating or exonerating — or both.[49]

The Supreme Court opinion in *Williams*, which held no Confrontation Clause right to examine the DNA laboratory technicians, has been subject to much criticism.

---

46. *Id.*
47. *Id.* at 295.
48. *Id.*
49. *Id.* at 296.

There are those who believe the Court was straining not to expand its prior cases on drug analysis and blood alcohol content to DNA.

Here is the final holding of the court in *Washington v. Griffin*, which followed the result in *Williams*:

> Considering the lack of clarity in the Supreme Court's Confrontation Clause jurisprudence, and in light of the factual similarities between *Williams* and the present case, this Court cannot hold that the state court's judgment — which mirrored the disposition in *Williams* — was an unreasonable application of clearly established Supreme Court precedent.[50]

However, a number of courts have more recently refused to follow *Williams*. In one of these, the circuit court for the District of Columbia[51] held contrary to the Supreme Court:

> Appellant Raymond Jenkins was convicted of first-degree murder while armed, first-degree burglary while armed, attempt to commit robbery while armed, two counts of first-degree felony murder while armed, and possession of a prohibited weapon, all in connection with the June 1999 stabbing death of Dennis Dolinger. In this appeal, appellant seeks reversal of his convictions on the ground that his rights under the Confrontation Clause of the Sixth Amendment were violated when the trial court permitted the government to present the entirety of its DNA evidence through the testimony of a single expert witness without making available for cross-examination the laboratory analysts who performed the underlying serological and DNA laboratory work.[52]

The defendant was located by running the DNA profile of blood found in the murdered man's home with a database of previous offenders in Virginia:

> [T]he government contacted the Virginia Department of Criminal Justice Services ("DCJS") requesting that DCJS run the profile of the unknown person [whose blood DNA was found in Dolinger's house] through Virginia's DNA database of 101,905 previously profiled offenders. Using only eight of the thirteen loci profiled by the FBI, the DCJS reported that the evidence sample was consistent with the eight-loci profile of Robert P. Garrett, a known alias of [appellant] Raymond Anthony Jenkins.[53]

The forensic expert testified as follows:

> At trial, Dr. Frank Baechtel, a forensic examiner and head of one of the FBI's DNA analysis laboratories, testified that the 13-loci DNA profile developed from appellant's blood sample matched at all loci the 13-loci DNA profiles that the laboratory had developed (before appellant became a suspect).

50. *Id.* at 297.
51. *Jenkins v. U.S.*, 75 A.3d 174 (D.C. Ct. App. 2013).
52. *Id.* at 176.
53. *Id.* at 178.

Dr. Baechtel testified, and his reports indicated, that he found a match between appellant's DNA and the DNA extracted from blood taken from the back of the gray shirt, from inside the pockets of the jeans discovered near Dolinger's body, from the towel and sink (a sink stopper and a swabbing of the sink itself) in the basement bathroom, and from the bannister swabbing. He testified that the likelihood of a merely coincidental match was at least 1 in 26 quadrillion in the African-American population, 1 in 870 quintillion in the Caucasian population, and 1 in 1,000 quintillion in the Southeastern Hispanic population.[54]

The court stated the law as follows:

In this jurisdiction, it is settled that "[f]orensic evidence, including DNA analysis, is not exempt from *Crawford*'s holding" that the Confrontation Clause of the Sixth Amendment bars the admission of testimonial hearsay against a criminal defendant at trial, unless the witness is unavailable and the defendant has had a prior opportunity to cross-examine him.

...

Although the Supreme Court has not agreed on the limitations of what it means to be testimonial, our own case law has established the principle that statements of DNA findings and analysis are testimonial if they are made primarily with an evidentiary purpose, regardless of their formality or any other particular criteria.[55]

Specifically referring to the Supreme Court opinion in *Williams*, the D.C. court declined to follow its result to admit DNA test reports without triggering the Confrontation Clause. It also quoted Justice Kagan's dissent in *Williams* for the proposition that the case gave no clear guidance on DNA testing:

Justice Kagan commented on the confusion that *Williams* would leave in its wake:

Before today's decision, a prosecutor wishing to admit the results of forensic testing had to produce the technician responsible for the analysis. That was the result of not one, but two decisions this Court issued in the last three years. But that clear rule is clear no longer.... What comes out of four Justices' desire to limit *Melendez-Diaz* and *Bullcoming* in whatever way possible, combined with one Justice's one-justice view of those holdings, is — to be frank — who knows what. Those decisions apparently no longer mean all that they say. Yet no one can tell in what way or to what extent they are altered because no proposed limitation commands the support of a majority ...

...

---

54. *Id.* at 178.
55. *Id.* at 180, 184.

We now hold that the splintered decision in *Williams*, which failed to produce a common view shared by at least five Justices, creates no new rule of law that we can apply in this case. Accordingly, we apply pre-*Williams* case law — both the Supreme Court's and our own — and conclude that the testimony and reports of the government's expert witness, Dr. Frank Baechtel, were admitted in violation of the Confrontation Clause. We further conclude that the error was not harmless, and we therefore reverse the judgment of the Superior Court and remand the case for a new trial.[56]

In a more recent case, *People v. M.F.*[57] in New York state court, the court also held that some of the DNA testing personnel must be present to be examined and it restricted the U.S. Supreme Court's opinion in *Williams* to its "narrowest grounds," which included that the DNA test was performed before the defendant was a suspect and submitted to a judge in a non-jury trial. It looked at the entire spectrum of people involved in the DNA test process to determine which ones must be present at trial. It explained the DNA test process in the case before it as follows:

> In the case before this Court, there were three phases to the production of the final report: 1) the initial visual inspection and analysis of the complainant's specimen; 2) the automated and computer imaging processes performed by four or five technicians to produce the DNA graphical profile; and 3) the comparison by a final analyst of the lab profile to the defendant's known DNA profile. The People have made an offer of proof of the OCME report and intend to call as both fact and expert witness a supervising analyst who reviewed the underlying data and drew the ultimate conclusion that the sample taken from the complainant's cervical specimen matched the defendant's known sample. This supervisor is a longtime OCME employee and familiar with the laboratory's procedures and testing protocols. She is competent to answer questions concerning the procedures utilized to produce the graphical data. Therefore, the People contend she may serve as a records witness for the admission of the report under the business records rule as well as offering her analysis and conclusions as an expert.

> Despite the supervising analyst's credentials and role in this case, the defense contends that each individual who conducted a task must be called because of the risk of contamination and the presumptions technicians make at each step of the testing process. This argument essentially represents the view of at least some of the dissenting Justices in *Williams*, namely that the practical difficulties of calling at trial every person in the testing process, regardless of his or her role, should be secondary to the defendant's confrontation rights.[58]

---

56. *Id.* at 185, 176.
57. *People v. M.F.*, 51 Misc.3d 327 (Sup. Ct 2016).
58. *Id.* at 332–3.

In this case, which involved a rape where the victim was unable to identify her assailant, the court decided that the first analyst, who made decisions about the evidence in the DNA rape kit, must be present to testify, as a supervisor had no direct knowledge of those decisions, which the court found to be "testimonial" in nature:

> The first analyst (Zhang) is also a witness to the completion of the chain of custody in the laboratory. Whether or not such analysis is always testimonial, in this instance there is also evidence in the report of procedural steps requiring decision-making and judgment by the analyst who received and opened the "rape kit." There was no involvement by the supervising analyst at that stage, and no way to "review" the specimens by simply reading the report. *See Bullcoming v. New Mexico*, 131 S.Ct. at 2719 [Sotomayor, J., concurring]. The initial analyst decided after a visual examination of the specimens to put only the cervical swab through testing, noting, "the most sperm seen on the cervical slide." In this sense, the defense is persuasive that the first analyst's role is not limited to application of a formula, but includes "assertive conduct."[59]

The court decided that the initial analyst must be present, but those who did the computer-testing did not:

> Given a laboratory with well-established protocols, in court testimony of every analyst who operated machinery is unnecessary. The People have made a sufficient offer of proof that a qualified expert from the laboratory that produced the report will be called to testify and be subject to challenge on her findings and conclusions ...
>
> ...
>
> In sum, the motion to bar admission of the DNA report in the absence of laboratory witnesses is separated into three distinct components: a) the initial analysis, in which the initial analyst took the alleged victim's cervical sample, b) the machine driven testing performed by several technicians and c) the analysis of the data and the report's conclusions as found by the supervising analyst. The initial analyst's work is deemed to be testimonial *and* the technical preparation of the DNA graphs is presumed not to be testimonial subject to contrary evidence elicited at trial. The data resulting from the testing protocols will be admissible through the testimony of the witness the People have proffered, the supervising analyst.[60]

What Objections Are Left to Refute DNA Profiles?

Today, few defendants argue that DNA testing is, of itself, objectionable. Therefore, defense objections must be restricted to the specifics of each case. The defense can always attack the following areas:

---

59. *Id.* at 334.
60. 51 Misc. 3d at 334.

1. Hire an expert to review the prosecution's DNA report to find any possible areas for objection.

2. Challenge the training and experience of the DNA investigator.

3. Challenge the laboratory conditions or present evidence of fraud in the lab.

4. Challenge the chain of custody of the genetic evidence.

5. Argue that the test cannot show when the DNA was deposited.

6. Remind the jury that of the prosecutor's fallacy — a DNA match does not equal guilt.

7. Argue that the DNA may have been either innocently transferred to the crime scene or may have been "planted" at the site by someone with a motive to frame the defendant.

8. Review the prosecution's DNA report for case-specific anomalies.

Blobs, noise, and stutter on a DNA chart can mask the true alleles.

Typically, the defendant in a case involving DNA will not hire a DNA expert to review the DNA reports created by law enforcement and offered by the prosecution. Although the public defender did contact an independent DNA expert in the *Grant* case, that expert did not testify at trial. One expert estimates that the software needed to even open the files provided by crime laboratories in discovery costs over $18,000.[61] Forensic Bioinformatic Services argues that defendants should focus on "case-specific issues and problems that greatly affect the quality and relevance of DNA test results, rendering DNA evidence far less probative than it might initially appear."[62] They discuss issues such as mixtures. They also explain how to identify degraded samples, how to interpret imbalances in which the peak height of one allele at a locus varies by more than 30% of the height of another, and how to identify "blobs, noise, and stutter," all of which appear to be alleles, but actually may mask a true allele. This company markets a software system which enables defendants to analyze a DNA profile without hiring an expert.

As one commentator has said:

Forensic evidence is only as good as the skill and integrity of the people who collect it. In a recent case in Illinois it was discovered that police officers claimed to have found the victim's blood on shoes belonging to the defendant. The defendant confessed. It was determined later that DNA evidence exonerated the accused. He was released from prison and declared innocent by the court. During civil litigation against the police who had framed him, the exoneree's lawyers discovered that the blood had been planted on his shoes — and that the shoes that they claimed belonged to the accused (a brand of Nike shoes) had not been manufactured at the time of the murder.[63]

Another commentator argues that DNA should not receive automatic deference:

61. Forensic Bioinformatic Services, www.bioforensics.com.
62. *Id.*
63. Stone, *supra.*

While the science of DNA testing is quite reliable, its use in a forensic setting is far less trustworthy. The crime scene is not the pristine laboratory. The use of databases is not the same as identification with certainty. In the laboratory, human error, contamination, mislabeling, and misinterpretation may cause DNA evidence to incriminate the innocent. Courts must not be blinded by the rhetoric of infallibility in the world of forensic DNA testimony. We must be ever vigilant to the possibility of error and the shame of wrongful convictions.[64]

Summary

The principle of DNA testing is that each person has a unique DNA profile. Scientists have proved this in the process of mapping the human genome. Currently, most DNA testing is done by examining the length of "alleles" at different locations or "loci" on specified chromosomes. These 13 loci have alleles that differ from person to person, but do not control for any known genetic trait. Thus, scientists assume that the length of an allele at each loci is independent from the length at any of the other 12.

The advent of the Polymerase Chain Reaction method of copying small amounts of DNA in order to yield a sample large enough for testing has vastly increased the ability of investigators to link crime scenes with suspects. DNA from a single hair root, for example, can yield a valuable DNA profile. Mitochondrial DNA, the latest form of DNA matching, can extract DNA from the mitochondria in a cell, which yields the DNA markers passed on through the mother's line. MtDNA, however, can be used in cases where DNA can no longer be extracted due to degradation or size of sample.

The phenomenon of reversals of convictions due to newly tested DNA is also a byproduct of DNA technology. Will DNA testing lead to fewer erroneous convictions and more confidence in the criminal justice system?

Although the National Research Council report in 2009 acknowledged that DNA was reliable science and did not need further testing, it called for improvements in accreditation, uniform standards across laboratories, and better training. It also noted the severe backlogs in many state laboratories, due in part to increased demand for DNA testing.

Although the STR method of DNA testing and the PCR method of copying small samples of DNA are both now pretty much uniformly accepted as meeting the *Daubert* test, DNA continues to evolve new practices that result in objections from defendants. The latest development is what is called "Touch DNA" or Low Copy Number (LCN) DNA, which is lifted typically from skin cells off weapons and the like. The objection

---

64. Jed Stone, "A Gold Standard Tarnished: How Reliable Is Forensic DNA Evidence?" *Utilizing Forensic Science in Criminal Cases* (Thompson Reuters, 2015).

results because greater amplification is needed than the PCR process uses, which results in DNA profiles with what is called "stutter," peaks that may not be real. No doubt this method will ultimately receive court approval, but there will probably continue to be new DNA technologies developed in the future, as the ability of DNA to link suspects to crimes is powerful. One such development is the Rapid DNA test kits designed to create a DNA profile in ninety minutes at a crime site or police station. No doubt results from these test kits will engender objections against admissibility.

Finally, the Confrontation Clause of the U.S. Constitution has led defendants to object that every person involved in the testing of DNA, from laboratory employee to supervisor, needs to be available for cross-examination. Although the U.S. Supreme Court in *Williams v. Illinois*[65] held in a plurality opinion that DNA test results were not "testimonial" and therefore did not trigger the Confrontation Clause, at least one court has restricted that opinion to its unusual facts and declined to follow it, holding that certain personnel involved in DNA testing must be present to testify. This issue can be expected to have widespread implications in the future.

Discussion Questions

1. How do probability statistics affect DNA expert testimony?

2. What is the CODIS? How does it affect how state law enforcement conducts DNA tests?

3. What are some differences between the history of use of fingerprint matching and DNA matching?

4. In the *Simpson* trial, the jury heard testimony from experts that blood drops at the scene of Nicole's death matched Simpson's DNA. They also heard testimony that blood on a sock found in Simpson's bedroom matched the DNA of Nicole. The jury acquitted O.J. What must the jury have concluded about the DNA evidence?

5. Explain the process of PCR. Why was it a major step forward in DNA testing?

6. What is mitochondrial DNA? Why is mtDNA match not as good as a DNA match?

7. Do most courts decide that deficiencies in lab conditions mean that DNA evidence should not be admitted? Why or why not?

8. What percentage of DNA is common among all humans? How many potential junk DNA loci could be tested? How can 13 sites create a reliable match?

9. What is the prosecutor's fallacy, and why do defendants worry about it?

10. Discuss the issues with admitting Low Copy Number or Touch DNA.

---

65. 132 S. Ct. 2221 (2012).

11. Understand the issues with whether DNA reports are testimonial in nature and how this affects whether the analysts must testify under the Confrontation Clause.

12. What possible objections can a defendant make to DNA evidence?

13. What was the objection to the DNA tests that Grant asserted in the gatekeeper hearing? How was it resolved?

Chapter 8

Firearms and Toolmarks

Overview

This area of forensic expertise is sometimes mistakenly referred to a "ballistics." Ballistics, however, is a separate discipline that analyzes the flight of a moving projectile. There is some ballistics in firearms, but not all firearms are ballistics.

Firearms and toolmarks are often taken together as one "area" of study, though they are markedly different. As a group, this area involves impression evidence. That is, forensic examination of impressions made when one object is impacted by another. In the case of firearms, it examines things like the impression a firing pin makes on a shotgun shell, or the marks made on bullet from the barrel of a weapon.

Historically, evidence involving impressions made by guns onto bullets or casing has been accepted by the courts, even prior to *Daubert*. Since the decision in *Daubert*, courts have generally held that such impression evidence meets the *Daubert* standard. The case of *U.S. v. Otero*, discussed below, provides a frame of reference on the admissibility of such testimony.

While similar, forensic examination of toolmarks stands on a different legal footing. This type of evidence involves, for example, the marks made by a crowbar used to open a locked cash register. One is hard-pressed to find case law regarding such evidence at all. And if found, it appears any *Daubert* analysis is limited at best.

Chapter Objectives

Based on this chapter, students will be able to:

1. Identify the class characteristics involved in firearm identification.

2. Identify the sub-class characteristics.

3. Identify the individual characteristics.

4. Have a working knowledge of how these characteristics help connect a particular projectile or casing to a particular weapon.

5. Understand how these characteristics can exclude a weapon from being the source of a projectile or casing.

6. Have a working knowledge of the National Integrated Ballistic Information Network and its operation.

7. Understand the role of gunshot residue.

8. Understand toolmark evidence.

9. Understand the utility and the legal difficulties associated with firearms and toolmark evidence.

Case Study

One can only imagine the despondency in the Raleigh, North Carolina, community from the spring of 2006 to the fall of 2007. Five people had been brutally murdered. It began on May 12, 2006, when Sam Haj-Hussein, a convenience store clerk, was shot and killed in his store.[1] The matter remained unsolved for over a year. Four more murders would occur, all unsolved, until a break in the case.[2] Prior to that "break," the North Carolina State Bureau of Investigation had made some progress in the case.[3] Bullets and shell casings from each of the murders had been submitted for examination to the state forensic laboratory. Upon examination, it was learned that each bullet and cartridge, all 9mm, was related to the others. Each bore distinctive markings relating it to each of the prior murders. The problem now was finding the weapon, and the person, that fired the bullets that killed the victims.

On November 21, 2007, Raleigh police arrested Samuel Cooper after a bank robbery. During Cooper's attempt to flee from law enforcement, he dropped a 9mm Ruger handgun. That gun was recovered by the police. Further investigation linked that gun to each of the unsolved murders.[4] Cooper would confess, and although his confession was challenged for legal reasons,[5] the result of the forensic testing played a key role in his conviction.

Firearms

Forensic study of firearms endeavors to match a particular bullet to a particular gun used in a particular crime. This is done through careful examination of the bullet and casing. Contrary to the portrayal in popular culture, identification of a bullet, and matching it to a particular firearm, is less common than might be expected.

---

1. Bureau of Alcohol, Tobacco, Firearms and Explosives, "NIBIN Leads to Life in Prison," www.atf.gov/firearms/nibin-leads-life-imprisonment.

2. *State v. Cooper*, N.C. Court of Appeals, No. COA11-809, March 6, 2012, www.aoc.state.nc.us/www/public/html/AR/CourtAppeals/2012/6_March_2012/11-809.pdf.

3. Testimony of Neil Moran, SBI agent, www.wral.com/news/local/video/72105786.

4. *Id.*

5. *See Cooper, supra.*

Bullets may be severely degraded or destroyed upon impact, and thus not readily available for comparison. Often it is the casing that proves to be the "smoking gun."

Class Characteristics

As with other types of evidence, bullets have characteristics particular to class, as well as to an individual firearm. While class characteristics may at first blush seem less important, these class characteristics can offer valuable clues. While class characteristics will not answer the question of whether a bullet was fired from a particular weapon, class characteristics can eliminate certain weapons from consideration.

Bullets are named by caliber. Caliber refers to the diameter of bullet in inches. Therefore, a .44 caliber bullet is 44/100 inches in diameter. Generally speaking, the caliber of the bullet matches the caliber of the gun. If there is evidence that a .22 caliber gun was used in a crime, the .357 caliber gun that law enforcement seized from a suspect is not likely the weapon used in the crime. If there is evidence that a .44 caliber gun was used in the commission of a crime, law enforcement's successful and proper seizure of a .44 caliber weapon does not mean it was in fact the weapon used. Nonetheless, that seized weapon cannot be ruled out as the one used in the crime. Thus, class characteristics such as caliber are important for rule-in/rule-out purposes. Further forensic testing is required to identify individual characteristics that would tend to prove whether this particular bullet was fired from this particular gun. In this respect, bullet caliber is similar to blood type. If a perpetrator's blood is left at the scene, it can be examined for type, and thus rule out everyone with a different type of blood and make suspect anyone with that blood type. Further forensic examination of the DNA can then locate individual characteristics to pinpoint a particular person.

Are class characteristics too general to be of any use? How might they be used?

Similarly, shotguns may likewise be identified by a particular class characteristic. This identifier is the "gauge" of the shotgun. Unlike rifles or handguns that discharge a single bullet when fired, shotguns propel a number of small round metal pellets, referred to as "shot." Gauge refers to the number of metal pellets in one pound of shot. The smaller the gauge of the shotgun, the larger the shot. Thus the pellets in a 12-gauge shotgun are larger than the pellets in a 20-gauge shotgun. The gauge of the shotgun shell matches the gauge of the shotgun.

Sub-Class Characteristics

There is a class of markings known as sub-class markings. Class characteristics are those that result from the manufacturing process. They are markings impressed from the manufacturing process. For example, as discussed below, a manufacturer will put grooves in a weapon's barrel that cause the bullet to spin. This leaves a distinctive mark on the bullet. The left- or right- direction of the groove is a class characteristic. Generally, it will be common to all guns of that type made by that particularly manufacturer.

By contrast, sub-class marks are unintended. In the manufacturing process, metals fatigue. The blades used to cut grooves dull. This leaves other marks, or perhaps has an effect on intended marks. But as a result of the manufacturing process, other marks are left on only some weapons. While the class characteristics remain, distinctive marks of a sub-class can appear.[6]

Individual Characteristics

How are accidental characteristics different from individual characteristics? Is it a distinction without a difference?

In the initial investigation, general class characteristics allow law enforcement to focus on a particular type of weapon. Further forensic testing can link a weapon to the bullet fired from it. By examining the particular marks made in a bullet as it travels down the barrel and exits the muzzle of the weapon, an examiner can determine with some certainty whether a particular bullet was fired from a particular gun. Similarly, by examining the imprints on a bullet or shell casing an examiner can make a similar determination.

Characteristics Based on Wear

These types of markings are also unintended. They arise perhaps over a short period of time. They can arise and appear because of use and abuse sustained by the weapon. Therefore, two casings or bullets, fired a lengthy period apart, may not have the same characteristics, although they were fired from the same weapon.

Bullets

Vagaries in the manufacturing process makes every firearm unique. Generally, however, a firearm manufacturer will place a spiral groove along the length of the barrel. Some manufacturers groove the barrel clockwise, others counterclockwise. The spiral grooves spin the bullet as it is ejected from the muzzle in order to increase stability and accuracy in flight. The process of imprinting spiral grooves is called "rifling." "Grooves" refer to the spiral cuts in a gun's barrel. "Lands" refers to the ridges between the grooves. The lands and grooves leave a distinctive pattern on a fired bullet. These marks are collectively referred to as "striations." They are individual characteristics, particular to a weapon.

If law enforcement is able to obtain a reasonably intact bullet, perhaps after an autopsy of a victim, that bullet can be compared against one test fired from the weapon thought to be used in the crime. The forensic firearm technician will fire a bullet from the potential weapon into a tank of water or gel. In this manner, the bullet maintains its essential characteristics and is not destroyed. The test bullet is then retrieved and compared to the bullet used in the crime by means of a comparison microscope. In so doing, the forensic examiner can now testify in court regarding the methods of testing and the results. Again, because of the nature of the manufacturing process,

---

6. *See* discussion in *U.S. v. Green*, 405 F. Supp. 2d 104 (D.Mass. 2005).

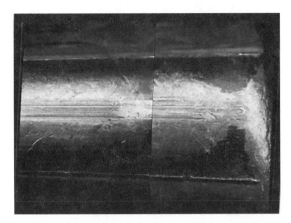

Figure 8.1 Comparing striations in a subject bullet to a test-fired bullet in a Leeds Forensic Systems LCF3 comparison microscope. Image courtesy of Leeds Forensic Systems.

bullets from different guns will be very different from one another, while bullets fired from the same gun will have identical, or nearly identical, striations.

Casings

Like bullets, a bullet's casing or shell can be examined for individual identifying characteristics. Examining casings and shells is far more common than examining bullets. Shells are rarely destroyed, and remain available for examination. But this is not without its problems.

Generally speaking, handguns are either revolvers or "automatic." A revolver operates by placing bullets in a cylinder that holds generally six or eight bullets. As a bullet is fired, the cylinder advances to the next position, so the gun can be quickly fired again. Once all of the bullets are fired, the shells must be emptied from the cylinder and new bullets inserted. This can be time consuming, particularly when a situation requires quick action. Conversely, revolvers are very reliable and do not malfunction, or "jam," as automatics may. For forensic investigators, the difficulty is that the shells remain in the revolver's cylinder. Unless the person firing the revolver empties the cylinder on site, the casing mays not be recovered.

The bullets in an automatic weapon are fed into the firing chamber though a spring-loaded "clip" or "magazine." Clips vary in size. The clip is placed into the handgun, often in the hand grip. The clip will continuously feed bullets into the firing chamber until there are no bullets remaining. As a bullet is fired, the shell is ejected from the gun. Thus, shells from automatic weapons are recoverable on scene, and can be used for comparison with test fires done in the forensic lab.

The operation of an automatic or semi-automatic handgun is generally that the complete cartridge, that is the intact bullet and casing, is pushed into the firing chamber from the magazine. When the trigger is pulled the hammer strikes a firing pin, which strikes the primer on the casing. This leaves a mark on the casing. The primer ignites and causes an explosion of the gunpowder located in the casing. That

Figure 8.2 Firing pin comparison. Image courtesy of firearmsID.com.

propels the bullet from gun. It also pushes the top portion of gun backwards. As the slide moves back into position, an extractor that has hooked onto the shell removes the shell from the chamber and pulls it back. The shell then comes into contact with an ejector, which is a static piece of metal that causes the shell to be ejected from the weapon. This process also leaves identifying marks on the casing.

Imprints left on the casing can be classified as either "static" or "sliding" marks. For example, when the firing pin strikes the primer, it leaves a static mark. The process of ejecting the shell from the weapon leaves sliding marks. These marks on the casing can be compared to those of a known weapon.

As stated, when a firing pin strikes the primer of a cartridge, it leaves a mark. Firing pins have different shapes, so the imprint it leaves will differ from weapon to weapon. Likewise, the firing pin of a particular weapon will strike the back of the bullet in a certain spot, usually fairly consistently. Therefore, the shape and the location of the firing pin imprint can be examined and compared. This individualized characteristic can link a particular weapon to a particular place.

Breech marks constitute another category of individualizing static impressions. When the bullet is fired from an automatic weapon, the upper portion of the weapon, the "slide," is forced backward. This is turn causes the bullet casing to strike the back of the breech (the firing chamber) and leaves an impression on the casing. These breech marks are very consistent to a particular weapon. This is the most common type of mark used by forensic scientists to identify a casing to a gun.

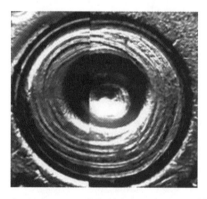

Figure 8.3 Breech mark comparison. Image courtesy of firearmsID.com.

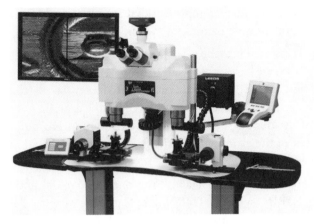

Figure 8.4 - Using a Leeds Forensic Systems LCF3 comparison microscope to compare breech marks of a known casing to exemplar casing. Image courtesy of Leeds Forensic Systems.

Ejector marks imprint on a casing as well. Because the casing is in motion at the time of firing, ejector marks can be either sliding or impressed. Despite their general reliability, there are times that an automatic weapon does not fire, perhaps because the firing pin did not strike the primer with sufficient force, or on point, or the primer was contaminated. These instances are referred to as a "dry fire." Dry fires result in a whole, intact bullet and cartridge being ejected from the gun. The ejection leaves sliding imprints on the casing. When the weapon is properly fired, and the bullet ejected, the impression left by the ejector on the casing is a static imprint. This type of static imprint tends to show that the bullet was actually fired by that particular weapon.

Other types of sliding marks include extractor marks, created when the extractor latches onto the shell. The firing pin can also leave sliding imprints. When the bullet is fired the force of the explosion causes the casing to move, even while the firing pin is still in place. These "drag marks" are readily identifiable and comparable. When a cartridge is loaded into the chamber, imperfections in the wall of the chamber can also leave marks on the cartridge casing that are also consistent and identifiable.

NIBIN

The National Integrated Ballistic Information Network (NIBIN) is both a tool and a machine, used by forensic investigators to examine and document marks on bullets and spent casings.[7] In some respects, it is similar to IAFIS, the fingerprint identification database described elsewhere in this text. There is a mechanical component, a

---

7. William King, William Wells, Charles Katz, Edward Maguire, and James Frank, *Opening the Black Box of NIBIN: A Descriptive Process and Outcome Evaluation of the Use of NIBIN and Its Effects on Criminal Investigations, Final Report*, Document No.: 243875, October 2013, https://www.ncjrs.gov/pdffiles1/nij/grants/243875.pdf.

mathematical component, and a component that requires the skill and ability of the examiner to determine if there is in fact a match.

A spent casing is inserted into the machine component of NIBIN, and is converted into a detailed 3D image. Proprietary algorithms are then employed to scan the database component of NIBIN to see if there are any potential matches with known weapons. If so, the potential matches are displayed for the examiner to review. NIBIN will not conclusively identify a match; that determination is a human one, based upon the judgment of the examiner. NIBIN has been instrumental in closing cases that had been previously unsolved.[8]

The Samuel Cooper case discussed above was one of the initial, and breakthrough, cases using the NIBIN system. The North Carolina forensic laboratory was instrumental in using NIBIN's predecessor, IBIS, the Integrated Ballistic Identification System. The U.S. Bureau of Alcohol, Tobacco, Firearms and Explosives deploys the IBIS platform to local law enforcement, and gathers the information developed into the central NIBIN database. NIBIN then scans the database for similar markings, and presents a set of data for the examiner to review in making a determination of a match.

The State of the Law

The matter of *U.S. v. Otero*[9] provides an excellent review of the application of the *Daubert* factors to firearms testimony. In that matter, the prosecution sought to introduce expert firearms examiner testimony linking cartridges found at a crime scene to guns recovered from the defendant. Defense counsel objected, claiming that such testimony lacked "established scientific methodology to support the opinion that a discharged bullet or shell was fired from a specific weapon."[10] The court took testimony from both sides, and in its decision discussed the *Daubert* factors at length. First, the court reviewed the AFTE standards discussed below, which provides that "sufficient agreement" exists between two toolmarks when the agreement is of such a quantity and quality that it is a practical impossibility that another tool could have made it.[11] In applying the *Daubert* factors the court found that the AFTE theory was testable, and had been tested, with sufficient validation studies having been conducted.[12] Further, the AFTE theory had been the subject of appropriate peer review and publication. Although a definitive error rate had not been established, the court found that, based on proficiency testing, the error rate was very low, likely 1-2%. The court further found that the testifying agency maintained a manual of

8. *See* for example "NIBIN Closes Cold Murder Case," https://www.atf.gov/firearms/nibin-closes-cold-murder-case; "Triple Murder Solved with NIBIN," https://www.atf.gov/firearms/triple-murder-solved-nibin.

9. 849 F. Supp. 2d 425 (D.N.J. 2012).

10. *Id.* at 429.

11. *Id.*

12. *Id.* at 432.

standards controlling the techniques for testing.[13] Finally, the court concluded, and noted that other courts have observed, that "the AFTE theory of firearms and toolmark identification is widely accepted in the forensic community and, specifically, in the community of firearm and toolmark examiners."[14] One wonders if that constitutes a sufficiently broad "scientific community," particularly if one believes that forensic science was developed by police agencies for use in policing and in the courts. The court further notes that the AFTE theory is widely accepted by courts as reliable, and such expert testimony to be admissible, with some limitations.[15]

The "limitations" are expounded upon in the matter of *U.S. v. Green*.[16] To the extent that the *Cooper* matter discussed above serves as an example of the appropriate use of forensic examination of ballistics markings, *Green* serves as an example of what is problematic in the field. That matter arose from alleged gang-related shootings in Boston. Due to extensive gun violence in the area, local and federal police began investigating the activities of a local street gang. Several undercover drug and weapon purchases were made.[17]

Within a week, police recovered several .38 caliber shell casings in two different areas in Boston. The locations were literally around the corner from one another. More than a year later, police recovered a loaded .38 caliber pistol in the front yard of a premises about one-half mile from where the casing were found.

Police investigating the scene compared the shell casings to one another, and to the weapon. A police sergeant was prepared to testify that all of the casings came from the same gun. Further, that the weapon from which the casings were ejected (and thus the bullets fired) was the gun recovered a year later, one-half mile from the scene. The police sergeant testified that the match between the casings and that particular gun could be made "to the exclusion of every other firearm in the world."[18]

The defense objected to the admission of the police's expert testimony, questioning among other things[19] the validity of the scientific evidence. In response to the defendant's objection, the court held a *Daubert* hearing to rule upon the admissibility of the law officer's testimony as scientific evidence. These are the concerns enumerated by the judge: neither the examiner nor the lab was certified by any professional organization; the examiner was never formally tested by a neutral proficiency examiner; the examiner could not cite any reliable report describing his own error

---

13. *Id.* at 434.

14. *Id.* at 435.

15. *Id.*

16. *United States v. Green*, 405 F. Supp. 2d 104 (D. Mass. 2005).

17. "Five Members of Dorchester Gang Charged in Federal Indictment with Racketeering, and Assault and Murder in Aid of Racketeering, Reports U.S. Attorney," *The Free Library*, 2002, PR Newswire Association, LLC, http://www.thefreelibrary.com/Five+Members+Of+Dorchester+ Gang+Charged+in+Federal+Indictment+With ... -a089147534.

18. The reader is cautioned to be skeptical of any result that claims 100% accuracy.

19. Research into this case reveals some other very interesting aspects, including the constitutionality of the makeup of the jury, and the propriety of bringing federal charges and seeking the death penalty, when Massachusetts has no death penalty remedy for state crimes.

rates, that of his lab, or that of the field. Additionally, there was no national or local database for the examiner to rely upon, and he repeated stated that he was relying on his own subjective judgment. The examiner did not fire any similar weapons for comparison purposes, only the suspect weapon. Of particular concern was the fact that the weapon and casings were tested over five years prior, but the examiner took no notes, kept no photos, and made no records. Finally, the judge questioned the finding of 100% accuracy.

The judge in *Green* indicated that, pursuant to *Daubert*, he was "obliged to critically evaluate toolmark and ballistics evidence, even though it has been accepted for years...."[20] He expressed serious concerns over many of the basic assumptions of firearms examination:

Do you agree with the concerns expressed by the judge? Why?

> 1) that each gun — like individual DNA — is unique, because it is made by a metal tool that changes over time; 2) the use of the gun by the consumer causes it to wear in a unique way; 3) the gun's unique signature will be transferred to the projectiles that emerge from it, imprinted on them through the firing pin; 4) an expert can identify that unique signature by visual comparison. There is no reason why these premises and observations cannot be tested under the *Daubert-Kumho* standards — using sound research methods yielding meaningful data on error rates. The problem is that they have never been tested in the field in general, or in this case in particular.[21]

Turning to the *Daubert* factors, the judge continued to express his concerns.

Is this not also true for fingerprint evidence? How could we ever know for certain that no two people's fingerprints are alike?

> The question of whether the expert's technique or theory is scientifically reliable is a specific one: The issue is not whether the field in general uses a reliable methodology, but the reliability of the expert's methodology *in the case at bar,* i.e., whether it is valid for the purposes for which it is being offered, or what the Court has described as a question of "fit." *Daubert,* 509 U.S. at 591, 113 S. Ct. 2786 (quoting *United States v. Downing,* 753 F.2d 1224, 1242 (3d Cir. 1985)). It may well be that each firearm produces a unique signature transferred onto a shell case and that it is possible to identify that signature using scientifically valid methods. The question is whether the approach used by the expert in this case allows for that identification "to the exclusion of every other firearm in the world."

Now we are getting to the crux of the issue. Can it be that *only this gun* fired that bullet? Is it so that such toolmarks on a spent shell casing are perfectly unique? Particularly since there was "no coherent database with which to compare the shell casings he was reviewing — neither a national database identifying the class and subclass characteristics of particular firearms or his own database from his experience with other weapons." Since the inception of the NIBIN database discussed above, are these concerns no longer an issue?

---

20. *Green* at 118.
21. *Id.*

On this *Daubert* factor, the judge opined that "[p]lainly, these issues — the reliability of the methods used and whether they can be tested — point against the admission of the [expert] testimony."

Moving on to the other *Daubert* factors, similar concerns are expressed, and again, bode against the admission of the expert testimony:

> Even if [the examiner's] approach did not account for observer bias, the Court and ultimately the jury could still evaluate the testimony by considering the error rates in the field and the error rates for this examiner. In other words, even if his approach may be flawed, if examiners in the field manage to overcome those flaws, or if this examiner had a low error rate, the evidence may still be reliable, and the jury can evaluate it. [citation omitted] Without information about error rates, the initial factfinder, this Court, and the ultimate one, the jury, have no accurate way of evaluating the testimony.

> Here, there was no credible testimony about the error rates of this examiner or in the field as a whole. O'Shea could not say that his work, his approach, his conclusions were certified by any neutral body to assure that he passed minimal standards. The Court had to rely solely on his testimony that he had examined hundreds of casings and guns. In effect, the jury would have to trust in his observational capacities, without knowing how often he was actually correct.

> These factors, the absence of testimony about error rates, certification, or proficiency testing, point against the admission of the testimony.[22]

There are, however, certain "checks and balances" available to defense counsel in addressing the expert testimony. Since the testing of the casing was not destructive, the defense was free to conduct its own test, with its own experts. Also, the defense is free to cross-examine the prosecution's expert and bring to light questionable issues. But,

> [t]his position does not completely address the threshold problem: the reliability of the testimony. Obviously, if the testimony is wholly unreliable, so as not to meet the *Daubert-Kumho* threshold, it would not matter how well the jury would understand it. Nevertheless, on balance, this factor tilts *in favor* of admission, so long as [certain] limits [on the extent of the testimony] are in place.[23]

It seems that history, however, weighs heavily as a deciding factor.

> There is apparently widespread acceptance in the courts of ballistics testing and toolmark analysis. True enough. Although the scholarly literature is extraordinarily critical, court after court has continued to allow the admission of this testimony.

> ...

---

22. *Id.* at 121–22.
23. *Id.* at 122.

Several court opinions rely upon the longstanding recognition of ballistics evidence in courts ...

...

Even the Supreme Court has weighed in on ballistics evidence. In *United States v. Scheffer*, the Court contrasted polygraph evidence with more acceptable forms of expert testimony, including ballistics, in which the expert "testif[ies] about factual matters outside the jurors' knowledge." 523 U.S. 303, 313, 118 S. Ct. 1261, 140 L. Ed. 2d 413 (1998). While this was merely a casual reference to ballistics, likely without any argument on the issue, many lower courts have cited this opinion as validating the use of ballistics experts.

...

State courts have similarly rejected *Daubert*-type challenges to ballistics testimony.

...

This reliance on longstanding use of ballistics evidence in the courts is troubling. It runs the risk of "grandfathering in irrationality," without reexamining it in the light of *Kumho* and *Daubert*. It arguably ignores the mandate of *Daubert*, especially where the courts are relying on pre-*Daubert* acceptance of a given scientific technique.[24]

One might think that, based on that record the judge would not allow the examiner to testify. One would be wrong. The judge went on to say that he felt "compelled" to allow the testimony, despite his "serious reservations." He did so, in part, because of his "confidence that any other decision will be rejected by appellate courts, in light of precedents across the county." He noted as well that "*every single court* post-*Daubert* has admitted this testimony."[25] With that, the judge put forth his own procedures, and refused to allow testimony that the shell casing came from a specific gun, "to the exclusion of every other firearm in the world."[26] Although he allowed the testimony, he did so with limitations on the expert's conclusions.[27]

There are certainly lessons to be learned here. Lack of professional certification, lack of national standards for "sorting out" types of markings, the premise of firearms markings being unique, the need for record-keeping, observer bias, lack of blind testing, and no data on error rates all contribute to potential compromise of data thought to be beyond reproach. Some of these concerns have been addressed through use of the NIBIN system. However, as in the *Cooper* case referred to above, the *Green* matter used the IBIS system, the forerunner to NIBIN. The *Green* court criticized its efficacy, noting that it is limited by the "detail with which departments have scanned" shell casings, and the accuracy of its algorithms in identifying matches. No IBIS data was sought to

---

24. *Id.* at 124.
25. *Id.* at 108.
26. *Id.* at 108–09.
27. *Id.* at 124.

be introduced. The examiner testified that even if IBIS suggested certain matches, he would not always check them all.[28] For the judge, this merely confirmed the examiner's bias: "Once he decides he has found a match" he will not go on to eliminate other alternatives.[29] Clearly the issue of examiner bias weighed heavily on the judge's mind.

The criticisms set forth in the *Green* decision are not unfounded. Other courts, around that same time, expressed similar misgivings.[30] These concerns were more particularly set out in an August 2009 report by the National Research Council.[31] The report cites a lack of mandatory standardization, certification, and accreditation. It criticizes the lack of a standard protocol for toolmark examination. As with other forensic disciplines, with the possible exception of DNA evidence, a reliable scientific methodology is needed, with less reliance on human interpretation.[32]

The battle regarding the science, or lack of it, in forensic firearm identification continues, and the arguments are myriad. Just by way of example, one side of the conflict argues that the very basis of forensic firearm identification is not valid. Citing an NRC report regarding the feasibility and accuracy of a ballistic imaging database,[33] Adina Schwartz argues that the fundamental assumption that firearms produce unique markings and that those markings are reproducible has not been scientifically established. On the other hand, Robert Thompson[34] advises that 100% certainty is not attainable.

The hypothesis is that toolmarks, in this case those made by firearms on bullets and casings, can be identified to a specific tool (gun) to the practical exclusion of all other tools. While human interpretation is certainly part of the process, the identification to a specific tool is inferred, based on experimentation and observation. While there is potential for random agreement, that agreement will generally not reach the quantity and quality shown between non-matches.

This standard is not acceptable to critics of the process.[35] They cite several areas of concern,[36] including a lack of certifications and standards, a lack of representative

---

28. *Id.* at 116–17.

29. *Id.*

30. *United States v. Monteiro*, 407 F. Supp. 2d 351 (D. Mass. 2006); *United States v. Glynn*, No. 07 Cr. 580, 2008 WL 4293317, at *6 (S.D.N.Y. Sept. 22, 2008).

31. National Research Council, *Strengthening Forensic Science in the United States: A Path Forward*, (The National Academies Press, August 2009), http://www.nap.edu/catalog/12589.html.

32. *Id.* at 154–55.

33. *Committee to Assess the Feasibility, Accuracy, and Technical Capability of a National Ballistics Database*, National Research Council, Ballistic Imaging (National Academies Press, 2008), http://books.nap.edu/catalog/12162.html.

34. Robert M. Thompson, *Firearm Identification in the Forensic Science Laboratory*, NDAA (2010), www.ndaa.org/pdf/Firearms_identify_NDAAsm.pdf.

35. *See e.g.*, Adina Schwartz, "Challenging Firearms and Toolmark Identification — Part One," *The Champion*, October 2008, https://www.nacdl.org/Champion.aspx?id=4927. *See also* Adina Schwartz, "A Systemic Challenge to the Reliability and Admissibility of Firearms and Toolmark Identification," *Columbia Science & Technology Law Review* 67 (2005), http://www.stlr.org/cite.cgi ?volume=6&article=2.

36. Association of Firearm and Tool Mark Examiners, afte.org/uploads/documents/ ppASadmisability.pps.

databases, lack of demonstrable error rates, and lack of methodology consistent with the scientific method.[37] Alternatively, the Association of Firearm and Tool Mark Examiners has taken the lead in promulgating standards of identification. This body is a professional organization, but it does not accredit examiners. Its "Theory of Identification" and its "Range of Conclusions," detailed below, appear to have wide acceptance. Whether that acceptance rises to the level of scientific acceptance required under the *Daubert* standard continues to be debated. Nonetheless, the AFTE "Theory of Identification" states:

1. The theory of identification as it pertains to the comparison of toolmarks enables opinions of common origin to be made when the unique surface contours of two toolmarks are in "sufficient agreement."

2. This "sufficient agreement" is related to the significant duplication of random toolmarks as evidence by the correspondence of a pattern or combination of patterns of surface contours. Significance is determined by the comparative examination of two or more sets of surface contour patterns comprised of individual peaks, ridges, and furrows. Specifically, the relative height or depth, width, curvature and spatial relationship of the individual peaks, ridges and furrows within one set of surface contours are defined and compared to the corresponding features in the second set of surface contours. Agreement is significant when the agreement in individual characteristics exceeds the best agreement demonstrated between toolmarks known to have been produced by different tools and is consistent with agreement demonstrated by toolmarks known to have been produced by the same tool. The statement that "sufficient agreement" exists between two toolmarks means that the agreement of individual characteristics is of a quantity and quality that the likelihood another tool could have made the mark is so remote as to be considered a practical impossibility.

3. Currently the interpretation of individualization/identification is subjective in nature, founded on scientific principles and based on the examiner's training and experience.[38]

As might be expected, critics of this standard argue that terms like "sufficient" and "significant" are far too subjective to live up to the rigors of the scientific method.[39] Proponents of the AFTE Standard stand by the method, maintaining that "[t]he AFTE Theory of Identification coupled with the comparative analysis and examination method upon which it is based, along with extensive studies in the literature and the individual training, experience, and expertise of examiners adequately addresses the primary question of the court — was this tool mark produced by this tool?"[40]

37. *Id.*

38. "AFTE Theory of Identification as It Relates to Toolmarks," https://afte.org/about-us/what-is-afte/afte-theory-of-identification.

39. *See Schwartz, supra,* and sources cited therein.

40. Ronald Nichols, *The Scientific Foundations of Firearms and Tool Mark Identification — A Response to Recent Challenges,* http://www.firearmsid.com/feature%20articles/nichols060915/AS%20Response%20110805.pdf.

In connection with the AFTE "Theory of Identification," a "Range of Conclusions" have been adopted. In examining firearm toolmark identification possibilities, the conclusions reached may be classified as:

1. **Identification**

   Agreement of a combination of individual characteristics and all discernible class characteristics where the extent of agreement exceeds that which can occur in the comparison of toolmarks made by different tools and is consistent with the agreement demonstrated by toolmarks known to have been produced by the same tool.

2. **Inconclusive**

   Some agreement of individual characteristics and all discernible class characteristics, but insufficient for an identification.

   Agreement of all discernible class characteristics without agreement or disagreement of individual characteristics due to an absence, insufficiency, or lack of reproducibility.

   Agreement of all discernible class characteristics and disagreement of individual characteristics, but insufficient for an elimination.

3. **Elimination**

   Significant disagreement of discernible class characteristics and/or individual characteristics.

4. **Unsuitable**

   Unsuitable for examination.[41]

With this background, the trend in allowing expert testimony on firearms toolmark identification seems to be to allow the testimony, but to limit the expert's opinion. The problem with the AFTE standard is succinctly stated in *U.S. v. Sebbern*, (E.D.N.Y. 2012), 2012 WL 5989813. Citing reports by the National Research Council of the National Academy of Sciences (the "NRC"), the court observed that

> AFTE standards acknowledged that ballistic comparisons "involve subjective qualitative judgments by examiners and that the accuracy of examiners' assessments is highly dependent on their skill and training." National Research Council, Committee on Identifying the Needs of the Forensic Sciences Community, *Strengthening Forensic Science in the United States: A Path Forward*, 5–20 (2009) (hereafter, the "NRC Report"). The NRC Report further stated that "a fundamental problem with toolmark and firearms analysis is the lack of a precisely defined process.... AFTE has adopted a theory of identification, but it does not provide a specific protocol." *Id.* at 5–21. The NRC Report concluded that, "[e]ven with more training and experience using new techniques, the decision of the toolmark examiner

---

41. "AFTE Range of Conclusions," https://afte.org/about-us/what-is-afte/afte-range-of-conclusions.

remains a subjective decision based on unarticulated standards and no statistical foundation for estimation of error rates." *Id.* at 5–20.

The 2009 NRC Report summarizes the state of the forensic science by saying:

> Because not enough is known about the variabilities among individual tools and guns, we are not able to specify how many points of similarity are necessary for a given level of confidence in the result. Sufficient studies have not been done to understand the reliability and repeatability of the methods. The committee agrees that class characteristics are helpful in narrowing the pool of tools that may have left a distinctive mark. Individual patterns from manufacture or from wear might, in some cases, be distinctive enough to suggest one particular source, but additional studies should be performed to make the process of individualization more precise and repeatable.[42]

The trend, then, is to allow the expert testimony, but to limit the extent of the expert's opinion. It appears that adherence to this standard, and particularly to these conclusions, would have been wise for the forensic examiner in the *Green* matter. As you may recall, he testified to 100% accuracy, to the exclusion of every other weapon in the world. Perhaps acknowledging the potential for error, and that testing was "consistent with" marks made by the same gun would have put the judge more at ease.

Similarly, in *U.S. v. Willock*[43] the court felt compelled to allow the expert testimony, albeit with limitations on the extent of the expert's opinion. The court had before it testimony from Baltimore County firearms examiner, Sgt. Mark Ensor, concluding that certain spent cartridges "matched" a particular weapon. The defense objected to the testimony, claiming that it was unreliable and scientifically invalid. The court overruled the objection, noting that allowing the testimony is consistent with every reported federal decision to have addressed the admissibility of toolmark identification evidence.[44] However, in light of two National Research Council studies cited above that call into question toolmark identification's status as "science," Judge Grimm concluded that toolmark examiners must be restricted in the degree of certainty with which they express their opinions. There will be no testimony indicating 100% certainty of a match, or that this weapon was used, to the exclusion of all other weapons. *U.S. v. Glynn*[45] reaches a similar conclusion, allowing the expert to testify only that it was "more likely than not" that a recovered casing came from a particular gun.

Even with such limitations the battle continues. And it is not helped by popular culture. Right around the time of this deluge of articles and research, *Popular Mechanics* magazine published an article entitled "CSI Myths: The Shaky Science Behind Forensics."[46] After going through the litany of wrongful convictions obtained

---

42. National Research Council, *Strengthening Forensic Science in the United States: A Path Forward* (The National Academies Press, 2009): 154.

43. 696 F. Supp. 2d 536 (D. Md. 2010).

44. *Willock*, at 556–57.

45. 578 F. Supp. 2d 567 (S.D.N.Y. 2008).

46. Brad Reagan, "CSI Myths: The Shaky Science Behind Forensics," *Popular Mechanics*, December 17, 2009, www.popularmechanics.com/science/health/a4535/4325774/.

by faulty forensic evidence, and realizing the concomitant result that people alleged to commit crimes remain on the street, the article points out that unlike other sciences, forensic science was created by police agencies, not scientists.

More recently, *The Atlantic* magazine published "CSI Is a Lie."[47] The litany in this article is of the various scandals that plague forensic evidence. It bears review at some length. The magazine cited as examples:

- At a Massachusetts drug lab, a chemist was sent to prison after admitting that she faked the results in perhaps tens of thousands of drug cases, calling into question thousands of drug convictions that ended with people in prison.

- In St. Paul, Minnesota, an independent review of the crime lab found "major errors in almost every area of the lab's work, including the fingerprint and crime scene evidence processing that has continued after the lab's drug testing was stopped in July. The failures include sloppy documentation, dirty equipment, faulty techniques and ignorance of basic scientific procedures. Lab employees even used Wikipedia as a 'technical reference' in at least one drug case ... The lab lacked any clean area designated for the review and collection of DNA evidence. The lab stored crime-scene photos on a computer that anyone could access without a password."

- In Colorado, the Office of the Attorney General documented inadequate training and alarming lapses at a lab that measured the amount of alcohol in blood.

- In Detroit, police shut down their crime laboratory "after an audit uncovered serious errors in numerous cases. The audit said sloppy work had probably resulted in wrongful convictions, and officials expect a wave of appeals ... auditors re-examined 200 randomly selected shooting cases and found serious errors in 19."

- In Philadelphia, "three trace-evidence technicians have flunked a routine test administered to uphold the police crime lab's accreditation, police brass announced Tuesday. Each technician tests hundreds of pieces of evidence a year for traces of blood and semen, so if investigators determine that the methods are problematic, it could throw countless court cases into question ..."

- In North Carolina, "agents withheld exculpatory evidence or distorted evidence in more than 230 cases over a 16-year period. Three of those cases resulted in execution. There was widespread lying, corruption, and pressure from prosecutors and other law-enforcement officials on

47. Conor Friedersdorf, "CSI Is a Lie," *The Atlantic*, April 20, 2015, http://www.theatlantic.com/politics/archive/2015/04/csi-is-a-lie/390897/.

crime lab analysts to produce results that would help secure convictions. And the pressure worked."

That is a *highly* incomplete sample from just the last decade....

Houston, already reeling from a scandal that has led to retesting of evidence in 360 cases, now faces a much larger crisis that could involve many thousands of cases over 25 years....[48]

While these examples do not necessarily implicate deficiencies in the area of firearms and toolmark evidence, they certainly call into question the role of the examiner. Similarly, they illustrate well the concerns expressed by judges and critics of the process, who call into question the subjective nature of examiner's findings. To alleviate some of these concerns, independent experts are recommended, or alternatively, funding for independent forensic review for the defense. Forensic laboratories are often paid for with state funds, so there may be some concern about bias in favor of the state.

Double-blind testing is appropriate. An examiner should not be told what bullet is thought to go with what gun. Rather, merely to match bullets with guns. That would address a concern expressed by the judge in *Green*, when he described the examiner's procedure as a ballistics "show-up." That is, there was only one bullet compared to only one gun. The recommendations set out in *The Atlantic* article mirror in many respects the recommendations made by other oversight authorities.

While this battle continues, academic researchers and commercial entities continue to attempt to find ways to put more science into the field. 2D and 3D imaging, along with automated comparisons, lessen the role of the individual examiner, and may take them out of the process entirely.[49] Enhanced algorithms to address matches are being explored.[50] Similarly, better statistical analysis is also being explored.[51] As these develop, and as the science gets better and databases of information are developed, the more likely toolmark evidence will be seen as being accepted in the scientific, not just law enforcement, community, and will comport with the *Daubert* standard for admissibility.

Other Firearms-Related Forensics

Forensic investigation of firearms also involves ballistics. That is, determining the flight path of the projectile, and the likely location from which the shot was fired.

---

48. *Id.*

49. *See* Intelligent Automation, Inc., "Computer Assisted 3D Analysis Tools for Forensic Applications," www.i-a-i.com/Pictures/Forensics%20Brochure.pdf; Francine Prokoski, *Use of Infrared Imaging, a Robust Matching Engine and Associated Algorithms to Enhance Identification of Both 2D and 3D Impressions*, Report to the U.S. Department of Justice, www.ncjrs.gov/pdffiles1/nij/grants/227933.pdf.

50. L. S. Chumbley and M. Morris. *Significance of Association in Tool Mark Characterization*, Report to the U.S. Department of Justice, www.ncjrs.gov/pdffiles1/nij/grants/243319.pdf.

51. Hoeksema, Amy B., "Statistical Methods for the Forensic Analysis of Striated Tool Marks," Graduate Theses and Dissertations, Paper 13383 (Iowa State University, 2013).

Generally speaking, there needs to be two points that can be connected to determine trajectory. That can be an entry and exit wound, or any other location where a bullet has entered and exited. The angle of the entry and exit locations are strung together, or sometimes rods or wooden dowels are used to calculate angles. If more than one entry and exit location can be found, the angles can be compared in an attempt to determine the location of the shooter when the shots were fired. This is somewhat similar to the stringing that occurs with blood spatter, which is also discussed in a separate chapter.

Another aspect of forensic firearms analysis involves trigger pull. In cases where there is an alleged "accidental" shooting, the amount of force necessary to pull the trigger can be important. A decidedly low-tech trigger pull gauge is used. It is a hanging scale. One end is attached to the trigger, and weights are placed on the other. The amount of weight needed to pull the trigger is documented on the scale.

Forensic analysis is also used to determine whether the gun is properly functioning. Similarly, forensic analysis can determine whether the safety is in good working order.

Despite a person's attempt to conceal a weapon's serial number, restoration is possible. Depending on the type of metal involved, chemically treating the area of an obliterated serial number may well restore it. Even if not completely restored, the partially restored number may give law enforcement a lead they would not have otherwise had.

Gunshot Residue

Forensic firearm examination also includes testing for gunshot residue, GSR. When a bullet is fired from a gun, the explosion that expels the bullet also discharges gunpowder from the muzzle of the weapon. The gunpowder may come in contact with the surrounding area, including the victim and the shooter. If the weapon is some distance away from the target, the gunpowder may be dispersed and there may not be any traces left.

However, if the weapon is in close proximity to the target, GSR may be recovered from the target. If the weapon is close to the victim, GSR will leave a tight pattern on the victim. If the weapon is farther away, the GSR pattern will be wider, until the weapon is so far away from the target that no GSR is recoverable from the target.

Forensic investigators test for GSR and are able to quantify the resulting pattern of GSR. Once the subject weapon is identified, tests can be performed to see the GSR pattern at various distances. Through the use of this data, forensic investigators can make some broad determination of the distance between the weapon and the target.

GSR testing can be useful in other ways, as well. In a revolver there is a small space between the cylinder and the frame, or the recoil shield, of the gun. GSR is emitted not only from the muzzle of the barrel, but also through this small gap. As such, testing for GSR can place a weapon in a certain location. For example, a shot fired with a revolver from an automobile may result in GSR being on the doorframe, dashboard,

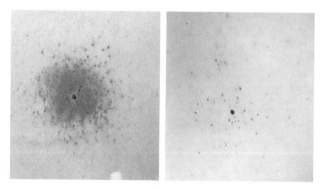

Figure 8.5 GSR test at 3″ (left) and at 15″ (right). Image courtesy of firearmID.com.

or steering wheel. Similarly, GSR testing may be done on the hands of an alleged suicide victim. This can be instrumental in determining whether the victim fired the weapon.

GSR is often sought to be used as an indication that a particular person fired a weapon. Certainly GSR would appear on the firing hand of a person who discharges a weapon. However, the presence of GSR is not conclusive. As the California Department of Justice Bureau of Forensic Services states:

> Gunshot residue (GSR) results from the discharge of a firearm. The residue escapes through openings in the weapon and the end of a barrel and is deposited on nearby surfaces. The actual amount of residue detected varies with the type of weapon, ammunition, conditions of discharge, and post-shooting activity. **GSR analysis does not determine whether or not an individual has discharged a firearm.**
>
> The presence of gunshot residue may occur for the following reasons:
>
> - The subject may have discharged a firearm or been in close proximity to the discharge of a firearm.
>
> - The subject may have handled a firearm or ammunition.
>
> - The subject may have been in contact with a surface bearing gunshot residue.
>
> The absence of gunshot residue may occur for the following reasons:
>
> - The subject did not discharge a firearm.
>
> - The subject may have discharged a firearm, but no GSR particles were deposited on the sampled area.
>
> - GSR particles were removed by washing, wiping, or other activity before the samples were collected.[52]

Similarly, the Federal Bureau of Investigation, although encouraged by recent scientific and technological advances in GSR, cautions:

---

52. California Department of Justice, Bureau of Forensic Services, "Gunshot Residue (GSR) Collection," *Physical Evidence Bulletin*, May 2014, http://oag.ca.gov/sites/all/files/agweb/pdfs/cci/reference/peb_15.pdf (emphasis in original).

In a GSR case, the submitting agency, attorneys, judge, and jury all want to know if the suspect fired a gun. Unfortunately, the presence or absence of GSR on a person's hands cannot answer that question. Rather, as the accepted practice, all positive gunshot residue reports include a qualifier, such as "The presence of primer residue on a person's hand is consistent with that person having discharged a firearm, having been in the vicinity of a firearm when it was discharged, or having handled an item with primer residue on it." Conversely, negative GSR reports often contain a qualifying statement, such as "The absence of gunshot residue on a person's hands does not eliminate that individual from having discharged a firearm." And, when GSR is found on an inanimate object, like clothing, a qualifier could be, "The presence of primer residue on an item is consistent with that item sometime having been in the vicinity of a firearm when it was discharged or having come in contact with primer residue on another item."[53]

To its credit, the FBI points to several cases where evidence regarding GSR may have been an unwarranted factor in obtaining a conviction. In examining the case of the actor Robert Blake, who in was acquitted in 2005 of killing his then-wife, it is noted that Robert Blake was tested for GSR, but not until the day after the murder. Initially, he was allowed to go home after police questioning. Although he was found to have GSR on his hands, that GSR could have come from another licensed revolver owned by the actor, or from cross-contamination.[54] Similarly, Barry George was convicted in 2001 of killing British celebrity Jill Dando in 1999. His conviction was overturned in 2007, with the appeals court judges saying that

> the jury might have reached a different verdict had they known of doubts about crucial gunshot evidence. The [trial court] had been told that a microscopic speck of firearms discharge residue, found in a pocket of George's coat, was linked to particles found in Miss Dando's hair and clothes.
>
> But scientists now say the particle was worthless as evidence. It was just as likely it came from innocent contamination in a police lab or from the general "environment" as that it came from the murder weapon.[55]

Toolmarks

The above discussion of static and sliding imprints on bullets and casing may be broadly characterized as "toolmark" evidence. As the name implies, toolmark evidence

---

53. Michael Trimpe, "The Current Status of GSR Examinations," *FBI Law Enforcement Bulletin*, May 2011, https://leb.fbi.gov/2011/may/the-current-status-of-gsr-examinations.

54. Lisa Sweetingham, "Expert: Gunshot Residue Does Not Mean Robert Blake Killed His Wife," Court TV, January 19, 2005, www.cnn.com/2005/LAW/01/19/blake.trial/.

55. Stephen Wright and Sam Greenhill, "Dando 'Killer' Barry George to Face Retrial after Winning Appeal," *Daily Mail*, November 16, 2007, http://www.dailymail.co.uk/news/article-494180/Dando-killer-Barry-George-face-retrial-winning-appeal.html#ixzz4Iqbgb9d1.

Figure 8.6 Toolmark comparison. Image courtesy of firearmsID.com.

involves circumstances where an object, often metal, inscribes or imprints on another object. It need not be guns imprinting on bullets and casing.

Similar to guns and bullets, however, even mass produced tools have minor variations that make them uniquely identifiable. Appropriately documenting a crime scene, including the location of the potential tool used, is vital. An untrained person, even in law enforcement, should never attempt to determine if a particular tool was used by placing it in the toolmark. This has the potential of destroying the evidence. The area on which the tool was used can be cast and tested against the tool at a later time in the appropriate setting. Additionally, the tool must be carefully and appropriately handled so as to preserve any fingerprint evidence that may be helpful later, and to preserve the chain of custody.

While cases involving firearms evidence are legion, those involving other sorts of toolmark evidence are not. Nonetheless, a bit of an overview and a couple of examples might be in order. In a motor vehicle theft case, the steering column had been broken open with a tool, in order to gain access to the ignition and disable the steering lock.[56] A suspect near the vehicle was found to have a screwdriver in his backpack. Casts were made from both the screwdriver and the marks on the steering column. You can see the result in Figure 8.6 above. This also points out some of the perceived difficulty with toolmark evidence. Is it so that no other screwdriver ever made could make these marks? If you are coming to a conclusion regarding a match, based on your own viewing of the photos, is that really an area for expert testimony? Are you already an expert?

The court in *U.S. v. Smallwood*[57] probably would not accept you as an expert. That case involved, among other thigs, a tire-slashing incident, in connection with other criminal activity. The prosecution proffered an expert to testify that a knife found on the desk of the defendant was the knife used to slash the tires. The defendant moved to exclude that testimony and a four-day *Daubert* hearing was conducted. The government's expert had significant experience in toolmark evidence, and testified that

> "her training in knives was limited to one class that did not solely cover knives, but rather 'covered an array of different tools and marks.'" She further

---

56. Jeffrey Scott Doyle, "Case Profile: Tool Mark ID," Firearms ID, www.firearmsid.com/Case%20Profiles/ToolmarkID/toolmark.htm.

57. 456 Fed. Appx. 563 (6th Cir. 2012).

testified that she had only looked at knife marks in tires on one occasion prior to this case, i.e., during that class. And she acknowledged that knife cases are rare in her lab, that she has never testified in a knife case before, and that she did not test any other knives for purposes of rendering her opinion in this case. The district court did not abuse its discretion in sustaining.... Notwithstanding [the expert's] significant experience with tool marks generally, her opinion that there is "sufficient agreement" between her test marks and the puncture marks found in the tires of the [victim's] vehicle is unreliable under the AFTE's own standard because she has virtually no basis for concluding that the alleged match exceeds the best agreement demonstrated between tool marks known to have been produced by different tools.[58]

Another interesting matter involving toolmark evidence is *State v. Emerick*.[59] In that matter, Emerick was convicted of the brutal killing of two people in connection with the robbery of a bar. Both had been bludgeoned to death. There was eyewitness testimony in the matter, but little forensic evidence. Specifically, there was no DNA evidence linking Emerick to the killings. What did link him, however, was toolmarks. There was a cigarette vending machine on the bar property that had been pried open with a tool. Police investigating the robbery and murder found a tire iron in Emerick's car. A forensic scientist testified at trial that the tire iron found in the car made the tool marks on the pried open cigarette machine, "to the exclusion of all other tools."[60] As discussed previously, 100% accuracy is hard to come by, and may well place that opinion in some jeopardy. Nonetheless, the defendant was convicted based on the weight of the evidence.

Sometimes toolmark evidence is called "impression" evidence. After all, the discipline deals with impressions made by an object, a "tool," onto another surface. The barrel of a firearm is tool, leaving an impression on a bullet. Thus, strictly speaking, toolmark/impression evidence may also include such things as tire marks, shoeprints,[61] and even bite marks. The latter, bite marks or forensic odontology, raises significant concerns.[62] In fact, as of this writing, the state of Texas has gone as far as banning forensic bite mark evidence.[63] The Texas Forensic Science Commission made the recommendation after a review of research, including some

---

58. *Id.* at 567.

59. 2011 Ohio 5543 (2011).

60. *Ohio v. Emerick*, Memorandum in Support of Jurisdiction of Appellant, the State of Ohio, www.sconet.state.oh.us/pdf_viewer/pdf_viewer.aspx?fpdf=698809.pdf.

61. *See*, for example, International Association for Identification, "Forensic Podiatry Discipline," theiai.org/disciplines/podiatry/index.php.

62. *See*, for example, Norm Pattis, "Forensic Gobbledygook and Criminal Law," February 26, 2009, www.pattisblog.com/blog.php?article=Forensic-Gobbledygood-And-Criminal-Law_879; *State v. Swinton*, 268 Conn. 781 (2004).

63. Joe Palazzolo, "Texas Commission Recommends Ban on Bite-Mark Evidence," Law Blog, *Wall Street Journal*, February 12, 2016, Blogs.wsj.com/law/2016/02/12/texas-commission-recommends-ban-on-bite-mark-evidence.

research wherein forensic dentists could not agree that an injury was the result of a bite mark.[64] Further, a recent report has gone so far as saying that bite mark analysis is "junk science."[65]

Summary

While there are undoubtedly some difficulties associated with firearm and toolmark evidence, the use of expert testimony in this area is well established in the legal community. At present, expert testimony is often allowed due to the weight of historical precedent, perhaps rather than the convincing nature of the science behind it. As the science develops and becomes more certain, the law will likely develop with it. Acceptance of such expert testimony as meeting the *Daubert* standard is far from a foregone certainty. Subjectivity in the process remains, and is integral to the process. Perhaps as the national computer database continues to grow, the human factor will diminish and the science will continue to become more focused, and generally accepted.

Discussion Questions

1. How are class characteristics determined?

2. What constitutes a class characteristic?

3. How do class characteristics differ from individual characteristics?

4. What is NIBIN and how is it used?

5. What role does ballistics play in firearms and toolmark identification?

6. What roles does gunshot residue play in firearms and toolmark identification?

7. How are firearms characteristics similar to toolmarks?

8. What other types of matters are examined in connection with firearm identification?

9. How can accidental characteristics prove or defend a matter?

10. Give an example of how non-firearm toolmarks are made. Are such marks helpful in proving a case?

---

64. *Id.*

65. Jordan Smith, "White House Report Concludes that Bite Mark Analysis Is Junk Science," *The Intercept*, September 7, 2016, https://theintercept.com/2016/09/07/white-house-report-concludes-that-bite-mark-analysis-is-junk-science/.

Chapter 9

Computer and Digital Forensics

Overview

Computers are ubiquitous. Your laptop computer is only one small example of the availability of computer processing power. In modern society, one can hardly touch something that is not connected to computer processing power. Your cell phone tracks you almost constantly and usually by default. The computing power in your car does something similar. Even your household appliances can contain computing power.

The information stored and handled by computers and cell phones is generally referred to as "digital evidence." The quantity of such information boggles the mind. As of this writing, 97% of Americans use text messaging at least once a day, accounting for over 6 billion text messages per day.[1] By some estimates, there are well over 4 billion email accounts worldwide, and that number is expected to grow dramatically.[2] Are those text messages and emails usable as evidence at trial? How can one be certain, if one can at all, that they are real? Or that they were sent by the person who claims to have sent them? It can be very material and relevant to issues that present at trial. It may even answer the age-old question: "Where were you on the night of ... ?"

But how do we go about obtaining this digital information? Where is it located? What are the circumstances under which it can be obtained? How do we ensure that it is what is purports to be? Do the rules, or for that matter the questions, differ for criminal prosecutions and civil actions? These are the questions that this chapter will address.

Chapter Objectives

Upon completion of this chapter, students will be able to:

1. Define digital evidence.

---

1. https://Teckst.com/19-text-messaging-stats-that-will-blow-your-mind/. Last accessed on April 27, 2016.
2. Statista, "Number of Active Email Accounts Worldwide from 2014 to 2019 (in Millions)," http://www.statista.com/statistics/456519/forecast-number-of-active-email-accounts-worldwide/.

2. Explain legal authenticity, as it applies to digital information.

3. Explain the types of information that digital evidence reveals.

4. Have a working knowledge of the storage of digital data.

5. Identify various types of computer data.

6. Discuss forensically sound acquisition and examination of digital evidence.

7. Explain what data can be recovered, what cannot be recovered, and the value of both.

Case Studies

There are myriad examples of law enforcement using digital data to capture criminals. Frequently, law enforcement will pose as a member of a vulnerable class, for example a minor seeking companionship. After some communication, often a meeting is arranged with the understanding that it will be for illicit purposes. At the time of the meeting, law enforcement then pounces on the offender and an arrest is made.

Similarly, law enforcement will monitor sites wherein child pornography is exchanged. Once able to trace the computers to which the images are sent, a search warrant can be obtained and appropriate enforcement action taken.

State v. Lasaga; U.S. v. Lasaga

The matter of Antonio Lasaga, former professor at Yale University, presents an interesting, if lamentable, series of facts.[3] Lasaga was employed at Yale in the geology and geophysics department. At some point, a graduate student in that department notified the person in charge of maintaining the department's computers that Lasaga had downloaded child pornography onto his office computer. The graduate student determined to continue monitoring Lasaga's computer activity, while the computer specialist remotely accessed the files that Lasaga had downloaded onto his office computer. He also installed a monitoring script that would alert him whenever Lasaga downloaded new files. When an alert came in, the computer specialist attempted to make certain that Lasaga was in fact in his office. While the door was shut, a student did confirm that Lasaga was in his office.

At that point, the geology department employees determined to contact law enforcement. An FBI agent applied for a search warrant to obtain the computer and related items, and that search warrant was executed by law enforcement the next day. Multiple items were seized, including the computer, discs and zip drives, and videotape. Based on the results of the search, Lasaga was charged under both Connecticut law and federal law. The federal court prosecution charged violations

---

3. The facts as set forth here are those reported in *State v. Lasaga*, 269 Conn. 454 (2004).

of the Child Pornography Prevention Act of 1996.[4] In that matter, he was sentenced to 180 months in prison. In addition to child pornography, information obtained through the search warrant revealed actual sexual contact with a minor. Lasagna was charged under state law for these crimes and was sentenced to 20 years in prison, to run concurrently with his federal sentence.

Several interesting issues arise from the actions of the parties surrounding Lasaga's conduct. Were the Yale employees acting as agents of the police at any time during the investigation? If so, does that effect the legal validity of the search warrant, such that Lasaga's conviction is unconstitutional? With respect to the allegations of possession of child pornography, how do we know it was actually Lasaga that was downloading the images? Might it have been someone else in the department using his computer? Perhaps someone logged in with his credentials. These types of questions face law enforcement and the courts frequently. Can digital evidence overcome any potential doubt?

Connecticut's Most Expensive Divorce

The type of information described above not only surfaces in criminal matters, but is also present in civil cases. The matter of *Tauck v. Tauck*,[5] perhaps Connecticut's longest running and most expensive divorce case, illustrates this point well.

Several matters were litigated during the course of this hotly contested 86-day trial. As with many such cases, child custody and visitation, as well as financial matters, were at issue. In the course of trial, it was disclosed by Mrs. Tauck that her husband had viewed child pornography on his computer. In fact, forensic examination of his computer revealed child pornography and related search queries. Certainly such a revelation, if proved, would significantly and negatively affect Mr. Tauck's ability to appropriately parent his children, would it not? How could a trial judge not consider such a revelation in ruling on issues of custody and visitation?

But how to prove such an allegation? It would seem simple enough, merely by viewing the subject computer. However, opening files on a computer may destroy evidence that lurks in the background and can be quite valuable. For example, your computer tracks dates and times when files are accessed. If the files are opened, that information is overwritten and lost. Locard's exchange principal, discussed elsewhere in this text, cautions that whenever an area is entered, one picks up something and leaves something behind. Although you might think of that in terms of scientific evidence, like DNA, it holds true for digital evidence as well. Therefore, investigators must be certain to minimize the likelihood that something is taken away, left behind, or otherwise destroyed. Those steps are discussed below. In the *Tauck* matter, one of the reasons the trial took as long as it did was to conduct searches for forensic

---

4. 18 U.S.C. §2251 *et seq.*

5. 2007 WL 3087962 (J.D. Middlesex, 2007). The author wishes to express his appreciation to the trial judge in that matter for her generosity is discussing these matters.

evidence on several computer hard drives, and this was how the child pornography was discovered.

Certainly, the possession of child pornography could be the proverbial "smoking gun" on which the court's decision rested. And in many respects it was, but certainly not in the way Mrs. Tauck might have anticipated.

Evidence was developed that Mr. Tauck travelled extensively for his business. The forensic investigation of Mr. Tauck's laptop computer showed that he was traveling at the time the child pornography was accessed. The evidence showed that he was on a ship at that time, and that there was no internet access. Furthermore, the laptop was left at home in Connecticut, and there was no indication of remote access to that computer. One of the various computer experts in the case testified that he

> ... was able to determine the location of the Toshiba I laptop on May 5, 2005. [The expert] observed what is commonly referred to as pop-ups as a result of access of adult web pages. The pop-up he found was for Adult Friend Finder. He explained that the pop-ups read the IP address that is responsible for access to pornography pages. It interprets the IP number (in essence a physical address of the computer) and offers an adult friend in that geographical area. [The expert] found several adult friend finder pop-ups and they all said the same thing, "find a partner in Westport tonight" for the date May 5, 2005. This indicated to [the expert] that the IP number associated with the computer browsing the website that created the pop-up, was showing an IP address associated with the Westport, CT, area.[6]

Clearly, computer IP and location data can truly make or break a case. In the *Tauck* matter, location data was particularly relevant and contributed a great deal to the determination of the case. Moreover, as alluded to above, unless a computer is biometrically enabled, can we really know who was using it? That is to say, although IP address information can tell us about the computer and its location, it cannot tell us who was actually sitting behind the computer at the time of the internet access.

Types of Cases

At this point, we will limit our inquiry to criminal matters. The types of crime that are facilitated by electronic means are almost boundless. And nearly every crime has some element of digital forensics attached to it. And it seems rather self-evident that if you have a computer, you are likely connected to the internet.

The Federal Bureau of Investigation's Internet Crime Complaint Center (the "IC3") deals with matters involving computer fraud. Their 2014 Internet Crime Report states that the most frequently reported internet crimes are auto fraud, government impersonation, intimidation/extortion scams, real estate fraud, and "romance" scams.

---

6. *Id.* at 25.

Social media has also become an increasingly popular platform for criminal activity.[7] The FBI lists as its key priorities computer and network intrusion, identity theft, and fraud.[8] Federal law found in Title 18 of the United States Code makes unauthorized computer intrusion, hacking, illegal and punishable by fine and imprisonment.[9] Interstate exchange of child pornography often forms the basis of federal criminal charges as well.[10]

In addition, as illustrated by the *Lasaga* matter, there may also be consequences pursuant to state law. States have similar computer crimes provisions with similarly harsh penalties. States also often see consequences of physical contact, or the attempt, that results from the electronic communication.

Digital forensics is also of concern in civil matters, where much evidence is in an electronic format. This will occupy our attention later.

Types of Data

Digital forensics can reveal information that is otherwise hidden. That information may consist of dates and times when certain internet sites were accessed or when files were created or downloaded, the location of the computer when sites were accessed, and actual contraband, even if the user has attempted to delete the data. And this is just a small sampling of the types of data available. That otherwise hidden, or deleted, information can be of substantial concern and has the ability to make or break a case.

Location Data and Identification Data

Your computer and your cell phone can provide critical information about the time and place of your activities. When time and location are important, digital forensics can provide an answer. At the time of this writing, police in Chicago were able to solve a murder in part by obtaining cell phone records that placed the perpetrator at the scene at the time of the act.[11]

IP Addresses

If a computer is connected to the internet, some company is providing internet service. That company is the "ISP," the internet service provider. When a computer accesses the internet, the ISP assigns a particular "address" to the computer. That address is referred to as the "IP address," or internet protocol address. Only one

---

7. Federal Bureau of Investigation, Internet Crime Complaint Center, *2014 Internet Crime Report*, www.ic3.gov/media/annualreport/2014_IC3Report.pdf.

8. www.fbi.gov/about-us/investigative/cyber/computer-intrusions

9. 18 U.S.C. § 1030.

10. 18 U.S.C. § 2256.

11. http://www.msn.com/en-us/news/crime/police-2-charged-in-killings-of-6-family-members-in-chicago/ar-BBtfx97?li=BBnbfcL

computer at a time can have that one unique IP address. Each time you access the internet, a new unique IP address is assigned. The ISP maintains a listing of what IP address are assigned at any particular time.

The ISP can be mandated through court order (subpoena) to provide subscriber information to the requesting party. The court order requests that the ISP provide the name and address of the subscriber at a particular IP address at a particular time. In effect, this allows the requesting party to know account information for who was using a computer at a particular time. While this also serves as identification data, IP addresses are also assigned according to general physical location of the computer. Thus, your IP address at home would be very different from your IP address when you are on vacation.

In the *Lasaga* matter, Professor Lasaga used the department's computer to access the illegal materials. When he logged on and accessed the internet, a unique IP address was assigned to that computer by the ISP. That IP and a shared folder the IP address of the computer used to access the illicit materials could be readily identified and traced. There could be no question that it was in fact his computer being used to obtain the illegal material. The question remains, however, was it in fact he who was using the computer? Is there a valid defense that it was someone else using his computer and his credentials when the illegal material was obtained? We will discuss this further when addressing the legal issue of *authentication* below.

EXIF Data

Pictures, too, often contain location information. When using your cell phone, and some digital cameras, the operating system will record information about the instrument used to take the photo, the location at which the phone was taken, and various other attributes. This information is readily accessible, and requires no special forensic tools.

By way of illustration, the picture in Figure 9.1 was taken using a cell phone. By merely downloading the image and opening the "properties," one is taken to a menu containing the details of the background information of the picture. The "details" tab contains the EXIF data. EXIF stands for exchangeable image file format. In essence, when you take a picture, the tool you used to take the picture, be it a camera, cell phone, tablet, or other item, inserts information about the picture into the picture itself. In the case above, the EXIF data contains very specific latitude and longitude information for where the picture was taken.

This background information, or "data about data," is sometimes called "metadata." Metadata is not restricted to pictures. It is found in all types of electronic data. If you have a portable music player, note what appears on the screen when you play your favorite song. Probably the album artwork; perhaps the artist and song title, maybe the number of "stars" you have given it. But that's not what you wanted when you clicked on "play"; you wanted to hear your song. The primary data is therefore the song; the metadata is other data attached to it that goes along with it. As you can see, it can contain some very important information. Sometimes getting to the metadata is as easy as a click. Other times, it takes specialized forensic tools to uncover it.

Figure 9.1 EXIF data, as viewed using Microsoft Windows Photo Viewer.

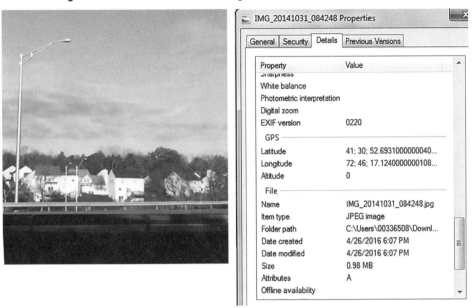

Substantive Evidence

Computer data can provide a wealth of information. Putting aside for a moment the obvious, that is, things that are illegal in and of themselves, what type of data can a forensic search yield?

Internet Searches

Internet search terms are recoverable with computer forensics. As every crime contains both physical and mental elements, internet search terms can be extremely helpful in trying to determine someone's state of mind. A person's list of favorites, or bookmarks, can also be recovered.

Importantly, even if a person has attempted to delete it, items downloaded onto the local computer can be recovered. This is particularly important in those circumstances where the material is itself contraband.

Consider the unfortunate matter of Casey Anthony, who was found not guilty of murdering her 2-year-old daughter. After trial, items came to light that might have shown Casey Anthony using a password protected site at her home, and entering a

Figure 9.2 Example of recovery of search term, using ProDiscover 7 Basic.

```
<html><head><meta HTTP-EQUIV="content-type" CONTENT="text/html; charset=UTF-
8"><title>Google Search: silencers glock model 30 </title><style><!--
body,td,div,.p,a{font-family:arial,sans-serif }
div,td{color:#000}
.f,.fl:link{color:#6f6f6f}
a:link,.w,a.w:link,.w a:link{color:#00c}
a:visited,.fl:visited{color:#551a8b}
a:active,.fl:active{color:#f00}
.t a:link,.t a:active,.t a:visited,.t{color:#000}
```

Google search term "fool-proof suffication [sic]." Shortly thereafter, there is access of a particular MySpace account, a service used by Ms. Anthony but not by others in the house.[12] Ms. Anthony's location in the home was determined by examining cell phone records, and seeing her phone was connecting to a cell tower closest to the home. Forensic recovery of location data and search information might have been more effectively used in the prosecution of the crime.

Private Browsing

Many internet browsers now contain a feature that allows a person to browse "privately." This privacy feature purports to limit the amount of browsing information retained by the computer. These privacy features in a browser made it more difficult for people to recover information from public computers. That is to say, if you have access to a library computer and open the browser, you may have access to login information and passwords for the previous user. Private browsing makes it far more difficult for the casual user to get hold of this information, but does not expunge it so as to prevent forensic recovery. Remnants of the information are still there and are recoverable with forensic tools.

Contrast private browsing with use of the Tor browser. Tor protects anonymity by "bouncing your communications around a distributed network of relays run by volunteers all around the world: it prevents somebody watching your Internet connection from learning what sites you visit, it prevents the sites you visit from learning your physical location, and it lets you access sites which are blocked."[13] Using the Tor browser is the only way to get access to the "dark web," a part of the web that is not accessible by traditional search engines and in which there alleged to be much nefarious activity.[14] Contrary to this not-so-aboveboard usage, Tor browser has been used as a platform for political discussion in geographic areas where such discussion may result in harsh, dire consequences.[15] While it may not be possible to recover the contents of searches conducted using the Tor browser, computer forensics will be able to tell if the Tor browser was used, even if it was run from a portable flash drive.

Contraband

Like in the *Lasaga* matter, computer forensics can aid in recovering materials that are in themselves illegal. Possessing child pornography can be readily proved with

12. Tony Pipitone, "Cops, Prosecutors Botched Casey Anthony Evidence," News 6, November 28, 2012, www.clickorlando.com/news/cops-prosecutors-botched-casey-anthony-evidence.

13. Tor, https://www.torproject.org/press/press.html.en.

14. Wikipedia, "Dark Web," https://en.wikipedia.org/wiki/Dark_web. Last visited May 7, 2016.

15. David Talbot, "Dissent Made Safer," *MIT Technology Review*, April 21, 2009, https://www.technologyreview.com/s/413091/dissent-made-safer/, as cited in https://blog.torproject.org/category/tags/arab-spring.

computer forensics. Similarly, chat logs in which lawbreakers attempt to lure children into harmful circumstances are valuable evidence, even if the "child" is a police officer's online persona. Evidence of drug possession, weapon possession, and identity theft can be found. Any crime facilitated by electronic communication will leave evidence on the computer, and will likely be able to be recovered.

Other Crimes

The list of crimes assisted by computer is nearly endless. Evidence of the following may be found:

- Harassment
- Stalking
- Threatening physical violence[16]
- Hate crimes
- Cyber-bullying
- Extortion

CMOS Data

The CMOS (complementary metal-oxide-semiconductor) is a small piece of memory located on the motherboard of the computer. The CMOS keeps the computer time and date settings, and the BIOS (basic input/output) settings that give the computer its initial boot-up instructions, including storing any password information needed for boot-up. If a computer's time and date settings have been altered, that information can be found here. There is a small battery on the motherboard that keeps power to the CMOS even when the computer is off, so that the time and date settings are maintained at all times. In addition, if a computer is password protected, removing the battery for the CMOS may also clear the stored password, making the computer accessible.

Evidence of Destruction

A client once opined that the only way to destroy evidence contained on a computer hard drive was to "grind it into a fine powder." While there is some truth to that adage, there are other methods of data destruction. As discussed, "delete" does not delete a file, it merely instructs the computer that the area of the memory in which the file is located is available to be written over. Until the data is in fact written over, the data is recoverable. "Wiping," on the other hand, is a process by which data is written over. As discussed below, at its most basic level all computer data consists of 1s and 0s. When a computer is "wiped" the computer memory is written-over

---

16. *See* for example Connecticut General Statue § 53a-182b; Virginia Code § 18.2-152.7:1; Florida Statutes § 784.048.

Figure 9.3 Evidence of "wiping."

```
000018E0   00 00 00 00 00 00 00 00   00 00 00 00 00 00 00 00
000018F0   00 00 00 00 00 00 00 00   00 00 00 00 00 00 00 00

00001900   00 00 00 00 00 00 00 00   00 00 00 00 00 00 00 00
00001910   00 00 00 00 00 00 00 00   00 00 00 00 00 00 00 00
00001920   00 00 00 00 00 00 00 00   00 00 00 00 00 00 00 00
00001930   00 00 00 00 00 00 00 00   00 00 00 00 00 00 00 00
00001940   00 00 00 00 00 00 00 00   00 00 00 00 00 00 00 00
00001950   00 00 00 00 00 00 00 00   00 00 00 00 00 00 00 00
00001960   00 00 00 00 00 00 00 00   00 00 00 00 00 00 00 00
00001970   00 00 00 00 00 00 00 00   00 00 00 00 00 00 00 00

00001980   00 00 00 00 00 00 00 00   00 00 00 00 00 00 00 00
00001990   00 00 00 00 00 00 00 00   00 00 00 00 00 00 00 00
000019A0   00 00 00 00 00 00 00 00   00 00 00 00 00 00 00 00
000019B0   00 00 00 00 00 00 00 00   00 00 00 00 00 00 00 00
000019C0   00 00 00 00 00 00 00 00   00 00 00 00 00 00 00 00
```

with all 1s or all 0s. While that data may not be recoverable, the evidence that a computer has been wiped may be valuable in its own right.

Obtaining the Data

Digital evidence can be found in a number of sources. For example, the "black box" in some cars can keep data about a car's speed, location, and whether brakes were applied in a particular instance. Our focus here will be on the two most prominent types of repositories of digital data: the personal computer and the cell phone. The type of data obtained from either or both can overlap and be common to both, or may be individual to that specific type of computer.

Legal Requirements

The first ten amendments to the United States Constitution are the Bill of Rights. The Bill of Rights governs the relationship between the people and the government. The Fourth Amendment prohibits the government from conducting "unreasonable searches and seizures."[17] That is to say, unless there is a very good reason, the law has a strong preference that a warrant issue before a search takes place. This requires that law enforcement state with particularity the need to seize and search any item, be it your car, your home, or your cell phone. That warrant must be presented to a judge for signature, in a system of checks and balances. And the ability to seize and search is not unlimited, either in scope or duration. Law enforcement cannot look in your dresser drawers if searching for a stolen car. Of course, there are exceptional circumstances in which a warrant may be not required, for example, when property may be readily destroyed or someone's safety is immediately in peril. Likewise, a warrant is not needed if a person consents to the search.

---

17. U.S. Const. amend. IV.

Figure 9.4 Forensic acquisition of an Apple Mac using a write-blocker (located in front of the Mac). Image courtesy of Mr. Paul A Henry, vNet Security, LLC.

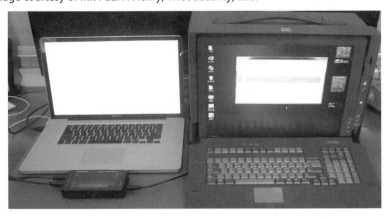

In order to gain access to a person's home for the purpose of seizing and securing a computer, a warrant generally must be obtained. The nature of the items sought on the computer must be stated with particularity. As discussed further below, if during the course of the search evidence of an entirely different crime is found, the search must stop and a new warrant be obtained.[18]

Forensic Recovery

Once the subject electronic device is properly secured, recovery of the data can begin. Although the material herein is presented in terms of a computer, similar steps obtain if the subject computer is a cell phone. Initially, a forensic duplicate of the computer hard drive is prepared. That is to be distinguished from a mere copy of the hard drive. A "copy" will provide only what resides on the hard drive. A forensic duplicate, by contrast, copies data on the hard but also "slack space" and internal operating system data. For example, a copy may not be able to show if the computer's clock has been "adjusted" to reflect a time more suited to the claims of one of the parties. A forensic duplicate will show that. With the proper software, the forensic duplicate can also recover deleted data.

A Word about Computer Operations

Computers are based on a binary system of 1s and 0s. In its most basic form, all computer data is a series of these 1s and 0s. Computers only understand "on" and "off," as represented by these 1s and 0s. This 1 or 0 is the smallest unit of data that a computer understands. It is called a "bit," short for "binary digit." Bits are grouped

---

18. *See* for example *U.S. v. Carey*, 172 F.3d 1268 (10th Cir. 1999). The warrant authorized search for drug distribution evidence. When police found suggestively named picture files, they were obliged to stop the search and obtain a warrant for a search of child pornography.

Figure 9.5 Text displayed in regular text, in hexadecimal format and in binary format. Image via unit-conversion.info.

Input data	The quick brown fox jumps over the lazy dog
Output:	01010100 01101000 01100101 00100000 01110001 01110101 01101001 01100011 01101011 00100000 01100010 01110010 01101111 01110111 01101110 00100000 01100110 01101111 01111000 00100000 01101010 01110101 01101101 01110000 01110011 00100000 01101111 01110110 01100101 01110010 00100000 01110100 01101000 01100101 00100000 01101100 01100001 01111010 01111001 00100000 01100100 01101111 01100111
Output:	54 68 65 20 71 75 69 63 6b 20 62 72 6f 77 6e 20 66 6f 78 20 6a 75 6d 70 73 20 6f 76 65 72 20 74 68 65 20 6c 61 7a 79 20 64 6f 67

together in groups of 8 to form a "byte." A byte is the smallest usable amount of information in computer data. Bytes are broken into 2 groups of 4, to form a hexadecimal, that is, a string of 8 bits reduced to 2 series of 4.

In turn, the hexadecimal code is converted to American Standard Code for Information Exchange (ASCII). There are 128 standard ASCII characters, corresponding to each of the characters on the keyboard. Each ASCII character uses only 7 bits of data. The eighth bit of data is reserved for Extended ASCII, which represents characters, commands, and other non-printable data. In many respects, computer forensics is very much about being able to recover the 1s and 0s, bits and bytes, and other hexadecimal codes to reconstruct and recover data.

In considering computer forensics, one must also be aware of the function of the "delete" key. As you may have guessed, "delete" does not actually remove data from the computer. The computer's operating system contains a File Allocation Table (the "FAT") whose function is to map out and help locate files in the computer's memory. It is sometimes likened to the table of contents in a book. When you delete a file from your computer, that space in the computer's memory is marked by the FAT for writing over. The information itself, that is, the file or picture or song or other date, is not removed. Rather, the space in which the file is located becomes available for use when there is a need to save other information. Thus, the "deleted" data remains in the computer's memory until it is written over by another file. You may have experienced this when you suffered a power outage or the like and thought you lost an entire document, only to have your computer provide you with a "recovered" document. It may not be exactly the same as the one you lost, but it's pretty close. And sure beats losing the whole thing.

Because of the structure of the computer's internal memory, files may be stored in more than one "sector" of memory. Or in only part of a sector. Computer forensics may not be able to recover the entirety of a deleted file, but may be able to recover

Figure 9.6 Partially over-written picture file. Photo by the author.

some portion of it. And that portion may be quite useful in proving, or defending, one's case.

Authentication

Simply stated, authentication is the process of ensuring that an item is what it purports to be. In order for an item to be entered into evidence in a legal proceeding, it must be authenticated. When an item is taken into evidence by law enforcement, it must be marked so that at the time of trial it can be identified and authenticated by the officer who obtained the evidence. If that evidence is a deadly weapon, it must be secured, placed in an appropriate container, and identifying information placed on the container. When the item is sought be introduced at the time of trial, the law enforcement official who obtained the evidence can identify it as the actual item that was found on scene.

These same procedures are in effect for digital evidence. The difficulty is that the evidence likely resides in digital format on a hard drive. Like in the *Lasaga* matter, law enforcement may obtain the computer through a search warrant, but the evidence needed resides on the hard drive of the computer itself. How can we ensure that the digital evidence obtained is actually that which came from the computer?

At the time a computer hard drive is duplicated, or "imaged," the hard drive is run through an algorithm and assigned a "hash" value to ensure its integrity. If done correctly, the hash value of the original hard drive and the hash value of the imaged drive are exactly the same. This is how the drive and its contents are authenticated, and able to be entered into evidence at trial. Anything can be run through an algorithm and assigned a hash value; a single picture, a file, a document, or an entire hard drive. Even the slightest changes to the item will result in an entirely different hash value. There are many different types of hash values, but those generally relied upon are the SHA1 hash and the MD5 hash. These are merely two different ways of obtaining a hash value for a particular item; there are many more. The MD5 hash creates a 32-digit hexadecimal number, the SHA1 hash creates a 40-digit hexadecimal number.

Figure 9.7 Two picture files with one pixel changed will result in entirely different hash values.

SHA1:82C7829C3DDEFC5E48883EF3982FEF0DBA8739E8

SHA1:C5C3E590A0787D3E82BD557735B7FBD6EDF70140

The computer forensic expert can then testify that the item of interest found on the drive she worked on is the same as what was on the accused's computer.

Acquiring the Data

Forensic analysis is in many respects aimed at recovering data that was thought to be deleted. There are a number of available forensic tools that will allow an examiner to recover data. The duplicated hard drive is examined with the use of these forensic tools, and a report is generated. This includes information concerning system data, for example whether a computer's time and date settings have been altered, recovery of deleted or hidden files, and recovery of internet searches. In a criminal matter, the recovery of this data is subject to constitutional limitation on unreasonable searches and seizures. If the warrant authorizing the computer search is limited to searching for evidence of criminal impersonation, and the examiner stumbles across evidence of illegal drug sales over the internet, the search must stop and a new warrant be obtained before searching further.

In conducting forensic data recovery, caution must be exercised. This is not a "do-it-yourself" project. If a person or agency comes into possession of computer hardware, and attempts to view the contents or recover data, in so doing important information may be destroyed. The computer's internal operating systems keeps track of each

Figure 9.8a Recovering deleted files using ProDiscover Basic 7.

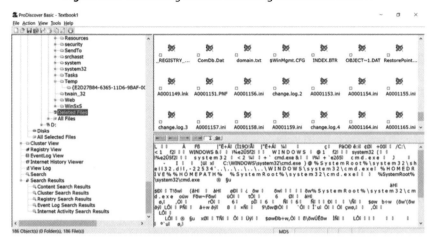

Figure 9.8b Recovery of an internet search in temporary internet files using ProDiscover Basic 7.

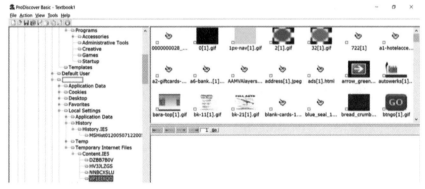

time a file is opened. If the date on which a file was acquired, or last viewed, is important, opening the file destroys that data behind the data. This is often referred to as "metadata." Metadata can make or break a case. More on this later.

First Responders

For the reasons set forth above, appropriately handling the computer or cell phone is key to preserving the data contained on it. In addition to the fact that opening a computer file can affect its metadata, someone having remote access to their electronics may be able to "wipe" the data from the computer or cell phone from a distance. Thus, appropriate measures must be taken to protect the data.

Upon entering the location where the computer equipment is located, law enforcement must secure the scene. At times, an "obliging" defendant may offer to "help" an unsuspecting officer with the computer equipment. Those not so computer savvy may be inclined to take them up on their "kind offer." Needless to say, that is not acceptable. The shrewd defendant may have the technical proficiency to have

In their haste to secure data, first responders are in a unique position to inadvertently destroy data.

created a "time bomb" in their computer, so by a few key strokes the entire hard drive can be wiped clean. Moreover, the defendant may be able to set off that program from a remote location or from their phone.[19]

On the scene, the computer, its contents, and potential loss of data are not the only concern. There will come a point where the computer has to be secured, unplugged, and removed from the scene. Whatever is on the screen will be lost. Therefore, law enforcement is frequently advised to take a picture of the computer display. It is wise to take a picture of the back of the computer as well, so to ensure that the appropriate reconnections can be made in a secure setting. Label all cables, and the locations into which they are inputted.

A Word about ROM and RAM

Generally speaking, computer memory is broken down into two general types, ROM and RAM. ROM is the "read-only memory." This is the permanent, generally unchanging memory in the computer. When you install a program on your computer, that program is stored in the ROM. RAM, or "random-access memory" is the memory that the computer uses to open and create things on-screen. When you shut down your computer, the RAM empties out. The ROM remains unchanged. One frequently hears the advice to regularly backup your data; this is why: If there is a power outage or if the dog gets wrapped up in a cord and unplugs the machine, all your work is lost. Your work was happening in the RAM, and again, it empties out when the computer is shut down. There are some limits on this, as you may have seen. Sometimes your computer is able to "recover" a lost document. This is generally a function of the automatic save feature, which backs up for you, even if you didn't think to do so. This is important for forensic recovery, because generally the information in the RAM will be lost as soon as the computer is unplugged.

Stopping remote access to the computer is also paramount in law enforcement's efforts to secure the computer and the data. Thus, disconnection from the internet is important. Any hard-wired connection to the internet needs to be disengaged. Of course, wireless connectivity must also be considered. Law enforcement may not want to turn off wireless access, for fear of disrupting evidence authentication and potential destruction of data. As such, the computer may be placed in a special container that stops signals from reaching the computer. This is commonly referred to as a Faraday bag. It need not be a bag, but can take the form of a box or another larger container. The idea is that that the bag stops signals from reaching the computer. As such, a suspect cannot use remote access to destroy the computer's contents.

---

19. *See* for example *U.S. v. Lloyd*, 269 F.3d 228 (3rd Cir. 2001), wherein a disgruntled employee planted a computer script that was enabled after his termination and resulted in millions of dollars in damages to the company.

Cell Phone Data

Like computers, cell phones can be seen as containers of data. The data can take many forms, including pictures (with EXIF data discussed above), text messages, and GPS data.

Substantive Evidence

Might your text messages incriminate you? Would you want your significant other scrolling through your text messages? Do you delete your text messages or just let them linger? Have you ever received a picture through text messaging that you downloaded to your cell phone hard drive? Have you ever taken a screen shot of a message that was in an app that "expires" your text messages?

As you can see, text message information can be very valuable and useful in both a criminal and civil context. Text messages can be used to prove the agreement necessary to show a conspiracy. In the matter of the June 12, 2016, mass murder at an Orlando nightclub, the killer was text messaging with his wife while on the shooting rampage. Had it been necessary, might the contents of those text messages be used to prove his intent? His sanity? His plan?

Similarly, the contents of a cell phone, and text messages, were very much at issue in the matter of the December 2, 2015, attack in San Bernardino, California. The FBI obtained cell phones belonging to the killers, but were unable to unlock them. A battle ensued between law enforcement and the phone's manufacturer, as the manufacturer refused to assist in the unlocking of the phone. Eventually, law enforcement was able to access the phone without the manufacturer's assistance.

Consider the types of information that might be on the phone. The text messages between the two killers; perhaps evidence of others in the community that assisted with the attack. Intent, sanity, and conspiracy information. We have yet to see how this all plays out.

Also worth noting is that cell carriers maintain the body of text messages, but only for a short time. The longest time a carrier will hold message is merely days. Legal process must be pursued quickly to have the carrier "hold" the contents of the text messages. However, every text you send is received by someone and may reside on their phone. Perhaps they do not delete their texts as assiduously as you do. And items that you download, be they pictures or texts or documents or the like, remain in your phone's memory and can be recovered.

As an aside, do you have information automatically uploaded from your phone to the "cloud"? Might it be recoverable there? As you may have guessed, it certainly is.

Identification Data

Without regard to data obtained from outside sources as discussed below, the cell phone itself contains data about the identity of its owner. The phone's contacts,

Figure 9.9 Forensic recovery of cell phone data. Image courtesy of the National Computer Forensics Institute.

photos, social media accounts and posts, email, and other settings can provide a wealth of information. If the phone itself is an instrumentality, or object, of a crime this data can help make the case. Consider the case of stolen cell phone. The thief insists that it is their phone. When the phone is turned on, however, a picture of the victim and their significant other appears on screen. This is something of a "smoking gun." There may also be apps connected to third-party cloud-based providers that may yield other important evidence, if obtained by appropriate legal means. This could include ownership information and information about relationships, as in the case of a conspiracy.

Location/GPS Data

Whether or not you are using your cell phone, your phone is continually looking to connect with a cell tower, wi-fi hotspot or both. Your cell phone carrier keeps this data. If you have a smart phone that is GPS capable, that location data is also available.

As your phone seeks a connection, it "pings" off of the closest cell tower. If you are traveling, your call is passed from cell tower to cell tower. The location of these towers is kept by longitude and latitude. Further, every cell tower is comprised of three 120° sectors. If you look at any cell tower, you will see it is basically in a triangular shape, with each side of the triangle covering a 120° area. The cell carrier keeps track

Figure 9.10 Cell tower array seen from below. Note the triangular configuration of the array. Photo by author.

of not only what tower your cell phone uses, but what sector in that tower. With that information, your location at any given time can be tracked, even if you are not using your phone.[20]

In the Casey Anthony matter referred to above, forensic examination showed that a cell phone belonging to Ms. Anthony was "pinging" off of the cell tower closest to her home. Is it possible that she simply left her phone behind when she left the house? Certainly. However, when we combine this information with evidence that a password-protected account which only she could open was accessed, perhaps a different inference can be drawn.

In *U.S. v. Adame*,[21] cell phone location data was used to prove the defendant's location at the time of an arson. In that matter, Adame was accused of setting a fire in his former girlfriend's apartment, after a particularly bad breakup. After a verbal altercation, Adame picked up another woman, Navarette, on the pretense of "going dancing."

> Navarette testified that once they got into her friend's car, Adame told her to stop for gas. Navarette thought the car had enough gas, but Adame insisted they stop for gas anyway. She drove to a gas station and Adame told Navarette to go inside and pay for $10 worth of gas. She did so, while Adame

---

20. The author commends the reader to http://www.zeit.de/datenschutz/malte-spitz-data-retention and https://www.ted.com/talks/malte_spitz_your_phone_company_is_watching?language=en, in which the German politician Malte Spitz obtained records from his cell phone carrier and used that data along with publicly available data to create a visual depiction tracking his location for a 6-month period.

21. No. 15-1196, 2016 WL 3536655 (7th Cir. 2016).

got out of the car and went to the gas pump. She stated that after she paid the cashier, she went back to the car and saw numbers going up on the machine, but did not see the gas nozzle inserted into the car's gas tank. Once the pump reached $10, Adame returned the nozzle and washed the car's windshield with his bare hands (despite the fact that it was winter), and dried his hands with the gas station towel. He then got in the car and put on his gloves.

Navarette testified that when they left the gas station, Adame told her he wanted to "pick up some things of his" before going dancing. He directed her down different streets, and eventually into an alley. He then had her park in the side parking lot of 4258 West 63rd Street. The parking lot was four buildings down from [Adame's former girlfriend's] apartment.[22]

How does cell phone location data differ from an IP address? Is there really a difference?

In addition to other evidence developed regarding the arson, the government called an FBI agent to testify regarding historical cell phone site analysis. The agent testified that while cell site analysis was not precise enough to determine that a person was "absolutely at a specific address," it could determine whether the phone was "in a general area." In ruling on the admissibility of the FBI agent's testimony, the court found

We recently examined the admissibility of historical cell site analysis under Federal Rule of Evidence 702. *See United States v. Hill*, 818 F.3d 289, 295 (7th Cir. 2016). In *Hill*, we noted that "historical cell-site analysis can show with sufficient reliability that a phone was in a general area, especially in a well-populated one. It shows the cell sites with which the person's cell phone connected, and the science is well understood." *Id.* at 298. But we noted that the expert witness should include a "disclaimer" regarding the accuracy of the analysis, and that the witness should not "overpromise[ ] on the technique's precision — or fail[ ] to account adequately for its potential flaws." *Id.* at 298–99.

In this case, Agent Raschke acknowledged that he was unable to tell from his historical cell site analysis whether Adame was at a "specific address" at any point during the evening of the fire. Rather, his testimony was that the data was "consistent with" Adame being present at different locations from January 13, 2012, to January 14, 2012. This testimony adheres to our opinion in *Hill* regarding the proper use of historical cell site analysis in trials. Further, Agent Raschke's specificity in his testimony that the data was consistent with Adame being present in Ortiz's apartment while Navarette was in the parking spot (and inconsistent with Adame being in the parking spot and Navarette being in the apartment) was adequately supported by his observations that cell phones at those two different locations utilized different cell towers, despite their close proximity.[23]

22. *Id.* at 3.
23. *Id.* at 6.

Cell phone location data was used in a similar manner in *U.S. v. Reynolds*.[24] The defendant Reynolds was accused of downloading child pornography. Reynolds alleged that, as he was not the only resident of the home, it could have been one or more of the other residents that downloaded the illegal materials. Forensic analysis of the computer identified the times during which the child pornography was downloaded. As in *Adame*, an FBI agent performed a historical cell site analysis. The analysis revealed that

> ... Cook made calls during the child-pornography download periods that connected to multiple cell towers in Dearborn and Inkster, all located between 10 and 15 miles away from the Reynolds residence; Arica made calls that connected to two cell towers in southwest Detroit, located approximately 20 miles away from the residence; and Andrew made calls that connected to two towers that were 6 to 8 miles away.[25]

Cell phones will not necessarily connect with the closest tower. This is referred to as "coarse granularity." Various factors affect the cell phone's connectivity, so that the phone may not necessarily connect to the best candidate. Nonetheless, it was recognized by the court that the phone is not likely to connect with a tower well out of its sector. With that, Reynolds had also made calls during the period of the downloads. His cell phone connected with

> two towers that were each approximately 1 mile away from his residence. Agent Hess's analysis concluded that, unlike the other three household members, the cell-site data *did not show* that Reynolds was *absent* from the home. Importantly, Agent Hess declined to draw a conclusion about Reynolds's location on the basis of cell-site data alone. The data was used to establish the absence of the other household members from Reynolds's residence. The data was also used to show that Reynolds's absence from the residence could not be demonstrated, permitting an inference that Reynolds was the only one out of four household members who was at the residence during the time child pornography was downloaded onto a desktop computer in that residence.[26]

Note that the opposite is true as well, in that cell phone location data can be used to provide a defense. The *Los Angeles Times* recently published a 6-part "mystery" entitled Framed.[27] It is an interesting read. At its core, it is the story of a wealthy couple who felt they were wronged by a volunteer at their child's school. In order to exact some measure of revenge, the couple was accused of devising a plan to plant illegal drugs in the volunteer's car and have her arrested while at work at the school.

---

24. 626 Fed. Appx. 610 (6th Cir. 2015).
25. *Id*. at 617.
26. *Id*. at 618.
27. Christopher Goffard, "Framed," *Los Angeles Times*, September 3, 2016, http://www.latimes.com/projects/la-me-framed/?utm_source=pocket&utm_medium=email&utm_campaign (last accessed Sept. 15, 2016).

Prior to her trial, the wife agreed to enter a guilty plea. This was part of plan to keep the husband, the breadwinner, from suffering drastic consequences. When the husband went on trial, his defense was that it was all his wife's idea. Therefore, he was not guilty. However, evidence showed that his cell phone "pinged" off of towers by the victim's residence, in the early morning hours the night before the illegal drugs were found in the victim's car. And his defense to this damning evidence? Why, his wife had taken *his* cell phone that evening! Suffice to say, the jury didn't buy it.[28] Nonetheless, this serves as a clear illustration that cell phone data can show where your cell phone is, but not necessarily where *you* are.

Pictures

"Crime scene photos" are not always what they appear. For example, posting pictures on social media of the marijuana you would like to sell. Or standing next to the car you just stole. Needless to say, posts on social media are easily discovered, particularly if the account owner does not bother to restrict those that may view the information. These difficulties arise in civil litigation as well, where unflattering posts affect the credibility of the claimant or the claim itself.[29] The law is still developing regarding whether social media posts are admissible in court and under what circumstances. At this point, it appears that if material is not restricted, it is fair game. If it is in fact restricted, a person may not fraudulently attempt to gain access by pretending they are someone else.

As intimated earlier, one must be careful that the technology does not get ahead of them. You may have a phone feature that automatically uploads pictures to the "cloud." If you have not disabled that feature, your photos can be recovered from the cloud provider. For example, in a matter where someone has pictures of child pornography on their phone and that phone is legally procured by law enforcement. When the phone's owner remotely "wiped" the contents of the phone, that did not destroy the photographs that had been automatically uploaded to the cloud. With proper legal process and identification of IP address information, those contraband photos could be placed in the possession of the phone owner.

EXIF Data

Through EXIF data, people posting pictures to social media sites may inadvertently provide others with the specifics of their location, even if they had hoped it would remain secret.

As discussed above, if your smart phone has GPS capability, it is more likely than not that your camera has geo-location enabled. Every time you take a picture using your cell phone, data about your phone is captured in that phone and embedded in the picture. By examining this data (and you can do so by right-clicking on the picture and viewing its details) one can also obtain the latitude and longitude of where the

---

28. *Id.*
29. *See* Ashby Jones, "The Latest Pitfall for Litigants: That Trove of Facebook Pictures," *Law Blog, Wall Street Journal*, January 28, 2011, blogs.wsj.com/law/2011/01/28/the-latest-pitfall-for-litigants-that-trove-of-facebook-pictures.

picture was taken. Plugging that information into a mapping program will reveal the location where the picture was taken, down to a few feet. Some picture viewing programs will take you right to the map, without the need to input the location coordinates. The details panel will also tell the make and model of the phone or camera taking the picture, the date and time the picture was taken, resolution, and other attributes.

Legal Issues

Authentication of Data

Authentication is the process of ensuring that a piece of evidence is what it purports to be. That frequently requires testimony. Authentication happens frequently through the creator of the evidence, who can testify that it is in fact the item they created. Think about a written document. The author of the document can testify that it is in fact the document they created and has not been altered. Similarly, the recipient of the document can testify that it is in fact the document they received and has not been altered. Other issues present with electronic data.

While an IP address can provide information about the account owner, it does not defeat a claim that someone else was using the device at that time. Threats via text message or instant message may have a valid legal basis, but how can one prove that the alleged actor was *in fact* the true actor? This issue was addressed in the *Tauck* decision. The question was raised regarding who was *in fact* the actual user of the computer at the time the illicit materials were obtained. In addressing the issue, the judge opined that

> there was no way of knowing who was actually logged on a computer at a particular date or time unless the computer is biometric capable. Biometrics is a method of using physical characteristics of an individual to authenticate that person for access to a facility or access to a device such as a computer. Typical biometrics, in secure facilities, include fingerprints or handprints. [This computer] did not have biometric capability.[30]

A similar issue was addressed in the *Lasaga* matter. When suspicions arose that Lasaga was obtaining child pornography on the office computer, the computer expert developed and implemented a "monitoring script" that would notify him of when Lasaga downloaded images to the computer. When so notified, the expert

> then attempted to confirm that the defendant [Lasaga] was in his office. [The expert] did not see the defendant in his office because the defendant's office door was closed, but a student informed [the expert] that he was in fact there.[31]

---

30. *Tauck, supra* at 18.
31. *State v. Lasaga*, 269 Conn. 454 (2004).

Does this leave open the possibility that Lasaga was not in fact the person using the computer at that time? It certainly does. Nonetheless, as evidence is developed and inferences are drawn from that evidence, a juror will arrive at their own conclusion. And such a possibility does not necessarily rise to the level of "reasonable doubt."

How might a non-expert authenticate digital evidence?

Likewise, digital images may be manipulated and changed to suit the needs of the possessor. Authentication of such images is very pertinent to the reliability of the evidence. Courts continue to grapple with such computer generated evidence.[32] Similarly, authentication of social media profiles and the potential evidence they contain are being addressed by the courts.[33] Have you ever met anyone (perhaps you!) with a fake social media profile?

Search and Seizure

The Fourth Amendment to the U.S. Constitution is interpreted to have a strong preference for the issuance of a search warrant prior to conducting a search.[34] Evidence obtained in violation of the Fourth Amendment, that is, by "unreasonable" search and seizure, is not admissible against the accused.[35] Incident to an arrest, police are generally authorized to search a person and their immediate surroundings, to prevent escape and destruction of evidence and for officer safety.[36] Items uncovered as a result of this warrantless "search incident to arrest" may be admissible in court.

During the course of an arrest, police would at times search the contents of the arrested person's cell phone. There developed a split among courts as to whether the results of such a cell phone search were admissible in court as "incident to arrest." Two such matters came to the attention of the U.S. Supreme Court and were addressed in the case of *Riley v. California*.[37] In each case, a person was arrested for a minor violation and a search of their respective cell phones yielded evidence of much more serious crimes. The U.S. Supreme Court unanimously held that the searches of the cell phones were not valid as searches incident to arrest. The police should have obtained a search warrant, and had ample time to do so, before searching the contents of the phone.[38] The Court did mention, however, that there may be "exigent circumstances" justifying the warrantless search of a cell phone.[39] For example, a

---

32. *See* Catherine Guthrie and Brittan Mitchell. "The Swinton Six: The Impact of *State v. Swinton* on the Authentication of Digital Images," *Stetson Law Review* 36 (2006): 661.

33. Julia Mehlman. "Facebook and MySpace in the Courtroom: Authentication of Social Networking Websites." *Criminal Law Brief* 8 (2012): 9.

34. *Mincey v. Arizona*, 437 U.S. 385 (1978); *Katz v. U.S.*, 389 U.S. 347 (1967).

35. *See e.g., Mapp v. Ohio*, 367 U.S. 643 (1961).

36. *See Chimel v. California*, 395 U.S. 752 (1969).

37. 134 S. Ct. 2473 (2014).

38. *Id.* at 2485.

39. *Id.* at 2494.

warrantless search is authorized for "exigent circumstances," that is, those emergency situations where the delay needed to obtain a warrant may result in the destruction of evidence.[40] It remains to be seen whether the possibility of "remote wiping" is a sufficient "exigent circumstance" such that the fruits of a warrantless search can be admitted in court.

Another exception to the warrant requirement is consent. That is to say, if a suspect gives the police consent, or permission, to search the police may do so, and the fruits of that search are admissible into evidence in court.[41] If the police request permission to examine the contents of a cell phone, and consent is given, whatever is found on the cell phone may be introduced into evidence at trial.

The "plain view" doctrine is another exception to the search warrant requirement. Assume a person is pulled over for a minor traffic violation. When the law enforcement officer shines a flashlight on the interior of the car and sees contraband or a weapon, the fact that there was no search warrant involved does not preclude the introduction of those items into evidence at trial later. Similarly, if the police view and read a text message that pops up on the screen of a cell phone, the lack of a search warrant will not prevent that image or text from coming into evidence later.

An interesting issue continues to be litigated regarding whether a court can compel an accused to turn over passwords to encrypted data.[42] Circumstances vary widely, with some courts viewing the provision of the password as a violation of the Fifth Amendment privilege against self-incrimination.[43] Other courts take the opposite view.[44]

Relevance

In order to be admitted into evidence, the evidence must be relevant to the case at hand.[45] That is, it must tend to make the existence of a fact more or less probable, and the fact that it addresses must have some import to the case.[46] Even then, if the evidence sought to be presented causes unfair prejudice, confuses the issues, is misleading, or is "needlessly cumulative," the evidence may be excluded.[47] For example,

---

40. *See* for example *Schmerber v. California*, 384 U.S. 757 (1966); *Kentucky v. King*, 131 S. Ct. 1849 (2011).

41. *See Schneckloth v. Bustamonte*, 412 U.S. 218 (1973).

42. *See* Doug Mataconis, "Court Rules Defendant Must Reveal Computer's Encryption Password," *Outside the Beltway*, July 1, 2014, www.outsidethebeltway.com/court-rules-defendant-must-reveal-computers-encryption-password/ and cases cited therein. *See also* Nathan K. McGregor, "The Weak Protection of Strong Encryption: Passwords, Privacy, and Fifth Amendment Privilege," *Vanderbilt Journal of Entertainment and Technology Law* 12 (2010): 581.

43. *See In the Matter of the Decryption of a Seized Data Storage System*, Case No. 13M449 (E.D. Wisc. 2013).

44. *See U.S. v. Fricosu*, Case 1:10-cr-00509 REB.

45. Fed. R. Evid. 401.

46. *Id.*

47. Fed. R. Evid. 403.

sometimes the law increases the severity of the crime based on the amount of illegal material in possession of the offender. A small amount of marijuana is punished far less harshly than is large amount. The same may hold true for possession of child pornography. Seeking to present evidence far in excess of what is necessary to prove the elements of the crime, though relevant, may still not be allowed.

Electronic Discovery

Electronic evidence has now made its way into civil law, as well. Civil law is the law of lawsuits. Given that substantial communications happen by electronic means, the contents of such communications can be very important to a lawsuit. In the course of a lawsuit, each party is entitled to information about what the other side knows. Unlike the way lawsuits are presented in popular culture, there is rarely an instance wherein one of the parties is surprised by something that comes out at trial. The procedures available in lawsuits are set up such that each party has access to the other party, to interview them on the record (deposition), to answer written questions under oath, and to obtain records in possession of other party. This process is called "discovery."

In the age of electronic communication, providing documentary evidence has become quite complicated. In an employment discrimination case, for example, were there electronic communications among those in charge concerning the employee? If so, they are discoverable. Did one of the parties attempt to delete an incriminating email? Not only may it be recoverable, but it may exist on the company's back-up tapes. Is that discoverable? It most certainly is. The real question, however, is how do we go about retrieving that information?

A brief description of two early cases describes the nature of the issue. *Zubulake v. UBS Warburg*[48] was an employment discrimination case of the sort described above. In that matter, the trial judge found that the defendant company willfully deleted relevant emails. As a consequence, she instructed the jury to assume that the destroyed emails would have been bad for the company and favorable to Ms. Zubulake. The jury awarded Ms. Zubulake more than $29 million in damages. Also of note, the court mentioned that the company's lawyer was partly at fault, for failing to instruct the company to cease any potential destruction of data.

Similarly, the issue in *Coleman (Parent) Holdings v. Morgan Stanley* involved the improper destruction of emails. In *Colman Holdings*, however, counsel certified that they had provided all the requested discovery when they had not. Forensic examination of the computer system revealed overwriting and failure to produce backups. The court found that the company intentionally thwarted discovery. The

---

48. 217 F.R.D. 309 (S.D.N.Y. 2003).

consequence in this case was an instruction to the jury to find that the facts alleged by the plaintiff had been established. The jury awarded nearly $1.5 billion in damages.[49]

Federal Rules of Civil Procedure

This process of discovery can be very lengthy and very expensive. To address these concerns, and to ensure full and fair discovery to all, there are rules governing the process. In the federal system, the Federal Rules of Civil Procedure ("FRCP") address discovery. Electronically stored information, or ESI, is specifically identified as being discoverable. In addition, four of the discovery rules have direct application to discovery of ESI.

The scope and purpose of the rules is set forth in Rule 1. It provides that the rules "should be construed, administered, and employed by the court and the parties to secure the just, speedy, and inexpensive determination of every action and proceeding." While this may sound like a gratuitous statement, the reality of its implications is apparent when read in context to the other rules.

FRCP 16 requires that the parties hold a scheduling conference to address various issues, include electronic discovery. The rule contemplates addressing the disclosure and preservation of electronically stored information, or ESI. There is imputed to the parties, and the attorneys, a duty to advise clients that routine destruction of emails must cease immediately, as soon as litigation is reasonably anticipated. No lawsuit need be filed to trigger the obligation to preserve evidence. Further, the committee notes to Rule 16 provide:

> How is computer forensics different from e-discovery? How are they alike, if at all? Do they overlap?

> Litigation involving complex issues, multiple parties, and large organizations, public or private, may be more likely to need extra time to establish meaningful collaboration between counsel and the people who can supply the information needed to participate in a useful way.

Thus, when an attorney attends a scheduling conference, she needs to be conversant in the client's computer systems, to be able to intelligently discuss the manner in which the discovery of ESI will be provided.

FRCP 26 really gets to the heart of the matter. In addressing the scope of discovery, the rule provides that discovery may be had for anything:

> relevant to any party's claim or defense and proportional to the needs of the case, considering the importance of the issues at stake in the action, the amount in controversy, the parties' relative access to relevant information, the parties' resources, the importance of the discovery in resolving the issues, and whether the burden or expense of the proposed discovery outweighs its

---

49. 2005 WL 674885 (Fla. Cir. Ct. Mar. 23, 2005). The judgment was later reversed on appeal on different grounds. *Morgan Stanley & Co., Inc. v. Coleman (Parent) Holdings, Inc.*, No. CA4D05-2606 (Fla. Ct. App. 4th Dist. 2007).

likely benefit. Information within this scope of discovery need not be admissible in evidence to be discoverable.

Note the "proportionality" rule. Because of the cost of discovery, judges are empowered to limit discovery, based on the amount at stake. A party may object to discovery as being unduly burdensome or costly, or being inaccessible. If a court finds that the information sought is available, but at great expense, the judge may portion out the costs among the parties.

The rule also allows that computer search technologies may have a dramatic effect on the cost of producing ESI. Technology assisted review, or TAR, is a method of "training" a computer program to recognize key words and concepts and to produce documents responsive to the party's discovery request. This has a dramatic cost reduction effect. And to those that would prefer human review, consider the number of mistakes to be made in having a human review or inspect 3,000,000 (or more) emails for a responsive document. One form of TAR is "predictive coding," which uses algorithms, key-word searches, and training documents to accomplish the task. TAR is gaining much wider acceptance in the legal community and is considered by some to be "the law."[50]

Finally, Rule 37 allows for sanctions for failure to provide the requested information. Before imposing any sanction, the court must find that the information sought cannot be otherwise restored or replaced. If it cannot, the court must find that not having the information caused harm to the party requesting it (prejudice). If there is prejudice, the court can order "measures not greater than necessary to cure the prejudice." If on the other hand, the court finds that a party acted intentionally in depriving another party information for use in litigation, the court may:

(A) presume that the lost information was unfavorable to the party;

(B) instruct the jury that it may or must presume the information was unfavorable to the party; or

(C) dismiss the action or enter a default judgment.[51]

Thus, the Federal Rules of Civil Procedure recognize and address the issue of electronic discovery in everyday litigation.

Methods

There are any number of ediscovery solution providers available, some with downloadable standalone products, others with cloud-based solutions. Many provide some method of culling down a large number of documents to a manageable number. Based on that result, there is some mechanism whereby responsive documents may be identified and singled out or otherwise "tagged." Reports with responsive documents can be generated. Problems of admissibility for authentication, and the

---

50. *See* for example *Da Silva Moore v. Publicis Groupe*, 868 F. Supp. 2d 137 (S.D.N.Y. 2012); *Rio Tinto PLC v. Vale S.A.*, No. 1:14-cv-03042 (S.D.N.Y. 2015).

51. FRCP 37.

Figure 9.11 Using Clustify to cull documents.

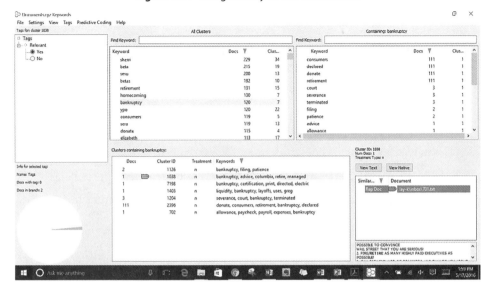

realization that in the copy process some things may be changed, are legal issues best addressed by the courts.

In beginning the process, appropriate search protocols must be established. This may be both a legal and business decision. There must be a mechanism in place for protecting information that should not be disclosed. For example, materials prepared in anticipation of litigation, and documents subject to the attorney-client privilege need not be disclosed, although they may be very relevant. Similarly, protected formulae, customer lists, and other trade secrets need not be disclosed. However, a log must be kept describing in general terms the items that a party holds back from producing. And courts recognize and enforce agreements whereby a party agrees to destroy or return protected information inadvertently disclosed (a "clawback" agreement).

Summary

The ubiquity and pervasiveness of electronic data permeates every aspect of life. That data may well become the object of the attention of law enforcement seeking to prove a case or of the private citizen seeking to defend themselves. Understanding both the practical and legal requirements to obtain and present digital evidence is a necessity for the legal professional. Failure to stay current on the law and the technology may well result in someone being quickly outmoded.

Discussion Questions

1. How might defense counsel claim innocence regarding illegal contraband found on their client's computer?

2. What methods might a prosecutor use to contradict such claims?

3. How is location data in a cell phone different from that in a laptop computer?

4. What legal issues surround search and seizure of computer data?

5. What is EXIF data, and how is it accessed? How is it used?

6. What concerns face first responders, in terms of the destruction of computer data?

7. What is required for computer data to be properly authenticated?

8. What issues surround destruction of digital data? Might it still be recovered?

9. How does "private browsing" effect the accessibility of computer data?

10. What is electronic discovery? How does it differ from computer forensics?

Chapter 10

Eyewitness Identification

Overview

When a witness identifies a suspect as the person who committed a crime, their testimony is direct evidence — the gold standard in criminal trials. The direct evidence of a personal identification is viewed by most people as far more powerful than a wealth of circumstantial evidence, facts which a jury must knit together by inference to conclude that a defendant is guilty.

> This is likely due to the fact, as the Supreme Court has observed, that 'despite its inherent unreliability, much eyewitness identification evidence has a powerful impact on juries'.... All evidence points rather strikingly to the conclusion that there is almost nothing more convincing than a live human being who takes the stand, points a finger at the defendant, and says, 'That's the one!' Yet, studies have repeatedly shown a roughly forty percent rate of mistaken identifications. In spite of this, nearly 80,000 suspects are targeted every year based on an eyewitness identification.[1]

Psychologists have shown through repeated experiments that eyewitness identifications are fragile and fallible. Their accuracy depends, not just on the lighting conditions or whether the witness normally wears eyeglasses, but on the ability of the brain to perceive, store, and retrieve information. Some of the factors that affect memory — such as the length of time the witness viewed the suspect or the time between the viewing and a later identification — are obvious to a juror. These issues have been held to be within the common knowledge of jurors by courts that exclude expert testimony on eyewitness identification problems. Other courts have noted the disagreement about experts on such issues as whether witnesses are subject to suggestions at lineups or photo arrays that change their memory of a perpetrator and have therefore concluded that such testimony is not generally accepted.

But the growing body of knowledge about how an eyewitness's memory of a face can be manipulated by later information or unconscious expectations or prejudices has demonstrated the need for testimony to educate and caution jurors. Some courts

---

1. Henry F. Fradella, "Why Judges Should Admit Expert Testimony on the Unreliability of Eyewitness Testimony," *Federal Courts Law Review* 3 (June 2006): 5.

have begun to admit eyewitness experts. As one court said: "Today, there is no question that many aspects of perception and memory are not within the common experience of most jurors, and in fact, many factors that affect memory are counter-intuitive."[2] Others have used their "bully pulpit" to threaten stern jury instructions cautioning jurors about the fallibility of eyewitness identifications unless local law enforcement adopts better lineup and identification procedures.[3]

Here is but one example of the psychological process of "misremembering." A photograph of two men standing and conversing in a subway car was shown to a wide variety of subjects. One was a black man. The other was white. The white man was holding a razor. Over half of the subjects reported that the black man had been holding the razor. "Effectively, expectations and stereotypes cause people to see and remember what they want or expect to see or to remember."[4]

The recent phenomenon of exonerations of prisoners by newly tested DNA evidence reveals that a majority were convicted based on erroneous eyewitness testimony. The Innocence Project, which successfully freed 197[5] defendants by early 2007, reported that approximately 75% to 85% of the convictions of innocent people were cases of mistaken eyewitness identification.[6]

There is now something of a feud brewing regarding the reliability of eyewitness testimony. One side of the debate is represented by Judge Alex Kozinski. In his preface to an article in the 2015 *Georgetown Law Review Annual Review of Criminal Procedure*, Judge Kozinski opines that, in the criminal justice system, "[a]lthough we pretend otherwise, much of what we do in the law is guesswork."[7] His first example of such "guesswork" is that eyewitnesses are highly reliable when in fact, they are not.

> This belief is so much part of our culture that one often hears talk of a "mere" circumstantial case as contrasted to a solid case based on eyewitness testimony. In fact, research shows that eyewitness identifications are highly unreliable, especially where the witness and the perpetrator are of different races. Eyewitness reliability is further compromised when the identification occurs under the stress of a violent crime, an accident or catastrophic event — which pretty much covers all situations where identity is in dispute at trial. In fact, mistaken eyewitness testimony was a factor in more than a third of wrongful conviction cases. Yet, courts have been slow in allowing defendants to present expert evidence on the fallibility of eyewitnesses; many courts still don't allow it. Few, if any, courts instruct juries on the pitfalls of eyewitness identification or caution them to be skeptical of eyewitness testimony.[8]

---

2. *United States v. Smithers*, 212 F.3d 306, 316 (6th Cir. 2000).

3. *State v. Ledbetter*, 275 Conn. 534 (2005).

4. Fradella, *supra*, p. 15, citing Elizabeth F. Loftus, *Eyewitness Testimony* 22 (1979).

5. Comments of Barry Scheck, The Innocence Project, March 19, 2007, University of Hartford.

6. www.InnocenceProject.org.

7. Alex Kozinski, "Criminal Law 2.0," *Georgetown. Law Journal Annual Review Of Criminal Procedure* 44 (2015): iii.

8. *Id.*

The other side of the debate is summed up nicely by Laurie N. Feldman of the Appellate Division of the Connecticut Office of the Chief State's Attorney. In response to Judge Kozinski, she asserts, among other things, that "there is no reliable basis in social science for generalizations about eyewitness identifications being unreliable." She concludes: "At best, the findings of eyewitness studies are dynamic, nuanced and limited in application to real crimes; at worst, they are policy preferences masquerading as science."[9]

The trend of the cases is to exclude expert testimony that is simply general in nature and not supported by specific scientific studies. However, recent cases have gone to great lengths to explore and understand the present state of scientific evidence on this important issue. Due to the possible prejudice, courts are also likely to ban such experts where there is other evidence identifying the defendant. Where, however, the expert testifies to a matter of high relevance, such as prejudicial lineup procedures, we are likely to see more and more courts admit this testimony. Eyewitness expert testimony is a good example of scientific research that is becoming more and more generally accepted, and has been found to meet the *Daubert* standards of testing, peer review, and error rate. As you will see, courts that have taken the time to review and understand the recent psychological studies into memory will allow such testimony, if the circumstances warrant, even without a *Daubert* hearing. At present, the science regarding memory is so well established and accepted in the scientific community that in many cases such testimony is not considered novel, and a *Daubert* hearing is not required.

Chapter Objectives

Based on this chapter, students will be able to:

1. Identify factors that make eyewitness testimony unreliable.

2. Describe both sides of the "debate" on the reliability of eyewitness testimony.

3. Describe circumstances where faulty eyewitness testimony has resulted in the conviction of an innocent person.

4. Describe the courts' use of scientific studies in determining how to approach eyewitness testimony.

5. Describe how memory works and factors that affect memory.

6. Identify and distinguish system variable and estimator variables, and describe the role of each in eyewitness identification.

7. Have a working knowledge of the various ways that courts allow attorneys to address the potential unreliability of eyewitness testimony.

---

9. Laurie N. Feldman, "The Unreliable Case Against the Reliability of Eyewitness Identifications: A Response to Judge Alex Kozinski," *Quinnipiac Law Review* 34, no. 3 (2016).

Why Is Eyewitness Testimony Unreliable?

Here are some of the psychological phenomena that affect eyewitness identifications:

- Expectations. A person's expectations influence the way he encodes details about an event in his mind. This was the factor at work in the experiment above with the white man holding the razor.

- Exposure to post-event misinformation can lead an eyewitness to encode the information into the original memory. In the case described more fully below, Jennifer Thompson's eyewitness identification of Ronald Cotton as her rapist led to his conviction. Cotton had been apprehended based on an anonymous tip that he resembled the artist's sketch based on the victim's description. Cotton was subsequently exonerated based on DNA, and the real rapist, Bobby Poole, was apprehended. Even though Jennifer Thompson now knows that it was Poole, and not Cotton, who raped her, she stills "sees" the face of Ronald Cotton as her rapist.[10]

- Stress. Contrary to popular belief, the stress of being exposed to a violent crime does not heighten perception and memory. "When people are concerned about personal safety, they tend to focus their attention on the details that most directly affect their safety, such as weapons and aggressive acts, and not on the personal characteristics of the suspect."[11] This has been called the "weapon focus" factor.

- Confidence Level. Finally, the reported confidence level of an eyewitness in his identification does not correlate with the rate of accuracy of his identification. Put another way, the confidence of an eyewitness that he has made a correct identification is not a good predictor of its accuracy, yet this is one factor likely to strongly impress a jury.

While it is frequently assumed that "everyone knows" the effects these factors have on a person's ability to recall, recent scientific advances seem to show otherwise. A good defense lawyer will ask to present evidence regarding the fallibility of human memory, in an attempt to show that the eyewitness identification of the defendant may not be accurate. Historically, courts relied on these factors as being within the common knowledge of jurors, and thus expert testimony was not necessary.

Eyewitness Errors in Exoneration Cases

A significant number of exonerations by DNA evidence were of convictions obtained based primarily on mistaken eyewitness identification. The Innocence Project maintains a website[12] on which it reports the details of the exonerated. Herman

---

10. WGBH Educational Foundation, *What Jennifer Saw*, www.pbs.org/wgbh/pages/frontline/shows/dna.

11. Fradella, *supra* at 13.

12. http://www.innocenceproject.org.

Atkins served more than eleven years of a forty-five year sentence for rape based on an eyewitness identification. The victim was raped at gunpoint in the shoe store where she worked. She identified Atkins after she saw a poster of him in the police station based on unrelated charges. After seeing the poster, she picked Atkins out of a lineup. But she was wrong.

Jennifer Thompson, who wrongly identified Joseph Cotton as the man who raped her when she was a college student, is now an activist for eyewitness reform. Thompson's identification of Cotton exemplifies the problems with lineups. She was raped by a black man who broke into her college apartment in 1984. Throughout the attack, she made a concerted effort to memorize his face. Thompson managed to escape after telling her attacker that she needed a glass of water. When she first spoke with police, she learned that a man with a similar description had committed a second rape shortly after hers. Based on an anonymous tip that a man named Ronald Cotton, who worked at a local seafood restaurant, resembled the composite sketch, the police put his photograph along with five other men with similar appearance, into a photo array.

Thompson was told that the man who raped her might or might not be in the array. She chose Cotton. And then the police said to her "We thought this might be the one," because he had a prior conviction for raping a 14-year-old white girl he knew.[13] From that point forward, Thompson was convinced the face she saw in the photo was the face of her rapist.

A second rape victim identified a different suspect, so prosecutors made the decision to try Cotton for just the rape of Thompson and not to tell the jury about the other rape. The police found a small piece of foam rubber under Cotton's bed that could have matched a piece of foam rubber left in Thompson's apartment. They also found a flashlight similar to the one she described. But there was little forensic evidence — no fingerprints, no hair. Blood typing of semen samples proved inconclusive. However, Cotton had given investigators three different false alibis, which hurt his credibility. Cotton did not take the stand, but his demeanor hurt him anyway. One juror said "he had no change of emotions for eight days. He never changed his facial expression. This was extremely strange to me and, as time went by, I expected to see him react and I never did. And so he seemed more guilty and guiltier and guiltier as time went by."[14] Cotton was convicted and sentenced to life.

> How do you think the factors cited above affected Jennifer Thompson's memory?

While in prison, Cotton became convinced that a fellow inmate — Bobby Poole — was actually the rapist. Poole had bragged of the crime to another inmate and the two looked very much alike. Two years later, Cotton was granted a new trial on the ground that the jury should have heard about the second rape, in which the victim did not identify him. However, she changed her mind and identified Cotton at trial. Poole testified that he did not rape anyone. Cotton was convicted a second time, and sentenced to serve two life sentences. Here is what Thompson said at the second trial about seeing Poole:

---

13. WGHB educational foundation, *supra*.
14. *Id.*

I never remember looking at Bobby Poole, thinking, 'Oh, I've got the wrong person!" I mean, "I've made a huge mistake." Now I remember that never — that never entered my head. It just didn't. Again, I thought, "Oh, this is just a game. This is just a game they're playing."[15]

Eight years later, Cotton's case came to the attention of a law professor, Rich Rosen, who noticed that there was no physical evidence of Cotton in Thompson's apartment. Given the length of time he had been in the house and the nature of the assaults, this surprised him. He asked for testing of the DNA from Thompson's rape. It excluded Cotton. However, it did match Poole, whose DNA had been entered into a database where samples from 20,000 violent offenders were kept.

Thompson's initial identification of Cotton from the photo array had been confirmed by the investigators, who said they thought this might be the one. Thompson admits that she felt a lot of pressure because her eyewitness testimony would be crucial to the trial. Cotton was released, and as of 1997, was working in the lab that had tested his DNA.

Thompson's initial identification of Cotton was reinforced to the extent that even today, she admits that she still sees Cotton's face as her rapist, even knowing now that he was not the man who raped her. Here is the ending from a program produced by Public Broadcasting System station WGBH called "What Jennifer Saw":

Ronald Cotton: What would I say to Miss Thompson? Well, I would like to know how she feels right now. What — what does she have to say in her own words, you know, to me?

Jennifer Thompson: I have to accept the answer that's been given to me and put faith in our system that the DNA tests, the science, tells me we had the wrong guy. I just wish I had some answers. I still see Ronald Cotton. And I'm not saying that to point a finger. I'm just saying that's who I see. And I would love to erase that face out of my mind. I would do anything to erase that face out of my mind, but I can't. It's just — it's in my head. Sometimes it's more fuzzy than others because my mind now says, "Well, it's Bobby Poole," But it's — it's still the face I see.[16]

The Historical Legal Standard for Eyewitness Identification

Recognizing the fallibility of memory and reliability of eyewitness identification is by no means a new phenomenon. Eyewitness's recollections have long been the subject of inquiry by defense counsel. Prior to *Daubert*, courts would exclude expert testimony on the fallibility of memory for a variety of reasons:

---

15. *Id.*
16. *Id.*

- The issue of eyewitness fallibility is within the common knowledge of jurors so no expert testimony is needed.
- The expert is not properly qualified.
- The testimony is general in nature and not supported by specific scientific research.
- Proper cross-examination can reveal any errors in the eyewitness identification.
- Scientific research demonstrating memory issues is not generally accepted.

Questions regarding the admissibility of eyewitness identification testimony, and the reliability of such testimony, began to be addressed by the United States Supreme Court in 1972, with the matter of *Neil v. Biggers*.[17] In that matter, the victim of a rape had given the police a general description of the suspect. Over the course of the next seven months, police brought various suspects to her to view at her home or at the police station. They also showed her between 30 and 40 photographs. She was not able to identify the suspect.

Finally, the victim was called to the police station to identify another person being held. The police attempted to construct an appropriate line-up, but were not able to get enough people to do so. Instead, they conducted a "showup," wherein only the suspect was presented. At the victim's request, the police had the suspect repeat a phrase used in the crime: "Shut up or I'll kill you." After the voice identification was made, the victim identified the suspect.

The question for the Supreme Court was whether the "showup" was so suggestive so as to violate the defendant's due process rights. In making its determination, the Supreme Court developed a "totality of the circumstances" rule. That is to say, even if the showup were suggestive, under all the circumstances was the identification reliable? If so, the identification testimony would be admitted. Interestingly, the Supreme Court also alludes to the fact that the trial court allowed expert testimony regarding the "relative reliability" of a line-up versus a showup.[18]

Totality of the circumstances remained the rule, and was affirmed by the Supreme Court in the case of *Manson v. Brathwaite*.[19] In that case, the Court determined that the "lynchpin" in determining the admissibility of identification testimony is reliability, with the primary concern being misidentification. If the police identification procedures were impermissibly suggestive, the identification could nonetheless be admitted. In so doing, courts should consider and weigh the five factors set out in *Biggers*. The Court determined that the courts should consider and weigh:

- The opportunity of the witness to view the criminal at the time of the crime,
- the witness' degree of attention,
- the accuracy of the witness' prior description of the criminal,
- the length of time between the crime and the confrontation,[20] and,

17. 409 U.S. 188.
18. *Id.* at 200.
19. 432 U.S. 98 (1977).
20. *Id.* at 114, citing *Biggers, supra,* at 199–200.

• the level of certainty demonstrated by the witness at the confrontation.

The level of certainty has long been an issue is courts. As noted by professor Elizabeth Loftus, there is nothing more convincing to a jury than a witness taking the stand, pointing a finger at the defendant and saying "That's the one!"[21] Of course, the follow up question by the prosecutor: "Are you sure?"

As you may have determined by now, certainty is no predictor or reliability. In 2002, a New York trial court, in *New York v. Legrand*,[22] held a pre-trial hearing on the reliability of testimony about errors in eyewitness identification and excluded the expert's testimony, holding it was not "generally accepted" under the *Frey* test, which was still used in New York. It evaluated competing research reports about the correlation between a witness's confidence in his identification and the accuracy of the identification, the impact of post-crime information on his level of confidence, and the effect of weapon focus accuracy.

New York v. Legrand, 747 N.Y.S.2d 733 (2002)

Seeking the admission of expert testimony concerning eyewitness identification, the defendant has requested a pretrial ruling allowing such evidence at his retrial, following the declaration of a mistrial, on a charge of Murder in the Second Degree. Specifically, what is sought to be introduced is the testimony of a psychologist, Professor Roy S. Malpass, Department of Psychology, University of Texas at El Paso, with regard to:

(1) the confidence-accuracy correlation;

(2) post-event information and confidence malleability; and

(3) weapon focus.

For the reasons set forth below, this application is denied.

...

At the outset, in order to avoid any misapprehensions, I believe it is necessary to recognize that these subjects or concepts are commonly defined as follows:

(1) Confidence-accuracy correlation refers to "the relation between the accuracy of an eyewitness's identification and the confidence that [the] eyewitness expresses in the identification"

(2) Postevent information refers to the proposition that "eyewitness testimony about an event often reflects not only what [the eyewitness] actually saw but information they obtained later on" ...

(3) Confidence malleability refers to the proposition that "an eyewitness's confidence can be influenced by factors that are unrelated to identification accuracy"; and

---

21. Elizabeth Loftus, *Eyewitness Testimony* 19 (1979), cited in *Watkins v. Sowders*, 449 U.S. 341, 352, 101 S. Ct. 654, 661, 66 L. Ed. 2d 549, 55859 (Brennan, J., dissenting).
22. *New York v. LeGrand*, 196 Misc. 2d 179, 747 N.Y.S.2d 733 (2002).

(4) Weapon focus refers to "the visual attention that eyewitnesses give to a perpetrator's weapon during the course of a crime."

FACTUAL AND PROCEDURAL BACKGROUND

At approximately 7:00 AM on June 15, 1991, a taxicab driver, Joaquin Liarano, was stabbed to death. Witnesses had heard the cab crash into a parked automobile, observed the victim and his assailant fighting both inside and outside the cab, saw the victim repeatedly being stabbed, and watched as the assailant then took property from the cab and fled the area. Almost immediately, they called 911; police officers responded to the scene, and the victim was taken to a hospital, where later that morning he died.

That same day one of the witnesses was taken to the 26th Precinct and shown photographs; however, he did not make an identification. The next day, that witness, and another witness, were shown additional photographs, but neither witness made an identification. Five days later, on June 20th at the Police Artist Unit, four witness — Pazmino, Foote, Gonzalez and Gomez — were present and a composite sketch was prepared. This sketch was incorporated into a wanted poster and circulated; however, for the next seven years no suspects were identified.

On April 5, 1998, the defendant was arrested in connection with burglary charges within the confines of the 26th Precinct, leading to a detective reopening the 1991 homicide investigation.... Thereafter, on May 9, 1998, Pazmino viewed a photo array, containing the defendant's photograph, and identified the defendant as the person who had committed the 1991 homicide. Then, on August 17, 1998, the detective traveled to Florida, where he displayed the photo array to Foote and Gonzalez. Each selected the defendant's photograph — to Foote it was a "close match"; to Gonzalez, it was similar.

A lineup was held on February 3, 1999, where the defendant was identified by Pazmino, which led to the defendant's indictment in April 1999. Just prior to the April 2001 trial, there was a defense motion seeking permission to call an eyewitness expert. The trial justice reserved decision until after Pazmino's testimony, and then after argument denied the application.

At that trial, Pazmino identified the defendant, as did Foote, noting that he was a "striking match." Gonzalez pointed out the defendant, stating that "it looks like he gained more weight." Other witnesses, including Gomez, did not identify the defendant. Because of the jury's inability to reach a unanimous verdict, a mistrial was declared, and the case was ultimately sent to me for retrial.

...

In addressing the general acceptability of the proffered expert testimony, it is not necessary that I determine whether the eyewitness identification discipline, in its entirety, is generally accepted. Rather, the issue that I must decide is whether the proposed testimony of the defense's witness, Dr. Malpass, which, specifically addresses the confidence-accuracy correlation, postevent information and confidence malleability, and weapon focus, is generally accepted as reliable within the relevant psychological community.

...

[The court determined that the testimony was both relevant and beyond common knowledge.] Thus, having affirmatively dealt with three parts of the *Frye* test, I will now turn to the last outstanding issue under *Frye*, which is whether the proffered expert testimony has gained general acceptance within the relevant psychological community.

I. CONFIDENCE-ACCURACY CORRELATION

First turning to the proffered expert testimony on confidence-accuracy, Dr. Malpass testified that twenty-five years of research has led psychologists to conclude that "there is a statistically significant, but very small correlation" between the confidence eyewitnesses express in the accuracy of their identifications, and the actual accuracy of those identifications. Dr. Malpass further testified that, according to a survey conducted by Saul M. Kassin, V. Anne Tubb, Harmon M. Hosch and Amina Memon, entitled "On the 'General Acceptance' of Eyewitness Testimony Research: A New Survey of the Experts," *American Psychologist* (2001), this relationship between confidence and accuracy is generally accepted within the relevant psychological community. This is based on the finding that 86.7% of the respondents found the proposition that "an eyewitness's confidence is not a good predictor of his or her identification accuracy" to be reliable.

...

Moreover, Professor Leippe testified, "that 'we don't always know what factors are influencing' an eyewitness," and that "a controversy existed in the area of the statistical probability of false identification, the one kind of information inaccessible to the average juror." Thus, it is evident that there is no consensus on the confidence-accuracy correlation.

...

For the foregoing reasons, I conclude that the confidence-accuracy correlation has not yet achieved general acceptability within the relevant scientific community.

II. POSTEVENT INFORMATION AND CONFIDENCE MALLEABILITY

Turning now to the proffered expert testimony on postevent information and confidence malleability: The defense seeks to introduce evidence "regarding studies investigating the impact of various types of suggestion, such as that involved in lineup and photo array procedures and post-identification feedback suggesting the identification was correct, on the witness's recollection of a perpetrator's appearance."

The defense further seeks to introduce evidence "that witnesses exposed to this type of post-event information tend to incorporate it into their memory of the actual event, that witnesses' confidence levels in an identification are higher when they chose a person pointed to by suggestion in an identification procedure, and that witnesses' confidence levels are enhanced by their receipt of post-event information which suggests to them that their initial identification was correct."

… [I]t is noteworthy that, as one study concluded: Failure to warn the eyewitness that the culprit might not be in the lineup resulted in 78% of the eyewitnesses attempting an identification from the culprit-absent lineup. This false identification rate dropped to 33% when the eyewitnesses were explicitly warned that the culprit might not be in the lineup.

Importantly, warning the eyewitnesses that the culprit might not be in the lineup still resulted in 87% of the eyewitnesses making accurate identifications when the culprit was in the lineup, indicating that this instruction does not merely reduce eyewitnesses' willingness to identify someone.

Results of this type reveal that eyewitnesses will simply select the person in the lineup whom they perceive is relatively more similar to the culprit than are the other lineup members if they approach the lineup with the presumption that the culprit is among the set.

. . .

The defense relies on the Kassin survey, according to which, 93.7% of the respondents found the proposition on postevent information, that "eyewitness testimony about an event often reflects not only what they actually saw but information they obtained later on," to be reliable. Moreover, according to the survey, 95.2% of the respondents found the proposition on confidence malleability, that "an eyewitness's confidence can be influenced by factors that are unrelated to identification accuracy," to be reliable.

. . .

More significantly, this apparent general consensus, as to the reliability of these propositions on postevent information and confidence malleability, is undermined by the survey's failure to adequately represent the relevant community of researchers in the eyewitness identification discipline, and the low response rate, of only 34.4%, from the people, to whom the questionnaire was sent. And, of course, as noted earlier, the survey failed to give an adequate description of who the respondents were, and their particular position in the forensic eyewitness identification debate.

For the foregoing reasons, I conclude that this proposed testimony on postevent information and confidence malleability, which includes the "Mock Witness Paradigm" experiment, has not been generally accepted.

III. WEAPON FOCUS

Finally, turning to weapon focus: Dr. Malpass testified concerning the effect of "weapon focus" on the accuracy of eyewitness identifications. Relying solely on Steblay's meta-analysis, he testified that it was generally accepted within the relevant psychological community that "witnesses to a crime in which the perpetrator is displaying a weapon tend to focus their attention on the weapon, and therefore are less accurate in identifying the perpetrator, relative to witnesses in equivalent situations where no weapon is displayed."

...

However, the allegedly general acceptability of this conclusion, which was drawn from Steblay's meta-analysis, does not adequately represent the majority of studies on weapon focus. According to the study, only six of the nineteen tests, which made up the meta-analysis, found a weapon focus effect, even though the mean effect size for the group of tests indicated otherwise.

...

For the foregoing reasons, I conclude that this proposed testimony on weapon focus is not generally acceptable.

LABORATORY vs. REALITY

One of the fundamental underpinnings of the disagreement concerns the question of whether it is generally acceptable for experts to extrapolate their research findings from laboratory studies to the testimonies of actual eyewitnesses in real life criminal events.

... Dr. Ebbesen has written that "not much is known about how these factors [stress, unconscious transference, confidence, retention interval, exposure duration, lineup fairness, racial similarity, and weapon focus] do interact" to affect eyewitness identification, which has, in turn, led to the question, "if not much is known, one wonders how defense experts can draw the sweeping conclusions that they do?"

Even Dr. Malpass testified that the research on the psychological state of witnesses (e.g., stress) is "messy," and therefore, he is unable to determine its application to a given situation. Thus, not only do the stress or arousal levels in the experimental studies dramatically differ from the real world, but there is apparently a lack of understanding of how that difference in stress or arousal levels will affect a witness's accuracy.

...

This is not a debate among experts about a generally accepted principle. Rather, it is a real controversy among the relevant experts concerning whether these principles are generally accepted. Thus, it is the current state of disagreement, and inconclusiveness, and the problems of external validity associated with the research, i.e., transposition to a courtroom setting, that leads me to conclude that this proffered evidence has not been generally accepted within the relevant psychological community.

Consequently, to allow this testimony to be received at trial would require jurors to determine whether the expert evidence is generally accepted as reliable, which is the role of the court, not the jury. And absent general acceptability, as Chief Justice Kaye once noted, "it is not for a court to take pioneering risks on promising new scientific techniques, because premature admission both prejudices litigants and short-circuits debate necessary to determination of the accuracy of a technique."

CONCLUSION

Accordingly, for the foregoing reasons, the defense motion to admit the proffered expert testimony on eyewitness identification is, in all respects, denied.

Jury Instructions

In a 2005 case, the Connecticut Supreme Court in *State v. Ledbetter*, reviewed problems with the lineup that resulted in an eyewitness identification and found them deficient. Although it upheld the conviction,[23] the court ruled that in the future, in any eyewitness identification in which an administrator failed to instruct the witness that the perpetrator might or might not be present, the defendant would be entitled to the following jury instruction:

In this case, the state has presented evidence that an eyewitness identified the defendant in connection with the crime charged. The identification was the result of an identification procedure in which the individual conducting the procedure either indicated to the witness that a suspect was present in the procedure or failed to warn the witness that the perpetrator may or may not be in the procedure.

Psychological studies have shown that indicating to a witness that a suspect is present in an identification procedure or failing to warn the witness that the perpetrator may or may not be in the procedure increases the likelihood that the witness will select one of the individuals in the procedure, even when the perpetrator is not present. Thus, such behavior on this part of the procedure administrator tends to increase the probability of a misidentification.

This information is not intended to direct you to give more or less weight to the eyewitness identification evidence offered by the state. It is your duty to determine whether that evidence is to be believed. You may, however, take into account the results of the psychological studies, as just explained to you, in making that determination.

---

23. *State v. Ledbetter*, 275 Con. 523, A.2d 290 (2005).

Problems with Lineup Procedures

Gary Wells, a psychologist who has conducted experiments in eyewitness identification, described a test of eyewitness identification error in 1993.[24] He summarized his findings as follows:

1. Victims under high stress are more likely to make mistakes in identification.

2. When a victim is not cautioned that the perpetrator might NOT be in the lineup, the victim tends to pick the person who looks the most like the perpetrator rather than concluding that the perpetrator is not present (the relative-judgment process).

3. In archival police lineups, eyewitnesses to actual crimes identified a known-innocent "filler" 24% of the time from live lineups.

4. Words, attitude, and even the presence of police at a line-up can influence the outcome.

An experiment was conducted in which a "staged crime" was shown to 200 witnesses.[25] The "perpetrator" was in the first lineup but not in the second one. Over 50% of the witnesses chose the correct perpetrator in the first lineup and 25% of them chose the person who was looked the most like the actual perpetrator. In the second lineup, in which the correct candidate was not present, 38% of the witnesses chose the next closest person. This showed that witnesses will choose a person who best fits their memory of the perpetrator, rather than choosing no one.

Using "sequential lineups," in which the witness is not able to compare one suspect against another, improves accuracy because the witness is not as tempted to choose the "best" candidate simply to make an identification.

Wells analyzed 30 studies including over 4,000 participants. He concluded that sequential lineups reduce false identifications, but also reduce accurate ones. He found that an administrator who knows which candidate is the suspect may consciously or unconsciously convey that knowledge to the eyewitness. Such feedback can affect whether the eyewitness picks any candidate and the perceived confidence level in the accuracy of his choice. Experiments have shown that the behavior of the administrator of the lineup influenced the outcome. In one experiment,[26] 352 people who made wrong identifications were put into two groups. One group received feedback that confirmed their choice; ("Good, you identified the actual suspect") the other received no feedback. Later, both groups were asked how certain they felt about their identification, and how good a view they got of the gunman's face. The group that were "confirmed" by the administrator were 35% more certain of their identifications than the other group. The first group also were more likely to say they got a clear view of the perpetrator's face.

---

24. Gary L. Wells, "Eyewitness Identification Evidence: Science and Reform," *The Champion* 29, no. 12 (April 2005).

25. *Id.*

26. Wells, *supra.*

This led Wells to conclude that the administrator of the lineup should not know which person in the lineup is the suspect (a "double-blind" administrator). The witness will stop looking for "cues" from the administrator.

Proposed Lineup Reforms

Wells proposed the following reforms:

1. Strict controls over lineups.
2. Double-blind lineups.
3. Sequential lineups.
4. Securing certainty statements from witnesses at the time of the identification.
5. Requiring detailed recording of the witness's statements or response to the lineup.
6. Some sort of probable cause before putting a suspect into a lineup.
7. Training police about eyewitness problems.
8. Improving how "fillers" are selected.
9. Warning instructions to juries.
10. Education for judges.

Are There Enough Experts on Eyewitness Error to Testify?

Wells, whose studies were reported earlier, does not favor using experts to explain the unreliability of eyewitness identifications. He acknowledges that an expert can explain what happens to eyewitnesses statistically, but the expert cannot state that those eyewitness phenomena happened in a particular case. Wells cautions there are only about 50 eyewitness identification scientists who could be potential experts, but well over 77,000 eyewitness identification cases per year. "The cost of expert testimony, and the arbitrariness with which cases will receive this benefit, make this solution ineffective given the magnitude of the problem."[27]

Wells argues instead for improvement in lineup procedures to minimize the rate of false identifications.

Admissibility of Composite Sketches

Many police departments use composite kits that contain hundreds of plastic overlays that can be combined for an eyewitness to examine.[28] These sketches are

---

27. Wells, *supra* at 10.
28. James Lang, "Hearsay and Relevancy Obstacles to the Admission of Composite Sketches in Criminal Trials," *Boston University Law Review* 64 (November 1984): 1101.

often circulated in canvassing for witnesses or suspects and publicized in newspapers or on TV in an effort to locate a suspect.

Traditionally, they were not admissible at trial, as once a suspect is arrested, the eyewitness can appear in person to identify the suspect. When a party tried to admit a composite as evidence of identity, as the prosecution did in the *Grant* case, some courts ruled the sketch inadmissible as hearsay.

Federal Rule of Evidence 801(d)(1)(C) and similar state laws now provide that a prior identification made in person or based on a photograph is admissible as proof of identification at trial if the witness is present in court and subject to cross-examination. The witness is referred to in the rule as a "declarant," indicating that he has "declared" a statement:

> A statement is not hearsay if ... [t]he declarant testifies at the trial or hearing and is subject to cross-examination concerning the statement, and the statement is ... one of identification of a person made after perceiving him."

In 1970 a New Jersey trial court decided that this rule would also permit admitting a composite sketch into evidence provided that the witness upon whose description it was based testifies at trial and is subject to cross-examination.[29]

Based on the consideration of those factors, even an impermissibly suggestive identification procedure might still be admitted into evidence.

Prior to the decision in Daubert, how might defense counsel go about challenging the reliability of eyewitness testimony? How does the Daubert decision change the analysis?

Those factors of witness reliability are still being debated and applied by courts. Defendants will seek to introduce expert testimony regarding the application of those factors, and how the mind processes and make memories. The contention is frequently that the application of the *Manson/Brathwaite* factors is not as self-evident as might appear at first blush. The frailties of human memory may well make this very powerful testimony far less reliable than initially thought, and for reasons outside of common knowledge. To address these concerns, attorneys have sought to introduce expert witnesses to testify about the frailty of human memory. While counsel has long sought to introduce such testimony, historically courts have been loath to allow it, instead relying on the *Manson/Brathwaite* factors. Due to advances in memory science, these concerns are now being addressed in court.

The Modern Approach after *Daubert*

Two courts have taken substantially similar steps to reach similar conclusions with respect to the admissibility in court of expert testimony on eyewitness identification. The court in *New Jersey v. Henderson*[30] commissioned a special master to receive scientific evidence in an attempt to determine if the historical approach described above still made sense in light of scientific advances and the *Daubert* criteria. The

---

29. *State v. Ginardi*, 268 A.2d 534 (N.J. Super. 1970), aff'd, 273 A.2d 353 (N.J. Sup. 1971).
30. 208 NJ 208, 27 A.3d 872 (2011).

Massachusetts Supreme Judicial Court commissioned a study group for the purpose of making recommendations on how to approach eyewitness identification testimony and to address jury instructions. Similar scientific evidence was received by both groups, with similar recommendations reached.

The "Special Master" Approach

The state of New Jersey has led the charge in allowing expert testimony regarding eyewitness identification. The *Henderson* matter has served as an example for other courts. The court in *Henderson* appointed a special master to receive testimony regarding the science and psychology of eyewitness identification so as to better address the legal framework for accepting such evidence. In that matter, Larry Henderson was charged for his role in a murder. The circumstances of his identification by the witness are certainly suspect. Henderson was named as an accomplice in the murder of Rodney Harper. James Womble and his girlfriend Vivian Williams were in William's apartment in during the early morning hours of January 1, 2003. They were drinking champagne and wine and smoking crack cocaine. Their friend James Harper was also present. At some point, both Williams and Harper left the apartment, leaving Womble there alone. Harper returned to the apartment around 2:30 a.m. Soon after,

> two men forcefully entered the apartment. Womble knew one of them, codefendant George Clark, who had come to collect $160 from Harper. The other man was a stranger to Womble. While Harper and Clark went to a different room, the stranger pointed a gun at Womble and told him, "Don't move, stay right here, you're not involved in this." He remained with the stranger in a small, narrow, dark hallway. Womble testified that he "got a look at" the stranger, but not "a real good look." Womble also described the gun pointed at his torso as a dark semiautomatic.

Womble heard Clark and Harper argue in another room and heard a gunshot. Womble walked into the room and saw that Harper had been shot, and Clark was holding a handgun. Clark told Womble, "Don't rat me out, I know where you live." Harper died from the gunshot wound to his chest on January 10, 2003.

Police interviewed Womble the next day. He was not truthful at his first interview, claiming that he was frightened by the threat made against him, and concerned for the safety of his elderly father. Womble was eventually brought to the prosecutor's office, where he was shown a photographic array. The officer administering the array did not know who the suspect was, and the photos were shown sequentially, one at a time. Womble was advised that the suspect might not be in the photo array, and that he was not expected to necessarily identify anyone.

Initially, Womble eliminated all of the photos except two. At that point, the two investigating officers entered the room in an effort to calm Womble down. They advised him to just focus and relax. After this short interaction, the administering officer re-shuffled the photos and presented them to Womble again. At that time, he identified Henderson as the person who had held the gun on him.

The trial court allowed the identification to be entered into evidence. After that, Womble testified that

> He had smoked two bags of crack cocaine with his girlfriend in the hours before the shooting; the two also consumed one bottle of champagne and one bottle of wine; the lighting was "pretty dark" in the hallway where Womble and defendant interacted; defendant shoved Womble during the incident; and Womble remembered looking at the gun pointed at his chest. Womble also admitted smoking about two bags of crack cocaine each day from the time of the shooting until speaking with police ten days later.

> At trial, Womble elaborated on his state of mind during the identification procedure. He testified that when he first looked at the photo array, he did not see anyone he recognized. As he explained, "[m]y mind was drawing a blank ... so I just started eliminating photos." To make a final identification, Womble said that he "really had to search deep." He was nonetheless "sure" of the identification. Womble had no difficulty identifying defendant at trial eighteen months later. From the witness stand, Womble agreed that he had no doubt that defendant — the man in the courtroom wearing "the white dress shirt" — "is the man who held [him] at bay with a gun to [his] chest."

On appeal, it was determined that the investigating officers' presence during the administration of the photo array created an "impermissible suggestive" procedure, pursuant to the *Manson* factors. The question, then, was whether or not the procedure was nonetheless reliable, applying the factors in *Brathwaite*. The matter was ordered to be sent back to the trial court for a hearing on that issue. The state then appealed that finding to the New Jersey Supreme Court. The court ordered an entirely new hearing on the issue of eyewitness identification

> It is ORDERED that the matter is remanded summarily to the trial court for a plenary hearing to consider and decide whether the assumptions and other factors reflected in the two-part *Manson*[...] test, as well as the five factors outlined in those cases to determine reliability, remain valid and appropriate in light of recent scientific and other evidence.

The *Henderson* court discusses the *Manson/Brathwaite* factors, noting first that "[v]irtually all scientific evidence" regarding human memory and eyewitness identification occurred *after* the *Manson* decision. The court concluded that there was a need to "test the current validity" of the current standards on the admissibility of eyewitness identification. To assist the court in making a determination on such validity, the court appointed a retired judge to serve as a special master to hear evidence regarding the validity of eyewitness identification as affected by human memory. Several expert witnesses gave testimony; 360 exhibits were submitted, including some 200 scientific studies.

The court's lengthy discussion regarding proof of misidentification shows the depth of their concern and their interest. They cite court cases as well as police standards indicating that eyewitness identification is one of the least reliable forms of evidence.[31] They describe at length the wrongful convictions obtained through misidentification. Nonetheless, the court remains cognizant of two important factors. First, people who make eyewitness identifications are not lying:

> We accept that eyewitnesses generally act in good faith. Most misidentifications stem from the fact that human memory is malleable; they are not the result of malice. As discussed below, an array of variables can affect and dilute eyewitness memory.

Nonetheless,

> we are mindful of the observation that "there is almost *nothing more convincing* [to a jury] than a live human being who takes the stand, points a finger at the defendant, and says 'That's the one!'" *Watkins v. Sowders*, 449 U.S. 341, 352, 101 S.Ct. 654, 661, 66 L.Ed.2d 549, 55859 (Brennan, J., dissenting) (quoting Elizabeth Loftus, *Eyewitness Testimony* 19 (1979)) (emphasis in original).[32]

The court went on to discuss memory science at length, and the variables that may affect memory. As shown above, the court was most cognizant of the effect of eyewitness identification testimony on a jury. It also understood that memory science makes clear the witnesses' memory could be faulty, and thus there is a need for checks and balances.

The "Study Group" Approach

Massachusetts has followed a similar path, but is noteworthy in the manner in which it was accomplished. Like the New Jersey court in *Henderson*, the Massachusetts Supreme Judicial Court was presented with a challenge to its model jury instruction regarding eyewitness identification. To address that concern, the court commissioned a special study group to make recommendations to the court.

The defendant in *Commonwealth v. Gomes*[33] was convicted of crimes surrounding the slashing of the face of the victim with a box cutter as the victim sat in his car. It appears as though the victim exchanged words with the defendant in a convenience store, but he was not previously known to the defendant. Five days after the attack, the victim went to the police station to review a photo array. The investigating officer had created a pool of 975 photos, which were shown to the victim on computer, 12 per page. Eventually he selected Gomes' picture, stating that he was "110% positive."[34] In a follow-up array of physical photos, in which the defendant was not present, the victim indicated that he did not see the perpetrator.

A few days later the victim went to purchase gas and saw the defendant at the station. A witness who was also with the victim saw the defendant. On returning to

---

31. *Id.* at 885–88 and sources cited therein.
32. *Id.*
33. *Commonwealth v. Gomes*, 470 Mass. 352 (2015)
34. *Id.* at 355.

the car the two conferred and agreed that it was in fact the assailant. They called the police, who stopped the defendant. The victim was called to the scene and identified the perpetrator in a "showup." As stated, the defendant was eventually convicted of various crimes related to the assault.

The defendant appealed his conviction claiming that the model jury instruction on eyewitness identification was inadequate. He asserted that he was entitled to a more robust instruction that would have informed the jurors about the various scientific principles affecting memory, as elucidated in *Henderson*. His request was denied, and the Supreme Judicial Court upheld his conviction. However …

In 2011, the Supreme Judicial Court convened a study group, whose purpose was to "offer guidance as to how our courts can most effectively deter unnecessarily suggestive identification procedures and minimize the risk of a wrongful conviction."[35] In a lengthy report, the committee reviewed considerable scientific evidence on memory, and offered recommendations in accordance with its mandate. They are, in brief:

Are any one of the reforms suggested more important for immediate implementation than another? Why?

- *Courts should take judicial notice of the science behind memory.* In so doing, the *Daubert* standard is met.

- *That best practices for police departments be adopted.* Practices should include such things as double-blind administration of line-ups in which the administrator does not know which person is the suspect.

- *Pretrial hearings.* Courts should conduct pretrial hearings in cases to determine whether, and to what extent, eyewitness identification evidence should be allowed at trial. Interestingly, the way in which the report phrases the recommendation appears to shift the burden. The recommendation seems to be that at such a hearing the side proffering the eyewitness identification needs to show why it should be allowed, rather than the defense seeking to suppress the eyewitness identification testimony.

- *More robust jury instructions.* The recommendation suggests that better jury instructions are needed in order to educate jurors, so that they might better assess the reliability of eyewitness testimony.

The report was delivered in 2013, sadly too late for Mr. Gomes. While his conviction was affirmed, the court took the opportunity to set out a recommended jury instruction, to be used in future cases. Those proposed instructions are set forth in detail below.

How Memory Works

The *Henderson* court described at length the scientific research on memory. The information below is gleaned from their opinion.

---

35. *Supreme Judicial Court Study Group on Eyewitness Evidence Report and Recommendations to the Justices*, submitted July 25, 2013, http://www.mass.gov/courts/docs/sjc/docs/eyewitness-evidence-report-2013.pdf.

The "process of memory" happens in three stages:

- Acquisition
- Retention
- Retrieval

"Acquisition" refers to the initial perception of the event. "Retention" describes the time that passes between the perception of the event and the recollection of the event. Finally, "retrieval" refers to the time when a person recalls stored information.[36] The court-appointed special master observed that

> [a]t each of those stages, the information ultimately offered as "memory" can be distorted, contaminated and even falsely imagined. The witness does not perceive all that a videotape would disclose, but rather "get[s] the gist of things" and constructs a "memory" on "bits of information ... and what seems plausible." The witness does not encode all the information that a videotape does; memory rapidly and continuously decays; retained memory can be unknowingly contaminated by postevent information; [and] the witness's retrieval of stored "memory" can be impaired and distorted by a variety of factors, including suggestive interviewing and identification procedures conducted by law enforcement personnel.[37]

Variables Affecting Memory

The *Henderson* court observed that two types of variables affect memory; system variables and estimator variables. We shall take each in turn. You will notice that there is some overlap among the variables.

System variables are those within the control of the criminal justice system. As such, they should be addressed appropriately by the police and prosecution. They are directed at the method in which a witness identification is made, and go to the makeup and administration of identification procedures.

- Blind administration of identifications. When presenting an array of photos to a witness, the administrator should not be aware of the identity of the suspect (double-blind administration). If the administrator does know who the suspect is, they should shield themselves from knowing where in the photo array the picture appears (blind administration). This will prevent any non-verbal cues to the witness. Even "seemingly innocuous" pauses, gestures, hesitations, or smiles can have an effect on the witness. Thus, blind- and double-blind administration has been described as the single most important characteristic that should apply to photo arrays. Even if only one administrator is available, double-blind administration can be accomplished by placing each photo in the array in its own single folder, and even having a few extra empty folders, and having the administrator observe from a location where he cannot see the photo within.

36. *Id.*, citing Elizabeth F. Loftus, *Eyewitness Testimony* 21 (2d ed.1996).
37. *Id.* at 894–95.

- Pre-identification instructions. When presented with a group of proposed suspects, people are likely to make a selection, even if the suspected person is not one of the choices. This is the concept of "relative judgment." People tend to select the person that looks *most like* the person they remember, even if the actual person is not in the lineup. This can be easily addressed by instructions.

- Lineup construction. The administrators of the lineup, be it in person or photographic, must ensure that the persons involved are relative look-alikes. People are more likely to simply "choose" a person who stands out from the rest.

- Avoiding feedback and recording confidence. Feedback from administrators can increase the confidence of an identification even if it is wrong. The administrator of a photo lineup indicating "yeah, we thought that was the guy" can increase misplaced confidence by a witness. Even feedback from non-state actors can have a confirming effect and increase confidence. In the Massachusetts case of *Commonwealth v. Gomes* discussed above, the victim and the witness conferred with one another before being "certain" of their eyewitness identification. A witness's level confidence in their identification must be recorded before any feedback.

In this same regard, a recent study reported that simply asking someone about their confidence level at the time they pick someone out of lineup, whether in a sequential or simultaneous lineup, improves the efficacy of lineups. The study was conducted using over 300 real lineups. In each case, the witnesses were asked to rate their confidence level as low, medium, or high. Of those cases wherein a suspect was identified, the most high-confidence identifications were of the suspect. The most low-confidence identifications were of "fillers."[38]

What steps can be taken to eliminate system variables? Have those steps changed from the earlier reforms?

- Multiple viewings. The reliability of an identification can be affected by viewing the suspect more than one time. "Successive views of the same person can make it difficult to know whether the later identification stems from a memory of the original event or a memory of the earlier identification procedure."[39]

Again, in the *Gomes* matter discussed above, how many times the witness saw the accused before his arrest matters. Was he recalling the awful event in which he was a victim, or seeing the face of this accused just as he had previously?

- Simultaneous vs. sequential lineups. This issue was left open by *Henderson*. Persuasive arguments exist for each. The defense claimed that relative judgment causes misidentification in simultaneous lineup procedures. The state claimed that sequential lineups were preferable, but noted that recent studies called that into question. The court made no recommendation in this regard.

Interestingly, the same study cited above that asked witnesses to rate their confidence level noted that there was little statistical difference between

---

38. Veronica Greenwood, "Are You Sure That's the Guy?," *Scientific American*, May 1, 2016, http://www.scientificamerican.com/article/are-you-sure-that-apos-s-the-guy/.

39. *Henderson, supra* at 900.

simultaneous and sequential lineups. However, the use of *sequential* lineups produced more confident identifications. So despite the "scientific findings" in *Henderson*, the simultaneous approach may have more usefulness.[40] In exactly what sort of cases it may be more useful, only time and science will tell.

- Composites. These are the drawings of the fabled "sketch artist." Now, such composites can also be computer generated.[41] In this area the science was similarly inconclusive. Aside from a recognition that composites produce "poor results," there was not sufficient evidence to make a determination on whether participating in the making of a composite has an effect on memory.

- Showups. Described by the court as a single-person lineup. The court noted that these are "inherently suggestive." When a suspect is brought to the location of a victim in a police car, and the victim is asked if "that's the one," it's hard to envision a situation more "inherently suggestive."[42] With the proper instruction that this may or may not be the person, a showup is acceptable. However, their reliability is diminished after two hours' post-event.

Estimator variables are those personal to the witness or circumstance, and thus outside of the control of the criminal justice system. While these may not be able to be controlled for, they may have a significant effect on a witnesses' memory and their ability to identify an actor.

- Stress. One may think it intuitive that in a high-stress situation one's senses and awareness are heightened. Scientific research has shown that not to be so. A criticism of this research is that the experiments making this determination are staged and thus not reflective of real life. That is a valid criticism. Nonetheless, such experiments show high stress levels significantly negatively affect a person's ability to recall people and details. In a field experiment, military personnel training in survival techniques were subject to high-stress interrogation. Only 30% were able to identify their interrogators 24 hours later.[43]

- Weapon focus. Return once again to *Gomes* discussed above. He provided an excellent description of the gun held to his chest, but a far poorer description of the person who held it. The presence of a visible weapon can affect the reliability of an identification, particularly if the duration of the event was short.

- Duration. Brief encounters tend to produce less accurate identifications. On the other hand, research indicates the lack of other distractions (see weapon focus, above) is more determinative of the accuracy of the identification.

- Distance and lighting. The greater the distance, and the poorer the lighting, the more diminished the reliability of identification.

---

40. Greenwood, "Are You Sure That's the Guy?," *supra.*
41. *See*, for example, sketchcop.com
42. Although we will address the inherent suggestiveness of first-time in court identifications.
43. *Henderson, supra*, at 904. *See also* Elizabeth Loftus, *The Fiction of Memory*, TED talk, www.youtube.com/watch?v=PB2Oegl6wvl.

What might a defense
counsel do to address
the effects of
estimator variable?
Can the prosecution
adequately counter?

- Witness characteristics. Witness intoxication and own-age bias may have an effect on reliability of identification, but there was not sufficient evidence in *Henderson* to warrant a special jury instruction on the topic.

- Characteristics of perpetrator. If facial features are altered, for example by growing a beard, reliability decreases. This may provide some scientific basis as to why a perpetrator may wear a disguise. Provided of course that the characteristic is not present at the time of the lineup.

- Memory decay. The longer the retention interval, the more memories fade. This decay is not reversible.

- Race-bias. Cross-racial identification is recognized as being particularly difficult, and thus affects the reliability of the identification.

- Private actors outside of the lineup. Private citizens can also have an effect on a witnesses' memory. Information coming to the attention of the witness after the event can be incorporated into the retention and retrieval process. What seems like a very real memory can be outside information that the mind has incorporated into the memory of the event. Newspaper reports, other witness feedback, and the like can affect memory. Even the manner in which questions are asked can create a false memory. For example, after a staged car crash, "witnesses" were asked questions about the scene. The question as to how fast the cars were going when they "hit" each other produced a series of answers. However, when the question was phrased that they "smashed into" each other, more witnesses remembered seeing broken glass on the scene, where there had in fact been none.

- Speed of identification. There is some indication, though not conclusively supported by scientific study, that the speed with which an identification is made is a good indicator of the reliability of the identification.

Juror Understanding

While all the science is impressive, expert testimony on a subject is not necessary if the subject to be addressed simply does not *need* expert testimony. For example, there is no need to elicit expert testimony on the issue that bad lighting results in bad identifications.

Do you think that the
issues raised by the
scientific studies are
within the knowledge
of the average juror,
such that expert
testimony is
unnecessary?

On the other hand, certain matters may seem "intuitive" to the average person (juror). The studies relied upon by the court in *Henderson* indicate that this is not always so. It is those matters that call for expert testimony, so that the jury may property consider. For example, many people think that a high-stress situation enhances their memory, or that they are the sort of person who "never forgets a face." As such, matters involving the reliability of human memory are not within the knowledge of the average juror. Therefore, it is appropriate for expert testimony to assist the jury.

Addressing Issues in Eyewitness Identification

Bear in mind that eyewitness identification is but one piece of evidence in a criminal trial, albeit powerful evidence. Even if a court concludes that eyewitness reliability is valid science and even if it concludes an eyewitness expert was wrongfully denied as a witness, a conviction may still be upheld on appeal due to other overwhelming evidence of guilt. One case that reversed a conviction due to denying an expert involved a bank robbery conviction based almost entirely on the eyewitness identification in court of three witnesses. The Sixth Circuit reversed the conviction in 2002 in *United States v. Smithers*,[44] rejecting the prosecution's argument that cross-examination of the witnesses would have been sufficient to reveal any weaknesses in their identifications.

Does your fingerprint or DNA at a crime scene prove that you committed the crime? Does your cell phone "pinging" off of a nearby cell tower prove that you were in the area? Of course not. Your fingerprint may provide evidence that you were there, but not that you committed a crime. Just because your cell phone was in a certain area it does not mean that you personally were there. How then, can defense counsel address the potential fallibility of eyewitness testimony?

Jury Instructions

One of the major reforms brought about by scientific evidence is a change to the instructions given to the jury at the end of the case, just before their deliberation. They are a powerful tool, again, in part because they are given by the judge and carry the weight of the judicial process behind them.

There are some limits to using only jury instructions to educate juries. As noted in *Guilbert*:

> [R]esearch has revealed that jury instructions that direct jurors in broad terms to exercise caution in evaluating eyewitness identifications are less effective than expert testimony in apprising the jury of the potential unreliability of eyewitness identification testimony...."[Generalized] instructions given at the end of what might be a long and fatiguing trial, and buried in an overall charge by the court, are unlikely to have much effect on the minds of [the jurors].... [Moreover], instructions may come too late to alter [a juror's] opinion of a witness whose testimony might have been heard days before. [Perhaps most important], even the best cautionary instructions tend to touch only generally on the empirical evidence. The judge may explain that certain factors are known to influence perception and memory ... but will not explain how this occurs or to what extent.

Therefore, focused and informative jury instructions on the fallibility of eyewitness identification evidence are best to address the issue.[45]

---

44. *United States v. Smithers*, 212 F.3d 306 (6th Cir. 2000).
45. *Guilbert, supra* at 735.

This lead the court in *Henderson* to call for the adoption of a very specific and focused instruction, taking into account the variables for which they found scientific support. The court in *Guilbert* agreed, noting as such and citing with approval their

> [a]gree[ment] with the New Jersey Supreme Court that the foregoing eight variables "are not exclusive. Nor are they intended to be frozen in time.... [S]cientific research relating to the reliability of eyewitness evidence is dynamic; the field is very different today than it was [three decades ago], and it will likely be quite different thirty years from now.... [T]rial courts [should not be limited] from reviewing evolving, substantial, and generally accepted scientific research. But to the extent ... [that] courts either consider variables differently or entertain new ones, they must rely on reliable scientific evidence that is generally accepted by experts in the community."[46]

The *Henderson* court also expressed particular concern with cross-racial identification. While New Jersey did have case law regarding cross-racial identification, indicating that a special instruction should be given

> only when ... identification is a critical issue in the case, and an eyewitness's cross-racial identification is not corroborated by other evidence giving it independent reliability.[47]

Since the holding in *Henderson*, the following jury instruction is now given, and it is noted that it must be given "whenever there is a cross-racial identification."

> Research has shown that people may have greater difficulty in accurately identifying members of a different race. You should consider whether the fact that the witness and the defendant are not of the same race may have influenced the accuracy of the witness's identification.

Here is the jury instruction proposed by the court in *Gomes*. The court cites the appropriate research at length, and the instruction serves as an excellent synopsis of the research and its application to the law:

> One of the most important issues in this case is whether the defendant is the person who committed [or participated in the commission of] the crime[s]. The Commonwealth has the burden of proving beyond a reasonable doubt that this defendant was in fact the perpetrator of the crime[s] alleged in the indictment[s].
>
> The identification of the defendant as the person who committed [or participated in the commission of] the crime[s] may be proved by direct evidence or circumstantial evidence, or by some combination of direct and circumstantial evidence, but it must be proved beyond a reasonable doubt. If you are not convinced beyond a reasonable doubt that the defendant is the person who committed [or participated in the commission of] the crime[s], you must find the defendant not guilty.

---

46. *Id.*, citing *State v. Henderson, supra*, 208 N.J. at 292.
47. *State v. Cromedy*, 158 N.J. 112, 132.

In evaluating eyewitness identification testimony, it is not essential that a witness be free from doubt as to the correctness of his or her identification of the defendant. However, you, the jury, must be satisfied beyond a reasonable doubt, based on all of the credible evidence, that this defendant is the person who committed [or participated in the commission of] the crime[s] before you may convict him/her.

As with any witness, you must determine the credibility of a witness identifying the defendant as the offender. If you conclude that the witness is not telling the truth regarding the person's identification, you shall disregard that testimony. If you conclude that the witness intended to tell the truth, you must also consider the possibility that the witness made a good faith error in identification. That is, you should consider whether the witness could be honestly mistaken in his or her identification of the defendant.

Human beings have the ability to recognize other people from past experiences and to identify them at a later time, but research has shown that people sometimes make mistakes in identification. That research has focused on the factors that may affect the accuracy of an identification, including the nature of human memory.

Research has shown that human memory is not like a video recording that a witness need only replay to remember what happened. Memory is far more complex. The process of remembering consists of three stages: first, a person sees or otherwise acquires information about the original event; second, the person stores in the brain the information about the event for a period of time until, third, the person attempts to recall that stored information. At each of these stages, memory can be affected by a variety of factors.

Relying on some of the research that has been done in this area, I am going to list some specific factors you should consider in determining whether the identification testimony is accurate.

By instructing you on the factors to consider, I am not expressing any opinion about the accuracy of any specific memory of any particular witness. You, the jury, must decide whether the witness's identification is accurate.

(1) The witness's opportunity to view the event. You should consider the opportunity the witness had to observe the offender at the time of the offense, how good a look the witness had of the offender, the degree of attention the witness was paying to the offender at that time, the distance between the witness and the offender, how good the lighting conditions were, and the length of time the witness had to observe the offender;

ADD ONLY IF RELEVANT TO THE EVIDENCE IN THE CASE:

[IF DISGUISE WAS INVOLVED OR FACE WAS OBSCURED] whether the offender was disguised or had his/her features obscured in some way;

[IF PERPETRATOR HAD DISTINCTIVE FACE OR FEATURE] whether the perpetrator had a distinctive face or feature;

[IF A WEAPON WAS INVOLVED] and whether the witness saw a weapon during the event — the visible presence of a weapon may reduce the reliability of an identification if the crime is of short duration, but the longer the event, the more time the witness has to adapt to the presence of the weapon.

2) Characteristics of the witness. You should also consider characteristics of the witness when the observation was made, such as the quality of the witness's eyesight, whether the witness knew the offender, and, if so, how well, and whether the witness was under a high degree of stress — high levels of stress, compared to low to medium levels, can reduce an eyewitness's ability to accurately perceive an event;

ADD ONLY IF RELEVANT TO THE EVIDENCE IN THE CASE:

[IF DRUGS OR ALCOHOL WERE INVOLVED] whether the witness at the time of the observation was under the influence of alcohol or drugs, and if so, to what degree;

[IF WITNESS AND OFFENDER ARE OF DIFFERENT RACES] and whether the witness and the offender are of different races — research has shown that people of all races may have greater difficulty in accurately identifying members of a different race than they do in identifying members of their own race.

(3) The time elapsed. You should consider how much time elapsed between the event observed and the identification. Generally, memory is most accurate right after the event and begins to fade thereafter.

(4) Witness's expressed certainty. Research shows that a witness's expressed certainty in an identification, standing alone, may not be a reliable indicator of the accuracy of the identification, especially where the witness did not describe that level of certainty when the witness first made the identification.

(5) Exposure to identification information from others. A person's memory may be affected by information the person received between the incident and the identification, as well as after the identification, and the person may not realize that his or her memory has been affected. You may consider whether the witness was exposed to identifications made by other witnesses, to opinions or descriptions given by others, including police officers, or to any other information or influence. Such exposure may affect the independence and reliability of a witness's identification, and may inflate the witness's confidence in the identification.

An identification that is the product of some suggestive conduct by the police or others should be scrutinized with special caution and care. The risk that suggestion will affect the identification is greater where the witness did not get so good a look at the offender, because a witness who got a good look is less likely to be influenced by suggestion.

ADD ONLY IF RELEVANT TO THE EVIDENCE IN THE CASE:

[IF THERE WAS A PHOTOGRAPHIC ARRAY OR LINEUP] An identification may occur as part of the police investigation through the showing of an array of photographs or through a lineup of individuals. You may take into account that any identification that was made by picking the defendant out of a group of similar individuals is generally more reliable than one which results from the presentation of the defendant alone to a witness.

You should consider whether the police in conducting the photographic array or lineup followed established or recommended procedures that are designed to diminish the risk of suggestiveness. If there was evidence that any of those procedures were not followed, you should evaluate the identification with particular care and consider whether the failure to follow the procedure affected the reliability of the identification.

Where a witness identified the defendant in a photographic array [or in a lineup], you should consider the number of photographs in the array [or individuals in the lineup], whether there was anything about the defendant's photograph [or the defendant's appearance in the lineup] that made him/her stand out from the others, whether the person administering the photographic array [or lineup] did know who was the suspect and therefore could not influence the witness's identification, and whether anything was said to the witness that would suggest that the suspect was among the persons shown in the photographic array [or lineup], or that would suggest that the witness should identify the suspect.

[IF THERE WAS A SHOWUP] An identification may occur as part of the police investigation through what is known as a showup, where a suspect is shown alone to a witness. An identification procedure in which a witness selects a person from a group of similar individuals in a photographic array or a lineup is generally less suggestive than a showup, which is to some degree inherently suggestive. You should consider how long after the initial event the showup took place, as a fresh memory of an event that occurred only a few hours earlier may reduce the risks arising from the inherently suggestive nature of a showup.

You should consider whether the police, in conducting the showup, followed established or recommended procedures that are designed to diminish the risk of suggestiveness. If any of those procedures were not followed, you should evaluate the identification with particular care and consider whether the failure to follow the procedure affected the reliability of the identification.

ADD ONLY IF RELEVANT TO THE EVIDENCE IN THE CASE:

[IF THERE WERE MULTIPLE VIEWINGS BY THE SAME WITNESS] You should consider whether the witness viewed the defendant in multiple identification procedures or events. When a witness views the same person in more than one identification procedure or event, it may be difficult to know whether a later identification comes from the witness's memory of the actual, original event, or from the witness's observation of the person at an earlier identification procedure or event.

(6) Failure to identify or inconsistent identification. You may take into account whether a witness ever tried and failed to make an identification of the defendant, or made an identification that was inconsistent with the identification that such witness made at trial.

(7) Totality of the evidence. You should consider all the relevant factors that I have discussed, viewed in the context of the totality of the evidence in this case, in evaluating the accuracy of a witness's identification testimony. Specifically, you should consider whether there was other evidence in the case, direct or circumstantial, that tends to support or not to support the accuracy of an identification. If you are not convinced beyond a reasonable doubt that the defendant was the person who committed [or participated in the commission of] the crime[s], you must find the defendant not guilty.

Cross-Examination

This was the traditional way to test a witnesses' recollection. During cross-examination, an attorney has the opportunity to question a witness about what he saw. A "vigorous" cross-examination was thought to provide the most effective weapon against faulty identification and memory.

While this remains true to some degree, witnesses are frequently quite certain of their identification of the perpetrator. Recall the matter of Ronald Cotton, and the other DNA exoneration cases where an eyewitness was wrong. In each case, the witness was certain of the identification, and was incorrect. Confident testimony by an aggrieved victim is considered credible by a jury.[48] The more confident the witness, the more likely a jury will consider his identification to be accurate.[49] Vigorous cross-examination may actually backfire. As the court noted in *Guilbert*:

> Cross-examination, the most common method, often is not as effective as expert testimony at identifying the weaknesses of eyewitness identification testimony because cross-examination is far better at exposing lies than at countering sincere but mistaken beliefs. An eyewitness who expresses confidence in the accuracy of his or her identification may of course believe sincerely that the identification is accurate. Furthermore, although cross-examination may expose the *existence* of factors that undermine the accuracy

---

48. Veronica Greenwood, "Confident Eyewitnesses Considered Credible," *Scientific American*, December 24, 2015, http://www.scientificamerican.com/article/confident-eyewitnesses-considered-credible/.

49. *Guilbert*, *supra*, at 724.

of eyewitness identifications, it cannot effectively educate the jury about the *import* of these factors.[50]

Similarly, cross-examination can be perceived as gamesmanship; merely one lawyer trying to outdo the other. Attorney questioning of a witness, no matter how scathing, does not bear the weight of an expert witness or a court instruction. Likewise, a witness cannot testify about the effects of weapon focus, accuracy of cross-racial identification, and the like.[51] Cross-examination cannot educate a jury about the significance of those and other factors.

Pretrial Hearings

The *Henderson* court fashioned a remedy in cases where a "system variable" may be at issue. Again, system variables are those that are within the control of the criminal justice system. If a defendant is identified with the intervention of state authorities, and the defendant wishes to question the identification, he may have the benefit of a pretrial hearing outside the view of the jury in order to show that the identification evidence should not be allowed in.

To obtain the hearing the defendant must first show evidence of suggestiveness in the identification procedure that could lead to mistaken identification. If successful, during the course of the hearing the burden is on the state to show that the witness who made the identification was reliable. If that burden is met, the burden again shifts to the defendant to show a "very substantial likelihood of irreparable misidentification." The defendant may cross-examine the witnesses proffered by the state, that is those administering the identification, in an attempt to meet that burden.

When all is said and done, the ultimate determination on whether the identification will be allowed is on the court. The court must look at the "totality of the circumstances," and if after doing so it determined there is a very substantial likelihood of misidentification, it may suppress the evidence. That is, it will not allow the evidence to be presented to the jury. Interestingly, the *Henderson* court also required that if the eyewitness identification evidence is allowed in, the court should provide a tailored jury instruction.

Expert Witnesses

Allowing expert witness testimony on the system and estimator variables discussed in *Henderson* appears to be the modern trend. For example, since the time of the *Ledbetter* and *McClendon* cases cited above, Connecticut has taken the major step of overruling its previous holding, and now expressly allowing expert testimony on the issue of eyewitness identification. Further, it holds that such expert testimony

---

50. *Id.* at 725–26.
51. *Id.*

meets the *Daubert* standard[52] as a matter of law, such that no hearing on admissibility is required.

The case of *State v. Guilbert* involved three significant assaults, two of which resulted in the death of the victim.

> At approximately 11:30 p.m. on October 8, 2004, Cedric Williams and Terry Ross arrived at a bar in New London known as Ernie's Cafe (bar). Before arriving at the bar, Ross had parked his Volvo station wagon in a nearby municipal parking lot. At approximately 11:45 p.m., William Robinson arrived at the bar. About one hour later, as Robinson walked to the restroom, he was shot in the face and suffered a life-threatening wound.
>
> …
>
> Before transporting him to the hospital, the police asked Robinson who had shot him. Robinson either did not respond to the question or stated that he did not know the identity of the shooter.
>
> …
>
> At approximately 12:51 a.m., the New London Police Department received a 911 call about a shooting at the intersection of Hope and Hempstead Streets in New London. Police officers responding to the call found Ross' Volvo station wagon crashed into a tree. Ross and Williams were inside the vehicle, and both had been shot in the head.

Brady Guilbert was apprehended a week after the shootings. He was initially identified as the shooter in the automobile case.

> [The witness Ms. Lashon] Baldwin saw the defendant's photograph in a newspaper and gave a statement to the New London police about the incident at the intersection of Hope and Hempstead Streets. At trial, Baldwin testified to the following. At the time of the shooting, Baldwin and her cousin, [Mr.] Jackie Gomez, were seated in a car parked on Hempstead Street. Baldwin saw a car traveling down Hempstead Street and, as the car reached Hope Street, she heard three "loud pops." The car then came to a stop after hitting another parked car, and the defendant exited through the back door on the driver's side. The defendant was wearing "a black flight [jacket]" and "a black skully hat." Baldwin recognized the defendant and knew him as "Fats" because she had seen him as a "regular customer" in a donut shop where she had worked for more than one and one-half years. Baldwin and Gomez left the area immediately. Shortly thereafter, Baldwin received telephone calls from family members indicating that Williams, who was Baldwin's cousin, had been in the car on Hempstead Street. Baldwin returned to the area and saw Williams' body in the car. Police were present, but Baldwin did not talk to them because she was "upset" and "scared."

---

52. As adopted by Connecticut in *State v. Porter*, 241 Conn. 57, 698 A.2d 739 (1997), cert. denied, 523 U.S. 1058, 118 S. Ct. 1384, 140 L. Ed. 2d 645 (1998).

Gomez gave a statement to the police nine days after the shooting. At trial, he testified to the following. At approximately 1 a.m. on October 9, 2004, Gomez was with Baldwin in the car on Hempstead Street when he heard three gunshots. He looked to see what was happening and saw a car drive up Hope Street and hit another car. A person wearing a "black hoodie" and "blue jeans" exited from the car and wiped the door handle with his sleeve. The person came toward the car that Gomez and Baldwin were in, and Gomez recognized him as the defendant. Gomez knew the defendant because they previously had lived together for "quite some time...." Gomez then left the area but returned upon learning that his cousin, Williams, had been shot. Although police were present, Gomez did not speak to them because he was "in shock."

Note that both witnesses knew the defendant prior to the crimes. This will be an important factor consideration by the court in this case, and in subsequent cases. Certainly, prior knowledge of a person would decrease the likelihood of a misidentification. Regarding the shooting at the bar, however:

Ten days after the shootings, Scott Lang, who had been at the bar when Robinson was shot, saw the defendant's photograph in a newspaper and recognized him as the person who had shot Robinson. Lang then went to the police and gave a statement. At trial, he testified to the following. On the night of the shooting, Lang was waiting in line to use the restroom at the bar when he was shoved against a door and a shot was fired. Lang was "shoulder to shoulder" with the shooter and observed that he was wearing "a black quilted jacket, possibly North Face." At trial, Lang identified the defendant as the shooter.

It appears that the witness Mr. Lang had no prior familiarity with the defendant.

At the time of trial, the defendant's attorneys indicated their intention to call an expert witness to testify to the reliability of eyewitnesses. The prosecution objected on the grounds that the reliability of eyewitness testimony was within the "common knowledge" of the jurors. The prosecution's argument was based in good law at the time. In 1999, the Connecticut Supreme Court held in *State v. McClendon*[53] that the trial court did not err when it refused to admit testimony by expert Michael Leippe, who questioned eyewitness identification and memory retention. It decided that Lieppe's testimony was all common knowledge and would not help the jurors resolve the case.

Leippe testified in general terms about memory retention and the various circumstances that can deter memory and recall. He testified, among other things, that the confidence of any eyewitness does not correlate to the accuracy of observation, that variables such as lighting, stress and time to observe have an impact on accuracy, that leading questions and the repetition

---

53. *State v. McClendon*, 248 Conn. 572 (1999).

of testimony can increase an eyewitness' confidence but not accuracy, that people remember faces best when they analyze many features and characteristics of the face rather than just one, that misleading police questions can alter memories, and that the most accurate descriptions are given immediately after a crime.[54]

The *Guilbert* court felt much differently. It held that the prior rule that expert testimony in eyewitness identification cases is generally inadmissible would no longer be the rule. *Guilbert* cited the *Henderson* case at length. The court held that the following eight propositions satisfy the *Daubert* standard and thus competent expert testimony predicated on these issues is admissible at trial, "[i]n light of the numerous scientifically valid studies cited":

(1) there is at best a weak correlation between a witness' confidence in his or her identification and the identification's accuracy;

(2) the reliability of an identification can be diminished by a witness' focus on a weapon;

(3) high stress at the time of observation may render a witness less able to retain an accurate perception and memory of the observed events;

(4) cross-racial identifications are considerably less accurate than identifications involving the same race;

(5) memory diminishes most rapidly in the hours immediately following an event and less dramatically in the days and weeks thereafter;

(6) an identification may be less reliable in the absence of a double-blind, sequential identification procedure;

(7) witnesses may develop unwarranted confidence in their identifications if they are privy to postevent or postidentification information about the event or the identification; and

(8) the accuracy of an eyewitness identification may be undermined by unconscious transference, which occurs when a person seen in one context is confused with a person seen in another.[55]

Nonetheless, an expert witness in this area is held to the same standards as expert witnesses in other areas. It is entirely up to the discretion of the court to allow or to disallow such expert testimony. The proffered witness must be qualified as an expert. If the court concludes that there is no scientific foundation for his testimony, the testimony may be excluded. Likewise, if the particular issue is in fact within the knowledge of the average juror, the court may exclude the testimony. Thus, a rule

---

54. "Eyewitness Identification Testimony Properly Excluded, Conn. Supreme Court Rules, 3–5," *Mealey's Daubert Reporter* 11 (1999).
55. *Guilbert, supra* at 733–34.

of nearly *per se* inadmissibility has been supplanted with a rule of sound judicial discretion, based on good scientific evidence.

Similarly, the role of the expert witness is to educate the jury in matters outside of their common knowledge. The expert is free to describe the various factors involved in identification and memory, and discuss the science behind it. The expert may not, however, opine as to whether any of those factors effecting memory were in play in this particular case.

In all, the *Guilbert* court found that expert testimony provided the best safeguard in eyewitness identification cases. While jury instructions, discussed above, carry the weight of the court behind them, they cannot explain the intricacies, and those matters that may be counter-intuitive to the average juror, as an expert witness can.

> [R]esearch has revealed that jury instructions that direct jurors in broad terms to exercise caution in evaluating eyewitness identifications are less effective than expert testimony in apprising the jury of the potential unreliability of eyewitness identification testimony. *See*, e.g., *State v. Clopten*, 223 P.3d 1103, 1110 (Utah 2009) (social scientists have found that cautionary instructions are not effective in helping jurors to spot mistaken identifications). "[Generalized] instructions given at the end of what might be a long and fatiguing trial, and buried in an overall charge by the court, are unlikely to have much effect on the minds of [the jurors].... [Moreover], instructions may come too late to alter [a juror's] opinion of a witness whose testimony might have been heard days before. [Perhaps most important], even the best cautionary instructions tend to touch only generally on the empirical evidence. The judge may explain that certain factors are known to influence perception and memory ... but will not explain how this occurs or to what extent." [Citation omitted; internal quotation marks omitted.] *see also* H. Fradella, "Why Judges Should Admit Expert Testimony on the Unreliability of Eyewitness Testimony," 2 Fed. Cts. L.Rev. 1, 25 (2007) ("Jury instructions do not explain the complexities about perception and memory in a way [that] a properly qualified person can. Expert testimony ... can do that far better than [a judge telling the jury about] the results of scientific research in a conclusory manner ... especially since jury instructions are given far too late in a trial to help jurors evaluate relevant eyewitness testimony with information beyond their common knowledge." [Internal quotation marks omitted.]); R. Wise et al., "A Tripartite Solution to Eyewitness Error," 97 J. Crim. L. & Criminology 807, 833 (2007) ("[J]ury instructions lack the flexibility and specificity of expert testimony.... [J]udges' instructions do not serve as an effective safeguard against mistaken identifications and convictions ... [56]

---

56. *Guilbert, supra* at 726–27.

Closing Argument

Another more traditional way to address eyewitness identification testimony is through counsel's closing argument to the jury. Although this remains a viable option, the court in *Guilbert* said it was not sufficient. It is most effective when used in conjunction with expert testimony.

> Defense counsel's closing argument to the jury that an eyewitness identification is unreliable also is an inadequate substitute for expert testimony. In the absence of evidentiary support, such an argument is likely to be viewed as little more than partisan rhetoric. See, e.g., *Forensic v. Birkett*, 501 F.3d 469, 482 (6th Cir.2007) ("The significance of [the proffered expert] testimony cannot be overstated. Without it, the jury ha[s] no basis beyond defense counsel's word to suspect the inherent unreliability of the [eyewitnesses'] identifications."). This is especially true if the argument relates to a factor that is counterintuitive.[57]

Disallow

This is an aspect of pre-trial hearings, discussed above. Judges always have the discretion to disallow the expert testimony if warranted. If it is determined, for instance, that the system variables at issues were handled very badly, a court can prevent the testimony from being heard.

> Finally, in rare cases, judges may use their discretion to redact parts of identification testimony, consistent with Rule 403. For example, if an eyewitness' confidence was not properly recorded soon after an identification procedure, and evidence revealed that the witness received confirmatory feedback from the police or a co-witness, the court can bar potentially distorted and unduly prejudicial statements about the witness' level of confidence from being introduced at trial.[58]

In-Court Identification for the First Time

What happens when the identification of the defendant as the perpetrator happens for the first time at trial, in front of the jury? The United States Supreme Court has not yet addressed the propriety and admissibility of such testimony. However, this may be the next frontier in eyewitness identification testimony. As discussed, the trend is for courts to make close examination of the scientific studies involving identification and memory. Once the science is explored, courts frequently find that the *Daubert* factors have been met: the theories have been tested; they are peer

---

57. *Id.* at 726.
58. *Henderson, supra*, at 925.

reviewed and published; there is a known error rate; there are appropriate standards in place, and; more and more, there is widespread acceptance in the scientific community. Some courts go as far as holding that the science is so well known and accepted, *Daubert* hearings are not required prior to the admission of the expert testimony.

We have seen that multiple viewings of a defendant can confirm a victim's identification, even if that identification is mistaken. We have likewise seen that confident, though mistaken, identifications made as a result of an inherently suggestive lineup. But what of first-time in court identifications?

In *State v. Dickenson*, the Connecticut Supreme Court was called upon to address this question. The background of the matter centers around a robbery that took place in connection with a proposed sale of an ATV. The "sellers" determined to rob the proposed purchasers of their money. At some point, during the course of the robbery, the defendant

> held a gun to [the victim] Weibel's head, threw him against a dumpster near the pickup and said, "You're a dead man." The defendant then shot Weibel in the leg and neck. Weibel was seriously injured but survived. When Lyles later asked the defendant why he had shot Weibel, the defendant replied, "because we didn't get any money."

It was not until one year after the shooting that the victim was presented with a photo array, in an attempt to identify the parties involved. Although the victim was able to identify other participants, he was not able to identify the defendant in that photo array. Ultimately, the defendant was arrested and charged with several crimes.

When the matter came up for trial the defendant's lawyer requested that the court preclude in-court identification. It was claimed that such "in-court identification of the defendant by Weibel would be so highly and unnecessarily suggestive and conducive to an irreparable misidentification of the defendant as to violate the defendant's due process rights under ... the Connecticut constitution."[59]

In ruling that the in-court identification should not have been allowed, the court distinguished between in-court identifications preceded by an unduly suggestive identification procedure and those that are not. The latter includes those circumstances where the prior out-of-court identification is not unduly suggestive, where there has been no out-of-court identification, and circumstances where the defendant was previously known to the victim.

The court applied a two-prong test to identification procedures. First, was the procedure unnecessarily suggestive? Second, if so, under the totality of the circumstances is the identification nonetheless reliable? In ruling, the court notes

---

59. *State v. Dickenson*, ___ Conn. ___ (SC 19385, August 2016).

that the U.S. Supreme Court has not yet passed on whether first time in-court identifications are unnecessarily suggestive. Further, the court pointed out that the question raised is one involving a defendant's due process rights.

> [W]e are hard-pressed to imagine how there could be a *more* suggestive identification procedure than placing a witness on the stand in open court, confronting the witness with the person who the state has accused of committing the crime, and then asking the witness if he can identify the person who committed the crime. If this procedure is not suggestive, then *no* procedure is suggestive. Indeed, the present case starkly demonstrates the problem, in that Weibel was unable to identify the defendant in a photographic array, but had absolutely no difficulty doing so when the defendant was sitting next to defense counsel in court and was one of only two African-American males in the room.

In order to comport with the requirements of due process protection, the court set forth a procedure for instances where in-court first identifications would be made. Initially, the court expressed a preference that nonsuggestive identification procedures occur as soon after the crime as possible. However, if there has been no pretrial identification, and the state intends to present a first-time in-court identification, the state must request the court's permission to do so. The court may allow the in-court identification if it determines that there is no dispute about the identity of the perpetrator or that the ability of the eyewitness to identify the defendant is not at issue.

> If the trial court determines that the state will not be allowed to conduct a first time identification in court, the state may request permission to conduct a nonsuggestive identification procedure, namely, at the state's option, an out-of-court lineup or photographic array, and the trial court ordinarily should grant the state's request. If the witness previously has been unable to identify the defendant in a nonsuggestive identification procedure, however, the court should not allow a second nonsuggestive identification procedure unless the state can provide a good reason why a second bite at the apple is warranted. If the eyewitness is able to identify the defendant in a nonsuggestive out-of-court procedure, the state may then ask the eyewitness to identify the defendant in court.

> If the trial court denies a request for a nonsuggestive procedure, the state declines to conduct one, or the eyewitness is unable to identify the defendant in such a procedure, a one-on-one in-court identification should not be allowed. The prosecutor may still examine the witness, however, about his or her observations of the perpetrator at the time of the crime, but the prosecutor should avoid asking the witness if the defendant resembles the perpetrator. *See United States v. Greene, supra,* 704 F.3d 304 ("if there is a line between resemblance and identification testimony it is admittedly thin" [internal quotation marks omitted]).

...

[A]s a general rule, if the state has conducted a nonsuggestive out-of-court identification procedure and the witness has identified the defendant, even with some uncertainty, the in-court identification need not be prescreened for admissibility and the witness' level of uncertainty at the initial procedure should go to the weight of the evidence.

...

[I]f the state requests ... [a jury instruction regarding the court's disallowing a first time in-court identification] the trial court may provide the jury with an accurate statement of the law, specifically, that an in-court identification was not permitted because inherently suggestive first time in-court identifications create a significant risk of misidentification and because either the state declined to pursue other, less suggestive means of obtaining the identification or the eyewitness was unable to provide one.

Despite the application of the new rule, the defendant's conviction was affirmed, on "other grounds."

The Future of Eyewitness Identification

As we can see, in the arena of eyewitness identification, there are at least two distinct competing forces at issue here. The first is the need for a fair trial, which means that identifications that are suggestive, and thus unduly prejudicial, should not be allowed into evidence.

On the other hand is the need to respect the victim and to provide an opportunity to be heard. Thus, a victim should be afforded the opportunity to take the stand, "point[] a finger at the defendant, and say[] 'That's the one!'" *Watkins v. Sowders*, 449 U.S. 341, 352, 101 S.Ct. 654, 661, 66 L.Ed.2d 549, 55859 (Brennan, J., dissenting) (quoting Elizabeth Loftus, *Eyewitness Testimony* 19 (1979)).

Facial Recognition Technology

Facial recognition technology, whereby a person's face is scanned and compared in a database of known faces, is rapidly advancing. Facial recognition technology became widely recognized as a result of a study done at a football stadium in 2001. Facial recognition scans were done as people entered the stadium. One hundred thousand people were scanned, and as a result some 19 petty criminals were identified. This experiment served as a proof of concept. Such technology was accurate and could be readily employed.[60]

---

60. Joseph Clarke Celentino, "Face-to-Face Facial Recognition Evidence," *Michigan Law Review* 114 (2016).

Since that time, the technology has been advancing rapidly. Algorithms are better, making the technology more accurate. Computer memory can maintain an almost unlimited amount of data. Data is available from public sources, including online social media.[61] More criminal cases involve pictures of people than DNA or latent fingerprint evidence.[62]

What needs to happen to ensure that facial recognition technology meets the admissibility standard of *Daubert*?

One author opines that admission under the *Daubert* standard is imminent. Facial recognition "technology's increasing accuracy and widespread use indicates that facial recognition evidence will soon — if it does not already — satisfy the requirements of the Federal Rules of Evidence." Of course, widespread use and increasing accuracy are not *Daubert* factors. However, these factors point toward *Daubert*, and indicate a potential reliability that comports with the standard. Known error rates have dropped, databases have grown. Since the "football stadium" test referred to above, testing continues, notably by government. The FBI has established the Next Generation Identification database; the Department of Defense seeks to create universal data standards. Government use is common. Thus, testing, error rates, standards, and peer review are in process, with widespread acceptance in the scientific community on its way.[63]

One commentator believes that the facial recognition technology should pass the *Daubert* test and will likely be admissible. However, although

> generally accepted by the scientific community, [i]t has the requisite reliability, but only barely. Until the technology becomes more widespread and accurate, it makes sense to open the door to its admissibility slowly.[64]

Unlike DNA evidence, a technologist could actually do the facial recognition scan right from the witness stand, in real time.[65]

There is little human involvement in facial recognition technology. In fact, some systems are fully automated.[66]

> The precise method of feature extraction will depend on the type of algorithm used, and thus this step may require more or less human input. Generally speaking, these algorithms operate by mapping data points on a subject's face and measuring vectors between these points. The goal of feature extraction is to isolate the "distinctive and repeatable" qualities of an individual's biometric pattern, while ignoring noise and imperfections in the data collected.

Does facial recognition technology remove the "human judgment" element from analysis?

> During pattern matching, the stored templates are compared against all others already stored in the database. "[T]he pattern matching process

61. *Id.*
62. *Id.*
63. *Id.*
64. *Id.*, citing John Nawara, "Machine Learning: Face Recognition Technology Evidence in Criminal Trials," *University of Louisville Law Review* 49 (2011): 601, 604–07 (describing the standards for admissibility of scientific evidence in federal court).
65. *Id.*
66. *Id.*

compares the present sample to multiple templates from the database one-at-a-time, as instructed by the decision subsystem, sending on a quantitative 'distance' measure for each comparison." Pattern matching also introduces a significant possibility of error into the facial recognition process. This is because "distances will rarely, if ever, be zero as there will always be some non-repeatable biometric-, presentation-, sensor- or transmission-related variation remaining after processing."[67]

Welcome to the new frontier.

Summary

Once thought to be an unassailable piece of evidence, eyewitness identification has become the subject of much scientific research and concomitant treatment by the courts. As the workings of human memory become better understood, courts strive to adapt and to implement the results of scientific research to ensure fair trial rights. While the approaches differ, modifications to jury instructions and allowing expert testimony on memory is more and more common.

Discussion Questions

1. What is the "common knowledge" about the validity of an eyewitness identification?

2. How do experts challenge that common knowledge?

3. What experiments have experts done to challenge eyewitness identifications?

4. What were the system variables identified in *State v. Henderson* that affect the validity of eyewitness identifications?

5. How do these differ from the estimator variables discussed in the same case?

6. How did Connecticut change its view regarding expert testimony in *Guilbert*?

7. How might a defendant's attorney attack a witness's eyewitness identification testimony?

8. How does the frequency of eyewitness misidentifications in exoneration cases affect your view of the reliability of eyewitness identifications?

9. What can be done to address system variables and estimator variables? Will that result in better identifications?

10. How might courts address the *Daubert* factors in future eyewitness identification cases?

---

67. *Id.*

Chapter 11

Blood Spatter Analysis

Overview

Blood spatter analysis is based on mathematics and physics, which can be used to determine the velocity and angle with which blood has hit a surface, as well as the direction from which it came. Experts can also determine what type of impact caused the blood, based on the size of the blood drops.

Once these basic facts are known, however, the job of the analyst becomes more complex. There may be blood drops from more than one source that are intermingled. As the analyst attempts to reconstruct the likely position of people and objects, the science of blood spatter analysis moves into a more speculative realm.

In 2009, the National Research Council identified bloodstain pattern analysis as an analysis that requires multiple types of scientific and experience qualifications:

- an appropriate scientific education;
- knowledge of the terminology employed (e.g., angle of impact, arterial spurting, back spatter, cast-off pattern);
- an understanding of the limitations of the measurement tools used to make bloodstain pattern measurements (e.g., calculators, software, lasers, protractors);
- an understanding of applied mathematics and the use of significant figures;
- an understanding of the physics of fluid transfer;
- an understanding of pathology of wounds; and
- an understanding of the general patterns blood makes after leaving the human body.[1]

Needless to say, most blood spatter "experts," particularly those who have gained experience as police officers, lack qualifications in all of these areas. However, today, most courts accept the reliability of blood spatter analysis and allow questions of qualifications to be handled by cross-examination. However, some courts have refused to let experts testify about blood spatter, when the conclusion of the expert seems speculative. Some experts are permitted to testify as to a hypothetical set of facts, but are not permitted to conclusively relate the reconstruction to the defendant.

---

1. NRC Report, *supra*, p. 177.

Blood spatter experts are frequently used when a defendant offers a version of facts, typically one in which the victim was the aggressor, which the blood spatter shows is inconsistent with the facts.

Experts are generally not permitted to testify about experiments they conduct to recreate the crime scene unless the court is satisfied that the conditions are exactly the same. Some police investigators have not been permitted to testify about crime scene blood on the theory that they lack training and experience in blood spatter.

Chapter Objectives

Based on the chapter, students will be able to:

1. Understand and explain how the measurement of blood spatter can identify angle and speed.

2. Explain the difference between low, medium, and high velocity blood spatter.

3. Define cast-off, arterial spurt, and transfer pattern.

4. Explain methods blood spatter experts use to reconstruct events at a crime scene.

5. Explain legal issues with admissibility of blood spatter testimony at trial.

6. Identify the reasoning behind cases that hold blood spatter testimony is reliable and those that hold it is not.

7. Find ways in which blood spatter testimony can refute a defense of self-defense.

8. Explain why the court in *Crawford v. County of Dauphin* admitted some blood spatter testimony and refused to admit other testimony.

9. Discuss the blood spatter issues in the case of Sam Sheppard.

What Is Blood Spatter?

We tend to think that blood spatter (that's spatter, not splatter) evidence is basically a matter of physics. The scientist measures the blood spots, determines the speed by which they were deposited and from what direction, and then can reconstruct the crime.

> Spattered blood is defined as a random distribution of bloodstains that vary in size and that may be produced by a variety of mechanisms. The quantity and size of spatters produced by a single mechanism can vary significantly, depending on the quantity of available blood.... Spatter is created when sufficient force is available to overcome the surface tension of the blood.[2]

---

2. Stuart H. James and Jon J. Nordby, *Forensic Science: An Introduction to Scientific and Investigative Techniques*, 2nd ed. (CRC Press, 2005), 195.

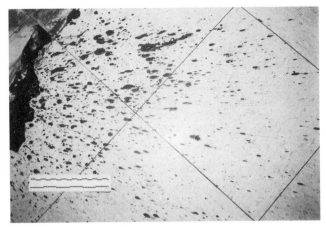

Figure 11.1 Low velocity blood spatter, courtesy Connecticut State Police, Department of Records.

In practice, the process is not so simple or certain. Here is what Louis L. Akin, a licensed professional investigator with 23 years' experience in crime scene reconstruction, says:

> [Blood spatter analysis is the term] most commonly used to describe the process of examining bloodstains at crime scenes for the purpose of determining what happened to who by whom.... However, the procedure is far more akin to a tracker reading a trail sign than a hematologist working in a lab. The analyst interprets the evidence at the scene just as if it were tracks in the same.
>
> In fact, the analyst uses every item of evidence at the scene, as well as the autopsy reports, the police reports, witness statements, and knowledge that he brings to the scene himself such as knowledge about the dynamics of the behavior of blood, knowledge of guns and ballistics, and knowledge of wounds to the human body. The analyst looks at the evidence, and based on what he sees in the blood spatter patterns and other evidence, makes a pronouncement about what he, or she, believes happened. Seen in this light, blood stain analysis is more of an art than a science and is always open to interpretation.[3]

This does not mean that the laws of physics are not important in the reconstruction, but it does mean that if the scientist is influenced by facts beyond the pattern of blood spatter itself, the results are going to be influenced by those facts.

Blood Spatter Analysis — What Is the Scientific Hypothesis?

All blood pattern analysts agree on certain fundamentals based on science and mathematics.

---

3. Louis L. Akin, *Interpretation of Blood Spatter for Defense Attorneys — Part II: Velocities of Blood Spatter*, *Champion* 26 (May 2005): 26, 28–29.

The shape of drops of blood reveals angle of impact and direction of motion.

The size of blood drops reveals speed of travel and likely weapon.

A free-falling drop forms a sphere or ball. The sphere breaks up when it strikes another object or when acted upon by some other force. The angle of impact can be determined by looking at the shape of the drop. A drop of blood striking a surface at right angles will produce a nearly circular stain. As the angle decreases, the stain appears more elongated. Therefore, the shape of blood drops can indicate the angle of impact. The tail of blood spatter drops will point in the direction of travel.

Therefore, just looking at the drops can tell the angle of impact and the direction from which the blood was moving.

Another part of the analysis of blood spatter involves the fact that blood travels through the air at different speeds, depending upon the force with which the blood is expelled from the body. The resulting size of the droplets will determine the speed, and therefore can be linked to the kind of weapon or object that produced the blood flow.

Blood spots are typically grouped into three types, depending on the different velocities at which the blood travels:

- Low velocity stains are produced by a force less than 5 feet per second (fps), which is the force of gravity. The resulting blood drops are 4 mm or larger and circular.

- Medium velocity stains result from a force between 5 fps and 25 fps. They are 1 to 3 mm in size. This kind of stain is commonly believed to result from blunt force trauma such as that caused by a fist or baseball bat.

Patterns can determine source and position of people and objects.

- High velocity spatter is produced by a force of greater than 100 fps. Those stains are generally less than 1 mm. This pattern is usually the result of a gunshot or explosive. As the drops are small, they do not travel far because of the resistance caused by the surrounding air.[4]

The size of the blood drops coupled with the impact pattern they create can help the investigator determine the object that caused the bleeding. In addition to the size of the drops, the analysts must examine the pattern of the drops:

- The first pattern is called "arterial spurt." Arterial spurts are squirted arcs of blood caused by blood being pumped from the left ventricle of the heart. It starts with low pressure, increasing and decreasing with the rhythm of the heart muscle, and generally is concentrated near the victim, who typically dies quickly from blood loss.

- Cast-off patterns typically result from blood being thrown off a weapon. After the first penetration, the assailant may yank the bloody knife blade out of the victim. As he does so, the victim's blood is cast off the blade, forming a pattern on items in the surrounding environment: perhaps a ceiling. Successive stab wounds will add to the number of separate spatter patterns. Analysis of these patterns can help determine how many blows were struck. The total will be one more than the spatter patterns, as the first blow will not create cast-off. The

---

4. Nordby and James, *supra*, 196.

pattern tends to be oval or elliptical as the weapon is swung in an arc. One of the most useful conclusions from cast-off analysis is based on finding a pattern in a place that is inconsistent with the defendant's version of what happened. For example, if the suspect says he was defending himself from attack, but has blood cast-off on the bottom of his shoes, the suspect was probably on his knees bending over a prone victim when the bleeding occurred.

- A transfer pattern occurs when a wet, bloody surface contacts another surface. The resulting pattern may indicate the source of the bloody surface. This is frequently the case with bloody fingerprints or handprints.

Investigators can reconstruct the crime by placing people and things at the scene based on the spatter patterns:

> There is a mathematical correlation between the length and the width of these blood spatters that can be measured. We can then determine what angle they came in at and by using a set of strings and thumbtacks and large protractor we are able to reconstruct the scenes of crimes many times and actually place people where they were at the time they were injured ... or shot.[5]

Of course, most blood scenes are not neat, and a variety of patterns can occur together, combined with smears or swipes as the victim or suspect touches blood, struggles, or wipes blood off on clothes or objects. Spatter patterns can help determine the location of objects, including the parties. For example, if a victim is surrounded by blood, but there is no blood under the body, the victim was probably killed in place.

Clotting time outside the body ranges from 3 to 15 minutes, so spattered clots indicate that time passed from initial bleeding. Coughing of clotted blood may indicate post-injury survival of the victim. Drying begins at the outside of the drop and proceeds inward. Drying time is affected by the surface type, amount of blood present, and climate.[6]

Methods of Determining Patterns

Blood spatter experts testify about the meaning of blood spatter patterns based on three methods of analysis.

- The first is an examination of the crime scene — generally by looking at photographs — and theorizing facts about the crime based on the patterns. This was the method used by Dr. Lee, who testified for the prosecution in the *Grant* case. See *Grant* Appendix.

- The second is by actually visiting the crime scene and measuring the distance from various points at the scene to the blood droplets, and drawing conclusions about the angles of impact and type of weapon.

---

5. *State v. Moore*, 458 N.W.2d 90, 96 (Minn. 1990).

6. Hugh Berryman, *Laboratory Demonstration of the Replication of Blood Stain Patterns*, Southern Institute of Forensic Science, 2005.

- The third method is by attempting to duplicate the blood patterns by experiments. One court opinion[7] criticized the "reenactment" method of blood spatter analysis as follows:

> "… blood spatter experiments are conducted using old blood received from blood banks. The blood is put into plastic bags and containers and dropped to the ground, or plastic bags filled with blood are strapped to one of the 'scientists' before they run into an object, such as a wall…."

This sort of analysis does not take into account factors such as the thickness of a victim's skin, or the presence of a large blood vessel, bone, or hair that may impede or accelerate the loss of blood by the victim. Also, blood spatter will look more circular if it falls on a hard, smooth surface, tending to become ragged at the edges if it falls on a rough or porous surface.[8]

> Blood spatter analysis requires linking the blood pattern to other known facts about the crime.

Is Blood Spatter Expert Testimony Reliable?

Most courts have held that the science of bloodstain shape, size, and movement is reliable in explaining the speed or trajectory of blood. However, expert testimony linking the blood spatter pattern to conclusions about how a crime occurred have sometimes been rejected on a number of grounds:

- the "expert" was not qualified to give an opinion. This has occurred most frequently when the expert was a police officer or criminologist without formal training.
- the opinion was speculative concerning the positions of people at the crime scene.
- the "expert" conducted his own experiment in attempting to reconstruct the crime, which went beyond testimony about the scene itself.

Reliability Rulings

A Texas court in 2004 concluded that the trial court erred in holding that blood spatter analysis was sufficiently reliable, in the absence of any testimony concerning the validity of the scientific techniques or whether they had been verified. On appeal, the court acknowledged that the parties had conducted a hearing on the testimony outside the jury's hearing, but said it was restricted to the qualifications of the expert, not the reliability of blood spatter testing itself. The court stated the test of reliability in Texas as follows:

> To be considered reliable, evidence derived from a scientific theory must satisfy three criteria:
>
> - The underlying scientific theory must be valid;
> - The technique applying the theory must be valid; and

---

7. *Idaho v. Rogers*, 812 P.2d 1208, 1216 (Id. 1991).
8. James and Nordby, *supra*, 192.

- The technique must have been properly applied on the occasion in question.

… This three-criteria test is not limited to novel scientific evidence; it applies to all scientific evidence…. The proponent of the scientific evidence has the burden to prove its reliability by clear and convincing evidence.[9]

The court reviewed cases from around the country and prior *Daubert* hearings on blood spatter evidence. It decided to take judicial notice of the scientific reliability of blood spatter testimony:

[T]he reliability of a scientific theory or technique can be judicially noticed in three ways: (1) when it is a matter of common knowledge, (2) when widely available court decisions show that reliability has been litigated elsewhere in fact-finding forums to a degree sufficient for the appellate court to conclude that reliability is well-established, and (3) when a prior determination of reliability has been made by an appellate court whose pronouncements are binding in the jurisdiction.[10]

In reviewing court decisions that had determined reliability, the court explained the scientific basis for bloodstain interpretation:

The geometric Blood Stain Interpretation is a method used to reconstruct the scene of the crime. Blood stains are uniform in character and conform to the laws of inertia, centrifugal force and physics. Study of the blood pattern along with its size and shape helps determine the source of the blood and any movement that might have occurred after the bloodshed began, including subsequent violent attacks upon the victim.[11]

As stated in the overview, the National Research Council report in 2009 cautioned that bloodstain analysis requires scientific knowledge in many areas:

- an appropriate scientific education;
- knowledge of the terminology employed (e.g., angle of impact, arterial spurting, back spatter, cast-off pattern);
- an understanding of the limitations of the measurement tools used to make bloodstain pattern measurements (e.g., calculators, software, lasers, protractors);
- an understanding of applied mathematics and the use of significant figures;
- an understanding of the physics of fluid transfer;
- an understanding of pathology of wounds; and
- an understanding of the general patterns blood makes after leaving the human body.[12]

---

9. *Holmes v. Texas*, 135 S.W.3d 178, 195 (Tex. App. 2004).
10. *Id.* at 187.
11. *Id.*
12. NRC Report, p. 177.

Understandably, then, the issue over admitting an expert often turns on the expert's qualifications. Because police crime scene investigators have years of experience processing crime scenes does not necessarily translate into all the required scientific expertise. The NRC specifically stated that experience is not a substitute for scientific education: "This emphasis on experience over scientific foundations seems misguided, given the importance of rigorous and objective hypothesis testing and the complex nature of fluid dynamics. In general, the opinions of bloodstain pattern analysts are more subjective than scientific."[13]

The NRC Report emphasized that, while some aspects of bloodstain pattern analysis can be scientifically proven, for example, the rate of bloodflow and the resulting spatter patterns, "some experts extrapolate far beyond what can be supported ... [E]xtra care must be given to the way in which the analyses are presented in court. The uncertainties associated with bloodstain pattern analysis are enormous."[14]

"The uncertainties associated with bloodstain pattern analysis are enormous."

Courts have agreed with the NRC Report about the reliability of all bloodstain analysis. Some judges caution that blood spatter testimony may not be as "scientific" as its proponents claim. For example, in *Idaho v. Rogers*,[15] the dissent stated: "If one reviews an article on blood spatter, it becomes quite clear that this is a new science in need of further research before it may be properly relied upon in a court of law. Note that in 1983, an article on the subject concluded that '[b]ackwards spatter of blood from gunshot wounds is a complex phenomenon which we do not presently understand completely.' ... Some experts have even testified that back spatter of blood from gunshot wounds does not exist."[16]

Bloodstain Analysis in Crime Reconstruction

The court in *Holmes v. Texas* reviewed cases around the country and found no court that had held blood spatter analysis to be unreliable. However, courts have excluded blood spatter experts and have held blood spatter analysis inadmissible *as applied*. In particular, courts have refused to admit expert conclusions or opinions, sometimes based on the expert's lack of qualifications and sometimes based on his experiments with bloodstains. For example, in *Franco v. Texas*,[17] the court held a police officer was not qualified to testify about the blood spatter in relation to the defendant's actions. In that case, a police officer testified that the blood spatter in the case showed that Franco was the aggressor and did not act in self-defense. The court stated:

> We can envision some circumstances where the trier of fact may quite properly be aided by some evidence of blood spatter analysis, but we are dubious of the claim in this record that blood spatter evidence can determine

13. *Id.* at 178.
14. *Id.*
15. 812 P.2d 1208 (Ida. 1991).
16. *Id.* at 1216.
17. *Franco v.* Texas, 25 S.W.3d 26 (Tex. App. 2000).

the aftermath of a violent incident of bloodshed and to try to determine the location of individuals before, during and after bloodshed and to try to determine, perhaps, a sequence of events that occurred based upon the bloodstain evidence at the scene.[18]

In this case, Carl, the victim, had been beaten with a cast iron skillet and stabbed seven or more times. The police arrested the defendant, Franco, based on a truck that had been stolen from the victim.

At the police station, Franco made a statement which was tape recorded. Franco said that Carl picked him up on the Andrews Highway and offered him a ride that Saturday night. They drove to Carl's home and went inside. Inside, Carl asked Franco to come to his bedroom where he attempted to take Franco's jeans off, ripping them in the process. Franco said that struggle began and moved from the bedroom, down the hall, and into the kitchen. Franco, who is 5'6" tall and weighing 130 pounds, insisted that he was defending himself against Carl, who was about 6' tall and weighed around 200 pounds.

When they entered the kitchen, Franco said he grabbed a frying pan and hit Carl in the head. Franco admitted that the handle broke off the pan when he hit Carl. Then Franco picked up a knife and stabbed Carl. Franco said that he stabbed Carl "everywhere because he kept comin' at me." Franco also stated that he kicked Carl in the head, and kept kicking Carl because he tried to get up. Franco did not leave the house until Carl stopped moving. When he left, Franco took Carl's wallet and pick up truck. Throughout his statement, Franco maintained that he only acted in self-defense. Franco stated that he was not injured in any way during the altercation.[19]

At trial, a police officer testified that the bloodstains painted a scenario in which Franco was the aggressor and the movement of the victim and Franco was away from the exit rather than toward the exit. Franco appealed, stating that the trial court did not conduct a *Kelly* hearing outside the jury's presence or require the state to show that the bloodstain testimony was reliable. The court agreed that this was error, adding that the testimony of a police officer would give the evidence an aura of reliability which could lead the jury to conclusions which were actually based on mere speculation. However, the court held that the error did not affect the verdict and so affirmed Franco's conviction.

"[T]he testimony of a police officer would give the evidence an aura of reliability which could lead the jury to conclusions which were actually based on mere speculation."

The Georgia Supreme Court came to a similar result. It held that the expert should not have been allowed to reconstruct the crime, but that the error was harmless:

An expert's testimony on issues to be decided by the jury is not admissible where the conclusion of the expert is one which jurors would ordinarily be

18. *Id.* at 29.
19. *Id.* at 27.

able to draw for themselves. In the instant case, it was permissible for Detective Gill to testify about his observations of the physical evidence at the Coleman residence. It was likewise allowable for him to assist the jury by stating his opinion that, based on his experience and training in the field of criminal investigation and crime scene reconstruction, the physical evidence was consistent with a hypothetical sequence of events surrounding the shooting.

Detective Gill should not have been allowed, however, to offer his factual conclusions concerning the victim's and defendant's locations when the victim was shot and whether she was holding a knife when shot. These conclusions were not beyond the ken of the jurors, once they were apprised of the physical evidence and the permissible conclusions of Detective Gill.[20]

Does a "Hypothetical Opinion" Solve the Problem?

The solution could be for the expert to give a "hypothetical opinion" rather than state with certainty based on the facts of the crime that he can tell what the defendant or the victim did. Given the technical nature of the testimony, however, it is doubtful that a jury could understand a lesson in both physics and mathematics sufficiently to draw its own conclusions about who stood where at the time of the crime.

The investigator can also use blood spatter analysis to corroborate and disprove a witness's statement. For example, in *Smith v. Virginia*,[21] the court held that blood spatter testimony was reliable in the murder trial of James Smith for the murder of Tracey Chandler, who was found in Smith's bedroom, lying on her back on the bed with her feet on the floor. Chandler had six bullet wounds, including one behind her right ear, in the right side of her chest, in her mouth, in her right hand, and above her left and right knee caps.

Smith testified that he killed Chandler in self defense when she attacked him with a needle during an argument over his drug use. The expert for the prosecution testified, based on blood spatter analysis, that Chandler was not standing when she was shot, thereby disproving Smith's defense. The court stated that bloodstain pattern analysis is a reliable science, composed of the application of principles of physics, chemistry, biology, and mathematics. The court also noted that the state of Minnesota had concluded that blood spatter science may be appropriate for judicial notice, which would mean that the proffering party would not need to prove the *Daubert* factors, although he would still need to prove that the testifying expert was qualified by experience or education to testify.

In the *Smith* case, investigators found 18 drops of blood on the leg of Chandler's pants and determined they were her blood. All but two of the spots were circular in shape, which indicated that the blood struck her pants at a perpendicular angle. As

---

20. *Coleman v. State*, 357 S.E.2d 566, 567 (Sup. Ga. 1987).
21. 576 S.E.2d 465 (Va. 2003).

there was no impact spatter on her pants below the knees, on the back of the pants, or on her shirt, the expert concluded that she was not standing when she was shot. At trial the expert explained the science to the jury: … "when a bullet enters the body and blood leaves the body through the entry wound, the type of bloodstain is known as impact spatter. The blood under these conditions, following 'the path of least resistance,' exits the entry wound in a conical pattern, and eventually falls to the ground. The greater the force of the impact, the smaller the droplets of blood that are expelled from the wound. [The expert] testified that when these droplets strike a surface at a perpendicular angle, the resulting blood-stain is circular. If the resulting blood-stain is elliptical in shape, it may be concluded that the blood droplet struck the surface at an angle."[22]

On cross-examination, the expert agreed that it was possible that the blood spatter on the pants could have come from Chandler's hand, but concluded it was unlikely because the bullet had entered the back of her right hand and exited at her palm. As exit wounds cause more spatter than entry wounds, the expert testified he would have expected to see more spatter on Chandler's pants and spatter below her knees and above her waistline.[23]

A number of factors can affect the blood patterns and mislead investigators. This is where the art and experience enter the picture. For example, blood that falls on different textures may result in different size droplets than normal. Drops can fall on top of each other, thus inflating their actual size. Blood patterns may support more than one plausible theory of the crime; yet the investigator may only see the most obvious one.[24]

In another case in which there were two drops of the victim's blood on the defendant's pants, the defense offered three different theories as to how the blood was deposited: they resulted from the defendant kneeling over the already-wounded victim, the victim and defendant had shaved and cut up vegetables together — perhaps this resulted in the blood spatter — or the victim may have mistaken the defendant's pants as his own.[25] The jury probably saw this as grasping at straws. In any event, they convicted the defendant of murder.

One fairly common defense to murder, when the defendant is found spattered with blood, is self defense. Using blood spatter analysis, experts can destroy this defense if they can show that the victim was not standing — and therefore could not be threatening the defendant — at the time of the murder.

Another common scenario when the defendant has the victim's blood on his body or clothes is to argue that he came upon the scene when the victim was already dead and got blood on his body or clothes by touching or trying to move the victim. This was the defense in the case of Jeffrey Hall, tried and convicted of killing his girlfriend

---

22. *Id.* at 467.
23. *Id.*
24. Akin, *supra*, Part I, *Champion* 29 (April 2005): 38.
25. *Tennessee v. Halake*, 102 S.W.3d 661, 672 (Tenn. Crim. App. 2001).

with a knife. He tried to convince the jury that he came upon the scene and found his girlfriend in a pool of blood and got blood on his clothes by dragging her body to get help. He ran to a neighbor's house holding the murder weapon, which he said he found by the body.

A criminalist who analyzed both the clothing and the murder weapon testified that the blood patterns on the defendant's clothes could only have been produced by blood spatter at a great velocity and could not have resulted from mere contact.[26] He also testified that certain blood on the defendant's pants was consistent with wiping a bloody knife on them. In addition, course blue fibers were identified on the knife, which were consistent with the defendant's corduroy pants. The court held the expert testimony was admissible:

> [T]he evidence offered to show the reliability of the bloodstain analysis included: (1) Professor MacDonnell's considerable experience and his status as the leading expert in the field; (2) the existence of national training programs; (3) the existence of national and state organizations for experts in the field; (4) the offering of courses on the subject in several major schools; (5) use by police departments throughout the country in their day-to-day operations; (6) the holding of annual seminars; and (7) the existence of specialized publications.[27]

Challenges to Expert Qualifications

The most likely challenge that succeeds is that the expert — generally a police officer — is not qualified to give the opinion. For example, in *Tennesee v. Halake*,[28] the court held that a police officer who testified that blood spatter on the victim's pants was "consistent with" gunshot blood spatter he had observed at other scenes, was held not qualified to give that opinion. The prosecution tried to rephrase the question so that the officer was not asked to testify about the actual crime scene, but instead about differences between the blood pattern from a gun shot victim and one who bleeds as the result of blunt force. The appellate court reversed the trial court's decision that a police officer who had observed one hundred crime scenes could testify to the limited question of whether the blood spots on the defendant's pants were consistent with blood spatter that the officer had observed as a result of other gunshot wounds.[29] The prosecution's attempt to qualify the officer as a "lay person" who could testify to his prior experience with gun shot wounds, but not offer an expert opinion was, in the appellate court's view, still prejudicial to the defendant and likely to be construed as expert testimony by the jury. It held the officer not qualified to testify as an expert.

---

26. *Iowa v. Hall*, 297 N.W.2d 80 (Iowa 1980).
27. *Id.* at 85.
28. *Supra.*
29. 102 S.W.3d 661, 670.

More recently, in a 2011 case,[30] defendant challenged the qualifications of a retired police officer who intended to testify about blood spatter. The court rejected defendant's claim and explained that although professional certifications were available, there is no requirement that an expert be certified in order to testify. This appears to be the trend: that experts are permitted to testify even where their level of training or education may not meet all the knowledge areas stated by the National Research Council in its report.

> ... there is no requirement that Mr. Sinke's expert testimony be based solely, or even partially, on formal training. *See* Fed.R.Evid. 702. The fact that Mr. Sinke's formal training in blood spatter analysis is by no means extensive does not, therefore, necessarily compel a finding that Mr. Sinke is unqualified to offer expert testimony on the subject. Defendants' other arguments are rejected for the same reason. There is simply no requirement that a witness be certified, licensed, or published before he can offer expert testimony on a subject. While these factors may, in certain cases, be relevant to a court's finding of qualification, their absence here does not discount Mr. Sinke's extensive practical experience in crime scene investigation generally and blood spatter analysis specifically. *See United States v. Locascio*, 6 F.3d 924, 937 (2d Cir.1993). Accordingly, the Court rules that Mr. Sinke is qualified to testify as an expert regarding blood spatter analysis. In so ruling, the Court stresses that it is not relying on any one factor in Mr. Sinke's background, but rather on the totality of Mr. Sinke's 30-plus years of experience.[31]

In 2011, a claim on appeal that the prisoner received a fundamentally unfair trial because he was denied a *Daubert* hearing and his attorney failed to cross-examine the prosecution's blood spatter expert was denied. There, the prisoner requested habeas corpus relief of the Ohio trial court for his murder conviction, arguing, among other things, that he requested and was unfairly denied a *Daubert* hearing about the expert bloodstain testimony and that his attorney failed to cross-examine the expert. In that case,[32] defendant Crawford was convicted of murder in the death of a man whom he admitted he shot while both were sitting in his car. His defense was self defense.

> Patrick Moran was a police officer who testified about the blood spatter and bullets in the Mercedes. Although Moran had been a criminologist for seven years, had attended a 40-hour blood-spatter course, and had testified about crime scenes and blood spatter on many occasions over the preceding seven years, he had not been specifically identified as an expert witness. Moran's testimony established that Wilson had been shot in the car while he was seated in the front passenger seat. Crawford's attorney did not cross-examine Moran.

> ...

---

30. *Rasmussen v. The City of New York*, 2011 WL 744522 (E.D.N.Y. 2011).
31. *Id.* at 2.
32. *Crawford v. Warden, Warren Correctional Institution*, 2011 WL 5307408 (S.D. Ohio 2011).

The court held that the blood spatter testimony was not prejudicial, regardless of whether Crawford's attorney had cross-examined the expert, because Crawford had admitted shooting the victim:

> Moran testified about his examination of evidence discovered in the interior of Wilson's Mercedes, including a gunshot hole in the right rear door, blood spatters and drips, a 9-millimeter Ruger cartridge recovered from under the front passenger seat, and other miscellaneous items found in the vehicle. With respect to the blood spatter evidence, Moran opined only that there was "high velocity blood spatter ... indicating a great deal of force such as a gunshot," and that it was his opinion that the blood came "from a person in the front right passenger seat."
>
> Contrary to petitioner's contention, neither Moran nor the other two police officers presented "highly damaging" testimony that arguably should have been subjected to cross-examination. Petitioner admitted at trial that he shot and killed Wilson and that the shooting occurred in Wilson's Mercedes when petitioner was sitting in the driver's seat and Wilson was sitting in the front passenger seat.[33]
>
> ...

The court also held that there was no requirement for the trial court to hold a *Daubert* hearing simply because it was requested.

> in an analogous habeas case, the Tenth Circuit stated: "Because *Daubert* does not set any specific constitutional floor on the admissibility of scientific evidence, the only relevant question is whether [the admission of such evidence] rendered the trial fundamentally unfair."); *Milone v. Camp*, 22 F.3d 693, 702 (7th Cir.1994) (similarly recognizing on habeas review of a state conviction that *Daubert* does not "purport[ ] to set a constitutional floor on the admissibility of scientific evidence").
>
> ...

Blood-spatter patterns involve a subject that lay people are not knowledgeable about. Moran had been a criminologist for seven years, had routinely examined and analyzed blood-spatter patterns, and had received both on-the-job and formal training. His testimony was based upon specialized information. The trial court did not err by allowing him to testify as an expert without a *Daubert* hearing.[34]

Blood Spatter "Experiments" Inadmissible

Here is one case that decided a certain experiment by the expert and his conclusions based on it were not reliable:

---

33. *Id.* at 28–29.
34. *Id.* at 30.

Crawford v. County of Dauphin, 1:CV-03-0693. 2006 U.S. Dist. LEXIS 15818 (M.D. Pa. April 4, 2006)

. . .

On January 9, 2006, plaintiff filed a motion *in limine* to preclude the expert testimony of blood spatter expert Herbert L. MacDonnell. After the matter was fully briefed, on January 30, 2006, we issued an order directing a *Daubert* hearing on the admissibility of MacDonnell's testimony before this court. A hearing was held on the afternoon of March 16, 2006. After the hearing both parties further briefed the matter and it is now ripe for our decision. For the following reasons we find that MacDonnell's proffered testimony is largely admissible under *Daubert*. However, we will preclude MacDonnell from testifying about his demonstrative of medium blunt force trauma overlaid onto human prints.

. . .

A court may qualify a witness as an expert based on his knowledge, skill, experience, training, or education. Fed. R. Evid. 702. In this case, neither the parties, nor the court, dispute that based on MacDonnell's professional and academic credentials, he qualifies as an expert in bloodstain pattern analysis and latent finger print identification.

. . .

Rather, it is the second prong, the reliability of MacDonnell's proffered testimony as applied to the facts of this case, that is the subject of the parties' dispute.

. . . In addition to those factors enumerated in *Daubert*, the United States Court of Appeals for the Third Circuit continues to apply a series of factors it enumerated prior to the *Daubert* decision. . . .

. . . [T]he factors *Daubert* and *Downing* have already deemed important include:

(1) whether a method consists of a testable hypothesis;

(2) whether the method has been subject to peer review;

(3) the known or potential rate of error;

(4) the existence and maintenance of standards controlling the technique's operation;

(5) whether the method is generally accepted;

(6) the relationship of the technique to methods which have been established to be reliable;

(7) the qualifications of the expert witness testifying based on the methodology; and

(8) the non-judicial uses to which the method has been put.

...

Plaintiff asserts that MacDonnell's expert testimony should be barred for several reasons. First, plaintiff argues that MacDonnell's methodology lacks reliability. Second, Crawford contends that the equipment used by MacDonnell to simulate a medium velocity blunt force trauma was never sufficiently demonstrated to have been calibrated, standardized, verified or ensured reliable by other methods. Likewise, plaintiff asserts that there is no known error rate for MacDonnell's methodology of simulating medium velocity blunt force trauma blood spatter on a human palm print. Next, plaintiff notes that MacDonnell's methodology in determining that medium velocity blunt force trauma blood spatter could repose in the valleys of a human print and the results of the subject test have never been published and subject to peer review. Plaintiff also argues that MacDonnell's methodology lacks general acceptance in the scientific community.

Finally, Crawford contends that MacDonnell's methodology and results in simulating the medium velocity blunt force trauma blood spatter on a human print were the product of subjective observations and methodologies.

The defendants initially assert that the "experiment" conducted by MacDonnell was not conducted in order to create data, but rather was a demonstration of known scientific principles of which MacDonnell was already aware, i.e., the relative sizes of blood spatter created by medium velocity impact as compared to the width of valleys of a human print. Essentially, defendants contend that although comparing the size of the blood spatter on the latent print via MacDonnell's blood spatter "experiment" is uncommon, comparing two known measurements does not involve unproven scientific method.

We agree with the defendants that MacDonnell sufficiently established that his testimony will be based on comparing the sizes of two objects. At the hearing, MacDonnell testified and cited numerous publications, which state that the size of blood spatter from medium velocity impact is in the range of 1 to 3 mm in diameter. MacDonnell testified that he measured the spacing between ridges on Crawford's print with a microscopic ruler as 0.53 mm. We agree with the central underpinning of the defendants' argument. MacDonnell's testimony will be based on the comparison of two sizes: (1) the range of sizes of microscopic blood spatter as generally accepted in the scientific community and (2) the size of the distance between the ridges of Crawford's print.

...

Therefore, we must turn to the reliability of MacDonnell's proffered testimony. We find that the expert qualifications of MacDonnell in the areas of blood spatter and fingerprint analysis and the wide publication of medium velocity blood spatter sizes along with his personal measurements of the space between the ridges on Crawford's print make his testimony regarding the two sizes reliable enough to be admissible for purposes of *Daubert*.

We now turn to the issue of whether MacDonnell should be allowed to present his demonstration of the medium velocity blunt force trauma blood spatter as measured against his own print. For the following reasons we will preclude MacDonnell from presenting the demonstrative to the jury.

Defendants argue that the device MacDonnell used to create the medium force trauma has been widely used by blood spatter experts and that at the hearing there was testimony regarding how high-speed strobe photography measured the device at 25 feet per second, the speed of medium velocity impact. The defendants also argue that it makes little difference that MacDonnell produced the blood spatter over his own hand print as he could have also easily produced the spatter on a blank piece of cardboard and compared it to the distance between ridges on Crawford's palm print.

...

We find that defendants have failed to produce by the preponderance of the evidence that MacDonnell's demonstrative has sufficient indicia of reliability.... we find that use of MacDonnell's own print and the circumstances on the whole of how he created his demonstrative lack the controls necessary to ensure reliable results. Although MacDonnell used his own print, which is presumably within the average of adult size, a demonstrative of Crawford's own print would be less confusing and more helpful to a jury.

Furthermore, the court is convinced that defendants failed to adequately demonstrate by a preponderance of the evidence that the demonstrative sufficiently captured the numerous factors at play at the scene of the crime, including the trajectory of the spatter, passage of time, climate, etc.

Because we cannot find by a preponderance of the evidence that MacDonnell's demonstrative offers sufficient indicia of reliability to be helpful to a jury, and because we find that the demonstrative might confuse a jury of the relevant issues we will preclude MacDonnell from testifying about the demonstrative.

The court ordered that MacDonnell could testify about the relative sizes of medium blunt force trauma blood spatter and the size of the space between ridges in the defendant's print, but was barred from presenting his experiment using his own handprint.[35]

"MacDonnell is precluded from presenting his demonstrative of medium blunt force trauma over his own handprint."

Case Study: The *Sam Sheppard* Case — Blood Spatter in a Brutal Killing

On July 4, 1954, Marilyn Sheppard, the wife of a prominent osteopathic physician, was found bludgeoned to death in her bed. Her husband, Dr. Sam Sheppard, was

---

35. *Id.*

arrested for her murder, and convicted of second degree murder and sentenced to life in prison. Sheppard maintained that he was downstairs when he heard his wife call out. He rushed upstairs and confronted a bushy-haired stranger, who knocked him out. After he regained consciousness, he followed the stranger out to his backyard, where he was again knocked out on the shore of the Lake Erie beach. Sheppard said that when he regained consciousness, he called his brother, who took him to the family osteopathic hospital for treatment. The story of the bushy-haired intruder was turned into a popular TV series called "The Fugitive," and later made into a film.

Sheppard exhausted all his appeals and finally, in 1966, he brought a habeas corpus petition, as a result of which the U.S. Supreme Court overturned his conviction on the ground that Sheppard had been denied a fair trial due to pretrial publicity and juror misconduct.[36] Sheppard was tried a second time in 1966 and was acquitted.[37] He died in 1970.

Blood spatter testimony was critical to Sheppard's conviction. The prosecutor's blood spatter expert testified that Marilyn Sheppard was beaten where her body was found, on the bed, whereas a defense expert testified that she had been bludgeoned elsewhere and her body repositioned on the bed and argued that she had been sexually assaulted by an unknown assailant. An additional piece of evidence was introduced late in the trial — a lamp that supposedly matched a bloodstain on Marilyn's pillow and could have been the murder weapon. A recent book on the *Sheppard* case concludes that this evidence was not disputed by the defense, although "the impression on the pillow was actually much smaller than the harp of the lamp that the government displayed."[38]

In addition to blood spatter in the bedroom, there was a trail of blood drops leading out of the bedroom, blood found on Sheppard's watch, which was in a green bag outside his house, and blood on his pants. The prosecution attempted to type the blood, but it was inconclusive.

In *Mortal Evidence*,[39] Dr. Cyril Wecht analyzes the blood evidence in the *Sheppard* case. At the time of the crime, the only blood test available was blood typing — A, B, AB, or O. Many pieces of blood-stained evidence were examined, but the only one tested was the bed sheet on which Marilyn Sheppard was lying. It was Type O, which was consistent with Marilyn's. None of the blood leading out of the house, the blood on Marilyn and Sam Sheppard's watches, or the blood spatters found on the bedroom wall were tested. Sheppard hired Dr. Paul Kirk, a professor of biochemistry and a criminalist at the University of California, to review the evidence.

Dr. Kirk, according to Wecht, found large amounts of spatter on the wall to Marilyn's right, and on the east wall, which also included a closet door. These were

---

36. *Sheppard v. Maxwell*, 384 U.S. 333 (1966).

37. Jonathan L. Entin, "Being the Government Means (Almost) Never Having to Say You're Sorry: The *Sam Sheppard* Case and the Meaning of Wrongful Imprisonment," *Akron Law Review* 38 (2005): 139, 148.

38. Entin, *supra*.

39. Cyril Wecht, Greg Saitz, and Mark Curriden, *Mortal Evidence* (Prometheus Books, 2003).

low-velocity drops, as opposed the high velocity spatter found throughout the rest of the room. Dr. Kirk concluded that the blood on the east wall must have been thrown off the murder weapon during its backswing, and based on the patterns, concluded that the murderer was left-handed.[40]

Kirk also found an area in the corner where the north and east walls met where there was no blood. He concluded that the blood was blocked by the body of the killer, who must have been standing at the foot of the bed on the east side, and would therefore have been covered with the blood spatter himself.[41]

At the first trial, Mary Cowan, a laboratory analyst at the corner's office, had testified that the blood on the watchband of Sheppard's watch, found in a green bag outside the house, was spatter. However, Kirk believed the blood looked more like smear that had been transferred by contact with something bloody, perhaps the hand of the killer.

Kirk also examined the blood trail leading out of the house. He disagreed that the stains came from blood dripping off the murder weapon and conducted experiments using different tools dipped in blood. Almost all of them shed all drops within fifteen feet and the drops were always small. But the blood trails in the house were longer and bigger. Kirk concluded that the killer was injured and the trail was in his blood,[42] the same conclusion that Henry Lee would draw in the case of *Grant*.

Sheppard moved for a new trial after his conviction on the ground of newly discovered evidence in the form of blood spatter experiments conducted by Kirk that were consistent with Sheppard's innocence. He argued that the prosecution had sealed off his house and that he had been denied access in order to conduct the experiments earlier. The court denied the motion on two grounds: first, it did not believe that Sheppard was refused access to his home to conduct these experiments prior to trial, and second, even if Sheppard had conducted such experiments, they would have been inadmissible because they were speculative and conducted under circumstances that were not similar to the conditions at the crime scene.[43]

Kirk's experiments involved the drying time for the blood on the watch, a series of experiments during which different instruments were used to strike a "skull" made of wood, rubber and plastic, evaluation of the "agglutination" of blood drops on the wardrobe and walls of the bedroom, and an examination of the blood trail.[44] He also offered his opinion that the murderer was left-handed, which had been argued to the jury at the trial.[45] The court reported Kirk's conclusions as follows:

> [Kirk] describes the distribution of blood on the walls, defendant's bed and the radiator. By determining the point of origin, he gives the opinion that

Sheppard's blood experiments, conducted after his conviction, were not newly discovered evidence and would not be admissible at trial because the conditions under which they were undertaken were unreliable.

40. *Id.* at 132.
41. *Id.*
42. *Id.*
43. *Ohio v. Sheppard*, 100 Ohio App. 399, 128 N.E.2d 504 (1955).
44. *Id.*
45. *Id.* at 415.

the head of the victim was essentially in the same position during all of the blows from which blood was spattered on the defendant's bed; that her head was on the sheet during most, if not all, of the beating that led to the blood spots; that probably all of the blood drops on the east wall were thrown there by the back swing of the weapon used; and that the blows on the victim's head came from swings of the weapon "which started low in a left hand swing, rising through an arc, and striking the victim a sidewise angular blow rather than one brought down vertically."

He then explains the *cause of distribution* and comes to the conclusion based on his experiments as described in Appendix I and his observation of the blood distribution in the bedroom that the blows were struck by a left-handed person. He then proceeds to explain the impact spatter, and the throw-off drops of certain weapons, and decides that the blood spots on the doors of the bedroom were drops made by the back-throw of the lethal weapon, and that a very large spot on the wardrobe door could not have come from the back-throw of the weapon.

This spot measured about one inch in diameter. He then expostulates that "this spot could not have come from impact spatter. It is highly improbable that it could have been thrown off a weapon," and that "it almost certainly came from a bleeding hand. The bleeding hand could only have belonged to the attacker.[46]

The Ohio Supreme Court affirmed Sheppard's conviction[47] in 1956, finding that there was sufficient evidence for the jury to have found guilt beyond a reasonable doubt. In a dissenting opinion, Judge Taft stated that in his opinion, the jury could not have used the blood evidence on Sheppard's pants to conclude guilt:

[T]he state established by its evidence facts and circumstances which cannot be reconciled with any reasonable hypothesis except that of defendant's innocence. For example, there was admittedly blood on the knee of defendant's pants which could have gotten there when he discovered his wife after she had been killed, because the knee was at about the height of the bed which was covered with her blood.

However, there was admittedly no other blood on those pants, although the evidence indicates without contradiction that defendant's wife's blood spurted all over the room. Certainly there would have been blood all over the pants of defendant if he had been her assailant.[48]

Twenty-five years after Sheppard's death, his son filed a civil suit to declare Sheppard innocent, which is a higher standard than "not guilty." A finding of innocence was then required in order to sue for damages for wrongful imprisonment.[49]

---

46. *Id.* at 414–415.
47. *Ohio v. Sheppard*, 165 Ohio St. 293 (Sup. Ct. Ohio 1956).
48. *Id.* at 307.
49. *Id.*

Sheppard's son hired Dr. Mohammad Tahir, an expert in DNA, to review the evidence once more. Tahir discovered that the bloodstains on Sheppard's pants were not from Marilyn, and as Sheppard had no open wounds right after the murder, the blood must have come from a third person. Tahir excluded Sheppard as the source of the sperm found in Marilyn's vagina and also excluded him as the source of the bloodstain on his pants.

Sheppard's defense team suspected that the murderer was Richard Eberling, a workman who had been in the Sheppard house shortly before the murder. When Eberling died in 1998, his autopsy showed a half-inch scar on the inside of his left wrist. Again, similar to the *Grant* case, the defense was looking for a wound that would have created enough blood to make the bloody trail.

In January of 2000, with both Sheppard and Eberling deceased, the jury refused to rule for Sheppard's estate that he had been innocent. Notwithstanding the new blood spatter evidence, a pregnant woman had died, and her husband was a womanizing socialite. In the end, it appeared that science could not overcome character evidence.

Blood Spatter in the *Grant* Case

The *Grant* trial involved blood spatter testimony that linked a blood trail in the parking garage to the white handkerchief that was found to contain Grant's DNA. It also involved an attempted crime scene reconstruction by Dr. Henry Lee at the request of the family. This can be found in detail in the *Grant* Appendix.

Summary

Blood spatter analysis depends upon mathematics and physics, which can be used to determine the velocity and angle with which blood has hit a surface, as well as the direction from which it came. The major variable in this type of analysis is the surface upon which the blood adheres, which can distort the size and shape of the drops somewhat.

Once these basic facts are known, however, the job of the analyst becomes more complex. There may be blood drops from more than one source that are intermingled. As the analyst attempts to reconstruct the likely position of people and objects, the science of blood spatter analysis moves into a more speculative realm.

Most courts accept the reliability of blood spatter analysis. Challenges to the qualification of blood spatter experts often result in the court permitting them to testify, with the issue of qualifications to be handled by cross-examination. However, some courts have refused to let experts testify about blood spatter, when their conclusion seems speculative. Some experts are permitted to testify as to a hypothetical set of facts, but are not permitted to conclusively relate the reconstruction to the defendant.

Blood spatter experts are frequently used when a defendant offers a version of facts, typically one in which the victim was the aggressor, which the blood spatter shows is inconsistent with the facts.

Experts are generally not permitted to testify about experiments they conduct to recreate the crime scene unless the court is satisfied that the conditions are exactly the same. Even in the case of Lee's review of the Serra murder in 1988, he could not duplicate the conditions in the garage at the time of the crime, due to alterations in the garage itself, among other factors.

Blood spatter testimony figured prominently in the conviction of Sam Sheppard for the murder of his wife, and his motion for a new trial based on experiments on blood conducted by an expert was denied. Blood spatter analysis also was important in reconstructing the facts in the *Grant* case, particularly the fact of how Serra's car was found on the 8th level of the garage, but her car keys and the handkerchief were found on the 7th level.

The NRC Report in 2009 concluded that blood spatter testimony requires knowledge of many areas of science and voiced concerns about its reliability. It stated that, while some aspects of bloodstain pattern analysis can be scientifically proven, for example, the rate of blood flow and the resulting spatter patterns, "some experts extrapolate far beyond what can be supported ... [E]xtra care must be given to the way in which the analyses are presented in court. The uncertainties associated with bloodstain pattern analysis are enormous."[50]

Discussion Questions

1. What information can examination of blood drops at a crime scene tell an investigator?

2. What would an investigator conclude if blood spatter drops were 3 mm in size versus if they were less than 1 mm in size?

3. How many wounds would likely have been inflicted if the investigator finds 4 cast-off patterns on the wall behind where the perpetrator stood?

4. What is a transfer pattern and what can it tell the investigator?

5. Why are courts likely to refuse to admit experiments with blood spatter in which an expert tries to duplicate crime scene conditions? What were the similarities between the blood spatter experiment in *Crawford v. County* and *Ohio v. Sheppard*?

6. On what grounds have trial courts refused to admit blood spatter opinion testimony from police? Explain the reasoning of the court in *Franco v. Texas*.

7. Have the courts all agreed that blood spatter analysis is reliable? Why or why not?

---

50. NRC Report at 179.

8. Are there any subjective elements to analyzing blood spatter? What are they?

9. How did Sam Sheppard hope that blood spatter analysis would constitute newly discovered evidence?

10. What was the NRC's main concern about the reliability of blood pattern testimony?

Chapter 12

Handwriting and Questioned Documents

Overview

Handwriting "experts" have testified in courts for many years about authorship and forgery. The basic premise used by handwriting experts is that handwriting, like fingerprints, is unique to the individual. Therefore, a person cannot disguise his or her handwriting from an expert who examines both a sample of the person's genuine handwriting and a purported forgery. Handwriting analysis is frequently used in courts to establish a number of issues:

1. Did an individual write a particular document in his or her "normal writing"?

2. Did an individual forge the writing of another person?

3. Did an individual write a document, attempting to disguise his or her normal writing?

The National Research Council, in its 2009 report, explained that the area of "Questioned Document Examination" involved comparison and analysis of documents and printing and writing instruments in order to identify or eliminate suspects as the source of the handwriting.

Although this chapter will focus primarily on handwriting analysis, the NRC noted that questioned document examination involved analysis of many factors:

- determining whether the document is the output of mechanical or electronic imaging devices such as printers, copying machines, and facsimile equipment;
- identifying or eliminating particular human or machine sources of handwriting, printing, or typewriting;
- identifying or eliminating ink, paper, and writing instrument;
- establishing the source, history, sequence of preparation, alterations or additions to documents, and relationships of documents;
- deciphering and restoring obscured, deleted, or damaged parts of documents;
- recognizing and preserving other physical evidence that may be present in documents; and

- determining the age of a document.[1]

The methods used to determine common authorship were developed by Albert Osbourn, Sr., in the early 1900s and have remained virtually unchanged. The examiner first views the suspected document and exemplars of the natural handwriting of the suspected author. If the examiner determines that he has enough writing to compare, he will first look for obvious differences, which might rule out the suspected author. Such differences include such "macro" features as line slant, pen pressure, and the like. If the suspect cannot be ruled out, the examiner will then proceed to examining "micro" features, such as the size and shape of particular letters. There is no set number of similarities that an examiner must find to determine a match.

Courts have admitted handwriting testimony for many years, but when confronted with the *Daubert* tests, some courts have determined that handwriting identification is not reliable. Experts cannot state which characteristics are most important, nor can they state that if a writer of a known document has x number of similarities, there is given probability that the writer wrote the questioned document.

In 2009, the National Research Council issued a "Summary Assessment" of the current status of handwriting analysis suggesting that the "scientific basis for handwriting comparisons needs to be strengthened."

> [R]ecent studies have increased our understanding of the individuality and consistency of handwriting and computer studies and suggests that there may be a scientific basis for handwriting comparison at least in the absence of intentional obfuscation or forgery. Although there has been only limited research to quantify the reliability or replicability of the practices used by trained document examiners, the committee agrees that there may be some value in handwriting analysis.[2]

All this may change with the advent of computer programs designed to compare questioned documents. One computer system has determined that handwriting is unique, by looking for a certain number of macro and micro features. In essence, it is similar to DNA testing in that it does not look at all possible match points, but the sample it examines is large enough to make probability estimates of common authorship.

Handwriting may well be a type of forensic science that does not meet *Daubert*, but that will lead to a form of computer analysis that will meet the tests in the near future.

Chapter Objectives

Based on this chapter, students will be able to:

1. Explain the different purposes for which handwriting comparison can be used.

---

1. NRC Report, *supra*, 163.
2. NRC Report, *supra*, 166–67.

2. Explain the scientific hypotheses about intra-writer and inter-writer handwriting.

3. Identify the different opinions a handwriting expert may give about common authorship.

4. Identify the 21 basic areas of macro characteristics experts look for in traditional handwriting analysis.

5. Understand the subjective elements of traditional handwriting analysis.

6. Explain the process involved in comparing handwriting as a forensic investigative device.

7. Explain how the admissibility of handwriting expert testimony has been viewed by the courts before and after *Daubert* and after the *Kuhmo* decision.

8. Evaluate whether traditional handwriting experts should be able to point out similarities and differences but not give an opinion as to authorship.

9. Evaluate the issues, including publicity and notoriety, which affected handwriting analysis in both the *Hauptmann* and the *Ramsey* ransom notes.

10. Explain how traditional handwriting analysis may be both generally accepted and yet still fail the remaining *Daubert* tests.

11. Evaluate the process of handwriting comparison when done by computer and compare with traditional handwriting analysis.

The Traditional Handwriting Analysis Process

The purpose of handwriting analysis is to determine whether a particular individual wrote a questioned document, based on examination and comparison of characteristics in his handwriting and that in the questioned document:

> The main goal of all forensic identification, including handwriting identification, is individualization. Individualization is the establishment that a person or object now held is the same person or object associated with a past event in a particular way, to the exclusion of all other candidates.[3]

Handwriting expert testimony can range from the routine cases, such as whether a defendant forged a check by "copying" the handwriting of someone else, to the highly dramatic. The best known handwriting cases have been ransom notes, in which the suspect has tried to disguise his writing. From the famous kidnapping of the Lindberg baby, in which Bruno Richard Hauptmann was executed based on evidence that included testimony about his authorship of the ransom note—to JonBenét Ramsey, in which officials have been unable to conclude that any known suspect wrote the ransom notes, continue to intrigue.

---

3. Michael Risinger, *Handwriting Identification in Modern Scientific Evidence: The Law and Science of Expert Testimony*, 2d ed. 2002 at 42.

Handwriting testimony has also undergone a transformation from the early days. At one point, the only "expert" permitted to testify in court was someone who had actually seen the writer's handwriting. Today, experts are people who generally have no first-hand knowledge of the writer, but have applied certain theories to determine authorship.

Traditional Handwriting Analysis Is a Subjective Process

Even handwriting experts agree that there is no identifiable "system" for analyzing handwriting and that the process depends on training and experience. Although the American Board of Forensic Document Examiners was established in 1977,[4] whose members include the American Society of Questioned Document Examiners,[5] there is no formal training to become a handwriting examiner. Most examiners have been trained at forensic laboratories.

> Unfortunately, as yet there is no program of reputable courses offered or training available in Canada or the United States to private persons who wish to enter the discipline. As a result, the few qualified private practicing examiners are, frequently, former employees of government forensic laboratories whose personal facilities for performing the work may be inadequate and may vary substantially.[6]

There are some who would argue that the 1910 text called *Questioned Documents*, written by Albert Osborn, is the definitive text on handwriting analysis. However, the book is currently out of print,[7] so it is doubtless not being used in any current training programs.

Handwriting analysis is subjective. Unlike fingerprints, there is no agreed upon number of points of comparison required to declare a "match." No one claims that handwriting analysis is a "science," although it has been called a "technique." After the *Daubert* standards were extended to "technical" experts by the Supreme Court in *Kuhmo*, some courts have attempted to apply these standards to handwriting. Most cases, however, seem to continue to accept handwriting expert testimony, even when it is challenged. The question we will examine is "why?" There appear to be three main reasons:

1. Handwriting expert testimony has been admitted since the early 1800s and therefore continues to be admitted because of its longevity,

2. Handwriting is "generally accepted" within the litigation community,

---

4. *See* http://www.abfde.org.

5. *See* http://www.asqde.org.

6. Roy A. Huber and A. M. Headrick, *Handwriting Identification: Facts and Fundamentals* (CRC Press, 1999).

7. Based on a search of amazon.com; later texts by the same author are available.

3. As the jury can examine the handwriting for themselves, there is little fear of prejudice from the expert opinions.[8]

Handwriting is one of those "unique" human characteristics that have been accepted as part of common wisdom. As we will see, there has never been a scientific study to confirm this common perception; nonetheless "experts" on handwriting have been permitted to testify in court both before and after *Daubert* virtually without challenge. Yet, how do we know that it is true that handwriting is unique? How does one become an expert in identifying handwriting? What techniques and methods do they use? Exactly how do they determine that a particular piece of handwriting originated from a particular person? What is the threshold of identification? And especially, what makes it possible to say with authority that this handwriting was produced by person A attempting to appear as if it were written by person B?

No one claims that handwriting analysis is a "science," although it has been called a "technique."

The Role of Training and Experience

Kenneth Zercie, retired assistant director of the State of Connecticut Forensic Science Laboratory, spent over twenty years examining handwriting. He believes handwriting can be individualized and handwriting analysis is "relatively reliable" as long as basic rules are followed.[9]

Is Handwriting Analysis a Reliable "Science"?

The scientific hypothesis underlying handwriting analysis has multiple components:

1. Each person's handwriting is unique.

2. Each writer will exhibit small variations within his writing.

3. Handwriting changes with age and over time and is affected by alcohol, drugs, and tiredness.

4. Handwriting is consistent from one piece of writing by one author to the next, assuming the pieces are written close together in time.

5. A certain number of similarities between one sample and another supports the conclusion of common authorship.

6. By examining a sufficient number of samples of a sufficient quality of writing, an expert can determine:
   - If two pieces of undisguised writing were written by the same person. For example, is a will written by person A genuine, based on other exemplars of person A's handwriting?

---

8. *United States v. Starzecpyzel*, 880 F. Supp. 1027 (S.D.N.Y. 1995).
9. Interview with the author, November 17, 2006, when Zercie was the assistant director.

- If one person has attempted to forge another person's signature or handwriting. For example, did person A forge person B's signature on a check?
- If one person, attempting to disguise his or her handwriting, can be identified from the disguised handwriting. For example, did person A write a ransom note or bank robbery note, attempting to avoid detection by disguising his handwriting?

By experience and training, an expert is in a better position to make these determinations than is a lay person.

Is There Any Proof That Handwriting Is Unique?

Whether each person's handwriting is unique would require a study of a large number of individuals. In addition, the study would need to determine which specific characteristics to include in the test. As there are literally hundreds of variations in handwriting, this might prove an impossible task. See some of the variables discussed below. Also, many Americans learned handwriting under a common instructional method in school. It is not known to what extent this promotes similarity of handwriting.

Students frequently cannot write all the letters of the alphabet in upper and lower case cursive script. Many do not write in cursive at all. Handwriting is becoming rare, as computer technology puts typewriting within the abilities of almost every writer. Some predict that in the future, there will be no handwriting experts, as documents will all be in type. Even signatures will rely on mechanical reproduction.

Some efforts have been made to study handwriting differences in large populations. A study was reported in 1977 that studied the characteristics of handwriting of 200 writers.[10] Almost 20 years later, Mary Wenderoth Kelly, a forensic document examiner with the Cleveland Forensic Laboratory and vice president of the American Board of Forensic Document Examiners, referred to the 1977 study as evidence of the uniqueness of handwriting and was unable to recall any more recent studies.[11]

The Connecticut Forensic Science Laboratory began a study in 2001 of 2,500 samples consisting of a letter and address on an envelope. The random samples were coded by age of writer, part of the country, sex, educational level, and handwriting method they learned in school. One study looked at the cursive letter "Q" and found that there were no identical Qs in the sample.[12]

---

10. J. Muehlberger, et al., "A Statistical Examination of Selected Handwriting Characteristics," *Journal of Forensic Science* 22 (1977): 206.
11. *U.S. v. Starzecpyzel, supra* at 1034.
12. Zercie, *supra.*

More recently, a computer program developed by Cedar-Fox has evaluated a number of characteristics of handwriting and determined that handwriting is unique, with a confidence level of over 90%. See the discussion at the end of this chapter.

What Characteristics Are Most Useful in Distinguishing Handwriting?

Even if one accepts on faith that handwriting is unique, which characteristics are the most important in matching one sample of handwriting to another? As we have seen with fingerprints, there are three class characteristics — arch, loop, and whorl. Are there certain "class characteristics" that handwriting examiners look at first? These would be characteristics shared by all handwriting, such as slant, alignment, connections, consistency of habits, and the frequency with which a given habit occurs. Is this the complete list? Should another factor be listed? A large sample size would perhaps answer this question.

What number of class characteristics must be found to "match" before the examiner will proceed to individual characteristics, rather than declaring exclusion? Again, there is no specific answer. Which characteristics are rarer and therefore more likely to distinguish between writers? We don't know. How many ways can one write a lowercase, cursive "e" or "i"? We do not know.

Most examiners tend to agree that one's handwriting can change over time, so it is important to evaluate two pieces of handwriting written over a short period. Illness, being tired, or intoxication can also affect one's handwriting, as one can attest simply from common knowledge. How does the examiner account for these variations?

In DNA testing, the examiner (or rather the DNA test kit) knows the relative frequency of different length alleles at each loci tested and also knows that the DNA sites do not control a specific genetic trait. If they did control a specific trait, they might not be truly independent. Many brown eyed people, for example, have brown hair. Therefore, if one were to test for the genes for eye color and hair color, one could not create independent statistics for the likelihood of a random match, as those two genes would not occur in mathematically random fashion. Because the loci in DNA testing are not associated with any known trait, there is not much possibility that an allele of a particular length at locus #1 would always occur with an allele of a particular length at locus #2. Is the same thing true for handwriting? In other words, are people who slant their letters to the right more likely to connect their letters? Again, no studies have been performed to answer this question.

Are More Common Characteristics Required in Identifying the Source of Disguised Writing?

Finally, is less skill needed to determine a match between two exemplars where the writer is not trying to disguise his handwriting than to determine a forgery (attempt to copy another's writing) or a ransom note (attempt to disguise one's own writing)? Logic would support the conclusion that it is far more difficult to determine writing when the author is deliberately trying not to write normally.

Gathering Exemplars

The process of comparison varies depending on whether the person suspected is available or not. If the person is available, such as in the case of Patsy Ramsey, the examiner will ask the suspect to write an exemplar of his or her "normal" handwriting. Generally, the expert will ask the suspect to write at least three exemplars of some length, on the theory that the suspect may try to write differently at the beginning, but will eventually lapse into familiar patterns. Many experts prefer ten exemplars written no more than six months prior to the questioned document.[13] In examining a known writing compared with a questioned document, they will first examine the questioned document to see if it is sufficient to continue investigating. There must be a sufficient amount of writing that is neither highly stylized nor in block letters.

Examine Pictorial Similarities

The next step is to make a general observation of pictorial similarities. Do the letters look alike? Are they in a similar style? Is the spatial relationship and slant similar? Is the format the same, either cursive, printing, or a combination? Are there obvious letter stylistics in common? At this point, an examiner may eliminate the suspect as the author of the questioned document.

Look for Individuating Characteristics

If not, then the examiner will look for individuating characteristics, beginning with the first letter and working forward. More than one person can share an individuating characteristic. Therefore, the issue of when the examiner has seen enough characteristics to make a conclusion is highly subjective.

Forgeries

When the questioned document is suspected to be a forgery, an examiner looks for a variety of indications. First, the writer was attempting to copy someone else's signature, and so was actually "drawing," not writing. This will be evident in the small motor skills, neuromuscular responses, and subconscious activity associated with drawing. Signs indicating forgery include: a lack of "feathering" on the introductory stroke. A writer will not touch the paper first with the writing instrument before beginning to write, but someone who is drawing will. The forger will also demonstrate abrupt pen lifts and an attempt to keep the signature on a baseline.[14]

---

13. Zercie, *supra.*
14. Zercie, *supra.*

Disguise

The second issue is whether the examiner is trying to match two pieces of writing, both of which were supposedly written without any effort at disguise, or whether one of the pieces of handwriting (as in a ransom note) was purposefully disguised. The task of comparing similarities between two pieces of undisguised writing is much simpler than to compare a sample of "normal" handwriting to one where the suspect is trying to disguise it. In that case, the examiner must determine how a person who writes as the suspect normally writes would write if that suspect were trying to disguise his or her handwriting. One can see immediately that this is a far more complex task. The theory is that even in a disguised writing, the suspect would still retain certain characteristics of his or her normal writing. But which ones?

The Handwriting Expert's Opinion

In rendering an opinion, a handwriting expert is limited to these conclusions:

- Common authorship;
- High probability;
- Probably;
- Inconclusive;
- No evidence.

What Characteristics Do Experts Look For?

According to one author, there are 21 basic areas which handwriting experts examine to determine handwriting matches.

1. **Elements of Style.** This includes arrangement, placement, and balance of text; dimensions and uniformity of margins; interlinear spacing; parallelism of lines; character and position of interlineations; depth of indentions; paragraphing; use of numerals and symbols in monetary amounts; location and nation of headings; location of signatures; and style, size, and position of addresses.
2. **Class of Allograph.** Cursive (letters are connected); script (letters are disconnected); hand lettering or block lettering; and composites of the above.
3. **Connections**
4. **Design of Allographs** and their construction, such as capitalization or use of two or more forms for the same letter.
5. **Dimensions**, such as relative heights.
6. **Slant, slope**
7. **Spacing**
8. **Abbreviations**
9. **Alignment**
10. **Commencements and terminations**

There are 21 basic areas which handwriting experts examine to determine handwriting matches.

11. **Punctuation and diacritics**

12. **Embellishments**, such as flourishes.

13. **Writing quality** and how legible the writing is.

14. **Line continuity.** Does the writer lift the pen or write continuously?

15. **Line quality,** from smooth to erratic.

16. **Pen control**, determined from ink level, pen position.

17. **Writing movement,** such as clockwise or not, more straight lines or curves.

18. **Consistency**

19. **Persistency**

20. **Lateral expansion.** Is the writing spread out or contracted?

21. **Word proportions.** Is the writing vertical or horizontal?[15]

The Admissibility of Handwriting Expert Testimony

Before the advent of the "expert" in handwriting analysis, courts accepted testimony concerning handwriting only from a witness who had actually seen the author write. So, for example, a witness who had seen a person write his will would be permitted to testify that the signature was, in fact, the testator's handwriting. Jurors would also be permitted to review the handwriting and make their own judgments.[16]

In 1836, a court in Massachusetts first allowed an expert to testify, stating that "it couldn't be any worse than what was traditionally relied on."[17] This is hardly a ringing endorsement of the science behind the field. This concept of relative benefit was echoed in 1995 by a New York court that accepted handwriting testimony as "nonscientific" expert testimony:

> While handwriting analysis may not be as scientifically accurate as fingerprint identification, it is, on the whole, probably no less reliable than eyewitness identification which is often made after a quick glance at a human face.[18]

Handwriting Analysis after *Daubert* but before *Kuhmo*

Many people believed that the *Daubert* decision applied only to forensic testimony based on science. If a "technique" were involved, then *Daubert* would not apply. The Supreme Court clarified this issue in the *Kuhmo* case, when it held that the *Daubert* standards applied to techniques as well — in that case testimony about the cause of a tire defect. Before the *Kuhmo* case was decided, however, a New York case called

---

15. Huber and Headrick, *supra*, at 136–38.

16. D. Michael Risinger with Michael J. Saks, "Science and Nonscience in the Courts: *Daubert* meets Handwriting Identification Expertise," *Iowa Law Review* 82 (October 1996): 21, 24.

17. *Id.* citing *Moody v. Rowell*, 34 Mass. 490 (1835).

18. *U.S. v. Starzecpyzel*, 880 F. Supp. 1027, 1043 (S.D.N.Y. 1995).

U.S. v. Starzecpyzel[19] evaluated handwriting testimony under the *Daubert* test. It found that handwriting failed *Daubert*, but it admitted it anyway on the ground that it was a technique, and at that time, *Daubert* did not apply to techniques. Its analysis of handwriting under *Daubert*, however, would prove helpful to later courts after *Kuhmo* was decided.

In *Starzecpyzel*, a husband and wife were charged with stealing paintings from the wife's elderly aunt by forging her name on deeds of gift.[20] The expert compared 224 samples of the aunt's known handwriting with her signature on two deeds made out to one of the defendants and determined that the deed signatures were not genuine. He pointed out to the jury that the letter "E" was slanted to the right in 219 of the genuine signatures but not on the deeds. Also, the "l" in "Ethel" was lower than the "B" in "Brownstone" in all 224 known signatures, but not on the deeds. The court said that this testimony would be helpful to the jury as it would save them the time of examining all the signatures themselves, but that the jury could come to its own conclusion after the similarities and differences were pointed out.

The court compared handwriting analysis to other nonscientific technical testimony such as carpenters, auto mechanics, drug sale experts, money laundering experts, pipe fitters, and dog trainers,[21] and found them of similar benefit:

> The problem arises from the likely perception by jurors that FDEs [forensic document examiners] are scientists, which would suggest far greater precision and reliability than was established by the *Daubert* hearing. This perception might arise from several sources, such as the appearance of the words "scientific" and "laboratory" in much of the relevant literature, and the overly precise manner in which FDEs describe their level of confidence in their opinions.[22]

The court was convinced that handwriting testimony would not meet *Daubert* based on a number of factors: the lack of studies demonstrating its reliability, the lack of peer review, and the lack of controlling standards. By far the most important factor to the court was the fact that the handwriting expert who testified at the *Daubert* hearing, Mary Kelly, a handwriting expert for the Cleveland police with over 10 years' experience, was unable to explain any objective standards for handwriting analysis. Here is an example of her testimony in the hearing:

> Q: [Osborn states that] a slight but persistent difference [in] slant in two documents of considerable length may be evidence that the writings are by two different writers, while a pronounced difference might be the result of intended disguise. What would be the difference between a slight but persistent difference and a profound difference in slant?

---

19. *Id.*
20. *Id.*
21. *Id.* at 1042.
22. *U.S. v. Starzecpyzel, supra.*

...

A: He is using it as a comparative between two different writers ...

Q: What degree of measure might be slight?

A: ... I wouldn't quantify it.

...

Q: To make that precise, let me give you an example. Suppose, let us say, that if we look at a known writing and a reasonably fair sample of known writing by a particular writer, that the writer's small L is always slanted between say 8 to 12 degrees to the right, you find that in an adequate sample of known writing, is there some numerical standard which a document examiner would apply to determine what degree of slant in the questioned document would lead to the conclusion that the questioned document is by a different author? Would you need 14 [degrees], 17, 19, is the real question.

...

A: I would say as a general rule, no, your Honor; there is no numerical measurement of that kind of slant.

The court stated that if the *Daubert* standards were applied, handwriting analysis would fail the test. However, it allowed the testimony anyway as "non-scientific" expert testimony on the ground that it would be helpful to the jury. This case was decided before *Kuhmo Tire v. Carmichael*,[23] in which the Supreme Court held that *Daubert* also applies to non-scientific testimony.

Admissibility after *Kuhmo*

After *Kuhmo*, one would assume that the New York courts would reject handwriting testimony, based on the detailed analysis under *Daubert* from the *Starzecpyzel* case. Yet, the Second Circuit Court of Appeals, which governs the New York court in *Starzecpyzel*, ruled in the *Brown* case that handwriting expert testimony is admissible under *Daubert*.[24] In that case, the defendant was charged with drug trafficking, and an expert testified that a mailing receipt was in his handwriting. The Second Circuit did not address the *Daubert* factors at all. It approved the trial court's admission of the testimony based on the grounds that other federal appellate courts were accepting it, and that the Second Circuit had "routinely alluded to expert handwriting analysis without expressing any reservation as to its admissibility." In addition, the court stated that if the admission of the testimony had been in error,

---

23. 526 U.S. 137 (1998).
24. *U.S. v. Brown*, No. 03-1542, 152 Fed. Appx. 59 (2d. Cir. 2005).

it was "harmless beyond a reasonable doubt," and therefore had not contributed to a wrongful conviction of the defendant.[25]

The standard for appeal from the trial judge's decision of whether to admit or deny an expert is "abuse of discretion." Therefore, unless the trial court was "clearly erroneous," the appeals court will generally let the trial court's decision stand.

So far, all the federal appellate courts have accepted handwriting testimony after *Daubert* and *Kuhmo*. Most of them conclude simply that handwriting testimony is "generally accepted" and therefore do not conduct a point-by-point *Daubert* analysis. The courts do not require a finding of controlling standards or error rate. One 2002 case admitted handwriting testimony, stating that it met *Daubert*.[26] However, the reason given was that handwriting testimony has a long history, is generally accepted in the expert community, and that it is primarily to draw the jury's attention to similarities between a known exemplar and a contested sample. Compared to the analysis in the cases above, this is not a rigorous *Daubert* analysis.

> Most courts conclude simply that handwriting testimony is "generally accepted" and therefore do not conduct a point-by-point *Daubert* analysis.

Most of the cases that discuss *Daubert* have been those where a defendant's writing is compared to his natural handwriting, either from exemplars or documents taken from another source. One example is drug shipments addressed by the defendant to himself or others. Others were based on a defendant accused of mailing an envelope containing a white substance to President Bush,[27] or where a defendant filed false tax returns.[28]

Two more recent federal appellate court cases confirm the continued acceptance of expert testimony in the area of expert handwriting analysis. *See, e.g., USA v. Dale*, 618 Fed. Appx. 494 (11th Cir. July 2, 2015) ["Defendant's] assertion that handwriting analysis is not reliable scientific evidence is without merit and has been squarely foreclosed by this court's precedent." [citation omitted]; and *USA v. Torres-Gonzalez*, 625 Fed. Appx. 331 (9th Cir. May 6, 2015).

Disguised Writing

The issue of comparing handwriting where the defendant is attempting a disguise is much more difficult. "Of course, where someone attempts to mimic the handwriting of another, there is a suppression of 'ordinary' inter-writer differences, which makes the [examiner's] task more difficult."[29] No court appears to have drawn a distinction between expert testimony where disguise is alleged versus the person's "natural handwriting." However, experts acknowledge that even one person's handwriting

---

25. *Id.*
26. *U.S. v. Crisp*, 324 F.3d 261 (4th Cir. 2003).
27. *U.S. v. Lewis*, 220 F. Supp. 2d 548 (S.D.W. Va. 2002).
28. *U.S. v. Hernandez*, 42 Fed. Appx. 172 (10th Cir. 2002).
29. *Starzecpyzel, supra* at 1032.

will vary because no one person will write exactly the same way when repeating (inter-writer differences). The same issue arises when the defendant is alleged to have forged the signature of another.

> To determine whether or not a signature is genuine is a very different problem from that of determining who actually wrote a forged signature. It is not often that the writer will put enough of his own writing qualities into it to identify himself. From this meager evidence it is of course just as presumptuous to say that the suspected writer did not write it.[30]

Rejections Based on Lack of Expert Qualifications or "Common Knowledge"

The courts that have rejected handwriting expert testimony have generally done so on the following grounds, where:

1. The expert was not qualified.

2. The jury could see for itself the similarities and differences, the expert would not be permitted to give an opinion as to authorship.

3. The expert did not explain his methodology in any detail.[31]

In one case, the expert testified that he had looked at two pieces of handwriting under a microscope and evaluated them based on "consistency, variation style, and peculiar or identifying characteristics."[32] The expert had also testified earlier that "there is no scientific methodology. It's a misnomer. There's not a scientific method in the sense of being a formal procedure. There is an analysis based upon the study of handwriting marks, including their length and width, the document, and sequence."[33] The court held that this was not sufficient to admit the testimony.

A few courts have barred handwriting testimony as not reliable in unique situations, such as one case in which a court barred expert testimony regarding printing by a defendant who learned to write in China.[34]

Expert May Point Out Differences, but Not Give an Opinion

Some courts have required that an expert simply point out similarities and dissimilarities between two pieces of handwriting, without giving an opinion as to authorship. The theory is that the expert is educating the jury to make up its own

---

30. *Id.* at 1043.
31. *Dracz v. American General Life Insurance Co.*, 426 F. Supp. 2d 1373 (M.D. Ga. 2006).
32. *Id.*
33. *Id.*
34. *U.S. v. Saelee*, 162 F. Supp. 2d 1097 (D. Ala. 2001).

mind, when it looks at the handwriting itself.[35] This was the same restriction put on fingerprint experts in the first of the *Llera Plaza* cases. That opinion was later retracted, so the ruling is no longer good law.

U.S. v. Hines, 55 F. Supp. 2d 62 (D. Mass. 1999)

This case raises questions concerning the application of *Daubert v. Merrell Dow Pharmaceuticals, Inc.*, to technical fields, that are not, strictly speaking, science.... Johannes Hines ("Hines") is charged under 18 U.S.C. §2113 for allegedly robbing the Broadway National Bank in Chelsea, Massachusetts, on January 27, 1997. The government's principal evidence consisted of the eyewitness identification of the teller who was robbed, Ms. Jeanne Dunne, and the handwriting analysis of the robbery note. In connection with the latter, the government offered Diana Harrison ("Harrison"), a document examiner with the Federal Bureau of Investigations, to testify as to the authorship of a "stick-up" note found at the scene of the crime.

Hines sought to exclude the handwriting analysis. This testimony, defense claims, notwithstanding its venerable history, does not meet the standards of *Daubert* and *Kumho*. In the alternative, if the court permitted the jury to hear the handwriting testimony, Hines sought to have his expert — Professor Mark Denbeaux ("Denbeaux") — testify as to the weaknesses of the methodology and the basis of Harrison's conclusions. The government, on the other hand, argued for its handwriting expert under the applicable tests, and rejects Denbeaux.... Our evidentiary rules put a premium on firsthand observations. Opinion testimony is disfavored except under certain circumstances; hearsay is generally excluded. The jury is to draw reasonable inferences from the firsthand data. When an expert witness is called upon to draw those inferences, several concerns are raised. The rules give expert witnesses greater latitude than is afforded other witnesses to testify based on data not otherwise admissible before the jury. In addition, a certain patina attaches to an expert's testimony unlike any other witness; this is "science," a professional's judgment, the jury may think, and give more credence to the testimony than it may deserve.

Accordingly, the trial court is supposed to review expert testimony carefully. The court is to admit the testimony not only where it is relevant to the issues at bar, the usual standard under Fed.R.Evid. 401, but when certain additional requirements are met under Fed.R.Evid. 702.

The first requirement has to do with the necessity for the testimony: expert testimony may be admitted where the inferences that are sought to be drawn

---

35. *U.S. v. Brown, supra.*

are inferences that a jury could not draw on its own. The inferences may be the product of specialized information, for example, beyond the ken of the lay jury.... For example, the subject looks like one the jury understands from every day life, but in fact, the inferences the jury may draw are erroneous. (As I describe below, eyewitness identification, and testimony about battered women syndrome fits uniquely into this category.)

The second requirement concerns the nature of the inferences to be drawn. In outlining the standards for admissibility, the *Daubert* Court noted the difference between information gleaned in a scientific setting and information presented in a courtroom. In the former, the decision makers are professionals; there is no need to come to a definitive conclusion; the decision making process comports with certain rules established by the professional scientific community. In the courtroom, the decision makers are lay, a jury; there is a need to come to a definitive conclusion; the decision making process has to satisfy norms of due process and fairness. In our tradition, for example, the adversary system and party examination and cross-examination are central.... Moreover, if the *Daubert* standard takes into account the unique trial setting — how well the lay trier will understand the testimony after examination and instructions — *Kumho* plainly does as well. In fact, cross-examination and limiting instructions may be more effective in "technical" fields because they are more accessible to the jury, than fields with the charisma of science.

Again, a mixed message: Apply *Daubert* to technical fields, even though the scientific method may not really fit, but be flexible. Moreover, in this setting, because few technical fields are as firmly established as traditional scientific ones, the new science/old science comparison is less clear. The court is plainly inviting a reexamination even of "generally accepted" venerable, technical fields.

Handwriting

Handwriting analysis is one such field. The Harrison testimony may be divided into two parts: Part 1 is Harrison's testimony with respect to similarities between the known handwriting of Hines, and the robbery note. Part 2 is Harrison's testimony with respect to the author of the note, that the author of the robbery note was indeed Hines. I concluded that Harrison could testify only as to the former.... Hines challenges Harrison's testimony under *Daubert/Kumho*. If I were to give special emphasis to "general acceptance" or to treat *Daubert/Kumho* as calling for a rigorous analysis only of new technical fields, not traditional ones, then handwriting analysis would largely pass muster. Handwriting analysis is perhaps the prototype of a technical field regularly admitted into evidence. But, if I were to apply the *Daubert/Kumho* standards rigorously, looking for such things as empirical testing, rate of error, etc., the testimony would have serious problems.

According to Denbeaux, handwriting analysis by experts suffers in two respects. It has never been subject to meaningful reliability or validity testing, comparing the results of the handwriting examiners' conclusions with actual outcomes. There is no peer review by a "competitive, unbiased community of practitioners and academics."

. . .

I do not believe that the government's expert, Kam, and the studies he has cited suggest otherwise. While Kam has conducted several interesting and important tests, purporting to validate handwriting analysis, they are not without criticism. They cannot be said to have "established" the validity of the field to any meaningful degree.

. . .

Handwriting analysis typically involves reviewing two samples, a known sample and an unknown one, to determine if they are similar. Both defense and government experts agree that unlike DNA or even fingerprints, one's handwriting is not at all unique in the sense that it remains the same over time, or uniquely separates one individual from another.

Everyone's handwriting changes from minute to minute, day to day. At the same time, our handwriting is sufficiently similar to one another so that people can read each other's writing. Given that variability, the "expert" is obliged to make judgments — these squiggles look more like these, these lines are shaped more like these, etc. And those judgments are, as Harrison conceded, subjective.

When a lay witness, the girlfriend of the defendant for example, says "this is my boyfriend's writing," her conclusion is based on having been exposed to her paramour's handwriting countless times. Without a lay witness with that kind of expertise, the government is obliged to offer the testimony of "experts" who have looked at, and studied handwriting for years. These are, essentially, "observational" experts, taxonomists — arguably qualified because they have seen so many examples over so long. It is not traditional, experimental science, to be sure, but *Kumho*'s gloss on *Daubert* suggests this is not necessary. I conclude that Harrison can testify to the ways in which she has found Hines' known handwriting similar to or dissimilar from the handwriting of the robbery note; part 1 of her testimony.

Part 2 of the Harrison testimony is, however, problematic. There is no data that suggests that handwriting analysts can say, like DNA experts, that this person is "the" author of the document. There are no meaningful, and accepted validity studies in the field. No one has shown me Harrison's error rate, the times she has been right, and the times she has been wrong.

There is no academic field known as handwriting analysis. This is a "field" that has little efficacy outside of a courtroom. There are no peer reviews of it. Nor can one compare the opinion reached by an examiner

Both defense and government experts agree that unlike DNA or even fingerprints, one's handwriting is not at all unique in the sense that it remains the same over time, or uniquely separates one individual from another.

with a standard protocol subject to validity testing, since there are no recognized standards. There is no agreement as to how many similarities it takes to declare a match, or how many differences it takes to rule it out.

...

The issue here is not only the validity and reliability of the expert testimony, but its validity and reliability in the context of this lay proceeding. Harrison's account of what is similar or not similar in the handwriting of Hines and the robber can be understood and evaluated by the jury. The witness can be cross-examined, as she was, about why this difference was not considered consequential, while this difference was, and the jury can draw their own conclusions. This is not rocket science, or higher math.[21]

...

The problem with ... handwriting is that there is no testing of the — no verification-type testing of these opinion results; and in addition, there has never been within the discipline of people who practice this skill — there has never been any agreement on how to express the results. There is no standardized nomenclature, you know.

Therefore, it seems to me that we should draw the distinction between somebody getting on the stand and saying 'Yeah, written by the same person,' or 'no, not written by the same person,' vs. 'these are the similarities or these are the dissimilarities'; and the jury can decide.

I find Harrison's testimony meets Fed. R. Evid. 702's requirements to the extent that she restricts her testimony to similarities or dissimilarities between the known exemplars and the robbery note. However, she may not render an ultimate conclusion on who penned the unknown writing....

This solution might be an ingenious compromise by courts that are unwilling to apply the strict *Daubert* standards. "But their solution may be, at its root, another attempt to evade the difficult question of whether handwriting experts offer genuine expertise."[36]

In addition, one court said that the fact that handwriting has been accepted for years as "generally accepted" does not mean that it should be generally accepted now.[37]

---

21. ... I am persuaded for now that the testimony involves more than just identifying what is similar and what is different in the same way a lay person would. It involves taking the next step — which this or that similarity matters, that it equals a general pattern. Presumably, the expert is helped in drawing general patterns by the numbers of exemplars she has seen, just like the spouse identifies the husband's handwriting because she has seen it numbers of times.

36. Jennifer L. Mnookin, "Comment: Scripting Expertise: The History of Handwriting Identification Evidence and the Judicial Construction of Reliability," *Virginia Law Review* 87 (December 2001): 1723, 1838.

37. *Saelee, supra* at 1105.

Reliability and Error Rate

Is handwriting comparison reliable? One court examined four studies attempting to distinguish between the results of experts versus lay people. Here is what it said.

> ... Mr. Cawley testified that there has been at least one empirical study concerning the reliability of handwriting comparison, conducted for the FBI by Moshe Kam. According to Mr. Cawley, the Kam study determined that a document examiner could do what he said he could do, i.e., compare a known document and a questioned document and offer an opinion about whether the writer of the known document was the writer of the questioned document.

> ... the Kam study concluded that document examiners had an error rate of 6.5% and laypersons had an error rate of 38.6%.... [there were 4 studies.] The first study found that experts outperformed non-experts but that the best non-experts did about as well as the experts.

> The second study found the rate of true positives to be almost identical for experts and non-experts, while experts committed fewer false positives.

> The third study found an unexplained 40% improvement in layperson's ability to avoid false positives. The fourth study tested the ability to determine whether a signature is genuine or not. Experts and laypersons had similar ability to detect forgeries.... [38]

In another federal court case, the court rejected expert testimony because the government had failed to meet its burden of showing that it was reliable based on reliability testing.[39] The defendant was convicted of sending a white powder through the mail addressed to President Bush. The defendant was charged with mailing five letters from Kanawha County, West Virginia, between January 2 and January 11, 2002, each of which contained a white powder, a cigarette butt, and a note. Four were identical copies and said "If I were you [sic], I'd change my attitude." The fifth note was sent to a private citizen, with a note saying "it is on." The return address on each envelope said "Gloria Fields," with her address incorrect. Ms. Fields admitted, however, that the notes were in her handwriting and that she had sent them to the defendant, her former boyfriend, Edward Lewis.

The defendant, Edward Lewis, moved to exclude the handwriting testimony before trial. The court denied the motion. On appeal, Lewis argued that the court failed to hold a *Daubert* hearing. The court agreed that the trial court could not refuse to apply the *Daubert* factors:

> While district courts have considerable leeway in determining how to assess reliability, they do not have the discretion to simply abandon their gate-keeping function by foregoing a reliability analysis.... Significantly, 'in a

---

38. *Id.* at 1102.
39. *U.S. v. Lewis*, 220 F. Supp. 2d 548 (S.D.W. Va. 2002).

particular case the failure to apply one or another of [the *Daubert* factors] may be unreasonable, and hence an abuse of discretion.'

… Handwriting analysis proposes a theory that each person's handwriting is unique, and involves a method by which a trained expert can identify each writing's author. The sufficiency of that theory and method can be tested through the basic factors set forth in *Daubert*.[40]

In a particular case, the failure to apply one or another of [the *Daubert* factors] may be unreasonable, and hence an abuse of discretion.

The expert in this case was John W. Cawley, III. Since 1977, he had been a forensic document analyst at the U.S. Postal Service, received a certificate after a two-year training with the post office and one year of internship training. He had testified approximately seventy times in the past. He attended annual meetings of the American Society of Questioned Document Examiners and passed annual proficiency tests with a 100% rating. He also referred to the Kam studies as demonstrating error rate, but didn't know of any other reliability studies, except for some vague references to some in other countries. The court decided that Cawley's statement that handwriting identification had been proven though studies was "inadequate to demonstrate testability and error rate."

The court was also troubled that Cawley and his fellow examiners always got 100% on their proficiency tests and always agreed with the first examiner when checking his results. Cawley also stated that twenty-five samples were necessary to compare handwriting, but could not say why.

Although the court decided that the handwriting evidence did not pass *Daubert*, it upheld the conviction because of the mass of other evidence that supported Lewis's guilt.

In *U.S. v. Crisp*, another bank robbery case,[41] the court admitted handwriting testimony about a note the defendant slipped to another convict in jail where he was awaiting trial. It asked the other man to lie and give him an alibi for the crime, stating "you know if you don't help me I am going to get life in prison, and you ain't going to get nothing. Really it's over for me if you don't change what you told them." Based on samples of the defendant's handwriting that the police got from his girlfriend, an expert with the North Carolina Bureau of Investigation testified that the defendant had written the note.

The trial held a *Daubert* hearing, but it did not strictly apply the criteria. First, it stated that all the other circuit courts admitted handwriting examiner testimony. The expert had twenty-four years of experience and referred to the Kam studies as evidence of error rates. His opinion that the defendant had written the note was based on the following:

Among the similarities … were the overall size and spacing of the letters and words in the documents; the unique shaping of the capital letter "L" in the

---

40. *Id.* at 550.
41. *U.S. v. Crisp, supra.*

name "Lamont"; the spacing between the capital letter "L" and the rest of the word; a peculiar shaping to the letters "o" and "n" when used in conjunction with one another; the v-like formation of the letter "u" in the word "you"; and the shape of the letter "t," including the horizontal stroke. ... Currin [the expert] also noted that the word "tomorrow" was misspelled in the same manner on both the known exemplar and the Note. He went on to testify that, in his opinion Crisp [the defendant] had authored the Note.[42]

The court concluded that the testimony was admissible given the fact that "handwriting comparison analysis has achieved widespread and lasting acceptance in the expert community ..." Here, Currin merely pointed out certain unique characteristics shared by the two writings. Though he opined that Crisp authored the Note in question, the jury was nonetheless left to examine the Note and decide for itself whether it agreed with the expert.[43]

> "Handwriting comparison analysis has achieved widespread and lasting acceptance in the expert community."

Judge Michael, of the three-judge panel, wrote a scathing dissent in this case. A dissent is not law that later cases must follow, but it does show what the courts could do to conduct a genuine *Daubert* hearing. Judge Michael first observed that the government has made no progress after *Daubert* in demonstrating that it complies and that "it should not be given a pass in this case."[44] Here is Judge Michael's evaluation of the *Daubert* factors.

1. **Has the science been tested?** " ... it appears that no one has ever assessed the validity of the basic tenets of handwriting comparison, namely, that no two individuals write in precisely the same fashion and that certain characteristics of an individual's writing remain constant when the writer attempts to disguise them."

2. **Has there been peer review and publication?** "Those within the field have failed to engage in any critical study of the basic principles and methods of handwriting analysis, and few objective outsiders have taken on this challenge.... Indeed, the field ... relies primarily on texts that were written fifty to one hundred years ago."

3. **What is the error rate?** The court looked at the few studies, including one that shows almost 25% of examiners misidentified the author of a forged document, and concluded the error rates were "disquieting to say the least."

4. **Are there standards or controls?** "There does not seem to be any list of universal, objective requirements for identifying an author.... the results are 'only as good as the unexaminable personal database of the practitioner and the practitioner's not-fully-explainable method of deriving answers.'" [quoting *Lewis*]

---

42. *Id.* at 271.
43. *Id.*
44. *Id.* at 272.

5. **Is the science generally accepted?** "general acceptance of handwriting analysis appears to come only from those within the field … and those within the field have not challenged or questioned its basic premises."[45]

Handwriting Testimony Found to Meet *Daubert* as Reliable

A federal appellate court ruled that admitting the testimony of a handwriting expert was not error, where the trial court applied all the *Daubert* factors and found the testimony reliable.

U.S. v. Prime, 431 F.3d 1147 (9th Cir. 2005)

Between April and June 2001, Prime, along with three co-conspirators, David Hiestand ("Hiestand"), Juan Ore-Lovera, and Jeffrey Hardy, sold non-existent items on eBay, purchased items using counterfeit money orders created by the group, sold pirated computer software, and stole credit card numbers from software purchasers. To facilitate this operation, Prime and his cohorts used a credit card encoder to input the stolen data on their own credit cards, set up post office boxes under false names, manufactured false identifications, and used a filter bank account to hide proceeds of the crimes.

At trial, numerous victims testified as to the details surrounding how they had been defrauded by Prime's various scams. In addition, co-conspirators Hiestand and Hardy both extensively testified as to the details of the conspiracy, implicating Prime in all of the crimes charged. The prosecution also elicited the expert opinion of Kathleen Storer ("Storer"), a forensic document examiner with the Secret Service. She testified that Prime was the author of as many as thirty-eight incriminating exhibits, including envelopes, postal forms, money orders, Post-it notes, express mail labels and postal box applications.

Prime took the stand in his own defense and claimed that despite all of the evidence linking him to the various scams, including admissions that his fingerprints were on several items linked to the crimes, he was simply attempting to engage in legal entrepreneurial ventures. Prime also confirmed that he had previously been convicted of first and second degree theft, two counts of possession of stolen property in the second degree, and forgery. The jury found Prime guilty on all counts.

Prime moved for a new trial based on the improper submission of extrinsic evidence to the jury. The district court denied the motion, and this appeal follows.

---

45. *Id.* at 280–81.

ADMISSIBILITY OF EXPERT TESTIMONY

Prime moved in limine to exclude Storer's expert testimony. The court held a *Daubert* hearing where both sides were allowed to offer voluminous materials and expert testimony regarding the reliability of the proposed testimony. After careful consideration, the court denied the motion, and Storer testified that, in her opinion, Prime's handwriting appeared on counterfeit money orders and other incriminating documents. On appeal, Prime contends that the admission of expert testimony regarding handwriting analysis was unreliable under *Daubert*, and thus the court abused its discretion by allowing Storer to testify.

...

1. Whether the theory or technique can be or has been tested.

Handwriting analysis is performed by comparing a known sample of handwriting to the document in question to determine if they were written by the same person. The government and Storer provided the court with ample support for the proposition that an individual's handwriting is so rarely identical that expert handwriting analysis can reliably gauge the likelihood that the same individual wrote two samples.

The most significant support came from Professor Sargur N. Srihari of the Center of Excellence for Document Analysis and Recognition at the State University of New York at Buffalo, who testified that the result of his published research was that "handwriting is individualistic."

With respect to this case in particular, the court noted that Storer's training credentials in the Secret Service as well as her certification by the American Board of Forensic Document Examiners were "impeccable." The court also believed that Storer's analysis in this case was reliable given the "extensive" 112 pages containing Prime's known handwriting.

2. Whether the technique has been subject to peer review and publication.

The court cited to numerous journals where articles in this area subject handwriting analysis to peer review by not only handwriting experts, but others in the forensic science community. Additionally, the Kam study, see infra, which evaluated the reliability of the technique employed by Storer of using known writing samples to determine who drafted a document of unknown authorship, was both published and subjected to peer review. The court also noted that the Secret Service has instituted a system of internal peer review whereby each document reviewed is subject to a second, independent examination.

3. The known or potential rate of error.

In concluding that the type of handwriting analysis Storer was asked to perform had an acceptable rate of error, the court relied on studies conducted by Professor Moshe Kam of the Electrical and Computer

Engineering Department at Drexel University. Professor Kam's studies demonstrated that expert handwriting analysts tend to be quite accurate at the specific task Storer was asked to perform — determining whether the author of a known writing sample is also the author of a questioned writing sample.

When the two samples were in fact written by the same person, professional handwriting analysts correctly arrived at that conclusion 87% of the time. On the other hand when the samples were written by different people, handwriting analysts erroneously associated them no more than 6.5% of the time. While Kam's study demonstrates some degree of error, handwriting analysis need not be flawless in order to be admissible.

Rather, the Court had in mind a flexible inquiry focused "solely on principles and methodology, not on the conclusions that they generate." As long as the process is generally reliable, any potential error can be brought to the attention of the jury through cross-examination and the testimony of other experts.

4. The existence and maintenance of standards controlling the technique's operation.

The court recognized that although this area has not been completely standardized, it is moving in the right direction. The Secret Service laboratory where Storer works has maintained its accreditation with the American Society of Crime Laboratory Directors since 1998, based on an external proficiency test. Furthermore, the standard nine-point scale used to express the degree to which the examiner believes the handwriting samples match was established under the auspices of the American Society for Testing and Materials ("ASTM"). The court reasonably concluded that any lack of standardization is not in and of itself a bar to admissibility in court.

5. General acceptance.

The court recognized the broad acceptance of handwriting analysis and specifically its use by such law enforcement agencies as the CIA, FBI, and the United States Postal Inspection Service.

Given the comprehensive inquiry into Storer's proffered testimony, we cannot say that the district court abused its discretion in admitting the expert handwriting analysis testimony. The district court's thorough and careful application of the *Daubert* factors was consistent with all six circuits that have addressed the admissibility of handwriting expert testimony, and determined that it can satisfy the reliability threshold.

Conviction AFFIRMED.[46]

---

46. *United States v. Prime*, 431 F.3d 1147 (9th Cir. 2005).

Does Scholarly Disagreement Show Lack of General Acceptance?

Although the court in *Prime* may be right that there has been little challenge among examiners themselves, a few professors have engaged in a long-standing debate about the validity of handwriting examination. Three law school professors, D. Michael Risinger, Mark P. Denbeaux, and Michael J. Saks, have publicly questioned[47] the opinion that handwriting analysis is valid with a fellow professor, Andre Moenssens. Moenssens has defended handwriting analysis as valid under "Osbornian" principles of identification and has referred to the Kam studies as support for their reliability.

Moenssens has argued that using the following procedures would ensure reliability.

- Accepted processes are stated in a professional literature.
- There are professional societies and associations to train and provide further education to examiners.
- Required courses of study and training.
- Education to be supervised by prominent professional in the discipline.
- A program of clinical experience supervised by such professionals.
- Any expert must show aptitude and proficiency by passing an examination board.
- The opposing party can retest the same materials with its own expert.[48]

Risinger and his colleagues challenge the conclusion that handwriting analysis is "science," and give their definition as follows:

> Science requires standardization of the conditions.... and a formal analytical system for their organization. A central condition that must be present is theoretical reproducibility of observation (two observers in the same position could perceive the same thing) with strong favor given to reports of observations that can be practically repeated by multiple observers ...
>
> A scientific hypothesis is a statement about inter-relationships between items of categories that is formulated in such a way that it can be subjected to empirical testing ...
>
> Handwriting identification ... doesn't even make it into the category of "science" in any tenable modern sense.... To apply the label "science" to the enterprise in general or to the practice of individual practitioners in particular would deprive the term of any defensible meaning.[49]

Risinger and his colleagues counter that Moenssens' standards will not screen out unreliable experts because all the "tests" would be supervised and conducted within

---

47. D. Michael Risinger, Mark P. Denbeaux, and Michael J. Saks, "Brave New 'Post-World' — A Reply to Professor Moenssens," *Seton Hall Law Review* 29 (1998): 405.

48. *Id.* at 444.

49. *Id.* at 440–41.

the handwriting community itself—a community with a vested interest in ensuring that the field be accepted.

Court Decisions after the NRC Report

Following the NRC Report and until more studies are conducted to determine (1) that all handwriting is unique and (2) that experts perform significantly better than non-experts in detecting handwriting written by a common writer, it likely that more courts will be confronted with requests for *Daubert* hearings. Although the courts have mostly admitted this testimony with a nod at *Daubert* and a comment that the science is generally accepted, we can expect more challenges arguing that the phrase "generally accepted" should not mean "generally admitted." To date, however, this approach has not been successful in the courts.

Even after the NRC Report in 2009, handwriting experts continue to be accepted by some courts, relying on earlier cases that have accepted handwriting experts to bolster their conclusion that handwriting is reliable. For example, in a 2015 case, *U.S. v. Dale*,[50] a case involving theft of public money, the Eleventh Circuit Court allowed a handwriting expert to testify about handwriting. Its analysis did not review the *Daubert* factors. Rather, the court decided the handwriting expert was well qualified and his testimony was helpful to the jury:

> Nor did the district court did abuse its discretion in admitting the testimony of Miller, the handwriting expert. Although Dale appears to argue that Miller was not qualified to testify as an expert in handwriting analysis, the record belies such a contention. Miller was properly qualified as an expert: he had been a forensic document examiner with the IRS for over ten years; he was certified with the American Board of Forensic Document Examiners; he had examined approximately 100,000 documents in his career; and he had twice previously been qualified as an expert in document examination in federal court. Further, Dale's assertion that handwriting analysis is not reliable scientific evidence is without merit and has been squarely foreclosed by this court's precedent. *See United States v. Paul*, 175 F.3d 906, 909–10 & n. 2 (11th Cir. 1999) (finding that the argument that "handwriting analysis does not qualify as reliable scientific evidence" is meritless).

> Finally, Miller's testimony was helpful to the jury in understanding how handwriting samples are compared and any danger of unfair prejudice from misleading the jury was mitigated by the fact that the jury was shown the handwriting, through the use of demonstrative aids, and was free to compare the handwriting for itself. *See Frazier*, 387 F.3d at 1262 (an expert's testimony is helpful to the trier of fact if the testimony "concerns matters that are beyond the understanding of the average lay person"). In sum, because Miller

---

50. 618 Fed. Appx. 494 (11th Cir. July 2, 2015).

was qualified to testify, handwriting analysis is a scientifically reliable methodology, and Miller's testimony was helpful to the jury, the court did not abuse its discretion in admitting Miller's testimony.[51]

But there continue to be courts that conclude that handwriting falls short of scientific reliability. For example, in *U.S. v. Johnsted*,[52] in a prosecution for threatening mail, the court held the handwriting expert could not testify because handwriting analysis falls far short of reliability as applied to an opinion about a hand-printed address. Although some may argue that the opinion should be restricted to the issue of hand-printing, the court's opinion is largely devoted to fundamental issues about the reliability of handwriting matching in general:

> [Defendant] Johnsted has moved to exclude the report and expert testimony of United States Postal Service handwriting analyst Gale Bolsover, who would opine that the hand printing on the communications at issue belong to the defendant. After reviewing Bolsover's proposed opinion testimony for relevance and reliability, as well as hearing evidence from the parties, the court finds that the science or art underlying handwriting analysis falls well short of a reliability threshold when applied to hand printing analysis. Because the government has not demonstrated that Bolsover's analysis is supported by principles and methodology that are scientifically valid, at least in light of the particular facts and circumstances of this case, the court will exclude Bolsover's testimony and report.[53]

> . . .

> In this case, both parties (and the government in particular) cite a large number of cases addressing whether hand *writing* analysis passes muster under *Daubert*. Given this court's obligation to inquire into the evidence's reliability, the court devotes most of this opinion to analyzing the expert testimony with reference to the *Daubert* factors, while maintaining an overarching focus on the scientific validity of the principles underlying the methodology of hand *printing* analysis, to determine their relevance and reliability "in light of the facts and circumstances of this particular case."[54]

> . . .

> Even accepting that studies have adequately tested the first principle — that all handwriting is unique — the government does not dispute the troubling lack of evidence testing or supporting the second fundamental premise of handwriting analysis. Even more troubling is an apparent lack of double blind studies demonstrating the ability of certified experts to distinguish between individual's handwriting or identify forgeries to any reliable degree of certainty. This lack of testing has serious repercussions on

---

51. *Id.* at 497.
52. 30 F. Supp.3d 814 (W.D. Wisc. 2013).
53. *Id.* at 816.
54. *Id.* at 817.

a practical level: because the entire premise of interpersonal individuality and intrapersonal variations of handwriting remains untested in reliable, double blind studies, the task of distinguishing a minor intrapersonal variation from a significant interpersonal difference — which is necessary for making an identification or exclusion — cannot be said to rest on scientifically valid principles.... With its underlying principles at best half-tested, handwriting analysis itself would appear to rest on a shaky foundation.[55]

The court in *Johnsted* specifically rejected the argument that appellate circuit courts have routinely approved trial courts' admission of handwriting experts, noting that the standard of review of the appellate court does not mean that the testimony should have been admitted in the first place:

> The government points out that every circuit court to review a district court's decision to admit handwriting analysis has affirmed that decision. *See Deputy*, 345 F.3d at 509 (collecting cases). But that argument is unavailing here. First, although circuit courts have affirmed lower courts' decisions to permit expert testimony on handwriting analysis, there remains "some divergence of opinion as to the soundness of handwriting analysis," and "[s]everal district courts ... have rejected handwriting analysis, finding it lacks scientific reliability." *Id.* (collecting cases). As defendant correctly points out, the circuit courts were also reviewing the district courts' decisions under deferential standards of review; they were not laying down a rule that handwriting analysis *must* always be admissible under Rule 702.[56]

Finally, the court specifically rejected the argument that cross-examination about reliability and methodology is sufficient to solve the problem of admitting handwriting testimony:

> The court is also aware that in general, "[v]igorous cross-examination, presentation of contrary evidence, and careful instruction on the burden of proof are the traditional and appropriate means of attacking shaky but admissible evidence" and that "[t]hese conventional devices ... are the appropriate safeguards where the basis of scientific testimony meets the standards of Rule 702." *Id.* at 596, 113 S.Ct. 2786. The proffered expert testimony here, however, does not even qualify as the "shaky but admissible" variety. It is testimony based on two fundamental principles, one of which has not been tested or proven, and neither of which have been proven sufficiently reliable to assist a lay jury beyond its own ability to assess the similarity and differences in the hand printing in this case. Because the government has not provided enough evidence to demonstrate the reliability of handwriting analysis to the hand printing in this case, Bolsover's expert analysis will be excluded at trial.[57]

---

55. *Id.* at 818.
56. *Id.* at 821.
57. *Id.* at 822.

Will Computer Handwriting Analysis Meet the *Daubert* Test?

The primary objections to handwriting analysis are that its scientific hypotheses have not been tested, that is, no one can prove what characteristics of handwriting are unique, either individually or in combination, or what number of characteristics could positively identify a writer. That may change with the advent of computer technology that can develop an objective set of characteristics to review and a large enough number of characteristics so that conclusions based on probability analysis could be as reliable as DNA analysis.

In 1999, the National Institute of Justice funded a project to determine if computers could prove, first, that handwriting is unique and second, that a sample of handwriting could be identified based on a computer program search of exemplars provided by a writer.

The results of the study were published in the *Journal of Forensic Science* in 2002.[58] The study included three copies of an identical handwriting sample from each of approximately 1,500 writers, randomly selected among gender, age, and ethnicity. The writing sample was a short letter to a doctor that incorporated 156 words, each letter of the alphabet at least once in each of upper and lower case, punctuation, all ten numerals and distinctive letter and number combinations.

The study examined both variations within the three samples for each writer (within-writer variance) and variations among all the writers (between-writer variance).

The study examined 11 "macro features," which are listed below correlated with the terminology used in conventional handwriting analysis:

Terminology from HW Analysis	Macro-Feature
pen pressure	1. entropy of grey values
	2. grey-level threshold
	3. number of black pixels
writing movement	4. number of interior contours
	5. number of exterior curves
stroke formation	6. number of vertical slopes
	7. number of horizontal slopes
	8. number of negative slopes
	9. number of positive slopes
slant	10. slant
word proportion	11. height

---

58. Sargur N. Srihari, Sung-Hyuk Cha, Hina Arora and Sangjik Lee, "Individuality of Handwriting" *Journal of Forensic Science* 47, no. 4 (July 2002).

The computer study also used certain "micro-features," such as gradient, structure, and concavity, all of which are evaluated based on the individual shape of letters. Cursive writing, for example, would have a greater number of interior contours and fewer exterior contours, whereas the opposite would be true for hand printing.

According to the authors, "in order to validate individuality among *n* writers, we would have to determine whether the samples form *n* distinct clusters, where samples of the same writer belong to the same cluster and samples of different writers belong to different clusters." The article reports: "Taking an approach that the results are statistically inferable over the entire population of the U.S., we were able to validate handwriting individuality with 95% confidence."[59]

In addition, the authors concluded that their software could determine the writer of a questioned document. The authors also analyzed the data to determine if they could identify the writer of the three samples based on their proximity in the criteria evaluated to each other. The prototype consisted of all of the exemplars written by all subjects, except for one exemplar removed from the set to "match." They report: "using character-level features of all eight characters of the word 'referred' in the exemplar, the correct writer was identified in 99% of the cases when all possible pairs of writers were considered. When there are five possible writers, the writer of the test document is correctly assigned with a 98% probability."

Figure 12.1 Cedar-Fox computer handwriting analysis image, courtesy Sargur Srihari.

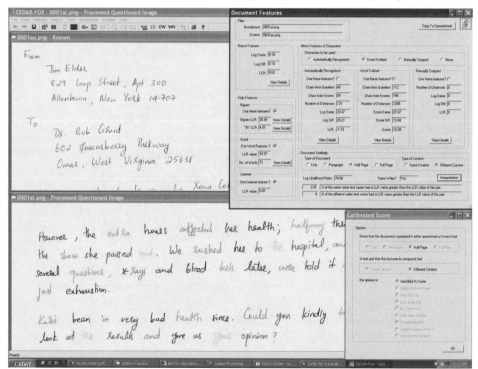

---

59. *Id.* at 16.

"Based on a few macro-features that capture global attributes from a handwritten document and micro-features at the character level from a few characters, we were able to establish with a 98% confidence that a writer can be identified." The computer screen in Figure 12.1 shows the results of analyzing the sample with the Cedar-Fox system.

The authors also attempted to determine whether two documents were written by the same writer. This process involved evaluating both within writer and between-writer distances. The verification accuracy was about 96%. A report by Sargur Srihari of the results of the Cedar-Fox testing is available at www.ncjrs.gov/pdffiles1/nij/grants/232745.pdf (2010).

The authors have marketed their system under the name Cedar-Fox. It has been used by law enforcement on a limited basis. According to the Srihari report cited above, its methods were cited in two federal cases, both of which admitted the handwriting experts.

Ransom Notes — From Lindberg to JonBenét

In 1935, Bruno Richard Hauptmann was convicted of one of the most notorious kidnapping and murders in history. He was accused of climbing up a ladder at the home of Charles A. Lindberg, the famous aviator, and kidnapping his almost two-year-old boy. On the window sill was a letter demanding a $50,000 ransom and referring to later instructions to come. The note said:

Dear Sir!
Have 50.000$ redy 25.000$ in 20$ bills 15.000in 10$ bills and 10.000$ in 5$ bills. After 2–4 days we will inform you were to deliver the Mony.
We warn you for making anyding public or for notify the polise the child is in gute care.
Idication for all letters are singnature and 3 holes.

The "signature" was two interlocking circles. The area within the overlap was solid red. The rest of the circles were outlined in blue. Three square holes pierced the symbol in a horizontal line.[60]

The note led to negotiations, and a number of additional notes. Hauptmann was captured at the meeting point for the supposed payoff. Eventually, it was determined that the baby died shortly after the kidnapping.

The nation followed the ordeal through the news. At the trial, Osborne, the famous author of the text referred to by every handwriting expert, testified that the notes were written by Hauptmann. He stated that his conclusion was "irresistible, unanswerable and overwhelming."[61] The testimony against Hauptmann included three experts who testified he wrote the kidnapping notes, one of whom said the

---

60. Dr. Henry Lee and Dr. Jerry Labriola, *Famous Crimes Revisited — From Sacco-Vanzetti to O.J. Simpson* (StrongBooks, 2001), 114.
61. *N.J. v. Hauptmann*, 180 A. 809 (Ct.App. N.J. 1935).

address of the package used to send the baby's sleeping suit was Hauptmann's. Hauptmann called John Trendley, a documents examiner from St. Louis, who said he did not believe Hauptmann wrote the ransom notes.

Hauptmann appealed his sentence, arguing, among other things, that the trial court gave a prejudicial instruction on the handwriting issue by emphasizing Osborn's testimony:

> A very important question in the case is, did the defendant, Hauptmann, write the original ransom note found on the window sill, and the other ransom notes which followed? Numerous experts in handwriting have testified, after exhaustive examination of the ransom letters, and comparison with the genuine writing of the defendant, that the defendant Hauptmann wrote every one of the ransom notes, and Mr. Osborn, senior, said that the conclusion was irresistible, unanswerable and overwhelming. On the other hand, the defendant denies that he wrote them, and a handwriting expert, called by him, so testified. And so the fact becomes one for your determination. The weight of the evidence to prove the genuineness of handwriting is wholly for the jury.[62]

Hauptmann also appealed on the ground that the trial court failed to give three jury instructions that he had proposed, which instructions stated that handwriting testimony was "proof of low degree," that it was "most unsatisfactory, very inconclusive, most unreliable and of the lowest probative force," and that a jury was not bound to accept an expert opinion. The court rejected the appeal. It said that although a judge in an earlier decision had referred to handwriting experts as of "a low order of testimony," the statement was not complete without the entire sentence, which defendant had not asked to charge:

"Handwriting is an art concerning which correctness of opinion is susceptible of demonstration ... Without such demonstration the opinion of an expert in handwriting is a low order of testimony."

> Handwriting is an art concerning which correctness of opinion is susceptible of demonstration, and I am fully convinced that the value of the opinion of every handwriting expert as evidence must depend upon the clearness with which the expert demonstrates its correctness ... Without such demonstration the opinion of an expert in handwriting is a low order of testimony.[63]

"Some authors and advocates argue that our legal system victimized Bruno Hauptmann because of the admission of questionable evidence: expert handwriting testimony. This controversy extends far beyond this infamous case, reaching the academic and judicial forum."[64] In reviewing a new book called *Using Great Cases to Think About the Criminal Justice System*, the authors note that Hauptmann could not afford to hire a lawyer and his head defense was paid by the Hearst newspapers, which stood to profit handsomely from the public's purchase of its papers.[65] Hauptmann's appeal was denied

---

62. *Id.* at 822.

63. *Id.* at 823.

64. Simone Ling Francini, "Expert Handwriting Testimony: Is the Writing Really on the Wall?," *Suffolk Journal of Trial & Appellate Advocacy* 11 (2006): 99.

65. Jonathan L. Entin, "Book Review: Using Great Cases to Think about the Criminal Justice System," *Journal Criminal Law & Criminology* 89 (Spring 1999): 1141.

and he was executed on April 3, 1936. His wife continued to declare that he was innocent.

In the year 2000, further evidence came to light casting doubt on whether Hauptmann had been guilty of the kidnapping. One of the claims was that "a document examiner for the U.S. Army and Secret Service" had concluded that Hauptmann was not the author of the ransom notes.[66]

Who Wrote the JonBenét Ramsey Ransom Note?

JonBenét Ramsey was a six-year-old found murdered on December 6, 1996, in her basement in Boulder, Colorado. The case, which as of this printing has not been solved, became famous because of its bizarre circumstances, the charges that the police compromised the crime scene, and the attempts to determine who wrote the ransom note. The note was found by Patsy Ramsey, JonBenét's mother, on the kitchen steps in the early morning of December 26. Patsy called 911 just before 6 a.m. JonBenét's body was found nearly seven hours later in the basement by her father at 1 p.m.

The ransom note was handwritten in printing on paper found in the basement. The note was addressed to "Mr. Ramsey" and demanded $118,000 in ransom money. It was signed "Victory! S.B.T.C." The following is the text of the note:

Mr. Ramsey,

Listen carefully! We are a group of individuals that represent a small foreign faction. We respect your business but not the country that it serves. At this time we have your daughter in our possession. She is safe and unharmed and if you want her to see 1997, you must follow our instructions to the letter.

You will withdraw $118,000.00 from your account. $100,000 will be in $100 bills and the remaining $18,000 in $20 bills. Make sure that you bring an adequate size attaché to the bank. When you get home you will put the money in a brown paper bag. I will call you between 8 and 10 am tomorrow to instruct you on delivery. The delivery will be exhausting so I advise you to be rested. If we monitor you getting the money early, we might call you early to arrange an earlier delivery of the money and hence a earlier pickup of your daughter.

Any deviation of my instructions will result in the immediate execution of your daughter. You will also be denied her remains for proper burial. The two gentlemen watching over your daughter do not particularly like you so I advise you not to provoke them. Speaking to anyone about your situation, such as Police, F.B.I., etc., will result in your daughter being beheaded. If we catch you talking to a stray dog, she dies. If you alert bank authorities, she

---

66. Jesse Leavenworth, "Questions Linger about 'Crime of the Century,'" *The Hartford Courant*, February 6, 2000.

dies. If the money is in any way marked or tampered with, she dies. You will be scanned for electronic devices and if any are found, she dies. You can try to deceive us but be warned that we are familiar with Law enforcement countermeasures and tactics. You stand a 99% chance of killing your daughter if you try to out smart us. Follow our instructions and you stand a 100% chance of getting her back. You and your family are under constant scrutiny as well as the authorities. Don't try to grow a brain John. You are not the only fat cat around so don't think that killing will be difficult. Don't underestimate us John. Use that good southern common sense of yours. It is up to you now John!

Victory!

S.B.T.C.

The immediate reaction to the ransom note was that it was a decoy to mislead the investigation. First, the note was three pages in length — far longer than required to state a ransom demand and of a length that would take considerable time to write. As it was written on paper found in the Ramsey home, the idea that an intruder would enter the home and write such a long note, risking detection, appeared ridiculous. The dollar amount was the same as Ramsey's year end bonus and it was much too small to indicate a real kidnapping. Authorities suspected that the murderer was a family member and the note was a ruse to make it look like a kidnapping gone bad.[67]

As the JonBenét Ramsey case shows, document analysis can include both handwriting and the content of the writing itself. For example, examiners have pointed out that the ransom note contained word choice and phrasings that would be highly unusual in a real kidnapping. For example, the note says that two men are "watching over" Ramsey's daughter. This sounded more like language from the Bible than a kidnapper, in the opinion of one author. He also noted that the phrase "and hence a earlier pickup of your daughter," used a word that is quite uncommon — hence. Yet the Ramseys' Christmas message at church used the word "hence."[68] The fact that $118,000 is an odd amount and coincidentally the amount of John Ramsey's bonus that year also raised suspicion.

Police hired four handwriting experts, and the Ramseys hired two. All of them concluded that Patsy Ramsey did not write the note, with a likelihood ranging from 4 to 4.5 out of 5 that she was excluded as the writer.

Both parties agree that the Ransom Note is not an ideal specimen for handwriting analysis, primarily due to the type of writing instrument, a broad fiber-tip pen, used to draft the note. This type of pen distorts and masks fine

---

67. Mark McClish, "JonBenét Ramsey Murder — The Ransom Note," Statement Analysis, July 2001, http://www.statementanalysis.com/ramseynote.

68. *Id.*

details to an extent not achievable by other types of pen, as for example a ball point pen.

In addition, the stroke direction used to construct certain letters and subtle hand printing features, such as hesitations and pen lifts, are difficult to ascertain because of the pen used in the Ransom Note. Finally, the handwriting in the original Ransom Note showed consistency throughout the entire writing.

One of the most common means to disguise one's handwriting is to attempt to make the script erratic throughout the text. In sum, for the above reasons, the Ransom Note is not an ideal specimen for handwriting analysis. Nevertheless, the writer does not appear to have been trying to disguise his or her handwriting.[69]

The handwriting note then became an issue in a lawsuit filed by Robert Wolf against John and Patsy Ramsey. Wolf was a local journalist who was investigated for a short time based on information from his girlfriend that he had been acting suspiciously. The Ramseys wrote a book and appeared on TV, denying their involvement in the murder and commenting that Wolf had been investigated as a suspect. Wolf then sued for libel stating that he had been falsely accused of murder. In order to win his case, Wolf needed to show that the Ramseys had acted with "actual malice" in accusing him as a suspect. The term actual malice in libel law means that the person making the statement knew it was untrue. The only way the Ramseys could know that Wolf was not the murderer was if one of them was, in fact, the murderer. Therefore, whether John or Patsy Ramsey wrote the ransom note, and knew that Wolf was not the murderer, was critical to Wolf's lawsuit.

Wolf claimed that Patsy Ramsey killed JonBenét in a fit of anger, possibly for wetting the bed, and smashed her head against the bathroom floor or tub. He then alleged that Patsy set up a cover-up to look like an intruder had killed JonBenét and wrote the ransom note. Two handwriting experts testified for Wolf on a motion by the Ramseys to dismiss the case. Both concluded the ransom note was written by Patsy Ramsey. The court ruled the first expert, Cina Wong Epstein, was unqualified because she had not taken any courses or tests. The second expert, Gideon Epstein, failed to provide any methodology for his conclusions. He was allowed to point out differences and similarities, but was not permitted to give his opinion that Mrs. Ramsey wrote the notes. Below is the court's analysis of the handwriting expert testimony.[70]

Plaintiff, however, asserts that his retained experts believe Mrs. Ramsey to be the author of the Ransom Note. Indeed, Gideon Epstein and Cina

---

69. *Wolf v. Ramsey*, 253 F. Supp.2d 1323, 1334 (N.D. Ga. 2003).
70. *Id.*

Wong, the handwriting experts proffered by plaintiff, opine that they are "100 percent certain" Mrs. Ramsey wrote the Ransom Note. In contrast to the experts relied upon by defendants and by the Boulder Police Department, however, neither of these experts have ever seen or examined the original Ransom Note.

. . .

Defendants' experts base their conclusion that Mrs. Ramsey is not the author of the Ransom Note on the "numerous significant dissimilarities" between the individual characteristics of Mrs. Ramsey's hand printing and of that used in the Ransom Note. For example, defendant asserts Mrs. Ramsey's written letter "u" consistently differs from the way the same letter is written throughout the Ransom Note. Plaintiff's experts respond that this variation may be due to a conscious effort by Mrs. Ramsey to change her handwriting or to her heightened stress level.

In support of their conclusion that Mrs. Ramsey authored the Ransom Note, plaintiff's experts assert that there are similarities between letters found in the Ransom Note and exemplars and that the note contains proof-reader marks of the kind often used by newspaper reporters and journalists. (Plaintiff also notes that Mrs. Ramsey was a journalism major in college.)

. . .

Other experts believe the Ransom Note may have been authored by other people. In addition to Mrs. Ramsey, there were other individuals "under suspicion" who had their handwriting analyzed and who were not eliminated as the possible author of the Ransom Note. For example, forensic document examiner Lloyd Cunningham cannot eliminate plaintiff as the author of the Ransom Note. Plaintiff's ex-girlfriend has also testified that she was "struck by how the handwriting in the note resembled [plaintiff's] own handwriting" and believes that he is the note's author. . . .

Defendants argue that the opinions of plaintiffs' expert should not be admitted because the field of forensic document examination is not sufficiently reliable. In their Brief in Support of the Motion in Limine, defendants argue that the "science" of handwriting analysis does not meet the reliability standards of Rule 702: as the theoretical bases underlying this science have never been tested; error rates are neither known nor measured; and the field lacks both controlling standards and meaningful peer review.

In examining defendants' contention, the Court notes that both parties agree that the field of forensic document examination is premised on the assumption that no two persons' handwriting is exactly alike; instead, each person has a unique handwriting pattern that allows the person to be identified through a comparison of proper handwriting specimens. Forensic document examination involves the subjective analysis and assessment of writing characteristics found in a person's handwriting or hand printing style, by examination of subtle and minute qualities of movement such as pen lifts, shading, pressure and letter forms.

Handwriting identification is an inexact endeavor that "cannot boast absolute certainty in all cases." Two or more handwriting experts can reach different conclusions of authorship, even when examining the same questioned document and handwriting exemplars.

Forensic document examiners are generally trained through a "guild-type" apprenticeship process, in which supervised trainees study methods of document examination described by the field's leading texts. The only recognized organization for accrediting forensic document examiners is the American Board of Forensic Document Examiners.

… The most reliable method of forensic document examination occurs when an examiner compares both historical writings and requests exemplars to the questioned document.

The recognized method for forensic document analysis occurs in several important steps. First, the expert determines whether a questioned document contains a sufficient amount of writing and enough individual characteristics to permit identification. After determining that the questioned document is identifiable, the expert examines the submitted handwriting specimens in the same manner. If both the questioned document and the specimens contain sufficient identifiable characteristics, then the expert compares those characteristics often through the use of a chart.

For example, the slant of the writing, the shapes of the letters, the letter connections, the height of the letters, the spacing between letters, the spacing between words, the "I" dots and "t" crosses are aspects of handwriting that can be used for comparison. Next, the expert weighs the evidence, considering both the similarities and the differences of handwriting, and determines whether or not there is a match.

Ignoring differences between characteristics is a frequent cause of error in handwriting identification. Similarly, dismissing differences as merely the product of intentional disguise is another common mistake made in the analysis. In addition, an examiner should not know the identity of the comparators and should consult more than one comparator to increase the reliability of his or her analysis.

"Ignoring differences between characteristics is a frequent cause of error in handwriting identification."

In addition to a recognized methodology, there are some accepted standards that should be employed when engaging in handwriting analysis. One standard is that the genuineness of the historical writing or request exemplar must be verified; that is, the forensic document examiner should ensure the purported author of the true and historical writing is indeed the author. In addition, any differences between the questioned document and the comparison writings are generally considered to be more significant than are similarities, when attempting to determine whether someone is the author of a questioned document.

The reason that similarity, by itself, is not dispositive is because most people are taught handwriting as children from the same or similar "notebook styles" and, therefore, many people will share common handwriting characteristics called "class characteristics."

The existence of even one consistent fundamental difference between writings, however, has historically been viewed as a legitimate basis for concluding that two writings were not produced by the same person. Finally, it is generally accepted that consistent characteristics present over the course of a long writing should be viewed as genuine characteristics of the author's handwriting, and not the product of an attempt to disguise.

. . .

The Reliability of Epstein's Proffered Testimony.

Although the Court has concluded, as a general matter, that Epstein is qualified to testify as a forensic documents examiner, it must still determine the parameters of his expertise with regard to the opinions he seeks to offer. Specifically, Epstein claims that he can state, with absolute certainty, that Mrs. Ramsey is the author of the Ransom Note. The Court, as gatekeeper, must therefore examine the methodology that he puts forward in support of such a categorical conclusion. First, Epstein states that he used the standard methodology of forensic document examiners when assessing the Ransom Note and Mrs. Ramsey's writing samples.

He initially determined that he had a sufficient amount of handwriting by Mrs. Ramsey to allow an examination. He then proceeded to examine the submitted materials for similarities and dissimilarities. After conducting the examination, he then determined that the original writing and the exemplars matched to a "one hundred percent" degree of certainty. Finally, he consulted other forensic document analysts who approved of his methodology and result.

Defendants move to exclude the testimony of Epstein because they assert that the methodology he employed does not meet the accepted standards of handwriting analysts. In particular, defendants argue that Epstein's opinions are not reliable because he did not consult the original Ransom Note, original handwriting exemplars of Mrs. Ramsey, nor original course-of-business writings of Mrs. Ramsey. . . .

Epstein's failure to consult the originals should go to the weight of his testimony, but should not bar its admission, completely. To hold otherwise could create a perverse incentive for individuals not to allow an opponent access to original documents, in order to render those expert's opinion inadmissible.

In short, the Court is satisfied as to Epstein's ability to testify concerning perceived similarities and differences in Mrs. Ramsey's known handwriting and the Ransom Note. Any criticism of Epstein's analysis by defendants goes to the weight of his testimony.

Of more concern to the Court, however, is the reliability of Epstein's ultimate conclusion concerning the identity of the writer of the Note. As noted, Epstein claims that he is "100 percent certain that Patsy Ramsey wrote the Ransom Note," and in his professional opinion "there is absolutely no doubt she is the author."

Nowhere in the submissions provided by plaintiffs is there any attempt to show by what methodology Mr. Epstein reaches a conclusion of absolute certainty that a given person is, in fact, the writer of a questioned document. Defendants persuasively argue that Epstein was unable to identify any unique characteristics of Mrs. Ramsey's handwriting that were mimicked in the Ransom Note. Instead, Epstein bases his conclusion on perceived similarities between the two. Yet, as noted by defendants, Epstein never indicates how many similarities or what kind of similarities are required before he can reach absolute certainty, 50% certainty, or no certainty, at all.

Further, as defendants also note, whenever encountering any differences between the known writing of Mrs. Ramsey and the Ransom Note, Epstein finds refuge in the explanation that Mrs. Ramsey must have been trying to disguise her handwriting.

While it is, of course, possible that differences between known writing and questioned documents are the result of a known writer's efforts to disguise her handwriting, it is just as plausible that the differences can occur because the known writer is not the author of the questioned matter. On that issue, Epstein offers no hint of the methodology that he employs to distinguish between disguised writing and writing that is simply being provided by two different people.

The underlying notion behind *Daubert*, and all good science, is that a given premise or principle should be capable of being tested to determine whether the principle is, in fact, sound. Thus, if Epstein indicated, for example, that whenever a writer of known material has x number of similarities, there is a given probability that the writer wrote the note — and if this methodology had been tested by reliable means in the past — then Epstein would have shown reliability in the methodology that he used to reach a determination of the likelihood of his Conclusion.

As it is, however, Epstein's explanation for his conclusion seems to be little more than "Trust me; I'm an expert." *Daubert* case law has indicated that such an assertion, which seems to be based more on intuition than on scientific reasoning, is insufficient.

Accordingly, the Court concludes that while Epstein can properly assist the trier of fact by pointing out marked differences and unusual similarities between Mrs. Ramsey's writing and the Ransom Note, he has not

"Epstein never indicates how many similarities or what kind of similarities are required before he can reach absolute certainty, 50% certainty, or no certainty, at all."

demonstrated a methodology whereby he can draw a conclusion, to an absolute certainty, that a given writer wrote the Note.

In a bizarre coda to the dispute over who wrote the ransom note, police finally apprehended a suspect, John Mark Karr, in the fall of 2006. Karr had been obsessed with the JonBenét Ramsey case and had made certain statements that he had been present at her death but that it had been an accident. In no time, a website appeared that compared Karr's handwriting from his high school yearbook to the ransom note, concluding "There is now no doubt that John Mark Karr wrote the JonBenét Ramsey ransom note. From the bottom kick on every 't' to the top loop of the 'a' to the concave of the semi-oval on the 'h', the handwriting samples match up almost perfectly."[71]

Karr's DNA was compared to the DNA samples found on JonBenét, and he was determined not to be a match.[72] The state of Colorado dropped all charges against Karr on August 28, 2006.[73] Clearly, Karr did not write the ransom note.

Summary

In 2009, the NRC Report issued a "Summary Assessment" of the current status of handwriting analysis suggesting that the "scientific basis for handwriting comparisons needs to be strengthened":

> recent studies have increased our understanding of the individuality and consistency of handwriting and computer studies and suggest that there may be a scientific basis for handwriting comparison at least in the absence of intentional obfuscation or forgery. Although there had been only limited research to quantify the reliability or replicability of the practices used by trained document examiners, the committee agrees that there may be some value in handwriting analysis.[74]

This report did not change most courts' response to handwriting experts, which permit them to testify if they are properly qualified, in particular as the jury can see the questioned handwriting for themselves and make their own conclusion.[75]

The methods used to determine common authorship were developed by Albert Osbourn, Sr., in the early 1900s and have remained virtually unchanged. The examiner first views the suspected document and exemplars of the natural handwriting of the suspected author. If the examiner determines that he has enough writing to compare, he will first look for obvious differences, which might rule out the suspected author. Such differences include such "macro" features as line slant, pen pressure, and the

---

71. http://www.powerwurks.com/john_mark_karr_handwriting.php.

72. "No DNA Match, No JonBenét Charges," October 23, 2006, http://www.cnn.com/2006/LAW/08/28/ramsey.arrest/index.html?iref=mpstoryview.

73. *People v. Karr*, No 2006 CR 1244, People's Motion to Quash Arrest Warrant.

74. NRC Report, *supra*, 167.

75. *U.S. v. Dale*, *supra*.

like. If the suspect cannot be ruled out, the examiner will then proceed to examining "micro" features, such as the size and shape of particular letters. There is no set number of similarities that an examiner must find to determine a match.

Courts have admitted handwriting testimony for many years, but when confronted with the *Daubert* tests, some courts have determined that handwriting identification is not reliable. Experts cannot state which characteristics are most important, nor can they state that if a writer of a known document has x number of similarities, there is a given probability that the writer wrote the questioned document. Courts that follow the general acceptance test frequently admit handwriting testimony. Some courts that follow *Daubert* permit the expert to point out similarities and differences to the jury, but not give an opinion as to authorship.

Handwriting experts have analyzed ransom notes in at least two highly publicized cases: the kidnapping and murder of the son of Lindberg and the murder of JonBenét Ramsey. Questions still remain as to whether Bruno Richard Hauptmann really wrote the Lindberg baby ransom note. Handwriting experts have disagreed as to whether John or Patsy Ramsey wrote the note found at the time of their daughter's death, but a content analysis of the style and words of the note raises many questions as to whether it was part of a hoax. The court in a libel case against Patsy Ramsey evaluated whether handwriting expert testimony met the *Daubert* test, and concluded that the methodology was not reliable enough to permit an expert to give his opinion about authorship. The most he could do was point out similarities and differences to the jury.

All this may change with the advent of computer programs to compare questioned documents. One computer system has determined that handwriting is unique, by looking for a certain number of macro and micro features. In essence, it is similar to DNA testing in that it does not look at all possible match points, but the sample it examines is large enough to make probability estimates of common authorship. The system has also demonstrated the ability to determine the writer of an unknown document.

Handwriting may well be a type of forensic science that does not meet *Daubert* but that will lead to a form of computer analysis that will meet the tests in the near future.

Discussion Questions

1. What are the scientific hypotheses of handwriting? Have any of these hypotheses been proved?

2. When was Osborn's *Questioned Documents* published and why do you think it is still viewed as an authority today?

3. Name at least three different purposes for which handwriting analysis can be used.

4. What are at least two assumptions in handwriting analysis?

5. What are the similarities and differences between fingerprint and handwriting evidence?

6. What are the subjective elements of handwriting analysis?

7. What are the main reasons why courts have admitted handwriting testimony?

8. How does the computer evaluating methodology developed by Cedar-Fox change your views about the scientific validity of handwriting comparison?

9. What effect did the *Kuhmo* case have on whether a *Daubert* hearing is required for handwriting testimony?

10. Does the disagreement among scholars demonstrate that handwriting analysis is not generally accepted?

11. Is the compromise strategy of allowing the expert to point out similarities and differences, but not give an opinion, a good idea? Refer to the opinion in *U.S. v. Hines* in your answer.

12. Do you agree with the court in *U.S. v. Prime* that handwriting analysis meets *Daubert*? Why or why not?

13. What has changed about the admissibility of handwriting analysis after the NRC Report in 2009?

14. How would you expect computer technologies such as that developed by Cedar-Fox to change handwriting analysis and admissibility?

15. What are the similarities and differences between the analysis of the ransom notes in the *Hauptmann* and *Ramsey* cases? How do these cases show what has changed in handwriting analysis from 1930 to today?

Chapter 13

Exonerations of the Wrongly Convicted

Overview

There are two organizations that report on the phenomenon of exonerations, a significant percentage of which have resulted from the testing of DNA that demonstrates the perpetrator was not the person convicted of the crime. The Innocence Project,[1] founded in 1992 at the Cardozo Law School, accepts a small percentage of petitions from the incarcerated requesting their help and as of 2016, report 344 exonerations based on DNA and 148 actual perpetrators found.[2] The Innocence Project accepts only DNA-related petitions and have terminated 30% of the cases they accepted due to lost or destroyed DNA. In addition, a majority of the prisoners who request testing of DNA evidence prove not to be innocent after all. Therefore, groups like The Innocence Project must carefully review and choose those prisoners whom they will represent.

The National Registry of Exonerations is a joint project of the University of Michigan School of Law and the Center on Wrongful Convictions at Northwestern University School of Law. It has a wider database than the Innocence Project because it does not limit itself to DNA cases only. It reported 2089 exonerations from January 1989 to September 2017, 420 of which involved DNA. As of 2012, mistaken eyewitness identifications (excluding deliberate misidentifications) accounted for 43% of exonerations.[3]

In 2014, the National Academy of Sciences (NAS) published *Identifying the Culprit: Assessing Eyewitness Identification*, which set forth proposed reforms that might reduce eyewitness identification errors.

A recent report states that the President's Council of Advisors on Science and Technology has concluded that bite-mark evidence is not scientifically valid. An online journal called *Intercept* notes that twenty-five wrongful arrests or convictions have been linked to bite-mark analysis.[4] On June 8, 2017, Alfred Swinton was

---

1. www.innocenceproject.org.

2. *Id.*

3. Fiona Leverick, "Jury Instructions on Eyewitness Identification Evidence: A Re-evaluation," *Creighton Law Review* 49 (June 2016): 555.

4. Jordan Smith, "White House Report Concludes that Bite Mark Analysis Is Junk Science," *The Intercept*, September 7, 2016, www.theintercept.com/2016/09/07/white-house-report-concludes-that-bite-mark-analysis-is-junk-science.

exonerated for a murder conviction in Connecticut and his sentence vacated. His conviction rested on bite-mark testimony by Dr. Gus Karazulas, former chief odontologist for the Connecticut State Police Forensic Science Laboratory. Karazulas acknowledged that bite-mark analysis had been repudiated. In addition, the use of "touch DNA" on the swabs taken from the victim's bite marks showed that the DNA was not Swinton's.[5]

The phenomenon of DNA exonerations has captured the public interest and has led many states to adopt legislation to help with exoneration requests. These laws cover issues such as:

- A requirement that states preserve DNA evidence after conviction for some period of time.
- A process to request post-conviction DNA for testing.
- Costs to be paid by the state if the prisoner cannot pay.
- A process for petitioning the court for exoneration.
- Compensation statutes for exonerees.
- Laws to provide post-exoneration social services.

Chapter Objectives

Based on this chapter, students will:

1. Understand the role that testing of DNA evidence plays in exonerating prisoners.

2. Explain the efforts of groups such as The Innocence Project in representing potential exonerees.

3. Appreciate the evolution of state responses to post-conviction exonerations, including legislation to create a process for requesting DNA testing.

4. Distinguish between pardons, dismissal of charges, and findings of actual innocence.

5. The importance of a finding of actual innocence as a prerequisite to suing for civil damages for wrongful incarceration.

6. Identify the role of habeas corpus petitions in the exoneration process.

7. Understand the effect of a prisoner's confession or plea to a lesser offense on a claim for exoneration.

8. Explain the legal test for motions for a new trial based on newly discovered evidence.

9. Appreciate the difficulty exonerees face in returning to society, the efforts of groups such as After Innocence, and proposed legislation to provide social services to exonerees.

---

5. www.innocenceproject.org

The Innocence Project

In 1989, Gary Dotson's conviction of a 1979 rape he did not commit was dismissed. Dotson had spent ten years in and out of prison as a result of this conviction. His was the first reported exoneration based on a testing of the DNA from the original rape kit. In 1994, Barry Scheck and John Newfeld founded The Innocence Project at Cordozo Law School in New York and began to review requests from prisoners for help in proving their innocence.

The Innocence Project has resulted in 344 post-conviction exonerations based on DNA forensic testing through 2016. Their website posts articles on research and activism for exonerations. In December of 2016, Congress passed the Justice for All Reauthorization Act of 2016, which provides funding for post-conviction DNA testing. As of 2012, all but eight states provided for some type of post-conviction relief,[6] but a process for relief without funding will not result in many exonerations.

Who Are the Exonerated?

The most well-known exonerations involve rape charges, simply because DNA can prove that semen from the rape kit did not belong to the prisoner. However, only 40% of those who request DNA testing are shown to be innocent. In other words, for 60% of prisoners, their DNA is actually present in the rape kit. And a number of prosecutors take the position that even if the semen did not belong to the defendant who was convicted, he could still be guilty of the rape.[7]

Although rape exonerations are the best known, one study reported that the total rape exonerations from 1989 to 2003 were 30%, compared with 60% for murder cases. In the vast majority of the rape cases, DNA testing was critical to the exoneration.

One reason that a majority of exonerations involve murder may be because attorneys are more likely to take on an exoneration claim for a high-profile case, particularly one that may involve the death penalty. Wrongful murder convictions have been shown to result from coerced confessions, police pressure to close terrible crimes, and testimony by the real killer that framed someone else for their crime. However, even in some of the murder cases, DNA has figured in the exoneration.

In the 2003 study referred to above, 121 of the 340 exonerations were for rape (36%), and 88% of those involved an eyewitness misidentification.[8] Two-thirds of the exonerated were African American or Hispanic.

We do not know how many innocent defendants agree to a plea to a lesser sentence to avoid serving long periods in prison before their case comes to trial, but there are

---

6. The holdout states as of 2012 with no post-conviction relief are Massachusetts, Alaska, Alabama, Mississippi, Oklahoma, South Carolina, South Dakota, and Wyoming.

7. Samuel R. Gross, Kristen Jacoby, Daniel J. Matheson, Nicholas Montgomery, and Sujata Patil, "Innocence in Capital Sentencing," *Criminal Law & Criminology* 95 (Winter 2005): 523, 524.

8. *Id.* at 530.

doubtless a fair number of innocent prisoners who have pled guilty. This presents another problem in exonerations, as most people assume that a defendant who had pled guilty is guilty.

In 2003, the top four states for exonerations were Illinois, New York, Texas, and California, which accounted for 40% of the exonerations reported by the study.

Laws to Preserve DNA Evidence

DNA is considered the gold standard of forensic evidence. A DNA profile of one person cannot wrongly implicate another. The statistics underlying DNA testing are such that the likelihood of a random person matching a defendant's DNA profile is generally greater than the entire U.S. population of over 300 million. Although defense counsel still argue to juries that poor testing procedures result in DNA profiles that are faulty, most scientists agree that a degraded or contaminated DNA sample will give no reading or a garbled reading, but it cannot give a false reading implicating another person. Of course, DNA from rape kits typically contains a mixture of DNA from the victim and the perpetrator, and in some cases, it may contain DNA from more than one sexual contact. However, DNA technicians can detect mixtures and determine the identity of the various contributors.

As a commentator who has argued for national standards for DNA storage argues:

> Currently, the FBI forensic laboratory in Quantico, Virginia, accepts evidence related to all crimes under investigation by the FBI, as well as evidence from violent crimes under investigation in federal, state, and local law enforcement agencies. These facilities include extensive long-term storage for DNA samples. As of May 2011, the FBI laboratory had over 712,000 DNA samples that required storage, which were stored in a "room in boxes stacked to the ceiling." At that time, the Department of Justice was looking into long-term storage alternatives, including off-site options. The Department of Justice was concerned about the option of storing DNA offsite because it would add complexity to the current storage and retrieval protocols and would increase risk regarding the maintenance of the samples. Currently there is no legislation to reform the way that the DNA samples are kept on the federal level.

> On the state level, DNA samples are kept in accordance with state law: some states require retention for particular crimes, others require retention for a certain period of time only, and some states do not have any evidence retention laws at all. This system is very fragmented and as a result, states have their own procedures and policies regarding evidence retention. This is reflective of the fragmentation of the criminal justice system, where positive progress is bogged down because of poor cooperation and communication between agencies.

> One of the main failings of the criminal justice system is its vast size and fragmentation. In order to ensure that appropriate systems are in place for

retention of DNA (as well as other real) evidence, cooperation and standardization among the federal, state, and local facilities is necessary.[9]

As of 2016, there were no national standards for statutes requiring law enforcement or courtroom personnel to retain DNA evidence after a conviction. The length of time to preserve the evidence, the types of crimes for which preservation is required, and the penalties for not preserving the evidence all vary from state to state. Sixteen states did not even have any form of evidence-retention statutes.[10] Of the states that have adopted DNA retention statutes the type of evidence varies from rape kits to hair, blood, or any other substance from which DNA may be extracted, including mitochondrial DNA.

Many murder exonerations result from either a confession by the true culprit or by other evidence connecting someone else to the crime. However, DNA evidence collected at the crime scene can corroborate the exoneration and sometimes lead to the real culprit. Some argue that the absence of DNA evidence is irrelevant to proving innocence; however the presence of DNA evidence that excludes the prisoner generally creates reasonable doubt of his guilt.

Also, there are prisoners who have been convicted of lesser crimes who might well be innocent and who might be cleared by DNA evidence. As these prisoners might well be released by the time the DNA evidence is finally tested, and as their cases are not nearly as high profile as death penalty cases, these prisoners stand little chance of being exonerated.

What Is the Process Leading to Exoneration?

The process of exoneration would seem to be simple. All the prisoner would need to do is request the original DNA evidence, arrange to have it retested, show it to the prosecutor, and then the prosecutor would drop the charges. It is seldom so simple. In the 340 exonerations examined in the 2003 study mentioned above, 42 were pardoned by governors or other state executives, 263 had the charges dismissed by the courts, 31 were acquitted after a retrial, and 4 were posthumously acknowledged to have been innocent.[11]

A finding of actual innocence, as opposed to a pardon or dropping of charges, is important, for in many states, the exoneree cannot sue for civil damages without a formal finding of innocence.

In the case of DNA exonerations, the defendant must first gain the attention of an attorney. This is often extremely difficult. The Innocence Project alone has file drawers of letters from prisoners asking for help. And in 60% of those cases,[12] retesting

---

9. Cristina Martin, "DNA Storage Banks: The Importance of Preserving DNA Evidence to Allow for Transparency and the Preservation of Justice," *Chicago-Kent Law Review* 91 (2016): 1173.

10. *Id.*

11. Gross et al. at 530.

12. Barry C. Scheck, Barry Scheck Lectures on Wrongful Convictions, 54 Drake L. Rev. 597, 601 (Spring 2006).

of DNA will not exonerate the defendant. Therefore, lawyers must choose carefully whom to represent in exoneration claims.

Next, the prisoner or his attorney must gain access to the DNA samples collected at trial and have them reexamined. There are three issues:

- Many samples have not been kept or are too degraded to test.
- The prisoner generally lacks funds to do the testing.
- He will have to convince the prosecutor who tried the case to release the evidence.

In December of 2016, Congress enacted the Justice for All Reauthorization Act of 2016, which provided funding for some post-conviction DNA testing. We will discuss below the various states that have also enacted legislation providing for a right to DNA for post-conviction testing. But where such rights do not exist, the prisoner would typically bring an action alleging that the state, through the action of the prosecutor, has deprived him of his Fourteenth Amendment right to due process.[13]

This step is not a request for exoneration; it is simply a request to obtain DNA for testing. Before 2000, only New York and Illinois had statutes that authorized post-conviction DNA testing. Although some sympathetic judges were willing to order relief in the interests of justice, particularly when a prosecutor joined in the petitioner's request,[14] the only formal avenue was to move for a new trial based on newly discovered evidence. If the time limit for moving for a new trial had run, the prisoner might have no recourse.

Even where a state has authorized applications for post-conviction DNA testing, the petition may not meet the requirements. The following case is an example of the legal hurdles a prisoner faces in attempting to obtain DNA test results.

Reddick v. Florida, 929 So.2d 34 (Fla.App. 2006)

The trial court denied the appellant's motion for postconviction DNA testing of evidence without a hearing, concluding that there was no reasonable probability that the movant would be acquitted or that he would have received a lesser sentence had the DNA testing occurred. We reverse, concluding that the appellant has alleged a facially sufficient claim.

The appellant, George Reddick, was convicted in 1985 of first degree murder and sexual battery of a seven-year-old girl who was staying in the same home as Reddick and several other people. No physical evidence was found linking Reddick to the crime. According to Reddick's motion, the sole testimony against him was the questionable identification of the victim's sister who testified that she saw Reddick take the victim out of a window.

---

13. Dylan Ruga, "Federal Court Adjudication of State Prisoner Claims for Post-Conviction DNA Testing: A Bifurcated Approach," *Pierce Law Review* 2 (March 2004): 35.
14. Margaret A. Berger, "The Impact of DNA Exonerations on the Criminal Justice System," *Journal of Law Medicine & Ethics* 34 (Summer 2006): 320.

However, this testimony was equivocal, as the witness apparently at first denied seeing anything, and at another time named another individual. Reddick maintained his innocence of the crime and asserted that another occupant of the home was the likely perpetrator.

In 2003, Reddick filed his motion for DNA testing pursuant to Florida Rule of Criminal Procedure 3.853. He recited the detailed facts and investigation of the case and listed the evidence for which he sought DNA testing. He also maintained his innocence and that the identity of the perpetrator was contested. He noted that in 1985 DNA testing was not available and none of the items had been tested other than for fingerprint analysis and semen analysis. Those tests failed to produce any results.

Reddick listed four categories of items to be tested for DNA:

(1) his clothing;

(2) items found near the victim's body, including beer cans, a plastic bottle, and a cup;

(3) sweepings of the victim's body, consisting of swabs of the vagina, rectum, and mouth; scalp hair, and fingernail clippings; and

(4) the victim's clothing, including her pajama bottoms, panties, etc.

As to his clothing, he stated that if DNA testing revealed no skin cells from the victim, it would exonerate him, as such cells would have to be on his clothing if he lifted her out of the house as the victim's sister testified. As to the items surrounding the victim's body, they might reveal that the victim was penetrated by a foreign object. DNA testing which did not reveal any of Reddick's DNA on such objects would create a reasonable probability that he was not in the area and did not use any of the objects to rape or murder the child.

With respect to the victim's clothing, he alleged that if they revealed no DNA from Reddick, this too would exonerate him of any rape, because skin cells would be present on the victim's pajamas if the perpetrator forcibly removed them, as was the testimony by experts. Finally, as to the victim's swabbings, these may reveal the DNA of the perpetrator, given the number of wounds and abrasions on the victim, particularly with respect to the fingernail clippings. Further, the rape of the victim would create DNA evidence, even if no semen was present.

The state responded, admitting the existence of the evidence sought to be tested. However, it claimed that Reddick's motion simply amounted to speculation that the clothing would have any DNA evidence on it or that the swabs would reveal any DNA. It suggested that the testing of Reddick's own clothing would not offer probative evidence in that the absence of the victim's DNA would be irrelevant. Finally, it also questioned the probative value of finding the victim's DNA on the bottles and cups around the victim's body.

Without conducting an evidentiary hearing, the court denied the motion. The court found that the items were available for testing and that the results would likely be admissible at trial. However, it concluded that there was no reasonable probability that Reddick would be acquitted or would receive a lesser sentence, adopting the state's response. It did not refer to the trial transcript or other portions of the record to support its conclusion.

In denying the motion without a hearing, the court must have assumed that it was legally insufficient for failing to show how the evidence would exonerate Reddick or lessen his sentence. However, as in *Schofield v. State*, we conclude that the motion was facially sufficient and alleged how he would be exonerated, at least as to some of the categories of evidence.

Identity was a disputed issue at trial, given the questionable eyewitness identification and the state's failure in its responses to refute that claim. With respect to the swabs of the victim's body and her clothes, the presence of the perpetrator's DNA is likely, as she was brutally beaten and sexually assaulted. If DNA testing confirms the presence of DNA of someone other than Reddick from the vagina, rectum, mouth or fingernail swabs, those results surely would create a reasonable probability that Reddick would be acquitted of the charges.

Although the state contends that there is no reason to suspect that testable skin cells or DNA would be found, that is not the criteria. What rule 3.853 requires the court to find is "whether it has been shown that physical evidence that may contain DNA still exists." Fla. R. Crim. P. 3.853(c)(5)(A) The court made that finding in its order.

As to DNA testing of Reddick's clothing, we agree that Reddick has failed to show how there would be a reasonable probability that he would be acquitted if the victim's DNA were not found on his clothing. Reddick has presented nothing to show that testable skin cells or other material would necessarily transfer to the clothing. Further, Reddick admits that his clothing was not delivered to the police until sometime significantly after the commencement of the investigation.

Even if there was no evidence of the victim's DNA on Reddick's clothing, given the passage of time and the possibility that the clothes were not in the same condition as they were on the night of the incident, it is apparent that this evidence would not reasonably result in an acquittal.

We also agree that Reddick did not adequately explain why the testing of the beer bottle, cup, and other material found around the body would exonerate him. The victim was found under a bush. No fingerprints were found on any of the surrounding items, nor were any of them tied to either the rape or the murder. In fact, there is nothing in the motion or the record before us which would indicate that these items were in any way connected to the crime, and instead were merely present under the bush when the body was found. We thus conclude that the motion was legally insufficient as to these items.

We therefore reverse and remand for further proceedings as the trial court erred in concluding that the motion was facially insufficient as to the testing of the victim's body sweepings and clothing.

Getting the Conviction Reversed

Assume that the prisoner does get access to DNA and the DNA is not his. Now the prisoner must convince a governor to pardon him, or a prosecutor to drop the charges, or a court to reverse his (most of the exonerated are men) conviction. Unless the DNA clearly implicates another known suspect, the prisoner may have a hard time convincing anyone that the DNA evidence should fully exonerate him.

Typically at this stage, the prisoner's state appeal rights have expired or all appeals have been denied. If he had brought a federal habeas corpus appeal, which is a collateral appeal to a federal court alleging a violation of a constitutional right, that right has also expired. A number of circuits have stated that the proper route to apply for exoneration is through a habeas petition.[15]

Habeas Corpus. A petition made to a federal court alleging a U.S. Constitution violation that justifies reversing a conviction.

A number of state legislatures have adopted or are considering laws that would give prisoners a right to post-conviction testing and would address how or when the prisoner might be released. In the absence of such legislation or the voluntary action of prosecutors, the prisoner, assuming the DNA exculpates him from the crime, must bring a writ of habeas corpus claiming that he is actually innocent of the charges and should be released from prison.

One State's Approach

Connecticut legislation prescribes a process for convicts to request post-conviction DNA testing and request exoneration. It enacted a statute that provides for a prisoner to obtain DNA for testing by petitioning the sentencing court if he states that the testing is related to his conviction and the evidence to be tested contains biological evidence.[16] After notice to the prosecutor's office and a hearing, the court shall order the DNA testing if it finds that:

1. A reasonable probability exists that the petitioner would not have been prosecuted or convicted if exculpatory results had been obtained through DNA testing;

2. The evidence is still in existence and is capable of being tested;

3. The evidence was never previously tested or the testing now may resolve an issue that was never previously resolved by testing; and

---

15. *Id.* at 39.
16. Conn Gen. Stat. § 54-102kk (2006).

4. the petition was filed to demonstrate the petitioner's innocence and not to delay the administration of evidence.[17]

The prisoner may also request such testing if there is a reasonable probability that it would have altered the verdict or reduced his sentence.

The cost of the testing shall be paid by the state or the petitioner as the court may order in the interests of justice. DNA testing may not be denied, however, if the petitioner cannot pay for it. The petitioner may also be represented by court-appointed counsel if he cannot pay for counsel.[18]

The law also requires erasure of the petitioner's criminal record if the petitioner is found not guilty of the charge or the charge is dismissed.[19] A prisoner can petition for a new trial based on DNA evidence that was not discoverable or available at the trial any time after the discovery or availability of such evidence.[20]

Federal Law

Required for exoneration of federal crime: the petitioner must swear that he is innocent and the evidence must have led to conviction as a career offender or the death penalty.

In October of 2004, the federal government passed the Innocence Protection Act of 2002, also called the Justice for All Act of 2004.[21] Under this act, an applicant who asserts that he is actually innocent of a federal offence for which he has been sentenced to prison or death may make a motion to the court that sentenced him if the petitioner swears that he is innocent and the evidence led to conviction as a career offender or the death penalty. The federal statute, therefore, is more restrictive than in states such as Connecticut, because it does not apply to all crimes.

The applicant must also have exhausted all other remedies, such as appeal to a state court, to request DNA testing, and the evidence must not have already been DNA tested, unless the applicant is requesting a new method of testing, the government still has the evidence, and the proposed testing is reasonable in scope.

Under the federal law, the identity of the perpetrator must have been an issue in the trial and the DNA testing would produce "material evidence" to support a defense and would "raise a reasonable probability that the applicant did not commit the offense."[22]

The standard for granting the motion is if the DNA test results, when considered with all other evidence in the case, establish by a preponderance of the evidence that a new trial would result in an acquittal.

The FBI is to conduct the testing, with costs to be paid by the applicant or the government, if the applicant is indigent. The government may also submit the testing results to the Combined DNA Index System ("CODIS"), and may use any results to match the petitioner with another offense.

If the testing excludes the applicant as the source of the DNA, the applicant may file a motion for a new trial or re-sentencing. The standard for granting the motion is "if the DNA test results, when considered with all other evidence in the case

---

17. *Id.*
18. *Id.*
19. Conn. Gen. Stat. § 54-142a (2006).
20. Conn. Gen. Stat. § 52-582 (2006).
21. 18 U.S.C.A. chapter 228A § 3600.
22. *Id.*

(regardless of whether such evidence was introduced at trial), establish by a preponderance of the evidence that a new trial would result in an acquittal."[23] The law specifically states that it does not authorize a habeas corpus proceeding. The Attorney General must file a report of all motions made under this act within two years of its enactment.

The Justice for All Act of 2004 has numerous provisions set on expanding forensic DNA databases and preserving DNA evidence, including:

(1) eliminating the backlog of DNA samples collected from crime scenes and convicted offenders; (2) expanding the Combined DNA Index System (CODIS); (3) improving and expanding DNA testing capacity of federal, state, and local crime laboratories; (4) increasing research and development of new DNA testing technologies; (5) developing new training programs for the collection and use of DNA evidence; (6) extending the statute of limitations for crimes where the suspect is linked to the crime through DNA evidence; (7) providing post-conviction DNA testing and the preservation of biological evidence.[24]

This Act was supplemented by the Justice for All Reauthorization Act of 2016, which extended funding to states for DNA testing. The Act expanded eligibility for post-conviction DNA testing in criminal proceedings other than the death penalty.

The Role of Eyewitness Misidentifications and Reform Efforts

By far the major explanation for the majority of wrongful rape convictions is false eyewitness identifications. There have been many recent studies of error in eyewitness identifications and calls for changes in the line-up and identification process used by law enforcement. About one-third of all rapes are committed by strangers, so the likelihood of a misidentification in those cases is great. In 85% of murder cases, the exonerated murder defendant knew the victim or at least one supposed eyewitness. In these cases, there is deliberate false evidence implicating the defendant, rather than a misidentification *per se*. As eyewitness misidentifications are often the cause of rape convictions from which prisoners are later exonerated, many commentators have called for reforms in the process of eyewitness identification. This was the topic of a national report in October of 2014 by the National Academy of Sciences, *Identifying the Culprit: Assessing Eyewitness Identification*. This topic is discussed in detail under Chapter 10, "Eyewitness Identifications." The link between eyewitness identifications and wrongful convictions cannot be denied.

---

23. *Id.* section (g) Post-Testing Procedures; Motion for New Trial or Re-sentencing.
24. Martin, *supra*, at 1180–1.

Are the New Statutes Too Little, Too Late?

Barry Scheck, a co-founder of the Innocence Project, delivered a speech at Drake University Law School on October 3, 2005,[25] in which he stated that his project of DNA exoneration was in a race against time. Although thirty-four states had adopted statutes to permit post-conviction DNA testing, he argued that less than ten percent of most serious felony cases have any biological evidence that would be susceptible to testing that could determine guilt or innocence. He added that the fact that there are innocent prisoners convicted of rapes or murders they did not commit means that the real perpetrator is still at large. "[I]n our cases where we have found the real assailant, in case after case it is a serial rapist. It is a serial murder. It is someone who has terrorized, pillaged, and hurt so many other people because of the wrongful conviction in the first place."[26]

Most DNA rape exonerations involve trials in which DNA evidence was not presented. As states now require DNA to be stored and kept, and as prosecutors routinely introduce DNA in trials, it is possible that fewer DNA exonerations will be brought in the future. Although this may reduce the number of wrongful convictions for rape, the issue of wrongful convictions for other crimes will likely persist, particularly in light of new studies demonstrating the fallibility of eyewitness identifications.

Claims Based on Failure to Test DNA Evidence

Some defendants have appealed, claiming they were denied effective counsel if DNA testing was not requested and presented at trial. As the standard for reversal based on ineffective counsel is very high, these appeals generally lose.

A 2005 Texas case dealt with an appeal based on the fact that no DNA testing had been done at trial and the evidence had subsequently been destroyed. The defendant had actually pled guilty at trial, which was why the DNA was destroyed. After conviction, he argued that he was entitled to have the DNA testing and that his conviction should be overturned because the DNA was no longer available. The court held that these claims did not justify relief under the Texas laws.

Lewis v. State, 191 S.W.3d 225 (Tex. App. 2005)

Matthew Raymond Lewis appeals the denial of his request for a court appointed attorney to assist him in filing a post-conviction motion for forensic DNA testing, and the denial of his motion for DNA testing. Because Lewis is unable to demonstrate reasonable grounds for filing his motion for DNA testing, we overrule his issues and affirm the trial court's order.

In 2002, Lewis was indicted for the sexual assault of a minor under the age of 17, and, in a separate count, for aggravated sexual assault of a second

---

25. Scheck, *supra*.
26. *Id.* at 603.

minor under the age of 14. Lewis entered a plea of guilty to both counts and was sentenced by the trial court to incarceration in the Texas Department of Criminal Justice, Institutional Division, for a period of eleven years.

Nineteen months later, on September 13, 2004, Lewis, acting pro se, filed a motion for DNA testing of evidence secured in relation to his conviction of sexual assault, a sworn affidavit in support of the motion, a request for the appointment of an attorney, a declaration of inability to pay costs and an affidavit of indigence. Lewis requested that all the motions be set for a hearing.

The trial court asked for a response from the district attorney's office in Kerr County. Sergeant John Lavender, the evidence officer for the Kerr County Sheriff's Office, and Ronald L. Sutton, the district attorney for Kerr County, filed sworn affidavits which stated, "The evidence in the above-mentioned case was destroyed after the Defendant's plea of guilty to one count of sexual abuse of a child and one count of aggravated sexual assault of a child with two different victims and the appeal time limit had expired."

Without holding a hearing, the trial court subsequently denied Lewis' motion for DNA testing, noting that Lewis entered a voluntary plea of guilty to the offenses and that there "was and is no issue of identity as required by Article 64 of the Texas Code of Criminal Procedure." The court further found, "based on the affidavit of John Lavender, evidence officer for the Kerr County Sheriff's Department, the evidence referenced in Defendant's motion no longer exists." Lewis filed a *pro se* appeal to this court.

We review the trial court's ruling on a post-conviction motion for forensic DNA testing under a bifurcated standard of review. We afford almost total deference to the "trial court's determination of issues of historical fact and application-of-law-to-fact issues that turn on credibility and demeanor, while we review de novo other application-of-law-to-fact issues."

In his first three issues, Lewis contends the trial court erred in denying his request for a court appointed attorney. To determine whether Lewis was entitled to appointed counsel to assist him in filing a post-conviction motion for DNA testing, we must examine the applicable statute. *See* TEX. CODE CRIM. PROC. ANN. art. 64.01(c) As originally written in 2001, article 64.01(c) stated that a defendant was entitled to the appointment of counsel merely upon requesting counsel and establishing indigence.... The legislature, however, amended article 64.01(c) effective September 1, 2003, to read, in relevant part, as follows:

> The convicting court shall appoint counsel for the convicted person if the person informs the court that the person wishes to submit a motion under this chapter, the court finds reasonable grounds for a motion to be filed, and the court determines that the person is indigent.

Because Lewis filed his motion for DNA testing after the effective date of the amendment, he had the additional burden of establishing "reasonable grounds for a motion to be filed" in order to qualify for appointed counsel. "Reasonable grounds" are not defined within the statute. Generally, in interpreting a statute, we give words their plain meaning unless the language is ambiguous or its plain meaning leads to an absurd result. Words and phrases are read in context and construed according to the rules of grammar and common usage.

...

In determining whether Lewis' motion sets forth reasonable grounds, we again examine the statute. Although anyone may request DNA testing, a court is required to order testing only if several statutory requirements are met. Two of those requirements are that the evidence "still exists" and that "identity was or is an issue in the case." TEX. CODE CRIM. PROC. ANN. art. 64.03(a)(1)(A)(i), (a)(1)(B). In its order denying Lewis' request for counsel, the trial court expressly found that Lewis failed to show both of these requirements.

As to the first of the requirements addressed by the trial court, the statute requires that the evidence still exists, and is in a condition to make DNA testing possible, before the court may order testing. TEX. CODE CRIM. PROC. ANN. art. 64.03(a)(1)(A)(i). Affidavit testimony from a relevant witness that no biological evidence from the case is maintained or possessed is sufficient, absent any contrary evidence, to support denial of a motion for forensic DNA testing. Such a determination may be made by the trial court without an evidentiary hearing.

Here, the trial court had before it the affidavits of the evidence officer and district attorney stating that "[t]he evidence in the above-mentioned case was destroyed after the Defendant's plea of guilty ... and the appeal time limit had expired." Therefore, on this record, the trial court could have reasonably concluded that the biological evidence referenced in Lewis' motion no longer exists.

"[T]he presence of another person's DNA at the crime scene will not, without more, constitute affirmative evidence of appellant's innocence."

As to the second requirement that identity "was or is" an issue, we note that Lewis' affidavit in support of his motion for DNA testing asserts that such testing is warranted because the minor was "sexually active" with other males, "lied about her age," and "did not want any sexual assault charges filed in this incident." Nowhere in his motion or affidavit does Lewis deny that he had sexual intercourse with the minor.

Instead, Lewis contends that no assault occurred because the minor was sexually promiscuous, lied about her age, and did not want to file sexual assault charges. Even if true, however, none of these claims exonerate Lewis. Assuming the minor was sexually promiscuous with other males, "[t]he presence of another person's DNA at the crime scene will not, without more, constitute affirmative evidence of appellant's innocence." Also, even assuming the minor lied about her age and did not want sexual assault charges filed in this incident, "[c]onsent is not an issue where the charged offense is sexual assault of a child because a victim under seventeen is legally incapable of consenting to the types of sexual relations described in the statute."

Moreover, Lewis confessed to the crime for which he was convicted; his identity was never an issue. Accordingly, the trial court could have reasonably concluded that there was and is no issue of identity in this case.

Because Lewis' motion for post conviction DNA testing fails to meet two of the preconditions to obtaining DNA testing under Chapter 64, specifically that the evidence still exists and that identity is or was an issue in the case, it also fails to demonstrate "reasonable grounds for a motion to be filed." We conclude that Lewis was not entitled to appointed counsel under article 64.01(c). We overrule Lewis' first three points of error.

In his fourth issue, Lewis claims the State violated the Texas Code of Criminal Procedure when it failed to preserve the biological evidence from his case, or notify him by mail before destroying the evidence. Lewis seeks reversal of his original conviction on the basis that such violations deprived him of his constitutional rights to due process and equal protection of the law.

In essence, Lewis seeks habeas corpus relief. The Code of Criminal Procedure does not authorize an appeal to a court of appeals for allegations that the State improperly destroyed DNA evidence; nor does a court of appeals have original jurisdiction to grant a writ of habeas corpus in criminal law matters. Accordingly, we have no jurisdiction to address Lewis' fourth issue.

In his fifth issue, Lewis complains that the trial court improperly denied his request for DNA testing based on his plea of guilty to the underlying charges. Lewis cites Chapter 64, which states in relevant part, "[a] convicted person who pleaded guilty or nolo contendere in the case may submit a motion under this chapter, and the convicting court is prohibited from finding that identity was not an issue in the case solely on the basis of that plea."

We disagree that the trial court improperly denied Lewis' motion. "Chapter 64 does not guarantee a person who pled guilty the right to DNA testing; it simply prohibits a convicting court from using a guilty plea to bar access to the filing of a motion for testing." Here, Lewis was not barred from filing his motion for DNA testing. In addition, the trial court did not deny Lewis' motion solely on the basis of his plea.

As previously discussed, the trial court reasonably found that Lewis' motion failed to meet two of the preconditions to obtaining post-conviction DNA testing under Chapter 64, specifically, that the evidence still exists and that identity is or was an issue in the case. Lewis' fifth issue is overruled.

Conclusion

The trial court's order denying Lewis' motion for post-conviction forensic DNA testing pursuant to Chapter 64 is affirmed.

House v. Bell — A Reversal Based on Improper Blood Testing

In *House v. Bell*,[27] pre-DNA blood serology was improperly performed at the trial and implicated the defendant House of murder of a woman on whom his alleged semen was found. Later DNA testing showed that the semen belonged to the victim's husband. Other evidence also showed that it was more likely the victim's husband, not House, who was the murderer.

The defendant had brought a habeas petition, which was denied by the Sixth Circuit on the ground that the prisoner failed to show actual innocence. The U.S. Supreme Court reversed, finding that the correct standard for granting a new trial was "whether it was more likely than not that no reasonable juror would not have reasonable doubt of the defendant's guilt after seeing the DNA evidence."

The case involved the murder of Carolyn Muncey in rural Tennessee in 1986. She was murdered outside her home in her nightgown and was found in some brush nearby. Although she was married to an abusive husband who had threatened her, the court convicted House based on a neighbor having seen House in the area on the night of the murder. House, when questioned, lied about spending the entire evening with his girlfriend. He had scratches on his arms and a bruise on his right ring finger. The girlfriend initially confirmed his alibi but recanted the next day, saying he left her trailer around 10 pm to go for a walk and returned some time later missing his shirt and shoes and hot and panting. House was not a particularly credible witness in light of his previous lies.

Investigators drove the evidence, consisting of Muncey's nightgown and House's pants, to the FBI for testing, a ten-hour drive. They packaged the pants, blood samples from the autopsy of Muncey, and other evidence in one box. The FBI stated that the semen was consistent with House's and that small bloodstains consistent with Muncey's blood but not House's appeared on his jeans. This conclusion, formed in 1986, was not based on DNA testing, but rather testing based on "serology," a study of the blood types of the blood and the blood type and "secretors" in the semen.

House, Mrs. Muncey, and Mr. Muncey all had Type A blood. The FBI found that the semen was from a contributor with Type A blood who was a "secretor," one who secretes ABO blood group substances in semen — a characteristic shared by 80 percent of the population, including House. The expert, Bigbee, testified he was unable to determine the secretor status of either Muncey.

---

27. 126 S. Ct. 2064 (June 12, 2006).

"Agent Bigbee found only the H blood-group substance, ... Agent Bigbee explained, however — using science an *amicus* sharply disputes ... that House's A antigens could have 'degraded' into H.... Agent Bigbee thus concluded that both semen deposits could have come from House, though he acknowledged that the H antigen could have come from Mrs. Muncey herself if she was a secretor — something he was not able to determine."[28]

Bigbee acknowledged that a saliva test would have answered the question, but the state did not provide a saliva sample. Bigbee testified that the blood spots on House's pants were Type A but had slight chemical traces consistent only with Mrs. Muncey's blood. Based on this, he concluded the blood could only have come from Mrs. Muncey. Muncey's shoes, found several months after the crime, had no blood on them.

The Supreme Court agreed with House's contention that the blood on the pants may well have come from a leak in the sample of Mrs. Muncey's blood that occurred during the 10-hour drive to the FBI lab. Four vials of Mrs. Muncey's blood were packed with the pants, but a vial and a half of the four vials were missing when it arrived for testing. There was also seepage of her blood in one corner of the packing box, and there was a forked streak of blood on a plastic bag with a label listing the pants.[29]

Later DNA testing confirmed that the semen had come from the victim's husband and not the defendant. The blood on the pants was too degraded to be tested, but the state's blood spatter expert testified that the majority of the stains were "transfer stains" resulting from "wiping across the surface of the pants" rather than seeping or spilling. The Supreme Court found that "the record before us contains credible testimony suggesting that the missing enzyme markers are generally better preserved on cloth than in poorly kept test tubes, and that principle could support House's spillage theory for the blood's origin."[30]

Additional witness testimony supported the view that Mr. Muncey had beaten his wife and threatened to kill her. The jury had not heard this evidence. The Court concluded:

> This is not a case of conclusive exoneration ... Yet the central forensic proof connecting House to the crime — the blood and the semen — has been called into question, and House has put forward substantial evidence pointing to a different suspect. Accordingly ... had the jury heard all the conflicting testimony — it is more likely than not that no reasonable juror viewing the record as a whole would lack reasonable doubt.[31]

The Court remanded the case for a new trial. Justice Roberts, joined by two other Supreme Court justices, wrote a dissenting opinion questioning the standard in the majority opinion for remand based on DNA testing:

---

28. *Id.*
29. *Id.* at 2080.
30. *Id.* at 2082.
31. *Id.* at 2086.

House must show more than just a "reasonable probability that ... the fact finder would have had a reasonable doubt respecting guilt ... House must present such compelling evidence of innocence that it becomes more likely than not that no single juror, acting reasonably, would vote to convict him.[32]

None of the justices concluded that the DNA evidence exonerated House. The only question was whether enough new evidence had been presented, including DNA testing of the semen and evidence about the source of blood on House's pants, to require a new trial in which the jury would hear all the evidence. Thus, we see the Supreme Court divided on what legal standard should be used where DNA retesting is not conclusive, but where it *may* affect the outcome of the case.

Here is part of the opinion in *House v. Bell*:

House v. Bell, 126 S. Ct. 2064 (June 12, 2006)

First, in direct contradiction of evidence presented at trial, DNA testing has established that the semen on Mrs. Muncey's nightgown and panties came from her husband, Mr. Muncey, not from House. The State, though conceding this point, insists this new evidence is immaterial. At the guilt phase at least, neither sexual contact nor motive were elements of the offense, so in the State's view the evidence, or lack of evidence, of sexual assault or sexual advance is of no consequence. We disagree. In fact we consider the new disclosure of central importance.

...

[W]e think the evidentiary disarray surrounding the blood, taken together with Dr. Blake's testimony and the limited rebuttal of it in the present record, would prevent reasonable jurors from placing significant reliance on the blood evidence. We now know, though the trial jury did not, that an Assistant Chief Medical Examiner believes the blood on House's jeans must have come from autopsy samples; that a vial and a quarter of autopsy blood is unaccounted for; that the blood was transported to the FBI together with the pants in conditions that could have caused vials to spill; that the blood did indeed spill at least once during its journey from Tennessee authorities through FBI hands to a defense expert; that the pants were stored in a plastic bag bearing both a large blood stain and a label with TBI Agent Scott's name; and that the styrofoam box containing the blood samples may well have been opened before it arrived at the FBI lab. Thus, whereas the bloodstains, emphasized by the prosecution, seemed strong evidence of House's guilt at trial, the record now raises substantial questions about the blood's origin.

A Different Suspect

Were House's challenge to the State's case limited to the questions he has raised about the blood and semen, the other evidence favoring the prosecution

---

32. *Id.* at 2096.

might well suffice to bar relief. There is, however, more; for in the post-trial proceedings House presented troubling evidence that Mr. Muncey, the victim's husband, himself could have been the murderer.

…

Conclusion

This is not a case of conclusive exoneration. Some aspects of the State's evidence — Lora Muncey's memory of a deep voice, House's bizarre evening walk, his lie to law enforcement, his appearance near the body, and the blood on his pants — still support an inference of guilt. Yet the central forensic proof connecting House to the crime — the blood and the semen — has been called into question, and House has put forward substantial evidence pointing to a different suspect.

Accordingly, and although the issue is close, we conclude that this is the rare case where — had the jury heard all the conflicting testimony — it is more likely than not that no reasonable juror viewing the record as a whole would lack reasonable doubt.

Exoneration and Post-Conviction Mitochondrial DNA Testing

The case of Mark Reid combines issues of expert testimony about hair analysis and subsequent mitochondrial testing of the hairs. Reid was convicted in 1997 of sexual assault and kidnapping. At trial, Kiti Settachatgul, a lead criminologist at the Connecticut Forensic Science Laboratory, testified that three pubic hairs taken from the victim's clothing were similar to the characteristics of hairs provided by the defendant. At Reid's appeal, he argued that the court improperly admitted the expert testimony without a *Daubert* hearing. The appeals court concluded that a *Daubert* hearing was unnecessary, as hair analysis, like shoeprint analysis, is a matter that is within the jury's common knowledge:

Settachatgul's testimony is akin to that of the podiatrist in *Hasan*. Although Settachatgul's training is based in science, he testified about a subject that simply required the jurors to use their own powers of observation and comparison. During his testimony, Settachatgul displayed an enlarged photograph of one of the defendant's hairs and one of the hairs recovered from the victim's clothing as they appeared side-by-side under the comparison microscope. Settachatgul explained to the jurors how the hairs were similar and what particular features of the hairs were visible.

He also drew a diagram of a hair on a courtroom blackboard for the jurors. The jurors were free to make their own determinations as to the weight they would accord the expert's testimony in the light of the photograph and their own powers of observation and comparison. The

"We conclude that this is the rare case where—had the jury heard all the conflicting testimony—it is more likely than not that no reasonable juror viewing the record as a whole would lack reasonable doubt."

jurors were not subject to confusing or obscure scientific evidence, but were able to use the testimony to guide them in their own determination of the similarity of the two hairs.

…

We conclude that microscopic hair analysis is not the type of evidence that we contemplated in *Porter* to be subject to the *Daubert* test. Accordingly, a hearing as to the admissibility of the evidence was not required by *Porter*, and the trial court properly admitted the evidence.[33]

Reid also challenged the admissibility of the hair comparison on the ground that the expert did not take measurements of the diameter or length of the hair, or quantify the density of pigment, the degree of curliness, or the color. The court held that these issues went to the weight of the evidence, but not its admissibility.

As a result of mtDNA testing, the trial testimony and visual comparison of the hairs which appeared to be identical was shown to be absolutely wrong.

Two years later, Reid petitioned for a new trial, alleging that mitochondrial DNA had excluded him as the source of the hair specimens. The Connecticut trial court granted the petition, and charges against Reid were subsequently dropped. The discussion of the mitochondrial DNA analysis appears under the DNA chapter.

The result in the *Reid* case is particularly troubling because it shows that the trial testimony and visual comparison of the hairs was absolutely wrong, yet it appeared to be correct. The mitochondrial evidence showed that any "similarity" between the hairs was prejudicial and highly misleading, as the hair was absolutely not the defendant's. Does this mean that no hair comparisons should be submitted to a jury without DNA or mtDNA testing? This is certainly one conclusion to be drawn from *Reid*.

Can Exonerees Sue for Money for Wrongful Imprisonment?

As states generally have statutory immunity from civil suits, exonerees generally cannot sue for civil damages unless they have been declared actually innocent (as opposed to being pardoned or a verdict of not guilty after a retrial) and the state adopts legislation permitting a suit or a statutory damage award.

An exoneree can sue under 42 U.S.C. § 1983, which is a civil suit against a public official for violation of a constitutional right. However, as one commentator points out, these suits are difficult to win:

[W]inning "1983 actions" is potentially difficult because many government officials — including judges and prosecutors and, perhaps to a lesser degree, police officers — are essentially immune. Winning these actions is also difficult because the plaintiff must prove all the elements of a constitutional violation. In *Heck v. Humphrey*, the U.S. Supreme Court held that damages under 1983

---

33. *State v. Reid*, 254 Conn. 540, 547–559 (Conn. 2000).

actions are barred when the plaintiff's original conviction (or sentence) has not been "reversed on direct appeal, expunged by executive order, declared invalid by a state tribunal authorized to make such determination, or called into question by a federal court's issuance of a writ of habeas corpus" (citation omitted). Otherwise, through the federal 2004 Innocence Protection Act, under the 2004 Justice for All Act, those wrongfully imprisoned may recover up to $50,000 per year (of imprisonment) under the federal compensation statutes.[34]

Although an exoneree can potentially demonstrate the loss of income from employment during imprisonment, damages for the "pain and suffering" resulting from unjust imprisonment could total millions. The family of Sam Sheppard, convicted of the murder of his wife, and held not guilty after a second trial showed flawed analysis both of blood spatter and DNA evidence proving a third party was at the crime scene, attempted to have a trial court declare Sheppard actually innocent in order to sue the state of Illinois for civil damages. Even though there was substantial evidence that Sheppard had not committed the crime, the suit was denied and the Sheppard heirs have never collected a dime for the many years that Sheppard spent behind bars.

On the other hand, Larry David Holdren, who spent fourteen years in prison for a crime he did not commit, received a substantial court award. In 1999, when Holden was 44, the court reversed his conviction and dismissed the indictment. He sued, and received $1,650,000, approximately $110,000 for each year in prison.[35]

In 1999, only fourteen states, the District of Columbia, and the federal government had laws to compensate individuals who had been unjustly convicted.[36] "Most offered compensation so skimpy as to be insulting. Many statutes were virtually inaccessible because they required a gubernatorial pardon."[37] Since 1999, more states have enacted compensation statutes, but some provide very low compensation. For example, Montana pays for tuition only. Ohio limits compensation to $40,333 per year, plus lost wages. Missouri proposed legislation that would limit economic loss to the amount the federal government regards as poverty level plus twenty percent.[38]

To receive such benefits, the exoneree must generally release the right to sue the state. However, a number of exonerees have refused the benefits and sued lawyers, police, prosecutors, and police departments under theories such as deprivation of civil rights under § 1983 of the federal code.

---

34. Charles L. Baum, "Calculating Economic Losses from Wrongful Incarceration," *Tennessee Bar Journal* 52, no. 7 (July 2016): 18, 19.

35. *Id.* at 709–710.

36. Adele Bernhard, "Justice Still Fails: A Review of Recent Efforts to Compensate Individuals Who Have Been Unjustly Convicted and Later Exonerated," *Drake Law Review* 52 (Summer 2004): 703.

37. *Id.* 703.

38. *Id.* at 606–712.

How Does the Exoneree Return to Society?

We Americans like a happy ending — we picture an exonerated prisoner, the iron prison doors clanging shut behind him, as he clutches a satchel containing his belongings and squints like a mole suddenly confronted with the sun. But what really happens after the exonerated returns to society? Does he receive job training, social services, medical treatment, therapy? Does he even get a formal apology? The answer is frequently "no." Unlike parolees, who generally receive these benefits, the exonerated do not qualify. After all, they're innocent.

A project called After Innocence has been formed to highlight this injustice and call for reform. The project produced a film tracking the lives of exonerees after release. Some are still viewed as pariahs in their community. Some are so angry about their treatment that they cannot move forward with their lives. Many cannot obtain a job because their primary years for learning a skill have been spent behind bars.

The film interviews Wilton Dedge, who spent twenty-two years in a Florida jail, serving two concurrent life sentences, until mitochondrial DNA tests proved that a hair found on the victim's bed and "matched" to him could not be his. Dedge fought for eight years to get the DNA testing that would eventually exonerate him. At the end of the film, he is shown returning to his childhood bedroom, decorated in boyish blue by his white-haired parents, the scene oddly sad for the homecoming of a man in his 40s.

Dennis Maher served nineteen years of a life sentence. The film shows him working fixing trucks and awaiting the birth of his first child. He's one of the lucky ones, willing to go out drinking in a local bar and listen with an inscrutable smile to his buddies rail at what they would do if they'd been wrongfully imprisoned.

Some are not so lucky. Scott Hornoff, a former police officer, whose only crime was a casual sexual affair with a woman who was later raped and murdered, was eventually exonerated. The film interviews his father, also a police officer, who believed his son was guilty and did not visit him once in prison. Hornoff tried to get his license as a cop reinstated. But the force was in no hurry to give him back his old life.

Others complain that they cannot get a job or housing with a criminal record. Their conviction is not automatically expunged. One exoneree discovers it would cost $6,000 to get the conviction removed.

As of 2015, thirty states, the District of Columbia and the federal government provided some sort of restitution or monetary award for wrongful imprisonment. In 2012, the Connecticut Bar Foundation, with private donors, established the Connecticut Innocence Fund to aid exonerees. Kenneth Ireland, exonerated in 2009 for a murder and sexual assault he did not commit, assisted in the fundraising efforts.[39]

---

39. www.ctbarfdn.org/ctinnocencefund.

Figure 13.1 Attorney Karen Goodrow, of the Connecticut Innocence Project, James C. Tillman, exonerated after 18 years for a crime he did not commit, and author Christine Lissitzyn. Tillman received $5 million in compensation from a special bill passed by the Connecticut State Legislature on May 21, 2007.

James Tillman

The state of Connecticut established an Innocence Project in 2004, when two public defenders — Brian Carlow (who defended Edward Grant) and Karen Goodrow — agreed to lead the project. They were instrumental in the release of Mark Reid, when mtDNA excluded him from the hairs introduced as a match at his trial for rape. By June of 2006, they had secured the release of James Tillman, who had been convicted in 1989 of rape.[40] Their first challenge was simply finding the evidence that had been used to secure Tillman's conviction. Fortunately, they were able to obtain the evidence used in the trial from a box stored in the back room of a local legal aid office that contained a dress and a pair of pantyhose — both had been exhibits in Tillman's trial.

Carlow and Goodrow then obtained a court order for new testing of the semen stains. The genetic profile categorically eliminated Tillman as the source. Tillman was granted a new trial on June 6, 2006. The judge found that had the jury known of the DNA results that showed Tillman was not the secretor of the six semen stains, it would have found him not guilty of the charges against him — the standard of law required for the granting of a new trial. At the pretrial conference on July 11, prosecutors "nolled"[41] the charges against Tillman and the judge then granted his motion for dismissal.

Nolle Prosequi is Latin for "we shall no longer prosecute." When the prosecution "nolles" a charge, it drops the charge.

---

40. Lisa Siegel, "A Criminal Justice 'Nightmare,'" *The Connecticut Law Tribune*, week of June 12, 2006.

41. The state chose not to re-try Tillman; it could have chosen to dismiss the indictment and acknowledge that Tillman was wrongfully charged, but it did not.

Although his attorneys acknowledged that prosecutors had not done anything underhanded at Tillman's trial, as DNA testing was not available at the time, the *Tillman* case illustrates the extent to which rape convictions of the innocent have depended upon false eyewitness identifications.

> The white victim testified that she was beaten, abducted and raped by an unknown black assailant, near Columbus Boulevard in Hartford. She testified that she focused during the attack on memorizing identifying details about the perpetrator. A few days after the attack, she was given photo books to look through by the Hartford police, who did not have a suspect at the time. After turning a few pages, she became emotionally distressed when she saw Tillman's photo. She identified him as the perpetrator, but said he looked younger than at the time of the attack.[42]

In December of 2015, Congress passed the Wrongful Convictions Tax Relief Act, excluding compensation for wrongful imprisonment from taxation.[43]

Summary

As of September of 2017, over 420 prisoners have reportedly been exonerated and released from prison since 1989 based on DNA testing and 2,089 exonerations, including all grounds, have occurred.[44] The phenomenon of DNA exonerations has captured the public interest and has led many states to adopt legislation to help with exoneration requests. These laws cover issues such as:

- A requirement that states preserve DNA evidence after conviction for some period of time.
- A process to request post-conviction DNA for testing.
- Costs to be paid by the state if the prisoner cannot pay.
- A process for petitioning the court for exoneration.
- Compensation statutes for exonerees.
- Laws to provide post-exoneration social services.

The legal standard for relief based on post-conviction testing remains high. The prisoner must show that no reasonable juror, if he had the results of the DNA test available, would have voted to convict.

We can expect DNA exonerations to decrease as trials today that involve DNA evidence will present the DNA test results in evidence. However, defendants will continue to be wrongfully convicted, particularly because of the problems with the reliability of eyewitness identification. These defendants may have a much more

---

42. Siegel, *supra.*

43. www.innocenceproject.org.

44. The National Registry of Exonerations, www.law.umich.edu/special/exoneration/Pages/about.aspx.

difficult time in proving their innocence, particularly if the public no longer perceives a major miscarriage in justice.

Discussion Questions

1. What does your state provide about whether DNA evidence must be kept?

2. Does your state have a process for requesting DNA for testing? For exoneration? For post-exoneration compensation?

3. With limited money and time, do you think it is better to open old cases and try to exonerate the wrongly convicted or to require that a defendant could not be convicted if DNA samples were available and had not been tested?

4. What is the legal standard required to petition for post-conviction testing in Connecticut? Give an example of what a prisoner would have to prove.

5. How does the federal law applicable to post-conviction testing differ from Connecticut's? Which do you think is the better law and why?

6. Do you believe federal legislation is required to standardize the storage periods of DNA?

7. What is a habeas corpus petition and why is it often used in post-conviction exoneration cases?

8. What are some of the actions the court can take based on a petition for post-conviction exoneration? Under what type of condition might the court order a new trial?

9. Why was a finding of "actual innocence" important to exonerees? Review the Chapter 11 on blood spatter and explain the result of the civil trial in which the family of Sam Sheppard attempted to have a court declare Sheppard actually innocent.

Appendix

The *Grant* Case Study and Record

Overview

In *State v. Grant*, Edward Grant was convicted in 2002 for the 1973 murder of Concetta "Penney" Serra in a New Haven, Connecticut, garage. Serra had driven her car into the garage and parked on the top floor. At some point, her attacker got into her car, a fight ensued with a knife, and his blood was left in the car and in a trail to where he had parked his car. (The blood was typed but DNA profiling was not yet invented.) Serra then fled across the lot and tried to escape up a staircase, which was locked at the top. Her body was found stabbed at the foot of the stairs. She was not raped and nothing was taken from her car. Based on these facts, investigators believed the murder was a "crime of passion" by someone Serra knew. They interviewed three former boyfriends and put them in a lineup for possible identification by some people who had been in the garage. A prior boyfriend of the victim was identified the following day in a lineup, but he was ruled out based on his blood type. Another was arrested and charged with the crime, but charges were dropped on the eve of trial when it turned out his blood type did not match the Type O blood trail either.

Investigators lifted one clear fingerprint from a tissue box on the floor behind the driver's seat. The print did not match any of the fingerprints on card files in New Haven at the time. (The Automated Fingerprint Identification System, AFIS, was not yet in operation.) They also found a handkerchief four flights down in the garage, which they initially thought was unconnected to the crime. They later connected it based on a blood trail in the garage which they believed was the attacker's as he searched the garage trying to find his own car.

The case remained a "cold case" for almost twenty-five years until Chris Grice, a fingerprint examiner in the Connecticut Forensic Science Laboratory (who had been involved as one of the investigators in New Haven twenty-five years prior), did a cold case run of the fingerprint from the tissue box through AFIS. As we saw in the fingerprint chapter, the AFIS report was a series of numbers identifying people. Grice then needed to pull actual prints and visually compare them. Ed Grant was not number 1 on the list. However, Grice eliminated the higher numerical "matches" and identified Grant as the print on the box.

The Investigation

Investigators initially targeted a boyfriend of the victim, who was identified the day after the crime in a lineup. He was subsequently excluded based on the fact that his blood type differed from blood stains believed to be the perpetrator's and left at the scene. They then turned to two other men the victim had known, because they believed that the victim had known her attacker.

None of the fingerprints found at the scene could be matched to anyone except family members of the victim. Blood typing showed the victim's blood type — A — was found where Serra was killed, but Type O blood, believed to be the attacker's, was present in a trail running through the garage. The prosecution's theory was that the attacker was wounded in the attack of Serra and bled as he ran through the garage Investigators took a fingerprint off a bloody tissue box found behind the driver's seat in the victim's car and compared it to the fingerprints cards on file in New Haven, but found no match.

Following the match of the fingerprint on the tissue box to Grant, investigators then got a warrant to take Grant's blood, which they subsequently matched to a small amount of genetic material, believed to be blood, on a handkerchief that had been found in the garage near Serra's discarded car keys. The DNA test of Grant's blood showed that he was the source of the genetic material on the handkerchief. However, none of the blood from the trail in the garage was testable. Serra's keys had been lost. Some of the witnesses had died.

The Trial and Appeal

Grant was tried in May of 2002 for Serra's murder. He did not take the stand. His defense was that he did not know Serra and did not commit the crime. The state was therefore required to prove each element of the crime of murder beyond a reasonable doubt.

The jury convicted Grant largely based on the two pieces of hard forensic evidence — his fingerprint on the tissue box and his genetic material on the handkerchief. His attorneys did not deny that the forensic tests were correct, but argued that there was no evidence to prove that the fingerprint was impressed on the tissue box at the time of the crime. Nor was there any testimony that proved the handkerchief was Grant's or that it was dropped at the time of the crime. They also questioned how only one small spot of "blood" could have remained testable after years of moving the handkerchief from place to place under conditions that deteriorated the rest of the spots beyond testing.

Grant made pretrial motions to exclude the DNA testing based on his argument that the DNA testing method — Short Tandem Repeat — was too new. The court denied the motion. He also made a post-trial motion for a new trial on the grounds of comments made by prosecutors and the failure to sanction the state for losing evidence. He lost that motion too. Grant was sentenced that August to 20 years in prison.

Penney Serra, Trial Exhibit 3.1

Car with Tissue Box on Back Floorboard
(Boxed), Trial Exhibit 2.3

Tissue Box with Blood Closeup,
Trial Exhibit 2.19

Latent Print on Tissue Box with Detective's Initials, Bottom, Trial Exhibit 2.21

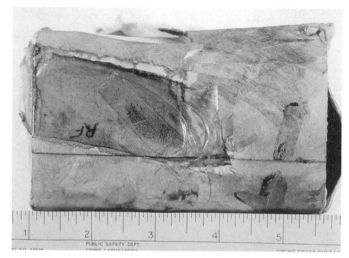

Latent Print on Tissue Box, Trial Exhibit 244

Handkerchief, Trial Exhibit 6.3

Crime Schematic
Temple St. Parking Garage, New Haven, CT

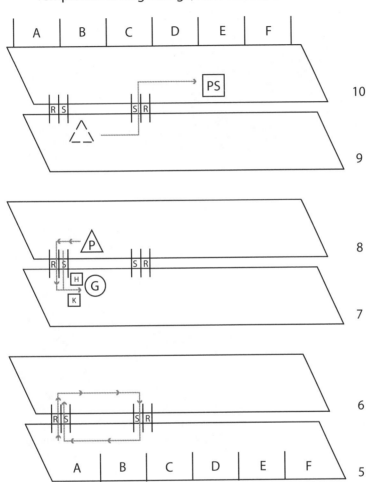

1. Serra's car is parked with Grant inside on level 9A; Serra runs out and up stairs to level 10, with Grant in pursuit; Serra is killed in stairwell from level 10 to roof.

2. Grant runs back to Serra's car on level 9A.

3. Grant drives Serra's car up to level 10 by mistake and then down to level 8A, looking for his own car. Grant exits Serra's car and proceeds on foot looking for his own car, leaving a blood trail as he walks.

4. Grant walks down to level 5 and then back up to level 7A, where he finds his car, leaving a trail of blood.

5. Grant enters his car, drops Serra's keys and his handkerchief and leaves the garage. Blood trail ends.

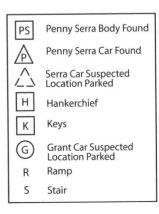

PS	Penny Serra Body Found
P	Penny Serra Car Found
Serra Car Suspected Location Parked
H	Hankerchief
K	Keys
G	Grant Car Suspected Location Parked
R	Ramp
S	Stair

Lineup Photo, Trial Exhibit 207 [circled: Phil DeLieto]

Photo of Grant with Composite Drawings,
Trial Exhibits 222.1, 208, 216, and 41.1

Selman Topciu, Trial Exhibit 1067

In August of 2006, Grant appealed his conviction. One of his main issues on appeal was that the affidavit used to get a warrant for his blood was defective because it did not disclose certain information about the fingerprint, including that the tissue box was moveable and therefore did not link him to the crime scene. The other was that a statement made by Grant after he was picked up by investigators in which he said "did you hear about the guy in Texas? They got him on a fingerprint too," violated his constitutional rights and was inadmissible.

The state responded that the affidavit for Grant's blood was not misleading and included all necessary information. It also responded that Grant's statement to investigators was made voluntarily and without any violation of law. Grant's appeal was denied by the Connecticut Supreme Court in 2008.

Detailed Record

The initial investigation disclosed the following facts:[1] On July 16, 1973, a worker in a New Haven garage discovered a dead woman in the stairwell leading to the 10th level. She was barefoot and dressed in a blue knit minidress with a large bloodstain on the bodice. Her body was curled in a fetal position. She had suffered a single stab wound to the left side of the chest which pierced the lower tip of the heart, causing death within a minute. Medical examination showed she had not been sexually molested. Her name was Concetta "Penney" Serra. She had apparently parked in the garage to shop in the attached mall.

Theory of the Case

The police report filed on July 16, 1973, contained a theory of the crime. Serra was shoeless because she often took her shoes off to drive. She was driving a 1972 Buick. The police surmised that the assailant arrived at the Temple Street Garage in a separate vehicle about four minutes before Serra, based on the entry and exit times stamped on his garage ticket. Serra and her assailant entered from different entrance points at different ends of the garage.[2]

There was a bloody trail at the scene, which detectives believed to be that of her attacker. The blood was later determined to be Type O. Serra was Type A. Police then concluded that the blood was probably the assailant's. The police suspected the attacker to be someone Serra knew, because she had apparently let him into her car. Her purse and possessions were untouched.

By tracing the blood drops evidently left by the assailant and looking at the placement of Serra's car, police theorized that the assailant got into Serra's car and they rode together to level 9 in her car. On level 9, Serra ran from the car and

---

1. Some of the facts are taken from the initial police report filed July 16, 1973.
2. *State v. Grant*, CR6-481390, State's Exhibit (hereinafter "Exhibit") No. 241.

attempted to leave by the stairwell. She ran up the stairs from level 9 to level 10. A wig or "fall" attached to her hair was found on level 9, where it apparently landed during her flight.

Once on level 10, Serra tried to go to the top level, but found the stairwell was a dead end. Both Serra and her assailant were apparently wounded when she was attacked. The police found a blood trail back down the stairway to level #9, where the blood drops disappeared. Police theorized that the murderer ran back from level 10 to level 9 and got in Serra's car, searching for his own. They found Serra's car on level 8, where it was abandoned in an erratic position. On level 7, the police found Serra's car keys and a man's handkerchief containing bloodstains and traces of an "unidentified substance."

Police found a blood trail from level 8, where the assailant abandoned Serra's car, down to level 5 and back to level 7, when it once again disappeared.

Semen

Experts concluded that there was evidence of semen on Serra's panties and slip. However, it was degraded and may have been residual after washing the garments.[3]

Suspects

Three men connected with Serra were questioned, but were all eventually eliminated as suspects:

1. Phil DeLieto, Serra's former fiancé.
2. Anthony Golino, a high school classmate of Serra's.
3. Selman Topciu, a patient at a dental practice where Serra had worked.

Serra and DeLieto had been in Rhode Island the weekend before she was murdered and had apparently quarreled the prior weekend. DeLieto was identified by an eyewitness in a lineup shortly after the crime, but was cleared based on both his blood type and an alibi.

Anthony Golino had been a classmate of Serra's at Wilbur Cross High School. Golino's wife, Melanie, told police in 1982 that her husband had threatened to kill her, saying essentially that "I will do to you what I did to Penney Serra."[4] Police questioned Golino, who had a one-inch scar on his left hand that he could not explain. They arrested him for the murder in 1984. In 1987, on the eve of trial, the state executed a search warrant for Golino's blood, which turned out to be Type A, the same as Serra's. This blood type excluded him as the source of the blood trail in the garage, which was Type O. The charges were dismissed.

---

3. Dr. Henry C. Lee with Thomas W. O'Neil, *Cracking More Cases* (Prometheus Books, 2004), 39.

4. *Cracking More Cases*, supra, 33.

Another suspect was Selman Topciu, a patient of the dental practice where Serra worked. Several invoices addressed to Topciu were found under the driver's side visor of Serra's car. Serra's father stated that they had not been there when his daughter had borrowed the car that morning. Topciu spoke with a foreign accent and had been seen at a diner when Penney was there. He also had a scar on his left wrist. His blood type was O, as was the blood found throughout the garage and in the car. Topciu's DQ Alpha DNA marker, which was based on an early form of DNA testing, matched the blood lifted from the car.[5] At the time of the crime, Topciu drove a brown Buick with license plate HN5533.[6] Christopher Fagan, the parking lot attendant, described the suspect who handed him a bloody parking ticket as driving a green or blue Chrysler or GM car with MR or MH as the first two letters on the license plate followed by four digits. The driver handed him a bloody ticket with his right hand in a "cross-body" motion. He did not see the driver, but said he spoke with a Hispanic accent.[7] Grant is not Hispanic. By the time of trial, the attendant had died and the ticket had been lost. New Haven detectives tried to obtain arrest warrants on two occasions after Topciu had moved out of Connecticut, but the court refused due to lack of evidence.[8]

Eyewitness Reports[9]

Two eyewitnesses on level 9 stated that they saw a man running toward the stairs with a "shiny object" and heard screaming. They also stated that the assailant later reappeared running, entered the victim's car and drove the length of level 9, apparently looking for the down ramp. He missed it, had to go up to level 10, where he was observed by a third witness who said the car was driving fast and erratically.

The eyewitness reports of the three witnesses inside the garage were somewhat conflicting. The assailant was variously described as "either white or Puerto Rican, 18–35 years of age," and was probably suffering from a cut on one hand or lower arm. One eyewitness created a composite sketch of the assailant and identified Phil DeLieto, Serra's former fiancé, at a lineup.

Forensic Evidence

The Weapon

Medical examination showed the weapon was a knife at least three inches long, which was never recovered.

---

5. Memorandum of Law in Support of Appeal of Edward Grant, filed August 14, 2006 (hereinafter "Appellant's Brief"), at 16.

6. *Id.* at 15.

7. *State of Connecticut v. Edward Grant*, CR6-481390, Trial Transcript (hereinafter "Transcript") May 1, 2002, p. 194.

8. *Cracking More Cases*, *supra*, 35.

9. *Cracking More Cases*, *supra*, 23–24.

Fingerprints

Three latent prints were lifted from the site — two within the car and one on a tissue box. Fingerprints were also lifted from envelopes under the visor of Serra's car.

The police did a visual search of all 70,000 fingerprints on file in New Haven. None matched. The police also recovered a handkerchief that appeared to have blood and perhaps red paint, or both, on it. DNA testing was not available at the time, but swatches were cut and showed that there was genetic material on the handkerchief.

There was no evidence that Grant had ever known Serra and no evidence of any possible motive for the crime. There were no recoverable prints on the steering wheel of Serra's car, although the prosecution's theory posited that Grant drove it. There was no evidence as to when the fingerprint was placed on the tissue box or how Grant could have reached the box from the front seat. There was no explanation as to why all genetic material on the handkerchief had deteriorated beyond the point of testing, except for the one spot that identified Grant. The entire incident, based on the time-stamped entry of Serra's and the perpetrator's parking tickets to the time the perpetrator left, was between 6 and 10 minutes.

Blood Spatter

The initial crime scene, the 10th floor stairwell leading to the elevator penthouse, was covered with blood from Serra, on her dress and on the floor. The police found her car on the 8th floor. The handkerchief was found on the ground of the 7th floor, about 9 feet from a set of car keys which had blood on the keys and on the white plastic key holder.[10] The investigating officer, Vincent Perricone, initially thought the keys had been thrown down from the 8th floor, where the car was located, to the 7th.[11]

The keys were subsequently lost and were therefore not introduced at trial. No testing for blood was done on them. Former Detective Louis Ranciato testified that he discovered a trail of blood leading from the Buick Serra drove, which was parked on the 8th floor, down various staircases and ramps leading down through the 7th, 6th, and 5th floors, then going across the 5th floor and back up the stairs ending on the 7th floor about 10 feet from where the bloody keys and handkerchief were found. The length of the trail was about 360 feet. It was photographed, and the photos were introduced at trial.

Serra's car, parked on the 8th floor, had visible blood on the driver's side door, window, handle, steering wheel, and seat. There was also blood covering a fingerprint found on a Pathmark-brand box of tissues found on the floor behind the driver's seat as well as other blood stained areas on the box where bloody fingers had touched it, but no identifiable prints were present.[12]

---

10. Appellant's Brief, at 4–5.
11. *Id.*
12. *Id.* at 11.

The police theorized that Grant, following the murder in the 10th floor stairwell, ran around looking for either his car or Serra's. He apparently found Serra's and then drove around looking for his own. He stopped her car on the 8th floor, and walked around the garage looking for his own car and leaving a trail of blood. When he finally found his car on the 7th floor, he dropped Serra's keys and his handkerchief, entered his car and left the garage. Police believed that Grant was wounded in the struggle in the stairwell, perhaps with his own knife, perhaps with the bread knife that Serra's mother testified she had given her daughter for a picnic. No knives were ever found.

The blood from the trail was typed and determined to be Type O. Penney Serra was Type A. There was no DNA testing at the time. By the time of trial almost thirty years later, none of the blood evidence had survived to the point of DNA testing except a small portion of a handkerchief which was found on the ground near Serra's car. Serra's blood was found only at the initial crime scene. Type O blood was identified on the Pathmark tissue box, on 5 of 6 tape liftings of blood from the Buick as well as on several items taken from the Buick. Type O was also identified on the handkerchief. No typing was done on the parking ticket. Type O was also identified in 3 of 4 tape liftings from the blood trail. About 45% of the U.S. Caucasian population has Type O blood. Both Grant and Selman Topciu, a patient of the dentist for whom Penney worked as bookkeeper and whose bills were found in the visor of the Buick, had Type O blood.

Crime Reconstruction

Dr. Henry Lee, director emeritus of the Connecticut Forensic Science Laboratory, was asked to complete a detailed analysis of the crime scene in 1989. He reviewed the police reports, the photographs, and toured the scene. He also completed an exercise in which similar cars were driven through the garage to attempt to validate the timeline from entrance to exit of Grant's car. He concluded in a book he wrote about the crime that it "meant that, in all probability, the sperm had been ejaculated outside the undergarments, the date of this deposit being impossible to determine."[13] Rape did not appear to be involved in the crime.

Lee determined in 1989 that Serra had been chased to and stabbed in the 10th floor stairwell. He concluded that either Serra and the perpetrator had been acquainted and the meeting at the top of the garage had been pre-arranged or they did not know each other and the meeting was by chance. Lee also concluded that the blood on the Buick meant the perpetrator had been injured on his left hand before he entered the driver's door. He concluded that there was no direct connection between the handkerchief and the crime.[14]

The prosecution called Lee to testify at trial to establish a link between Serra, her car, and the suspect. The location of the car was a secondary crime site and as

---

13. *Cracking More Cases, supra*, at 39.
14. *Id.* at 12.

the handkerchief and fingerprint were found there, the state needed to link them to the crime.

The defense, on cross-examination, attempted to show that Lee never viewed the actual crime scene, and relied on reports of witness accounts as written in the original police report.

Blood Testing

In 1988, a tape lift of blood from the car was tested using an early form of DNA testing known as DQ Alpha and was found to have the profile 1.2, 3. Five percent of the Caucasian population with Type O blood has profile 1.2, 3. As Topicu was determined to have this profile, he continued to be investigated for the murder. Lee examined photos of the blood-like stains on the driver's side and stated that the stains on the metal trim are consistent with medium velocity impact blood spatters. He explained: "means somebody hand maybe move, like move the hand, now it's not the contact, it becomes spatter. If I have some liquid or blood on my hand, I'm doing that, deposit on exterior surface of the window and the car, so that's called medium velocity."[15]

Lee was asked on cross-examination whether he could measure the size of the blood stain from the photos, and he said he could not: "since there is no close-up, just a distance photo, I could only see transfer of blood."[16] He further identified stains on the left portion of the driver's seat as drop-like patterns. However, he admitted on cross-examination that his opinions were limited to what he could see on the photographs and that he did not see a photo of the blood trail, the handkerchief, or the keys.

Lee stated that as part of his reconstruction, he took cars and drove them around the garage to see if they could meet the timing of the crime. However, he did not reach any conclusions because the garage had been altered after the murder and prior to Lee's examination. Lee denied relying on witness statements, stating "I have to base on my independent result of police officers'[17] [statements and records]." Here is the process of reconstruction as he explained it:

> My reconstruction basically the first group is the police report. Second group is reexamination of the physical evidence. Third group is interpretation of the photograph. The fourth section, talk about reenactment. The fifth is conclusion. Conclusion basically based on my interpretation of the photograph, look at the scene and reexamine evidence. So witnesses, I did not use their statement to put my report together.[18]

Although Lee stated that he did not allow witness statements to affect his reconstruction, it is clear that he did allow the DNA testing on the handkerchief to alter his conclusion as to whether the handkerchief was connected to the crime.

---

15. *Id.* at 77.
16. *Id.*
17. *Id.* at 88.
18. *Id.*

By the time Grant was arrested, none of the blood spots from the car or trail could be DNA typed, as they had all degraded beyond the point of being tested. The only DNA test linking Grant to the crime was that on some genetic material found on a small spot on the handkerchief, which could have been blood, nasal mucus, or some other form of genetic material.[19]

At trial, Lee was called as an expert witness to testify about the blood on the tissue box and his reconstruction of the crime based on the blood trail. Lee testified that the bloody fingerprint resulted from blood being placed over the existing fingerprint. On cross-examination, he said that he could not tell when the fingerprint had been put on the tissue box. It could have been hours, days, or months. As to the other blood stains on the box, Lee testified that the person who picked up the box must have picked it up and then turned it around in order to get a thumb print where it was located.[20]

Lee testified that the photos he examined did not include a photo of the handkerchief or keys and the blood trail was in black and white. The prosecution then presented Lee with a detailed "hypothetical" in order to have Lee recreate the crime scene. Counsel asked Lee to assume the following:

- Serra's car was found on level 8 parked skewed.
- There was O type blood in the car and no A type.
- A trail of blood starts at the driver's side door and runs down to 7A, down to 6A, and across to the next stairway.
- It then goes down to 5, comes up from 5 to 6, 7 and ends with a large number of drops which increase in number and closeness to each other right next to the space where Serra's car is parked.

Counsel then asked Lee, "Is the car and the blood trail connected?" Lee said it was. He was then asked if the handkerchief was connected:

> The handkerchief on the seventh floor and the key looks like a direct line. The blood drops in this area, which suggest the vehicle more likely parking this side and if those, in fact, those keys have blood, handkerchief we know have Type O blood, and those blood drops, I don't know those drop, they lift it or not, if those are Type O, and, again, shows continuous. [Dr. Lee is a native Chinese speaker.]

> Q: Given the additional information that you learned since 1988 concerning the DNA on the handkerchief, the identity of the fingerprint, the fact that the fingerprint owner has O and the DQ Alpha 1.2, 3, which is from a spot inside the car, and all of this stuff about the blood trail, is that handkerchief connected to that crime, to the car itself in this case?

> A: Indicative this handkerchief is associate to the car, associate to this crime.

19. *Id.* at 10.
20. Transcript, May 9, 2002, p. 36.

Lee was then asked if the bloody ticket helped him reconstruct the crime. He replied, "Judge from all that evidence we have, this is a multiple location crime scene. It's not a single location on the tenth floor where the victim was stabbed, it's kind of continuation of the crime scene involving tenth floor, tenth level, ninth level, seventh level, five, six level, and then finally exits Frontage Road exit."[21]

Counsel then asked Lee why he said there was no connection with the handkerchief back in 1988. Lee replied that he was looking for paint on the handkerchief to associate with a garage. Also "we found Type O human where victim is Type A. I cannot make an association between — that's not victim's blood type."[22] So at the time, Lee was assuming the blood trail was the victim's, not the perpetrator's, and the blood type ruled this out. Lee did not change his testimony that the blood on the tissue box was over, not under, the fingerprint linked to Grant.

Counsel then asked Lee if he had an opinion on the amount of pressure used to make the fingerprint, but all he could say is that the fingerprint was a "stationary contact," not a sliding motion.

The defense concentrated on the discrepancy between Lee's written report in 1988 that decided the handkerchief was not connected to the crime and his subsequent reversal of that opinion at the time of trial. Lee's reconstruction did not add much to the original speculation in the police report. He had reviewed only black and white partial photographs, had done no testing on any of the blood, and did not give any opinion as to where the perpetrator may have been injured.

In the end, the jury apparently did not believe that these two facts created reasonable doubt: first, that Dr. Lee initially did not connect the handkerchief with the crime scene, and second, that he testified the fingerprint on the tissue box had been placed on it before blood was smeared on top.

Fingerprint Testimony

The crime scene had yielded four sets of latent fingerprints that could not be identified, plus a bloody print on the parking ticket, which had been lost by the time of trial. None of the prints were ever identified, other than the one print on the tissue box. At trial, Christopher Grice of the New Haven police stated that the partial fingerprint on the tissue box matched Grant's.

> I found that the same person who made the latent impression on the tissue box was the same person who left his left thumb print on an ink card ... the card was in the name of Edward Grant.[23] [You can see photos of Grant's fingerprints in Chapter 6, "Fingerprint Analysis."]

Grice acknowledged under cross-examination that there were other fingerprints in evidence that were not identifiable. He also said that it was impossible to establish

---

21. *Id.* at 46–47.

22. *Id.*

23. Christa Lee Rock, "No Motive Offered," *New Haven Register*, May 15, 2002.

when, how, or why the left thumbprint matching Edward Grant's got on the tissue box.[24]

The defense argued that the state had lifted several prints from Serra's car that had never been identified. There were no identifiable prints on the steering wheel or on the bloody parking ticket. The public defender planned to use Kenneth Moses, a fingerprint expert, to testify that the fingerprint was on the box before blood spattered on top of it.[25] However, Lee acknowledged this was true on cross-examination, so it was unnecessary for the defense to call an additional witness.

DNA

Carll Ladd, a DNA lab technician who worked for the Connecticut Forensic Science Laboratory, testified that the DNA on the handkerchief matched Grant's DNA. The significance of a match is a statistical probability that someone other than the defendant could have contributed the specimen. The Connecticut Forensic Science Laboratory at that time used the figure of 1 in 300 million, roughly the population then of the United States, even if the actual probability exceeds this ratio, as it did in the *Grant* case. In other words, if only 1 person in 300 million could have been the source of the DNA, and it matches Grant's DNA, theoretically there would be no one else in the entire country who would match that profile.

The lab acknowledged that the handkerchief and tissue box had been moved from one location to another over the 30 years, and at one point were stored in a basement near a furnace.[26] Heat is known to degrade DNA.

The defense did not contest the validity of the DNA match; however, the state's expert agreed that there was no test that could tell when the blood was put on the handkerchief. The defense raised the inference that, as only one drop of blood had not degraded beyond the point of being tested, the drop of blood may have been planted by the crime lab, eager to close a long outstanding murder case. There was no question that the case had remained in the public view; Serra's father had made it his life mission to find his daughter's killer.[27] The prosecution's expert also agreed under cross-examination that the fingerprint could have been placed on the tissue box in another location entirely.[28]

In addition to the genetic material found on the handkerchief, which could have been blood or saliva, Dr. Virginia Maxwell, a forensic chemist, testified that there were additional paint stains consistent with paint used at auto-body shops. Grant was employed at a body shop at the time of the killing.

24. *Cracking More Cases*, 55.

25. Christa Lee Rock, "No Motive Offered," *New Haven Register*, May 15, 2002.

26. Colleen Van Tassell, "Penney's Ghost: Blood Never Lies. Does It?" *New Haven Advocate*, May 17, 2002, http://old.newhavenadvocate.com/articles/penny.html.

27. Paul Bass, "After 29 Years, Phil DeLieto Tells His Side of the Serra Case," *The New Haven Register*, May 2003.

28. Transcript, May 21, 2003.

Eyewitness Testimony

No one saw Grant murder Serra. Although the state introduced either live testimony or written statements from five witnesses who stated that they saw Grant, the testimony was about seeing a man running after a woman, seeing a man running with "something shiny" in his hands, seeing a man driving by "fast" in a car, and a description of a man who handed a bloody parking ticket to a parking attendant.

No witness at trial was asked to identify Ed Grant in person. Of course, Grant looked much different in 2002 than he had in 1973. Also, none of the eyewitnesses were shown a photograph of Grant from 1973, although the photograph was presented to the jury and to several other witnesses, and the prosecution commented on the "uncanny resemblance" between the composite and Grant's 1973 photo in its closing remarks.

Jane Merold and Gary Hyrb were smoking marijuana on level ten on their lunch break from their jobs. Shortly before 1 pm as they were going down to level nine to return to work, they saw a blue car traveling fast up to level ten. Merold testified that she saw a car come careening by in the garage. She said she did not see who was driving. Hyrb went to the police that afternoon and gave a statement to Detective Donald Beausejour. Hyrb described the driver as a white male, 21 to 27 years old, 180 pounds, medium build, 5 feet, 10 inches tall, with collar length black or brown hair, a neat mustache and wearing dark trousers and a white shirt.[29] In the meantime, detectives had questioned Phil DeLieto, Serra's former fiancé. Later that evening, Hyrb picked Phil DeLieto's photo out of an array and later identified him in a lineup. Unfortunately, he had seen DeLieto on his way into the station, so his identification may well have been compromised.[30]

Timothy Woodstock and his cousin Frederick Petzold had parked their car on level eight to go shopping. As they returned shortly before 1 pm, they could see through the half level wall to a commotion on the next floor up. Woodstock said he saw a female chased by a white man, heard a long scream and a few seconds after the couple disappeared from sight, he saw the man running back to the blue Buick Electra, carrying a shiny object that was five to six inches long. Woodstock described the man as in his 20s, 5 feet, 8 inches tall, slim build, fair complexion, medium length black hair combed slick with hair tonic. The man had no facial hair and was wearing light green trousers, a white or light colored "golf-type" shirt and black dress shoes.[31]

Petzold said the man was in his early 20s, slim, slightly taller than 5 feet, 9 inches, with dark hair and an olive or darker skin tone, possible Hispanic. The man was wearing a blue short-sleeve shirt.[32] Both Woodstock and Petzold worked with a sketch artist to develop composite drawings.

---

29. Appellant Brief, at 6.
30. Transcript, May 6, 2002, p. 122–26.
31. Appellant Brief, at 2.
32. *Id.*

Christopher Fagan, the parking lot attendant who took a bloody parking ticket from the perpetrator as he fled the scene, was deceased at the time of trial. His statement was admitted as an exhibit, in which he testified that the driver was 21, with olive skin, perhaps Puerto Rican or Italian, with black medium length hair. Fagan said the driver spoke in a foreign accent. When Fagan asked if the driver needed assistance, he said "no thank." The car Grant drove at the time — an orange Jeep Wagoneer — did not match the description given by the parking attendant of the car he was driving in the garage.[33] Selman Topciu, a later suspect, drove a brown Buick with registration number HN5533.[34] No eyewitness expert testified at trial.

The police initially suspected DeLieto, because they believed that the perpetrator was someone known to the victim and that the murder was a crime of passion. They seriously interviewed Phil DeLieto, Selman Topciu, and Anthony Golino. All of these men apparently looked close enough to the composite sketch to lead investigators to question them further. DeLieto had Type O blood, which was the type found throughout the crime scene.[35] In 1992 and 1993, DQ Alpha DNA tests were done on the blood samples from Phil Delieto and Selman Topciu, another suspect. DQ Alpha is one locus now included in standard DNA testing. The test excluded DeLieto as the source of the blood in the garage, but it included Topciu, along with about 5% of the population.[36] De Lieto also had an alibi that was confirmed by investigators.

Although this evidence was not presented to the jury, Golino was actually arrested for the murder and not until the eve of trial, when blood testing excluded him, was he released from suspicion. Golino actually created a disturbance at Grant's trial, shouting that Grant was innocent too.[37]

At trial, the defense presented "third party culprit" evidence that the real killer could have been DeLieto or Topciu. DeLieto had been excluded in 1993 by the DQ Alpha DNA test, but Topciu had not. The DNA testing done pursuant to a warrant for Grant's blood identified him as the source of the blood on the handkerchief and excluded both DeLieto and Topciu. However, by that time, none of the other crime scene blood could be tested.

The evidence against Topciu connected him with Serra. First, he had been a patient in a dental practice where Serra had worked, and two bills for dental service, sealed and stamped but not postmarked, were found in the visor of the car Serra was driving.[38] No one could give any explanation as to how the bills got there, but Serra's father testified that they had not been there when his daughter had picked up the car from him that morning. The bills inside, dated May 1 and April 20, would have been typed by Serra to be sent to Topciu. A co-worker of Serra's at the dentist's office said

---

33. Transcript, May 20, 2002, p. 172.

34. Appellant Brief, at 15.

35. 45% of the population has O type; 40% has A, 11% B, and 4% A/B.

36. Appellant Brief, at 16.

37. Colleen Van Tassell, "Penney's Ghost: Blood Never Lies. Does It?" *New Haven Register*, May 17, 2002.

38. Appellant Brief, at 14.

that she recalled seeing Topciu at a diner where she and Penney would go for lunch.[39] A photo of Topciu from 1973 was introduced into evidence as well as photos of his left wrist, showing what defense lawyers called a very noticeable scar.[40] Topciu also spoke with a foreign accent. However, two different Connecticut superior court judges refused to issue arrest warrants for Topciu in 1994 and 1995 due to lack of probable cause.[41]

At the trial, the prosecutor showed the jury the "uncanny similarity"[42] between the artist's sketch and Ed Grant's photograph at the time.

Composite Sketch

Police artists frequently make a composite sketch based on a description by an eyewitness shortly after a crime has occurred. Traditionally, composite sketches were made by police artists, but this required a trained artist and sufficient time to create the sketch. Today, many police departments use composite kits that contain hundreds of plastic overlays that can be combined for an eyewitness to examine.[43] These sketches are often circulated in canvassing for witnesses or suspects, publicized in newspapers or on TV in an effort to locate a suspect.

Two composite sketches were introduced in court, although no eyewitness was asked if the photograph of Ed Grant taken around 1973 was the man they saw. A photograph of the lineup that included Phil DeLieto and a photograph of Selman Topciu were also introduced as trial exhibits.

The prosecution claimed in closing arguments that the photograph of Ed Grant looked just like the composites. The defense claimed just the opposite. If the eyewitness descriptions had been a major part of the state's evidence, it is conceivable that the parties would have relied on eyewitness experts. After all, the eyewitnesses saw only fleeting images of a man either running after a woman at some distance, or driving by very fast, or in the case of the parking lot attendant, handing a bloody ticket to him when leaving the garage. Was it more likely that Christopher Fagan was looking at the bloody ticket than at the suspect's face? With such strong forensic evidence, the issue of eyewitness reliability was not important enough to create reasonable doubt.

Grant's Character

Grant did not take the stand, as was his right; his defense was that the prosecution had arrested the wrong man and had not proved his guilt beyond a reasonable doubt. The jury did not have an opportunity to assess his credibility as a witness. They were

---

39. *Id.* at 15.
40. *Id.* at 16.
41. Appellee Brief, at 29.
42. Transcript, May 22, 2002.
43. James Lang, "Hearsay and Relevancy Obstacles to the Admission of Composite Sketches in Criminal Trials," *Boston University Law Review* 64 (November 1984): 1101.

therefore free to form their own opinion of what kind of a man Grant was. One family witness testified Grant was a violent man. Another testified that he was a loving family man. Here is what Lee said in his book:

> In the summer of 1994, Edward R. Grant of Waterbury beat his then-fiancee so fiercely that she was hospitalized. This victim reported Grant's assault to the local police, and he was arrested. Subsequently, Edward Grant was fingerprinted. Grant was then fifty-one and had worked most of his adult life at his family's auto repair and towing business in Waterbury.

> In 1971, already married, Grant had been a member of the Connecticut National Guard and, while on his six months of active duty in South Carolina during the Vietnam War, has been injured in a Jeep accident. Depending on who is telling the tale, the intoxicated Grant was driving the Jeep or was simply a passenger when the vehicle rolled over. The injuries that Grant sustained resulted in a steel plate being placed in his head, and he was given an administrative discharge from the service. Grant returned to his home in Waterbury and went back to work for his family's successful business. The long-term effects of his injury were that he suffered from memory loss and severe mood swings.

> … The identification of [Grant's] print electrified those of us who had been waiting for years to catch a break in this case. Edward Grant's age, occupation, and track record for violence with women further galvanized investigators.[44]

In light of Lee's conclusions above, one can see why Grant would not want to take the stand and risk cross-examination.

No Alibi Evidence

The defense originally planned to introduce evidence that Grant was at his cabin at the time of the murder, detained there due to local summer flooding from violent thunderstorms. However, the defense discovered evidence that the storms took place after the murder, and this evidence was not introduced.[45]

Press Coverage of the Trial

The trial was covered daily, with much speculation about the evidence and guilt. The public learned background information the jury would not hear, either because the information was not admissible or because counsel chose not to bring it up. The evidence presented to the jury inside the courtroom did not reveal all the facts, which is always the case. Rules of court exclude evidence that is not relevant or may be prejudicial to the defendant. Also, if the defendant does not take the stand, the jury never hears him speak or gets to assess his credibility.

---

44. *Cracking More Cases*, at 44.
45. *Cracking More Cases*, at 49.

The press also covered the various "side stories," such as Golino's claims of having been unjustly accused and his assertion that Grant was innocent, as well as Serra's father's obsession with finding his daughter's killer, and interviews with friends and neighbors about Grant being a nice old guy who just liked to go fishing.

The "Lost" Evidence

In the *Grant* case, certain evidence had been lost — the bloodstained parking ticket, the wig or "fall" Serra had been wearing, and a bloodstained key chain. Some pieces of evidence were altered, such as the handkerchief that had many holes chopped out of it, as police did testing over the years. The "chain of custody" of all these items was confused, as the evidence had been moved from one location to another and the numbering system had been changed. Some of the lost evidence then appeared, including some nasal hairs recovered from the handkerchief and a "negroid" hair in Serra's wig. The nasal hairs, according to a 1980 forensics report, still contained roots, which could have been tested for DNA.[46] However, although the defense requested that the hairs be tested, they did not have enough roots left for DNA testing, in part because they had been stored between glass slides.[47] Prosecution witness Dr. Kimberlyn Nelson, testified that she had conducted mitochondrial DNA tests on three nasal hairs but her results were "inconclusive."

Written Statements Read at Trial

Courts generally exclude evidence of the statements made by witnesses who are unavailable. In other words, if a person cannot appear in person at trial, the court will not allow a written statement, letter, or earlier sworn testimony to be read to the jury. But in this case, the trial judge allowed the jury to hear statements both by Serra's father and Chris Fagan, the parking lot attendant. Both had died before trial. Both men, according to defense attorneys, had given statements to police implicating Selman Topciu in the crime.[48] Serra's father had insisted that the bills addressed to Topciu, a patient at the dental office where Serra worked, had not been under the sun visor when he loaned Serra his Buick around 12:15 pm on the day of her murder.

In addition, Topciu had a long scar on his left hand. Police believe the killer was injured on his left side during the incident. Grant had no scar. Topciu also spoke with an Albanian accent, and Chris Fagan, the lot attendant, had testified the man who handed him the bloody ticket spoke with a Hispanic accent. The defense won its motion to allow the jury to hear that Topciu was initially investigated for the murder.

Although the jury did not hear the possibly prejudicial evidence that Grant's fingerprint was obtained from an arrest for domestic abuse in 1994, they also did

---

46. Christa Lee Rock, "New Twist in 28-year-old Serra Murder Case," *New Haven Register*, January 22, 2002.
47. Christa Lee Rock, "Hair Test Sought in Serra Mystery," *New Haven Register*, January 23, 2002.
48. Christa Lee Rock, "Serra's Grave Won't Speak," *New Haven Register*, February 10, 2002.

not hear the possibly positive fact that he had never been convicted of a crime or committed any act of violence. Two ex-wives of Grant refused to testify about his alleged abusive past.[49] Grant had no criminal record and neighbors said he was quiet and loved fishing and fixing cars, but the jury never heard about it.

George Oliver, a friend of Grant's, stated out of court that Grant was in Groton, not New Haven, the day Serra was killed. However, he did not testify as an alibi witness for Grant.[50] This left the jury with no possible explanation of where Grant had been on the day of the murder.

Lack of Motive

No evidence of motive was presented. Because proof of motive is not one of the legal elements required to find murder, the jury could find Grant guilty without evidence of why he might have killed the victim.

How the Fingerprint Got on the Box

Dr. Lee testified as a blood pattern expert for the prosecution. Although Lee's testimony about how he believed the fingerprint was deposited on the box was somewhat disjointed at trial, he summarizes it as follows in his book:

> [Following the stabbing of Serra,] [a]fter running back to the lower level, the murderer got into the victim's car. He wanted to stanch the bleeding from a wound on his left hand, so he reached behind him as he started to drive the car through the garage. The tissue box must have been lying face down, so the murderer had to reach around the car's bucket seat to flip the box over in order to extract tissues to stop the bleeding.
>
> In this dynamic flipping motion, the assailant had left behind three bloody finger marks, due to direct contact, none of which yielded any readable ridges for fingerprint comparison. But in gripping the upright portion of the tissue box, the killer left the one clear fingerprint, his left thumbprint. Subsequent to this, the assailant also transferred some blood from his wound up on top of this print.[51]

Lee did not give an opinion as to what happened to the bloody wad of tissues, or why the assailant would have either left the box on the backseat floor or deliberately put it in the backseat, given his obvious frantic activity in the aftermath of the crime. It is also unclear whether in the reenactment of the crime led by Lee in 1989, someone of the probable height and build of the assailant tried to reach a tissue box on the floor behind the driver's seat from the front of a 1971 Buick Electra.

---

49. Christa Lee Rock, "Portrait of a Complex Suspect," *New Haven Register*, April 28, 2002.

50. *Id.*

51. *Cracking More Cases*, at 52.

Motions

Motion to Exclude DNA Results

In the *Grant* case, there were many motions (or requests made to the trial judge) to exclude particular pieces of evidence. The defense wanted the DNA evidence excluded on the ground that the form of DNA testing known as Short Tandem Repeat ("STR") testing was not yet proven reliable. The defense also made a motion to exclude the handkerchief based on chain of custody, on the ground that the tissue box had been moved from place to place since 1973 without a proper "chain of custody." They lost both motions. See Chapter 2, "The Court Process."

The DNA evidence identified Grant based on statistics cited by Dr. Carll Ladd that the chance of someone other than Grant being the source of the genetic material on the handkerchief was less than one out of 300 million. Public Defender Brian Carlow argued that the DNA profile was fatally flawed because it failed to detect certain "gene pairs" in blood on the handkerchief and because there was DNA from multiple sources on the sample. The court ruled against the defense and allowed the evidence following a detailed hearing in which it examined the Short Tandem Repeat form of DNA testing and found it to be reliable.

Motion to Exclude Statement Made by Grant to Police

Grant made the following comment to investigators at the police barracks:

Did you read about the guy in Texas who killed all those people? They got him on a fingerprint, too.[52]

Prosecutors wanted the jury to hear the statement because it appeared that Grant acknowledged that Grant was guilty "too." Grant's lawyers argued Grant's statement was not a knowing and intelligent waiver of the defendant's privilege against self incrimination. The judge disagreed and admitted the statement.

Grant had also told investigators about his working in a family auto body shop in Waterbury in the 1970s and apparently stated that he had suffered frequent blackouts due to an Army injury and sometimes couldn't remember where he had been or what he had done.[53]

The defense won its motion to allow the jury to hear that the police had investigated both Philip DeLieto, Serra's ex-fiance, and Selman Topciu, a former restauranteur whose dental bills had been found in Serrra's car. In support of its point, the defense argued that one of the eyewitnesses, Gary Hryb, had identified DeLieto out of a lineup within 12 hours of the murder.

---

52. Christa Lee Rock, "'Too' Key Word in Slay Case," *New Haven Register*, January 12, 2002.
53. *Id.*

Motion During Trial for a "Mistrial"

When retired New Haven Police Detective Vincent Perricone testified that the fingerprint on the tissue box had been "fresh" and told the jury that there are factors you can use to approximate how long ago a suspect left his prints behind, the defense moved for a mistrial on the ground that the state was offering an expert opinion from Perricone without giving the defense notice of its expert, which it is required to do. The defense also argued that there was no scientific proof that a fingerprint could be dated. The court denied the motion.[54]

Closing Arguments

Overview

Trial lawyers on both sides regard closing arguments as a vital component of their respective cases. These arguments occur after all of the evidence has been presented to the jury, and just before the judge gives his or her instructions to the jury before its deliberations. Closing arguments provide each side with the opportunity to summarize all of the testimony which it believes is important in persuading the jury of the strength of its case. The attorneys may not refer to any evidence that was not presented at trial in their closing arguments.

In *Grant*, the prosecution's closing argument listed all of the inferences which the jury was entitled to draw based on the circumstantial evidence presented in the case. The defense listed all of the issues that would give the jury reason to find reasonable doubt.

There are actually three closing arguments in a criminal trial. The prosecution goes first and presents its side of the case. Its goal is to summarize the evidence from trial and fit the evidence into the legal elements of the crime that it must prove beyond a reasonable doubt. Then the defense makes its closing argument, also referring to the evidence and the issues where the defense argues there is reasonable doubt of guilt. Finally, the prosecution has the opportunity to respond to (or rebut) the points made in the defense's presentation.

By the end of the *Grant* case, both prosecution and defense offered detailed closing arguments. The prosecution summarized all of the testimony to support its theory of how the crime occurred and to convince the jury — beyond a reasonable doubt — that Grant was the murderer. The prosecution's closing was simply a story of what happened, with abundant references to the forensic evidence (presented by the prosecution's expert witnesses) and the eyewitnesses who supported its theory of the case.

---

54. Christa Lee Rock, "Mistrial Denied," *New Haven Register*, May 3, 2002.

In contrast, the defense had one job: to convince the jury that there were enough holes in the prosecution's evidence to create a reasonable doubt as to Grant's guilt. If the defense could accomplish that, then Grant must be acquitted. Certainly, there was a lot of confusion about the eyewitness testimony. Among other points, the defense was able to raise questions based on the fact that two different suspects were investigated before Grant was charged. The lack of motive was also helpful to the defense. But motive is not an element of the crime of murder and, therefore, the prosecution did not have to prove Grant's motive.

In summary, the defense conceded that the two pieces of incriminating forensic evidence were accurate. That is, the fingerprint was Grant's and the DNA found at the crime scene matched Grant's DNA. But the defense strongly suggested that the DNA evidence was planted by the police at the crime scene, or was altered thereafter, in an effort to implicate Grant and solve a high-profile cold case. However, the defense did not say this directly. Rather, counsel simply said "something is not right with the handkerchief."[55] He pointed out that the bloody parking ticket had needed two days for the blood to dry, but the handkerchief was "bone dry" when it was picked up from the garage floor on the day of the murder.

The Prosecution's Initial Closing Argument

Here is what the prosecution told the jury at the end of the case. His job was to summarize the evidence and convince the jury that it had proved guilt beyond a reasonable doubt. The prosecution must simply refer to the evidence and not offer its own opinions. It must not offer any facts that do not appear in the record.

> The elements of murder. This is what the State has to prove.... [The] first one [is] the intent to cause the death of another person. Intent is necessary pretty much in any crime and certainly all the serious ones. Intent can be proven in a number of ways. Normally, we can't crawl into somebody's head and understand what that person was actually thinking to determine their intent. So the Judge is going to tell you, common sense, that normally we infer intent from the actions that we see somebody take. Common sense tells you that we usually mean to do what we do.
>
> And what did this killer do? Chase the barefoot Penney Serra from her car or at least the direction of her car, caught her in the stairwell ... and stabbed her to death directly in her heart. Does common sense tell you that's intent to kill? Of course it does. In fact, the medical examiner told you that his thrust was so efficient into her heart that even if she had been stabbed on the steps of St. Raphael's Hospital, [to which Serra was taken], she would not have survived.

---

55. Transcript, May 22, 2002, p. 53.

Second element. There will be a lot of discussion about this one. The defendant has to be shown beyond a reasonable doubt to be the person who committed this crime.

And the third element is that he caused the death of Penney Serra, and there is clearly no doubt that that is what happened.

Three elements, that's it. Those are the elements of murder. That's what has been charged. That's what you have to find.

Did we prove those three things beyond a reasonable doubt? And I submit that there is going to be very little, if any, challenge to the ones on top and bottom because the question here is who was the killer.

And to know the answer to that question, you have to look at what happened between 12:37, when the killer entered the garage, and 1:01, when he handed the bloody ticket across his body to Christopher Fagan and drove out. And some of that, what happened in that period of time, you're never going to know. Some things only Penney Serra knew and the killer knows.

So, while it would be extremely interesting to know everything that happened in that garage on July 16, 1973, it's unlikely that you will. But if it's not part of those three elements, we don't have to prove it.

And I submit that the evidence you have is sufficient for you to make your decision without knowing everything that happened in that garage. And any suggestions that you do know what happened, for instance, between the time that the parking ticket was checked in at the entrance, where you all stood the other day, and the car was seen in approximately that location by Mr. Petzold and Mr. Woodstock, is pure speculation.

...

We don't know exactly how it happened and we don't know exactly what the murder weapon is, and we don't have to prove that. But you do know that there was a knife in her car from a week earlier, that that knife was never returned to the Hurleys. In fact, you have an exhibit which is an exact copy from the same set of that same knife. Is that the weapon she was killed with? You will probably never know, but we don't have to prove that. And certainly it's an inference that you could draw, that that is not only the knife that killed her, but the knife that injured him.

...

Now, one thing you don't have any direct evidence of in this case is the motive for this crime. And one of the things that the Judge is going to tell you is that is not an element. You know, you might not like it. You might even find that the lack of motive is something that is really important to you. You might find that it raised reasonable doubt. But you've got to look at the issue of motive, was there a lack of motive completely in this case? Was there a motive that you could infer? And even if there isn't, the Judge will tell you that if you find the case proved otherwise beyond a reasonable doubt, then that's okay because it isn't an element of the crime.

But you know this about motive; you know that that killer had some reason to kill Penney Serra. You may not ever know what the motive was. But he stabbed her in the heart, most likely after she cut him, and you know that or you could conclude that from the evidence because you got blood on the left-hand side coming down here, and you have those two blood spots on the back of her dress completely consistent with a lunge to grab her, the location of where her fall would have been because there are two O blood spots, that's the only non-A blood on her dress.

And the cuttings are there, they are the only holes in the back of that dress and they are right there where your hand would be if you grabbed for that wig and contacted the dress. Whether it was at the car or as he stabbed her, it's not an element of the crime. You could make your own decisions. Like many of the other things that you can't know the details, that you can't know, motive may be one of them.

But you know this, that every important piece of evidence in this case points to Edward Grant as being at the scene and it points to no one else.

...

So, what points to Ed Grant as the person who murdered Penney Serra? There are some things you know for sure and these may not be seriously challenged. You know that the killer stabbed Penney Serra with a knife. You know that the killer drove Penney Serra's Buick and, therefore, was in the car. You know that the killer had to have the keys to that car because he drove the car. You know that the killer had O type blood. You know that the killer left O type blood that had this DQ Alpha, this one in 20 at 1.2, 3. You know the killer touched the tissue box because there are all these bloody fingerprints on it — fingermarks, not fingerprints. You know the killer left a blood trail from the car to the keys that he had to be carrying because he drove the car to that location. Those things you know about this killer, whoever he is.

And then you've got to ask yourself, whose fingerprints are on the bloody tissue box? Edward Grant.

Who has O type blood? Edward Grant. Who has DQ Alpha 1.2, 3? Edward Grant. Who carries a handkerchief, according to his own sister, just like his father did? Edward Grant.

Whose DNA is on the bloody handkerchief which has Type O blood on it next to the blood trail which is Type O in every place it was tested six to eight feet from the keys to the car that the killer had to have? Edward Grant.

And whose DNA is on it in the level of certainty of one in six trillion? Edward Grant.

And who looked stunningly like the drawings taken, done in 1973 by the only two people who got a clear view of this killer? Edward Grant.

You know this evidence is overwhelming that the killer could only be Edward Grant. And that's a lot more than proof beyond a reasonable doubt because of the power of this evidence. There may be lots of stuff that happened around that time, but none of it can contradict this evidence at any level.

In a moment you are going to hear the defense argue to you and you may hear suggestions that you should look at one piece of evidence and say, well, that doesn't prove guilt beyond a reasonable doubt, and then some other piece of evidence, and that doesn't prove guilt beyond a reasonable doubt or some relatively innocuous fact that for some reason you are going to be told you should conclude that raises a reasonable doubt.

Judge Blue, though, is going to tell you that it's not one at a time, that the determination, and you have heard this instruction in voir dire, it was awhile ago, the determination of guilt in any case has to do with every piece of evidence, and to use your common sense and your knowledge of the way things work and your understanding of how this crime scene developed to say those things can't all happen by coincidence in the real world that we have lived in all our lives that developed our common sense. The patterns of Edward Grant's guilt are clear in all this evidence.

And there are two other things that are also clear. There is not one shred of evidence in this case offering an innocent explanation for Edward Grant's fingerprint being on that tissue box. And there is not one shred of evidence offering an innocent explanation for his DNA being on that bloody handkerchief.[56]

The Defense's Closing Statement

What follows are portions of the closing statement made by the defense. After the defense closing argument, the prosecution has the right to "rebut" the argument, which it did. The prosecution has the last word. Here is part of what Grant's attorneys said:

… Your job is to assess the evidence and decide whether or not you are convinced beyond any reasonable doubt that Edward Grant, not anybody else, but Edward Grant is the one on July 16th who caused Penney Serra's death.

That "beyond a reasonable doubt," the term, we talked about that with you during jury selection. And I think we told you that if you were selected you would hear more about that concept and you would have that explained to you at the end of the trial.

I just want to point out a couple of different pieces of what I think the Court's instruction is going to be. You are going to be able to hear what he

---

56. Transcript, May 22, 2002, p. 16–34.

has to say and you will also have it in the jury room with you so you could take a look at it as well, but I have been listening to similar instructions for probably now about 16 years.

One of the parts that I think helps understand exactly what that concept means is this idea, and his Honor will tell you that a reasonable doubt is a doubt which has its foundation, it's basic in either the evidence you hear or the lack of evidence. The lack of evidence in a case is just as important in terms of that concept as the evidence itself. You are allowed to focus on both. You are required to focus on both. And if the evidence causes you to have a reasonable doubt or the lack of evidence, including such things as motive, causes you to have a reasonable doubt, that is sufficient and requires a verdict of not guilty.

We talked in jury selection about this concept beyond a reasonable doubt and how certain you need to be and it's more certain than a possibility. We even talked it's more certain than even probabilities. That in a criminal case, when someone is on trial facing a criminal charge, in this case or any criminal case, you have to be more certain than that.

Is there evidence which points towards Edward Grant? Of course there is. But the evidence has to be such that you are convinced beyond any reasonable doubt that it was Edward Grant that caused Penney Serra's death. You will hear part of the instruction when his Honor talks about reasonable doubt; that beyond a reasonable doubt is proof that precludes any reasonable hypothesis consistent with innocence.

So, if you have several, based upon these facts, several different hypotheses that you think might have happened, if any of those are not consistent with Ed Grant having done this crime, if they are consistent with Phil DeLieto having done this crime, consistent with Selman Topciu having done this crime or someone we don't know about having done this crime, if any of those are reasonable, based upon this evidence, the law requires you to come back and say not guilty. It's not kind of balancing, here is Phil DeLieto, here is Selamn Topciu, here is Ed Grant, which one do we think fits best.

You have to be convinced beyond any reasonable doubt that it was Ed Grant to the exclusion of every other person on this planet. That is the level of certainty that is required, that is mandated in a criminal case.

I am going to talk with you about some of the evidence. I'm going to talk with you, as probably most of you could guess, about the science in the course of this case because I was talking with witnesses about science. When Dr. Nelson was on the stand the other day, at the end of his questions, Mr. Clark asked her a question, and basically the bottom line of the question was, look, your conclusion is that these hairs are inconclusive? She said, yes.

And then he said, so that any other conclusion or if people try to kind of draw more out of it — I suppose he was suggesting either us or me — draw more out of it, that would be inappropriate? And she said, yes, because the science can tell us this and it can't tell us more.

The physical evidence in the case, one of the issues that I think is important to understand is the storage of the physical evidence. And I think that it's probably fair to say — and understand we're not blaming folks from 1973 or four or five, they didn't know that these advances in technology were coming. But I think it's fair to say that the manner in which this evidence was stored during the course of almost three decades really until it got into Carll Ladd's hand or maybe the advent of the new building at the State Police Forensic Crime Lab in 1994 was awful. Bill Petzold, who used to work in the lab, and Elaine Pagliaro told you that he was the one, one of the two people assigned to be the custodian of this evidence, he told you how that was stored. And we heard from every expert witness, you got to keep it cool, you got to keep it dry.

The evidence in the case, the tissue box, the tissue box has blood on it. The tissue box has a fingerprint on it. The fingerprint is a latent print, Mr. Grant's print is a latent print; that means it is not visible, it has to be processed to be observed and compared. There is some blood on top of that print.

The evidence from Chris Grice is as clear as it could conceivably be. There is absolutely no way to date that fingerprint, whether it was on a particular day, a particular month or a particular year. There is a stipulation the court read into the record in terms of that too, that science does not allow one to date a latent fingerprint, it simply cannot be done.

The handkerchief, it was tested by Dr. Maxwell and she came up with some paint-like substances, I think tested in about the last year or so. I think you have the report, maybe you could check on that in terms of the dates. Paint-like substances used for cars, repainting, respraying, also used for household applications, exterior trim for any areas in the house that have a lot of — a lot of business is not the right word. But a lot of activity, bathrooms, kitchens, that's what she could tell you about that.

Five stains were tested on that handkerchief by Dr. Ladd. Let me start right off, there is no contest here to either Dr. Ladd's qualifications, the work that he did and how he did it. He told you how meticulously they handled this evidence to make sure that it's not contaminated. So, I think that we could all feel comfortable from December, 2000, when Dr. Ladd was requested to do work on the handkerchief, until his work was done, that that handkerchief was handled in precisely the way we would all hope it would have been handled for the 30 years, but we know it wasn't handled that way before that. It is not an issue of Dr. Ladd's work and Dr. Ladd's conclusions.

He does five stains; from those 5 stains Selman Topciu and Phillip DeLieto are excluded. Ed Grant is included. The State talks a lot about G4, one of the four — five stains because G1, G3 and G5 have some other DNA in there, they are mixtures, some of it requires some interpretation, Dr. Ladd said. He gave his best interpretations. But the State focuses on G4, the clean stain. How do we know they focus on G4 when they are having people like Dr. Kidd come in and talk about numbers or having people like Ed Blake look at the numbers? They are talking about G4, that one stain, so we could talk about G4.

Dr. Ladd in his work on G4 says that the probability of that DNA profile in the random population is one in 300 million. He also said that science cannot tell you how it was deposited, under what circumstances it was deposited, and most critically when it was deposited. The science can't tell you that.

The State's theory is July 16, 1973, but the science can't answer the question.

Mr. Clark indicated there is blood all over the seat. There is O blood in a variety of locations and I jotted them down because I didn't want to miss them, but the tissue box has blood, the tissue next to the tissue box has blood, the steering column and floor pedal have blood, the outside door handle has blood, small white envelope has blood, pink rag on the floor has blood, metal trim of the left door, metal trim of the left seat, metal door handle, debris from the floor has blood, blood from the blood trail in three different locations, and the back of the dress had blood, all those locations have Type O blood.

Mr. Clark talked about the fact that the blood on the back of the dress was consistent with whoever was reaching their hand dripping blood onto the back of the dress.

So, we have all that Type O blood all over the seat, all of it would include Phillip DeLieto, Edward Grant and Selman Topciu, no way to distinguish between them.

The items I talked about, I'll talk about them further. The storage of those items and the manner in which they were stored and the handling of those items and the manner in which they were handled destroy the ability of present science to tell us who was the source or who was a potential source of all that evidence. And we're talking about blood on the tissue box, blood in the car, blood on the tissue next to the tissue box, blood on the back of Penney Serra's dress, that the storage, and just the awful way in which this evidence was handled, will not change one to another, but will destroy your ability to have information that will tell us about the source of that DNA.

There is something just not right about the handkerchief. That's the centerpiece of the State's DNA case. And there is something that is just not right about it. We heard that although the parking ticket needed to dry for two days, the handkerchief in the parking lot was bone dry. And we know that former detective or former Lieutenant Perricone told you that. And the reason he could even remember that now because it was immediately put in a plastic bag, and he said he would never do that with even something that was remotely damp. The handkerchief was bone dry.

According to the State, the DNA on that handkerchief has been there for 28 plus years, about 28 years from what Dr. Ladd testified. The DNA on that handkerchief was then subjected to the age factor in degradation, just as every other piece of evidence was. All the other old blood I talked about, the blood in the car, the same degradation factors in terms of age. So, as those other items would degrade, so would the DNA on the handkerchief. The same environmental insult is what they call it, but the heat, the humidity, the dampness, the handkerchief was exposed to all those variables just like every other piece of evidence in this case, no difference. The handkerchief yields us results in 2001 of one in 6.9 trillion.

All other evidence was available, in terms of the blood on the dress, the tissue box, all of that that I mentioned so far was subjected to the same technology, that PCR technology that they talked about which takes minute amounts of DNA and makes copies, copies, and millions of copies so you could test it. All this blood is so degraded that technology, as advanced as it is, can't give them anything, not even a partial profile, it can't even give them a profile. But this handkerchief somehow maintains its integrity for 29 years and is able to give us numbers of one in 6.9 trillion. Something is just not right about that handkerchief.

What motive does Ed Grant have to kill Penney Serra? There is not a shred of evidence that gives you any indication regarding that. The State tries to downplay motive in the case, it is not an element of the crime, but motive drives what happens in criminal cases. And the lack of a motive, as you will hear in an instruction from the Court, can create on its own a reasonable doubt. And that makes some sense because crimes aren't committed out of the blue, there are reasons for things happening; not a shred of evidence in this case.

What's the relationship or association that Ed Grant has with Penney Serra? None. There isn't a shred of evidence regarding such an association or a relationship. Why? Because Ed Grant is not the killer of Penney Serra, that's why.

Everything in this case points towards the direction that the person who killed Penney Serra knew her. I'm going to start going through some of that for you.

The suspect is — there is a range of times here that the suspect could have entered the building. It says here that the range of time between the suspect's entry and the victim's entry is between three and five minutes. In fact, I think if you compute this, it's two to six minutes. It's an extremely short window of time for two strangers to get in touch with each other and meet somewhere above, extremely short. It almost seems like it was a planned meeting.

The suspect comes into the garage. You were there, George Street passes underneath the garage. And as you are looking one way on George Street,

Macy's is on the left and Malley's is on the right. The suspect's vehicle enters the George Street entrance north going towards Crown Street, the northern end of the building, that's the way that ramp takes you at that point in time, that's why it says George Street.

Miss Serra is coming in from the connector, from the East Haven area, Morris Cove area, and comes in the Frontage Street entrance, the southern end of the building. You were there at both the southern entrance, Frontage Street, and also the exit where the perpetrator left. They are in two completely different ends of the building, about anywhere from two to six minutes apart.

The suspect's car ends up on 7B, assuming the keys and the handkerchief lead you to the car. Miss Serra's car ends up on 9C, 9D, up on the top of the garage where Mr. Petzold and Woodstock see them. How did these two get together in that short window of time? How does that happen without some planned meeting? Was the planned meeting on 7B where both cars parked and then the vehicle went upstairs? It doesn't make any sense in terms of the time, the time that they have to get together. Clearly, it's not a situation where some guy is sitting there for hours watching who is coming, watching who is parking, watching who is coming back from shopping, none of that is taking place. There is not enough time for that to happen. But they end up in completely different places from where they actually entered the building.

Why is she up on the ninth floor? July 16th, we heard the testimony; it's a summer, sunny, beautiful day. Normally she parks anywhere from the third to fifth level, I think the testimony was. This is not a packed building that day. Why is she going up there? To meet somebody.

Now, Mr. Petzold and Mr. Woodstock are sitting in the vehicle, here is what their description is when they see the guy chasing the woman, among other things, male, early twenties, 5'10" tall, dark-skinned, Hispanic male, Mr. Petzold says under oath at a proceeding, and also in this statement and in a pre-hypnotic session that he had later on. I mean, we talk about these witnesses, they were all very young, but every one of them spent hours with the police attempting to help the police in this case. Really, if you think about it, they are all 17-, 18-year-old kids, happened to be in the wrong place at the wrong time. They went to the police department, they gave statements, they did their best. And this is what they come out with: Mr. Woodstock, he has the male chasing the woman in a Polo shirt, described as the same kind of shirt that he was wearing, a golf-type shirt or Polo shirt; we all know what they are. He has him dressed in black dress shoes, I don't know how he could see that, that's what he said, black dress shoes.

Now, Mr. Clark will lead you back, as he already has, to the composites in this case, and how much they look like Ed Grant back in '73. So, what I want you to do is every time you think or he flashes that composite or you take a look at that composite, think about a dark-skinned Hispanic male, think about what it doesn't show you of all the other features, 5'10", these are the descriptions, think about that.

Now, Jane Merold and Gary Hyrb, they are smoking pot up there, and that vehicle, as they are about to go back to Malley's and work, that vehicle comes by. We heard Jane Merold's testimony; Hyrb is either in front of her or immediately to the right when that car comes by.

What we do know about what Gary Hyrb observed? Well, Don Beausejour from the police department, Beausejour told us. Mr. Beausejour after the homicide is looking for evidence in the case. Maybe two hours after the body had been found, no one has discovered the car, the police are scouring the garage, but they haven't found this vehicle yet. They do not know the identity of the victim. And Mr. Hyrb approaches Mr. Beausejour and tells him that he thinks he saw something. And Mr. Beausejour testifies that Gary Hyrb said that he saw the driver of the vehicle on two separate occasions, one upstairs and one downstairs when the vehicle was parked. And who is the person who leads the police to the Buick? Gary Hyrb. Up until the point that Gary Hyrb shows up, I'm sure they would have found it at some point, but up until Gary Hyrb gets there, they have not found the car. And when Don Beausejour is led to that car by Gary Hyrb, he sees the blood all over the place and he knows immediately that this car is involved. And that's when the dispatches go out to everybody. And that's when they open the car and find the pocketbook in the back on the floor.

Gary Hyrb. When Don Beausejour testified here, he told you what Gary Hyrb's description of the driver of the vehicle was and the person who got out of the vehicle. What was that description? White male, 21 to 27 years of age, 5'10", 180 to 185 pounds, medium build, dark complexion, again, and heavy, well-trimmed mustache, well-groomed.

We questioned you very carefully about Dr. Lee. And we asked you, you know, he is obviously a well-known individual, can you critically look at his testimony?

Let me go over for a moment his theory about the tissue box and the print. Mr. Clark referred to that. The killer gets into this vehicle. He is obviously getting out of the area quick. The car is described by Jane Merold as speeding by. He is sitting in that front seat, the tissue — he is bleeding from the left hand, he is driving with his one hand. He has got to lean back. First of all, he has to know that the tissue box is upside down. I guess he scanned the whole car when getting in because his theory has to be that the tissue box is upside down in order for those three smudge prints to get on there.

Now, the person has to put their hand behind, you saw the demonstration, has to flip — he is driving, he has to flip the box over, flipping a box going in the other direction. This is not a car with bucket seats where you could lean around, that seat goes all the way across. Look at the photographs. He flips it over and now he has to pick it up and bring it around. Look at the photographs in terms of the space that is between that seat and the door closed while you are driving, it doesn't make any sense. It makes assumptions about where that box was prior to sitting in that position.

Who knows where the box was? It could have been in front. It could have been in the back, we just don't know that answer. But those assumptions would cause you, if you grab it the way he has suggested; it would make you find some blood underneath where you have to grab it with your other fingers. Picture that in your mind as you walk through that. I don't think it sits well, and I think there is all kinds of different explanations. And it's really disturbing that that theory was expounded here on the stand for the first time.

There are remaining fingerprints in the car that have never been identified, and I'll just briefly mention it. There is LP2, this was testified to by Christopher Grice, one on the right passenger window in the interior, not the defendant's. One on — LP3, one on the right passenger window, interior. LP4, right window exterior, AFIS quality print. To this day they are running that print to see if they could identify it. Is it the killer or is it just some other person? I don't know.

Of course, we do not have, as you remember, we do not have close-up photographs of this handkerchief, none were taken at the garage, none were taken at the police department. Does this look like the handkerchief to you? That's the blow-up of that. Even looking at that picture, it does not look like the handkerchief. It does not come close. It looks like a shirt; it looks like it has sleeves. It looks like it could be a towel. Look at the bulk on this picture of this object. And remember the handkerchief that was — the picture of the handkerchief that was introduced when Ken Zercie was on the stand, it was a photograph that they said the range of the photograph could have been anywhere from late '73 to 1980.

Remember the nature of the stains that were on that photograph, they were dark. Whether they were blood or paint or whatever it was, where is that? You don't even see a trace of that in these photographs. Please look at those photographs. That is not a handkerchief.

How do all these details differ from Ed Grant? Ed Grant is 30 years old at the time, born in 1942. He works at Midway, a family business in Waterbury. He is fair-skinned. When you look at that picture from '73, he is fair-skinned. He is not a dark-skinned individual. He has no scars, they specifically looked for it. He doesn't speak in broken English or a foreign accent.

Here are the distinctions that are relevant:

- White male, Hispanic male, that's reasonable doubt.
- Dark-skinned versus light-skinned or fair-skinned, that's reasonable doubt. 5'10" versus 5'6", according to Mr. Hanahan, that's reasonable doubt.

- Foreign language or broken English versus English, that's reasonable doubt.
- Substantial injury occurred during the incident, no scars or cuts, that's reasonable doubt.
- Polo shirt versus work uniform, completely different description, that's reasonable doubt.
- Dark blue pants versus light green dressier pants, that's reasonable doubt. Short sleeved shirt described by several people at the scene, whereas the work shirt is a long sleeved shirt with a logo.
- And look at the shirt that he is wearing in the 1973 photo. Even on July 16th of '73, they are rolling up the sleeves; there is no short sleeved shirts, reasonable doubt.
- Description of the perpetrator, early twenties, Edward Grant, 30 years old on July 16th of 1973, reasonable doubt.

Here is what we don't know: Where did Penney Serra and the killer meet? Was it a planned meeting? Are they both in the car? What happens in the car? Is there any sexual activity or attempted sexual activity? If so, is it consensual or coerced? How did the male DNA get on the underpants and the slip? Is it connected to this killing in some way or not? Whose Type O blood is all over the items inside the car, backside of the—outside of the car, inside of the car, the blood trail, backside of the dress? Ninth floor, tenth floor, whose blood is that? Where does the weapon come from? How does it come into play to begin with? How did the dental bills get into the car? Was it that morning? By whom?

Whose fingerprint is on L4? Whose fingerprint is on the chrome strip on the side of the seat? Whose are the other fingerprints where they are—where they are identifiable characteristics? Some are not, but there are some that are. Are they the killer's or someone else's? We know that they are not Ed Grant's. Whose palm print was it on the Jeep upstairs? Whose palm print was it on the railing upstairs? When did the biological material get on the handkerchief?

What connection does Ed Grant have to New Haven? What connection does Ed Grant have to Penney Serra? Where is the accent or broken English who is the person that has it? Where is the scar from this substantial injury that was inflicted by Penney Serra? Who owns the vehicle with the MR license plate? Why did DeLieto not attend the funeral or pay any respects? Why doesn't DeLieto acknowledge the Liberos when he sees them at the police department when the Liberos are there and they see Phil DeLieto? What does the father say at the time? Why is she getting dressed up to buy some patio furniture? What is she doing on the ninth floor on the day where you would expect her to park far below? What is Ed Grant's motive to kill? Why is he in New Haven?

There are more holes in this, the State's case, than there are holes in the handkerchief.

In order for you to believe that Ed Grant did this, here is what you have to believe: That Ed Grant, a married man with two children three years old and 18 months old, living in the city of Waterbury, goes to work in the City of Waterbury at a family business, that he has to drive, he drives his vehicle to work every day, an orange or gold colored Jeep Wagoneer, goes to work in his work clothes every day, dark blue pants, light blue shirt with the logo on it.

You have to believe that at some point in time he drives to a city that he usually doesn't work in and he drives in a vehicle that he doesn't drive, a blue car with an MR license plate on it. And at some point he has to change his clothes and then get into some kind of a Polo shirt and dress shoes, and at some point he has to pick out the Temple Street garage for some unknown reason to arrive there, and then he has to meet a complete stranger virtually.

And then at some point Ed Grant has to chase her for some unknown reason and kill her for some unknown reason. And then he has to get back into her car and he has to put on his Phil DeLieto mask because that's how he is described after that. And then he has to park that car, get back into this foreign car, assume a foreign accent, real remarkable for someone who has received this substantial wound on his left arm, side, hand or wrist and drive off. And in the meantime, look like he is a dark-skinned Hispanic male. That's what has to happen.

And he has to go back to Waterbury. After 26 years, nothing comes up. He raises his kids. You heard he was at the Christening for his grandchildren in December of 2000 or 1999. Every time he is approached by the police, he is at work. The last time when he was arrested, he is working on a car in the driveway of his house. That's the set of facts that have to happen for him to be the killer in this case. It's totally preposterous.[57]

...

The Prosecution's Rebuttal to the Defense's Closing Argument

Here are excerpts of the Prosecution's Rebuttal argument:

You know the killer had a motive. You know that he got in Penney Serra's Buick and he drove it from the scene of the crime and then he abandoned it. Did he abandon it because he was driving the wrong way and was going to have to go back up to another level or did he plan to abandon it on the eighth level? Was he taking the car from the ninth level because he wanted the car? There is not a clear answer to that question, but there is an inference that you could draw if you choose to, that that could be the motive ...

---

57. Transcript, May 22, 2002, p. 34–87.

You are supposed to look at pictures that witnesses have come in and sworn under oath were taken of the handkerchief that you have in evidence that has the DNA on it, and because those photographs look weird, because of the way the handkerchief was dried, you are supposed to say it's not the handkerchief, given all of that evidence.

It is absolutely correct the only testimony in this case is that you cannot scientifically date a fingerprint. And nobody suggests that you can. But common sense and logic and reason can cause you to draw a conclusion about when the fingerprint was put on that tissue box and that's different, and you know what? That all it takes is common sense and logic to do that ...

There are no prints from anybody except Edward Grant. There are no prints from the stock boys at Pathmark. There is only one print that was identifiable on that whole box, and it's Edward Grant's, the same guy whose DNA matched.

You also know that his access to the box innocently was essentially eliminated in this case, that's why they've got to talk about Pathmark, I guess because on June 29th that box went into Penney Serra's father's car when Mrs. Hurley gave it to them to go to Florida, it then went to Florida. It came back on the 8th of July, there were three days when Mr. Serra was driving the car before it then goes to Rhode Island. Mr. Serra went, according to Rosemary Serra, to work and back, to work and back, to work and back because Penney was home after being away for awhile and he wanted to get home quickly to spend time with her ...

Sure, Phil DeLieto was drawn and he sure doesn't meet any of those criteria, except the blood. But that's not all the evidence you have ... You also have the blood trail. And so far all of it matches Mr. Grant, doesn't it? And you have the keys to the car next to the handkerchief. And you've got the handkerchief and you have ... spray paint ... [a]nd the only evidence that you have of Mr. Grant that was spraying any paint was in the shop. And that paint is consistent with shop paint ...

And you have this ... You have just been arrested on a murder and your mind goes to the other murder that you have just read about and you say this word, they got him on a fingerprint "too." That's not a nothing. That's not a nothing. That's not what you would have said if you brought up Raphael Ramirez. You would say, well, they picked him up because they found his fingerprint, not that they picked him up because they found his fingerprint "too."

Mr. Grant had been waiting 26 years, he thought he had gotten away with it, and here they are knocking on his door saying that he was under the arrest for the murder of Penney Serra ...

When you look at all this evidence, Mr. Ullmann asked you to be sure that justice was done, that is your job. And your job isn't an easy one in the sense that you have to make a decision which is a very weighty decision, but I submit to you that this evidence is over-whelming of the defendant's guilt and in that sense your decision is easier than it might have been.

When you finish, you, like Dr. Kidd, will be virtually certain that the killer is up there on the board with his victim [referring to the trial exhibits] and that you will come back and find this defendant, Edward Grant, guilty of the murder of Penney Serra.[58]

Objections Made in Closing Arguments

During the prosecution's closing statements, defense attorneys objected to a number of statements, thus preserving those issues as possible prejudice on appeal. First, they objected to the state suggesting that Grant may have had a motive to steal Serra's car, as there was no evidence at trial on this issue. Second, the defense objected to a statement that the jurors would have to disbelieve the crime scene investigators to believe the defendant's arguments about the evidence. Connecticut courts have held that it is error for a party to suggest that a witness may have lied.[59]

The defense also renewed its request for the court to give the jury an instruction that the fact that Serra's keys were lost should be held against the state — that the jury should draw an "adverse inference on the missing property, particularly because of the manner in which the State highlighted the keys during its final argument."[60]

Jury Instructions

Here is a portion of the judge's instructions to the jury:

Ladies and gentlemen, you heard the evidence presented in this case and it's now my duty to charge you on the law that you are to apply to the facts that you find from the evidence.

You, as the jury, and I, as the Judge, have separate functions. It's your function to find what the facts are in this case. With respect to the facts, you and you alone are charged with that responsibility.

My function is to charge you on the law to be applied to the facts that you find in order to decide this case.

With respect to the law, what I say to you is binding on you and you must follow all of my instructions. The parties are entitled to have this case decided pursuant to established legal standards that are the same for

---

58. Transcript, May 22, 2002, p. 88–122.
59. *State v. Singh*, 259 Conn. 693 (2002).
60. Transcript, May 22, 2002, p. 128.

everybody. Those are the standards that I will give you and that you must follow.

Elements of the Crime of Murder

The statute cited in the information, Connecticut General Statute Section 53a-54a defines the crime of murder. The statute provides that, and again I'll quote, "A person is guilty of murder when, with intent to cause the death of another person, he causes the death of such person," end of quote.

For you to find the defendant guilty of this charge, the State must prove each of three elements beyond a reasonable doubt:

One, that it was the defendant and not some other person who was the perpetrator.

Two, that the defendant intended to cause the death of another person.

And three, that in accordance with that intent, the defendant caused the death of that person.

The State must prove beyond a reasonable doubt that it was the defendant and not some other perpetrator who committed the crime alleged in the Information.

You must be satisfied beyond a reasonable doubt that the defendant was the perpetrator of the crime in question before you may convict him.

Was Grant the Perpetrator?

The element of identity or, more simply put, who committed the crime, is obviously a disputed issue in the case. The identity of the perpetrator is a question of fact for you to decide after a full consideration of all the evidence including the testimony of witnesses, the full exhibits and your observations during the view.

The State has the burden of proving beyond a reasonable doubt that it was the defendant, Edward Grant, who committee this crime.

Intent

[W]hat a person's purpose or intent has been is ordinarily a matter of inference. The nature of the wound inflicted and the instrument used may be considered as evidence of the perpetrator's intent and from such evidence an inference may be drawn that the perpetrator had an intent to kill or to cause death. This is an inference of fact that you are permitted to draw after a consideration of all the evidence in accordance with my instructions.

You may draw reasonable and logical inferences from the conduct that you find in light of all the surrounding circumstances, and from this determine whether the State has proven the element of intent beyond a reasonable doubt. This inference is permissive rather than required. You are not required to infer a specific intent from the conduct that you find, but it's an inference that you may draw if you find that it's reasonable and logical and in accordance with the instructions on circumstantial evidence.

The State has the burden of proving the specific intent to cause death. If you find that the State has proven beyond a reasonable doubt each of the elements of the crime of murder, you must find the defendant guilty.

Lack of Motive

Motive is not an element of either the crime of murder or the crime of manslaughter in the first degree. And the State is not required to prove or show motive.

Evidence of a motive may strengthen the State's case. An absence of evidence of motive may tend to raise a reasonable doubt of the guilt of the defendant, but even a total lack of evidence of motive would not necessarily raise a reasonable doubt as to the guilt of the defendant as long as there is other evidence produced that is sufficient to prove guilt beyond a reasonable doubt.

If the absence of an apparent motive does not raise a reasonable doubt that the defendant is guilty, then the mere fact that the State has been unable to prove what the motive of the defendant actually was does not prevent you from returning a verdict of guilty.

Circumstantial Evidence

You may consider both direct and circumstantial evidence. Direct evidence is testimony by a witness about what that witness personally saw or heard of did. Circumstantial evidence is evidence involving inferences reasonable and logically drawn from proven facts.

Let me give you an example of what I mean by direct and circumstantial evidence. If you wake up in the morning and see water on the sidewalk, that is direct evidence that there is water on the sidewalk. It is also circumstantial evidence that it rained during the night. Of course, other evidence such as a turned on garden hose may explain the water on the sidewalk.[61]

...

Meaning of Reasonable Doubt

The defendant does not have to prove his innocence in any way or present any evidence to disprove the charge against him. The state must prove each and every element necessary to constitute the crime charged beyond a reasonable doubt.

The meaning of reasonable doubt can be arrived at by emphasizing the word "reasonable." It is not a surmise, a guess or a mere conjecture. It is not hesitation springing from any feelings of pity or sympathy for the accused or any other persons who might be affected by your decision.

---

61. Transcript, May 22, 2002, p. 134.

It is a real doubt, an honest doubt, a doubt that has its foundation in the evidence or lack of evidence. It is doubt that is honestly entertained and is reasonable in light of the evidence after a fair comparison and careful examination of the entire evidence.

Proof beyond a reasonable doubt does not mean proof beyond all doubt. The law does not require absolute certainty on the part of a jury before it returns a verdict of guilty. The law requires that after hearing all of the evidence, if there is something in the evidence or lack of evidence that leaves in the minds of the jurors as reasonable men and women a reasonable doubt as to the guilt of the accused, then the accused must be given the benefit of that doubt and acquitted.

Proof beyond a reasonable doubt is proof that precludes every reasonable hypothesis except guilt and is inconsistent with any other rational conclusion. If you can in reason reconcile all of the facts proved with any reasonable theory consistent with the innocence of the accused, then you cannot find him guilty....

Credibility of Witnesses

Now, the credibility of witnesses and the weight to be given their testimony are matters for you to determine, however, there are some principles that you should keep in mind. You may believe all, none or any part of any witness's testimony ...

You must consider all of the evidence in the case. You may decide that the testimony of a smaller number of witnesses on one side has greater weight than that of a larger number of the other side. It's the quality and not the quantity of evidence that controls. All of these are factors that you may consider in finding the facts....

Police officers and other officials have testified in this case. You must determine the credibility of these witnesses in the same way and by the same standards that you would use to evaluate the testimony of ordinary witnesses.

The testimony of a police officer or other official is entitled to no special or exclusive weight merely because it is from an official. You should recall the witness's demeanor on the stand and manner of testifying and weigh and balance the testimony just as carefully as the testimony of any other witness. You should neither believe nor disbelieve the testimony of a police officer or any other official just because the witness is an official.

Expert Opinions

You have heard some testimony of witnesses who have testified as expert witnesses. Expert witnesses are witnesses who, because of their training, skill, education and experience, are permitted not only to testify about facts that they have personally observed, but to state their opinions. However, the fact that a witness has qualified as an expert does not mean that you have to accept that witness's opinion. You could accept an expert witness's opinion or reject it in whole or in part.

In making your decision whether to believe an expert's opinion, you should consider the expert's education, training and experience in the particular field, the information available to the expert, including the facts the expert had and the documents or other physical evidence available to the expert, the expert's opportunity and ability to examine those things, the completeness or incompleteness of the expert's report, the expert's ability to recollect the facts that form the basis for the opinion, and the expert's ability to tell you accurately about the basis for the opinion.

You should ask yourselves about the methods employed by the expert and the reliability of the result. You should further consider whether the opinions stated by the expert have a rational and reasonable basis in the evidence.

Based on all of these things together with your general observation and assessment of the witness, it's up to you to decide whether or not to accept the opinion. You may believe all, some or none of the testimony of an expert witness. An expert's testimony is subject to your review like that of any other witness.[62]

. . .

Conviction

The jury returned with a verdict of guilty on May 28, 2002. On September 27, 2002, Grant was sentenced to 20 years to life. At his sentencing, Grant spoke in court for the first time, saying:

I'm sorry for the pain, sorrow and loss of the Serra family. I can't begin to imagine it. I had no part in this tragic event. However, the jury has convicted me, and I ask for leniency. I lived my entire life trying to make life better for my family. I'm devastated by the jury's decision.[63]

Judge Blue made the following statement in sentencing Grant:

No one can deny that someone killed Penney Serra and thrust a knife in her heart. Someone left that beautiful young woman dead or dying in a dirty stairwell in a parking garage. No one can deny what the evidence shows beyond any doubt—that someone was you.[64]

---

62. Transcript, May 22, 2002, p. 129–161.
63. Michelle Tuccitto, "Grant Gets '20-to-Life' in Serra Murder," *New Haven Register*, September 28, 2002.
64. *Id.*

The judge took Grant's lack of a criminal record into account, but refused leniency because Grant did not come forward when another suspect was arrested and because of Grant's "refusal to accept responsibility and apologize" for the murder.

Public Defender Brian Carlow, who represented Grant, in speaking about the case following Grant's conviction, maintained his client's innocence. He said:

Grant is the unluckiest man in the world.[65]

Carlow believed the jury would have acquitted if it had been presented with just the fingerprint or the blood spot. But the two together convinced the jury that Grant was guilty.

Post Trial Motions

Following the verdict, Grant's attorneys moved for a new trial, citing such errors as the prosecution's offering a possible motive in their closing statement that Grant was trying to steal Serra's car, although no evidence to that effect had been introduced. The motion also argued that the prosecution had impermissibly stated that the jury would have to believe two investigators had lied to acquit. Finally, it asserted error because of the judge's failure to sanction the state for losing significant pieces of evidence.[66] The motion was denied.

* * *

Appeal

Grant filed his appeal brief on August 14, 2006 — four years from his sentencing and imprisonment. As in his court trial, he was represented by the public defender's office. Grant properly filed his notice of appeal within the time period required by law; however, his appeal brief was not due until 60 days following the delivery of the last page of the trial transcript, which accounted for the delay.

The appeals court does not hear any testimony from witnesses. It must accept the written transcript of the trial as the only facts in the case. Appeals are based on legal arguments presented in appeal briefs with references to the testimony from the actual trial transcript of the witness testimony and exhibits and evidence admitted at trial.

Grant's appeal asked the appellate court to grant a new trial based on certain errors of law he asserted were made at the trial level.

The fundamental remedy that Grant's appeal requested was a new trial. "This Court should declare that there was error below and order a new trial."[67] The

---

65. Interview of Brian Carlow with the author, October 2004.

66. Christa Lee Rock, "*Citing Misconduct, Grant's Lawyers Seek New Trial,*" *New Haven Register,* June 4, 2002.

67. Appellant Brief, at 69.

prosecution could re-try him, if it wishes. Of course, if the appeals court remands the case for a new trial, but the prosecution decides not to retry him, Grant would be a free man.

The Grounds for Grant's Appeal

The major legal issues were these:

- Did the warrant to take Grant's blood lack probable cause because certain facts were not included in the affidavit submitted to obtain the warrant?

- Should certain statements made by Grant have been kept from the jury because they violated his *Miranda* rights to be informed that any statement he made could be used against him in a court of law?

- Was there an improper "foundation" laid for testimony about blood without actual testing to show the substance was blood?

- Did the prosecution commit misconduct in the closing arguments by referring to a possible motive for the killing, when no evidence about motive had been submitted at trial?

Grant also argued that his attorneys were wrongly denied a hearing on the issue of whether certain material facts had been improperly omitted from the affidavit used by the police to secure the warrant. Specifically, he asserted the affidavit failed to connect either Grant or his blood to the crime scene or to the perpetrator of the crime. It stated that the lab "determined that [the victim's] blood type is 'A' and that blood scrapings taken from the scene and believed to be that of the perpetrator is Type 'O.'[68] The brief argued that as 45% of the population has Type O blood, that fact, by itself, did not show probable cause to connect Grant with the crime. As to whether the fingerprint, by itself, is sufficient to show probable cause, the brief stated that, given the fact that no one can state when the fingerprint was placed on the tissue box and given also that a tissue box is highly moveable, the fingerprint did not establish probable cause. In other words, even if the defense admitted that the fingerprint was Grant's and therefore Grant touched the box at some point, there is no evidence that he touched the box *at the time of the crime* because the box is an easily moveable item. Grant's appellate brief said:

> This proves that the person whose fingerprint it is touched the outside of the box, but given the *portability* of the box, it does not even prove the tissue box was touched while [in the car] as opposed to at some other time prior to the tissue box being put [in the car.] Does the print on the tissue box provide probable cause that the person who made it is [the burglar?] Not if the fingerprint belongs to anyone who touched the box before the burglary at any of its many prior locations before it ended up on the [car.][69]

---

68. Appellant's Brief, at 2.
69. Appellant's Brief, at 26–27.

Grant's attorneys also argued that, as there was no fingerprint of Grant's anywhere on the car itself, including on the bloody steering wheel or any of the car handles, there is no way to place him in the car as a result of a fingerprint match on the tissue box.

Wrongful Admission of Statement by Grant to Police

Another ground for appeal is the admission as evidence of the following statement made by Grant to Officer Rouella after he was booked and after Grant said that he was not waiving his rights (under *Miranda*) and would wait for his attorney. According to Rouella, he and Grant were sitting in silence at the table where the booking was done, when Grant said to him, "Did you read about the guy in Texas that killed all those people? They got him on a fingerprint too." The statement was admitted to the jury over a defense objection. Grant's appeal argued that once a defendant is in custody, no questioning can take place unless the requirements of *Miranda* are met. Therefore, the statement made without counsel was inadmissible.

Prosecutorial Misconduct

Grant also contended that the prosecutor committed misconduct in statements made during the closing argument, including his statement about a possible motive for Serra's death being that Grant may have wanted to steal her car. There was no evidence of motive at trial, so counsel was not permitted to speculate about it in his closing.

* * *

The State's Response

The state of Connecticut contended in its brief that there was no error in granting the warrant for Grant's blood.

- The State argued that none of the statements Grant argued should have been in the affidavit supporting probable cause were required. Statements such as the fact that other fingerprints were found in Serra's car or that other suspects had been investigated were not relevant at the time of the warrant, and even if they were, the result was harmless error. The state argued that the facts were not material to granting the warrant and were not omitted with any intent to mislead the judge who signed the warrant.

Grant's first claim on appeal was that the warrant for his blood was issued in error because the affidavit upon which it was based omitted material facts. The State's Reply Brief summarized the omissions Grant claims were made from the warrant as follows:

1. several identifiable fingerprints were located in or on the Serra vehicle and were identified *not* to be the defendant's;

2. that the affiants omitted a statement from a 1992 affidavit directed against another suspect, Selman Topciu, that "it has never been substantiated that the latent prints lifted from the Serra vehicle belong to the perpetrator";

3. that "a microscopic examination of the fingerprint lifted from the tissue box showed that it was placed there prior to the time the blood was deposited";

4. "information regarding how long the tissue box had been in the Serra vehicle";

5. certain eyewitness descriptions of the perpetrator that "do not match that of the defendant";

6. the opinion of certain investigators that "the perpetrator had suffered a serious injury to his left hand and that the perpetrator would thus be likely to have a significant scar in that area" and that "there was no evidence of any scar" on Grant;

7. that another suspect, Philip DeLieto, had been confidently identified by an eyewitness and had had "some domestic disputes" with the victim shortly before her death;

8. that the reference in ¶ 14 of the affidavit to the "suspect under investigation whose blood has genetic markings that are consistent with those of the perpetrator's blood" was to Selman Topciu, not Grant.[70]

The State argued that none of these statements were required and that even if they were, the result was harmless error. Grant's attorneys had moved before trial for a *Franks* hearing to ask the court to hear these issues; the motion was denied on January 7, 2002.

Here is the standard for a *Franks* hearing, according to the State:

> Before a defendant is entitled to a *Franks* hearing, he "must make a substantial preliminary showing that the information was (1) omitted with the intent to make, or in reckless disregard of whether it made, the affidavit misleading to the judge, and (2) material to the determination of probable cause.
>
> Not all omissions, even if intentional, will invalidate an affidavit. An affiant may "pick and choose" the information that he includes in the affidavit and he may omit facts that he believes to be either immaterial or unsubstantiated. Cases like this one, which involve allegedly material omissions, are "less likely to present a question of impermissible official conduct" than those which involve "allegedly material false inclusions."[71]

The state specifically rejected Grant's claims about omissions of information as follows:

---

70. Appellee's Brief, at 22.
71. *Id.* at 20.

As to the issue of the fingerprint on the tissue box being under the blood and therefore possibly placed there days before the commission of the crime, the state responds that even had "Dr. Lee's statement ... been included in the affidavit, it would not have defeated a finding of probable cause because it was entirely consistent with the inference implicitly drawn by the issuing judge, based on the totality of the other information in the affidavit, that the defendant's [bloody] and admittedly inexplicable fingerprint could have been deposited on the tissue box during the commission of the crime or its immediate aftermath."[72]

The failure to describe in detail conflicting eyewitness descriptions of the perpetrator was not material because all the eyewitnesses described a white man between 5 feet 8 inches and 5 feet 10 inches in height. As to the likelihood that the perpetrator would have a significant scar on his left wrist, the state responded "[c]ommon experience, moreover, dictates that not all injuries, even substantial ones that result in bleeding, leave a permanent visible scar."[73]

The failure to disclose that Phil DeLieto had been identified earlier by an eyewitness and that Selman Topciu had been investigated and arrest warrants sought against him were irrelevant, argued the state, because by the time of the Grant warrant, both had been eliminated as suspects.

- Grant's appeal brief contended it was error to admit Grant's statement: "did you read about the guy in Texas that killed all those people? They got him on a fingerprint too." The state responded that Grant's statement was voluntary, not in response to a question from authorities, but that the trial court correctly concluded that "Grant wanted to talk and that the police allowed him to do so."[74] The state also claims that, even if the statement had violated Grant's constitutional rights, it was "harmless error" because the "properly admitted evidence" showed beyond a reasonable doubt that Grant was guilty.

The state then summarized its view of the evidence that "overwhelmingly established guilt":

1. the defendant's admittedly unexplained bloody fingerprint on the tissue box.

2. the defendant's unique DNA profile on the handkerchief found near the terminus of the Type O human blood trail;

3. Type O human blood bearing the defendant's DQ Alpha genotype on a trim piece inside the Buick;

4. composite drawings of the killer that both bear remarkable similarities to the 1973 photo of the defendant; and

5. the traces of aftermarket automotive paint on the handkerchief.[75]

---

72. *Id.* at 24.
73. *Id.* at 28.
74. Appellee Brief, at 37–38.
75. *Id.* at 44.

Grant also appealed that certain testimony should have been excluded at trial, specifically any reference to "blood" unless there had been independent evidence that the substance had in fact been tested and found to be blood. The state's brief sets out the legal standard for claims that evidence has been improperly admitted:

> The trial court has broad discretion in ruling on the admissibility of evidence. A reviewing court must make every reasonable presumption in favor of upholding a trial court's evidentiary ruling and will overturn it only upon a clear and manifest abuse of discretion.
>
> > Relevant evidence is evidence that has a logical tendency to aid the trier in the determination of an issue....
> >
> > [E]vidence need not exclude all other possibilities [to be relevant]; it is sufficient if it tends to support the conclusion [for which it is offered], even to a slight degree.... [T]he fact that evidence is susceptible of different explanations or would support various inferences does not affect its admissibility, although it obviously bears upon its weight. So long as the evidence may reasonably be construed in such a manner that it would be relevant, it is admissible.[76]

Finally, as to Grant's argument that certain statements made by the prosecution were misconduct, the state contended:

> The standard to be followed in analyzing claims that allege prosecutorial misconduct is the fairness of the trial rather than the culpability of the prosecutor. This Court does not scrutinize each comment in a vacuum, but rather examines the comments both in the context of the entire trial and in the context in which they were made.... A prosecutor may argue the state's case forcefully, provided the argument is fair and based upon the facts in evidence and the reasonable inferences to be drawn therefrom.[77]

Appeal Denied

After oral argument before the Connecticut Supreme Court, Grant's appeal was denied:

> In most of the cases relied on by the defendant, the courts held that fingerprint evidence with a possible innocent explanation was insufficient to support a finding of guilt *beyond a reasonable doubt*. The mere possibility of an innocent explanation for evidence connecting a defendant with a crime does not, however, preclude a finding of probable cause. *See Johnson v. Lewis*, 120 Cal. App. 4th 443, 453, 15 Cal. Rptr. 3d 507 (2004) (possibility of innocent explanation does not vitiate probable cause);

---

76. *Id.* at 46.
77. *Id.* at 51.

Peterkin v. United States, 281 A.2d 567, 569 (D.C. App. 1971) (mere possibility of innocent explanation does not negate finding of probable cause); *People v. Hartman*, 294 App. Div. 2d 446, 447-48, 744 N.Y.S.2d 38 (2002) (because probable cause does not require proof beyond reasonable doubt, possibility of innocent explanation does not preclude finding of probable cause). In the present case, the search warrant affidavit contained sufficient facts for an impartial and reasonable mind to weigh the probability of an innocent explanation for the fingerprint and reasonably to support a belief that such an explanation was no more likely than the defendant's presence in the Buick at the time of the murder, for which there was *no* apparent innocent explanation. Accordingly, we conclude that the trial court properly determined that the search warrant was supported by probable cause.

286 Conn. 499, 518, 944 A.2d 947, 962 (2008).

Comments from the Jury

The jury found Edward Grant guilty. They were not required to state the reasons for their decision and they did not. However, one of my students tracked down one of the jurors and asked her a series of questions. What she answered says a lot about the jury system:

What was your opinion of the DNA evidence that was collected? Since the evidence was so old, were there times that you felt that the evidence would not prevail?

I felt the DNA evidence was certainly adequate. I'm sure we all would have loved to have had the bloody parking ticket in evidence, as well, but there was plenty of genetic material on hand for identification. Once we'd heard expert testimony regarding the DNA evidence, I had no worries about its age or quantity.

Whose expert testimony did you rely on the most? Why?

I relied heavily on the prosecution's DNA expert and the prosecution's fingerprint expert in making my decision. In the end I think that's what convinced all of the jurors in their decisions. You can't argue with facts, and the prosecution's expert witnesses left no doubt in my mind that both the DNA and the fingerprint combined matched with no one other than Ed Grant.

What is your most memorable moment?

It would have to be the time I held Penney's bloody blue dress in my hands.... The dress was so small, she'd been a petite little girl. There was so much blood—Penney's blood—and the fabric was slashed right where her heart had been. There were several smaller holes in the dress where samples had been taken for blood analysis. And that tiny blue dress had been examined by the hands and the eyes of so many strangers, and put on display so many times, — it seemed a horrible invasion of an innocent girl's privacy, and disrespectful somehow. It was the last thing she picked out to wear on the last day of her too-short life. It was all too human.

One juror, Linda Linsky, said that she became convinced that Grant had murdered Serra as she watched the fingerprint testimony. Joe Braychak, another juror who was an engineer said:

> We just started with the evidence ... I'm an engineer, or was an engineer, and everything I do has to have a logical basis. So I went to the crime scene, and [Grant's] blood type was there, but that's not enough to convince me. Then I went through the blood trail, his blood was there, too. I went into the car and his fingerprint was there. And once I looked at the handkerchief and it has his DNA on it, I said 'You know, there's nobody else on the planet that has that.'"[78]

The *New Haven Register* published a poll of 14 citizens following the trial, asking "Do you agree with the verdict in the Penney Serra murder case?" Nine of the fourteen felt the state had not proved Grant guilty. Two disagreed. The other three did not express an opinion. Given the substantial coverage of the trial in the New Haven papers, it is interesting to realize that if these 14 people had been jurors, Grant would not have been convicted.

In a subsequent letter to the editor, William Doriss of New Haven said:

> There is no way a murder case with as many unanswered questions as this can be solved on the basis of one and only one 29-year-old fingerprint, which in and of itself is debatable. His thumbprint looks exactly like mine, and I didn't do it. This is a sad day for criminal justice in Connecticut.[79]

People v. Grant came down essentially to a case of forensic evidence — at least that is the way the juror quoted above saw it. Although she appeared to be emotionally swayed by Penney's dress and a desire to find her killer, she made it clear that her decision was based on expert testimony about one fingerprint and one drop of blood. The eyewitness testimony was confused and contradictory. There was no evidence of motive. The timeline of the crime, eight minutes from entry into the garage to exit, seems almost unbelievable. But as one New Haven reporter put it, "Blood doesn't lie."

---

78. Christa Lee Rock, "Serra Jurors Talk Evidence Pointed Only to Grant," *New Haven Register*, May 30, 2002.

79. "Serra Trial Raised Reasonable Doubts," letter to the editor, *New Haven Register*, June 1, 2002.

Index